Mercedes

Rainer W. Schlegelmilch

Hartmut Lehbrink · Jochen von Osterroth

Mercedes

h.f.ullmann

Contents · Inhalt · Sommaire

Benz Patent-Motorwagen 1886 — 16	Mercedes-Benz Nürburg 1929 — 94	Mercedes-Benz 300 S 1951 — 148
Daimler Motorkutsche 1886 — 20	Mercedes-Benz 170 1931 — 98	Mercedes-Benz *Ponton* 1953 — 154
Daimler Stahlradwagen 1889 — 24	Mercedes-Benz 500 K & 540 K 1934 — 102	Mercedes-Benz 300 SL 1954 — 158
Benz Victoria 1893 — 28	Mercedes-Benz 130 H–170 H 1934 — 110	Mercedes-Benz 219–220 SE 1954 — 166
Benz Velo 1894 — 34	Mercedes-Benz 170 V 1936 — 112	Mercedes-Benz 190 SL 1955 — 170
Benz Dos-à-Dos 1899 — 40	Mercedes-Benz 260 D 1936 — 116	Mercedes-Benz *Heckflosse* 1959 — 176
Mercedes Simplex 1902 — 42	Mercedes-Benz 320 1937 — 120	Mercedes-Benz *Pagode* 1963 — 188
Benz Spider 1902 — 48	*Großer Mercedes* 770 1938 — 124	Mercedes-Benz 600 1963 — 192
Mercedes 28/95 PS 1914 — 50	Mercedes-Benz 230 1938 — 128	Mercedes-Benz S-Klasse 1965 — 196
Mercedes 400–630 K 1924 — 54	Mercedes-Benz 170 V 1946 — 130	Mercedes-Benz /8 1967 — 200
Mercedes-Benz S–SSKL 1927 — 58	Mercedes-Benz 170 S 1949 — 134	Mercedes-Benz SL & SLC 1971 — 204
Mercedes-Benz Stuttgart 1928 — 86	Mercedes-Benz 220 1951 — 140	Mercedes-Benz S-Klasse 1972 — 210
Mercedes-Benz Mannheim 1929 — 90	Mercedes-Benz *Adenauer* 1951 — 144	Mercedes-Benz 200 D–280 CE 1976 — 214

	Bruno Sacco: Fascination Mercedes 6	Bibliography · Bibliografie · Bibliographie 406
Mercedes-Benz S-Klasse 1979 **222**	Glittering years—but not always Lichtjahre – aber nicht immer Des années de lumière – mais avec des zones d'ombre 10	Acknowledgements, Photo credits · Danksagung, Fotonachweis · Remerciements, Crédits photographiques 407
Mercedes-Benz 190 1982 **228**	Mercedes-Benz C-Klasse Sportcoupé / CLC 2000 **298**	Mercedes-Benz GL 2006 **356**
Mercedes-Benz E-Klasse 1984 **232**	Mercedes-Benz SL 2001 **304**	Mercedes-Benz CL 2006 **360**
Mercedes-Benz SL 1988 **244**	Mercedes-Benz E-Klasse 2002 **310**	Mercedes-Benz C-Klasse 2007 **364**
Mercedes-Benz S-Klasse & SEC/CL 1991 **248**	Mercedes-Benz CLK 2002 **314**	Mercedes-Benz GLK 2008 **368**
Mercedes-Benz C-Klasse 1993 **254**	Maybach 2002 **318**	Mercedes-Benz E-Klasse 2009 **372**
Mercedes-Benz E-Klasse 1995 **260**	Mercedes-Benz SLR McLaren 2003 **324**	Mercedes-Benz SLS-AMG 2009 **376**
Mercedes-Benz SLK 1996 **264**	Mercedes-Benz SLK 2004 **330**	Mercedes-Benz CLS 2011 **380**
Mercedes-Benz CLK 1997 **270**	Mercedes-Benz CLS 2004 **336**	Mercedes-Benz SLK 2011 **384**
Mercedes-Benz A-Klasse 1997 **276**	Mercedes-Benz B-Klasse 2005 **340**	Mercedes-Benz M-Klasse 2011 **388**
Mercedes-Benz ML 1997 **284**	Mercedes-Benz R-Klasse 2005 **344**	Mercedes-Benz B-Klasse 2011 **392**
Mercedes-Benz S-Klasse & CL 1998 **288**	Mercedes-Benz S-Klasse 2005 **348**	Mercedes-Benz SL 2012 **396**
Mercedes-Benz C-Klasse 2000 **294**	Mercedes-Benz ML 2005 **352**	Mercedes-Benz A-Klasse 2012 **400**

Bruno Sacco: Fascination Mercedes

Highway 405, en route to Los Angeles Airport. It's 19 August 1997, around 9 AM. The link is OK, and Mr. S... is on the other end of the line. The book is already in production, he explains, almost ready to go to press. It's planned as a photographic record of the most interesting and beautiful Mercedes vehicles. He's a photographic designer. Only at the second time of asking do I get his name: Rainer Schlegelmilch. I'm familiar with his pictures for the Car Museum in Untertürkheim. They're good.

Hartmut Lehbrink is responsible for the text. Would I like to write a foreword? I call back ten minutes later. I'll do it.

I've been a devotee of Mercedes cars since 1952, which seems a long time ago now. What happened in 1952? A one-two in the Le Mans 24 Hour race. And the Carrera Panamericana. And then, in 1954 in Reims, "veni, vidi, vici," the rest of the world had to give best to the new Mercedes phalanx of Nallinger, Uhlenhaut and Neubauer with worldclass drivers like Fangio, Herrmann and Kling at the wheel. The same year saw the launch of the 300 SL, one of the most beautiful cars of all time. So it was then I joined Mercedes in 1958. And I've remained faithful to Mercedes ever since. Why? The answer lies in the fascination that Mercedes cars exerted and still exert on me, naturally at different levels of perception. It was Leo Levine who said in 1988: "Why cars look the way they do, and why Mereedes-Benz automobiles look the way they do, are fascinating subjects."[1] How right he was!

The history of the invention of the motor car undoubtedly began long before Karl Benz and Gottlieb Daimler. However, Karl Benz and Gottlieb Daimler were the first to build "machines" that really ran and were therefore usable. One fact which is of great importance in historical terms too is that neither of them was a mere tinkerer who had managed to create some one-day wonder or other. They were experienced engineers who had arrived separately at their goal as a result of methodical work and then continued to refine and improve their inventions and eventually bring them to industrial fruition. They produced the first saleable products of this type, even if the manufacturing process used for these cars was not comparable with that of what we would now term production cars: these earliest models were lovingly built by highly-specialized craftsmen who overcame all kinds of difficulties in the process.

Your next question will be: What is fascinating? Let's take the example of Benz's three-wheeler (1885/86), Daimler's motor carriage (1886) and their direct derivatives such as the Daimler Stahlradwagen. With these models I would refer to the fascination of the spirit of invention. What's next? The Benz Victorias and Velos, and the Daimler Riemenwagen and Phoenix. Not the most visually attractive of cars, if we're honest. However, what

Highway 405, auf dem Weg zum Flughafen Los Angeles. Es ist der 19. August 1997, so um 9 Uhr vormittags herum. Die Verbindung funktioniert, auf der anderen Seite der Leitung Herr S... Das Buch befindet sich bereits in der Herstellungsphase, ist sozusagen »im Druck«. Es soll ein Bildband über die interessantesten und schönsten Mercedes-Fahrzeuge werden. Er sei Fotodesigner. Erst beim zweiten Anlauf verstehe ich seinen Namen: Rainer Schlegelmilch. Ich kenne seine Aufnahmen für das Untertürkheimer Automobil-Museum. Gute Arbeiten.

Den Text soll Hartmut Lehbrink verfassen. Ob ich doch ein Vorwort schreiben möchte? Nach zehn Minuten rufe ich zurück. Ich werde es schreiben.

Mercedes-Fahrzeuge haben mich in ihren Bann gezogen seit dem inzwischen fernen 1952. Was war geschehen? 1. und 2. Platz bei den 24 Stunden in Le Mans. Und die Carrera Panamericana. Und dann, 1954 in Reims, »veni, vidi, vici«, der Rest der Welt musste sich der neuen Mercedes-Phalanx der Nallinger, Uhlenhaut und Neubauer beugen, gefahren von Weltklasse-Piloten wie Fangio, Herrmann und Kling. Dann erschien im selben Jahr der 300 SL. Eines der schönsten Sportwagen aller Zeiten. So kam ich zu Mercedes 1958. – Und blieb auch Mercedes treu. – Warum eigentlich? Die Antwort liegt in der Faszination die Mercedes-Automobile, natürlich auf unterschiedlichen Ebenen des Wahrnehmbaren, auf mich ausübten und noch ausüben. Sagte doch Leo Levine 1988: »Why cars look the way they do, and why Mercedes-Benz automobiles look the way they do, are fascinating subjects«[1] – wie recht er hatte!

Die Geschichte der Erfindung des Automobils beginnt sicher lange vor Karl Benz und Gottlieb Daimler. – Es waren aber Karl Benz und Gottlieb Daimler die ersten, die wirklich laufende und somit brauchbare »Maschinen« schafften. Was auch historisch betrachtet sehr wichtig ist: beide waren keine Tüftler, die irgendwelche Eintagsfliegen zusammenbastelten. Sie waren erfahrene Ingenieure, die methodisch arbeitend – getrennt – zum Ziel gekommen waren und Schritt für Schritt ihre Erfindungen weiterentwickelten, verbesserten und schließlich bis zur industriellen Reife führten. Sie erzeugten die ersten verkäuflichen Produkte dieser Gattung, auch wenn diese Automobile in ihrem Herstellungsprozess nicht vergleichbar waren mit sogenannten Serienautos: Handwerker mit hohem Spezialisierungsgrad bauten diese ersten Stücke liebevoll und unter Überwindung allerlei Schwierigkeiten zusammen.

Sie werden nun fragen: Was ist faszinierend? Nehmen wir doch das Dreirad von Benz (1885/86), die Motorkutsche von Daimler (1886) und ihre unmittelbaren Derivate, wie z.B. der Daimler-Stahlradwagen. Bei diesen Objekten würde ich von Faszination durch den Erfindergeist sprechen. Was kommt danach? Es sind die Benz Victorias und Velos, die Daimler Riemenwagen und Phoenix. Eigentlich keine optisch absolut begehrenswerten Automobile. Es ist aber

Autoroute 405, je suis en route vers l'aéroport de Los Angeles. Nous sommes le 19 août 1997, vers neuf heures du matin. Le téléphone sonne, c'est un certain monsieur S… qui m'appelle. Le livre est déjà en cours de réalisation, pour ainsi dire «en phase d'impression», dit-il. Il s'agira d'un ouvrage photographique sur les plus intéressantes et les plus belles des Mercedes. Il est photographe, ajoute-t-il. Ce n'est qu'après coup que je comprends son nom: Rainer Schlegelmilch. Je connais les photos qu'il a faites pour le musée de l'Automobile d'Untertürkheim. Du bon travail.

Le texte sera signé Hartmut Lehbrink. Ne pourrais-je pas écrire une introduction? Après dix minutes de réflexion, je le rappelle. Je l'écrirai.

Je suis tombé sous le charme des Mercedes un jour qui remonte déjà loin, c'était en 1952. Que s'est-il passé?

Première et deuxième places aux 24 Heures du Mans. Et la Carrera Panamericana. Puis en 1954, à Reims, *veni, vidi, vici*, le reste du monde a dû plier l'échine sous les coups de boutoir de la nouvelle phalange de Mercedes réunie par les Nallinger, Uhlenhaut et Neubauer, dont les voitures sont conduites par des pilotes d'exception comme Fangio, Herrmann et Kling. C'est alors qu'apparaît, la même année, la 300 SL, l'une des plus belles voitures de sport de tous les temps. Et c'est ainsi que je me suis retrouvé chez Mercedes en 1958, et que j'y suis resté fidèle. Pourquoi? En raison de la fascination que les voitures de chez Mercedes ont exercée sur moi, et exercent encore. N'était-ce pas Leo Levine qui disait, en 1988: *« Why cars look the way they do, and why Mercedes-Benz automobiles look the way they do, are fascinating subjects[1] »* – comme il avait raison!

L'histoire de l'invention de l'automobile aura sans doute commencé longtemps avant Karl Benz et Gottlieb Daimler. Ils furent pourtant les premiers à réaliser des «machines» qui roulaient réellement, donc viables. Autre considération très importante sur le plan historique: les deux hommes n'étaient pas du genre «bricoleur». Ingénieurs expérimentés, ils travaillaient avec méthode – séparément – et ont atteint leur objectif puis, pas à pas, ont perfectionné leurs inventions, les ont améliorées, jusqu'à ce qu'elles parviennent enfin à la maturité industrielle. Constructeurs, ils sont aussi les premiers véritables vendeurs automobiles, même si leurs engins n'étaient en rien comparables avec ce que l'on pourrait appeler des voitures de série, de par leur processus de fabrication: des artisans doués d'un haut niveau de spécialisation construisaient ces premiers exemplaires avec amour et ingéniosité pour surmonter toutes les difficultés.

Vous allez maintenant me demander: Qu'y a-t-il de passionnant? L'invention et la nouveauté que représentent le tricycle de Benz, mû par un moteur à essence (1885–1886), la calèche à moteur de Daimler (1886) et ses dérivés directs,

is fascinating about them is that they represent the clear progression from the original spirit-of-adventure prototypes to very saleable cars built in factories in small series. Just take a moment to consider the almost insurmountable variety of difficulties that these two inventors must have encountered. Everything was new, and even certain borrowings from coachbuilding techniques of the time cannot lessen these enormous achievements. The fascination, therefore, of skillful problem-solving and consolidation.

I don't wish to repeat the genesis of the first "Mercedes" here. One thing is clear, however: in addition to providing the name for the small series of cars which he had ordered, Emil Jellinek undoubtedly prompted the first modern car of the emerging century. A delicate masterpiece of engineering esthetics, which is sadly missing from the company's own museum. On the instructions of Prof. Werner Breitschwerdt, the then senior designer, I commissioned the museum's 1:4 scale model from the late modelmaker Carlo Brianza. The first Mercedes had a very clearly defined structure: the axles, the drive, the very low, horizontally configured floor, the seat bases, the front bulkhead, the steering gear, everything was in its "correct" place in the considered overall architectural plan.

The artistic freedom granted to the designer in putting together the SLK shows on the one hand the positive points of the sports car design of 1901 while, on the other, the photo provides the clearest evidence of just what a long route there was to the thoroughbred sports car of 1996. Wilhelm Maybach, the designer responsible at that time at Daimler, developed this car series. These "Mercedes" overshadowed everything else when they appeared and raced in Nice in 1901. It was the dawn of a new automotive era. The fascination of innovation!

From then on, it was a constant cavalcade. To name but a few models, take the Mercedes-Simplex, the Benz-Parsifal, the brilliant Blitzen-Benz, the Mercedes 38/100. Everything would probably have continued like this as Daimler unveiled a new racing car in 1914 which left all others in its wake on the track in Reims (where Mercedes took a 1-2-3), but then the First World War broke out. An obligatory break therefore ensued. After the war things picked up and proceeded again slowly, and the sedan body designs throughout the world came to resemble each other very closely. Daimler and Benz then merged. The newly formed company was an absolute world-beater in three fields:

1. The victorious racing car of 1914 was like the initial charge for a series of thoroughbred sports cars which were gradually developed over the years, i.e. up to about 1939, into imposing touring cars. I'm referring here to the "S," the "K," the "SSK," the "SSKL," and then the 500 K and 540 K series. The fascination of this group is based on power and restrained beauty. Some 500 K models fitted with "Sindelfingen bodies" are now amongst the most successful cars at the most prestigious concours d'élégance around the world.

der klare Schritt von den einstigen Erfindergeist-Prototypen zu den manufakturell in kleinen Serien zusammengebauten, durchaus verkäuflichen Automobilen, der für Faszination sorgen muss. Man denke an die fast unüberwindbare Vielfalt von Schwierigkeiten, die diesen beiden Erfindern begegnet sein müssen! Es war alles neu und selbst gewisse Anleihen an den damaligen Kutschenbau können diese gigantischen Leistungen nicht schmälern. Also: Faszination durch gekonnte Problemlösung und Konsolidierung.

Ich möchte hier die Geschichte der Entstehung des ersten »Mercedes« nicht wiederholen. Eines ist aber klar: Neben der Namensgebung für die von ihm bestellte kleine Serie von Fahrzeugen hat Emil Jellinek zweifellos den Anstoß zum ersten modernen Automobil des aufbrechenden Jahrhunderts gegeben. Ein delikates Meisterwerk der technischen Ästhetik, welches im werkseigenen Museum fehlt. Das Automobil im Maßstab 1:4 hatte ich im Auftrag von Prof. Werner Breitschwerdt, damals noch Entwicklungschef, beim inzwischen verstorbenen Modellbauer Carlo Brianza

bauen lassen. Der erste Mercedes war klar gegliedert, die Achsen, der Antrieb, der sehr tief liegende und horizontal verlaufende Wagenboden, die Sitzböcke, die vordere Trennwand, die Lenkung, alles lag in einer durchdachten architektonischen Gesamtkonzeption am »richtigen« Platz.

Die künstlerische Freiheit des Autors bei der Zusammenstellung mit dem SLK zeigt einerseits, was in diesem Sportwagenkonzept von 1901 »drin« steckte, andererseits liefert diese Aufnahme den besten Beweis dafür, wie weit der Weg bis zum reinrassigen Sportwagen von 1996 doch noch gewesen wäre. Wilhelm Maybach, der damalige verantwortliche Konstrukteur bei Daimler, entwickelte diese Fahrzeugserie. Bei ihrem Erscheinen und Renneinsatz in Nizza stellten diese »Mercedes« alles in den Schatten. Eine neue Automobilära war eingeleitet worden. – Faszination durch Innovation!

Von da an geht es weiter wie ein Feuerwerk, es seien lediglich einige Fahrzeugtypen genannt, wie z. B. der Mercedes-Simplex, der Benz-Parsifal, der fulminante Blitzen-Benz, der Mercedes 38/100. Alles wäre wahrscheinlich auch so weitergegangen, 1914 stellte Daimler einen neuen Rennwagen vor, der auf dem Rundkurs von Reims alle anderen hinter sich ließ (1., 2., 3. Platz: Mercedes!) – aber dann brach die Erste Weltkrieg aus. Es gab somit eine Zwangspause. Nach diesem Krieg ging es langsam wieder weiter, die Karosserieformen der Limousinen ähnelten sich stark

par exemple la voiture à roues d'acier de Daimler. Évoquant ces objets, je les qualifierais de fascinants eu égard au génie inventeur dont ils relèvent. Ensuite? Ce sont les Benz Victoria et Velo, les voitures à courroie et Phoenix de Daimler. Des voitures qui, à proprement parler, n'ont esthétiquement rien qui puisse les rendre si désirables. Mais c'est le passage sans équivoque des anciens prototypes issus d'un génie créateur aux automobiles tout à fait commercialisables et construites en petites séries dans des manufactures, c'est ce passage qui engendre la fascination. Imaginons seulement le nombre presque incalculable de difficultés auxquelles ces deux inventeurs ont dû être confrontés! Tout était nouveau, alors, et ce ne sont pas quelques emprunts à la construction de calèches de cette époque qui peuvent minimiser leur immense mérite. Autrement dit: fascination par la maîtrise à résoudre les problèmes techniques et par la consolidation.

Il n'est pas dans mes intentions de réécrire ici l'histoire de la première « Mercedes ». Mais une chose est sûre: outre le nom de baptême donné à la petite série de voitures qu'il avait commandées, Emil Jellinek a sans aucun doute donné l'impulsion pour la première voiture moderne d'un siècle encore tout jeune. Un chef-d'œuvre raffiné d'esthétique technique dont on regrette l'absence dans notre propre musée. Sur ordre du professeur Werner Breitschwerdt, alors encore chef du développement, j'avais fait construire la voiture à l'échelle 1:4 chez le maquettiste Carlo Brianza, décédé entre-temps. La première Mercedes était clairement structurée, les essieux, la chaîne cinématique, le plancher de voiture très bas et horizontal, les banquettes, l'auvent antérieur, la direction, tout était au « bon » endroit dans une conception générale pensée dans les derniers détails sur le plan architectural.

La liberté artistique accordée à l'auteur pour le dessin de la SLK montre tout ce que renfermait déjà ce concept de voiture de sport de 1901. Mais aussi, rétrospectivement, combien le chemin allait encore être long jusqu'à la voiture de sport racée de 1996. Wilhelm Maybach, alors chef constructeur chez Daimler, a conçu cette série de voitures. Lors de leur sortie et de leur première participation à une course, à Nice en 1901, ces « Mercedes » ont ridiculisé le reste du plateau. Une nouvelle ère automobile venait d'être inaugurée. Fascination par l'innovation!

Dès lors, c'est un véritable feu d'artifice qui s'ensuit et nous nous contenterons de citer quelques types de voitures tels que la Mercedes-Simplex, la Benz-Parsifal, la météorique Blitzen-Benz, la Mercedes 38/100. Tout aurait probablement continué ainsi – en 1914, Daimler dévoila une nouvelle voiture de course qui, sur le circuit de Reims, domina toutes les autres voitures de la tête et des épaules (1re, 2e et 3e places à Mercedes!) –, mais c'est alors qu'éclata la Première Guerre mondiale. Toute compétition cessa séance tenante. Après la fin des hostilités, les choses ne redémarrèrent que lentement et les carrosseries des berlines se ressemblaient toutes dans le monde entier. C'est alors que Daimler et Benz fusionnèrent. La nouvelle firme

2. Daimler-Benz became one of the few specialists in the development and production of prestige cars. The rather conservative Stuttgart model was followed by the legendary Nürburg (Pope Pius XII's and Emperor Hirohito's Nürburgs can be admired in the Daimler-Benz Museum in Stuttgart). But the 770 K series was also highly suitable as an official car. I would claim the "fascination of authority" for this particular type of automotive monument.

3. If the victorious racing car of 1914 can be regarded as the precursor for the road-going sports car, straightforward refinement of its design would not have been quite enough to yield the spectacular W25, W25 and W54 series. These required an almost unimaginable research and development effort. This must be termed the "fascination of the will to win, accompanied by technological superiority." From 1935 to 1940 these cars dominated the racetracks of Europe, but the outbreak of the Second World War in 1939 brought this era to an abrupt close.

After 1945 the company had to adapt to new market conditions. The age of the 540 K had been ended once and for all by the devastating events of the war. The chosen vehicle for Daimler-Benz's new start was a pre-war car, a four-door sedan designated the 170 V. Different bodies were added, and new series (220, 300) expanded the range. The 300 was the new high-status car for Germany. Attractive body variations, e.g. the cabriolet and coupé, were also built. Although these cars were still reminiscent of the style of pre-war designs, they had a fascination founded on solidity and reliability. From 1952 onwards Mercedes cars once again set new standards. Having dealt in some detail with this period which was of such significance for the starmarque cars (and for myself) above, I don't intend to say much more. I shall merely summarize as follows: 1952 the 300 SL road-going sports car, 1954 the racing cars, the 300 SL Gullwing Coupé, 1957 the 300 SL Roadster. In short: fascination upon fascination.

W120 and W180, the new, modern sedans with the monocoque body using the more contemporary unibody construction are also products of this time. The fascination did not, understandably, reach the pinnacles of the sports cars. But the W120 and W180 enabled Daimler-Benz to further strengthen its reputation as a manufacturer of highclass, high-quality automobiles. The fascination of consolidation.

1959 saw the launch of the W111, now better known as the "Fin" to lay admirers and specialists alike. This was actually the first modern top-of-the-range Mercedes sedan, the true "King of the Road." The coupé was unveiled two years later: "The 1961 220 SE Coupé is one of the most beautiful Mercedes ever designed, but not only that: it is one of the most beautiful cars ever designed anywhere," I stated in 1988 in Pebble Beach to an audience of 20 leading North American motoring journalists, and none ventured any contradiction. This was followed by the "Pagoda," the W113. Then the 600 (W100), again a car for prestigious official roles. After that there was the W108, the stylistically more

auf der ganzen Welt. Daimler und Benz fusionierten. Auf drei Gebieten entwickelte sich die neu entstandene Firma Daimler-Benz zur absoluten Spitze:

1. Der siegreiche Rennwagen von 1914 war wie eine Initialzündung bei einer Reihe von reinrassigen Sportwagen, die im Laufe der Zeit, d.h. bis etwa 1939, allmählich zu imposanten Tourenwagen hin entwickelt wurden. Ich meine damit die »S«, die »K«, die »SSK«, die »SSKL«, danach die 500 K und die 540 K Baureihen. Bei dieser Gruppe kann man von Faszination durch Kraft und kühle Schönheit sprechen. Einige 500 K mit der sogenannten »Sindelfinger Karosserie« gehören zu den meist ausgezeichneten Autos auf den prestigeträchtigsten Concours d'Elegance weltweit.

2. Daimler-Benz wurde einer der wenigen Spezialisten bei der Entwicklung und beim Bau von repräsentativen Fahrzeugen. Auf den etwas bieder anmutenden Typ Stuttgart folgte der legendäre Nürburg (Papst Pius' XII und Kaiser Hirohitos Nürburgs können im Stuttgarter Daimler-Benz-Museum bewundert werden). Aber auch die Baureihe 770 K eignete sich bestens als Repräsentationsfahrzeug. Bei dieser Gattung von Automobil-Denkmälern würde ich für »Faszination durch Autorität« plädieren.

3. Wenn der siegreiche Rennwagen von 1914 als Vorläufer für die Straßensportwagen gelten kann, so wäre seine Konzeption nicht ganz geeignet gewesen, um durch einfache Weiterentwicklung zu den spektakulären W25, W125 und W154 gelangen zu können. Dafür wurde eine fast unvorstellbare Entwicklungs- und Forschungsarbeit geleistet. Hier hat man von »Faszination durch Siegeswillen, flankiert von erreichter technologischer Führerschaft« zu sprechen. Von 1935 bis 1940 waren das die Protagonisten auf den Rennstrecken Europas. Diese Ära ging mit dem Ausbruch des Zweiten Weltkrieges 1939 abrupt zu Ende.

Nach 1945 musste man sich den neuen Gegebenheiten des Marktes anpassen. Die Zeit der 540 K war endgültig durch die verheerenden Kriegsereignisse weggewischt worden. Daimler-Benz begann wieder mit dem Bau eines Vorkriegs-Fahrzeugs, einer viertürigen Limousine mit der Typbezeichnung 170 V. Es kamen Karosserievarianten dazu, neue Baureihen (220, 300) ergänzten das Programm. Der 300er war der neue »high status car« für Deutschland. Davon wurden auch schöne Karosserievarianten als Cabriolet bzw. als Coupé gebaut. Stilistisch noch an den Fahrzeugen der Vorkriegszeit orientiert, faszinieren diese Autos hauptsächlich ihrer Solidität und Zuverlässigkeit wegen. Ab 1952 setzen Mercedes-Autos wieder neue Zeichen. Ich werde mich an dieser Stelle nicht länger fassen; ich habe zu Beginn meiner Ausführungen über diese, für die Autos mit dem Stern (und für mich) so bedeutende Zeit ausführlich berichtet. Ich fasse nur zusammen: 1952 die 300 SL Straßensportwagen, 1954 die Rennwagen, das 300 SL Flügeltüren-Coupé, 1957 der 300 SL Roadster. In Summa: Faszination über Faszination.

W120 und W180, die neuen, modernen Limousinen mit selbsttragender Karosserie und in der zeitgemäßen Pontonform sind auch Produkte dieser Zeit, die Faszination

baptisée Daimler-Benz devint ensuite championne absolue dans trois domaines:

1. Les voitures de course victorieuses de 1914 ont constitué le premier jalon de toute une série de voitures de sport racées qui, au fil du temps, c'est-à-dire jusqu'aux environs de 1939, se sont muées graduellement en d'imposantes voitures de tourisme. Je fais allusion ici aux S, K, SSK, SSKL, ainsi qu'aux séries 500 K et 540 K. Pour ces voitures, on peut parler de fascination par la force et la beauté froide. Quelques 500 K avec la « carrosserie de Sindelfingen » comptent parmi les voitures qui remportent le plus souvent des distinctions lors des concours d'élégance les plus prestigieux du monde.

2. Daimler-Benz est devenu l'un des rares spécialistes pour la conception et la construction de voitures de représentation. La Stuttgart aux lignes plutôt bourgeoises a été suivie par la légendaire Nürburg (les Nürburg du pape Pie XII et de l'empereur Hirohito peuvent être admirées au musée Daimler-Benz de Stuttgart). Mais la gamme 770 K, aussi, a été une base idéale pour les voitures de représentation. Pour cette catégorie de « monuments automobiles », je parlerai de « fascination par l'autorité ».

3. À quiconque prétend que la voiture de course victorieuse de 1914 est le précurseur des voitures de sport routières, on pourrait rétorquer que sa conception n'était pas parfaite au point de donner naissance, par simple perfectionnement, aux spectaculaires W25, W125 et W154. Il a fallu pour cela accomplir des efforts difficilement imaginables de développement et de recherche. Ici, on peut parler de « fascination par la volonté de vaincre, avec comme facteur concomitant le leadership technologique acquis ». De 1935 à 1940, elles furent de grands acteurs sur les circuits d'Europe. Cette ère s'acheva brutalement lorsque éclata la Seconde Guerre mondiale, en 1939.

Après 1945, il a fallu s'adapter aux nouvelles donnes du marché. Les hostilités et leurs séquelles traumatiques mirent un point final aussi définitif que brutal à l'ère de la 540 K. Faisant feu de tout bois, Daimler-Benz a redémarré sur la base d'une voiture d'avant-guerre, une berline à quatre portes appelée 170 V. Elle reçut différentes variantes de carrosserie et des gammes nouvelles (220, 300) vinrent compléter le programme. La 300 était la *high status car* (nouvelle voiture de haut standing) de l'Allemagne. On en construisit aussi de magnifiques dérivés en tant que cabriolets et coupés. Esthétiquement encore très proches des voitures de l'avant-guerre, ces automobiles fascinent essentiellement par leur solidité et leur fiabilité. Pour Mercedes et ses voitures, 1952 est l'année inaugurale d'une ère nouvelle. Résumons: en 1952, les 300 SL, de sport pour la route; en 1954, les voitures de course, le coupé 300 SL à ailes papillon et, en 1957, la 300 SL Roadster. *Summa summarum*: fascination et encore fascination.

Les W120 et W180, les nouvelles limousines modernes à carrosserie autoporteuse et à la forme ponton plus moderne sont aussi des produits de cette époque, mais la fascination n'atteint bien évidemment pas les sommets de celle des voitures de sport. Toutefois, avec ces limou-

convincing replacement for the "Fin." W115/114; C111/I and C111/II, the Wankel prototypes; R and C107, the SL Roadster and Coupé; the W116 as the new S-Class; the W123 with its coupé and station wagon variants.

A long period, from 1959 to 1977. What is the fascination of the cars from this period based on? One thing is certain: Daimler-Benz was able to further consolidate, expand and indeed claim as its own the role of the developer and manufacturer of unique cars in terms of safety, reliability and stability of value. The fascination of mastery of its art?

The 1977 C111/III prototype had been developed as a design study in aerodynamics. The W126, the S-Class of 1979 and a number of other cars developed subsequently, such as the 1981 S-Class coupé (the SEC), the 1983 190 series (W201), and the W124 (the "mid-range" series with all its variants) from 1985 onwards, profited from this. This period would be summed up for me by "the fascination of a perfect marriage of function and form."

The "fascination of a successfully interpreted myth" characterized the new SL (R129) in 1989. No more needs to be said.

The "fascination of authority" already encountered with reference to the Nürburg and 770 K models also applies to the S-Class and the S-Class coupé of 1991/92. With regard to the C-Class and the station wagon derived from it, I would refer to the "fascination of restraint." With the E-Class, by contrast, I would prefer to speak of the "fascination of freshness and innovation."

SLK, CLK and A-Class: three very different cars but which have one thing in common, the "fascination of design."

Bruno Alfieri wrote: "Mercedes-Benz cars can irrefutably be considered the most recent, and the most exciting, metamorphosis of the Classicist idea, even though viewed in a global creative scenario which includes art, architecture, photography, fashion, cinema, scenography and industrial design."[2]

---

[1] Leo Levine, head of press of Mercedes-Benz of North America in the 1980s (until 1989). Quote from an MBNA brochure, *Mercedes-Benz Design,* by Bruno Sacco, 1988.
[2] Bruno Alfieri, automobile historian, editor of automotive literature. Quote from *Form. Mercedes-Benz,* Automobilia, 1995, Milan.

[1] Leo Levine, Presseleiter von Mercedes-Benz of North America in den 1980er Jahren (bis 1989). Das Zitat stammt aus einer Broschüre der MBNA, *Mercedes-Benz Design,* by Bruno Sacco, 1988.
[2] Bruno Alfieri, Automobilhistoriker, Herausgeber von Automobilliteratur. Zitat aus *Form. Mercedes-Benz,* Automobilia, 1995, Mailand.

[1] Leo Levine, attaché de presse de Mercedes-Benz of North America en 1980 (jusqu'en 1989). La citation est tirée de MBNA, *Mercedes-Benz Design, by Bruno Sacco,* 1988.
[2] Bruno Alfieri, historien de l'automobile, éditeur de livres sur l'automobile. Citation tirée de *Form. Mercedes-Benz,* Automobilia, 1995, Milan.

---

erreicht die Spitzen der Sportwagen nicht, begreiflicherweise. Aber mit dem W120 und dem W180 konnte Daimler-Benz seinen Ruf als Erbauer hochklassiger, hochwertiger Automobile weiter stärken. Faszination durch Festigung der Positionen.

1959 wird der W111 vorgestellt. Inzwischen als »die Heckflosse« besser bei Laien und Spezialisten bekannt. In der Tat die erste moderne Mercedes-Limousine der Oberklasse. Die wahre »Königin der Autobahn«. Zwei Jahre später kommt das Coupé: »The 1961 220 SE coupé is one of the most beautiful Mercedes ever designed, but not only that: it is one of the most beautiful cars ever designed anywhere«, sagte ich 1988 in Pebble Beach vor 20 fahrenden nordamerikanischen Journalisten, ohne auf irgendeinen Widerspruch zu stoßen. Dann kommt die »Pagode«, der W113. Danach der 600er (W100), wieder ein Auto für die große Repräsentation. Dann der W108, die stilistisch überzeugendere Ablösung der »Heckflosse«. W115/114; C111/I und C111/II, die Wankel-Prototypen; R und C107, die SL-Roadster und Coupé; der W116 als neue »S-Klasse«; der W123 mit seinen Varianten als Coupé und Stationswagen.

Eine lange Periode, von 1959 bis 1977. Worin besteht die Faszination, die aus den Automobilen dieser Zeit hervorgehen soll? Eines ist schon klar: Daimler-Benz konnte die Rolle des Entwicklers und Herstellers einzigartiger Fahrzeuge in Punkto Sicherheit, Zuverlässigkeit und Wertbeständigkeit weiter ausbauen, stärken und für sich in Anspruch nehmen. Faszination durch Beherrschung?

Der Prototyp C111/III von 1977 war als Aerodynamik-orientierte Designstudie entwickelt worden. Der W126, die S-Klasse von 1979 und mehrere danach entwickelte Autos, wie z. B. das Coupé der S-Klasse 1981 (der SEC), der 190er 1983 (W201), der W124 (die »Mittelklasse« mit allen Varianten) ab 1985, profitierten davon. Für diese Periode würde für mich gelten: »Faszination durch perfekte Abstimmung von Form und Funktion«.

»Faszination durch gelungene Interpretation eines Mythos« charakterisiert 1989 den neuen SL (R129). Weitere Worte wären hier überflüssig.

Die uns bereits bei den Nürburgs und 770 K begegnete »Faszination durch Autorität« trifft auch für die S-Klasse und das Coupé der S-Klasse von 1991/92 zu. Bei der C-Klasse und dem davon abgeleiteten Stationswagen würde ich »Faszination durch Zurückhaltung« feststellen. Nicht so bei der E-Klasse, da möchte ich von »Faszination durch Frische und Innovation« sprechen.

SLK, CLK und A-Klasse: Drei sehr verschiedene Automobile. Eines haben sie gemeinsam: »Faszination durch Design«.

Zitat von Bruno Alfieri: »Es ist unwiderlegbar, dass Mercedes-Benz-Automobile als die jüngste und offensichtlichste Metamorphose der Klassik bezeichnet werden können; dies gilt auch, wenn man sie im Hinblick auf das gesamte kreative Umfeld betrachtet, das sich aus Kunst, Architektur, Fotografie, Mode, Film, Bühnenbild und Industriedesign zusammensetzt.«[2]

---

sines, Daimler-Benz a pu encore cimenter sa réputation de constructeurs d'automobiles de très grande qualité et de très grande valeur. La fascination par la consolidation de sa réputation.

Année 1959: présentation de la W111, entre-temps mieux connue des profanes et des spécialistes sous le surnom de «Mercedes à ailerons». En fait, la première berline Mercedes moderne du segment supérieur. La véritable «reine de l'autoroute». Deux ans plus tard arrive le coupé: «Le Coupé 220 SE de 1961 est l'une des plus belles Mercedes jamais conçues, mais pas seulement: c'est l'une des plus belles voitures jamais conçues dans le monde», ai-je déclaré en 1988 à Pebble Beach devant vingt des plus grands journalistes automobiles d'Amérique du Nord, sans rencontrer la moindre contradiction. Vint ensuite la «Pagode», la W113. Et, après elle, la 600 (W100), encore une voiture de grand standing. Puis la W108, remplaçante, autrement plus séduisante sur le plan esthétique, de la «Mercedes à ailerons», et les W115/114, C111/I et C111/II; les prototypes Wankel; la R et C107, la SL roadster et coupé; la W116 comme nouvelle «Classe S»; la W123 avec ses variantes coupé et break.

C'est une longue période, qui s'étend de 1959 à 1977. En quoi consiste la fascination censée émaner des voitures de cette époque? Une chose est déjà claire: Daimler-Benz a pu accentuer, renforcer et revendiquer pour elle-même le rôle de concepteur et de constructeur de voitures uniques en leur genre en termes de sécurité, de fiabilité et de stabilité de leur valeur. Fascination par la maîtrise?

Le prototype C111/III de 1977 a été conçu en tant qu'étude de style privilégiant l'aérodynamique. La W126, la Classe S de 1979 et plusieurs autres voitures mises au point plus tard, par exemple le coupé SEC de la Classe S de 1981, la 190 de 1983 (W201), la W124 (la «classe intermédiaire» avec toutes ses variantes) à partir de 1985 en ont profité. Pour cette période, j'invoquerais la devise: «Fascination par l'harmonie parfaite de la forme et de la fonction.»

«Fascination par l'interprétation réussie d'un mythe», voici ce qui caractérise, en 1989, la nouvelle SL (R129). Tout autre commentaire est ici superflu.

La «fascination par l'autorité» que nous avons déjà évoquée pour les Nürburg et 770 K vaut aussi pour la Classe S et la version coupé de la Classe S de 1991–1992. Pour la Classe C et les breaks qui en sont les dérivés, je parlerais de «fascination par la discrétion». Cela n'est pas le cas de la Classe E, pour laquelle je pense plutôt à la «fascination par la fraîcheur et l'innovation».

SLK, CLK et Classe A: trois automobiles en aucun point comparables, sauf un: la «fascination par le design».

Citons Bruno Alfieri: «Que les automobiles Mercedes-Benz puissent être considérées comme la métamorphose la plus récente et la plus manifeste de l'idée du classicisme ne peut guère être contesté, même si elles sont vues dans le panorama créateur global comprenant l'art, l'architecture, la photographie, la mode, le cinéma, la scénographie et le design industriel[2].»

Glittering years—but not always
Lichtjahre – aber nicht immer
Des années de lumière – mais avec des zones d'ombre

In many ways the history of Mercedes-Benz is synonymous with the history of the automobile, from its chugging, awkward beginnings to the most technologically sophisticated forms of the vehicle, which has given us unprecedented mobility in unprecedented measure. In addition, Mercedes cars were always witnesses to their age—just as the brand in turn shaped that age. Even their ever-changing names represent different phases, identify key players, and reveal change, continuity in change, and sometimes wrong turnings.

The Benz & Cie. Rheinische Gasmotorenfabrik AG, Mannheim, was launched into the world on 8 May 1899. Founding father Karl Benz (1844–1929) had received the Reich patent number 37,435 for his "Patent Motor Car" on 29 January 1886. This spindly three-wheeler became famous thanks to the bold ride taken by his wife Berta Benz to Pforzheim on a fine August day in 1888, rigorous proof that the self-moving vehicle worked, and a demonstration of what it could do. Berta's pioneering feat was inspirational: by 1900, Benz & Cie. had become the largest car factory in the world. In 1904, profits gently started rolling in. In March 1914, Benz shares were introduced onto the stock exchange, and were already being traded in the free market at 226 percent. With the outbreak of the First World War, production folded. The firm emerged reasonably unscathed from the trials and tribulations of inflation in the early twenties, because a car with the reputation of a Benz was a good investment. Nevertheless, the business could not on its own save itself from the octopus arms of the speculator Jakob Schapiro, who by 1924 had contrived to become the major shareholder, with 60 percent of the shares.

So, too, the Daimler-Motoren-Gesellschaft was notarized on 28 November 1890. The titular saint was Gottlieb Daimler (1834–1900). Whereas Karl Benz thought of himself as the steward of the vehicle as an organically knit unit, Daimler worked as an exponent of the high-speed internal combustion engine, with which he helped an American-type four-wheeled carriage make its first independent leap in the fall of 1886. The symbiosis of engine and chassis, however, was proceeding apace, with Daimler's congenial partner Wilhelm Maybach (1846–1929) as the

In vielerlei Hinsicht ist die Geschichte von Mercedes-Benz synonym mit der Geschichte des Automobils, von den tuckernd-unbeholfenen Anfängen bis hin zu den technisch ausgefeiltesten Ausformungen des Fahrzeugs, das uns individuelle Beweglichkeit in nie gekanntem Maße geschenkt hat. Immer auch waren Autos von Mercedes Zeugnisse der Zeit – so wie die Marke ihrerseits die Zeit geprägt hat. Schon ihre sich wandelnden Namen bilden Aggregatzustände ab, benennen Schlüsselfiguren, Wechsel, Dauer im Wechsel und sogar Irrwege.

Da ist die Benz & Cie. Rheinische Gasmotorenfabrik AG, Mannheim, in dieser Form ins Leben gerufen am 8. Mai 1899. Gründervater Karl Benz (1844–1929) hat das Reichspatent Nr. 37435 für seinen »Patent-Motorwagen« am 29. Januar 1886 erhalten. Berühmt wird das spillerige Dreirad durch den kühnen Ausritt von Benz-Gattin Berta nach Pforzheim an einem schönen Augusttag des Jahres 1888, stringenter Beweis dafür, dass das selbstbewegliche Vehikel funktioniert und wozu es fähig ist. Bertas Pioniertat zündet: 1900 ist die Benz & Cie die größte Autofabrik der Welt. 1904 beginnen sich sanfte Gewinne einzustellen. Im März 1914 wird an der Börse die Benz-Aktie eingeführt, im freien Verkehr bereits für 226 Prozent gehandelt. Mit Kriegsbeginn knickt die Produktion ein. Die Irrungen und Wirrungen der Inflation Anfang der Zwanziger übersteht man halbwegs unbeschadet, weil ein Auto vom Renommee eines Benz eine gute Kapitalanlage ist. Dennoch kann sich das Unternehmen nicht aus eigener Kraft aus den Krakenarmen des Spekulanten Jakob Schapiro befreien, der sich 1924 mit 60 Prozent der Anteile zum Großaktionär emporgemogelt hat.

Da ist die Daimler-Motoren-Gesellschaft, notariell beurkundet am 28. November 1890. Namenspatron ist Gottlieb Daimler (1834–1900). Wo sich Karl Benz als Sachwalter des Kraftwagens als organisch zusammengewachsener Einheit versteht, wirkt Daimler als Exponent des schnell laufenden Verbrennungsmotors, mit dem er im Herbst 1886 einer vierrädrigen Kutsche Typ Americain auf die eigenständigen Sprünge hilft. Die Symbiose von Trieb- und Fahrwerk schreitet indessen zügig voran, mit Daimlers kongenialem Partner Wilhelm Maybach

À bien des égards, l'histoire de Mercedes-Benz correspond à celle de l'automobile, depuis ses débuts poussifs jusqu'à la conception de véhicules dotés de formes approchant la perfection technique et offrant une liberté de mouvement inconnue jusqu'alors. Les voitures Mercedes ont toujours été les témoins de leur temps, tout comme la marque elle-même a fait époque. Ses différentes appellations évoquent des situations, des personnages clés, des changements, la durée dans le changement et même des erreurs de parcours.

La Benz & Cie Rheinische Gasmotorenfabrik AG à Mannheim fut fondée le 8 mai 1899. Le père fondateur, Karl Benz (1844–1929), avait obtenu le brevet impérial n° 37 435 pour son «Patent-Motorwagen», le 29 janvier 1886. Le frêle tricycle devint célèbre grâce à l'audacieuse promenade de Berta, l'épouse de Benz, qui la mena à Pforzheim par une belle journée d'août 1888, preuve évidente que le véhicule automobile fonctionnait et qu'il était performant. L'acte pionnier de Berta créa l'étincelle: en 1900, Benz & Cie était la plus grande usine automobile au monde. En 1904, de faibles bénéfices commencèrent à apparaître. En mars 1914, l'action Benz fut introduite en bourse; sur le marché libre, elle était déjà négociée à 226 % de sa valeur. Cependant, le début de la guerre entraîna une chute de la production. Au début des années 1920, les erreurs et la confusion résultant de l'inflation furent surmontées sans trop de difficultés car une voiture jouissant de la renommée de la Benz était un bon placement. Toutefois, l'entreprise ne put se libérer seule des tentacules du spéculateur Jakob Schapiro qui, s'étant approprié 60 % des parts en 1924, était devenu le plus gros actionnaire.

La Daimler-Motoren-Gesellschaft fut enregistrée par acte notarié le 28 novembre 1890. Le patron était Gottlieb Daimler (1834–1900). Alors que Karl Benz envisageait l'automobile comme une unité constituée d'éléments interactifs et indissociables, Daimler, considéré comme le chef de file du moteur à combustion rapide, n'hésita pas à équiper un buggy américain à quatre roues et le rendit autonome, à l'automne 1886. La symbiose entre le moteur et le châssis progressa rapidement sous la houlette du partenaire de Daimler, le génial Wilhelm Maybach (1846–1929). Sa gamme Simplex, en particulier,

Gottlieb Daimler (1834–1900) testing a "first practicable four-wheeled automobile" in 1886.

Gottlieb Daimler (1834–1900) erprobt 1886 ein »erstes vierrädriges gebrauchsfähiges Automobil«.

Gottlieb Daimler (1834–1900) expérimente en 1886 une « première automobile viable à quatre roues ».

The genius who preferred to stay out of the limelight: Wilhelm Maybach (1846–1929).

Der Genius, der lieber im Hintergrund wirkt: Wilhelm Maybach (1846–1929).

Le génie qui ne s'est jamais placé sous les feux de la rampe : Wilhelm Maybach (1846–1929).

Lest we forget: even 50 years after the death of the founding father, it was a privilege to work "at Benz."

In wacher Erinnerung: Noch 50 Jahre nach dem Tod des Gründervaters ist es ein Privileg, »beim Benz« zu arbeiten.

Toujours présent dans les esprits : 50 ans après la mort du père fondateur, travailler « chez Benz » est un privilège.

driving force. Above all, his Simplex series was already producing real cars that were flat, wide, strong, and fast. It made a spectacular debut thanks to the convincing appearance of its predecessor "Sports and Touring Car 35 hp" at the Nice-Salon-Nice race of 1901, as the model launched by the bustling consul Emil Jellinek. The brand name "Mercedes"—originally the sonorous name of Jellinek's little daughter—had been protected by law since 1902.

Between 1910 and 1913, Daimler-Motoren-Gesellschaft generated a net profit of 8.66 million marks. 70 percent of all Mercedes were exported. The triple success of the white Daimler racing car 18/100 at the Grand Prix de France on 4 July 1914 was the icing on the cake. The First World War spurred uninhibited growth, if only because of military requirements, but things did not continue so well in the twenties. The DMG clumsily planned a route into the market with expensive supercharger models. In the end it felt the need for support, and remembered (without any particular feelings of affection) its old rival, Benz. Not only was the hyphenated name sealed after two years of engagement, with the wedding of the weakened giant on 28 June 1926, but also the common emblem created, into which the two brand names merged. The Daimler laurel, including the new company name, Mercedes-Benz, now encircled the Benz star, standing for man's power over air, water, and earth.

Wilhelm Kissel, architect of the integration, developed the firm on the basis of rationalization. The phalanx

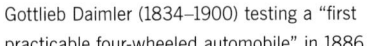

1916

(1846–1929) als treibender Kraft. Vor allem seine Baureihe Simplex bringt schon richtige Autos hervor, flach, breit, stark und schnell. Sie wird spektakulär in Szene gesetzt durch den überzeugenden Auftritt ihres Vorläufers »Sport- und Tourenwagen 35 PS« beim Rennen Nizza-Salon-Nizza von 1901, wie das Modell selber angestoßen von dem umtriebigen Konsul Emil Jellinek. Die Wortmarke Mercedes – ursprünglich der klangvolle Name von Jellineks Töchterchen – ist seit 1902 gesetzlich geschützt.

Zwischen 1910 und 1913 erwirtschaftet die DMG einen Reingewinn von 8,66 Millionen Mark. 70 Prozent aller Mercedes werden exportiert. Der Dreifach-Sieg der weißen Daimler-Renner 18/100 beim Grand Prix de France am 4. Juli 1914 wirkt wie ein Ausrufezeichen unter etwas, das ohnehin schon jedermann weiß. Dem Ersten Weltkrieg vermag man schon wegen des Heeresbedarfs schier ungehemmtes Wachstum abzugewinnen, beweist indessen in den zwanziger Jahren nicht immer ein glückliches Händchen. So plant die DMG etwa mit teuren Kompressormodellen ungeschickt am Markt vorbei. Am Ende ist auch sie stark anlehnungsbedürftig und entsinnt sich ohne sonderliche Zärtlichkeit des alten Rivalen Benz. Nicht nur der Bindestrich besiegelt nach zweijähriger Verlobungszeit die Hochzeit der geschwächten Elefanten am 28. Juni 1926, sondern auch das gemeinsame Emblem, zu dem die Markenzeichen verschmelzen: Der Daimler-Lorbeer, in den der neue Firmenname

1926

était déjà constituée de véritables automobiles, basses, larges, robustes et rapides. Elle fut mise en scène de façon spectaculaire par la prestation du modèle précurseur, la « Voiture de sport et de tourisme 35 hp » – comme le modèle conduit par l'actif consul austro-hongrois Emil Jellinek en personne –, lors de la course Nice-Salon-Nice de 1901. Dès 1902, la marque Mercedes – prénom aux consonances mélodieuses de la fille de Jellinek – fut déposée. Entre 1910 et 1913, la DMG généra un bénéfice net de 8,66 millions de Marks. 70 % des Mercedes étaient alors exportées. La triple victoire des bolides blancs Daimler 18/100 lors du Grand Prix de France, le 4 juillet 1914, accentua ce que, de toute façon, tout le monde savait déjà. En raison des seuls besoins de l'armée, la Première Guerre mondiale généra une croissance presque sans limites de l'entreprise ; en revanche, dans les années 1920, quelques maladresses furent commises. Ainsi, DMG ne convainquit pas le marché avec ses coûteux modèles à compresseur. Finalement, ayant besoin de soutien, DMG se souvint sans tendresse particulière de son vieux rival Benz. Le 28 juin 1926, après deux ans de fiançailles, le mariage des deux éléphants affaiblis fut scellé. Un trait d'union liait désormais les deux noms ainsi qu'un emblème commun, constitué des deux logos jadis autonomes : les lauriers de Daimler dans lesquels était inscrit le nouveau nom de la firme, Mercedes-Benz, cernaient désormais l'étoile Benz, synonyme de la puissance de l'homme, dans les airs, sur l'eau et sur terre.

Berta Benz stopping to refuel at a drugstore in Wiesloch during her long journey in 1888.

Während ihrer Fernfahrt 1888 legt Berta Benz an einer Apotheke in Wiesloch einen Tankhalt ein.

Durant son excursion de 1888, Berta Benz refait le plein devant une pharmacie de Wiesloch.

of 18,124 employees in 1927 had shrunk to a smaller band of 8,850 by 1932. Automobile production had long since been concentrated in Untertürkheim, with lorry manufacturing in Gaggenau and body work in Sindelfingen. Even selection had been streamlined, to the detriment of the dowry brought by Benz, which was completely scuttled. For reasons of prestige, the supercharger stayed in the program. When its creator and co-designer Ferdinand

Mercedes-Benz eingelassen ist, umkränzt nun den Benz-Stern, der für die Macht des Menschen über Luft, Wasser und Erde steht.

Wilhelm Kissel, Architekt der Integration, baut auf Rationalisierung. Die Phalanx von 18 124 Beschäftigten anno 1927 schrumpft bis 1932 zum Fähnlein von 8850. Da sind längst die Pkw-Produktion in Untertürkheim, die Lkw-Fertigung in Gaggenau, der Karosseriebau in Sindelfingen konzentriert. Auch das Sortiment wird verschlankt, zu Lasten der Benz-Mitgift, die vollständig in der Versenkung verschwindet. Aus Prestigegründen belässt man die Kompressorwagen im Programm. Als ihr Schöpfer und Mitgestalter Ferdinand Porsche (1875–1951) seinen Dienst bei Daimler-Benz 1928 im Zorn quittiert, bleiben als Vermächtnis die aufgeladenen Modelle 400 und 630 K sowie die gefeierte Typenreihe S, SS und SSK. Am 25. Oktober 1929 kollabieren die Börsen. Mercedes-Benz lässt inmitten der allgemeinen Misere zunächst relativ wenig Federn: Jeder zehnte Wagen im Reich trägt den Stern. Überdies rundet man auf dem Pariser Salon 1931 die Produktpalette nach unten mit dem Hoffnungsträger Typ 170 ab, Premiere zugleich für die Schwingachse. Ende 1932 jedoch weist die DBAG Verluste von 13,4 Millionen aus, rund ein Drittel des Grundkapitals.

Mit der Machtergreifung am 30. Januar 1933 beginnt ein regelrechter Boom, von Auto-Freund Adolf Hitler mit Steuervergünstigungen, Sportförderung und dem Ausblick auf üppigen Straßenbau angefacht. Vorstandsvorsitzer Kissel fährt einen kalkulierten Schmusekurs, belohnt etwa am 20. April 1939 des »Führers« Vorliebe für die Stuttgarter Firma und die tatkräftige Unterstützung des Systems im Rennsport zu dessen 50. Geburtstag mit dem Großen Mercedes 770 offen, noch ein paar hierarchische Stufen über den Pracht-Mobilen 500 K und 540 K. Die beiden neuen Stars im Sortiment auf der Berliner Automobil-Ausstellung im Februar 1936 geben sich eher volksnah: der derb gewirkte 170 V und der gleichermaßen knorrige und vernehmlich dieselnde 260 D. 1938, an der Schwelle zum

Joint advertising by Daimler and Benz.

Gemeinsame Werbung von Daimler und Benz.

Publicité commune de Daimler et Benz.

Wilhelm Kissel, acteur de la fusion, se basait sur la rationalisation et les 18 124 employés de 1927 ne furent plus que 8850 en 1932. Depuis longtemps, la production était concentrée à Untertürkheim pour les voitures, à Gaggenau pour les camions et à Sindelfingen pour les carrosseries. Les gammes furent également réduites au détriment de la dot de Benz qui fut totalement engloutie. Pour des raisons de prestige, les voitures à compresseur furent cependant conservées au catalogue. Lorsque Ferdinand Porsche (1875–1951) quitta, furieux, Daimler-Benz en 1928, il laissa en héritage les puissants modèles 400 et 630 K, ainsi que les

German officers during the Russian campaign in a Mercedes-Benz L1500A. They obviously seem in high spirits.

Deutsche Offiziere während des Russlandfeldzugs in einem Mercedes-Benz L1500A. Die Laune ist offenbar glänzend.

Officiers allemands pendant la campagne de Russie à bord d'un Mercedes-Benz L1500A. L'humeur est apparemment joyeuse.

Untertürkheim factory after the air raid on 5 September 1944.

Werk Untertürkheim nach dem Angriff am 5. September 1944.

L'usine d'Untertürkheim après les bombardements du 5 septembre 1944

Porsche (1875–1951) left his service with Daimler-Benz in 1928 after a huge row, he bequeathed the supercharged models 400 and 630 K as well as the acclaimed series s, ss, and ssk. On 25 October 1929, the stock exchanges collapsed. In the midst of general misery, the feathers of Mercedes-Benz at first remained relatively unruffled: one in ten cars in the country carried the Mercedes star. Moreover, at the Paris Salon of 1931, the product range was extended downward with the type 170, bearer of hope; the oscillation axis was also premiered. At the end of 1932, however, DBAG showed losses of 13.4 million marks, approximately one third of the capital stock.

With Hitler's seizure of power on 30 January 1933 a boom time began, fuelled by the car-friendly Führer, with tax breaks, the promotion of sport, and a lavish road building program. Board chairman Kissel adopted a calculated stance of friendship toward Hitler and on 20 April 1939 rewarded the preference of the Führer for the Stuttgart-based company and his active support of the system on the 50th anniversary of motor racing with the Großer Mercedes 770, another level or two above the de luxe mobiles 500 K and 540 K. The two new stars in the range displayed at the Berlin Motor Show in February 1936 had an appearance that suited them more to ordinary folk: there was the coarsely modeled 170 V, and the equally gnarled and distinctly diesel model 260 D. In 1938, on the threshold of the Second World War, 42,687 Mercedes vehicles rolled off the production lines. In 1944, however, passenger car production of DBAG amounted to one vehicle. In the meantime, production had covered the entire gamut of fighting craft. In the second half of that year, the knock-out blow finally arrived: after heavy Allied bombing raids, Kissel's successor Wilhelm Haspel looked out over a smoldering wasteland of ruins. Between the rise and fall of Daimler-Benz AG, not even 20 years had elapsed.

The new beginning was based on a tried and tested formula: the models 170 S and D turned out to be

Now we are someone again: the Mercedes range of 1952 also reveals growing prosperity.

Wir sind wieder wer: Die Mercedes-Palette von 1952 bildet auch wachsenden Wohlstand ab.

Nous sommes de nouveau quelqu'un: le programme Mercedes 1952 est aussi le reflet d'une prospérité croissante.

Jahrhundert-Desaster Nummer zwei, verlassen 42 687 Mercedes-Fahrzeuge die Bänder. 1944 hingegen wird sich die Pkw-Produktion der DBAG auf ein Fahrzeug belaufen. In der Zwischenzeit hat die Fertigung die ganze Klaviatur des Kampfhandwerks abgedeckt. In der zweiten Hälfte jenes Jahres folgt schließlich der Knock-out: Kissel-Nachfolger Wilhelm Haspel blickt nach schweren alliierten Bombenangriffen auf eine schwelende Trümmerwüste. Zwischen Aufstieg und Fall der Daimler-Benz AG lagen nicht einmal 20 Jahre.

Der Neubeginn fußt auf Bewährtem: Als wahre Renner in der Gunst des Publikums erweisen sich die Modelle 170 S und D auf der Internationalen Exportmesse Hannover 1949. Die Sechszylinder 220 und 300 auf der Frankfurter IAA 1951 hingegen gehören schon zu den gehobenen Requisiten des knospenden Wirtschaftswunders, während Juan Manuel Fangios Formel-1-Titel 1954

gammes S, SS et SSK, qu'il avait conçues. Le 25 octobre 1929, les bourses s'effondrèrent. Au cœur de la misère générale, Mercedes-Benz souffrit relativement peu: dans le Reich, une voiture sur dix portait l'étoile. En outre, lors du salon de Paris de 1931, la gamme de produits fut limitée à la série 170 porteuse d'espoir – les premières automobiles à essieu oscillant. À la fin de 1932, le déficit de DBAG s'élevait à 13,4 millions de Marks, environ un tiers du capital social.

La prise du pouvoir par Adolf Hitler, amateur d'automobiles, le 30 janvier 1933, donna lieu à un véritable boom, favorisé par des avantages fiscaux, la promotion du sport et la perspective d'un réseau routier bien structuré. Le PDG Kissel courtisa le régime de façon calculée et en fut notamment récompensé le 20 avril 1939 par la préférence du «Führer» pour l'entreprise de Stuttgart. Pour son 50e anniversaire, avec la Grosser Mercedes 770, quelques échelons hiérarchiques au-dessus des voitures de luxe 500 K et 540 K, la firme gagna ouvertement le soutien actif du régime dans la course automobile. Les deux nouvelles stars, la 170 V à l'aspect robuste et la tout aussi sévère 260 D fonctionnant au diesel, présentées au salon de l'automobile de Berlin en février 1936, se voulaient proches du peuple. En 1938, à la veille du deuxième désastre du siècle, 42 687 véhicules Mercedes sortirent des chaînes de montage. En revanche, en 1944, la fabrication de voitures de DBAG se limita à un véhicule. Entre-temps, la production avait couvert tout le registre de l'armement. Durant la seconde moitié de cette année-là, ce fut finalement la débâcle: après un important bombardement allié, c'est un champ de ruines que le successeur de Kissel, Wilhelm Haspel, fut amené à contempler. Entre l'essor et la chute de Daimler-Benz AG, il s'était écoulé moins de vingt ans.

Le nouveau départ s'appuya sur les valeurs sûres: les véritables succès auprès du public furent les modèles 170 S et D présentés lors du salon international de l'exportation à Hanovre en 1949. Lors de l'IAA à Francfort en 1951, les six cylindres 220 et 300 comptaient déjà parmi les facteurs hauts de gamme d'un miracle économique débutant. En

Sustainable solutions: series L 319 transporters in 1955 and an LK 338 truck from the short-hood series introduced in 1959.

Tragfähige Lösungen: Transporter der Baureihe L 319 anno 1955 und ein LK 338 Kipper der 1959 eingeführten Baureihe mit Kurzhaube.

Moyens de transport: Fourgons de la série L 319 de 1955 et un camion benne de la série LK 338 à capot court introduite en 1959.

Introduction   13

In 1973, Mercedes-Benz extends its range of diesel cars with the 240 D, *the* money spinner in the taxi trade.

1973 erweitert Mercedes-Benz das Spektrum seiner Diesel-PKW mit dem 240 D. Er wird ein Renner im Taxi-Gewerbe.

En 1973, Mercedes-Benz élargit sa gamme de diesel avec la 240 D, un franc succès auprès des chauffeurs de taxi.

real favorites in public opinion at the 1949 Hanover International Export Trade Fair. The six-cylinder 220 and 300 at the Frankfurt International Motor Show of 1951, however, were already among the most sophisticated contributions to the budding economic miracle, while Juan Manuel Fangio's Formula 1 title in 1954 and 1955 in Mercedes-Benz cars bore witness to the possibilities dormant in the renaissance of the company. The Pontoon Pioneer Type 180 became a technical landmark and milestone in 1953. The philosophy of the product rested on two pillars: whereas in the case of commercial vehicles the whole range, from light- through heavy-duty trucks, was developed, passenger cars were aimed squarely at the upper-middle and upper classes. Only much later did the range extend to lower social strata with the 190 E (1982), the A-Class (1997), and the Smart (1998). Between 1950 and 1960, passenger car production increased from 33,609 cars to 122,684. In the sixties, Daimler-Benz AG floated almost intact across the swelling waves. Domestic sales grew from 1.444 billion marks in

Columbus's egg: the tiny space miracle, Smart.

Ei des Kolumbus: das winzige Raumwunder Smart

L'œuf de Colomb: la miraculeuse et minuscule Smart.

und 1955 auf Mercedes-Benz von den Möglichkeiten zeugen, die in der Renaissance der Firma schlummern. Zum technischen Mark- und Meilenstein wird der Ponton-Pionier Typ 180 von 1953. Die Produkt-Philosophie ruht auf zwei Säulen: Während man bei den Nutzfahrzeugen die ganze Bandbreite zwischen dem Leicht-Laster und dem Schwertransporter bespielt, hat man bei den Pkw die obere Mittelklasse und die Oberklasse im Visier. Erst viel später wird man mit dem 190 E (1982), der A-Klasse (1997) und dem Smart (1998) nach unten anbauen. Zwischen 1950 und 1960 steigt die Pkw-Produktion von 33 609 auf 122 684 Einheiten. In den Sechzigern schwebt die Daimler-Benz AG fast unversehrt über wogenden Wassern. Der Inlandsumsatz wächst von 1,444 Milliarden Mark 1960 (bei einem Grundkapital von 270 Millionen) auf 6,473 Milliarden 1970 (Grundkapital 761 Millionen).

Unterdessen gebiert die chronische Raumnot der Marke mit dem Stern einen weiträumigen Polyzentrismus, belegt etwa durch die Lkw-Filiale in Wörth ab Juli 1965. Er wächst sich schließlich aus zum merkantilen Weltreich: Der Geschäftsbericht von 1983 merkt an, man wolle »nicht nur auf Schwerpunktmärkten, sondern in allen Ländern vertreten sein«. Zwei Jahre später wird der Stuttgarter Stern in 200 Staaten repräsentiert, schaffen 123 Generalvertreter zum Wohle der Firma, gibt es 21 eigene Vertriebsgesellschaften und Montagebetriebe vornehmlich in der Dritten Welt sowie 25 Werke, die eigenständig produzieren. Ein Eiland im Archipel Daimler-Benz: Das Werk Bremen, in dem ab Herbst 1982 die Kompakten 190 und 190 E vom Band rollen, ein anderes: das Werk Tuscaloosa, Alabama, ab 1997 Wiege des SUV namens ML. Im Februar 1988 begießt man den zehnmillionsten Mercedes-Pkw seit Kriegsende, im Mai 1990 den millionsten Transporter Düsseldorfer Provenienz.

Am 29. Juni 1989 indessen kristallisiert sich der Ausbau der einst reinrassigen Auto-Manufaktur zum integrierten Technologiekonzern in einer neuen Organisationsform. Unter dem Dach der Daimler-Benz AG als geschäftsführender Holding hausen fortan die

The 230G 'Popemobile'—two of them were made in 1980 for the visit of Pope John Paul II to Germany.

»Papamobil« 230G, 1980 für den Deutschlandbesuch von Papst Johannes Paul II. in zwei Exemplaren angefertigt.

La 230G « Papamobile », fabriquée à deux exemplaires en 1980 pour la visite du pape Jean-Paul II.

outre, les titres de Juan Manuel Fangio en Formule 1 sur Mercedes-Benz en 1954 et 1955 prouvèrent les capacités à renaître de l'entreprise. La première Ponton 180 de 1953, étape technique importante, fit date. La philosophie du produit reposait sur deux éléments : alors que pour les véhicules utilitaires on jouait entre les petits gabarits et les convois exceptionnels, pour les véhicules de tourisme, on visait les classes moyennes et supérieures. Ce n'est que bien plus tard, avec la 190 E (1982), la Classe A (1997) et la Smart (1998), que la gamme s'étendit aux petits modèles. Entre 1950 et 1960, la production de véhicules de tourisme passa de 33 609 à 122 684 unités. Dans les années 1960, Daimler-Benz AG navigua efficacement sur des eaux houleuses. Le chiffre d'affaires passa de 1,444 milliard de marks en 1960 (pour un capital social de 270 millions) à 6,473 milliards en 1970 (pour un capital social de 761 millions).

Dans l'intervalle, le manque de rayonnement chronique de la marque à l'étoile entraîna une large diversification, notamment par la création de la filiale poids lourds de Wörth en juillet 1965. L'entreprise devint finalement un empire commercial mondial : le rapport de l'exercice de 1983 indique qu'elle souhaitait « non seulement opérer sur les marchés prioritaires mais aussi être représentée dans tous les pays ». Deux ans plus tard, l'étoile de Stuttgart brillait dans 200 pays, 123 importateurs contribuaient à la bonne santé de l'entreprise, 21 sociétés de distribution et usines de montage étaient dédiées à la marque, particulièrement dans le tiers monde, et 25 usines produisaient de façon autonome. Un îlot dans l'archipel Daimler-Benz : l'usine de Brême d'où les compactes 190 et 190 E sortirent de la chaîne à partir de l'automne 1982. Il en était de même de l'usine de Tuscaloosa dans l'Alabama, berceau du SUV ML. En février 1988 fut fêté la dix millionième VP Mercedes depuis la fin de la guerre et, en mai 1990, le millionième camion provenant de Düsseldorf. Le 29 juin 1989, la transformation de l'ancienne manufacture automobile pure en un groupe technologique se concrétisa dans une nouvelle

1960 (capital, 270 million) to 6.473 billion in 1970 (capital, 761 million).

Meanwhile, the chronic shortage of space suffered by Mercedes gave birth to a far-flung, many-centered domain, as evidenced by the lorry subsidiary in Wörth, from July 1965 onward. It eventually grew into a mercantile empire. The annual report of 1983 noted that the firm wanted to be "represented not only on essential markets, but in all countries." Two years later, Mercedes was represented in 200 countries; 123 general representatives were working for the company, there were 21 of its sales companies and assembly plants, mainly in the Third World, as well as 25 plants producing independently. One island in the Daimler-Benz archipelago was the Bremen factory, from whose assembly belts there rolled off, in the fall of 1982, the compact 190 and 190 E. Another was the plant in Tuscaloosa, Alabama—from 1997 the cradle of the SUV called the ML. In February 1988, a toast was raised to the ten millionth Mercedes car since the war, and in May 1990 to the millionth transport vehicle from Düsseldorf.

On 29 June 1989, however, the expansion of the once purely auto-manufacturing concern crystallized in the shape of an integrated technology company with a new form of organization. Under the umbrella of Daimler-Benz AG as a managing holding company, there now coexisted Mercedes-Benz AG, AEG AG, Deutsche Aerospace AG (DASA), and Daimler-Benz InterServices AG (debis). Integral calculus did not inevitably bring better results: loss-making parts of the company, such as AEG and Fokker, had to be shed in the second half of the nineties.

The marriage of convenience with the Chrysler Corporation was not much more of a success. When, on 21 December 1998, the merger was registered in the Stuttgart trade register, Daimler-Benz AG ceased to exist. With the ugly compound noun DaimlerChrysler, one man—bitterly mourned by the purists—was left out: Karl Benz. On 4 October 2007, the disparate intercontinental union faded away like a ghost. The Extraordinary General Meeting of DaimlerChrysler AG agreed to the renaming of the company as Daimler AG. The occasion was the sale of 80.1 percent to the Chrysler Holding LLC. Stakes in the Far Eastern car-makers Hyundai Motor Company and Mitsubishi Motors Corporation did not really help, too, and were soon sold.

Unaffected by all that, tradition flourishes and anything worth preserving is retained. The new Mercedes-Benz Museum opened in Stuttgart-Untertürkheim on 19 May 2006—a spectacular sight. Daimler AG survived the global crisis—and the associated serious decline in automobile sales—relatively unscathed. By 2011, the situation had started to improve, with the first signs of a growth in car sales. Mercedes shone with the C-Class, and celebrated a fabulous start to its small van series with the new B-Class. The first quarter of 2012 brought more good news for the brand in the form of a 30-percent increase in the highly-competitive US market.

The future has already begun: Mercedes-Benz F125—study of a zero-emission luxury automobile with a range of 620 miles.

Die Zukunft hat schon begonnen: Mercedes-Benz F125 – Studie eines emissionsfreien Luxusmobils mit einer Reichweite von 1000 Kilometern.

L'avenir est déjà en marche : la Mercedes-Benz F125, étude d'une voiture de luxe sans émission d'une autonomie de 1000 kilomètres.

Mercedes-Benz AG, die AEG AG, die Deutsche Aerospace AG (DASA) sowie die Daimler-Benz InterServices AG (debis). Die Integral-Rechnung geht nicht unbedingt auf: Verlust bringende Firmenteile wie AEG und Fokker müssen schon in der zweiten Hälfte der Neunziger wieder abgestoßen werden.

Nicht viel besser ergeht es der Zweckehe mit der Chrysler Corporation. Als am 21. Dezember 1998 die Verschmelzung ins Stuttgarter Handelsregister eingetragen wird, erlischt die Daimler-Benz AG. Mit dem hässlichen Klebewort DaimlerChrysler bleibt, von den Puristen bitterlich beweint, ein Mann der ersten Stunde auf der Strecke: Karl Benz. Die angeschlagene Chrysler Group zu sanieren und salonfähig zu machen, entpuppt sich als Herausforderung, an der man schließlich scheitern wird. Am 4. Oktober 2007 ist der disparate Interkontinental-Bund wie ein Spuk vorbei. Die außerordentliche Hauptversammlung der DaimlerChrysler AG stimmt der Umbenennung des Unternehmens in Daimler AG zu. Anlass ist die Veräußerung von 80,1 Prozent an die Chrysler Holding LLC. Auch die Beteiligung an den Fernost-Autobauern Hyundai Motor Company und Mitsubishi Motors Corporation erweist sich als wenig erquicklich und findet ein frühes Ende.

Von all dem unberührt blühen Tradition und die Pflege des Bewahrenswerten. Am 19. Mai 2006 wird das neue Mercedes-Benz-Museum in Stuttgart-Untertürkheim eröffnet, ein spektakulärer Blickfang. Relativ unbeschadet übersteht die Daimler AG die globale Krise, die 2009 von erheblichen Absatzrückgängen in der Autoindustrie begleitet wird. Doch bereits 2011 folgen bei den Pkw-Segmenten Zuwächse. So brilliert Mercedes-Benz bei der C-Klasse und feiert mit der neuen B-Klasse einen fantastischen Einstieg bei den kleinen Vans. Das erste Quartal 2012 beschert der Stuttgarter Marke eine weitere Sternstunde: Auf dem heiß umkämpften US-Markt erzielt sie ein Plus von 30 Prozent.

forme d'organisation. Sous le toit de Daimler-Benz AG, société mère, furent accueillies la Mercedes-Benz AG, l'AEG AG, la Deutsche Aerospace AG (DASA) ainsi que la Daimler-Benz InterServices AG (debis). La stratégie d'intégration n'apporta pas les résultats escomptés : les filiales AEG et Fokker, générant du déficit, durent être liquidées dès la seconde moitié des années 1990.

Le succès ne fut pas non plus au rendez-vous avec le mariage de convenance avec Chrysler Corporation. Lorsque la fusion fut inscrite au registre du commerce de Stuttgart, le 21 décembre 1998, Daimler-Benz AG cessa d'exister. Avec le nom composé peu attractif DaimlerChrysler, un homme de la première heure, amèrement pleuré par les puristes, resta sur le carreau : Karl Benz. Assainir le groupe Chrysler mal en point et le rendre attrayant se révéla un défi qui ne fut pas relevé. Le 4 octobre 2007, l'alliance intercontinentale disparate n'était plus qu'un fantôme. L'assemblée générale extraordinaire de DaimlerChrysler AG décida de rebaptiser l'entreprise Daimler AG. Le motif était la cession de 80,1 % à la Chrysler Holding LLC. Les participations dans les groupes extrême-orientaux de construction automobile Hyundai Motor Company et Mitsubishi Motors Corporation furent peu rentables et cessèrent rapidement.

Inchangés malgré les aléas, la tradition et l'entretien des valeurs traditionnelles s'épanouissent. Le nouveau musée Mercedes-Benz, ouvert le 19 mai 2006 à Stuttgart-Untertürkheim, séduit au-delà de toute espérance. La société Daimler AG surmonte relativement bien la crise mondiale qui, en 2009, s'accompagne d'un recul considérable des ventes dans l'industrie automobile. Pourtant, dès 2011, le segment des voitures de tourisme connaît une certaine croissance. Mercedes-Benz s'illustre ainsi avec la Classe C et, avec la nouvelle Classe B, fait une entrée triomphale dans le secteur des monospaces compacts. Le premier trimestre 2012 offre une nouvelle heure de gloire au constructeur allemand : il enregistre une croissance de 30 % sur le marché américain sur lequel règne une concurrence féroce.

The essential factor that made this vehicle worthy of the German Imperial Patent 37,435, dated 29 January 1886, was its sheer functionality. The first motor car ever, designed by Karl Benz, was not simply a carriage with an engine bolted to it. Instead the motor, chassis, and drive train formed an integrated unit. Its first public appearance—on Mannheim's "Circular Road" which was constructed on the fragments of the earlier city wall—certainly disturbed the quiet of that Sunday: 3 July 1886.

Any onlookers had a treat. The passengers sat on a double bench seat perilously exposed to the vagaries of the weather. Those first spectators also had a clear view of the technology that was at work. The heart of the car was a compact, fast-running four-stroke engine, which, much later, was evaluated at the Technical University of Stuttgart and found to produce 0.9 bhp at 400 rpm. A water boiler projecting above the engine was Benz's solution to the problem of the single cylinder overheating—the effect of evaporation cooling prevented it.

Ligroin bought direct from the chemist's was used as the fuel, but no tank was provided for it. The surface carburetor held ⅜ gal and to replenish it Benz's son, Eugen, had to trot alongside the vehicle and top it up from a bottle every 6–9 miles. The flywheel on the original model rotated horizontally. Benz believed that a vertical arrangement would adversely affect the steering of the vehicle due to gyrostatic effect.

Sadly Model 1 saw out the remainder of the century in a dismantled and neglected condition, and it was immaculately restored only as a result of Daimler-Motoren-Gesellschaft's claim to have produced the world's first motor car. Initially Model 2 received similarly neglectful treatment but it then served as a four-wheeled test vehicle for the investigation of swiveling-axle, and later stub-axle, steering. Model 3 (from 1886 onwards) was very advanced, having two forward gears, a more powerful engine with a vertical flywheel, wooden-spoke wheels and solid rubber tires (first only on the front but later also on the rear wheels). It was available in a half-roof and dickey-seat version.

Evidence of Benz's pride in this vehicle can be found in a brochure which stated that the third-generation car should be benevolently regarded as a "pleasing carriage and mountain climbing machine."

Was ihn des Deutschen Reichs-Patents 37 435 vom 29. Januar 1886 würdig macht, ist seine Funktionalität: Der automobile Erstling von Karl Benz ist keine Kutsche, in die man ein Triebwerk hineingeschraubt hat, sondern Motor, Fahrgestell und Antrieb finden sich zu einem Guss zusammen. Sein erstes Erscheinen auf einer öffentlichen Straße, dem Mannheimer »Ring« auf den Parzellen des früheren Stadtwalls, stört indes erst die sonntägliche Ruhe des 3. Juli 1886.

Der spärliche Zuschauerflor bekommt einen Fall für zwei zu sehen: Auf einer Doppelbank sind die Passagiere den Wechselfällen der Witterung schutzlos preisgegeben. Durch nichts behindert wird auch der Blick des neugierigen Betrachters auf die Technik hinter ihnen, Herzstück: ein kompakter, schnelllaufender Viertakter. Viel später misst man an der Technischen Hochschule Stuttgart 0,9 PS bei 400/min. Über der Maschine ragt ein Wasserkessel auf: Möglicher Überhitzung des Einzylinders hat Karl Benz mit Kühlung durch Verdampfung vorgebeugt.

Für den Treibstoff Ligroin, erhältlich in Apotheken, findet sich indes kein Behältnis: 1,5 Liter fasst der Oberflächenvergaser, und notfalls muss Benz' Filius Eugen das väterliche Fahrzeug in lockerem Trab begleiten und alle zehn bis 15 Kilometer aus einer Flasche nachfüllen. Das Schwungrad rotiert am Ur-Typ horizontal. Senkrechte Anordnung, meint Benz, würde wegen unerwünschter Kreiselwirkung die Lenkbarkeit beeinträchtigen.

Modell 1 erlebt den Rest des Jahrhunderts zerlegt und vernachlässigt und wird erst dann untadelig restauriert, als auch die Daimler-Motoren-Gesellschaft den Anspruch darauf erhebt, das erste Auto in die Welt gesetzt zu haben. Ein Modell 2 erfährt zunächst ebenfalls stiefväterliche Behandlung, dient aber dann mit vier Rädern als Versuchsträger für eine Drehschemel- und später für eine Achsschenkellenkung. Das Modell 3 (ab 1886) gibt sich durchaus fortschrittlich, mit zwei Vorwärtsgängen, stärkerem Motor mit vertikalem Schwungrad, Holzspeichenrädern, Vollgummireifen erst vorn und später auch hinten. Es ist lieferbar mit Halbverdeck und Notbank als Option.

In einem Prospekt artikuliert sich verschämt Vaterstolz: Der Motorwagen der dritten Generation wird der geneigten Aufmerksamkeit als »gefälliges Fuhrwerk und als Bergsteigerapparat« empfohlen.

Ce qui la rend digne du brevet du Reich allemand n° 37 435 du 29 janvier 1886, c'est son caractère fonctionnel: la première création automobile de Karl Benz n'est pas une calèche sur laquelle on a greffé un moteur. Châssis, moteur et chaîne cinématique constituent une entité. Cela n'empêche pas que sa première apparition sur une route publique, sur le « ring » de Mannheim, ait troublé le calme dominical du 3 juillet 1886.

Peu nombreux, les spectateurs découvrent deux courageux pionniers: juchés sur une banquette double, les passagers sont exposés sans la moindre protection aux aléas des intempéries. Rien n'entrave, non plus, la vue du curieux sur la mécanique derrière eux avec, comme morceau de bravoure, un compact moteur à quatre temps à régime rapide. Beaucoup plus tard, à l'université technique de Stuttgart, on mesurera une puissance de 0,9 ch à 400 tr/min. Un réservoir d'eau trône sur le moteur: Karl Benz a paré à toute éventualité de surchauffe du monocylindre avec un refroidissement par vaporisation.

Pour le carburant, de la ligroïne en vente en pharmacie; on ne trouve pas en revanche de réservoir: le carburateur de surface a une capacité de 1,5 litre et, en cas de besoin, le fils de Benz, Eugen, doit accompagner le véhicule de son père en le suivant au pas de course pour refaire le plein, tous les dix à quinze kilomètres, à l'aide d'une bouteille. Sur le modèle original, le volant-moteur est horizontal. Une position verticale, pense Benz, porterait préjudice à la maniabilité en raison de la force centrifuge indésirable.

Le modèle 1 vécut le reste du siècle démonté et abandonné dans un coin et il n'est alors restauré à la perfection que lorsque la Daimler-Motoren-Gesellschaft revendique d'avoir construit la première voiture du monde. Un modèle 2 est tout d'abord, lui aussi, traité en cousin pauvre avant de servir ensuite de véhicule expérimental à quatre roues pour une direction à boggie et, plus tard, à fusée. Le modèle 3 (à partir de 1886) comporte déjà de nombreux progrès avec deux rapports avant, un moteur plus puissant à volant-moteur vertical, des roues à rayons en bois, des pneus en caoutchouc plein tout d'abord à l'avant et, plus tard, aussi à l'arrière. Il est livrable avec une demi-capote et une banquette de dépannage en option.

La fierté paternelle transparaît à deux niveaux dans le prospectus: la voiture à moteur de la troisième génération est recommandée aux intéressés potentiels comme « véhicule séduisant ou appareil à escalader les montagnes ».

Benz Patent-Motorwagen 1886

Great things cast long shadows. The overhead view reveals the compact dimensions and the strict functionalism of the Benz three-wheeler. Nothing was ornamental: everything served a purpose.

Große Dinge werfen ihre Schatten voraus: Der Blick von oben zeigt die kompakten Dimensionen und die strenge Zweckmäßigkeit des Benzschen Tricycles: Alles ist Funktion, nichts Ornament.

Les grands événements jettent leur ombre longtemps à l'avance : compacité et fonctionnalité sévère du tricycle de Benz vu d'en haut : tout est fonction, rien n'est fioriture.

Benz Patent-Motorwagen 1886

The flywheel was fitted horizontally because the inventor feared that, had it been mounted vertically, the gyrostatic effect might have adversely affected cornering stability.

Das Schwungrad ist liegend angeordnet. Der Erfinder fürchtete, senkrecht könne es infolge seiner Kreiselwirkung die Kurvenstabilität beeinträchtigen.

Le vélomoteur est horizontal. L'inventeur craignait que la force centrifuge d'un vélomoteur vertical porte préjudice à la stabilité en virage.

Benz Patent-Motorwagen 1886

On 8 March 1886 Gottlieb Daimler ordered an Americain carriage from coachbuilder Wilhelm Wimpff & Sohn in Stuttgart. It was delivered in August at a price of 795 goldmarks. The manufacturer generously guaranteed the axles, springs, and wheels for two years.

What seems to have been conceived as a present for the approaching birthday of Daimler's wife, Berta, meanwhile developed its own dynamic—literally. The carriage was taken to the Maschinenfabrik Esslingen where, under Daimler's precise guidance, it developed into the automobile. First of all, the shaft was removed—an act of historical significance. The passengers in the second row of seats had to share footspace with Daimler's fast-running combustion engine which developed 1.1 bhp at 650 rpm. The unit functioned proudly and efficiently, and was nicknamed the "grandfather clock" in company parlance because of its resemblance to that stately timepiece. The single cylinder was fired by glow-tube ignition, a system protected by German Imperial Patent 28,022 of 16 December 1883. A small externally-heated tube projected into the combustion chamber. The piston compressed the gas mixture until it ignited at the correct moment, so avoiding misfires which would cause the piston to blow back before it reached the cylinder's top dead center. This was a provision that the man who operated the starting handle could be profoundly grateful for—a misfire could have easily resulted in a broken arm.

The "grandfather clock" was fed by Wilhelm Maybach's surface carburetor. The carburetor float ensured that the air was continuously mixed with a consistent quantity of fuel and so the composition of the resulting mixture remained constant. A multi-plate cooler of tinplate behind the rear seat kept the engine operating at a comfortable and stable temperature. Swiveling-axle steering, actuated by a toothed quadrant, ensured that the front wheels of the motor carriage pointed in the required direction. The driver had two gears available. The belt pulley of the engine drove differently sized pulleys on a countershaft, which drove the rear wheels through pinion crown gears on both sides of the vehicle. Gear changing was performed manually and required the belts to be changed over while the vehicle was stationary.

The horseless four-seater managed a bare 12½ mph. The first excursion in it of the creative team of Gottlieb Daimler and Wilhelm Maybach in April 1887 was greeted with mixed emotions by the citizens of Esslingen, Bad Cannstatt, and Untertürkheim. Popular opinion held that it was the work of the devil and general bewilderment reigned.

Am 8. März 1886 bestellt Gottlieb Daimler bei der Wagenbaufabrik Wilhelm Wimpff & Sohn in Stuttgart eine Kutsche vom Typ Americain, die im August um den Preis von 795 Goldmark geliefert wird. Der Hersteller gewährt generös eine Zweijahres-Garantie auf Achsen, Federn und Räder.

Was ein Geschenk zum bevorstehenden Geburtstag von Daimlers Gattin Berta zu sein scheint, entwickelt indes seine eigene Dynamik – buchstäblich. Die Kutsche wird nämlich zur Maschinenfabrik Esslingen gebracht und mutiert dort nach Daimlers genauer Anleitung zum Automobil. Als erstes entfernt man die Deichsel – eine Tat von historischer Tragweite. Die Passagiere in der zweiten Reihe müssen sich den Fußraum mit Daimlers schnell laufendem Verbrennungsmotor von 1,1 PS bei 650/min teilen, der dort seiner Tätigkeit stolz und aufrecht nachgeht, im Hausjargon wegen der unverkennbaren Ähnlichkeit die »Standuhr« genannt. Befeuert wird der Einzylinder von einer Glührohrzündung, urheberrechtlich geschützt durch das Deutsche Reichspatent 28 022 vom 16. Dezember 1883. Ein von außen erhitztes Röhrchen ragt in den Verbrennungsraum. Der Kolben quetscht das Gasgemisch zusammen, bis es termingerecht entflammt. Fehlzündungen, die ihn vor dem Erreichen des oberen Totpunkts zurückwerfen würden, werden solchermaßen vermieden. Es dankt der Mann an der Anlasserkurbel – ihm könnte das schon mal den Arm brechen.

Verpflegt wird die »Standuhr« durch Wilhelm Maybachs Oberflächenvergaser. Dessen Schwimmer gewährleistet, dass die Luft eine ständig gleich dicke Kraftstoffschicht durchmisst und das entstehende Gemisch konstant zusammengesetzt bleibt. Ein Lamellenkühler aus Weißblech hinter dem Rücksitz hält die Maschine bei Laune und bei angenehmen Betriebstemperaturen, eine Drehschemellenkung, betätigt über ein Zahnbogensegment, sorgt dafür, dass die Vorderräder der Motorkutsche in die gewünschte Richtung zeigen. Ihr Lenker gebietet über zwei Gänge: Die Riemenscheibe des Motors treibt verschieden große Scheiben einer Vorlegewelle an. Diese bewegt durch beidseitige Ritzel Zahnkränze an den Hinterrädern. Per Handarbeit wird der Gangwechsel vorgenommen – das Umlegen der Riemen bei stehendem Fahrzeug.

Der pferdelose Viersitzer läuft knapp 20 Stundenkilometer, und erste Ausfahrten der kreativen Herren-Riege Gottlieb Daimler und Wilhelm Maybach im April 1887 nehmen die Bürger von Esslingen, Bad Cannstatt und Untertürkheim mit gemischten Gefühlen zur Kenntnis. Der Gedanke an Teufelswerk drängt sich auf, so dass Bestürzung überwiegt.

Le 8 mars 1886, Gottlieb Daimler commande à l'usine de construction de voitures Wilhelm Wimpff & Sohn à Stuttgart une calèche type Américain qui lui est livrée en août au prix de 795 marks or. Le fabricant accorde généreusement une garantie de deux ans sur les essieux, les ressorts et les roues.

Ce que l'on croit être un cadeau pour l'anniversaire imminent de Berta, l'épouse de Daimler, génère en réalité sa propre dynamique – au sens propre du mot. La calèche est en effet amenée à l'usine de machines d'Esslingen où elle se mue, selon les instructions exactes de Daimler, en une automobile. On commence par éloigner le timon – une action d'une portée historique. Les passagers de la deuxième rangée doivent partager l'espace pour les jambes avec le moteur thermique à régime rapide de Daimler, qui développe 1,1 ch à 650 tr/min et s'attelle là à la tâche verticalement et avec fierté, ce qui lui a valu dans le jargon maison, en raison d'une évidente similitude, le surnom d'« horloge ». Le monocylindre est actionné par un allumage à tube incandescent, système déposé par le brevet du Reich allemand n° 28 022 du 16 décembre 1883. Un petit tube chauffé de l'extérieur fait saillie dans la chambre de combustion. Le piston comprime le mélange gazeux jusqu'à ce qu'il s'enflamme au bon moment. Cela permet d'éviter tout raté d'allumage qui le ferait revenir en arrière avant qu'il n'ait atteint le point mort supérieur. Cela épargne un retour de manivelle à l'homme qui démarre le moteur – cela pourrait lui briser net le bras.

L'« horloge » est alimentée par le carburateur à surface de Wilhelm Maybach. Son flotteur garantit que l'air traverse toujours une couche de carburant à l'épaisseur identique et que le mélange ainsi formé reste d'une composition constante. Un radiateur à lamelles en tôle étamée derrière le siège arrière maintient le moteur de bonne humeur et à une température de fonctionnement agréable, une direction à boggie actionnée par un secteur denté garantissant que les roues avant de la calèche à moteur sont orientées dans la direction souhaitée. Son conducteur est maître de deux rapports: le disque de courroie du moteur entraîne les disques de diamètre différent d'un arbre intermédiaire. Grâce à des pignons des deux côtés, celui-ci entraîne des couronnes dentées se trouvant sur les roues arrière. Le changement de vitesses s'effectue à la main – on déplace les courroies une fois la voiture arrêtée.

Cette quatre-places sans chevaux frise les 20 km/h et les premières excursions des ingénieux Gottlieb Daimler et Wilhelm Maybach, en avril 1887, suscitent des sentiments mitigés parmi les citoyens d'Esslingen, Bad Cannstatt et Untertürkheim. Ils y voient surtout une machine infernale et c'est donc l'effroi qui prédomine.

Daimler Motorkutsche 1886

The resemblance of the motor carriage to its horse-drawn antecedent was unmistakable, though the shaft, like the horse itself, had become redundant, and horsepower was generated by the vehicle itself.

An der Verwandtschaft der Motorkutsche zum Pferdefuhrwerk kommt kein Zweifel auf. Nur: Wie das Pferd selbst ist auch die Deichsel entbehrlich geworden, und die Pferdestärken erzeugt das Fahrzeug selbst.

La parenté est évidente entre la calèche à moteur et le char à bancs. À cela près que, avec le cheval, le timon lui aussi est devenu superflu et que les chevaux sont produits par le véhicule lui-même.

Details: engine spur at the rear, parts of the suspension, carriage lamp for nocturnal outings.

Details: Ausläufer des Motors im Fond, Teile der Aufhängung, die Kutschenlampe für nächtliche Eskapaden.

Détails: l'environnement du moteur à l'arrière. La lampe de calèche pour les escapades nocturnes, des éléments de la suspension.

Front and rear suspension consisted of a rigid axle with double elliptical springs. The swiveling-axle steering worked by means of a toothed quadrant and a pinion.

Die Aufhängung, vorn wie hinten: eine Starrachse mit Vollelliptikfedern. DieDrehschemellenkung wirkt über ein Zahnbogensegment und Ritzel.

La suspension, identique à l'avant et à l'arrière : un essieu rigide à ressorts complètement elliptique. La direction à sellette agit par le biais d'un segment à secteur denté et pignon.

The 89 million visitors to the World Exhibition in Paris in 1889 gazed in wonder at the Eiffel Tower, showed polite interest in two boats powered by Daimler engines plying the Seine, but frankly regarded the steel-wheel car from the same company as a bizarre detour into a technical no-man's-land. However, the graceful conveyance did have something to offer because, like Benz's three-wheeler, the sum of its parts amounted to a complete automobile.

Because Gottlieb Daimler was a man of enduring convictions, his partner Wilhelm Maybach had to exert all his persuasive powers to convince him of the worth of new ideas. While Daimler liked to feel that his engines were suitable for all kinds of applications and was content with a quiet evolution of the carriage, Maybach opted for a tubular steel frame which also served as a duct for cooling water. The front wheels ran in bicycle-wheel forks which were aligned by means of a common steering rod. The chassis was manufactured by Neckarsulmer Strickmaschinen-Fabrik AG, a company which later became famously known as NSU. Where Daimler considered the belt drive of the motor car of 1886 still capable of development and advancement, Maybach pointed the way to the future with a 4-speed transmission. A relaxed journey to Paris, a bold adventure undertaken without any unbecoming fuss, was convincing proof of the validity of this solution. At a top speed of 11 mph, the beauty and variety of the French landscape could really be appreciated.

The steel-wheel car was of two-cylinder type with the v-engine set at an angle of 17 degrees, configured—as usual—vertically under the driver and the front passenger seat, a double "grandfather clock" so to speak. Careful examination of this rare powerplant in 1961 showed that its designer had managed to extract 1.65 bhp at 920 rpm from a cubic capacity of 565 cc. The surface carburetor also acted as a reservoir holding half a gallon of fuel. An enclosed bevel gear differential was mounted in the rear axle next to the right-hand wheel and the left-hand rear wheel was provided with an external band brake that was operated from the driver's seat.

This development ended after two show models had been built; Gottlieb Daimler simply lost all interest in the project. A further twelve vehicles, known as Schroedter cars, were sold by the Daimler-Motoren-Gesellschaft between 1892 and 1895. They were named after the new Technical Director of the company as by this time both creators of the Paris model had temporarily turned their backs on the business in disgruntlement. What had been hailed as the latest craze had simply become antiquated. One particular feature of the original is absent from the reconstructed model—its wheels are made of wood, not steel.

Die 89 Millionen Besucher der Pariser Weltausstellung von 1889 bestaunen den Eiffelturm, zollen zwei Booten auf der Seine mit Motoren von Daimler höfliches Interesse, tun jedoch den Stahlradwagen aus dem gleichen Hause als skurrilen Abstecher in technisches Niemandsland ab. Dabei hat das grazile Gefährt einiges zu bieten: Auch in ihm bildet wie am Dreirad von Benz die Summe der Teile ein automobiles Ganzes.

Da Gottlieb Daimler ein Mann bewahrender Denkungsart ist, hat Partner Wilhelm Maybach streckenweise echte Überzeugungsarbeit zu leisten. Wo jener seine Motoren allen möglichen Verwendungen zugeführt sehen und sich mit einer sanften Evolution der Kutsche begnügen möchte, setzt dieser auf einen Rahmen aus Stahlrohren, durch die zugleich das Kühlwasser strömt. Die Vorderräder laufen in Fahrradgabeln, welche mittels einer gemeinsamen Lenkstange gleichgerichtet werden. Gefertigt wird das Chassis von der Neckarsulmer Strickmaschinen-Fabrik AG, die später unter dem Namen NSU firmieren wird. Wo jener meint, das Riemengetriebe des Motorwagens von 1886 sei noch durchaus entwicklungs- und ausbaufähig, zeigt dieser mit einem Viergang-Zahnradgetriebe den Weg in die Zukunft. Von den Qualitäten dieser Lösung überzeugt man sich bereits schmunzelnd anlässlich der Anreise nach Paris, einem Unterfangen ohne ungebührliche Hektik: Bei Tempo 18 Spitze kommen Schönheit und Vielfalt französischer Landschaften noch so recht zur Geltung.

Der Stahlradwagen ist ein Zweizylinder: Unter der Sitzbank für Fahrer und Beifahrer steht gewohnt aufrecht ein V-Motor im Winkel von 17 Grad, eine doppelte »Standuhr« gewissermaßen. Eine penible Prüfung dieses Leitfossils ergibt 1961, dass seine Väter aus 565 cm³ Hubraum 1,65 PS bei 920/min mobilisiert haben. Der Oberflächenvergaser bildet zugleich ein Reservoir für zwei Liter Kraftstoff. Neben dem rechten Rad findet sich in der Hinterachse ein gekapseltes Kegelrad-Differential, im linken Hinterrad eine Außenbandbremse, vom Fahrersitz aus zu betätigen.

Zunächst hat es mit zwei Show-Exemplaren sein Bewenden, wohl auch, weil Gottlieb Daimler dem Projekt mit zäher Unlust begegnet. Weitere zwölf werden von der Daimler-Motoren-Gesellschaft zwischen 1892 und 1895 vertrieben, bekannt als Schroedter-Wagen. Sie heißen so nach dem neuen Technischen Direktor der Firma, denn die beiden Schöpfer des Pariser Exponats haben dem Unternehmen zeitweise verstimmt den Rücken gekehrt. Was damals der letzte Schrei war, ist indessen nun einfach alt. Unter anderen charakteristischen Merkmalen des Originals fehlt der Kopie vor allem eines: Ihre Speichen sind aus Holz.

Les 89 millions de visiteurs de l'Exposition universelle de Paris, en 1889, admirent bouche bée la tour Eiffel, portent un intérêt poli à deux bateaux à moteurs Daimler se trouvant sur la Seine, mais considèrent en revanche la voiture à roues d'acier de la même maison comme un bizarre représentant de la technique. Et pourtant, le gracile engin ne manque pas d'élégance: comme le tricycle de Benz, lui aussi constitue, avec la somme de ses pièces, une entité automobile.

Comme Gottlieb Daimler est un homme à l'esprit conservateur, son associé Wilhelm Maybach doit parfois faire preuve d'un grand pouvoir de persuasion. Là où le premier préférerait voir ses moteurs affectés à toutes les utilisations possibles et souhaiterait se contenter d'une évolution modérée de la calèche, le second impose un cadre en tubes d'acier à travers lesquels circule l'eau de refroidissement. Les roues avant sont montées dans des fourches de vélo qui sont orientées dans la même direction grâce à une bielle de direction commune. Le châssis est fabriqué par la Neckarsulmer Strickmaschinen-Fabrik AG, qui deviendra plus tard célèbre sous l'abréviation NSU.

Là où le premier pense que la boîte de vitesses à courroies de la voiture à moteur de 1886 mériterait encore parfaitement d'être perfectionnée, le second s'engage dans la voie de l'avenir avec une boîte de vitesses à engrenages à quatre rapports. On peut déjà se convaincre en souriant des qualités de cette solution à l'occasion du voyage à Paris, entreprise exempte de toute nervosité: à 18 km/h, on peut encore vraiment admirer la beauté et la diversité des paysages français.

La voiture à roues d'acier est une bicylindre: sous la banquette du conducteur et du passager se trouve – à la verticale comme d'habitude – un moteur en V à 17 degrés, une «double horloge», en quelque sorte. Un examen minutieux de ce fossile a révélé en 1961 que ses pères avaient mobilisé 1,65 ch à 920 tr/min à partir d'une cylindrée de 565 cm³. Le carburateur à surface constitue simultanément un réservoir pour deux litres de carburant.

À côté de la roue droite se trouve, dans le train arrière, un différentiel à roue conique encapsulé et, dans la roue arrière gauche, un frein à bande extérieur, à actionner depuis le siège conducteur.

Il en exista tout d'abord seulement deux exemplaires de démonstration, pour une bonne partie parce que Gottlieb Daimler ne s'attaqua à ce projet qu'avec un empressement mitigé. Douze autres modèles seront vendus par la Daimler-Motoren-Gesellschaft entre 1892 et 1895, sous le nom de voiture de Schroedter. Elles portent le nom du nouveau directeur technique de la société, car les deux créateurs de la voiture exposée à Paris ont provisoirement quitté l'entreprise par suite de divergences de vues. Ce qui était alors le dernier cri est maintenant tout simplement démodé. Entre autres caractéristiques de l'original, on déplore, sur la copie, surtout l'absence d'une chose: leurs rayons sont en bois.

Daimler Stahlradwagen 1889

The Stahlradwagen or steel-wheel car was a light four-wheeled carriage with its engine located in front of the rear axle underneath the seat. After its première at the Paris World Fair in 1889, it remained in France.

Der Stahlradwagen: eine leichte Vierradkutsche mit Motor vor der Hinterachse stehend unter dem Sitz. Nach seiner Premiere auf der Pariser Weltausstellung 1889 bleibt er in Frankreich.

La Stahlradwagen ou la voiture à roues en acier: une légère calèche à quatre roues avec moteur vertical sous le siège devant le train arrière. Après sa première à l'Exposition universelle de Paris en 1889, elle reste en France.

The drive came via gear wheels in direct contact with the rear axles, and the V-engine's power was transmitted by a 4-speed gear mechanism. The half-gallon fuel supply in the surface carburetor was soon exhausted.

Der Antrieb erfolgt über Zahnräder direkt auf die Hinterachse. Vermittelt wird die Kraft des V-Motors durch ein Viergang-Zahnradgetriebe. Der Kraftstoffvorrat von zwei Litern im Oberflächenvergaser ist rasch aufgezehrt.

L'essieu arrière est entraîné directement via des engrenages. La puissance du moteur en V est transmise par une boîte de vitesses à engrenages à quatre rapports. La réserve de carburant, de deux litres, dans le carburateur à surface, est rapidement consommée.

"Victoria" is what Karl Benz is supposed to have rejoiced in Latin when he invented stub-axle steering. In the winter of 1892–93 he patented it as a "car steering device with steering circles to be set tangential to the wheels." The main advantage of this innovation was that the front wheels on the inside and the outside of the curve could now run at different angles to the direction of travel. On 28 February 1893 he was awarded Imperial Patent 73,151 for this invention.

With a jubilant cry of relief Benz at the same time celebrated victory over the three-wheeler—from now on four wheels were to be the norm on a motor car. Many doubt this etymology of the car's name—Victoria is also understood to have been the name of an ordinary carriage with two seats. Nevertheless, whatever the derivation, this is what Karl Benz named his first four-wheeler, which progressively became more powerful and faster. In 1893 the rear-mounted, single-cylinder engine with its vertical flywheel produced 3 bhp from 1730 cc, in 1894 4 bhp from 1990 cc, 5 bhp from 2650 cc in 1895 and 6 bhp from 2915 cc from 1898 onwards.

Despite its heavy appearance, the Victoria was in fact quite light, weighing not more than 1345 lbs in total. The flat belt drive had two gears, sometimes with a supplementary planetary gear, and from 1896 onwards it had three forward gears and one reverse. The gears were changed by shifting the belts from one of the two stepped pulleys of the engine to the fixed pulleys or idling pulleys of the countershaft to which the differential was also connected. The rear wheels were driven by chains. The family resemblance to the carriage was always evident, whether the Victoria was a Two-seater, Vis-à-Vis, Phaeton or Landau. At first only the small front wheels bore solid rubber tires but later they were also fitted to the large rear wheels. Of all Benz's creations, the Victoria was his favorite, "because its solid tires gave it protection from the normal tire defects and the high seating position was clear of road dust." Pride in the product was evident in the advertising literature produced by the very successful French Benz agent Émile Roger. It described it as "horseless carriage driven by a special petroleum engine … elegance, solidity, comfort, great simplicity, no shaking, upkeep with ease."

But the reality was not quite so rosy. The car ran 11¾ miles per gallon of gasoline and 1½ miles to the gallon of water to keep going. This did not deter Theodor Freiherr von Liebig from covering the considerable distance from Reichenberg in Bohemia via Mannheim to Reims in France and back in 1894 in a Victoria. Although the look on the nobleman's face when he reached his destination was one of quiet dignity, it is likely that among his circle of close friends he would also have admitted to a feeling of relief.

Victoria« soll Karl Benz auf lateinisch frohlockt haben, als er die Achsschenkellenkung erfand. Im Winter 1892/93 meldet er sie zum Patent an, als »Wagenlenkvorrichtung mit tangential zu den Rädern zu stellenden Lenkkreisen«. Hauptvorteil dieser Novität: Kurveninneres und kurvenäußeres Vorderrad können nun in unterschiedlichen Winkeln zur bisherigen Fahrtrichtung laufen. Am 28. Februar 1893 wird ihm dafür das Reichspatent 73 151 zugeteilt.

Mit dem Jubelschrei der Erleichterung feiert Benz zugleich den Sieg über das Dreirad – vier Räder sind von Stund an die Norm. Manche zweifeln diese Etymologie aus dem Hochgefühl des glücklichen Augenblicks heraus an – Victoria habe auch ein landläufiger Kutschentyp mit zwei Sitzen geheißen. Immerhin nennt Karl Benz seinen ersten Vierradler so, der im Laufe seiner Modellgeschichte immer kräftiger und immer schneller wird: Drei Pferdestärken und 1730 cm³ hat der hinten liegend eingebaute Einzylinder mit stehendem Schwungrad 1893, vier PS aus 1990 cm³ 1894, fünf PS aus 2650 cm³ 1895 und sechs PS aus 2915 cm³ ab 1898. Der Victoria sieht klobig aus, ist aber leicht: ganze 610 Kilogramm. Zwei Gänge hat sein Flachriemengetriebe, gegebenenfalls mit zusätzlichem Planetengetriebe, drei Fahrstufen vorwärts und eine rückwärts ab 1896. Der Wechsel der Gänge vollzieht sich durch Verschieben der Riemen von den beiden Stufenscheiben des Motors zu den Festscheiben oder Leerscheiben der Vorgelegewelle, auf der auch das Differential angesiedelt ist. Die Hinterräder werden durch Ketten in Marsch gesetzt und am Laufen gehalten.

Immer präsent ist die Familienähnlichkeit zur Kutsche, ob der Victoria nun als Zweisitzer, Vis-à-Vis, Phaeton oder Landauer daherkommt. Erst sind nur die kleinen Vorderräder vollgummibereift, später auch die großen Hinterräder. Von all seinen Kreationen ist Karl Benz der Victoria die liebste, »da seine Vollreifen vor den üblichen Reifendefekten schützten und durch den hohen Sitz der Straßenstaub abgehalten wurde«. Der Stolz auf das Produkt schlägt sich etwa in den Werbetexten des sehr erfolgreichen französischen Benz-Agenten Émile Roger nieder. Er verheißt »pferdelose Wagen, durch Spezial-Petroleum-Motoren angetrieben … Eleganz, Solidität, Bequemlichkeit, große Einfachheit, keine Erschütterungen, große Leichtigkeit der Unterhaltung«.

Ganz so rosig sehen die Dinge jedoch realiter nicht aus: Das Auto möchte immerhin mit 20 Litern Benzin und 160 Litern Wasser je hundert Kilometer bei Laune gehalten werden. Das bringt Theodor Freiherr von Liebig indes nicht davon ab, 1894 mit einem Victoria die beträchtliche Entfernung von Reichenberg in Böhmen über Mannheim nach Reims und retour zurückzulegen. Obwohl die Gesichtszüge des Edelmannes bei der Zieldurchfahrt eine Art verklärter Würde ausdrücken, wird er in kleinem Kreise auch Erleichterung eingestanden haben.

Victoria » se serait écrié Karl Benz en latin, après avoir découvert la direction à fusée de roue. Durant l'hiver 1892–1893, il fait déposer pour elle un brevet en tant que « dispositif de braquage de voiture avec cercles de braquage tangentiels aux roues ». Avantage majeur de cette innovation : la roue intérieure au virage et la roue extérieure au virage peuvent désormais tourner en prenant des angles différents par rapport à la direction initiale. Le 28 février 1893, on lui décerne le brevet du Reich 73 151.

Avec ce cri de joie et de soulagement, Benz fête simultanément la victoire sur le tricycle – dorénavant, quatre roues sont la norme. Certains mettent en doute l'étymologie et son lien à l'instant de bonheur – il y aurait aussi eu un type répandu de calèches à deux sièges appelé Victoria. C'est en tout cas ainsi que Karl Benz baptise sa première voiture à quatre roues qui, au cours de son histoire, devient de plus en plus puissante et de plus en plus rapide : le monocylindre en position horizontale à l'arrière avec volant-moteur vertical de 1893 a trois chevaux et une cylindrée de 1730 cm³; celui de 1894 en tire quatre à partir de 1990 cm³, celui de 1895, cinq de 2650 cm³ et celui de 1898, six chevaux à partir de 2915 cm³. La Victoria a l'air massif, mais c'est trompeur : elle ne pèse que 610 kg. Sa boîte de vitesses plate à deux rapports, parfois avec engrenage planétaire supplémentaire, trois rapports avant et une marche arrière à partir de 1896. Le changement des rapports s'effectue en déplaçant les courroies de la poulie étagée du moteur vers les disques fixes ou disques vides de l'arbre intermédiaire, sur lequel se trouve aussi le différentiel. Les roues arrière sont entraînées par chaînes.

La Victoria présente encore une similitude avec la calèche, qu'elle soit carrossée en Biplace, Vis-à-Vis, Phaeton ou Landau. Au début, seules les petites roues avant ont des bandages à caoutchouc plein. Ce ne sera, aussi, le cas des grandes roues arrière que plus tard. De toutes ses créations, c'est la Victoria que Karl Benz préfère, « car ses pneus pleins ne sont pas sujet aux défaillances des pneus courants et que, grâce aux sièges élevés, la poussière de la route n'est pas soulevée ». L'agent de Benz en France, Émile Roger, remporte un très grand succès en faisant de la fierté du propriétaire un argument de vente. Il évoque dans ses publicités « des voitures sans chevaux, propulsées par des moteurs à pétrole spécial … Élégance, solidité, confort, grande simplicité, pas de secousses, entretien d'une grande facilité ».

Dans la réalité, les choses ne sont pourtant pas aussi simples : la voiture tient tout de même à se sustenter avec 20 litres d'essence et 160 litres d'eau tous les 100 km. Cela n'empêche pas le comte Theodor von Liebig de couvrir, en 1894, avec une Victoria, la distance considérable de Reichenberg, en Bohême, à Reims, en passant par Mannheim et retour. Bien que les traits du visage du noble aient traduit une espèce de dignité rayonnante lors de son arrivée, il n'en aura sans doute pas moins exprimé son soulagement à huis clos.

Benz Victoria 1893

The seat backs in the front of the car and the armrests reveal that in the Vis-à-Vis you sat face to face, just as Karl Benz and his wife Berta once did.

Die Rücklehne vorn und die Armstützen zeigen es: Im Vis-à-Vis sitzt man einander Auge in Auge gegenüber wie einst Karl Benz und Gattin Berta.

Le dossier du siège avant et les accoudoirs le prouvent: dans la Vis-à-Vis, on se fait face comme jadis Karl Benz et son épouse Berta.

Benz Victoria 1893

A technical puzzle made up of components which, working in unison, made it possible for people to travel under their own steam, albeit slowly and not exactly in comfort. The steering wheel crank sat on a vertical steering column in the middle of the vehicle, leading to an innovative stub-axle steering system. Karl Benz is said to have shouted "Victoria!" when the idea came to him. As at the rear, the front wheels were suspended from a rigid axle by double elliptical springs. The bodywork was wooden and frameless. Parts of the stub-axle steering can clearly be seen.

Ein technisches Puzzle aus Teilen, die in ihrer Summe menschliche Fortbewegung aus eigener Kraft ermöglichen, gemächlich noch und wenig komfortabel, aber immerhin. Die Lenkradkurbel auf einer senkrechten Säule in der Wagenmitte führt zu der innovativen Achsschenkellenkung, deren Erfindung Karl Benz den Freudenschrei »Victoria« entlockt haben soll. Wie auch hinten sind die Räder vorn an einer Starrachse mit Vollelliptikfedern aufgehängt. Der Aufbau: rahmenlos aus Holz. Deutlich zu erkennen sind Elemente der Achsschenkellenkung.

Un vrai puzzle technique qui permet à l'homme de se mouvoir de sa propre force, lentement encore et de façon peu confortable, certes. La manivelle de volant sur une colonne verticale au centre de la voiture entraîne une direction novatrice à fusée, dont la découverte aurait fait pousser à Karl Benz le cri de joie « Victoria! » À l'arrière, comme à l'avant, les roues sont suspendues à un essieu rigide avec ressorts complètement elliptiques. La carrosserie, tout en bois, ne comporte aucun cadre. On reconnaît aisément les éléments de la direction à fusée.

The top speed of the Benz-Laudaulet was 18½ mph, making the horn an important supplement to the driver's shouts. With its modern-looking folding roof, the Landaulet could be used both as a coupé and as a cabriolet—a sensible concession to the German climate. The doors and roof could be completely removed.

Das Benz-Laudaulet von 1898 läuft bis zu 30 Stundenkilometern. Da ist die Hupe schon eine willkommene Ergänzung zu den Zurufen des Fahrers. Mit seinem modern anmutenden Klappverdeck ist das Landaulet als Coupé wie als Cabriolet universell verwendbar – eine kluge Konzession an deutsche Witterungsverhältnisse. Türen und Dach lassen sich komplett herausnehmen.

Le Landaulet-Benz de 1898 peut rouler jusqu'à 30 km/h. Le klaxon est donc un complément bienvenu aux cris du conducteur. Avec sa capote rabattable d'allure moderne, le Landaulet peut se présenter en coupé comme en cabriolet – une concession intelligente aux aléas du temps en Allemagne. Les portières et le toit se démontent complètement.

Benz Victoria 1893

Benz Victoria 1893

The impetus for the development of this light, inexpensive vehicle came from Josef Brecht who was Karl Benz's business advisor. The Benz Veloziped, known as Velo for short, was built with that specification in mind. The melodious and unassuming name is a reminder of the origins of the self-propelled vehicle.

That was exactly what its inventor had in mind, as was its silhouette that recalled a carriage with its small front wheels and large rear wheels. Even up to the mid 1890s, Benz stressed the kinship of his creation with the horse-drawn carriage in his advertising literature, until Benz cars took the lead in emancipated design. The Velo was in fact very light and at 127 lbs a seductive offer, even to the many doubters of the day. According to a contemporary brochure, the Veloziped cost 2000 marks "complete with the finest fittings with lamps, or 2200 marks fitted out with a half roof and grained leather." Customers flocked to buy it in huge numbers. Between October 1894 and October 1895, 125 Velos were sold. Together with the improved Comfortable version from 1898 (available with pneumatic tires), 1200 cars were sold. Thus the production car was born. One third of this number went to customers in Germany and France (under the name Éclair, "lightning" in English) and the remainder to other countries.

Initially, the single-cylinder engine produced 1.5 bhp at 450 rpm from a good 1-liter capacity, and 3.5 bhp at 800 rpm by the end of its production in 1901. Benz never tired of making changes to the Veloziped, first offering it with flat belt gearing and later with planetary gears—three forward gears and one reverse. An unusually advanced detail was its float carburetor. A gas-air quantity regulator on the inlet manifold operating together with a throttle valve and adjustment of the ignition produced more flexible engine running.

The advanced variant, the Ideal, whose cooling-water tank somewhat resembled an engine bonnet, and its offshoots, the Duc and Charette, proved difficult to sell. In 1902, its last year of production, the Ideal was offered with a commanding 8 bhp powerplant. Lateral thinker Benz had fitted it with a special kind of two-cylinder engine which he called the Contra Engine. In fact this was none other than a flat boxer engine which gave the "small two-seater car" a powerful advantage. Although Karl Benz had a healthy aversion to power and speed, the last generation Ideal was capable of up to 31 mph.

Die Anregung für ein leichtes und preiswürdiges Fahrzeug kommt von Josef Brecht, der Karl Benz in kaufmännischen Dingen beratend zur Seite steht. Nach diesen Parametern entsteht das Benz Veloziped, kurz Velo geheißen. Der Name ist klangvoll und bescheiden, und er gemahnt an die Ursprünge des Selbstbewegers.

Das ist ganz im Sinne des Erfinders, ebenso wie die kaum verhohlene Kutschen-Silhouette mit kleinen Rädern vorn und großen Rädern hinten. Noch bis Mitte der 1890er-Jahre hebt Benz in den Werbeschriften der Firma die Affinität seiner Kreationen zum Pferde-Fuhrwerk hervor, bis Benz-Automobile führend werden in emanzipatorischem Design. Ein Leichtgewicht ist der Velo in der Tat mit seinen 280 Kilogramm und ein verführerisches Angebot dazu, selbst an die zahlreichen Auto-Muffel der Zeit: »Preis komplett in feinster Ausstattung mit Laternen Mark 2000. Mit Halbverdeck und Spritzleder ausgestattet kostet das Veloziped Mark 2200«, steht in einem zeitgenössischen Prospekt zu lesen. Kunden in ungewöhnlicher Zahl wissen das zu würdigen. Zwischen dem Oktober 1894 und dem gleichen Monat im folgenden Jahr allein werden 125 Velos verkauft. Zusammen mit der verbesserten Version Comfortable ab 1898 (mit Luftreifen) bringt man 1200 Exemplare unter die Leute: Soeben ist das Serienauto geboren worden. Je ein Drittel geht nach Deutschland, Frankreich (unter dem Namen Éclair, zu deutsch Blitz) und ins restliche Ausland.

1,5 PS bei 450/min leistet der Einzylinder von reichlich einem Liter Inhalt am Anfang, 3,5 PS bei 800/min am Ende seiner Produktion 1901, und auch sonst unterzieht Benz das Veloziped nimmermüder Modellpflege, bietet es etwa zunächst mit Flachriemengetriebe und später mit einem Planetengetriebe an, mit drei Fahrstufen und einem Rückwärtsgang. Ein ungemein fortschrittliches Detail ist sein Schwimmervergaser. Ein Gas-Luft-Mengenregler am Ansaugrohr reguliert gemeinsam mit einer Drosselklappe und einer Verstellung des Zündzeitpunkts den Motorlauf flexibler.

Schwer verkäuflich bleiben die Sublimationsstufe Ideal, deren Umkleidung für den Kühlwasserbehälter vorn den Anschein erweckt, es handele sich um eine Motorhaube, und ihre Varianten Duc und Charette. Im letzten Jahr seiner Fertigung 1902 kommt der Ideal mit stattlichen acht PS daher. Querdenker Benz hat ihm einen Zweizylinder der besonderen Art spendiert. Was er Contra-Motor nennt, ist nichts anderes als ein Boxertriebwerk, das dem »Kleinen zweisitzigen Kutschierwagen« mächtig auf die Sprünge hilft: Obwohl Karl Benz eine gesunde Abneigung gegen Kraft und Tempo hegt, ist der Ideal der letzten Generation fähig zu Tempo 50.

C'est Josef Brecht, le conseiller de Karl Benz pour les questions commerciales, qui suggéra de produire un véhicule léger et peu coûteux. C'est selon ce cahier des charges que naît le vélocipède Benz, familièrement appelé Velo. Le nom sonne bien, est modeste, et il rappelle les origines de l'automobile.

Cela est tout à fait dans l'esprit de l'inventeur, au même titre que la silhouette à peine masquée de calèche avec de petites roues à l'avant et de grandes à l'arrière. Jusque vers le milieu des années 1890, encore, Benz souligne, dans les prospectus de la firme, l'affinité de ses créations avec les calèches jusqu'à ce que ses voitures deviennent les pionniers d'un design émancipateur. Avec ses 280 kg, le Velo est vraiment un poids plume et, qui plus est, une nouvelle option, même pour les nombreux adversaires de l'automobile de cette époque : « Prix complet en finition de luxe avec lanternes, 2000 marks. Avec semi-capote et cuir antiprojections, le Vélocipède coûte 2200 marks », peut-on lire dans un prospectus de cette époque. Un nombre inhabituel de clients l'auront apprécié personnellement. D'octobre 1894 à octobre 1895, Benz ne vend pas moins de 125 véhicules. Conjointement avec la version améliorée, baptisée « Comfortable » à partir de 1898 (avec pneus à chambre à air), ce ne sont pas moins de 1200 exemplaires qui trouvent preneur : le véhicule de série venait de naître. Un tiers a été vendu en Allemagne et en France (sous le nom d'Éclair), le reste, dans les autres pays étrangers.

Le monocylindre d'un bon litre de cylindrée développe au début 1,5 ch à 450 tr/min puis 3,5 ch à 800 tr/min, à la fin de sa production, en 1901. D'ailleurs, Benz ne ménage aucun effort pour maintenir son vélocipède toujours au goût du jour. Ainsi le propose-t-il tout d'abord avec une boîte de vitesses à courroies plates et, plus tard, avec une boîte de vitesses planétaire à trois rapports avant et une marche arrière. Son carburateur à flotteur est une caractéristique qui représente un très grand progrès. Conjointement avec une vis papillon et un décalage de l'allumage, un régulateur du volume gaz-air dans le tube d'aspiration rend plus harmonieux le fonctionnement du moteur.

Ultime extrapolation, l'Ideal, dont le carénage du réservoir d'eau de refroidissement à l'avant incite à penser qu'il s'agit d'un capot moteur, avec ses variantes Duc et Charette qui s'avèrent difficiles à vendre. Lors de sa dernière année de production, en 1902, l'Ideal a la puissance respectable de huit chevaux. Esprit fertile, Benz l'a doté d'un bicylindre d'un type particulier. Ce qu'il appelle moteur Contra n'est rien d'autre qu'un moteur à plat qui donne des ailes à la « petite calèche à deux places » : bien que Karl Benz nourrisse une profonde méfiance à l'égard de la puissance et de la vitesse, l'Ideal de la dernière génération est capable d'atteindre les 50 km/h.

Benz Velo 1894

The small Comfortable, manufactured from 1898, was technically the same as the Velo. As the name suggests, however, it offered greater comfort and had a nicely rounded hood.

Der kleine Comfortable ab 1898 entspricht technisch dem Velo. Er bietet aber, wie der Name sagt, mehr Komfort und hat eine gefällig gerundete Motorhaube.

La petite Comfortable, construite à partir de 1898, correspond techniquement au Velo. Mais, comme son nom l'indique, elle offre plus de confort et un élégant capot moteur arrondi.

The Veloziped Comfortable was driven by a four-stroke single cylinder engine with an upright flywheel. It first justified its name in 1896 with the addition of pneumatic tires. The family resemblance to the horse-drawn carriage is still clearly apparent.

Angetrieben wird das Veloziped Comfortable durch einen Viertakt-Einzylinder mit stehendem Schwungrad. Luftreifen gereichen seinem Namen erst ab 1896 zur Ehre. Die Familienähnlichkeit zur Kutsche ist immer noch deutlich.

Le vélocipède Comfortable est propulsé par un monocylindre à quatre temps avec volant-moteur vertical. Il ne mérite son nom qu'en 1896 avec l'adjonction de pneus. La parenté avec la calèche est encore manifeste.

Parts of the front suspension and the mountain safety bar which could be let down to brake the car on steep roads, a necessary precaution since the outer band brakes only worked when moving in a forward direction.

Teile der Vorderradaufhängung und die Bergstütze. Sie muss den Wagen an Steigungen halten, weil die Außenbandbremsen nur in Vorwärtsfahrt greifen.

Parties de la suspension avant et du frein de montagne que l'on peut faire descendre sur les routes escarpées. Le système retient la voiture en montée car le frein courroie extérieur agit seulement en marche avant.

Benz Velo 1894

The next evolutionary development, the Velo Ideal, proved hard to sell despite the obvious advances. The bodywork was now mounted on a sectional steel frame, whereas its forerunner still used wood. The hood opened in one piece from above to reveal the four-stroke, one-cylinder engine. Under the front lid with the ventilation slits was the cooling water tank.

Als schwer verkäuflich erweist sich die Velo-Evolutionsstufe Ideal trotz manifester Fortschritte: Die Karosserie lagert nun auf einem Rahmen aus Profilstahl, wo beim Vorgänger noch Holz herhalten musste. Aus einem Stück: die nach oben zu öffnende Motorhaube über dem Viertakt-Einzylinder. Unter dem vorderen Deckel, durch Luftschlitze aufgebrochen, verbirgt sich der Behälter für das Kühlwasser.

Le Velo Ideal s'avère difficilement vendable malgré des progrès manifestes: la carrosserie repose maintenant sur un cadre en profilé d'acier là où sa devancière comportait encore du bois. D'un seul jet: le capot moteur s'ouvrant vers le haut au-dessus du monocylindre à quatre temps. Sous le carénage avant, interrompu par des fentes d'aération, se trouve le réservoir d'eau de refroidissement.

Details of the driver's cockpit. The photographs show the oil supply and the drip-feed lubricator with the outlets to the lubrication points (right), and the accelerator handle, ignition timing handle, and mixture controller (left).

Details aus dem Führerstand. Ölvorrat und Tropfölerapparat mit Abgängen an die Schmierstellen (rechts), Handgashebel, Zündverstellhebel und Gemischregler (links).

Détails du poste de pilotage. À droite, le réservoir à huile et ses sorties vers les points de lubrification; à gauche, l'accélérateur à main et le levier de réglage de l'allumage et la régulation du mélange.

In the early years of motoring history, it was not just the silhouettes of vehicles which provided a reminder of their lineage, it was also their names. A Phaeton, named after the son of Helios, the sun god in Greek mythology, was originally a light, four-wheeled carriage, a Tonneau was a two-wheeled bassinet with a pair of shafts which you entered from the rear, a Break was a light, open carriage.

The terms Vis-à-Vis and Dos-à-Dos refer to the arrangement of the passengers relative to one another, a situation that also determined the degree of sociability which travelers could enjoy as a consequence. In the Vis-à-Vis the occupants sat facing one another—in early cars of this type a stoical composure was always clearly maintained by the passengers as numerous contemporary pictures show. The driver was somewhat handicapped in having to look past the passengers in the front row. In the Dos-à-Dos the occupants sat back to back, an arrangement which helped the driver to concentrate on the road ahead, but made conversation between the occupants of the two rows of seats rather difficult.

In 1899 the Benz range was extended by the Mylord, Break and Dos-à-Dos model types all equipped with opposed two-cylinder flat engines (in company jargon: Contra Engines). The first of these cars had 5 bhp, 1710 cc engines which doubled the top speed of the Mannheim cars from a sluggish 15½ to a brisk 31 mph. The most powerful of these boxer engines, a 20 bhp unit, was produced in 1901 but was never actually installed. In that year the standard Dos-à-Dos had a 10 bhp, 2690 cc engine, and, depending on its equipment, it was available for up to 7800 marks. The power was transmitted via a 3-speed box with reverse gear, through a belt to the countershaft and by chains to the rear wheels.

From 1897 onwards, pneumatic tires promised a more comfortable ride but they were not without their problems. A journey might frequently be interrupted by the explosive hiss of suddenly escaping air, much to the annoyance of the chauffeur who at that time could still be readily recognized by his dirty hands. A tire change required tedious dismantling work. It was not until 1908 that the first removable rims appeared, and not until just before the First World War that wheel changing became relatively straightforward. But by this time the principle of the Dos-à-Dos was outmoded. It did not surface again until after the Second World War—this time in the form of the poor man's car, the Zündapp Janus.

Nicht nur die Silhouette erinnert in den Babyjahren des Automobils an die Mutter Kutsche, sondern auch die Namensgebung. So ist ein Phaeton, benannt nach dem Sohn des Sonnengotts im griechischen Mythos, ursprünglich ein leichter vierrädriger Kutschwagen, ein Tonneau ein zweirädriger Korbwagen mit Gabeldeichsel sowie Einstieg von hinten, ein Break ein leichter, offener Wagen.

Die Begriffe Vis-à-Vis und Dos-à-Dos bezeichnen die Anordnung der Passagiere zueinander und umreißen zugleich das Maß an Geselligkeit, die diese Gefährte gestatten. Im Vis-à-Vis sitzt man einander Auge in Auge gegenüber, in frühen Autos dieses Typs offenbar stets in stoischer Gelassenheit, wie zahlreiche zeitgenössische Abbildungen bezeugen. Leicht behindert wird der Fahrer, der an den Reisenden im ersten Glied vorbeischauen muss. Im Dos-à-Dos indessen kehrt man einander den Rücken zu, was der Konzentration des Piloten auf den Weg vor ihm förderlich ist, aber die Kommunikation zwischen Reihe eins und Reihe zwei erschwert.

Im Jahre 1899 wird die Benz-Palette erweitert um die Modellfamilien Mylord, Break und Dos-à-Dos, allesamt ausgestattet mit Zweizylinder-Flachtriebwerken (Hausjargon: Contra-Motoren) von zunächst 1710 cm³ und fünf Pferdestärken, was die Spitzengeschwindigkeit der Mobile aus Mannheim umgehend von müden 25 auf muntere 50 Stundenkilometer verdoppelt. Die mit 20 PS stärkste dieser Boxermaschinen entsteht 1901, gelangt indes wohl nie zum Einbau. In jenem Jahr hat der Dos-à-Dos à la carte, je nach Ausstattung feil für bis zu 7800 Mark, bereits 2690 cm³ und zehn Pferdestärken. Sie werden vermittelt über ein Dreiganggetriebe mit Rückwärtsgang – per Riemen auf das Vorgelege, via Ketten zu den Hinterrädern.

Für vermehrten Fahrkomfort sorgen ab 1897 Luftreifen. Aber sie gereichen nicht nur zu ungetrübter Freude: Häufig unterbricht das Zischen schlagartig entweichender Luft die Fahrt, zum Leidwesen der Chauffeure, die man zu jener Zeit noch an ihren schwärzlichen Händen erkennen kann. Umständliche Demontagearbeiten sind die Folge, erst 1908 gibt es abnehmbare Felgen, erst kurz vor dem ersten Weltkrieg vergleichsweise bequem zu entfernende Räder. Da aber gehört das Prinzip Dos-à-Dos längst der Vergangenheit an und feiert erst nach dem zweiten Weltkrieg fröhliche Urständ – in der Form des Armeleute-Autos Zündapp Janus.

Lors des premiers pas de l'automobile, il n'y a pas que la silhouette, mais aussi le nom qui rappelle ses origines, la calèche. Ainsi un Phaeton, nommé d'après le fils du dieu du Soleil dans la mythologie grecque, est-il à l'origine une légère calèche à quatre roues alors qu'une Tonneau est une voiture compacte à deux roues à carrosserie tressée et brancard à fourche ainsi qu'accès depuis l'arrière, un Break étant une voiture légère et découverte.

Les dénominations Vis-à-Vis et Dos-à-Dos font allusion à l'agencement des sièges passagers et donnent simultanément un aperçu de la convivialité autorisée par ces véhicules : dans la Vis-à-Vis, on peut se regarder les yeux dans les yeux ; dans les premières voitures de ce type, une décontraction stoïque était de mise ainsi que le prouvent d'innombrables illustrations contemporaines. Le conducteur est légèrement handicapé, car le passager assis devant lui se trouve exactement dans son champ de vision. Dans la Dos-à-Dos, si la position conforme au nom est bénéfique à la concentration du pilote, elle l'est beaucoup moins à la communication.

En 1899, la gamme Benz s'enrichit de la famille Mylord, Break et Dos-à-Dos, toutes propulsées par des moteurs bicylindriques à courroies plates (en jargon maison : moteurs Contra) de tout d'abord 1710 cm³ de cylindrée et cinq chevaux, ce qui fait instantanément passer la vitesse de pointe des automobiles de Mannheim d'un lymphatique 25 km/h à un fringant 50. Le 20 ch, le plus puissant de ces moteurs boxer, naît en 1901, mais ne sera en réalité jamais installé dans une voiture. Cette année-là, la Dos-à-Dos proposée à un prix pouvant aller jusqu'à 7800 marks selon son équipement à la carte, a déjà une cylindrée de 2690 cm³ et 10 ch. Ceux-ci sont transmis à la route via une boîte à trois vitesses avec marche arrière – par courroies à l'arbre intermédiaire et par chaînes aux roues arrière.

À partir de 1897, les pneus à chambre à air confèrent un meilleur confort. Mais ils ne sont pas toujours une source de plaisir sans faille : il est fréquent que le sifflement de l'air qui s'échappe inopinément interrompe le voyage, au grand dam des chauffeurs que l'on peut reconnaître encore à cette époque à leurs mains noires. Cela impose de laborieux travaux de démontage, car la première jante interchangeable n'apparaît qu'en 1908 et les roues relativement faciles à remplacer, tout juste avant la Première Guerre mondiale. Mais, à ce moment-là, le principe de la Dos-à-Dos appartient depuis longtemps à une époque révolue et il ne connaîtra un regain de popularité qu'après la Seconde Guerre mondiale – sous la forme de la Zündapp Janus, voiture pour conducteurs à revenus modestes.

Benz Dos-à-Dos 1899

Benz Dos-à-Dos 1899

The Benz Dos-à-Dos (French for back to back) demonstrated that carmakers at that time were still experimenting with seating arrangements. It was not until the turn of the century that today's well-nigh universal arrangement became customary. Above: a view of parts of the power train with the seats and floor removed.

Der Benz Dos-à-Dos (für Rücken an Rücken) zeigt, dass man noch mit der Sitzanordnung experimentiert. Erst im neuen Jahrhundert setzt sich die bis heute übliche Verteilung durch. Oben: Unter der entfernten Sitzfläche Teile der Kraftübertragung.

La Benz Dos-à-Dos montre que l'on fait encore des expériences avec l'agencement des sièges à cette époque. Il faudra attendre le XXe siècle pour que la répartition aujourd'hui courante s'impose. Ci-dessus: sous les sièges, des parties de la transmission.

The visitors to the fifth Automobile and Bicycle exhibition in the Paris Grand Palais were witnesses to the first instance of mass imitation in the history of the car. The Mercedes Simplex was the original and there was an abundance of copies. No manufacturer was able to resist the trend towards a modern car which now bore less and less resemblance to the original carriage. Mercedes has revolutionized the world of the car intoned the chorus of reviewers of the show, while some cheeky individuals among them dared to ponder the question "can the car really be further improved?" "But of course" was the response from Wilhelm Maybach who, since the death of Gottlieb Daimler in March 1900, was solely responsible for engineering at Daimler-Motoren-Gesellschaft. He indicated those areas which still offered room for improvement. Tire technology was one example. The 60 kph (37 mph) barrier had long been passed but motor journeys were still bedevilled by irritating punctures with depressing regularity. Meanwhile, engines had not only become more powerful, they had also grown louder.

The Mercedes Simplex really did have something to offer. The Daimler cars had been called Mercedes ever since Emil Jellinek had so named them after his favorite daughter, and he used them in a positively imperial round of presentations of the company to potential customers in Austria-Hungary, France, Belgium, and the United States. Jellinek was the driving force behind the 35 PS sports and touring car of 1901, which, between 1901 and 1905, became the basis of the multi-variant Simplex dynasty with engines ranging from 28 bhp (at 5315 cc capacity) to 60 bhp (at 9235 cc capacity) with various wheelbases and bodies. The cars were called Simplex because of the simplicity with which they could be operated.

The outstanding features of these cars were their long shape, low center of gravity, and light weight. No effort had been spared on the four-cylinder engine which now weighed 408 lbs. It was constructed of alloy and the cylinders consisted of two units each in a single casting. The cylinder head and block were cast as one unit. The chassis of the first Simplex weighed only 2200 lbs. Maybach's honeycomb radiator consisted of rectangular tubes and it enabled the power of the engine to increase as required while at the same time substantially reducing the amount of cooling water it needed. In 1898 a 5 bhp car required 4¾ gallons of cooling water; the winning car at Nice in 1901 still required 2⅜ gal, whereas a Simplex 28/32 PS of the same year required a mere 1⅞ gal.

The numerical code forming part of the car's name in those days provided two pieces of information. The numbers before the slash showed the rated horsepower of the engine, while the actual power was shown after the slash. Power was to increase rapidly—in the second decade of Maybach's leadership "at Daimler" it increased sixtyfold.

Die Besucher der v. Automobil- und Fahrradausstellung im Pariser Grand Palais werden zu Augenzeugen des ersten Massen-Mimikrys der Autogeschichte. Original ist der Mercedes Simplex, Kopien gibt es in Hülle und Fülle. Kein Hersteller mag sich dem Zug der Zeit zum modernen Mobil entziehen, das sich auch visuell immer mehr von der Mutter Kutsche entfernt. Mercedes, so intoniert der Chor der Rezensenten der Show, habe die Autowelt umgekrempelt. Und kecke Solisten wagen die nachdenkliche Frage: »Kann das Kraftfahrzeug überhaupt noch verbessert werden?« »Aber gewiss«, antwortet ihnen Wilhelm Maybach, der seit dem Tod Gottlieb Daimlers im März 1900 die alleinige technische Verantwortung in der Daimler-Motoren-Gesellschaft trägt, und nennt auch gleich Felder, auf denen dem Fortschritt noch Spielräume offenstehen. In der Reifentechnik zum Beispiel: Die 60-Stundenkilometer-Mauer ist längst geschleift, und ärgerliche Pneu-Pannen säumen nach wie vor den Pfad der Automobilisten mit bedrückender Regelmäßigkeit. Und die Motoren sind nicht nur immer stärker, sondern auch immer lauter geworden.

Der Mercedes Simplex indes hat in der Tat einiges zu bieten. Mercedes heißen die Daimler-Wagen, seitdem Emil Jellinek ihnen den Namen seiner Lieblingstochter gegeben hat und sie in ein regelrechtes Imperium von Vertretungen der Firma ausführt, nach Österreich-Ungarn, Frankreich, Belgien und den Vereinigten Staaten. Jellinek ist der Anreger hinter dem Daimler Sport- und Tourenwagen 35 PS von 1901, und dieser wird zum Vorbild der weitverzweigten Simplex-Dynastie zwischen 1901 und 1905 mit Maschinen zwischen 28 PS (bei 5315 cm³ Hubraum) und 60 PS (Hubraum: 9235 cm³) mit diversen Radständen und Aufbauten, Simplex geheißen, weil ihre Bedienung so simpel ist.

Markante Merkmale sind die gestreckte Form, der niedrige Schwerpunkt, die Leichtigkeit: Vor allem an den nun 185 Kilo schweren Vierzylindern hat man abgespeckt. Sie bestehen aus Leichtmetall, und jeweils zwei Zylinder sind zusammengegossen. Kopf und Block bilden eine Einheit. Das Fahrgestell des ersten Simplex wiegt nur noch 1000 Kilogramm. Maybachs Bienenwabenkühler ist komponiert aus eckigen Röhrchen und erlaubt, die Kraft der Maschinen nach Belieben zu steigern sowie die Kühlwassermenge erheblich zu reduzieren: 1898 werden für einen Wagen mit fünf Pferdestärken noch 18 Liter benötigt, für den Siegerwagen von Nizza 1901 noch neun Liter, für einen Simplex 28/32 PS aus dem gleichen Jahr lediglich sieben.

Der Zahlencode, der die Autonamen in dieser Zeit begleitet, enthält eine doppelte Information: vor dem schrägen Querstrich die Steuer-PS, abgeleitet vom Hubraum, dahinter die tatsächliche Leistung. Sie eskaliert zügig: In den zwei Jahrzehnten von Maybachs Stabführung »beim Daimler« auf das Sechzigfache.

Les visiteurs du 5ᵉ Salon de l'automobile et du cycle, au Grand Palais de Paris, sont témoins du premier plagiat industriel dans l'histoire de l'automobile. L'original est la Mercedes Simplex et il en existe des copies par dizaines. Aucun constructeur ne peut se payer le luxe de négliger la mode de la voiture moderne, qui présente également de moins en moins de similitudes avec la calèche à ses origines. Mercedes, déclarent encore les journalistes présents à l'exposition, a révolutionné le monde de l'automobile. Et quelques plumes effrontées posent même une question qui fait réfléchir: « L'automobile peut-elle même être encore améliorée? » « Mais bien sûr », leur répond Wilhelm Maybach qui, depuis la mort de Gottlieb Daimler en mars 1900, assume la responsabilité technique exclusive dans la Daimler-Motoren-Gesellschaft et cite aussi, immédiatement, des domaines dans lesquels il y a encore une certaine marge de progrès. Dans la technique des pneumatiques, par exemple: il y a des lustres que l'on a franchi le mur des 60 km/h et les ennuyantes crevaisons bornent toujours le sentier des automobilistes avec une déprimante régularité. Quant aux moteurs, ils ne sont pas seulement devenus toujours plus puissants, mais aussi toujours plus bruyants.

La Mercedes Simplex ne manque réellement pas d'atouts percutants. Les voitures de Daimler s'appellent Mercedes depuis qu'Emil Jellinek leur a donné le nom de sa fille préférée et les exporte pour les distribuer dans le véritable empire de concessions de sa firme en Autriche-Hongrie, France, Belgique et aux États-Unis. Jellinek est l'initiateur de la voiture de sport et de tourisme Daimler 35 ch de 1901, qui sert régulièrement d'exemple pour la généalogie Simplex, très ramifiée, entre 1901 et 1905 avec des moteurs allant de 28 ch (pour une cylindrée de 5315 cm³) à 60 ch (cylindrée: 9235 cm³) avec divers empattements et de multiples carrosseries, baptisées Simplex parce que leur maniement était d'une grande simplicité.

Parmi les caractéristiques marquantes, la forme allongée, le centre de gravité bas, la légèreté: ce sont surtout les quatre-cylindres, qui pèsent maintenant 185 kg, qui ont perdu du poids. Ils sont en alliage léger et deux cylindres sont respectivement coulés ensemble. La culasse et le bloc moteur constituent une entité. Le châssis de la première Simplex ne pèse plus qu'une tonne. Le radiateur Maybach à nid d'abeilles est une mosaïque de petites tubulures anguleuses qui permet de majorer à volonté la puissance des moteurs et de réduire considérablement la quantité d'eau de refroidissement: en 1898, il fallait encore 18 litres pour une voiture de 5 ch alors que la voiture victorieuse à Nice en 1901 se contente de neuf litres et qu'une Simplex de 28/32 ch de la même année n'en a besoin que de sept.

Signification du code numérique: les chevaux fiscaux, calculés sur la base de la cylindrée, précèdent la barre oblique, les deux autres chiffres indiquent la puissance réelle; celle-ci est multipliée par soixante durant les vingt ans passés par Maybach à la direction « chez Daimler ».

Mercedes Simplex 1902

The 1903 Mercedes Simplex 60 PS: undoubtedly an elegant motor vehicle which had shrugged off the past and which pointed the way far into the future, both as a complete design and in its details.

Der Mercedes Simplex 60 PS, 1903: zweifellos eine stattliche Auto-Erscheinung, die sich von der Vergangenheit gelöst hat und im Ganzen wie im Detail weit in die Zukunft weist.

La Mercedes Simplex 60 ch de 1903: un modèle élégant et précurseur, aussi bien dans la ligne générale que dans les détails.

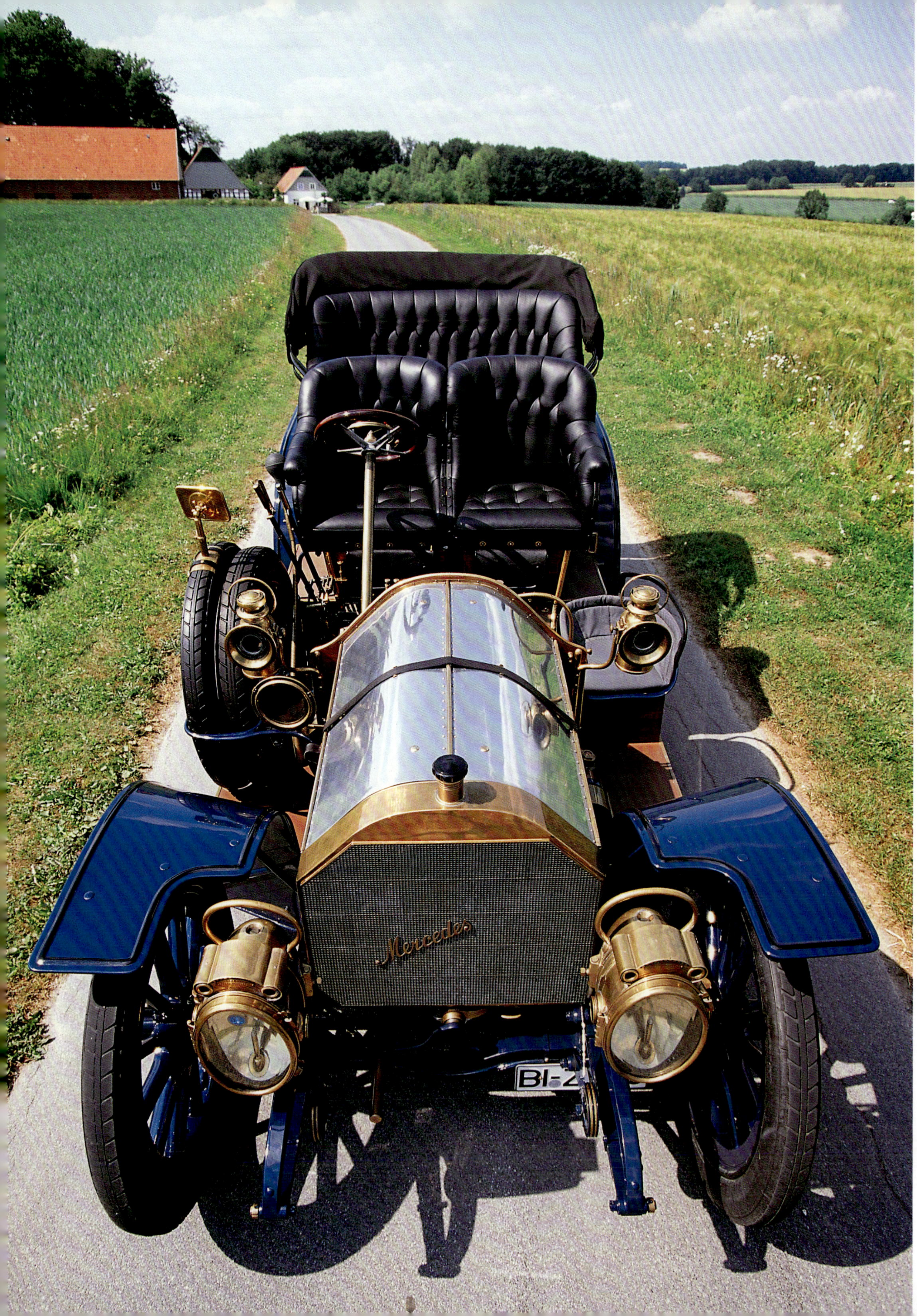
Mercedes

The view from above reveals the character of the Simplex, a machine that transported its occupants in considerable comfort.

Die Perspektive von vorn offenbart den Charakter des Simplex: eine Maschine, die mit elementarem Komfort aufwartet.

La vue de l'avant illustre le caractère de la Simplex : un engin présentant un grand confort.

Variations on the seating theme: the touring car's front passenger seat opens a quarter turn outwards to allow access to the rear seats. The seats in the racing version of the Simplex are relatively spartan, and there is no rear seating.

Variationen: Der Beifahrersitz im Tourenwagen eröffnet auf eine Vierteldrehung hin den Zugang nach hinten. Vergleichsweise spartanisch sind die Schalen in der Rennausführung des Simplex ohne Aufsatz für die Fond-Passagiere.

Variations : le siège passager de la voiture de tourisme libère en un quart de tour l'accès à l'arrière. Dans la version course de la Simplex, les baquets dépourvus de rembourrage pour les passagers arrière sont plutôt spartiates.

What the driver sees—glass inspection panels for the drip-feed lubricators and a large glass oil jar for additional lubrication of the clutch and crankshaft. On the right next to the clock is the speedometer.

Im Blickfeld des Fahrers: Schaugläschen für die Tropföler, ein großes Ölglas für die Zusatzschmierung von Kupplung und Kurbelwelle. Rechts neben der Uhr der Tachometer.

Dans le champ de vision du conducteur: un petit voyant pour le graisseur à gouttes, un grand voyant pour la lubrification supplémentaire de l'embrayage et du vilebrequin. À droite, à côté de la montre, le tachymètre.

Left: a hefty oil tank for pressure feed lubrication.
Right: the Simplex engine which consumed oil in copious quantities.

Links: voluminöser Vorratsbehälter für die Druckschmierung.
Rechts das Triebwerk des Simplex, das Öl als Grundnahrungsmittel zu sich nimmt.

À gauche, le volumineux réservoir d'huile pour la lubrification sous pression.
À droite, le gourmand moteur de la Simplex.

Bright yellow in color, it now stands in the Mercedes Museum in Stuttgart-Untertürkheim, a remarkable fossil that was literally dug out of the sediment of automobile history.

Its curiosity value begins with its name. Today we associate the word spider with cars that are low and wide and rounded, whereas this Benz is of a slender, angular build. But this is what open, two-seater vehicles were called at the turn of the century. In fact, by using suitable accessories, the Benz Spider could easily be converted into a four-seater that was available for 8500 marks. It had a horizontal, opposed two-cylinder engine mounted in the front, unlike earlier practice, a configuration which is reminiscent of today's underfloor construction. With a capacity of 2945 cc, it produced 15 bhp at 1100 rpm, making it quite fast for its time. This yellow car could do 37 mph and take up to a 20 per cent gradient without the passenger having to get out and push.

There is also a certain romanticism attached to the history of the permanent exhibit in Stuttgart. For a long time the Spider slept under an Irish coalheap, jealously concealed from the eyes of the world. There it was discovered by an English enthusiast who kissed the sleeping beauty awake, fastidiously restored it and sold it to hotelier R. G. Sloan. He proved the unbroken roadworthiness of his acquisition by taking part in the veteran London to Brighton rally, where the short Benz car soon became a regular participant. When asked how long he intended to keep this gem of a car, Sloan would answer that it had become the love of his life. However, when he later had an opportunity to buy a larger hotel, he needed cash and agreed to sell the car to Daimler-Benz, being consoled by the knowledge that this slice of recovered automobile history was in good hands.

On 16 January 1969 the Benz Spider arrived in Stuttgart in a special waggon of the German Railways, in the illustrious company of an SSK. Since then many people have had the opportunity to see and marvel at what was once buried under a coalheap.

Poppig-postgelb steht er heute im Mercedes-Museum in Stuttgart-Untertürkheim, ein drolliges Leitfossil, das aus den Sedimenten der Automobilgeschichte gegraben wurde – buchstäblich.

Seine Kuriosität beginnt beim Namen: Mit dem Wort Spider verknüpfen wir heute Begriffe wie flach und breit und rundlich, wo doch dieser Benz von schmalem und eckigem Hochwuchs ist. Um die Jahrhundertwende nennt man so zweisitzige Fahrzeuge ohne Verdeck, nur dass der Benz Spider durch geeignete Anbauten ohne Schwierigkeiten in einen Vierplätzer verwandelt werden kann, der für 8500 Mark käuflich ist. Er hat einen liegend angeordneten Zweizylinder-Contra-Motor, entgegen früheren Gepflogenheiten im Wagenbug untergebracht in einer Art, die an die heutige Unterflurbauweise erinnert. Sein Hubraum beträgt 2945 cm³, und 15 Pferdestärken bei 1100/min machen ihn ganz schön flott: 60 Stundenkilometer läuft der Gelbe, und er steigt bis zu 20 Prozent, ohne dass der Beifahrer schieben muss.

Die Vita des Stuttgarter Dauer-Exponats trägt romanhafte Züge: Lange Zeit schlummert der Spider unter einer irischen Kohlehalde, von irgendjemand eifersüchtig versteckt vor dem Zugriff dieser Welt. Dort entdeckt ihn ein englischer Enthusiast, küsst ihn wach aus seinem Dornröschenschlaf, restauriert ihn pingelig und veräußert ihn an den Hotelier R. G. Sloan. Dieser bestätigt die ungebrochene Fahrtauglichkeit seiner Akquisition, indem er an der Veteranen-Rallye London–Brighton teilnimmt, wo der kurze Benz bald zum lebenden Inventar zählt. Auf die Frage, wie lange er diese automobile Gemme zu behalten gedenke, pflegt Sloan zu antworten, mit ihr verbinde ihn schon eine Liebe auf Lebenszeit. Schließlich wird ihm jedoch ein größeres Hotel zum Kauf angeboten. Er benötigt Bares, wird sich handelseinig mit Daimler-Benz und hat zugleich die tröstliche Gewissheit, die Fundsache komme in gute Hände.

Am 16. Januar 1969 trifft der Benz Spider in einem Spezialwagen der Bundesbahn in Stuttgart ein, in der illustren Begleitung eines SSK. Viele haben seitdem gesehen, was einst unter einem Haufen Kohle verborgen war.

Jaune bouton d'or, elle trône aujourd'hui au musée Mercedes de Stuttgart-Untertürkheim, étrange fossile exhumé – littéralement – des sédiments de l'histoire de l'automobile.

Les bizarreries commencent déjà avec son nom: par Spider, on entend aujourd'hui des qualificatifs comme bas, large et rond alors que cette Benz est de haute stature, étroite et anguleuse. À la charnière du siècle, c'est le nom que l'on donne aux véhicules biplaces sans capote, à cette différence près que la Benz Spider peut sans difficulté se transformer en une quatre places, facturée 8500 marks, grâce à des carrosseries appropriées. Elle possède un bicylindre à plat horizontal qui, contrairement à la coutume, est monté dans la proue de la voiture selon une architecture qui rappelle les moteurs sous plancher d'aujourd'hui. Sa cylindrée est de 2945 cm³ et ses 15 ch à 1100 tr/min lui confèrent de bonnes performances: notre voiture jaune atteint les 60 km/h et est capable de grimper des pentes à 20 % sans que le passager n'ait à la pousser.

L'historique de cet hôte permanent du musée de Stuttgart a des caractères romanesques: longtemps, le Spider a croupi sous un tas de charbon irlandais. Jusqu'à ce qu'il soit découvert un jour par un Anglais enthousiaste qui le réveilla de son sommeil de Belle au bois dormant et le restaura avec une minutie incroyable avant de le céder à l'hôtelier R. G. Sloan. Celui-ci confirma la vitalité de sa nouvelle acquisition en participant au rallye de voitures anciennes Londres–Brighton, auquel la courte Benz participe régulièrement désormais. À ceux qui lui demandaient combien de temps il entendait conserver ce joyau automobile, Sloan avait coutume de répondre qu'il ressentait pour lui déjà un amour éternel. Finalement, on lui proposa l'achat d'un grand hôtel, pour lequel il manquait de liquidités: il passa un marché avec Daimler-Benz et eut simultanément la certitude consolante que son bijou serait désormais en de bonnes mains.

Le 16 janvier 1969, la Benz Spider arrive à Stuttgart dans un wagon spécial de la Bundesbahn avec l'illustre escorte d'une SSK. Depuis, beaucoup ont admiré ce que jadis un tas de charbon avait soustrait à la vue de tous.

Benz Spider 1902

Benz Spider 1902

Back in the light of day—this Benz Spider spent many years beneath a coalheap in Ireland. As can be seen, the car, now a museum piece, survived its ordeal in fine condition.

Durch Nacht zum Licht: Viele Jahre verbrachte der Benz Spider unter einer irischen Kohlehalde. Wie man sieht, hat das heutige Museumsstück das Exil glänzend überstanden.

La lumière au bout de la nuit : cette Benz Spider a passé de longues années sous un tas de charbon irlandais. Comme on peut le constater, ce véhicule exposé aujourd'hui dans un musée a fort bien survécu à cet enfouissement.

This was the first of an illustrious series of powerful and distinguished high-performance cars encompassing both sports cars and thoroughbred racers, a series which ranged from K through S, SS, SSK, SSKL up to the 500 K and 540 K. Distinctive features of this model were the pointed radiator with its two star badges, and the exhaust routed externally on both the left and the right of the car with the exhaust pipes wrapped in metal hose. This had been an extra-cost option on Mercedes models from 1912, but it was now a standard feature for the first time. Displaying the exhaust prominently outside the car as a styling element was to become a feature of the supercharged cars from Stuttgart-Untertürkheim.

The distinctive image of the status-symbol 28/95 PS Mercedes hinted at its hidden qualities. This was particularly the six-cylinder 7280 cc engine which produced 90 bhp at 1800 rpm. It had an overhead camshaft driven by a vertical shaft. This engine had its origin in the Kaiser Prize, an award promised in May 1912 for the best aero engine. Such engines would have to be economical, powerful, and light. Paul Daimler responded with an engine which was intentionally lightweight, with pistons and crankcase made of aluminum. Steel pistons and a welded water jacket were employed. The valves were arranged in a V configuration.

First place went to Daimler's competitor, Benz. Daimler-Motoren-Gesellschaft had to be content with second place, but it still made the best of it. Of the four Mercedes on the starting line in the 1913 Sarthe Grand Prix in Le Mans two had the Kaiser Prize aero engines bearing the code DF80 under their bonnets. Suitably modified, this engine was also used in tourers and it drew remarkable performances from the 28/95 PS. To exploit these qualities fully required a driver with power, courage, and skill. The job was not easy in other respects also—the operating instructions warned that 23 lubrication points needed daily attention, and a further ten needed similar treatment at the end of each week.

Only 25 production models were produced during the 1914 and 1915 war years, with a further 565 between 1920 and 1924. Anyone with the means to purchase a 28/95 PS was indeed faced with an agonizing choice. The model was available as a two-seater and sports and racing two-seater, as Phaeton and Sport Phaeton, as a sedan, as a town coupé, a touring car or sport sedan. And added to this, it still held its own on dusty race tracks. Mercedes driver Max Sailer completed the first of the four 104-mile-long circuits of the 12th Targa Florio on 29 May 1921 in his white two-seater 28/95 PS, finishing second and having notched up the fastest lap.

Er steht am Anfang einer illustren Reihe von kraftvollen und vornehmen Spitzenautomobilen mit sportlichem Akzent einschließlich reinrassiger Rennfahrzeuge, vom K über die S, SS, SSK, SSKL bis hin zu den 500 K und 540 K. Gattungsmerkmale sind der Spitzkühler mit den zwei Stern-Emblemen rechts und links sowie nach außen verlegte, mit Metallschläuchen umwundene Auspuffrohre, aufpreispflichtige Option bereits an Mercedes-Modellen von 1912, nun erstmals serienmäßig. Dass der Auspuff als Stilelement für jedermann sichtbar ausgelagert ist, gehört später zum Image der Kompressorwagen aus Stuttgart-Untertürkheim.

Das gediegene Erscheinungsbild des Status-Symbols Mercedes 28/95 PS lässt auf innere Werte schließen. Korrelat ist vor allem sein Sechszylinder mit 7280 cm³ und 90 PS bei 1800/min, mit einer obenliegenden Nockenwelle, die von einer Königswelle angetrieben wird. Seine Genese: Im Mai 1912 wird der Kaiserpreis ausgelobt für den besten Flugmotor. Sparsam soll er sein und stark und leicht. Paul Daimler antwortet mit einem Triebwerk, das auf Leichtbau abgestellt ist: Kolben und Kurbelgehäuse sind aus Aluminium. Überdies verwendet man Stahlkolben und einen aufgeschweißten Kühlwassermantel. Die Ventile hängen v-förmig.

Den ersten Platz erringt Konkurrent Benz. Die Daimler-Motoren-Gesellschaft muss sich mit Rang zwei bescheiden, macht indessen das Beste daraus. Von den vier Mercedes, die 1913 beim Sarthe Grand Prix in Le Mans zum Start rollen, haben zwei das Kaiserpreis-Flugtriebwerk mit dem Code DF80 unter der Haube. Mit entsprechenden Modifikationen wird es auch für den Einsatz im Tourenwagen vorbereitet und beflügelt etwa den 28/95 PS zu bemerkenswerten Fahrleistungen. Diese voll auszuschöpfen erfordert einen Chauffeur, der Kraft, Mut und Können mitbringen muss. Auch sonst ist der Job nicht einfach: Die Gebrauchsanleitung mahnt an, 23 Schmierstellen bedürften täglicher Zuwendung, am Ende der Woche noch einmal zehn weitere.

Lediglich 25 Serienexemplare entstehen in den Kriegsjahren 1914 und 1915, weitere 565 zwischen 1920 und 1924. Wer sich für einen 28/95 PS entscheidet und die nötigen Mittel mitbringt, hat fürwahr die Qual der Wahl: Es gibt ihn als Zweisitzer und Sport- und Rennsport-Zweiplätzer, als Phaeton und Sport-Phaeton, als Limousine, Stadt-Coupé, Touring Car sowie Sport Sedan. Selbst auf staubigen Pisten steht er seinen Mann: Die erste von vier 167 Kilometer langen Durchgängen der 12. Targa Florio am 29. Mai 1921 führt Mercedes-Pilot Max Sailer mit seinem weißen zweisitzigen 28/95 PS, wird am Ende zweiter und fährt auch die schnellste Runde.

Elle est au début d'une illustre série de puissantes et prestigieuses voitures de très grand standing à l'accent sportif, y compris d'authentiques voitures de compétition, de la K aux 500 K et 540 K en passant par les S, SS, SSK et SSKL. Une caractéristique génétique est le radiateur pointu avec deux étoiles servant d'emblème à droite et à gauche ainsi que les tuyaux d'échappement placés à l'extérieur du capot traversant des tubulures de métal, option matière à supplément de prix dès les modèles Mercedes de 1912, mais désormais proposée en série. Le pot d'échappement placé bien visible par chacun comme élément de style sera plus tard un signe distinctif des voitures à compresseur de Stuttgart-Untertürkheim.

La prestance imposante et luxueuse de la voiture phare qu'est la Mercedes 28/95 ch est le reflet de ce qui se cache sous son capot. Il s'agit surtout, en l'occurrence, de son six-cylindres de 7280 cm³ et 90 ch à 1800 tr/min, avec un arbre à cames en tête entraîné par un arbre à renvoi. Sa genèse est intéressante : en mai 1912, le Prix de l'Empereur est décerné pour le meilleur moteur d'avion. Il doit être économique, mais aussi puissant et léger. La réponse de Paul Daimler est un moteur dédié à la légèreté de construction : pistons et carter-moteur sont en aluminium. Il utilise en outre des pistons en acier et un manteau d'eau de refroidissement soudé. Les soupapes sont suspendues en v.

C'est le concurrent Benz qui remporte la première place. La Daimler-Motoren-Gesellschaft doit se contenter du rang de dauphin, mais en tire le meilleur profit. Sur les quatre Mercedes qui prennent le départ du Grand Prix de la Sarthe au Mans, en 1913, deux, avec le code DF80, ont sous le capot le moteur d'avion du Prix de l'Empereur. Il suffit de le modifier en conséquence pour l'installer aussi dans les voitures de compétition : il permet à la 28/95 ch d'afficher des performances enviables. Pour en exploiter à fond tout le potentiel, il faut un chauffeur qui possède force, courage et savoir-faire. Mais quoi qu'il en soit, le travail n'est pas simple : le mode d'emploi cite 23 points de graissage qui doivent recevoir leurs soins quotidiens, sans compter dix autres échus à la fin de la semaine.

25 exemplaires de série seulement seront construits durant les années de guerre 1914 et 1915, suivis de 565 autres entre 1920 et 1924. Quiconque opte pour une 28/95 ch, à condition d'avoir les moyens, n'a vraiment que l'embarras du choix : elle est proposée en biplace ou biplace de sport et de compétition, en Phaeton et Phaeton-Sport, en berline, coupé de ville, Touring Car et Sport Sedan. Même sur les pistes poussiéreuses, elle fait honneur à son nom : le 29 mai 1921, le pilote de Mercedes, Max Sailer, avec sa 28/95 ch biplace blanche, couvre en tête le premier des quatre tours de 167 km de long de la 12e Targa Florio. Finalement, il termine deuxième et signe aussi le meilleur tour.

Mercedes 28/95 PS   1914

The front-mounted radiator of the 1922 Sport Phaeton contained square pipes soldered together. The metal used was still brass, though this was later replaced by nickel and chrome. Incidentally, this striking design has survived right up to the present day and has almost become part of the Mercedes-Benz emblem.

Im Spitzkühler des Sport-Phaeton von 1922 sind quadratische Rohre miteinander verlötet. Noch ist das Material Messing. Es wird erst später durch Nickel und Chrom ersetzt. Das markante Design hat sich andeutungsweise bis auf den heutigen Tag erhalten und wurde praktisch Teil des Firmenemblems.

Des tubes de section carrée sont soudés les uns aux autres dans le radiateur du Phaeton-Sport de 1922. Le matériau est encore du laiton, mais il sera remplacé plus tard par du nickel et du chrome. Ce design spécifique a été en partie préservé jusqu'à aujourd'hui et est pratiquement devenu un élément constitutif de l'emblème de la firme.

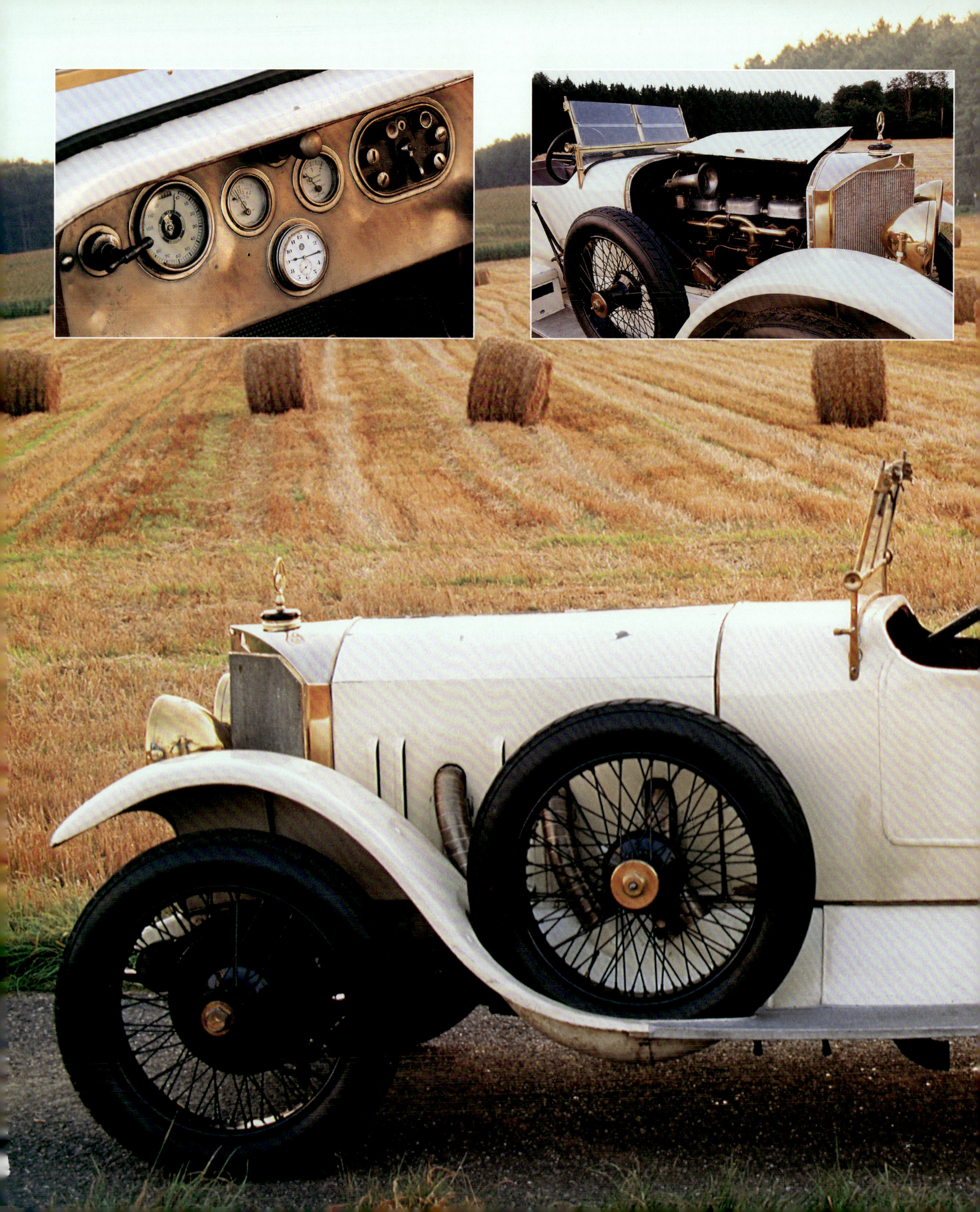

A blast from the past: on 23 March 1922 this 28/95 was despatched to one Señor Villota in Spain. However, it was ordered by Rudolf Ullstein of Berlin. Characteristic feature: the dashboard switch box for electrical instruments.

Zeichen aus der Vergangenheit: Am 23. März 1922 wurde dieser 28/95 an einen Señor Villota nach Spanien ausgeliefert. Besteller war allerdings Rudolf Ullstein in Berlin. Typisch: der Schaltkasten für elektrische Funktionen am Armaturenbrett.

Signe du passé: le 23 mars 1922, cette 28/95 a été livrée à un certain Señor Villota en Espagne. L'auteur de la commande était toutefois Rudolf Ullstein de Berlin. Caractéristique typique: le boîtier à fusibles pour les fonctions électriques au tableau de bord.

Shake-ups and intrigue are not just a feature of the modern Formula One racing scene; they have been part of the history of the car right from the very start. Egos have always clashed. Both success and failure have always been embodied in one outstanding figure, and constructors' heads have invariably rolled as the price for the failure of designs and concepts.

And of course Daimler-Motoren-Gesellschaft was no Arcadian haven in this Darwinian jungle. After all one man's meat is another man's poison. Paul Daimler left the company in 1922 to build an eight-cylinder engine for competitor Horch, which the Daimler board, with an ever watchful eye trained on the average car buyer, had turned down. Ferdinand Porsche became equally obsessed with the idea of the supercharger. But he contented himself with the realization that supercharged engines were fit only for racing cars and one-offs. Two of these, 15/70/100 PS and the 24/100/140 PS, completed the DMG program after a gestation period of two years and were greeted by the chorus of critics as crowning works of world-class production. After the merger of Daimler and Benz in 1926, they were simply called the 400 and 630. The multiple-digit slash code indicated the rated horsepower and the power of the engine blown and unblown.

Many variants were derived from this single master. Some chassis were fitted with Sindelfingen bodies while others were fitted out by coachbuilders such as Erdmann & Rossi, Reutter, Papler, Balzer, Million Guiet, or the Farina stable to suit their customers' taste. The series was crowned by a third variant, the type K (*kurz*, for short wheelbase) in 1926. This came as sporty two- and four-seaters equipped with the 6.3-liter engine of the 24/100/140 PS and a wheelbase shortened from 12 ft 4 in to 11 ft 2 in. The total length was reduced from 17 ft 5 in to 15 ft 6 in on the K variant, an abbreviation that did not detract from its stately appearance. The three hefty metal exhaust pipes sweeping extravagantly out of the right side of the bonnet were also incorporated in the autumn of 1927 in the sister models, the 400 and 630. In this configuration the 630 K was the fastest tourer in the world with a top speed of 90 mph. In 1928 Porsche and his team went even further and produced the ultimate version of the K which delivered 110 bhp unblown and 160 bhp blown. The more powerful engine was still available as an option—even for the standard 630. An average mileage of 9.4 mpg was easily achieved and could be readily exceeded, but, after all, a good 4400 lbs of car had to be shifted. And in any case fuel economy mattered little to the well-heeled clientele of the Twenties—their small talk did not include money.

Revirement und Personal-Rochade gehören nicht erst ins Repertoire der modernen Formel 1, sondern begleiten die Geschichte des Automobils von Anbeginn an. Schon immer knirschen Egos aufeinander. Schon immer knüpfen sich Erfolg und Misserfolg an herausragende einzelne. Schon immer rollen Konstrukteurs-Köpfe für das Scheitern von Konstruktionen und Konzepten.

Die Daimler-Motoren-Gesellschaft bleibt da kein Arkadien inmitten eines darwinistischen Dschungels. Indes: Des einen Eule ist oft des anderen Nachtigall. Paul Daimler geht 1922, um für den Konkurrenten Horch die Achtzylinder zu bauen, die ihm der Daimler-Vorstand mit wachem Blick auf den Mittelstand der Autokäufer verwehrt. Ferdinand Porsche kommt, gleichermaßen besessen von der Idee des Kompressors. Aber er bescheidet sich: Aufgeladene Maschinen taugen nur für Rennfahrzeuge und Repräsentationswagen. Zwei von letzteren runden nach einer Inkubationszeit von zwei Jahren das DMG-Programm nach oben ab, vom Chor der Kritiker zugleich willkommen geheißen als Spitzen-Werke der Weltproduktion, der 15/70/100 PS und der 24/100/140 PS. Nach der Fusion von Daimler und Benz 1926 werden sie schlicht 400 und 630 genannt. Die dreiteiligen Schrägstrich-Kürzel geben Auskunft über Steuer-PS sowie die Leistung ohne und mit Kompressor.

Die Modellreihe wird zum Tummelplatz des Unikats: Viele Fahrgestelle sind mit Sindelfinger Aufbauten erhältlich, andere werden von Karosseriewerken wie Erdmann & Rossi, Reutter, Papler, Balzer, Million Guiet oder den Stabilimenti Farina eingekleidet, ganz nach Gusto ihrer Kunden. 1926 krönt eine dritte Variante die Baureihe, der Typ K (für kurzer Radstand). Sie umspannt sportive Zwei- und Viersitzer mit dem 6,3-Liter-Triebwerk des 24/100/140 PS, dessen Radstand von 3750 auf 3400 Millimeter verringert wird. Wo die Gesamtlänge sonst monumentale 5320 Millimeter betragen mag, tun es für den K deren 4735, ohne dass seinem stattlichen Auftritt Abbruch getan würde. Die drei fetten Metallschläuche, die aus der rechten Seite seiner Motorhaube wuchern, werden im Herbst 1927 auch den Schwestermodellen 400 und 630 spendiert. Bereits in dieser Form ist der 630 K mit einer Spitze von 145 Stundenkilometern der schnellste Tourenwagen der Welt. 1928 satteln Porsche & Cie. noch einmal drauf: 110 PS ohne und 160 PS mit Kompressor leistet der K in dieser ultimativen Version. Auf Wunsch ist die stärkere Maschine auch für den Normal-630 erhältlich. Ein durchschnittlicher Verbrauch von 25 Litern ist rasch erreicht und wird mühelos überschritten – immerhin wollen gut und gerne 2000 Kilogramm in Schwung und bei Laune gehalten werden. Für die verehrte Klientel gilt ohnehin, was im Small Talk der Zwanziger so locker dahingesagt wird: Geld, davon spricht man nicht, man hat es.

Les revirements et échanges de personnel ne figurent pas seulement au répertoire de la Formule 1 moderne. Ils ont accompagné l'histoire de l'automobile dès ses tout débuts. Les ego sont toujours entrés en collision. Succès et échecs ont toujours été liés à des personnalités individuelles éminentes. Des têtes d'ingénieurs sont toujours tombées lorsque les constructions et les concepts se sont soldés par un échec.

La Daimler-Motoren-Gesellschaft ne constitue pas un pays d'Arcadie au cœur d'une jungle darwinienne. Néanmoins, chacun voit midi à sa porte. Paul Daimler s'en va en 1922 pour aller construire, chez le concurrent Porsche, le huit-cylindres que la direction de Daimler lui refuse, parfaitement consciente de ce que les acheteurs de voitures appartiennent le plus souvent aux classes moyennes. Ferdinand Porsche arrive, littéralement obsédé par l'idée du compresseur. Mais il fait preuve de modestie: selon lui, les moteurs suralimentés ne sont idéaux que pour les voitures de course ou de représentation. Après une période d'incubation de deux ans, deux de ces dernières couronnent le programme de la DMG, accompagnées par le chœur enthousiaste des critiques qui les classent parmi les meilleures réalisations de la production mondiale, la 15/70/100 ch et la 24/100/140 ch. Après la fusion de Daimler et de Benz en 1926, elles sont tout simplement rebaptisées 400 et 630. La kyrielle de chiffres indique les chevaux fiscaux ainsi que la puissance sans et avec compresseur.

La gamme se mue en royaume du spécimen unique: de nombreux châssis sont disponibles avec des carrosseries de Sindelfingen alors que d'autres sont habillés par des carrossiers tels Erdmann & Rossi, Reutter, Papler, Balzer, Million Guiet ou le Stabilimenti Farina. Le client est roi. En 1926, une troisième version couronne la gamme, la K (pour empattement court). Elle se compose de deux et quatre places sportives avec le moteur de 6,3 litres de la 24/100/140 ch, dont l'empattement est raccourci de 3750 à 3400 mm. Là où la longueur hors tout atteint, sinon, le chiffre monumental de 5320 mm, pour la K, 4735 « suffisent ». Les trois gros flexibles en métal dont est affublé le côté droit de son capot moteur font aussi leur apparition, à l'automne 1927, sur les modèles jumeaux, la 400 et la 630. Sous cette forme, déjà, la 630 K est, avec une vitesse de pointe de 145 km/h, la voiture de tourisme la plus rapide du monde. En 1928, Porsche & Cie ajoutent du piment: dans cette version ultime, la K développe 110 ch sans compresseur et 160 avec. Pour celui qui le désire, le moteur plus puissant est aussi disponible pour la 630 normale. Une consommation moyenne de 25 litres aux 100 km est tout à fait banale et facile à dépasser – il faut, en effet, faire conserver leur rythme et leur élan à deux bonnes tonnes. Pour l'honorable clientèle, la consommation de carburant est un sujet mineur dans les conversations des années 1920 puisque l'argent, si on n'en parle pas, ne manque pas.

Mercedes 400–630 K   1924

A wide variety of functions were brought together on the steering wheel of the open-top 630 K tourer of 1926. Pressing the instrument ring sounded the horn, while lifting it activated the dipped beam, the handle on the left was a hand throttle, and the handle on the right operated the ignition. The gas pedal was in the middle, a characteristic feature of models K to SSKL.

Am Lenkrad des offenen Tourers 630 K von 1926 sind viele Funktionen versammelt. Das Drücken des Signalrings löst die Hupe aus, das Heben das Abblendlicht, der Hebel links Handgas, der Hebel rechts die Zündverstellung. Das Gaspedal steht in der Mitte, typisch für die Modelle K bis SSKL.

De nombreuses fonctions ont été rapprochées du volant de la Tourer 630 K de 1926. Pour klaxonner, il faut appuyer sur l'anneau de signal et le relever pour enclencher les feux de croisement. Le levier à gauche est l'accélérateur manuel, le levier à droite, celui du réglage de l'allumage. L'accélérateur se trouve au centre, détail typique des modèles K à SSKL.

The 630 K still had separate lamps for main (the upper pair of lamps) and dipped headlights. The practical luggage compartment consisted of a detachable trunk. The spare canister on the running board was for oil, which early automobiles dripped over the countryside in copious amounts.

Für Fernlicht und Abblendlicht gibt es im 630 K noch verschiedene Leuchten. Das Gepäckabteil besteht praktischerweise aus einem abnehmbaren Koffer. Der Ersatzkanister auf dem Trittbrett ist vorzugsweise für den Transport von Öl gedacht, das die Automobile der Frühzeit noch liberal auf die Landschaft tröpfeln ließen.

La 630 K comporte encore des phares différents pour les phares de route (en haut) et les feux de croisement. Le coffre à bagages consiste en une malle démontable, ce qui est bien pratique. Le jerrican sur le marchepied est destiné de préférence au transport d'huile, que les voitures des débuts de l'automobile écoulaient encore avec libéralité sur les routes.

Fabrik-Marke
Trade-Mark
Mädler-Koffer
Mädler-Koffer

NR-EK 27

The day 19 June 1927 developed into a German festival of patriotic celebration. At the opening event on the Nürburgring, three Mercedes were lined up on the first row, two s-types driven by Rudolf Caracciola and Adolf Rosenberger and a 630 K with retired cavalry captain Oskar von Mosch at the wheel.

The similarities between the cars were obvious, but there could be no doubt as to which model was the antecedent and which the successor. The s-type had the shortened chassis of the K, lowered between the axles and deeply curved over them. This lowered the center of gravity and improved roadholding. The engine was more powerful, constructed of silumin, an alloy of aluminum and 13 per cent silicon, with race linings and gray cast-iron cylinder heads. A two-vane supercharger geared to run at three times engine speed blew additional air as required through two pressure carburetors and boosted the power of the monumental six-cylinder engine from 60 to 70 bhp. It was activated by pressing the throttle hard to the floor—a professional signature of the men on the racetrack. The engines idled at a quiet rumble, punctuated by isolated gas surges, then at half-past ten the start of the race was signaled by a shattering crescendo of engine noise which died away as the cars went into the dip of the south loop. They swept into view again on the return straight and then all was stillness, broken 18 minutes later by the rising whine of compressors coming from the direction of Antoniusbuche. The Mercedes were in the lead. Their headlong speed, the blurred merging of the white bodywork into the red of the upholstery—this was the stuff of dreams.

The s model, the masterpiece of Professor Ferdinand Porsche during his time at Daimler-Benz, and its derivatives are among the cars of the century which still fascinate us to this day. One reason for this is their sheer size, the result solely of the massive size of the engine with its 6800 cc capacity, which was increased to 7065 cc from the ss onwards. Only half the 290 units were used for racing; others were acquired for everyday use taking advantage of their utterly solid and tractable engines which produced full power at low rpm. Their type codes mark their journey into legend and are themselves already legends: s for *Sport*, ss (from 1928) for *Super Sport*, ssk (from 1929) for *Super Sport Kurz* (Short), because the wheelbase had been shortened from 11 ft 2 in to 9 ft 8 in, sskl (from 1931 onwards) for *Super Sport Kurz Leicht* (Short Light), so-called because engineers Hans Nibel and Max Wagner had drilled away material wherever possible to save weight. The combination of numbers associated with these magical letters denote the escalation of elegant, controlled power according to the established sequence of the rated horsepower/unblown horsepower/blown horsepower: 26/120/180 (s), 27/170/225 (ss), 27/180/250 (ssk), and 27/240/300 (sskl). It is sometimes difficult to identify exactly which was the original model. Older cars were frequently updated to the latest specification and the type sskl is not to be found

Der 19. Juni 1927 wird zum Fest vaterländischen Hochgefühls: Bei der Eröffnungsveranstaltung auf dem Nürburgring stehen drei Mercedes in der ersten Reihe, die beiden s von Rudolf Caracciola und Adolf Rosenberger und ein 630 K, den der Rittmeister a. D. Oskar von Mosch lenkt.

Man sieht die Ähnlichkeit, kein Zweifel aber auch, welches Modell Vorgänger und welches Nachfolger ist: Der s hat den verkürzten Rahmen des K, näher zur Fahrbahn zwischen den Achsen, stärker hochgekröpft über ihnen. So liegt der Schwerpunkt tiefer, ist die Straßenlage besser. Noch kräftiger sind die Motoren, aus Silumin, einer Legierung aus Aluminium und 13 Prozent Silizium, mit Laufbüchsen und abnehmbaren Zylinderköpfen aus Grauguss. Ein Zweiflügel-Gebläse, das mit dreifacher Motordrehzahl läuft, beschickt bei Bedarf zwei Druckvergaser mit zusätzlicher Luft und bläst dem monumentalen Sechszylinder dann mehr Leistung ein, 60 bis 70 PS. Es wird aktiviert durch beherztes Durchtreten des Gaspedals, Berufsmerkmal der Männer am Ring. Maschinen grollen im Leerlauf, vereinzelte Gasstöße folgen. Schließlich, gegen halb elf, kündet wütendes Crescendo vom Start des Rennens, verebbt im Gefälle der Südschleife. Noch einmal erscheinen die Wagen auf der Gegengeraden, dann herrscht Stille, bis nach 18 Minuten aus Richtung Antoniusbuche das hohe Weinen der Kompressoren anschwillt. Die Mercedes führen. Ihre rasende Passage, das verschwimmende Ineinander vom Weiß der Karosserie und vom Rot der Polster, ist der Stoff, aus dem die Träume sind.

Der s, Meister-Stück des Professors Ferdinand Porsche während seiner Dienstzeit bei Daimler-Benz, und seine Derivate sind Jahrhundertautos, deren Faszination sich bis auf den heutigen Tag mitteilt. Ein Grund dafür liegt in ihrer schieren Größe, bedingt allein schon von der stattlichen Bauhöhe des Triebwerks mit seinen 6800 cm³, vom ss an 7065 cm³. Nur etwa die Hälfte der 290 Exemplare wird in Rennen eingesetzt, uneingeschränkt alltagstauglich, auch sie mit ursoliden und geschmeidigen Motoren, die ihre volle Leistung bei niedrigen Drehzahlen abgeben. Ihre Typenkürzel markieren ihren Weg in die Legende und sind selbst schon Legende: s steht für Sport, ss (ab 1928) für Super Sport, ssk (ab 1929) für Super Sport Kurz, denn der Radstand ist von 3400 auf 2950 Millimeter verknappt worden, sskl (ab 1931) für Super Sport Kurz Leicht, weil die Ingenieure Hans Nibel und Max Wagner Substanz herausgedrillt haben, wo immer das vertretbar war. Die Zahlenkombinationen aber, die diesen magischen Lettern zugeordnet sind, zeichnen die Eskalation elegant gebändigter Gewalt nach, jeweils in der Reihenfolge zu versteuernde PS, PS ohne Kompressor, PS mit Kompressor: 26/120/180 (s), 27/170/225 (ss), 27/180/250 (ssk) und 27/240/300 (sskl). Genau zu orten, um welches Modell es sich ursprünglich handelt, ist manchmal schwierig: Ältere Fahrzeuge wurden häufig auf den letzten Stand der Dinge gebracht, und der Typ sskl ist in den

Le 19 juin 1927 fait vibrer la fibre patriotique des spectateurs: lors de l'inauguration solennelle du Nürburgring, trois Mercedes figurent en première ligne au départ, les deux s de Rudolf Caracciola et Adolf Rosenberger et une 630 K, pilotée par le noble Oskar von Mosch.

On reconnaît la similitude, mais sans le moindre doute aussi la filiation entre chacun des modèles: la s a le cadre raccourci de la K avec moins de garde au sol entre les essieux, plus fortement galbé au-dessus de ceux-ci. Le centre de gravité est, ainsi, plus bas et la tenue de route, meilleure. Les moteurs sont encore plus puissants, en silumi, un alliage d'aluminium et de 13 % de silicium, avec des chemises et des culasses démontables en fonte grise. Un compresseur à doubles ailettes tournant à un régime triple de celui du moteur envoie en cas de besoin de l'air supplémentaire à deux carburateurs à pression et insuffle alors au monumental six-cylindres environ 60 à 70 chevaux supplémentaires. On actionne le compresseur en enfonçant brutalement l'accélérateur – déformation professionnelle des hommes forts du Nürburgring. Au ralenti, les moteurs émettent des borborygmes suivis de coups d'accélérateur nerveux. Enfin, vers 10 h 30, le crescendo furieux annonce le départ de la course avant de s'évanouir peu à peu dans la descente de la boucle Sud. Les voitures font leur réapparition, puis c'est le silence total jusqu'à ce que, 18 minutes plus tard, en direction d'Antoniusbuche, la plainte stridente des compresseurs reprenne de l'ampleur. Les Mercedes sont en tête. Leur passage météorique, la mosaïque floue des flancs de leur carrosserie et du rouge des capitonnages est la substance dont sont faits les rêves.

La s, chef-d'œuvre du professeur Ferdinand Porsche durant son passage chez Daimler-Benz, et ses dérivés sont des autos qui ont marqué leur siècle et à la fascination desquelles nous succombons aujourd'hui encore. L'un des motifs est leur taille inimaginable, due, déjà, à l'énorme encombrement en hauteur du moteur avec ses 6800 cm³ de cylindrée, ou 7065 pour la ss. La moitié seulement, environ, des 290 exemplaires a été engagée en course, sans la moindre restriction quant à une utilisation quotidienne, elles aussi avec des moteurs indestructibles et ronronnants qui délivrent toute leur puissance à bas régime. Les dénominations sont des étapes sur la route de la légende et elles font elles-mêmes déjà légende: s signifie Sport, ss (à partir de 1928) Super Sport, ssk (à partir de 1929) Super Sport Court, car l'empattement a été ramené de 3400 à 2950 mm, sskl (à partir de 1931) pour Super Sport Court Léger, parce que les ingénieurs Hans Nibel et Max Wagner ont fait la chasse aux kilogrammes superflus partout où cela était raisonnable. Mais les combinaisons de chiffres qui précèdent ces lettres magiques sont le symbole d'une course à la puissance maîtrisée avec élégance, toujours dans la chronologie des chevaux fiscaux, chevaux sans compresseur et chevaux avec compresseur: 26/120/180 (s), 27/170/225 (ss), 27/180/250 (ssk) et 27/240/300 (sskl). Il est parfois difficile

Mercedes-Benz S–SSKL   1927

on the order books of Mercedes, even though at least one works car was built.

Even though the chassis of an ss cost 31,000 reichsmarks and the sports four-seater 44,000 reichsmarks, no profit was made from the construction of the series. Its function was rather that of an artistically-designed tavern sign. The car itself earned nothing, but its advertising value was considerable.

Kommissionsbüchern von Mercedes nicht nachzuweisen, obwohl es mindestens einen Werkswagen gab.

Obwohl etwa das Fahrgestell eines ss 31 000 und der Sport-Viersitzer 44 000 Reichsmark kosten, ist mit der Baureihe kein Profit zu machen. Sie erfüllt eher die Funktion eines kunstvoll gestalteten Wirtshausschildes: Es bringt selbst nichts ein, aber die Werbewirkung ist beträchtlich.

de savoir avec exactitude de quel modèle il s'agissait à l'origine : les modèles anciens sont fréquemment restaurés, au gré des évolutions techniques, mais la sskl ne figure pas dans les livres de commissions de Mercedes bien qu'il en ait existé au moins une voiture d'usine.

Bien qu'un châssis de ss coûte 31 000 reichsmarks et la quatre-places Sport, 44 000 reichsmarks, il n'est pas possible de faire des bénéfices avec cette gamme. Elle a surtout pour fonction de donner un lustre supplémentaire à une marque dont l'image est déjà prestigieuse : elle ne rapporte rien elle-même, mais l'effet médiatique est considérable.

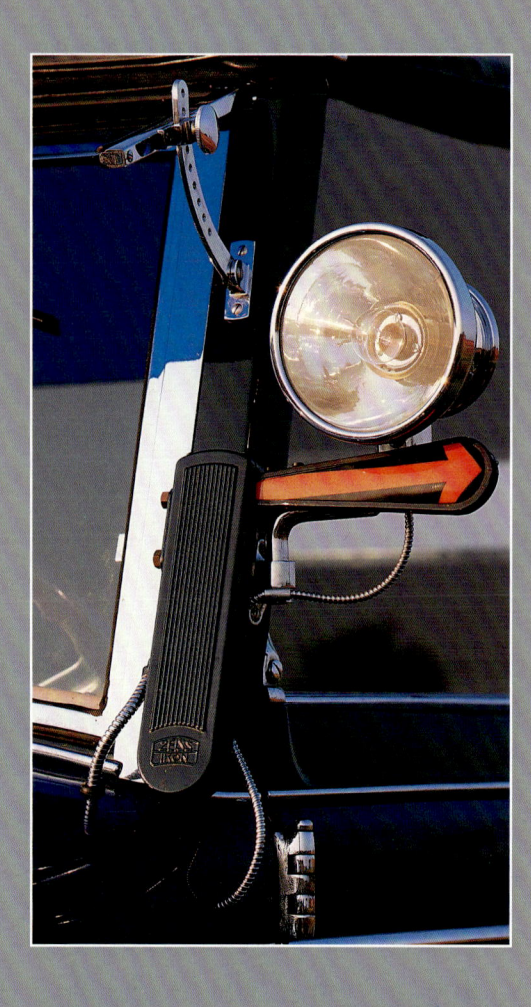

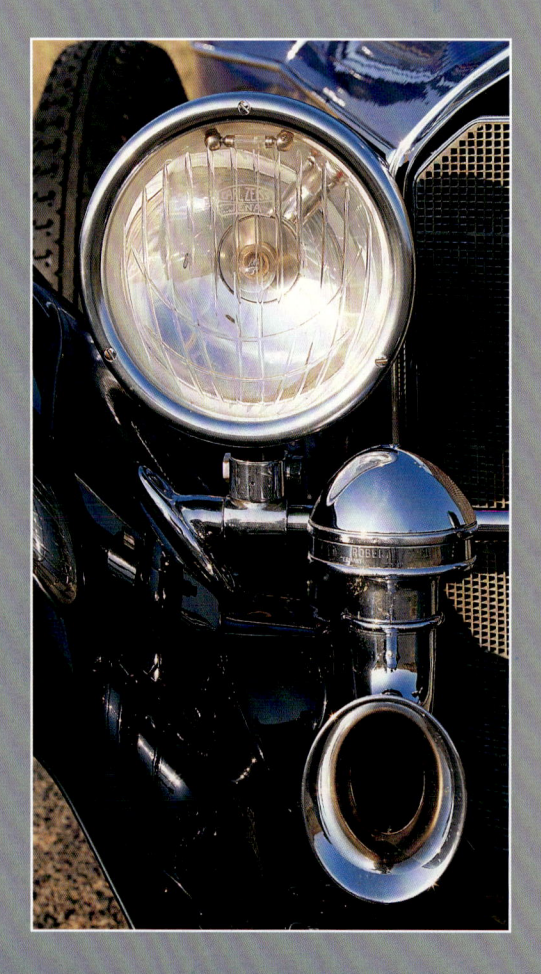

The lights were from Zeiss, and the horn from Bosch. The body of the four-seater S cabriolet from 1929 was the work of the Berlin-based coachbuilders Erdmann & Rossi. Only about half of all chassis had a works-built body.

Die Lampen kommen von Zeiss, das Horn steuert Bosch bei. Der Aufbau des viersitzigen S-Cabriolets aus dem Jahr 1929 stammt von der Berliner Karosseriefabrik Erdmann & Rossi. Nur etwa die Hälfte aller Chassis werden vom Werk eingekleidet.

Les phares sont signés Zeiss, le klaxon est de Bosch. La carrosserie du cabriolet S à quatre places de 1929 est l'œuvre du styliste berlinois Erdmann & Rossi. Environ la moitié, seulement, de tous les châssis ont été habillés par l'usine.

Mercedes-Benz S–SSKL 1927

It came, it saw—and it conquered: the winning car in the opening race at the Nürburgring on 19 June 1927, an S-model racing car. The small door ahead of the rear wheels was a concession to the rules and was not functional.

Er kam, sah – und gewann: Der Siegerwagen des Eröffnungsrennens am Nürburgring am 19. Juni 1927, ein S-Rennsport. Die kleine Tür vor den Hinterrädern ist ein Zugeständnis an das Reglement und wurde nicht benutzt.

Veni, vidi, vici: la voiture victorieuse de la course inaugurale du Nürburgring, le 19 juin 1927, un Cabriolet S. La petite porte devant les roues arrière est une concession au règlement qui n'était pas utilisable.

Mercedes-Benz S–SSKL 1927

This four-seater, open-top S tourer from 1928 is fitted with a body from Sindelfingen. The stick-on cellophane side-screens hardly protected this sporting tourer against the rigors of the weather. It had a detaachable trunk. Under the bonnet the two carburetors are visible, while the adjustable supercharger was mounted vertically at the front of the engine. At the head of it all, the radiator cap surmounted by the Mercedes star with a thermometer in its base.

Dieser viersitzige offene S-Tourer von 1928 ist mit einer Karosserie aus Sindelfingen bekleidet. Selbst mit seitlichen Steckscheiben aus Zellophan ist der Tourer kaum gegen die Unbilden der Witterung gewappnet, ein sportliches Reisefahrzeug mit abnehmbarem Koffer. Jenseits der Motorhaube werden seine zwei Vergaser sichtbar. Der zuschaltbare Kompressor steht vorn senkrecht. Beherrschend der Kühlerverschluss: der Mercedes-Stern mit einem Thermometer im Sockel.

Cette Tourer S décapotable à quatre places de 1928 possède une carrosserie réalisée à Sindelfingen. Même avec les vitres latérales démontables en Cellophane, la Tourer n'est presque pas protégée contre les aléas du temps. Elle possède une malle démontable à l'arrière. Sous le capot apparaissent, bien visibles, les deux carburateurs. Le compresseur débrayable se trouve à la verticale, à l'avant. Notez le magnifique bouchon de radiateur : l'étoile Mercedes avec un thermomètre dans le socle.

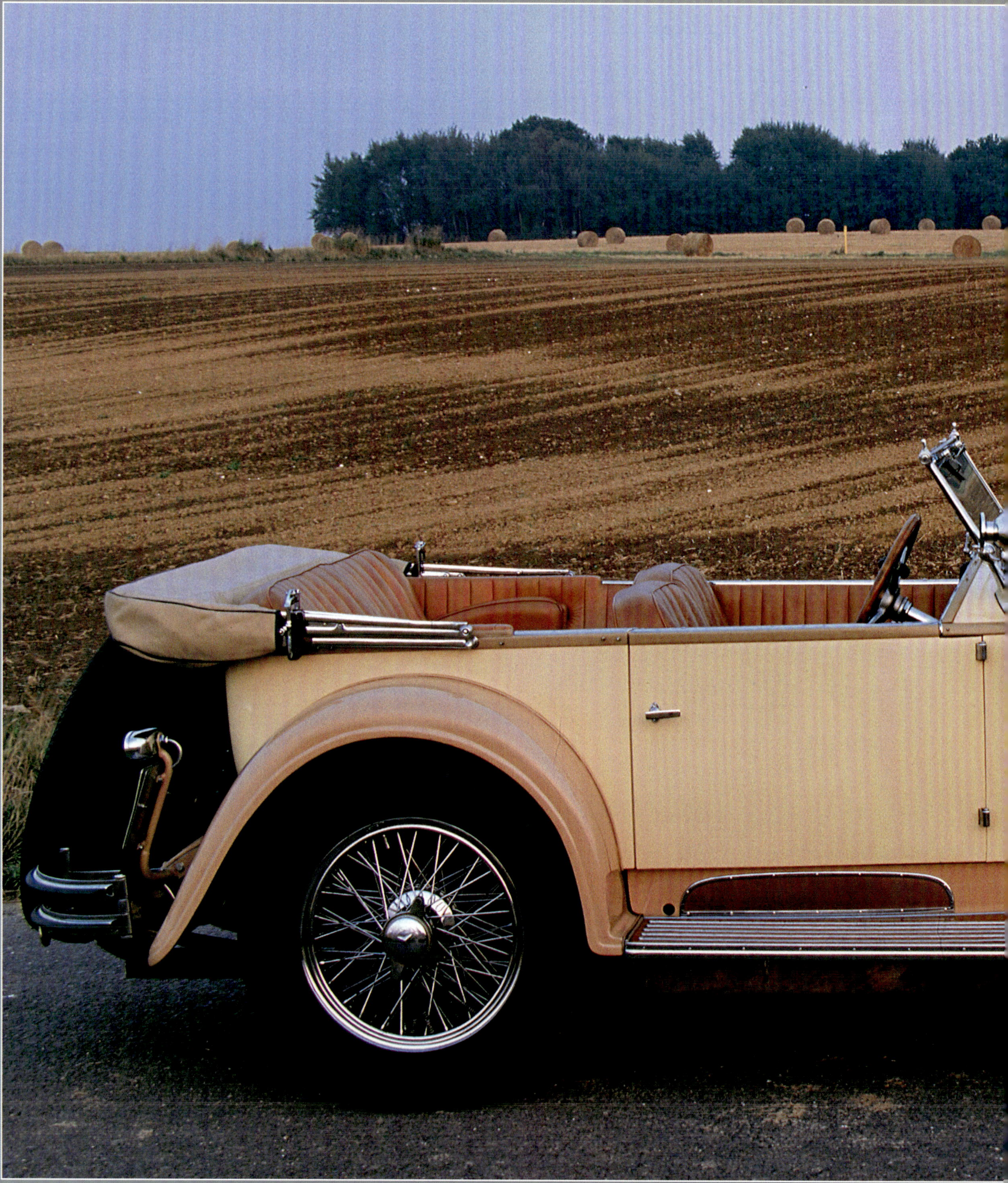

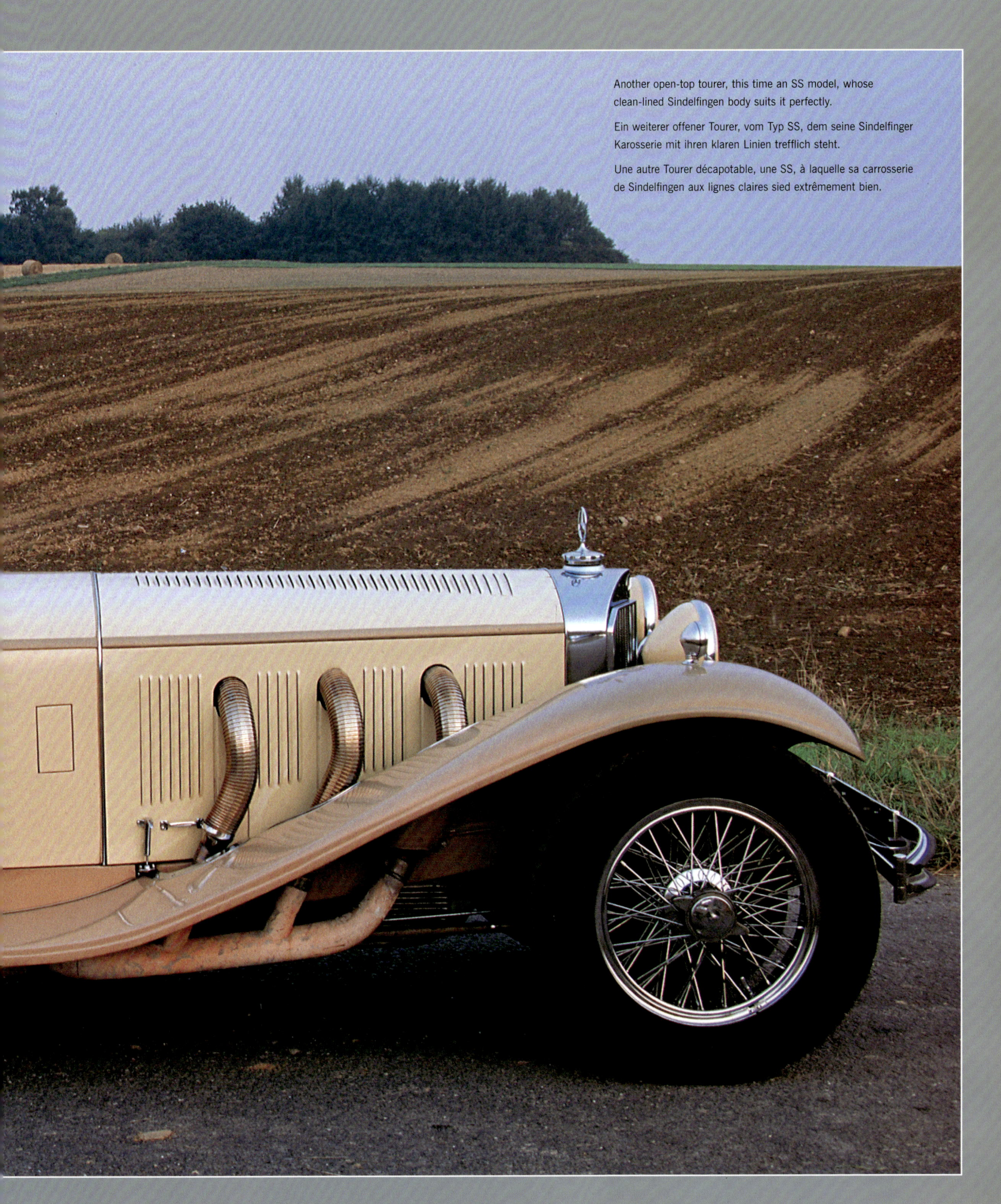

Another open-top tourer, this time an SS model, whose clean-lined Sindelfingen body suits it perfectly.

Ein weiterer offener Tourer, vom Typ SS, dem seine Sindelfinger Karosserie mit ihren klaren Linien trefflich steht.

Une autre Tourer décapotable, une SS, à laquelle sa carrosserie de Sindelfingen aux lignes claires sied extrêmement bien.

At the end of the Roaring Twenties the exuberance of the times demanded extravagant status symbols. The SS Tourer was a majestic motor vehicle which met this need to perfection, with its high radiator, masses of chrome, and impressive dimensions.

Am Ende der Roaring Twenties verlangt ein gesteigertes Lebensgefühl nach manifester Statussymbolik. Der SS-Tourer eignet sich glänzend dazu, ein majestätisches Automobil mit höherem Kühler, viel Chrom und einschüchternden Dimensionen.

À la fin des Roaring Twenties, années d'exubérance, les signes extérieurs de richesse sont essentiels. La SS Tourer, automobile majestueuse s'il en est, satisfait cette exigence de perfection, avec un radiateur plus élevé, des chromes omniprésents et de larges dimensions.

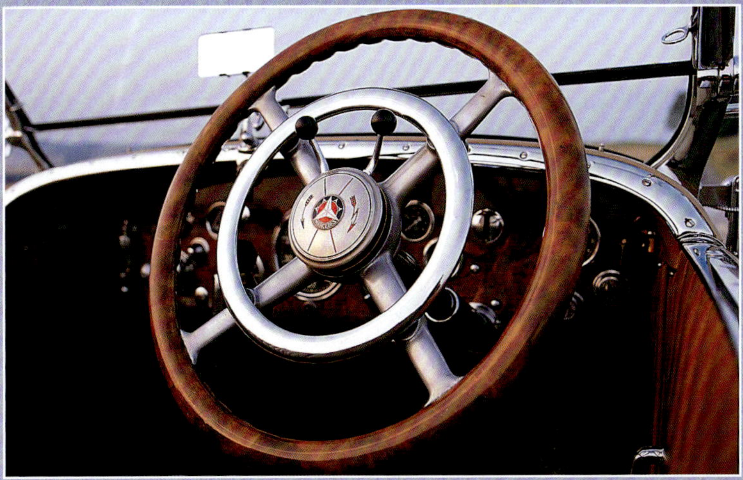

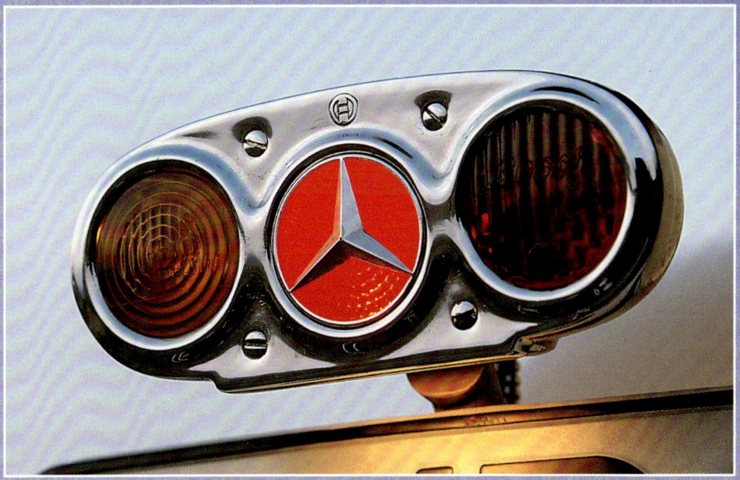

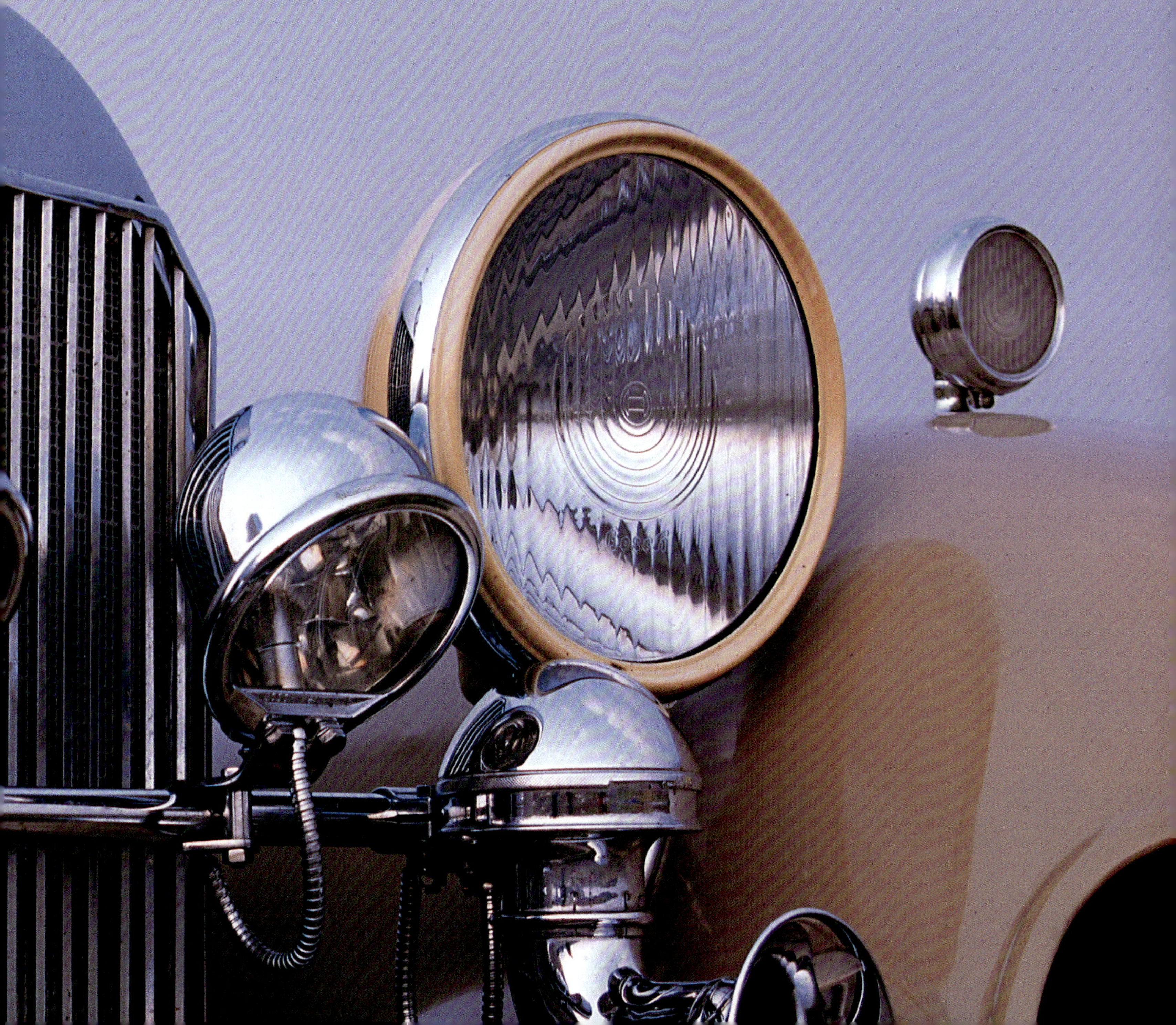

Mercedes-Benz S–SSKL 1927

After its win, with Rudi Caracciola at the wheel, in the 1929 Tourist Trophy, the SS Rennsport depicted here was purchased by wealthy amateur racing driver Earl Howe. He commissioned the English firm Barker to fit it with new bodywork which was fairly similar to the original works version. However, the ash frame was replaced by a light aluminum structure.

Nach seinem Sieg unter Rudi Caracciola bei der Tourist Trophy 1929 wird der abgebildete SS Rennsport von dem wohlhabenden Herrenfahrer Earl Howe erstanden. Der lässt ihm eine englische Barker-Karosserie verpassen, nicht unähnlich dem ursprünglichen Werksaufbau. Allerdings ersetzt man das Eschengestell durch eine leichte Aluminiumkonstruktion.

Après sa victoire avec Rudi Caracciola au Tourist Trophy de 1929, la SS Rennsport illustrée ici est achetée par un *gentleman driver* aisé, Earl Howe. Il la dote d'une carrosserie anglaise Barker, assez semblable à la carrosserie d'origine. En revanche, il fait remplacer le cadre en frêne par une construction plus légère, en aluminium.

The license plate is from the time of Earl Howe. However, the German origin of the vehicle is betrayed by its left-hand drive.

Das Kennzeichen stammt aus der Zeit des Earl Howe. Die deutschen Ursprünge des Autos verrät allerdings noch seine Linkslenkung.

La plaque minéralogique remonte à l'époque de Earl Howe. Sa direction à gauche trahit toutefois les origines allemandes de la voiture.

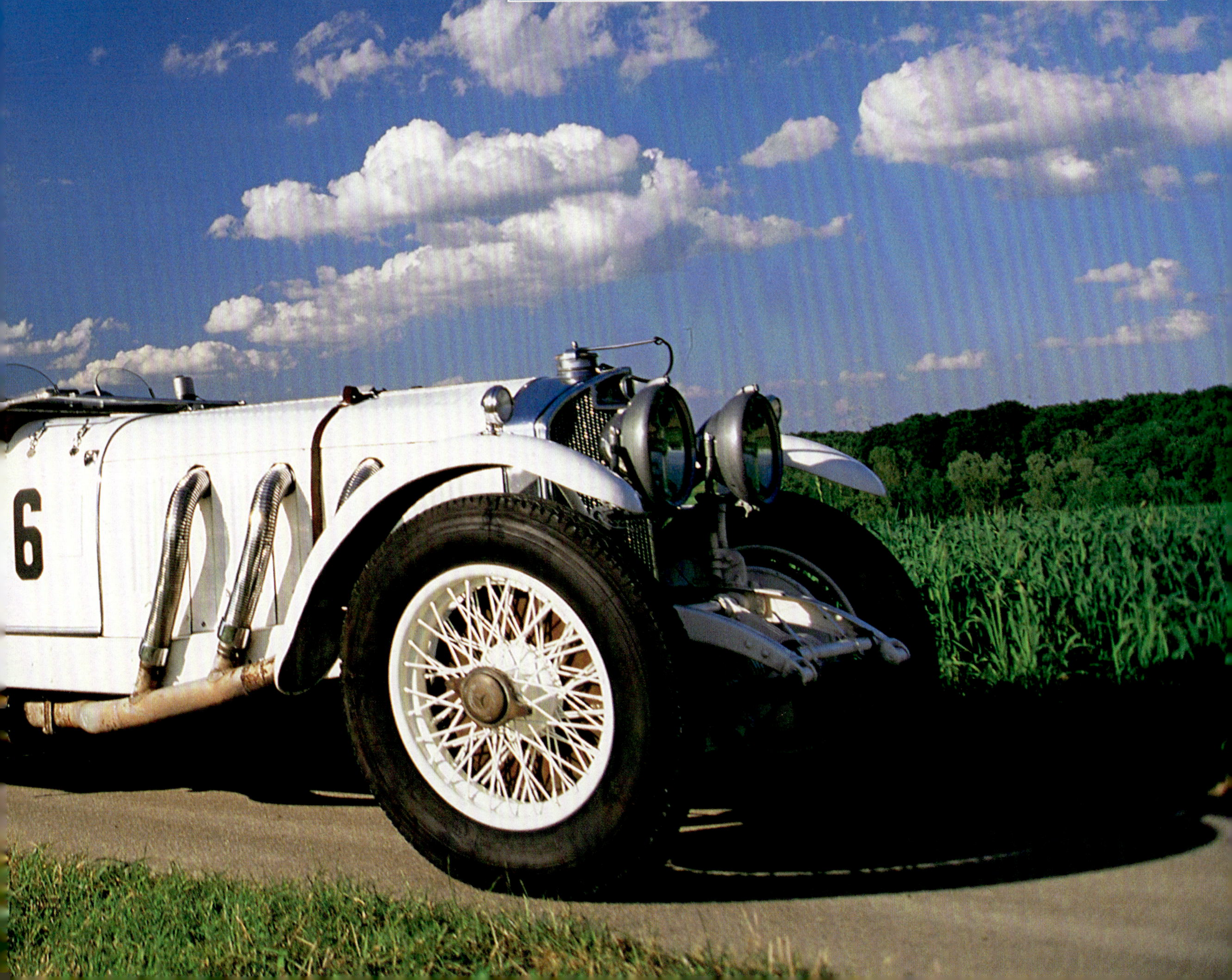
6
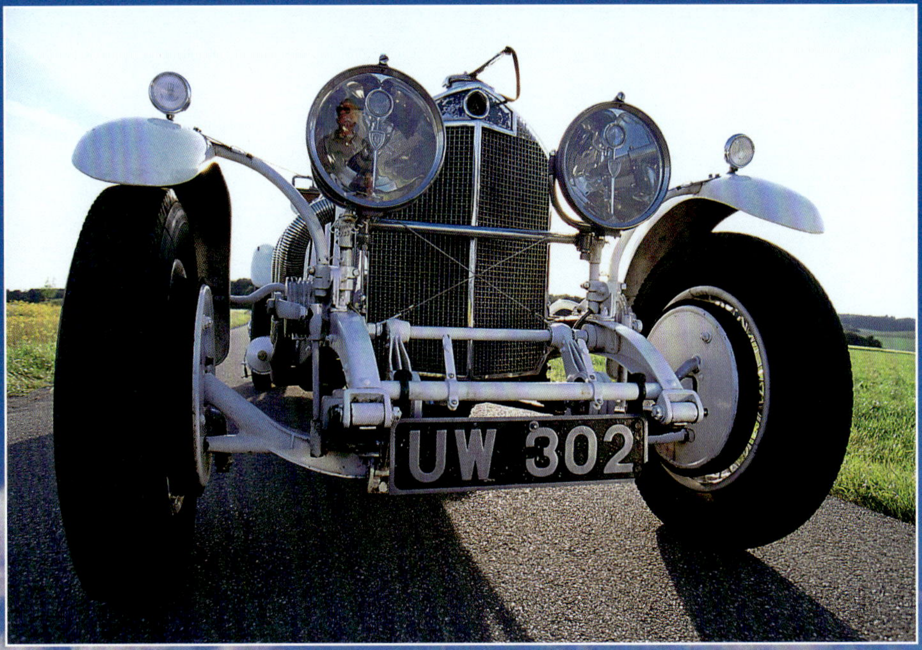
UW 302

Record-breaking British driver Malcolm Campbell was so taken by Caracciola's success in the 1929 Tourist Trophy that he ordered an SS for the following year, with standard bodywork and right-hand drive. His GP10 license plate became famous, not least because of his successes with the car on the Brooklands racetrack.

Der britische Rekordfahrer Malcolm Campbell ist so begeistert von Caracciolas Erfolg bei der Tourist Trophy 1929, dass er sich fürs nächste Jahr einen SS bestellt, mit Werkskarosserie und Rechtslenkung. Nicht zuletzt durch seine Erfolge auf der Bahn von Brooklands wird sein Nummernschild berühmt: GP10.

Le pilote de record britannique Malcolm Campbell est si enthousiasmé par le succès de Caracciola lors du Tourist Trophy 1929 qu'il se commande pour l'année suivante une SS avec carrosserie d'usine et conduite à droite. Sa plaque minéralogique – GP10 – deviendra célèbre, notamment grâce à ses succès sur les pistes de Brooklands.

Mercedes-Benz S–SSKL 1927

Mercedes-Benz S–SSKL 1927

The soft top of the SS Rennsport is a makeshift feature in a car lacking side windows. The mighty six-cylinder engine looks all the more impressive, a monument in itself. Loving details: Mercedes star with thermometer, adjustable windshield to reduce wind resistance.

Das Stoffverdeck des SS Rennsport ist fürwahr eine Notlösung. Nicht einmal Seitenscheiben sind vorgesehen. Um so eindrucksvoller der riesige Sechszylinder, ein Monument seiner selbst. Liebe zum Detail: Stern mit Thermometer, umlegbare Windschutzscheibe zur Verringerung des Luftwiderstands.

La capote en tissu de la SS Rennsport n'est qu'une solution de dépannage sur un véhicule qui ne comporte même pas de vitres latérales. D'autant plus impressionnant, le gigantesque six-cylindres, un monument dédié à lui-même. L'amour du détail : le bouchon de réservoir à l'anglaise, l'étoile avec thermomètre, le pare-brise rabattable pour diminuer la résistance aérodynamique.

Mercedes-Benz S–SSKL 1927

Mercedes-Benz S–SSKL 1927

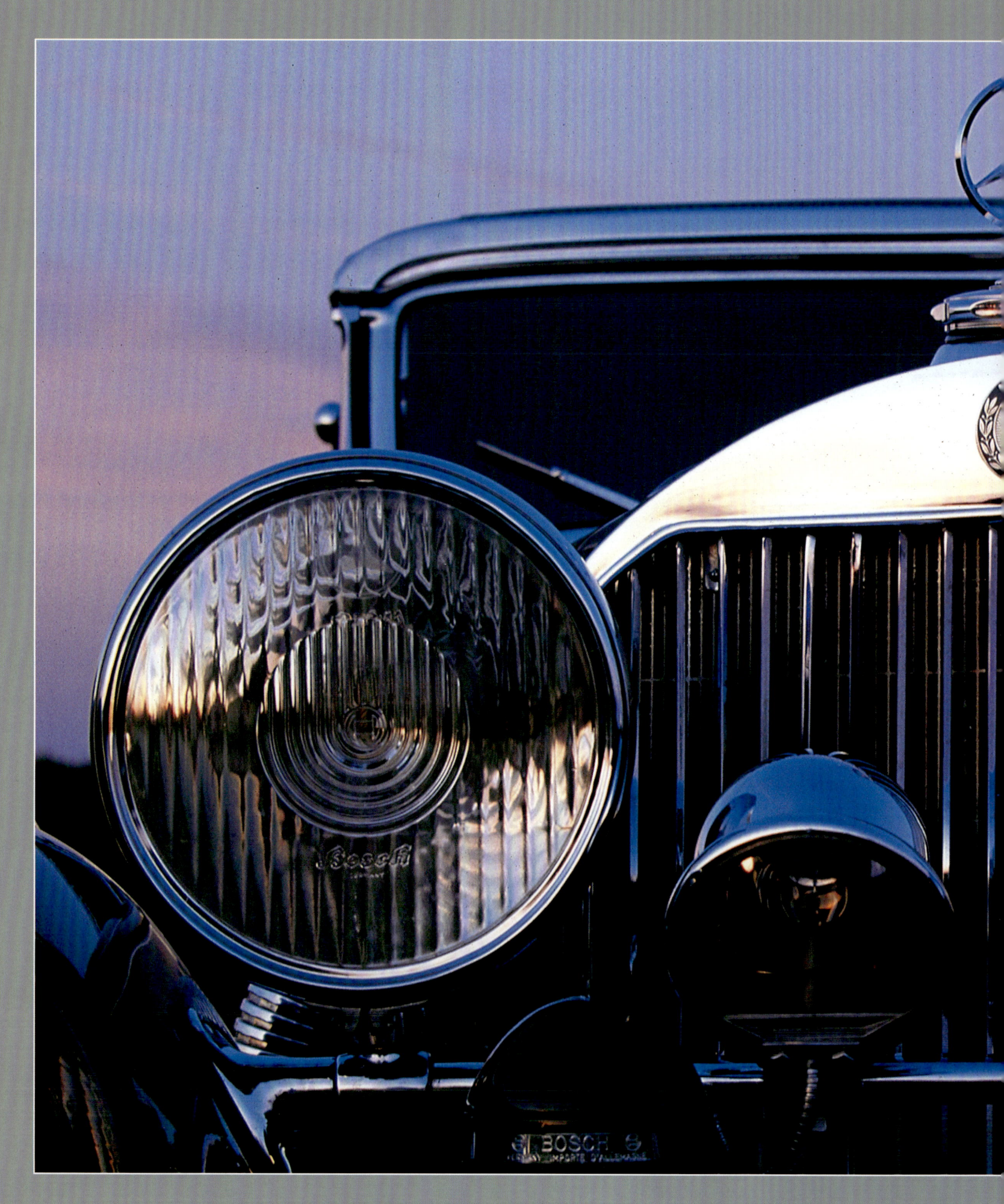

Stylistically this two seater SS cabriolet with in-house coachwork, the only one of its type, was a precursor of the future 500 series. Power and ambition are embodied in its aristocratic appearance.

Stilistisch weist dieses zweisitzige SS-Cabriolet, einziges seiner Art, bereits auf die zukünftige Baureihe 500 vor. Die Karosserie wurde im Werk geschaffen. In seinem aristokratischen Auftreten manifestieren sich Macht und Anspruch.

Sur le plan esthétique, ce cabriolet SS deux places, le seul en son genre, préfigure déjà la future série 500. La carrosserie a été réalisée à l'usine. Dans sa démarche aristocratique, elle incarne pouvoir et ambition.

Enormous two-seater: the semi-circular wings merging with the running boards were a striking feature. Also noteworthy are the chrome-plated counterbalance weights. The characteristic instrument ring with throttle and ignition handles was still fitted on the steering wheel. The engine was identical to that of the racing version.

Monumentaler Zweisitzer mit markanten Radlaufkotflügeln. Bemerkenswert: die Chromhülsen der Auswuchtgewichte. Vor sich hat der Pilot aufwändige Armaturen. Auf dem Lenkrad sitzt wieder der typische Signalring mit Hebeln für Handgas und Zündverstellung. Der Motor ist identisch mit dem der Wettbewerbswagen.

Détail typique : les ailes qui couvrent un demi-cercle de la roue avant de se fondre dans les marchepieds. À remarquer : les manchons chromés des masses d'équilibrage. Le pilote a de quoi se distraire avec ces nombreux cadrans. Au volant, on retrouve le typique anneau avec leviers pour l'accélérateur manuel et le réglage de l'allumage. Le moteur est identique à celui de la version course.

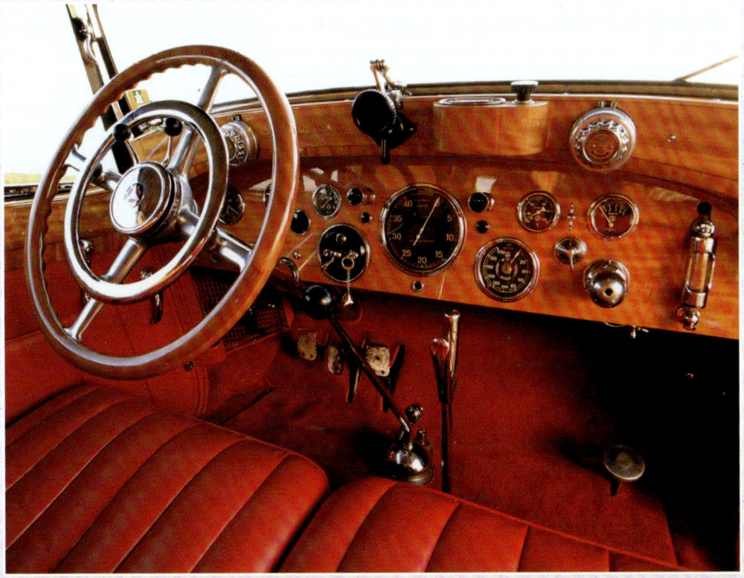
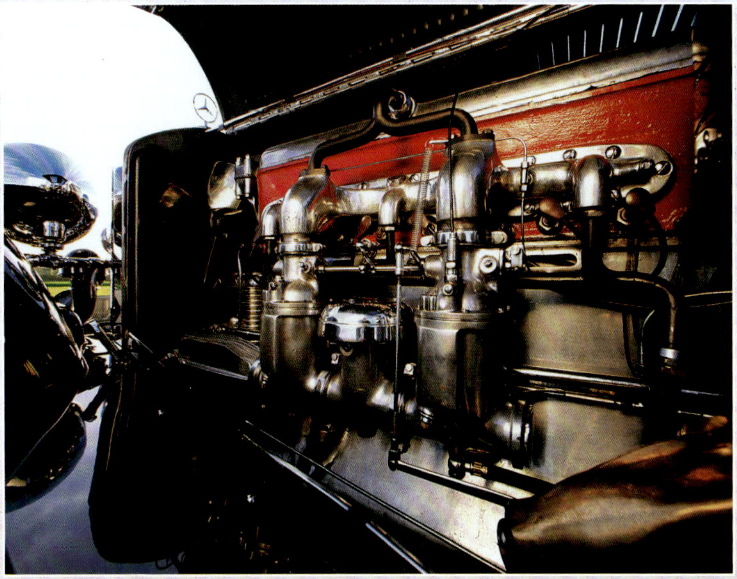
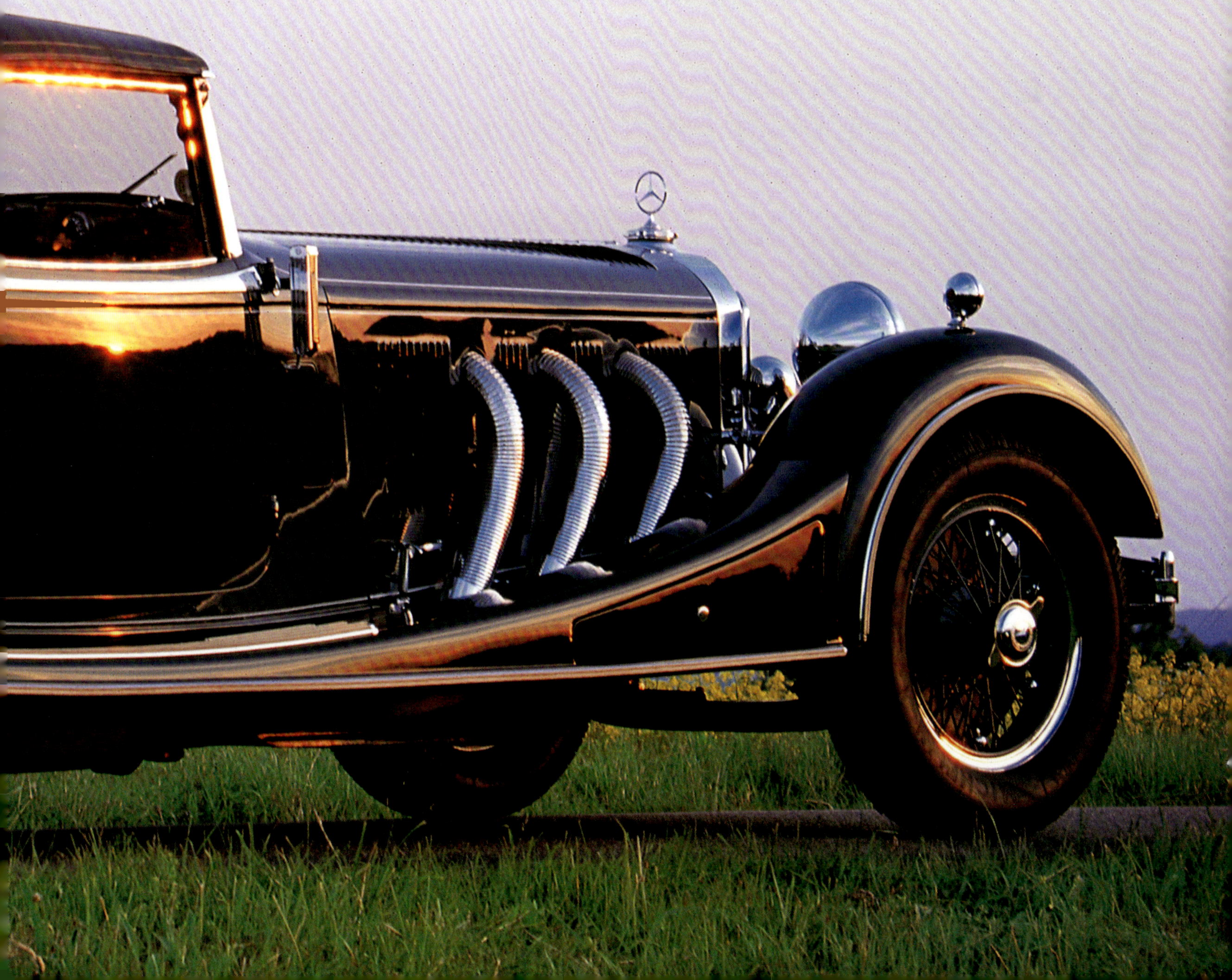

The unmistakable SSK, the K standing for *kurz* (short). Note the two-seater sports-car bodywork without doors, wings housing the wheels, and the small windshield to which the roof attached by two cord loops.

Unverkennbar SSK, mit K für kurz: zweisitzige Sportkarosserie ohne Türen, Radlaufkotflügel, die kleine Windschutzscheibe, an der das Notdach nur mittels zweier Ösen festgezurrt werden kann.

Incontestablement une SSK, avec un K comme *kurz* («court»): carrosserie sport biplace sans portières, pare-boue enveloppants sur les roues, petit pare-brise sur lequel la capote de dépannage ne peut être attachée qu'à l'aide de deux œillets.

Mercedes-Benz S–SSKL 1927

In order to assist "privateers" like Hans Stuck and Rudi Caracciola, Mercedes engineers Hans Nibel and Max Wagner reduced the weight of the SSK wherever possible. The result was the SSKL, of which there were probably only ever three examples.

Um »Privatfahrer« wie Hans Stuck und Rudi Caracciola zu unterstützen, erleichtern die Mercedes-Ingenieure Hans Nibel und Max Wagner den SSK, wo es geht. Das Ergebnis ist der SSKL. Wahrscheinlich gab es nicht mehr als drei.

Pour soutenir les pilotes « privés » comme Hans Stuck et Rudi Caracciola, les ingénieurs de Mercedes Hans Nibel et Max Wagner allègent autant que possible la SSK : cela donne la SSKL. Il n'y en aura vraisemblablement pas eu plus de trois exemplaires.

Mercedes-Benz S–SSKL 1927

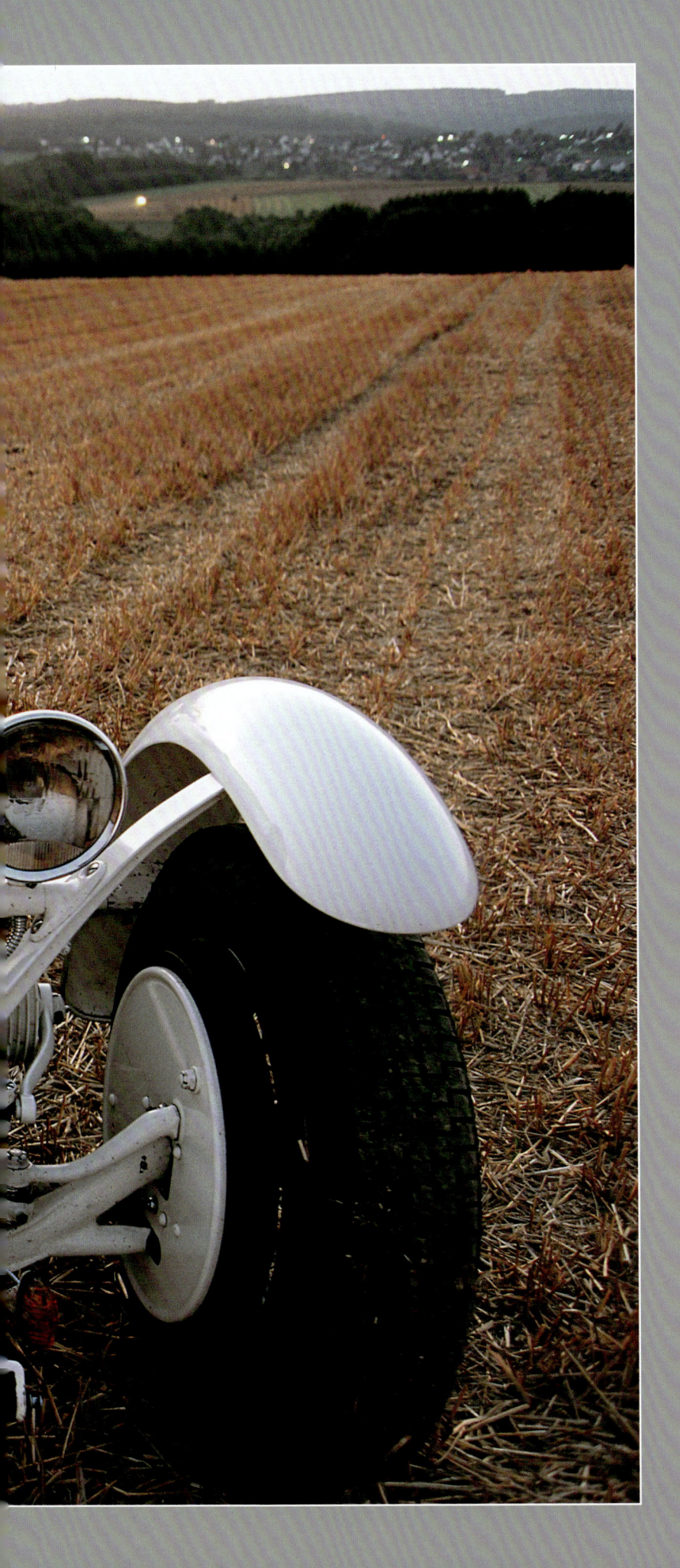

Of course, large supercharged cars were the most glamorous exhibits at the Berlin Automobile Exhibition of October 1926, but for the ordinary man in the street they remained objects of pure platonic worship. The straight six, 2-liter type 8/38 PS attracted far greater customer attention. Nevertheless, the angular mid-range Mercedes proved difficult to sell. The prices of 7800 reichsmarks for the tourer and 8600 reichsmarks for the two-door sedan were pitched far too high. The fact that the model was offered a year later for a good deal less led to the suspicion that it was being sold off cheaply because of numerous teething problems. In the end, even the designer Ferdinand Porsche came to grief over the 8/38 PS project and left Daimler-Benz AG in 1928 on the worst of terms.

His successor Hans Nibel, who did not become the technical director officially responsible for design and engineering until the beginning of 1929, gladly took the problem child under his wing. He ironed out problems in the detail and made it look more appealing. In the autumn of 1928 it was given the name Stuttgart 200, and in January 1929 it was fitted with a 2.6-liter engine under the designation of Stuttgart 260 (10/50 PS). Drawing on the company's good reputation, the price was set just a little higher than that of its competitors, such as the Adler Favorit and the Opel 8/40 PS. The gamble paid off and the Stuttgart type became the backbone of Mercedes production for years. It was manufactured exclusively in Untertürkheim with the coachwork carried out in Sindelfingen. There were many variants: sedans, cabriolets and roadsters, a Pullman version with six seats and a stretched chassis, taxis and hire cars, and delivery vehicles for commercial purposes. In the first half of the Thirties, jeeps based on the Stuttgart 260, which were as solid, robust, and tough as the entire range, became standard equipment with the Reichswehr and Wehrmacht military forces.

And this was no surprise, as it was a classic example of conventional and well-tried vehicle construction. It had U-section framework, rigid axles with semi-elliptical springs and band shock absorbers front and rear, mechanical brakes on all four wheels, a cardan shaft with a centrally-mounted ball-joint gearshift, engines with seven-bearing crankshafts, vibration dampers, and three-point mounting, as well as upright valves controlled by a lateral camshaft. From the middle of 1930 onwards, a cruise or overdrive gear could be added to the existing three gears. But the performance remained rather sluggish—the Stuttgart 200 was capable of 50 mph, but the Stuttgart 260 was 6 mph faster.

Mercedes-Benz Stuttgart 1928

The Stuttgart was the first reasonably-priced mid-range Mercedes, and despite its largely rectangular lines it had a pleasing appearance. Its simple exterior concealed tried and tested technology.

Der Stuttgart wird zum ersten preiswürdigen Mercedes in der Mittelklasse, zumeist eine Domäne des rechten Winkels und gleichwohl gefällig anzusehen. Im schlichten Gewand verbirgt sich gestandene Technik.

La Stuttgart est la première Mercedes à prix calculé au plus juste dans le segment intermédiaire, un modèle caractérisé par l'angle droit mais néanmoins d'une allure assez séduisante. Une mécanique à toute épreuve se dissimule sous une présentation sobre.

Manufacturers and drivers alike have always used symbols or numbers and letters to draw attention to features of their vehicles which are not immediately apparent. In this case the logo boasted of the mechanical four-wheel braking system (*Bremse* = brake).

Schon immer wiesen Werke oder Kunden durch Sigel oder Symbole auf verborgene Errungenschaften ihrer Fahrzeuge hin. Hier manifestiert sich der Stolz auf die mechanische Vierradbremse.

Depuis toujours, constructeurs et conducteurs ont attiré l'attention sur les caractéristiques méconnues de leurs véhicules à l'aide de chiffres, de lettres ou de symboles. Celui-ci représente la particularité du frein mécanique sur les quatre roues (*Bremse* = «frein»).

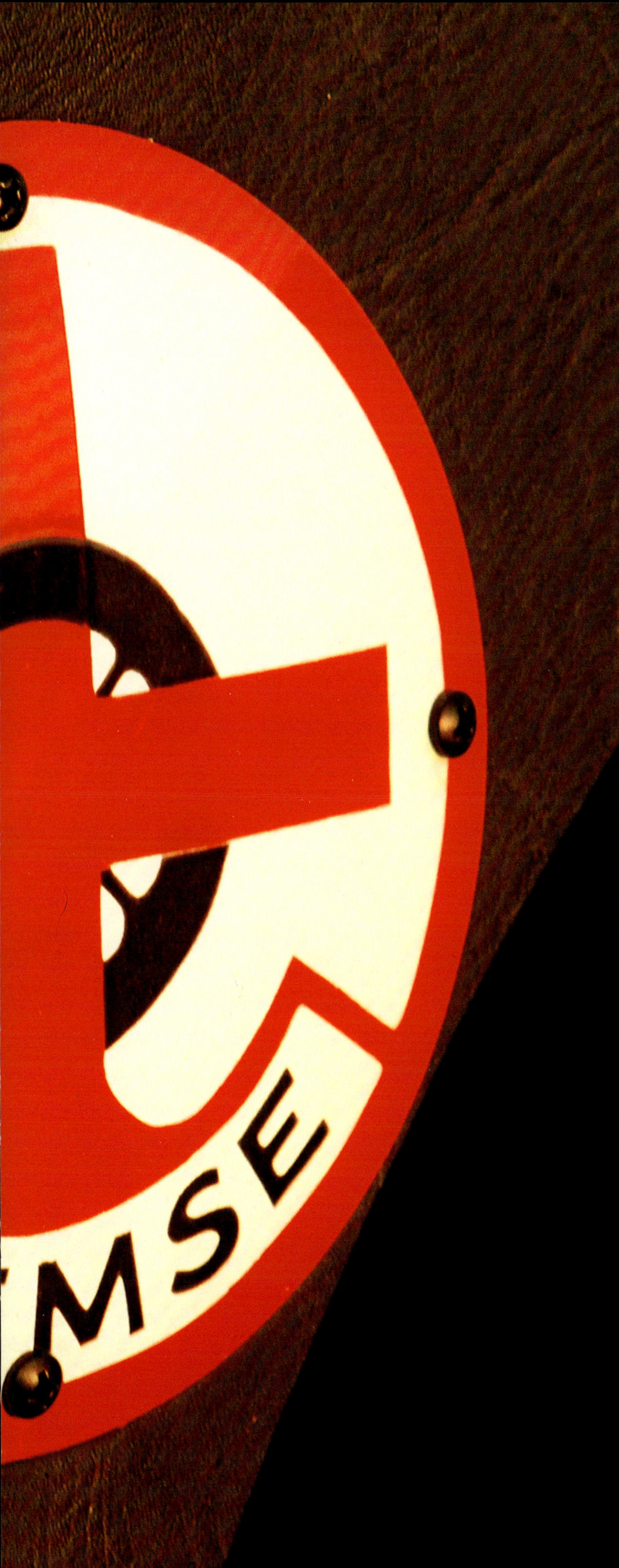
MSE

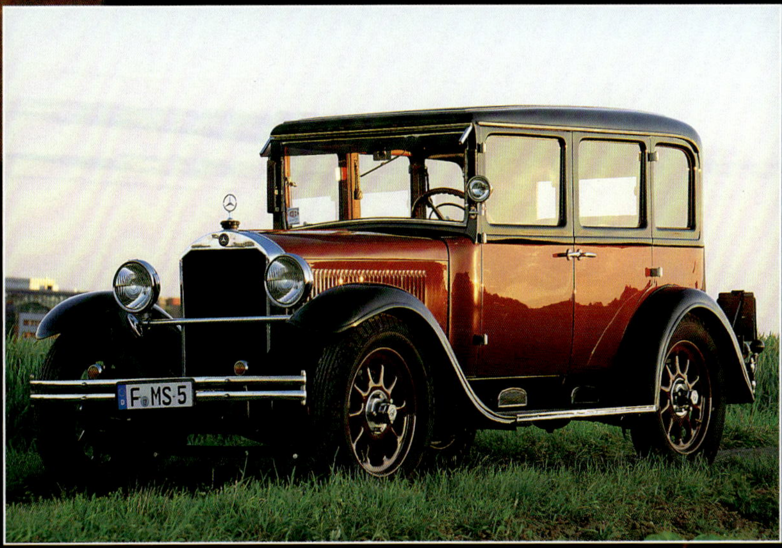
F MS 5

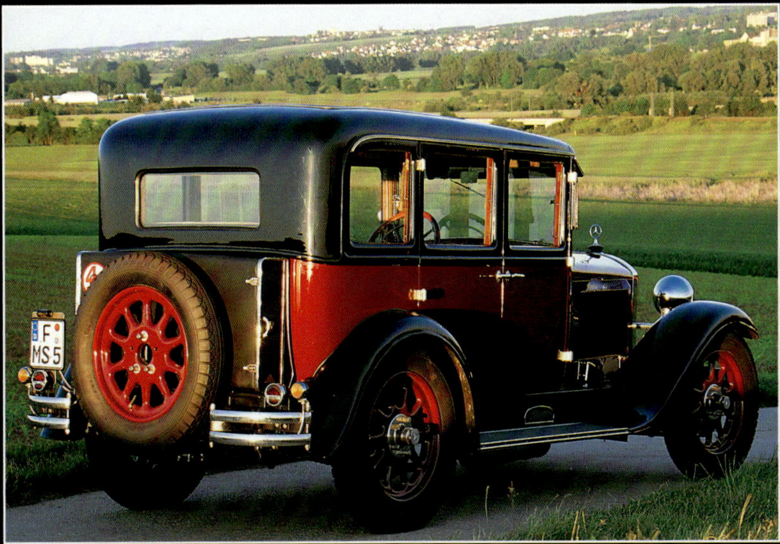
F MS 5

It was remarkable how the careers of Ferdinand Porsche and Hans Nibel, his successor as technical director at Daimler-Benz, intersected. Nibel officially arrived on 1 January 1929, on the same day that Porsche became the overall technical director of Steyr-Werke. At the same time Nibel rented Porsche's villa in Feuerbacher Weg, Stuttgart.

The German had actually become involved somewhat earlier and had sorted out a couple of serious problems that he inherited from the grumpy Austrian genius, such as the model 8/38 PS which Nibel developed into the Stuttgart. The case of the structurally-similar, Porsche-designed, Mercedes-Benz 300, which was unveiled as an upper mid-range car at the 1926 Berlin Motor Show, turned out to be quite similar. Such terms are relative. Although this "stagecoach," which seemed massive and impractical, was equipped in rapid succession with large 3-, 3.2- and 3.5-liter six-cylinder engines, the favorites of the contemporary motoring upper-class, such as the types s and ss, simply had much more cubic capacity to offer.

Nibel gave Porsche's luckless and dull creation more sensible dimensions and an appealing appearance, and he named the remodeled and restyled version the Mannheim in honor of the old Benz team. The Mannheim 350 (or 14/70 PS) of 1929 was followed in the same year by the 370 (or 15/75 PS), and then a year later by the 370 K—for *kurz* (short) as the wheelbase had been reduced from 10 ft 6 in to 9 ft 11 in—and the 370 s (for Sport), with a wheelbase again reduced to a bare 9 ft 4 in.

The 370 s, exclusively built as a roadster and cabriolet, became the star of the series and, costed at 12,800 or 13,800 reichsmarks, was seen as a reasonably-priced alternative for those who could not afford the sinfully-expensive s models. With only 183 units built, it was neither particularly powerful nor particularly fast, however. With a top speed of 71 mph, the 370 s still rolled along at a leisurely pace. In 1932 the 380 s (or 15/80 PS) was produced, again available only as a cabriolet. Production of the model was shared between the Daimler-Benz sites at Stuttgart and Mannheim. The 350 and 370 were produced in Mannheim, and the K and s versions in Stuttgart.

Merkwürdig, wie sich die Lebensläufe von Ferdinand Porsche und Hans Nibel, seinem Nachfolger als technischer Direktor bei Daimler-Benz, überkreuzen. Nibel tritt diese Stelle am 1. Januar 1929 an, am gleichen Tag wird Porsche technischer Gesamtleiter der Steyr-Werke. Zugleich pachtet Nibel Porsches Villa am Stuttgarter Feuerbacher Weg.

Schon vorher hat der Deutsche ein paar Hypotheken übernommen und abgetragen, die der grantig-geniale Österreicher hinterlassen hat, wie das Modell 8/38 PS, aus dem Nibel den Stuttgart sublimiert. Ganz ähnlich ist der Fall des konstruktiv fast gleichen Porsche-Opus Mercedes-Benz 300 gelagert, seit der Berliner Automobil-Ausstellung 1926 Offerte der Stuttgarter in der gehobenen Mittelklasse. Solche Begriffe sind relativ: Obwohl diese ein wenig klobig und unbeholfen wirkenden Karossen in rascher Folge mit voluminösen Sechszylindern von 3, 3,2 und 3,5 Litern ausgestattet werden, haben Exponenten der zeitgenössischen automobilen Oberkaste, wie etwa die Typen s und ss, einfach noch viel mehr Hubraum.

Nibel verhilft Porsches glück- und glanzloser Schöpfung zu vernünftigen Dimensionen und einem ansprechenderen Erscheinungsbild und nennt die überarbeitete und retuschierte Version Mannheim, zu Ehren der alten Benz-Garnison. Auf den Mannheim 350 (oder 14/70 PS) von 1929 folgt noch im gleichen Jahr der 370 (oder 15/75 PS), ein Jahr später der 370 K (für kurz: Der Radstand wurde von 3200 auf 3025 Millimeter zurückgenommen) und der 370 s (für Sport, mit nochmals auf 2850 Millimeter verknapptem Radstand).

Der 370 s, ausschließlich als Roadster und als Cabriolet gebaut, wird zum Star der Baureihe, für 12 800 beziehungsweise 13 800 Reichsmark eine preiswürdige Alternative für alle, die sich die sündhaft teuren s-Modelle nicht leisten können. In nur 183 Exemplaren hergestellt, ist er allerdings weder besonders stark noch sonderlich schnell: Mit 115 Stundenkilometern Spitzengeschwindigkeit rollt ein 370 s doch relativ gemächlich dahin. 1932 sattelt man noch mit dem 380 s (oder 15/80 PS) drauf, der wiederum lediglich als Cabriolet erhältlich ist. Die Fertigung des Modells schultern die Daimler-Benz-Standorte Stuttgart und Mannheim arbeitsteilig: In Mannheim werden 350 und 370 hergestellt, in Stuttgart die Versionen K und s.

Il est étonnant de voir combien les vies de Ferdinand Porsche et de Hans Nibel, son successeur comme directeur technique chez Daimler-Benz, se recoupent. Nibel le remplace le 1er janvier 1929, jour même où Porsche est nommé directeur technique général des usines Steyr. Au même moment, Nibel loue la villa de Porsche située Feuerbacher Weg à Stuttgart.

Auparavant, déjà, l'Allemand a repris et payé quelques hypothèques laissées par le bourru mais génial Autrichien, par exemple la 8/38 ch que Nibel sublime pour donner naissance à la Stuttgart. Leurs carrières vont encore se croiser avec la Mercedes-Benz 300, œuvre de Porsche presque identique sur le plan mécanique à la Stuttgart, et qui sera présentée au Salon de l'Automobile de Berlin de 1926, lors duquel Nibel se présente en défenseur des voitures de classe moyenne supérieure. Toutefois, bien que ces berlines un peu imposantes et peu gracieuses se succèdent rapidement avec de volumineux six-cylindres de 3, 3,2 et 3,5 litres, les représentantes de la classe automobile supérieure de cette époque, par exemple les types s et ss, ont tout simplement encore plus de cylindrée.

Nibel redonne des dimensions raisonnables à la création peu réussie et peu séduisante de Porsche. En l'honneur de la vieille ville de garnison de Benz, il donne à cette version retravaillée et retouchée, au style plus agréable, le nom de Mannheim. La Mannheim 350 (ou 14/70 ch) de 1929 est encore suivie, la même année, par la 370 (ou 15/75 ch), un an plus tard par la 370 K pour *kurz* («court»: l'empattement a été ramené de 3200 à 3025 mm) et par la 370 s (pour sport, avec empattement encore raccourci à 2850 mm).

La 370 s, construite exclusivement en roadster et cabriolet, devient la vedette de la gamme, avec un prix respectif de 12 800 et 13 800 reichsmarks, un choix à la portée de tous ceux qui ne peuvent pas se payer le luxe des séries s, d'un coût astronomique. Construite à raison de seulement 183 exemplaires, elle n'est toutefois ni particulièrement puissante ni extrêmement rapide: avec une vitesse de pointe de 115 km/h, une 370 s est donc relativement lente. En 1932, elle est remplacée par la 380 s (ou 15/80 ch), qui est, elle aussi, disponible seulement en cabriolet. Les sites de production de Daimler-Benz, à Stuttgart et à Mannheim, se partagent le travail pour fabriquer ce modèle: Mannheim fabrique les 350 et 370 alors que Stuttgart se consacre aux versions K et s.

Mercedes-Benz Mannheim 1929

Despite its impressive size, the Mannheim
was an upper mid-range model.

Bei durchaus stattlichen Dimensionen zählt der Typ
Mannheim gleichwohl zur gehobenen Mittelklasse.

Malgré des dimensions assez imposantes, la Mannheim
appartient néanmoins au segment intermédiaire supérieur.

Views of the elegantly designed dashboard and the six-cylinder engine. The factory recommendation was that the pressure differential between the studded tires on the same axle "should not exceed 0.1 atmospheres."

Freier Durchblick auf das aufwändig gestaltete Armaturenbrett und den Sechszylinder. Das Werk schreibt vor, der Druckunterschied der Ballon-Stahlseilreifen auf einer Achse dürfe »nicht größer als 0,1 atm« sein.

Vue du tableau sophistiqué et du moteur six-cylindres. L'usine prescrit que la différence de pression entre les pneus ballons à fil d'acier d'un même essieu ne doit pas « être supérieure à 0,1 bar ».

The 1929 Mannheim 350 model touring car offers plenty of places in the sun. The spare wheels on the right and left and the trunk were all situated outside the passenger compartment and it was all just a little bit drafty.

Viel Platz an der Sonne: im Tourenwagen Typ Mannheim 350 von 1929. Kofferraum sowie Reserveräder links und rechts sind ausgelagert, und es zieht schon mal ein bisschen.

Beaucoup de place au soleil: dans la voiture de tourisme Mannheim 350 de 1929, les roues de secours placées sur les côtés à l'avant et le coffre à l'arrière dégagent de l'espace. Seul défaut: on est parfois exposé aux courants d'air.

Some of the visions which inspired Ferdinand Porsche during his six-year period as head of the design department of Daimler and Daimler-Benz seem to have belonged somewhat in the past. This applies to the 8/38 PS and 12/55 type 300, as well as the 18/80 PS type 460, also called the Nürburg, which occupied a slightly higher place in the automobile hierarchy. Even at its première in the autumn of 1928 it appeared quite old-fashioned, or classical if one preferred a more generous term. Classic in its form, classic in its chassis with a high framework of U-sections, rigid axles, and semi-elliptical springs. Nevertheless, the eight-cylinder inline engine was an innovation, similar in concept to the six-cylinder engines of both other models, with side-operated valves and cast-iron cylinders cast as a unit with the top section of the crankshaft housing. The alloy bottom section also served as the oil sump for the pressure-circulated lubrication system. The dynamic image conjured up by the name Nürburg turned out in reality to be mere sound and smoke. In its quickest version, the venerable two-tonner could not manage more than 68 mph. It did however prove its durability in a two-week 8000-mile endurance marathon on the Eifel circuit.

By an irony of fate, Paul Daimler, who had broken away from the Daimler management because of a disagreement regarding an eight-cylinder engine, was now building the Horch 8 for manufacturing competitor Horch. And in this category the car was the benchmark, more than a match for Mercedes in all respects, attractive, outstandingly engineered, technically more advanced, and better priced. Even a total revamp from which the Nürburg 460 emerged visually rejuvenated and embellished was not enough to enable Hans Nibel to turn this situation around. His short variant K with its 11 ft 3 in—as opposed to the normal 12 ft 4 in—wheelbase was designed principally as a four- to five-seater with production fittings and special bodywork. Numerous cabriolets tailored by fashionable coachbuilders such as Gläser, Papler, or Erdmann & Rossi were also available. Customers, however, almost always preferred the long version, simply because it was hardly any more expensive to buy.

The Nürburg 500 (or 19/100 PS), later simply called the type 500, with an engine capacity of 4918 cc, followed in 1931. To the confusion of historians, a few examples of the 460 were fitted out as Pullman limousines with the coachwork of the Großer Mercedes 770. One of these became part of the Pope's automobile fleet, surely the equivalent of the elevation of an automobile to the peerage.

Mercedes-Benz Nürburg 1929

The Nürburg 500 Pullman limousine was certainly one of the most elegant motor cars to appear on German roads. This two-and-a-half ton giant's fuel tank needed refilling with a gallon every 7.8 miles. The Nürburg depicted here, 17 ft 8 in long by six feet in height and width, was first delivered to the German Embassy in London in 1936, two years after its construction.

Die Pullman-Limousine vom Typ Nürburg 500 gehört gewiss zu den hochherrschaftlichen Auto-Erscheinungen auf deutschen Rollbahnen. Dafür möchte der Zweieinhalbtonner mit bis zu 30 Litern Treibstoff je 100 Kilometer bei Laune gehalten werden. 5380 Millimeter lang und mit 1820 Millimetern ebenso hoch wie breit, wurde der abgebildete Nürburg 500 erst 1936 zwei Jahre nach seinem Bau an die deutsche Botschaft in London ausgeliefert.

La limousine Pullman Nürburg 500 figure incontestablement parmi les voitures de très grand luxe les plus imposantes des routes allemandes. En revanche, ce pachyderme de 2,5 tonnes pouvait consommer jusqu'à 30 litres de carburant aux 100 km. 5380 mm de long pour 1820 mm de haut et de large : la Nürburg 500 représentée ici n'a été livrée qu'en 1936, deux ans après sa construction, à l'ambassade d'Allemagne à Londres.

The three rows of seats of this classy Mercedes offered varying degrees of comfort for six or seven passengers. The rear-view mirror was mounted on the spare wheel. The four-wheel-brakes logo on the trunk served the additional purpose of warning following drivers: don't mess with this car!

Auf drei Sitzreihen offeriert der Nobel-Mercedes durchaus unterschiedlichen Komfort für sechs bis sieben Passagiere. Der Rückspiegel thront auf dem Reserverad. Der Hinweis auf die Vierradbremse auf dem Koffer dient auch als Warnung an Nachfolgende: Mit diesem Auto ist nicht zu spaßen.

Sur trois rangées de sièges, cette Mercedes grand luxe offre un confort assez variable pour six ou sept passagers. Le rétroviseur trône sur la roue de secours. Sur la malle, le logo rappelant la présence de freins sur les quatre roues fait office de mise en garde pour les véhicules qui suivent : il est recommandé de se méfier de cette voiture.

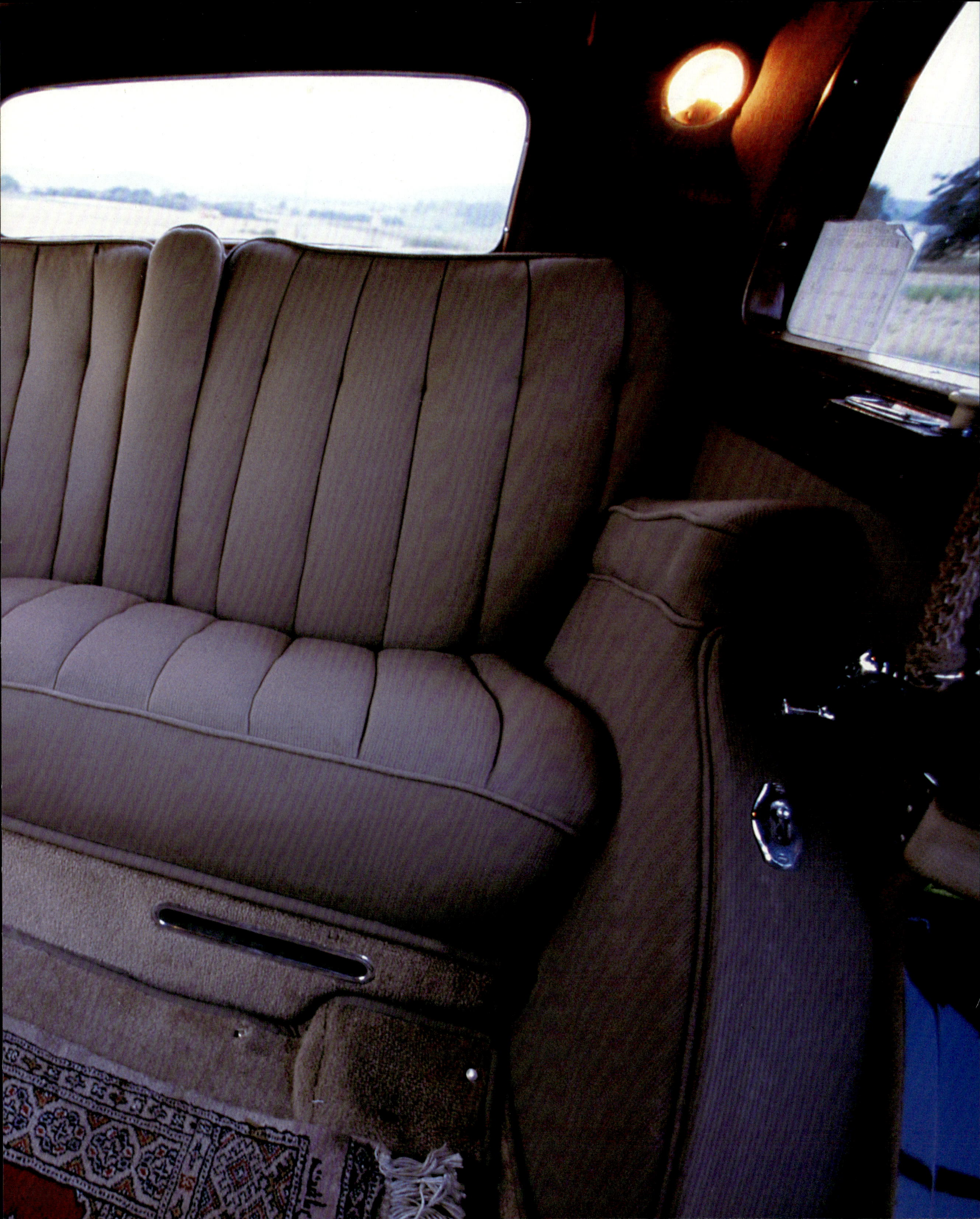

At the start of his career with the company, chief designer Hans Nibel had been mainly engaged in sorting out his predecessor's creations and bringing them to a level which everyone expected of a Mercedes. At the Paris Automobile Exhibition in October 1931 he presented his own masterpiece. The new car, which fitted in well with the existing range of models, precisely matched the market conditions created by the world economic crisis. It was compact, economical, well built, and most reasonably priced for a six-cylinder vehicle. In the year in which it appeared, with standard production equipment, which even included an ignition steering lock as a precaution against theft, the 170 (or 7/32 PS) cost 4400 reichsmarks, 1580 marks less than the Stuttgart 200 from the same stable.

Nibel had also been working on independent suspension since 1924. The 170 with its front and rear independent suspension was the forerunner of what was to become a standard in future Mercedes and which established a new yardstick with regard to safer roadholding for many years to come. The front wheels were mounted on two transverse springs and the rear wheels on double coil springs. The engine delivered 32 bhp from 1692 cc at an average mileage of 21 mpg taken from its 8¾-gal tank. As the advertising proclaimed, such fuel consumption was assisted by its overdrive and economy gear in addition to the normal three gears. The concept was so successful and the technical standard of the 170 so high that a mere four major design changes were made in the six years of its production. It was first delivered with a separate trunk ¾ inch from the rear enclosure of the bodywork. This was followed in 1934 by a mounted trunk, and an integrated luggage compartment in 1935. In the same year, the U-section frame was replaced by a box-section, pressed-steel lower frame. A softly-angled wedge-shaped radiator replaced the previous flat radiator in February of the following year. A revised and updated instrument panel was also more ergonomical in design. The 170 was presented as a two-door model at the Berlin Automobile Exhibition in that month and this clearly anticipated the rounded lines of the 170 V of 1936.

The pretty cabriolet, a roadster and the type L 300 delivery van, 126 of which were used mainly for commercial purposes from 1932 onwards, were also members of the family of the smallest Mercedes. It was not simply that the type 170 was the right car for the Depression era after the Wall Street crash, it also carried Daimler-Benz AG through the lean years of the early Thirties. It was a favorite with the public and 4481 of the models were sold in its first year, more than the complete production of the company in the previous year. A total of 13,775 of the first generation Mercedes 170 s were produced, which set a new record.

Bisher ist Chefkonstrukteur Hans Nibel vor allem damit beschäftigt gewesen, die Kreationen seines Vorgängers formal zu entrümpeln und auf das Niveau zu heben, das jedermann von einem Mercedes erwartet. Auf der Pariser Autoschau im Oktober 1931 meldet er sich mit einem eigenen Meisterstück zu Wort. Der Neue, der sich von unten an die bestehende Modellpalette anlagert, passt genau in das Umfeld, das die Weltwirtschaftskrise geschaffen hat: kompakt, sparsam, von trotziger Qualität und höchst erschwinglich für einen Sechszylinder. Im Jahr seines Erscheinens kostet der 170 (oder 7/32 PS) mit einer Serienausstattung, die sogar ein Zünd-Lenkschloss als Diebstahlvorsorge umfasst, 4400 Reichsmark – 1580 Mark weniger als ein Stuttgart 200 aus demselben Hause.

Schon seit 1924 hat sich Nibel mit der Einzelradaufhängung beschäftigt. In dieser Hinsicht wird der 170 zum Pilotauto, mit Schwingachsen vorn und hinten, die künftig Mercedes-Norm werden und für lange Zeit neue Maßstäbe hinsichtlich hoher Fahrsicherheit setzen. Seine Vorderräder sind an zwei Querfedern, die Hinterräder an doppelten Schraubenfedern aufgehängt. Sein Triebwerk leistet 32 PS aus 1692 cm³ und entzieht dem 33-Liter-Tank im Schnitt elf Liter Kraftstoff auf 100 Kilometer. Zu den Punkten, die die Werbung herausstellt, zählt sein Schnell- und Spargang zusätzlich zu den normalen drei Fahrstufen. So gelungen ist das Konzept, so hoch der technische Standard des 170, dass in den sechs Jahren seiner Fertigung lediglich vier größere Retuschen fällig werden. Er wird zunächst mit einem freistehenden Koffer ausgeliefert, zwei Zentimeter von der hinteren Karosseriewand entfernt. An diese schließt sich 1934 ein angebauter Koffer und 1935 ein integriertes Gepäckabteil an. Im gleichen Jahr ersetzt man den bisherigen U-Profilrahmen durch einen Kastenprofil-Pressstahl-Niederrahmen. Im Februar des folgenden Jahres findet sich ein Kühler in sanft gewinkelter Keilform an der Stelle des bisherigen Flachkühlers. Überarbeitet und auf den neuesten Stand gebracht bietet sich auch die Armaturentafel dem Auge und der Hand dar. Auf der Berliner Automobil-Ausstellung im selben Monat wird der 170 als Zweitürer präsentiert und nimmt bereits die rundlicheren Linien des 170 V von 1936 vorweg.

Zur Familie des kleinsten Mercedes gehören schmucke Cabriolets, ein Roadster sowie der Kastenwagen vom Typ L 300, der ab 1932 in 126 Exemplaren vornehmlich gewerblichen Zwecken dient. Nicht nur, dass der Typ 170 wie gemacht scheint für die Zeit der Flaute nach dem Wall Street Crash, er trägt die Daimler-Benz AG auch durch die mageren Jahre Anfang der Dreißiger hindurch, ein Liebling des Publikums: Schon im ersten Jahr seines Modell-Lebens wird er in 4481 Einheiten unter die Leute gebracht, mehr als die gesamte Produktion der Firma im Jahr vorher. Insgesamt entstehen 13775 Mercedes 170 der ersten Generation – das ist eine neue Rekordmarke.

Jusqu'alors, le chef constructeur Hans Nibel s'est surtout consacré à épurer esthétiquement les créations de son prédécesseur et à les élever au niveau que chacun attend d'une Mercedes. Au Salon de l'automobile de Paris, en octobre 1931, il fait pour la première fois parler de lui avec son propre chef-d'œuvre. Le nouveau modèle, qui s'ajoute au bas de gamme existant, intègre à la perfection l'environnement généré par la crise économique mondiale: compacte, économique, de très bonne qualité et d'un prix vraiment très bas pour une six-cylindres. L'année de sa sortie, la 170 (ou 7/32 ch) coûte, avec un équipement de série qui comporte même une clef de contact comme prévention antivol, 4400 reichsmarks – soit 1580 marks de moins qu'une Stuttgart 200 de la même écurie.

En 1924 déjà, Nibel s'était penché sur la suspension à roue indépendante. Dans cette perspective, la 170 jouait le rôle de voiture expérimentale, avec essieux oscillants à l'avant et à l'arrière qui allaient devenir la norme chez Mercedes à l'avenir et poser pendant longtemps de nouveaux jalons en ce qui concerne une sécurité de conduite optimale. Ses roues avant sont suspendues à deux ressorts transversaux et les roues arrière, à des ressorts hélicoïdaux doubles. Son moteur développe 32 ch à partir de 1692 cm³ et prélève en moyenne 11 litres de carburant aux 100 km dans le réservoir de 33 litres. Parmi les points mis en exergue par la publicité figure sa vitesse surmultipliée en sus des trois rapports avant normaux. Le concept est si bien étudié et le niveau technique de la 170 si sophistiqué que seules quatre retouches importantes seront nécessaires durant les six années de sa fabrication. Elle est tout d'abord livrée avec un coffre de malle séparé et éloigné de la paroi de carrosserie arrière de deux centimètres. En 1934, le coffre de malle est contigu à celle-ci et, en 1935, il est transformé en un coffre à bagages intégré.

La même année, le cadre profilé en U utilisé jusqu'ici est remplacé par un cadre bas en acier soudé à profilés en forme de caisson. En février 1936, un radiateur de forme légèrement cunéiforme remplace l'ancien radiateur plat. Le tableau de bord est, lui aussi, plus séduisant pour l'œil et plus pratique depuis qu'il a été retravaillé et incarne dès lors l'état de la technique. Au Salon de l'automobile de Berlin, le même mois, la 170 est présentée en deux portes et anticipe d'ores et déjà les lignes plus arrondies de la 170 V de 1936.

La famille de la plus petite Mercedes comporte de jolis cabriolets, un roadster ainsi que la fourgonnette type L 300 fabriquée à 126 exemplaires à partir de 1932 et qui sert essentiellement d'utilitaire. Absolument idéale pour l'époque de marasme suivant le krach de Wall Street, la 170 aide aussi Daimler-Benz AG à franchir les années de vaches maigres du début des années 1930. Véritable coqueluche du public, dès sa première année, elle est vendue à 4481 exemplaires, plus que toute la production de la firme de l'année précédente. Au total, ce sont 13775 Mercedes-Benz 170 de la première génération qui seront construites – et c'est un nouveau record.

Mercedes-Benz 170   1931

The long life of a motor vehicle has its highs and lows. During the 1960s this 1931 170 found itself serving as a chicken coop near the Czech town of Budweis.

Auch ein langes Autoleben hat seine Höhen und Tiefen: In den 1960er-Jahren musste dieser 170 von 1931 in der Nähe des tschechischen Budweis als Hühnerstall herhalten.

Une longue vie de voiture a aussi ses hauts et ses bas : dans les années 1960, cette 170 de 1931 a servi de poulailler non loin de Budweis, en Tchéquie.

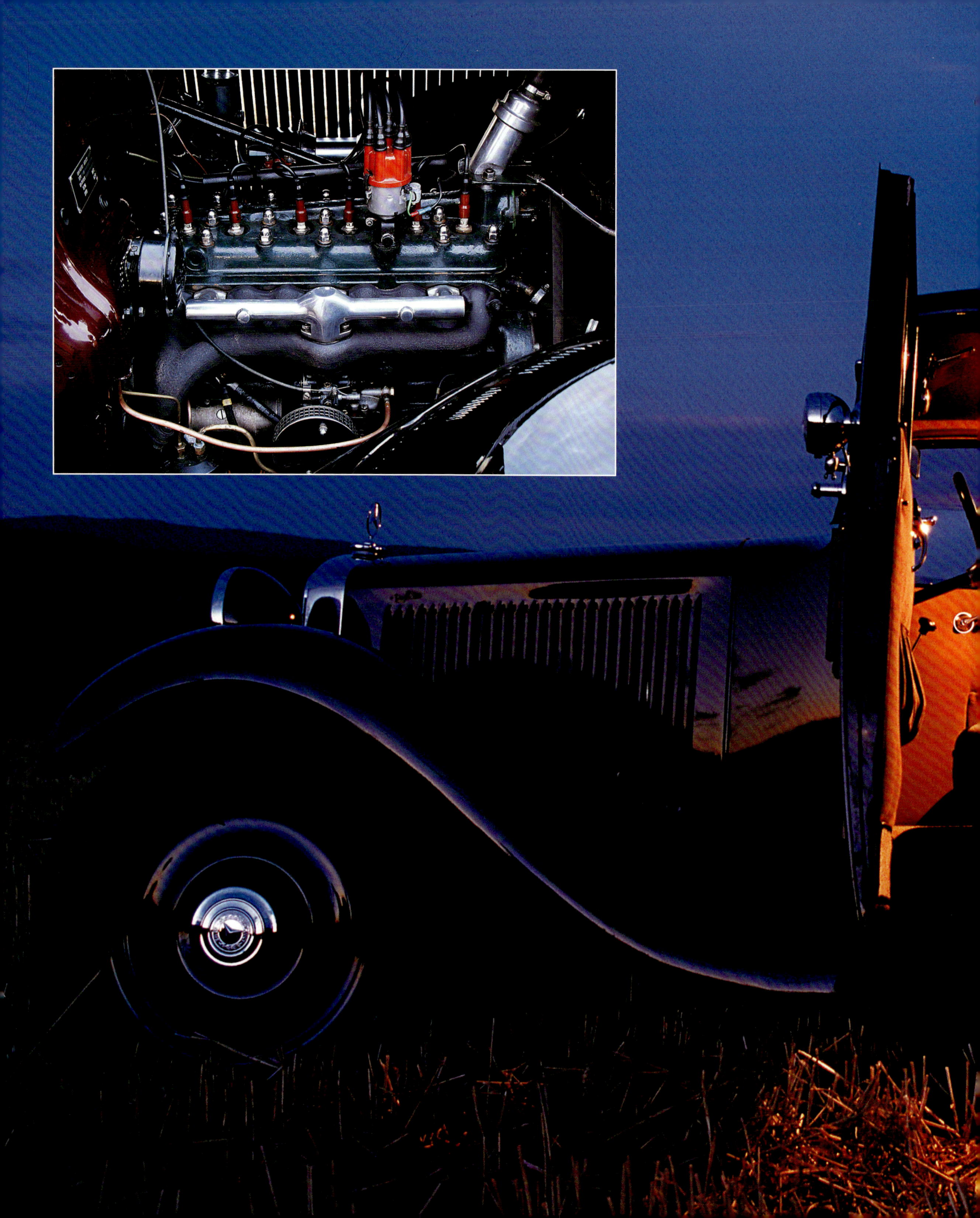

An open invitation: lit by its interior lights in twilight's last gleaming, the 170 seems to take on a life of its own.

Einladend geöffnet: Im letzten Licht des Abends und traulich illuminiert durch die Bordbeleuchtung scheint der 170 eigenes Leben zu entwickeln.

Accueillante: sous les derniers rayons du crépuscule et avec l'éclairage intime de bord, la 170 dévoile un habitacle cossu.

The 500 K and its derivatives are firmly rooted in the great tradition of supercharged Mercedes cars, of which the S to SSKL series was the first blossoming. While the latter certainly met the purpose of getting quickly from A to B, free of the need for unnecessary adornment and elaborate fittings, with form distinctly subordinate to function and (where necessary) race-winning performance, the 500 and its derivatives still displayed definite elements of the majestic, extravagant baroque styling, even the gigantic, reflecting the changed consciousness of Germany in the Thirties. A particular example of this was (in company jargon up to 1935) the "Chassis for sports cars" which later came to be known as the "Chassis with set-back engine." This had a standard wheelbase of 10 ft 10 in and the radiator, engine and cockpit were moved back 7 in, affording the mighty inline eight-cylinder engine its "Lebensraum" under the seemingly endless bonnet.

The series was to produce its most beautiful blossoms twice. One was the Special Roadster which cost 6000 reichsmarks (the equivalent price of a four-door type 230 sedan) over and above the generously priced 22,000 reichsmarks for most of the other models, and the other the Autobahnkurier at 24,000 reichsmarks which paid homage to the current vogue for pseudo-streamlining. These were dream cars and much talked-about spirits of their time. When the Second World War broke out, the series had made a great evolutionary leap, but had nowhere to go. The 5018 cc 500 K, which produced 100 bhp unblown or 160 bhp blown and was shown at the Berlin Motor Show in February 1934, was followed by the 540 K (115/180 bhp from 5401 cc) at the Paris Salon in October 1936. A 580 K (130/200 bhp from 5800 cc) was brought to production standard by 1940 but the project then petered out because new priorities had intervened. Max Sailer, manager of the Design Office of Daimler-Benz after the death of Hans Nibel, was already responsible for the 540 K. Only after a change in engine capacity did the showpiece Mercedes gain a power unit with the dynamism to match its visual appeal. Just the bare chassis alone weighed 4000 lbs and with bodywork it tipped the scales at a good 5500 lbs, with the special armored type weighing even more at 6800 lbs. Its fuel consumption resembled the appetite of a gluttonous Renaissance prince—8 mpg was quickly reached, and even exceeded if the 540 K's 106 mph top speed was attained.

Ten styles of bodywork were available ex-works, among them various tourers, sedans, coupés and cabriolets. The Sindelfingen stylists proved to be surprisingly imaginative and were willing to meet the special requirements of a distinctive clientele, provided they were ready to meet the extra cost. In all a total of 342 of the 500 K and 319 of the 540 K models were produced. This clientele included the famous and mighty from around the world. An Indian Maharajah used a 540 K to hunt tigers. And of course the powerful charisma of this giant was not lost

Mercedes-Benz 500 K & 540 K   1934

on the Nazi high command. After the attack on Reinhard Heydrich, Reichsprotektor of Bohemia and Moravia, 20 type 770 and 20 type 540 K armored versions were ordered from Daimler-Benz for their protection and that of allies in other countries. Those who doubted their own popularity preferred, it seems, to ride in bullet-proof security.

540 K – bereitwillig ein, vorausgesetzt, diese ist bereit, entsprechende Aufpreise zu entrichten. Die Klientel: die Prominenten und Mächtigen dieser Welt. Ein indischer Maharadscha verwendet einen 540 K zur Tigerjagd. Natürlich bleibt auch der Nazi-Nomenklatura das robuste Charisma des Kolossalischen nicht verborgen. Nach dem Attentat auf Reinhard Heydrich zum Beispiel, Reichsprotektor über Böhmen und Mähren, gibt man bei Daimler-Benz 20 Einheiten des Typs 770 und 20 Exemplare des 540 K in Auftrag, gepanzert, zum eigenen Schutz und zu dem von Freunden im Ausland. Wo man an der eigenen Beliebtheit zweifelt, reist man doch lieber kugelfest.

de ce monde – soit disposée à payer les suppléments de prix exigés.

Un maharadjah indien utilise une 540 K pour aller chasser le tigre ! Le charisme irrésistible de tout ce qui est colossal n'échappe pas non plus à la nomenklatura nazie. Après l'attentat perpétré contre Reinhard Heydrich, Protecteur du Reich en Bohême et Moravie, par exemple, Daimler-Benz reçoit une commande pour vingt exemplaires de la 770 et vingt de la 540 K, blindés, pour la protection des dignitaires nazis et celle de leurs amis à l'étranger. Là où l'on doute que l'on soit populaire, il est en effet recommandé de bien se protéger.

The two-seater Cabriolet A was unmistakable with its low windshield, low waistline, and recessed radiator. The bodywork was that of the 500 K, the powerplant came from the 540 K, an interim model with only five units manufactured. The externally mounted spare wheels could be removed without tools thanks to the flanged retaining nut. The 5.4-liter, eight-cylinder engine with laterally actuated valves and horizontally mounted, two-stage Roots supercharger was the epitome of power and magnificence.

Unverkennbar das zweisitzige Cabriolet A: mit niedriger Windschutzscheibe, niedriger Gürtellinie, zurückgesetztem Kühler. Die Karosserie ist die des 500 K, das Triebwerk vom 540 K, ein Interimsmodell, in nur fünf Exemplaren gefertigt. Die hinten außen liegenden Reserveräder können dank einer Knebelmutter rasch und ohne Werkzeug entfernt werden. Der 5,4-Liter-Achtzylinder mit seitengesteuerten Ventilen und liegendem zuschaltbarem Zweiflügel-Roots-Gebläse ist Inbegriff von Macht und Herrlichkeit.

L'inconfondable Cabriolet A à deux places: avec un pare-brise bas, une ligne de ceinture basse et un radiateur reculé. La carrosserie est celle de la 500 K, le moteur celui de la 540 K, modèle intérimaire réalisé à cinq exemplaires seulement. A l'extérieur, à l'arrière, les roues de secours peuvent être démontées rapidement et sans outil grâce à un écrou papillon. Le huit-cylindres de 5,4 litres à soupapes à commande latérale et compresseur Roots à doubles ailettes horizontales débrayables est l'incarnation même de la puissance et de la magnificence.

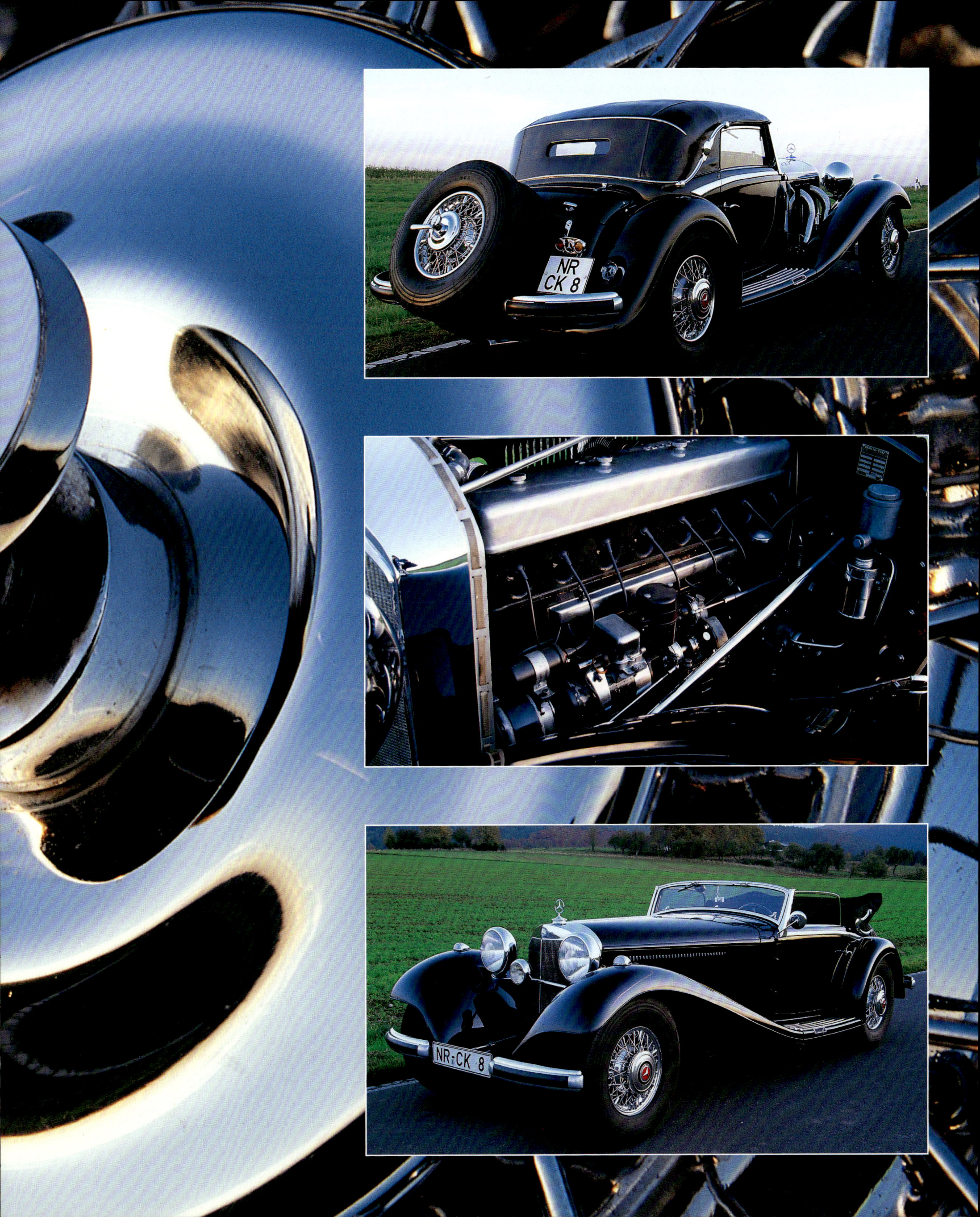
NR
CK 8
NR-CK 8

The Cabriolet A of the 540K was a car of seductively virile beauty, acquisition and ownership of which was reserved for just a few lucky souls. The engine seemed to go on for ever. Characteristic were the two large front headlights and the central fog lamp. The license plate at the rear was mounted under a transparent cover.

Das Cabriolet A des 540K besticht mit viriler Schönheit, deren Erwerb und Besitz nur einigen wenigen Glücklichen vorbehalten war. Der Motortrakt scheint nicht zu enden. Typisch: die beiden großen Scheinwerfer vorn und die zentrale Nebellampe. Das Nummernschild hinten findet sich im Anschluss an eine transparente Abdeckung.

Le Cabriolet A de la 540K séduit par sa beauté virile, mais le posséder n'est l'apanage que d'un petit nombre d'heureux élus. Le capot du moteur semble interminable. Typique : les deux grands phares avant et le phare antibrouillard central. La plaque minéralogique arrière se trouve juste derrière une protection transparente.

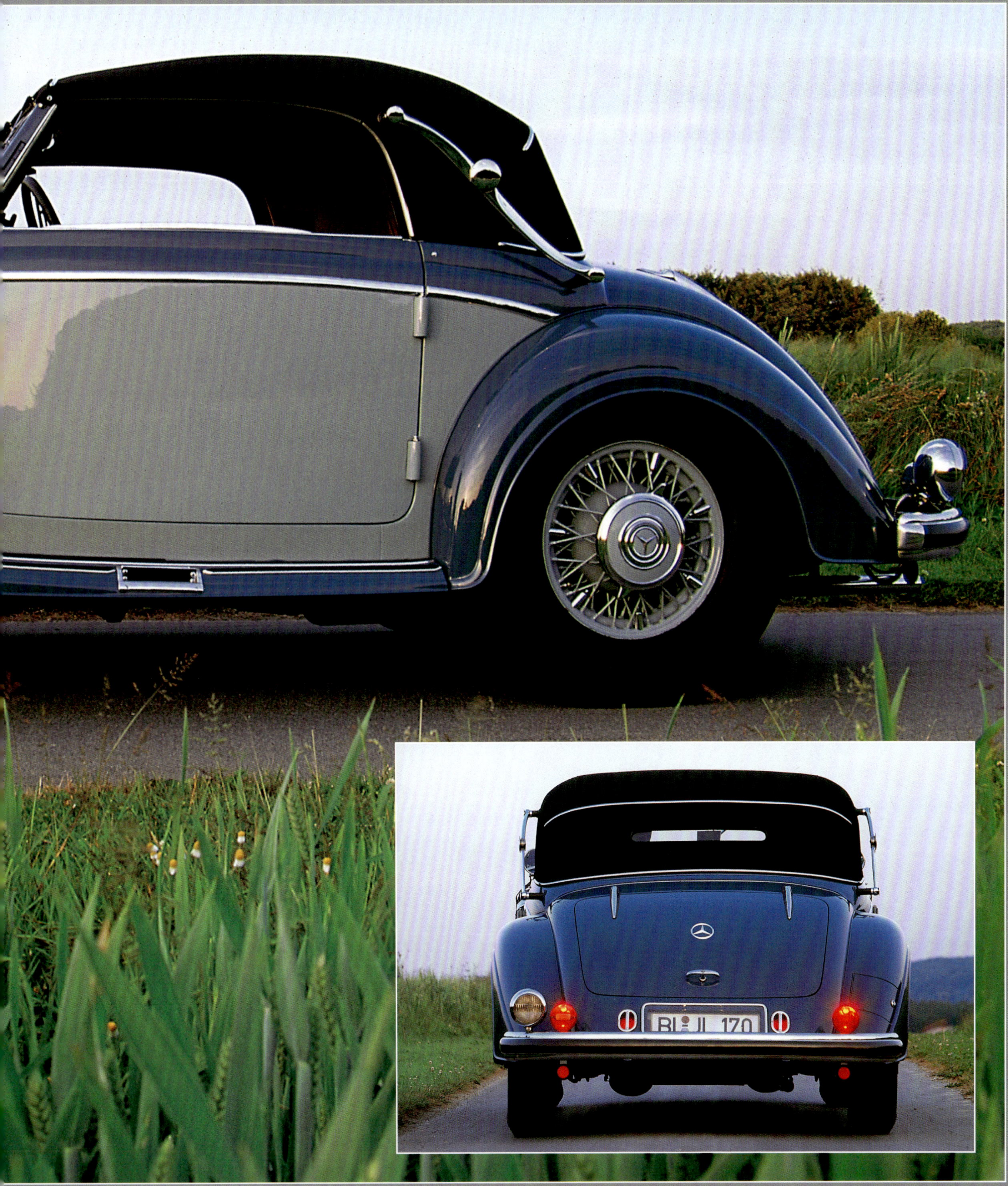

Easy access: the impressive polished chrome mount for the spare wheel and the rear-view mirror mounted on top of the spare wheel, which was also finished in polished chrome.

Schnelle Lösungen: die einprägsam geformte Halterung für das Ersatzrad, der Rückspiegel rittlings auf diesem, Chromglanz hingegen wie für die Ewigkeit.

D'un accès aisé : le support de la roue de secours orné de l'emblème et le rétroviseur qui chevauche celle-ci, des chromes brillants pour l'éternité.

Mercedes-Benz 500 K & 540 K   1934

The Bosch two-tone horn underneath the huge hood also helped establish the right tone. The series' distinctive dashboard was inlaid with mother-of-pearl.

Für den guten Ton sorgt ein Bosch-Zweiklanghorn unter der gewaltigen Haube. Das für die Baureihe markante Armaturenbrett ist mit Perlmutt hinterlegt.

Un klaxon Bosch à deux tons sous le gigantesque capot libère la voie en fanfare. Le tableau de bord spécifique de cette série est décoré de nacre.

This was an oddity, a strange model ill-suited to the Mercedes range, and one destined to have a short, unfulfilled lifespan. The type 130 reflected the fashion of the time—streamlining, or what at that time passed for streamlining. The design created a lot of space at the back of the car so that it seemed appropriate to move the engine to the rear for the car's first trials. The fact that Daimler-Benz spent any time on it passed generally unnoticed. The forerunners of the 130, such as the W17 of 1931 with its 1.2-liter, four-cylinder boxer engine, or the W25D of 1933, which drew a passable performance from its three-cylinder, 30 bhp diesel engine flourished and disappeared unremarked. Consequently, the 130 attracted considerable attention at the Berlin Motor Show in February 1934 because of its shape and the technology it incorporated. Its backbone was a central supporting tube on which the wheels were independently suspended. Its 1308 cc, inline, four-cylinder engine produced 26 bhp and was supported on rubber mountings behind the rear axle.

But soon talk of flaws and handling problems emerged. Two thirds of the vehicle's weight was at the back and this meant that the little car was as treacherous as a roused rattlesnake, a backslider which could only be held in check by masterful driving, and, all in all, rather a handful. Six 1498 cc, 55 bhp type 150 Sport Sedans prepared for the popular 2000 km rally of that year behaved rather more agreeably because their engines were relocated forward of the rear axle. This early interpretation of the mid-engine principle, however, meant that two seats were sacrificed. A sporty roadster built in 1935 on the same chassis, although clearly eye-catching and appealing, proved decidedly too expensive at a purchase price of 6600 marks compared with 3900 marks for a 130 cabrio sedan. It also already had a notorious reputation because of its difficult handling. Its trunk was barely worthy to bear the Mercedes name. The 150 therefore shared the fate of the 130 and disappeared from the sales catalogue in 1936.

Meanwhile the 170 H had been developed in Untertürkheim in parallel with the 170 V and was launched in February 1936. The 38 bhp car with a capacity of 1697 cc was distinctly more civilized than the earlier rear-engined models. And yet while the front-engined 170 blossomed in the market place, the 170 H withered away like a wallflower and was deleted from the range in 1939. It did, however, achieve late honors after the war as some new (unused) examples were still available, only now they were as exclusive as they should have been when first marketed. In all a total of only 5805 units of the 130 and 170 series were produced—it proved to be an excursion which ended in a cul de sac.

Mercedes-Benz 130 H–170 H   1934

A short front and long rear with the 1.5-liter straight four breathing down the passengers' neck. The lines of the 150 type sport roadster conjured up speed, but due to its glaring faults, it enjoyed little success. The 150 was an eye-catching car, but its roadholding was diabolical.

Wenig Bug, viel Heck mit dem Reihenvierzylinder von 1,5 Litern im Nacken der Insassen. Die Silhouette des Sportroadsters Typ 150 mutet zwar rasant an, gleichwohl findet das Auto wenig Anklang wegen seiner evidenten Untugenden. Ein Blickfang ist der 150 gewiss. Aber seine Straßenlage ist teuflisch.

Une proue discrète, mais une poupe allongée avec les quatre-cylindres en ligne de 1,5 litre placés dans le dos des passagers. Le roadster sport 150 présente une silhouette plutôt sportive, mais la voiture a cependant remporté peu de succès en raison de ses défauts. La 150 a certes fière allure, mais sa tenue de route est déficiente.

When this model was shown at the Berlin Motor Show in February 1936 as a successor to the six-cylinder 170, it was already destined for a success which was to carry it through almost two decades. The 170 V was economical, and at a price of 3750 reichsmarks for the two-door sedan it was unusually good value for money. It was as strong as a battletank, both as a unit and in its individual components, and it was designed to a technically conservative brief. It had an unobtrusive style, far removed from the contemporary fashion, in whichever variant it was offered, i.e., as a two- or four-door sedan, two- or four-seat cabriolet, roadster and cabrio-sedan, open tourer, delivery van—of either pickup or box type, and ambulance or patrol car. Such a great variety of types could be offered because of its mixed construction technique of steel sheet cladding over a wooden framework. When in 1946 the 170 V was reintroduced completely in steel, the options shrunk decidedly. Its construction was based on a cruciform oval tubular frame. The rear swing axle was supported on both sides by coil springs attaching it to the frame. The front wheels, as on its predecessor, were independently suspended on a pair of transverse leaf-springs. The 1697 cc engine was hardly overworked in producing just 38 bhp and, being resiliently-mounted at two points, was remarkable for its unprecedentedly quiet running. Initially only the two top gears were synchromeshed, but from 1940 all four were.

The concept was so comprehensively engineered and developed that very few changes were necessary. The star badge, first fixed to the radiator frame, again crowned the radiator cap from 1937 onwards. The structure of the Cabriolet B's top was changed in April 1937 and the additional pillars between the side windows were removed at the same time. The fuel tank in the engine compartment was first of 8.7-gal capacity. From 1939 this was increased by 2.6 gal, which was quite enough for the thrifty 170 V with its average mileage of 23.5 mpg.

Following contemporary practice, the model was used in several different guises for long distance events such as the 1938 Motor Vehicle Winter Rally. This was not so much because of sporting considerations, but so as to verify its suitability for war use. While the off-road 200 V two-seater of 1938 bore only a faint resemblance to the original, the jeep used by the Wehrmacht owed much to the series. The 16,315 examples amounted to one fifth of the total of 86,615 units produced between 1935 and 1942. This made the 170 V the most-produced Mercedes of this period, and it was also a step in the direction of the concept of "people's motoring" demanded by Adolf Hitler.

There is no doubt that in this respect the ruling regime performed a service for the common good.

Mercedes-Benz 170 V 1936

Unlike the 170/6 series with its seven relatively similar models, the 1936 170 came in seven very different designs. The cabrio both drew on the past and pointed the way to the future.

Im Unterschied zum 170/6 mit seinen sieben ziemlich uniformen Varianten hat der 170 von 1936 sieben sehr verschiedene Karosserieformen zu bieten. Das Cabrio nimmt Motive von gestern auf und weist weit über morgen hinaus.

À la différence de la 170/6 avec ses sept variantes plutôt similaires, la 170 de 1936 propose sept formes de carrosserie très différentes. Le cabriolet reprend des motifs d'hier mais se montre tout autant avant-gardiste.

There were some fine members of this series, such as the Cabriolet A, which featured nice design details. Generating just 38 bhp, the four-cylinder engine was a sedate performer.

Die Modellfamilie hat schöne Angehörige wie das Cabriolet A mit schönen Details. Mit bescheidenen 38 PS ermöglicht der Vierzylinder geruhsame Fortbewegung.

Cette famille de modèles a de beaux rejetons comme le Cabriolet A aux jolis détails. Avec ses modestes 38 ch, le quatre-cylindres n'autorise qu'une mobilité décontractée.

Mercedes-Benz 170V 1936

The chrome-trimmed dashboard included fuel and oil pressure gauges, speedometer, and clock. The external semaphore indicator is only permitted today if supplemented by blinkers.

In Chrom gefasste Armaturentafel mit Instrumenten für Benzin und Öldruck, Tachometer und Zeituhr (von links). Der Winker ist heute nur zusätzlich zum Blinker erlaubt.

Tableau de bord avec des cadrans cernés de chromes pour les jauges d'essence et d'huile, le tachymètre et l'horloge (de gauche à droite). Aujourd'hui, le bras de changement de direction n'est autorisé qu'en complément au clignotant.

The spotlights-cum-rear-view mirrors and the additional brake lights came as extras.

Extras sind der Suchscheinwerfer mit Rückspiegel und die zusätzliche Bremsleuchte.

Le projecteur orientable avec rétroviseur et le voyant de frein supplémentaire sont facultatifs.

Mercedes-Benz 170 V 1936

Among the Mercedes exhibits at the Berlin Motor Show of 1936, the one which particularly caught the public eye was the 260 D. Its message was that Daimler-Benz had managed to produce a diesel engine suitable for passenger cars. What no one could predict was that the company had at the same time laid the foundation stone of an empire that would dominate the market in hackney carriages, taxis, and hire cars from then until the present day.

But this achievement did not come easily, the road was rough, strewn with mantraps and pitfalls. The high compression of the diesel engine with its similarly sized combustion units gave rise to two problems. One was that the thicker cylinder walls meant more weight, and the other was that, compared with a gasoline engine, higher inertial forces at the same speed led to uneven engine running. This caused headaches for the engineers in the new Development Department in the Gaggenau Works, and gave one or two of them sleepless nights. In the autumn of 1933 two Mannheim-type diesel sedans were taken from production and mounted on a test rig. These had six-cylinder, 3.8-liter engines producing a stately 80 bhp at 2800 rpm. The tests showed that the transmission was being hammered by the vibration of the engine. A battle had been lost, but not the war.

Three things helped to solve the problem. The use of the Bosch injection pump meant that the path of the fuel up to the injection nozzle could be checked. An inlet chamber system divided the combustion process into two phases so that some of the impulse stressing of the bearings was removed. Then in November 1934 two cylinders were removed from the existing engine resulting in a 2.6-liter unit producing a modest 45 bhp at 3200 rpm which proved to be relatively quiet, smoke-free, and unusually tough and economical. It ran an average of 24.8 mpg compared with the 18.1 mpg of a comparable 2300 cc gasoline engine. Furthermore, diesel fuel at that time cost 17 pfennigs per liter compared with 38 pfennigs for gasoline. A field trial for the new four-cylinder model was first run with 170 models clad in the unprepossessing habit of the type 200/230 landaulet six-seater, used almost exclusively as taxis. The new kid on the block was still rough, but the results were encouraging. The vehicles which had dominated the taxi business up to that point, the Adler Favorit and Adler Standard 6, were soon displaced, especially as their manufacturer Adler had no equivalent car to offer at the time. The second-generation 260 D, which was launched in 1937 in the guise of the type 230 as a six-seater with a wider body, was better behaved. A four-seater sedan and two cabriolets B and D then followed for private owners who wanted, one might say, the automotive equivalent of being seated in a box at the theater. Driving a diesel was a declaration of a certain world view, in addition to being a recognition of commercial utility; this view, however, was shared by only 2000 customers between 1936 and 1940.

Zu den Mercedes-Exponaten, die sich auf der Berliner Automobil-Ausstellung 1936 der besonderen Aufmerksamkeit des Publikums empfehlen, zählt der 260 D. Seine Botschaft: dass es Daimler-Benz gelungen ist, dem Personenwagen den Dieselmotor zugänglich zu machen. Was noch niemand weiß: dass die Stuttgarter zugleich den Grundstein gelegt haben zu einer souveränen Herrschaft über den Markt im Droschken-, Taxi- und Mietwagengewerbe, die bis auf den heutigen Tag andauert.

Der Weg dorthin ist allerdings holprig gewesen, übersät gleichsam mit Fußangeln und Selbstschüssen. Die hohe Verdichtung am Diesel-Triebwerk bei gleichen Abmessungen der Verbrennungseinheiten wirft zweierlei Probleme auf. Zum einen führen dickere Zylinderwände zu mehr Gewicht. Zum anderen wirken bei gleichen Drehzahlen wie beim Benziner höhere Massenkräfte, was unruhigen Motorlauf zur Folge hat. Dies bereitet den Ingenieuren einer eigens ins Leben gerufenen Entwicklungsabteilung im Werk Gaggenau einiges Kopfzerbrechen und die eine oder andere schlaflose Nacht. Dort stehen seit dem Herbst 1933 zwei aus der Serie abgezweigte Limousinen vom Typ Mannheim dieselnd auf dem Prüfstand, mit Sechszylindern von 3,8 Litern, die bei 2800/min stattliche 80 PS leisten. Wie sich erweist, wird das Fahrwerk von den Schwingungen der Maschine zerrüttet und zermürbt. Man hat eine Schlacht, nicht aber den Krieg verloren.

Drei Dinge helfen: Durch die Verwendung der Bosch-Einspritzpumpe lassen sich die Wege des Kraftstoffs bis zur Einspritzdüse kontrollieren. Ein Vorkammer-System unterteilt den Verbrennungsablauf in zwei Phasen, so dass etwa die stoßweise Belastung der Lager entfällt. Und: Man amputiert im November 1934 zwei Zylinder aus dem bestehenden Triebwerk. Ein 2,6 Liter mit bescheidenen 45 PS bei 3200/min entsteht, der sich als relativ leise, rauchfrei, ungemein zählebig und sparsam erweist: Er verbraucht im Schnitt 9,5 Liter gegenüber den 13 Litern eines vergleichbaren Benzinmotors von 2300 cm³. Überdies kostet Dieselkraftstoff zu jener Zeit 17 Pfennige, Benzin aber 38 Pfennige pro Liter. Der neue Vierzylinder wird zunächst im unscheinbaren Habit des Landaulet Sechssitzers vom Typ 200/230 in 170 Exemplaren einem Feldversuch zugeführt, fast ausschließlich im Taxigewerbe. Noch immer gibt sich der Debütant knorrig und rauh, aber die Ergebnisse ermutigen. Rasch bleiben die bisherigen Platzhirsche im Taxigewerbe, Adler Favorit und Adler Standard 6, auf der Strecke, zumal der Konkurrent Adler im Augenblick nichts Gleichwertiges anzubieten hat. Schon feinere Manieren erzieht man dem 260 D der zweiten Generation an, der 1937 im Gewand des Modells 230 mit einem breiteren Aufbau als Sechssitzer präsentiert wird. Eine viersitzige Limousine und zwei Cabriolets B und D folgen als Offerte an eine private Kundschaft mit Logencharakter. Einen Diesel zu fahren, das verrät jenseits seiner kommerziellen Nutzbarkeit zugleich eine gewisse Weltanschauung, die zwischen 1936 und 1940 nur 2000 Kunden teilen.

L'une des Mercedes exposées au Salon de l'automobile de Berlin de 1936 qui ont surtout attiré l'attention du public est la 260 D. Elle véhicule un message: que Mercedes a réussi à civiliser le moteur diesel pour la voiture de tourisme. Mais nul ne sait encore que le constructeur de Stuttgart vient de poser la première pierre d'un monopole incontesté sur le marché des taxis et voitures de location, monopole qui perdure aujourd'hui encore.

Mais pour y parvenir, il aura fallu contourner de nombreux obstacles et pièges. Le taux de compression élevé des moteurs diesel, pour des chambres de combustion aux cotes identiques, pose un double problème. Premièrement, les parois de cylindres, plus épaisses, sont aussi plus lourdes. Deuxièmement, à un régime identique à celui d'un moteur à essence, les masses en mouvement sont plus importantes et le moteur ne tourne donc pas aussi rond. Ce qui a occassionné bien des migraines et des nuits blanches aux ingénieurs du service de développement spécialement créé à cette fin à l'usine de Gaggenau. Depuis l'automne 1933, deux berlines Mannheim prélevées sur la série s'y trouvent au banc d'essais des moteurs diesel, avec des six-cylindres de 3,8 litres développant la puissance respectable de 80 ch à 2800 tr/min. Comme prévu, le châssis ne résiste pas aux oscillations provenant du moteur et se brise. Si l'on a perdu une bataille, on n'a pas perdu la guerre pour autant.

Trois remèdes sont trouvés: l'utilisation de la pompe à injection Bosch permet de contrôler l'écoulement du carburant jusqu'aux injecteurs. Un système à préchambre subdivise le processus de combustion en deux phases distinctes, si bien que les charges brutales subies par les paliers disparaissent. Et, en novembre 1934, on ampute le moteur existant de deux cylindres. On obtient ainsi un 2,6 litres à la puissance modérée de 45 ch à 3200 tr/min, relativement léger, peu polluant, d'une longévité incroyable et sobre: il consomme en moyenne 9,5 litres alors qu'un moteur à essence comparable de 2,3 litres en brûle 13 litres. En outre, à cette époque-là, le litre de gazole coûte moins de la moitié du litre d'essence. Le nouveau quatre-cylindres subit tout d'abord des premiers essais grandeur nature dans l'anonymat le plus complet du Landaulet six places de la série 200/230 avec 170 exemplaires, presque tous des taxis. Le moteur est encore rugueux et fruste, mais les résultats sont encourageants. Les anciennes dominatrices de l'industrie du taxi, l'Adler Favorit et l'Adler Standard 6, sont vite réduites à la défensive, d'autant plus qu'Adler n'a rien d'équivalent à opposer. La 260 D de la deuxième génération, présentée en 1937 sous la forme de la 230 à carrosserie plus large, a déjà affiné ses manières. Une berline à quatre places et deux cabriolets B et D la suivent pour briguer les faveurs d'une clientèle privée qui n'hésite pas à faire parler d'elle. Outre les aspects purement économiques, conduire un diesel à cette époque était aussi le symbole d'un certain état d'esprit qu'entre 1936 et 1940 ne partagent que 2000 clients.

Mercedes-Benz 260 D   1936

The conventional appearance of the 260 D masks a technical innovation: it was the first production car with a diesel engine. The use of diesel was particularly favourable in the mid-1930s: a liter of petrol cost 38 pfennigs, while a liter of diesel fuel was less than half that sum. This sturdy auto-igniting vehicle spoils its owners with its economical fuel consumption, roomy interior and high degree of comfort. These features made it ideal for the taxi trade.

Das eher biedere Gewand des 260 D verhüllt eine technische Premiere: den ersten serienmäßigen Dieselmotor in einem Pkw. Seine Genügsamkeit ist höchst willkommen. Ein Liter Benzin kostet Mitte der Dreißiger 38 Pfennige, ein Liter Dieselöl weniger als die Hälfte. Trotz kernigen Nagelns verwöhnt der stämmige Selbstzünder seine Besitzer, mit günstigem Verbrauch, viel Innenraum und hohem Komfort. Das prädestiniert ihn für das Taxigewerbe.

La robe plutôt banale de la 260 D dissimule une première technique : le premier moteur diesel équipant en série une VP. Sa sobriété est un atout bienvenu. Vers le milieu des années 1930, un litre d'essence coûte 38 pfennigs, alors qu'un litre de gazole n'en coûte que 17. Malgré les claquements, le vigoureux moteur à auto-allumage comble ses propriétaires par une consommation peu élevée, avantage qui s'ajoute à la grande habitabilité et au confort de son intérieur. Un véhicule prédestiné aux compagnies de taxis.

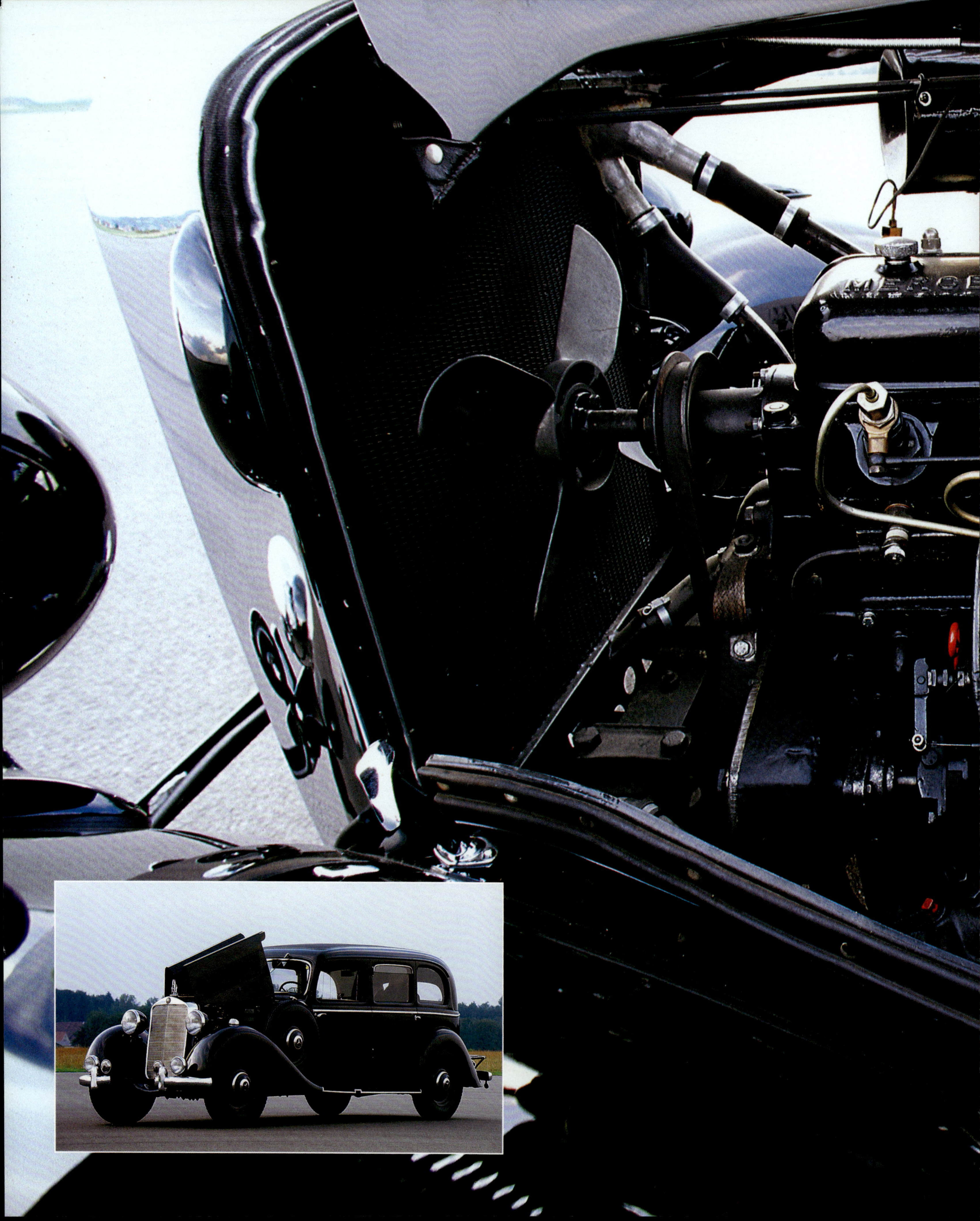

The 260 D's 4-cylinder engine was designed
by Fritz Nallinger. The fuel is delivered to the
combustion chamber via a pre-chamber. The patent for
this process was first issued to Benz & Cie. in March 1909.

Der Vierzylinder des 260 D ist eine Konstruktion von Fritz Nallinger. Der
Kraftstoff gelangt über eine Vorkammer in den Verbrennungsraum. Das Patent
zu diesem Verfahren wurde bereits im März 1909 an Benz & Cie. erteilt.

Le quatre-cylindres de la 260 D est l'œuvre de Fritz Nallinger. Le carburant
arrive dans la chambre de combustion après avoir transité par une préchambre.
Le brevet pour ce procédé a été décerné à Benz & Cie. dès mars 1909.

Introduced in February 1937, the Mercedes-Benz 320 was a comfortable car available in a huge range of bodywork configurations, from a four-door sedan costing 8950 marks, via a six-seater touring car, a number of cabriolets and a roadster, up to a streamlined sedan available for 14,550 marks.

The most distinctive form of this series, based on a shortened chassis, was a two-seater, like the 540 K in pocket-book format, which was available as a cabrio or a coupé whose solid top could be replaced by a light fabric hood. This was an early precursor of the hardtop. This Proteus in automobile form was termed a convertible coupé or convertible car by Mercedes. With only 5097 cars sold, the 320 was never a particularly common car, and its performance was hardly electric: its inline six-cylinder engine developed 78 bhp but had to propel a vehicle weighing up to 4300 lbs. Nonetheless, its running gear consisting of coil springs all round and a rear swing axle was a state-of-the-art design and coped wonderfully well even with difficult conditions.

In the autumn of 1938 its 3208 cc displacement was increased to 3405 cc to compensate for the deteriorating fuel quality. At the same time the Pullman version was fitted with a huge trunk as standard. The power output and the type designation of 320, which indicated a 3.2-liter engine, remained unchanged. The four gears provided hitherto were then supplemented by an overdrive from Zahnradfabrik Friedrichshafen so that the top speed of 78 mph was also the cruising speed. Owners appreciated this on the steadily growing motorway network which measured 1305 miles by the end of the war.

Im Februar 1937 eingeführt, ist der Mercedes-Benz 320 ein kommodes Reiseauto in den unterschiedlichsten Karosserie-Konfigurationen, von der viertürigen Limousine für 8950 Mark über einen sechssitzigen Tourenwagen, etliche Cabriolets und einen Roadster bis hin zu einer Limousine in aktueller Stromlinie für 14 550 Mark.

Die apartste Ausformung der Baureihe, auf verkürztem Fahrgestell: ein Zweisitzer, gleichsam ein 540 K im Taschenbuchformat, als Cabrio zu haben oder als Coupé, dessen Festdach gegen ein leichtes Stoffverdeck ausgewechselt werden kann. Das Hardtop grüßt von ferne, aber die Namensgebung ist aus heutiger Sicht verwirrend – Kombinations-Coupé oder Kombinationswagen nennt man diesen automobilen Proteus bei Mercedes. Insgesamt bleibt der 320 mit 5097 Exemplaren recht schwach verbreitet. Ein Ausbund an Feuer ist er nicht: Sein Reihen-Sechszylinder mit 78 PS muss es mit bis zu 1950 Kilogramm Wagengewicht aufnehmen. Gleichwohl auf dem letzten Stand der Dinge, kommt sein Fahrwerk mit Schraubenfedern ringsum und Pendelachse hinten auch mit schwierigeren Umständen glänzend zurecht.

Im Herbst 1938 wird sein Hubraum von 3208 cm³ auf 3405 cm³ vergrößert, um mindere Treibstoffqualität aufzufangen. Zugleich erhält die Pullman-Version serienmäßig einen voluminösen Außenkoffer. Unverändert bleiben die Leistung und auch die Typenbezeichnung 320, die ja auf einen 3,2 Liter hinweist. Den vier Fahrstufen bisher kann indessen ein »Ferngang« der Zahnradfabrik Friedrichshafen zugeschaltet werden, so dass die Höchstgeschwindigkeit von 126 Stundenkilometern auch als Dauer-Tempo genutzt werden kann. Auf dem stetig sich erweiternden Autobahnnetz – bei Kriegsende 2100 Kilometer – wissen die Kunden das zu würdigen.

Présentée en février 1937, la Mercedes-Benz 320 est une confortable voiture de voyage proposée dans les configurations de carrosseries les plus diverses, de la berline à quatre portes pour 8950 marks à la berline à carrosserie aérodynamique en vente pour 14 550 marks en passant par la voiture de tourisme à six places, de nombreux cabriolets et un roadster.

Modèle le plus élégant de la gamme sur châssis raccourci: une biplace, espèce de 540 K miniaturisée, disponible en cabriolet ou coupé dont le toit en dur peut être échangé contre une légère capote en tissu. C'est l'ancêtre du *hard-top*, mais son nom nous semble peu approprié aujourd'hui. Mercedes baptise ce Protée « coupé convertible » ou « voiture convertible ». Avec au total 5097 exemplaires, la 320 ne connaît pas une très grande diffusion. Elle ne brille pas non plus particulièrement par ses performances: son six-cylindres en ligne de 78 ch doit en effet mouvoir jusqu'à 1950 kg. En revanche, ses trains roulants à ressorts hélicoïdaux sur les quatre roues et essieu brisé à l'arrière s'en tirent très honorablement même dans les circonstances difficiles.

À l'automne 1938, sa cylindrée passe de 3208 à 3405 cm³ pour compenser la moindre qualité de certains carburants. À cette occasion, la version Pullman reçoit en série un volumineux coffre à bagages extérieur. La puissance et la dénomination, 320, qui indiquent l'existence d'un moteur de 3,2 litres, restent inchangées. Après les quatre rapports actuels, on peut en revanche enclencher une « surmultipliée » de Zahnradfabrik Friedrichshafen qui a l'avantage de transformer la vitesse maximale de 126 km/h en une authentique vitesse de croisière. Le réseau autoroutier devient de plus en plus dense – il compte 2100 km à la fin de la guerre – et les clients l'apprécient à sa juste valeur.

Mercedes-Benz 320   1937

The streamlined type 320 sedan used the same bodywork and chassis as its predecessor, the type 290. Aerodynamic lines were all the rage; streamlined 500K and 540K coupés were also available.

Karosserie und Chassis übernimmt die Stromlinienlimousine Typ 320 von ihrem Vorgänger Typ 290. Windschnittig zu sein ist der letzte Schrei: Auch 500K und 540K gibt es als Stromlinien-Coupés.

La berline 320 aux lignes fluides reprend de sa devancière, la 290, la carrosserie et le châssis. Son aérodynamisme est du dernier cri. La 500K et la 540K sont aussi proposées en coupés très profilés.

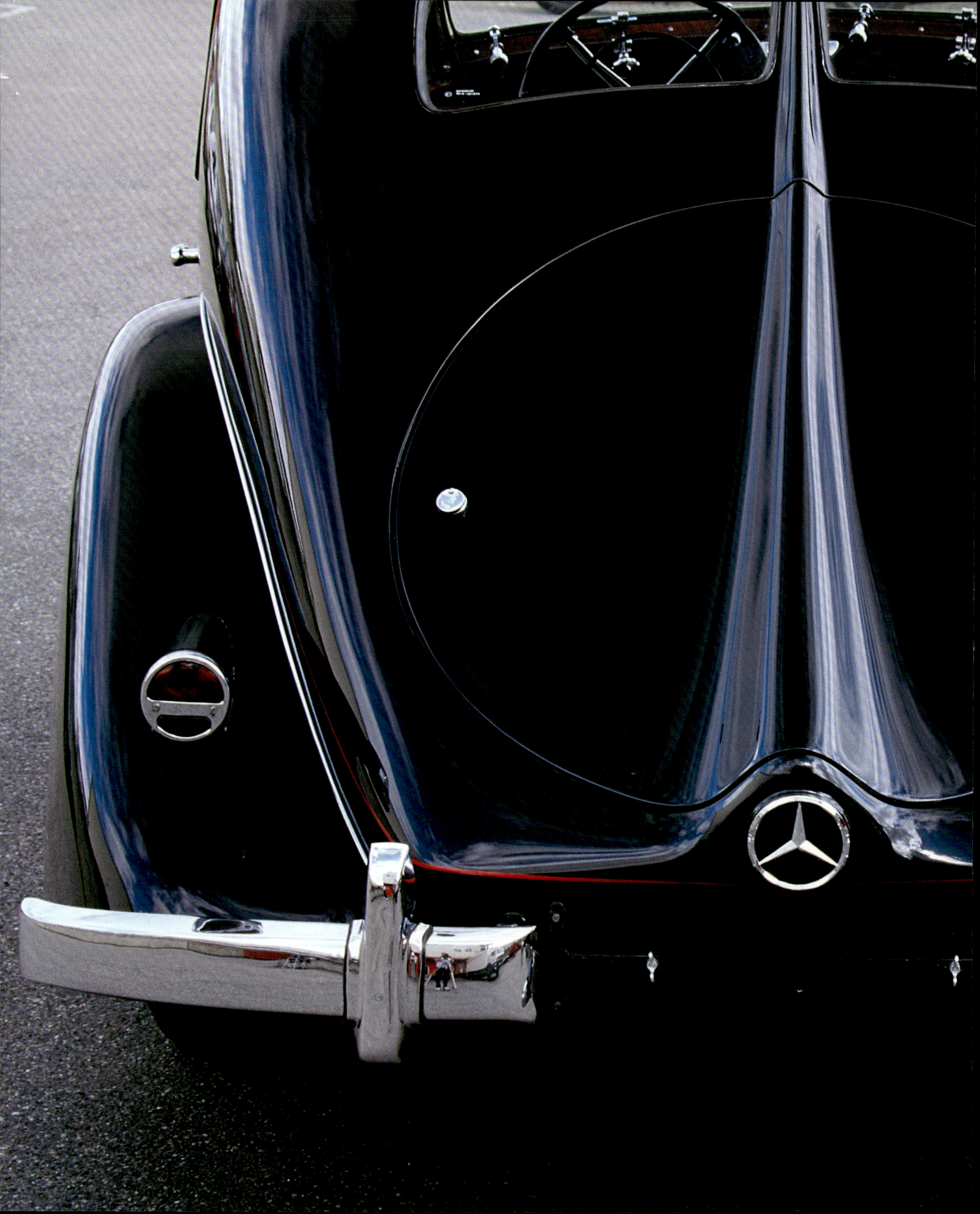

Before Professor Kamm's principle of the aerodynamic efficiency of the smallest possible cross section became generally accepted, long sweeping curves were regarded as the ideal solution.

Bevor sich die Lehre des Professors Kamm von der Effizienz des kleinsten Abreißquerschnitts durchsetzt, gilt ein lang ausschwingendes Heck als der Weisheit letzter Schluss.

Avant que la doctrine du professeur Kamm ne s'impose (soit l'efficacité du moindre maître-couple), une longue poupe effilée était considérée comme le summum de l'aérodynamique.

Since 1971 an exhibit in the Mercedes Museum in Untertürkheim has borne witness to the presence of giants in the history of the car, namely a Pullman type 770 limousine from the Emperor of Japan's fleet whose emblem—a chrysanthemum—appears on its red doors. This species, manufactured from 1930 onwards in Stuttgart, would quickly have become extinct if it had not been kept alive by the excited interest of the leadership of Nazi Germany exhibiting its characteristic passion for the gigantic. So it was that a new edition even appeared in 1938. The 117 first-generation models were then followed by a further 88, including one chassis without bodywork.

The main features of the early "Großer Mercedes" were: it was, above all, big with an inline eight-cylinder engine of 7655 cc and 150 bhp without or 200 bhp with supercharger, a 3-speed gearbox with a semi-automatic overdrive, a pressed-steel low-frame chassis with U-sections and cross-bracing, rigid axles and semi-elliptic springs front and rear. The later models were the epitome of contemporary high-tech state-of-the-art manufacture. The alloy engine of unchanged capacity used a combination of battery and magneto ignition with two spark plugs per cylinder and developed 155 bhp without and 230 bhp with the fitted Roots supercharger, power which was transmitted to the rear axle via five synchromeshed gears. The chassis consisted of an oval-tube frame with double wishbones and coil springs at the front and a double-pivot axle with coil springs (from 1939 onwards interlocking double coil springs) at the rear. The ample power which was available even at a low engine speed had to shift a heavy load: the bare chassis weighed 4600 lbs, while the complete car which was capable of 106 mph tipped the scales at up to 8000 lbs.

The armor-plated special version of the 770 in which politicians of the time used to keep themselves far from the madding crowd weighed in at 10,600 lbs, as a result of the 1½ in-thick bulletproof glass and ¾ in-thick armor plate steel with which it was shielded. To make up for this, a slight weight saving was achieved on the wings which were constructed of aluminum. The factory recommended that this heavyweight should not be taken above 50 mph as it was possible that the tires might fail above this speed. This special version achieved 5.9 mpg whereas the series version rolled two extra miles (7.8 mpg). Would-be owners had to splash out 44,000 reichsmarks for the Pullman version, 46,000 reichsmarks for the four-door Cabriolet D, or 47,500 reichsmarks for the six-seater Cabriolet F. This pricing structure inevitably reduced the circle of potential purchasers of the "Großer Mercedes." In the end, interest in the armored version increased—in inverse proportion to the decreasing popularity of its occupants.

Seit 1971 kündet ein Exponat des Mercedes-Museums in Untertürkheim vom Vorkommen von Riesen in der Geschichte des Automobils, eine Pullman-Limousine des Typs 770 aus dem Fuhrpark des japanischen Kaisers, dessen Emblem sie auf den roten Türen trägt: eine Chrysantheme. Diese Spezies, in Stuttgart ab 1930 gefertigt, wäre schon bald ausgestorben, hätte sie nicht das lebhafte Interesse der politischen Führungskaste des nationalsozialistischen Deutschlands mit ihrer arteigenen Gigantomanie am Leben gehalten. So kommt es 1938 sogar zu einer Neuauflage: Auf 117 Exemplare der ersten Generation folgen noch einmal 88 weitere, davon ein unbekleidetes Fahrgestell.

Der frühe »Große Mercedes«: vor allem groß, mit einem Reihen-Achtzylinder von 7655 cm³ und 150 PS ohne oder 200 PS mit Kompressor, Dreigang-Getriebe mit halbautomatischem Schnellgang, einem Pressstahl-Niederrahmen mit U-Profilen und Kreuzverstrebungen, Starrachsen und Halbfedern vorn und hinten. Der späte: ein Ausbund von High-Tech auf dem Stande der Zeit. Sein Leichtmetall-Triebwerk mit unverändertem Volumen, befeuert von einer kombinierten Batterie- und Magnetzündung mit zwei Kerzen je Zylinder, leistet 155 PS ohne und 230 PS mit zugeschaltetem Roots-Gebläse, die von fünf synchronisierten Fahrstufen an die Hinterachse vermittelt werden. Das Chassis: ein Ovalrohrrahmen mit Doppel-Querlenkern und Schraubenfedern vorn und einer Doppelgelenkachse mit Schraubenfedern (ab 1939 ineinanderliegenden Doppelschraubenfedern) hinten. Die üppig bemessenen und bereits bei niedrigen Drehzahlen verfügbaren Pferdestärken haben auch ordentlich zu schleppen: 2100 Kilogramm wiegt das bloße Fahrgestell, bis zu 3600 Kilogramm das ganze Auto, das zu 170 Stundenkilometern fähig ist.

In der gepanzerten Sonderausführung, mit der sich führende Politiker der Zeit vor dem Zugriff der Menge schützen, bringt der Typ 770 bis zu 4800 Kilogramm auf die Waage, bedingt durch Panzerglas von 40 Millimetern und Panzerstahl von 18 Millimetern Dicke. An den Kotflügeln hat man dafür leicht eingespart – sie sind aus Aluminium. Das Werk empfiehlt, diesem Schwergewichtler höchstens Tempo 80 zuzumuten, da darüber die Reifen nicht mehr mitspielen könnten. Ihn verlangt es nach 40 Litern Treibstoff je 100 Kilometer, wo sich die Serienausführung mit zehn Litern weniger begnügt. Für die Pullman-Version muss die Klientel 44000 Reichsmark auf den Tisch legen, für das viertürige Cabriolet D 46000, für das sechssitzige Cabriolet F 47500 Reichsmark. Diese Preisgestaltung engt den Kreis der Bezieher des »Großen Mercedes« zwangsläufig ein. Am Ende nimmt das Interesse an der Panzer-Variante zu – umgekehrt proportional zu der abnehmenden Popularität seiner Insassen…

Depuis 1971, une voiture exposée au musée Mercedes d'Untertürkheim témoigne de l'existence de titans dans l'histoire de l'automobile, une limousine Pullman 770 de la flotte de l'empereur japonais, dont elle arbore l'emblème sur ses portes rouges: un chrysanthème. Cette espèce fabriquée à Stuttgart à partir de 1930 se serait rapidement éteinte si le vif intérêt manifesté par la classe politique de l'Allemagne nazie, connue pour sa folie des grandeurs, ne l'avait pas maintenue en vie. Ainsi une nouvelle série en est même produite en 1938: les 117 exemplaires de la première génération sont suivis, un peu plus tard, par 88 autres, dont un châssis nu.

L'ancienne «Grosser Mercedes»: surtout grosse, avec un huit-cylindres en ligne de 7655 cm³ et 150 ch sans compresseur ou 200 ch avec boîte à trois vitesses avec surmultipliée semi-automatique, châssis surbaissé en acier extrudé avec profilés en U et renforts en X, essieux rigides et ressorts semi-elliptiques à l'avant et à l'arrière. La seconde «Grosser Mercedes»: un parangon de haute technologie qui tutoie les sommets de la technique. Son moteur en alliage léger, d'une cylindrée inchangée, est alimenté par un allumage mixte à batterie et magnétique, à deux bougies par cylindre développant 155 ch, et 230 ch avec le compresseur Roots en action, une cavalerie transmise aux roues arrière par cinq vitesses synchronisées. Le châssis est formé d'un cadre en tubes ovales à doubles bras transversaux et ressorts hélicoïdaux à l'avant ainsi qu'essieu à double articulation et ressorts hélicoïdaux (à partir de 1939, avec doubles ressorts hélicoïdaux concentriques) à l'arrière. Pléthoriques et disponibles dès les bas régimes, les chevaux n'ont pas une tâche enviable: le châssis nu pèse déjà 2100 kg et la voiture peut atteindre jusqu'à 3600 kg alors qu'elle est capable de rouler à 170 km/h.

Dans la version blindée spéciale, destinée principalement aux hommes politiques de l'époque lors de leurs déplacements, la 770 peut accuser jusqu'à 4800 kg, tribut du verre blindé de 40 mm et de l'acier blindé de 18 mm d'épaisseur. Économie symbolique de poids: les ailes sont en aluminium. L'usine recommande de ne pas faire rouler ce «poids lourd» à plus de 80 km/h, car, au-delà, les pneus risqueraient de ne plus jouer le jeu. Sa voracité est extraordinaire: 40 litres de carburant aux 100 km alors que la version de série se contente de 30 litres. Pour la version Pullman, la clientèle doit débourser 44000 reichsmarks, 46000 pour le cabriolet D à quatre portes et même 47500 pour le cabriolet F six places. Un tel tarif limite évidemment le nombre de clients potentiels de la «Grosser Mercedes». En fin de compte, l'intérêt suscité par la version blindée augmente – de façon inversement proportionnelle à la popularité en régression de ses passagers.

Großer Mercedes 770 1938

The many people who could not afford one nicknamed the *Großer Mercedes* "the express train of the roads." Hardly surprising: no expense was spared in the manufacture of this prestige automobile.

Dem »Großen Mercedes« legen die vielen, die ihn sich nicht leisten können, den Spitznamen »D-Zug der Landstraße« bei. Kein Wunder: Er ist ein Prestigeautomobil, das ohne Rücksicht auf Kosten gebaut wird.

Tous ceux qui ne pouvaient se l'offrir ont affublé la « Grosser Mercedes » du surnom de « train express de la route ». Ce n'est pas étonnant : c'est une voiture de prestige construite sans égard envers les coûts.

Open touring cars like this formed part of the Reich Chancellery's fleet. Somewhat illogically, the passengers of this 4.5-ton vehicle were protected by armor-plating—but only up to shoulder height. This rolling fortress was powered by an inline eight-cylinder engine with a fitted Roots supercharger and a colossal 7600 cc, generating 230 bhp at 3200 rpm.

Offene Tourenwagen wie dieser zählen zum Fuhrpark der Reichskanzlei. Ein Widersinn ist, dass die Panzerung des 4,5-Tonners seine Insassen bestenfalls bis auf Schulterhöhe vor Unheil behütet. Für die Fortbewegung der rollenden Festung zuständig ist ein Achtzylinder-Reihenmotor mit zuschaltbarem Roots-Gebläse und dem kolossalen Hubraum von 7600 cm³. Er leistet 230 PS bei 3200/min.

Des voitures de tourisme décapotables comme celle-ci figuraient dans la flotte de la chancellerie du Reich. Erreur de conception? Le blindage de cette voiture de 4,5 tonnes protège au maximum ses passagers jusqu'à hauteur des épaules! Un huit-cylindres en ligne à compresseur Roots débrayable avec la cylindrée colossale de 7600 cm³ assure la propulsion de cette citadelle roulante. Il développe 230 ch à 3200 tr/min.

Its appearance at the Berlin Automobile Exhibition seemed simultaneously to signal an investment in a great future, and a declaration of war. In the sophisticated mid-range market, the new Mercedes 230 with its 2.3-liter, straight six-cylinder engine generating 55 bhp was challenging tried and tested competition such as the Adler 2.5 Liter and the Opel Kapitän. But it was not to be: against the ominous backdrop of the Second World War the latest creation from Stuttgart withered like a spring flower, and only 4210 were ever produced. However, the Mercedes 230 sedan and its cabriolet A, B, and D variants did perform one service. Its design was so timeless and handsome, and its chassis with its cruciform oval tubular frame, as with the 170 V, was so modern, that ten years later it formed their basis for the design of the post-war models 170 S and 220.

Seine Vorstellung auf der Berliner Automobil-Ausstellung wirkt wie eine Anzahlung auf eine schöne Zukunft und ist zugleich eine Kampfansage: In der gehobenen Mittelklasse stößt der neue Mercedes 230 mit seinem Sechszylinder-Reihenmotor von 2,3 Litern und 55 PS auf gestandene Konkurrenten wie den Adler 2,5 Liter und den Opel Kapitän. Aber es soll nicht sein: Vor dem Hintergrund des Zweiten Weltkriegs verkümmert die jüngste Kreation aus Stuttgart in einer Auflage von lediglich 4210 Exemplaren zum Mauerblümchen. Ein Verdienst indessen bleibt dem Mercedes 230 in den Varianten Limousine und Cabriolet A, B und D unbenommen: So schön und zeitlos sind seine Formen, so modern ist sein Fahrgestell mit einem x-förmigen Ovalrohrrahmen wie beim 170 V, dass man sich noch zehn Jahre später bei der Konzeption der Nachkriegsmodelle 170 S und 220 an ihnen orientiert.

Sa présentation au Salon de l'automobile de Berlin fait figure d'acompte sur un futur tout en rose, mais est aussi, simultanément, une déclaration de guerre: dans le segment intermédiaire supérieur, la nouvelle Mercedes 230 doit faire face, avec son six-cylindres en ligne de 2,3 litres et 55 ch, à une concurrence aussi forte que l'Adler 2,5 Liter et l'Opel Kapitän. Mais il n'en sera rien: dans l'ombre de la Seconde Guerre mondiale, imminente, la toute dernière création de Stuttgart connaîtra un destin peu enviable. Elle ne sera produite qu'à 4210 exemplaires. Elle a en revanche des mérites qu'on ne peut lui contester: en versions berline et cabriolet A, B et D, ses formes sont si belles et si intemporelles, son châssis est si moderne avec son cadre en tubes ovales en forme de x, comme pour la 170 V, que, dix ans plus tard, pour la conception des modèles d'après-guerre, la 170 S et la 220, on s'en inspirera encore.

Mercedes-Benz 230   1938

The type 230 Cabriolet D began its long life in 1939 as a service vehicle for the NSFK (Nationalsozialistisches Flieger-Korps or National Socialist Flyers Corps) at the Kassel garrison. After a long exile in Czechoslovakia, it finally returned to Germany in 1986.

Das abgebildete Cabriolet D vom Typ 230 beginnt sein langes Leben 1939 wie andere auch als Dienstfahrzeug beim NSFK (für Nationalsozialistisches Flieger-Korps) mit Garnison Kassel und kehrt 1986 nach langem Exil in der Tschechoslowakei nach Deutschland zurück.

Le Cabriolet D 230 représenté ici entame sa longue carrière en 1939 comme d'autres également en tant que voiture de fonction auprès du NSFK (Nationalsozialistisches Flieger-Korps ou corps national-socialiste d'aviateurs) de la garnison de Cassel et reviendra en Allemagne en 1986 après un long exil en Tchécoslovaquie.

With its rough, classless solidity, it was just made for difficult times. So it was that the Mercedes-Benz W136, better known by its model name, the 170 V, ensured continuity for the star marque from the last years of peace, through the Second World War and the turmoil of reconstruction, to the burgeoning post-war economic miracle. And, with 169,805 units sold, it carried Daimler-Benz AG from catastrophe, with its nadir in corporate destruction, to resurrection at the beginning of the Fifties, as the bestseller up to that time in the company's history.

The new beginning started out modestly; in 1946 various small vans were produced using very crude bodies made by Hägele, a Stuttgart-based coachbuilder, simply because there was always something needing transport at that time. A four-door sedan built all of steel appeared in July 1947. In manufacturing this, the Mercedes engineers of the immediate post-war period were fortunate in that the large deep-drawing press in Sindelfingen had survived the war almost unscathed. At the Hanover Technical Export Fair in May 1949 the 170 D was introduced alongside the 170 V. Like the 170 V, this had a 1697 cc engine developing 38 bhp, but it used diesel fuel which was available everywhere without rationing. The characteristic feature of the 170 D was its robust, knocking engine sound. In May 1950 the twins were given a thorough makeover. This involved increasing the engine size (1767 cc) and the power (45 bhp for the gasoline model, 40 bhp for the diesel), modifications to the running gear in the form of telescopic shock absorbers, a broader rear track and better brakes, and greater comfort provided by wider seats and more elbow-room. A further facelift in May 1952 also brought about distinct changes: a further-increased rear track, one-piece bumpers, a larger windshield, and a few horizontally inset ventilation slits in the hood which had previously sported a number of vertically inclined vents.

7358 chassis were exported throughout the world, for example to Argentina, where they were shipped in "CKD" (completely knocked down) form. The Bochum-based Daimler-Benz agent and coachbuilder Lueg fitted various special bodies to the chassis. In 1951 and 1952 the German Federal Border Guard took delivery of 530 units of the semi-military OTP version (Open-top Police Touring Car), a 170 D with four doors, a lightweight fold-down top, top-hung windows at the side, and a windshield that could pivot forwards. The collectible status later enjoyed by this model—many people think it is a relic from Hitler's army fleet—is not always justified.

In seiner knorrig-klassenlosen Solidität ist er wie geschaffen für schwierige Zeiten. Also sorgt der Mercedes-Benz W136, besser bekannt unter seinem Modellnamen 170 V, für Kontinuität im Zeichen des Sterns, von den letzten Friedensjahren über den Zweiten Weltkrieg und die Wirren des Wiederaufbaus bis hinein in das werdende Wirtschaftswunder. Und er trägt die Daimler-Benz AG vom Fall mit dem Tiefpunkt der Zerstörung des Konzerns in den Aufstieg Anfang der Fünfziger, als vorläufiger Bestseller in der Firmengeschichte mit 169 805 Exemplaren.

Der Neubeginn lässt sich indessen bescheiden an: 1946 entstehen mit reichlich kruden Aufbauten des Stuttgarter Karosseriefabrikanten Hägele diverse Kleinlaster, schon weil es in jenen Jahren immer irgend etwas zu transportieren gibt. Eine viertürige Limousine in Ganzstahlbauweise stellt sich im Juli 1947 ein, wobei den Mercedes-Männern der ersten Stunde zugute kommt, dass die große Tiefziehpresse in Sindelfingen den Krieg fast unversehrt überstanden hat. Auf der Technischen Exportmesse Hannover im Mai 1949 rollt dem 170 V der 170 D zur Seite, wie dieser 38 PS stark bei einem Motorvolumen von 1697 cm³, aber mit Dieselkraftstoff gespeist, der überall uneingeschränkt gezapft werden kann. Der 170 D ist vor allem erkennbar durch kerniges Nageln. Im Mai 1950 lässt man den Zwillingen eine energische Modellpflege angedeihen. Sie umspannt mehr Hubraum (1767 cm³) und mehr Leistung (45 PS für den Benziner, 40 PS für den Diesel), Retuschen am Fahrwerk wie Teleskop-Stoßdämpfer, eine erweiterte hintere Spur und bessere Bremsen sowie ein Plus an Komfort durch breitere Sitze und zusätzliche Freiheit für den Ellenbogen. Auch ein weiteres Facelifting im Mai 1952 hinterlässt deutliche Veränderungen: noch mehr Spurweite hinten, einteilige Stoßstangen, eine größere Frontscheibe sowie wenige waagerecht eingeschnittene Lüftungsschlitze in der Motorhaube, die bislang schräg senkrecht vielfach aufgebrochen war.

7358 Fahrgestelle werden zum Teil in alle Welt exportiert, zum Beispiel nach Argentinien, wohin sie als Teilesätze (»CKD«, für *completely knocked down*) reisen. Zahlreiche Sonderaufbauten stülpt dem Chassis der Bochumer Daimler-Benz-Agent und Karosseriebauer Lueg über. 1951 und 1952 erhält der Bundesgrenzschutz 530 Einheiten der halbmilitärischen Version OTP (für Offener Polizei-Tourenwagen), ein 170 D mit vier Türen, einem leichten Klappverdeck, seitlichen Steckfenstern und einer Frontscheibe, die sich nach vorn umlegen lässt. Der Sammlerwert, der dieser Spezies später beigemessen wird, ist nicht immer gerechtfertigt: Viele halten sie für Relikte aus dem Fuhrpark der Wehrmacht.

Par ses lignes banales qui échappent à toute classification sociale, elle est comme prédestinée aux temps difficiles. La Mercedes-Benz W136, mieux connue sous son nom de série 170 V, garantit donc la continuité sous l'emblème de l'étoile, des dernières années de paix en passant par la Seconde Guerre mondiale et les aléas de la reconstruction jusqu'aux débuts du miracle économique. Et, avec 169 805 exemplaires, elle porte Daimler-Benz AG depuis sa chute et la destruction du groupe jusqu'à son essor du début des années 1950, en tant que best-seller provisoire dans l'histoire de la firme.

Ces nouveaux débuts s'effectuent toutefois dans la plus grande modestie : en 1946 avec les carrosseries, dénuées de tout charme, du carrossier de Stuttgart, Hägele, Daimler-Benz produit divers petits camions car, au cours de ces années, le transport est une activité en plein essor. Une berline à quatre portes avec carrosserie tout acier n'apparaît qu'en juillet 1947. Les ouvriers de la première heure de chez Mercedes ont profité de ce que la grosse presse emboutisseuse de Sindelfingen a survécu à la guerre sans dommages notables. Lors du Salon des exportations techniques de Hanovre, en mai 1949, la 170 V est rejointe par la 170 D, qui possède comme celle-ci un moteur de 38 ch et 1697 cm³, mais diesel, le gazole étant désormais un carburant que l'on peut se procurer sans restriction. La 170 D se reconnaît notamment à ses claquements marqués. En mai 1950, les deux jumelles bénéficient d'une modernisation poussée. Leur cylindrée augmente (1767 cm³) et leur puissance aussi (45 ch pour le moteur à essence, 40 ch pour le diesel), leur châssis est retouché avec des amortisseurs télescopiques, des voies plus larges à l'arrière et de meilleurs freins tandis que le confort s'améliore grâce à des sièges plus larges et à une plus grande liberté de mouvement à hauteur des coudes. Un nouveau lifting, en mai 1952, laisse lui aussi des traces sensibles : la voie arrière est encore élargie, les pare-chocs sont d'une pièce, le pare-brise de plus grandes dimensions et un petit nombre de fentes d'aération horizontales ornent le capot moteur à la place des multiples fentes diagonales de l'ancien modèle.

Sur 7358 châssis, une partie a été exportée dans le monde entier, par exemple en Argentine où ils s'en vont en pièces détachées. Lueg, concessionnaire Daimler-Benz et carrossier de Bochum, habille les châssis de nombreuses carrosseries spéciales. En 1951 et 1952, la Protection fédérale des frontières prend possession de 530 exemplaires de la version semi-militaire OTP (pour voiture de tourisme de police décapotée). Il s'agit d'une 170 D à quatre portes, avec capote légère, fenêtres latérales à insérer et pare-brise rabattable vers l'avant. La valeur que les collectionneurs attacheront plus tard à ce modèle n'est pas toujours justifiée : beaucoup les considèrent comme des survivantes du parc automobile de la Wehrmacht.

Mercedes-Benz 170 V 1946

The 170 V's simple lines and, after a few teething troubles were sorted out, its virtual indestructibility ensured that one of the better products of pre-war Germany remained available for the first seven years after the war.

Eine schlichte Erscheinung und nach den Anlaufschwierigkeiten der Anfangsphase schier unzerstörbar, rettet der 170 V ein gutes Stück Vorkriegsdeutschland in die ersten sieben Nachkriegsjahre hinüber.

D'une grande sobriété extérieure et, après correction de ses défauts de jeunesse, absolument indestructible, la 170 V réincarne l'Allemagne de l'avant-guerre au cours des sept premières années de l'après-guerre.

Mercedes-Benz 170 V 1946

Even minor details like the windshield wipers, which worked from above, betray the pre-war provenance of the 170 V. The trunk lid hinges together with the spare-wheel cover were at the bottom. Modest improvements in 1950 saw the seats increased in size, and the interior widened. The various switches, levers, handles, and other controls had a comfortingly solid feel to them.

Auch Kleinigkeiten wie die Scheibenwischer, die ihre Arbeit von oben verrichten, verraten die Vorkriegs-Provenienz des 170 V. Die Scharniere des Kofferraumdeckels mit der Verkleidung des Reserverads sind unten angesiedelt. Im Zuge sanfter Modellpflege werden 1950 Sitze und Innenbreite vergrößert. Schalter, Hebel, Kurbeln und andere Bedienungselemente sind von knackiger Solidität.

De petits détails comme les essuie-glace articulés en haut du pare-brise montrent que la 170 V remonte à l'avant-guerre. Les charnières du couvercle de malle comportant le carénage de la roue de secours sont placées en bas. Lors d'une remise au goût du jour modérée, en 1950, sièges et espace intérieur s'agrandissent. Les manettes, leviers et autres éléments de commande dégagent une impression de grande solidité.

Mercedes-Benz 170 V 1946

It did not exactly flaunt its charms, but nonetheless it appealed to those who were enjoying the first blossoming of renewed affluence in Germany and were keen to show off what they had achieved. In its style and design the 170 s, which was launched at the Hanover Technical Export Fair in May 1949, was derived from the pre-war model 230, though two prestigious cylinders had been ditched en route. In engineering terms it was based on the 170 v whose power unit delivered 52 bhp in the smoother bodywork of the new car. An important innovation in the running gear revealed the hand of the gifted engineer Rudolf Uhlenhaut: forged double wishbones at the front with coil springs and an anti-roll bar.

The 170s initiated the post-war tradition of the slightly more refined Mercedes whose special status was already hinted at in the simple suffix "s." Its introductory price (which was later to fall) was 9850 marks. That was already quite a sum. However, Joe Average did not have a hope of affording the two cabriolets—the B (four-seater, 12,850 marks) and A (a well-designed two-seater, 15,800 marks), 830 of which were sold alongside the sedan between 1949 and November 1951. In January 1952 the original version was replaced by the revamped 170 sb which can be recognized by its larger rear screen, internal hinges on the trunk lid, steering-column-mounted gear lever, hypoid rear axle, camshaft drive via a duplex chain, wider track, and more effective heating. It was in production until August 1953, matching the lifespan of the diesel model, which was slightly damaging to the supposed exclusivity of the series. Even more damaging was the despicable attempt to play the modular card in 1953 when the Mercedes strategists planned to help their aging star stand out against the type 180 by means of lower prices. The s and ds were simply transplanted onto the 170 v and d chassis, giving birth to the 170 s-v and s-d hybrids. Most buyers opted for the diesel version whose 11,800 sales between 1953 and 1955 decisively outstripped the 3002 gasoline-engined units. Connoisseurs recognize the two cut-down models by the lack of chrome trim strips on the air vents in the hood, a grab handle instead of a twist handle on the trunk lid, and the fact that the bumpers were no longer reinforced with overriders. And that put paid to the refined image of the 170 s, especially as all manner of third-party bodies were foisted upon it to allow it to be used for more mundane purposes than the transport of bosses, professors, and ministers.

Er versteckt seinen noblen Charme gewissermaßen in der hohlen Hand und kommt dennoch dem Wunsch des frühen bundesrepublikanischen Wohlstandsbürgers entgegen, Errungenes auch zur Schau zu stellen. Im Stil und seiner Konzeption nach leitet sich der 170 s, präsentiert auf der Technischen Exportmesse zu Hannover im Mai 1949, vom Vorkriegsmodell 230 her, nur dass zwei prestigeträchtige Zylinder auf der Strecke geblieben sind. Technisch fußt er auf dem 170 v, dessen Triebwerk sich im glatteren Gewande des Neuen zu 52 PS aufschwingt. Eine wichtige Innovation im Bereich des Fahrwerks verrät die Hand des begnadeten Ingenieurs Rudolf Uhlenhaut: geschmiedete Doppel-Querlenker vorn mit Schraubenfedern und einem Stabilisator.

Der 170 s begründet die Tradition der noch etwas feineren Mercedes nach dem Kriege, deren besonderer Status sich bereits an dem bloßen Buchstaben »s« kristallisiert. Sein Einstandspreis, der später nach unten tendiert: 9850 Mark. Das ist schon eine ganze Menge. Aber vollends unerreichbar für Otto Normalverbraucher sind die beiden Cabriolets B (mit vier Sitzen, 12 850 Mark) und A (ein wohlgeformter Zweisitzer, 15 800 Mark), welche die Limousine zwischen 1949 und dem November 1951 in einer Verbreitung von zusammen 830 Exemplaren flankieren. Im Januar 1952 wird die ursprüngliche Version abgelöst vom vielfältig retuschierten 170 sb, erkennbar an seiner größeren Heckscheibe, nach innen verlegten Scharnieren des Kofferraumdeckels, Lenkradschaltung, hypoidverzahnter Hinterachse, Nockenwellenantrieb durch Duplex-Rollenkette, breiterer Spur und wirksamerer Heizung. Er wird bis zum August 1953 gebaut, zeitgleich mit der Diesel-Variante, die der bisherigen Exklusivität der Baureihe ein wenig zum Schaden gereicht. Noch mehr tut dies ein schnöder Griff in die Baukästen, als die Mercedes-Strategen 1953 den alternden Star durch Minderpreise gegen den Typ 180 abheben wollen: s und ds werden kurzerhand auf die Fahrgestelle von 170 v und d gesetzt, so dass die Hybriden 170 s-v und s-d entstehen. Die Mehrzahl der Klientel entscheidet sich für den Diesel, der mit 11 800 Einheiten zwischen 1953 und 1955 gegenüber den 3002 Benzinern entschieden die Oberhand hat. Kundige erkennen die beiden Mager-Modelle daran, dass die Chromleisten an den Lüftungsschlitzen der Motorhaube fehlen, ein Haltebügel den Drehgriff am Kofferraumdeckel ablöst und die Stoßstangen nicht mehr mit Hörnern bewehrt sind. Um das feine Image des 170 s ist es damit endgültig geschehen, zumal er auch mit zahlreichen extern gefertigten Sonderaufbauten profaneren Verwendungen zugeführt wird als dem Transport von Bossen, Professoren und Ministern.

Elle incarne à sa manière le charme discret de la bourgeoisie et répond au désir du citoyen prospère d'Allemagne fédérale d'afficher sa réussite. Par son style et sa conception, la 170 s présentée lors du Salon des exportations techniques de Hanovre en mai 1949 dérive de la 230 d'avant-guerre. À cette différence près que deux cylindres, signe de prestige, lui ont été enlevés. Sur le plan mécanique, elle est extrapolée de la 170 v, et le moteur sous la carrosserie du nouveau modèle aux lignes plus lisses développe maintenant 52 ch. Une innovation importante dans le domaine des trains roulants porte la signature du talentueux ingénieur Rudolf Uhlenhaut : les doubles bras transversaux forgés à l'avant avec ressorts hélicoïdaux et barre antiroulis.

La 170 s instaure la tradition des Mercedes encore un peu plus luxueuses après la guerre, dont le statut particulier est déjà mis en exergue avec la simple lettre « s ». Son prix d'achat, qui sera plus tard revu à la baisse, est de 9850 marks, montant qui représente déjà une certaine somme pour l'époque. Mais les deux cabriolets, le B (quatre places, 12 850 marks) et le A (une biplace élégante, 15 800 marks) qui viennent épauler la berline de 1949 à novembre 1951, en étant diffusés à eux deux à 830 exemplaires, sont financièrement tout à fait hors de portée de l'Allemand moyen. En janvier 1952, la version originelle est remplacée par la 170 sb retouchée dans de nombreux domaines et reconnaissable à sa lunette arrière de plus grandes dimensions, aux charnières du coffre à bagages désormais placées à l'intérieur de la malle, au levier de changement de vitesses au volant, avec l'essieu arrière à engrenages hypoïdes, l'entraînement de l'arbre à cames par chaîne à rouleau double, les voies plus larges et un chauffage plus efficace. Elle sera construite jusqu'en août 1953, parallèlement à la version diesel qui – il faut bien l'avouer – entache un peu l'exclusivité qu'avait la gamme auparavant. En cette même année, les stratèges de Mercedes, souhaitant relooker le modèle, revoient à la baisse les prix de la star vieillissante qui doit faire face à la concurrence de la nouvelle 180 : les s et ds sont en un tour de main montées sur des châssis de 170 v et d, donnant naissance aux 170 s-v et s-d.

La majorité des acheteurs opte pour la diesel qui, avec 11 800 exemplaires vendus de 1953 à 1955, bat à plates coutures la version à essence vendue seulement 3002 fois. Les initiés reconnaissent les deux modèles économiques à l'absence de joncs chromés le long des ouïes d'aération du capot moteur, à l'étrier qui remplace la poignée tournante sur le couvercle de malle et au pare-chocs désormais sans cornes. L'image raffinée de la 170 s a donc totalement disparu, surtout à partir du moment où de nombreuses carrosseries spéciales fabriquées à l'extérieur lui donnent des applications beaucoup moins « nobles » que le transport de managers de l'économie, de professeurs et de ministres.

Mercedes-Benz 170 s   1949

The 170S was available in Cabriolet A or B form from its launch year in 1949. It was time to live again, particularly when it only took a few movements to let in the summer sun.

Bereits in seinem Geburtsjahr 1949 ist der 170S als Cabriolet A oder B erhältlich. Die Lebensgeister erwachen wieder, vor allem, wenn man Sommer und Sonne mit ein paar Handgriffen Einlass verschaffen kann.

Dès sa naissance, en 1949, la 170S est disponible en Cabriolet A ou B. On commence à reprendre goût à la vie, notamment quand quelques gestes suffisent pour faire entrer à flots l'été et le soleil.

At a price of 15,800 marks (compared with 9450 marks for the sedan), the 1950 Cabriolet A would remain a pipe dream for the man in the street. You can see why. The whitewall tires were a popular luxury accessory.

Mit einem Preis von 15 800 Mark (Limousine: 9450 Mark) ist das Cabriolet A anno 1950 ein Auto, an dem der Normalverbraucher allenfalls seine Wünsche und Träume festmachen kann. Man sieht warum. Ein beliebtes Luxus-Accessoire: die Weißwandreifen.

Avec un prix de 15 800 marks (9450 marks pour la berline), le Cabriolet A de 1950 est une voiture dont l'Allemand moyen ne peut, dans le meilleur des cas, que rêver. On comprend pourquoi. Un accessoire de luxe apprécié à cette époque: les pneus à flancs blancs.

Mercedes-Benz 170 S 1949

Mercedes-Benz 170 S 1949   137

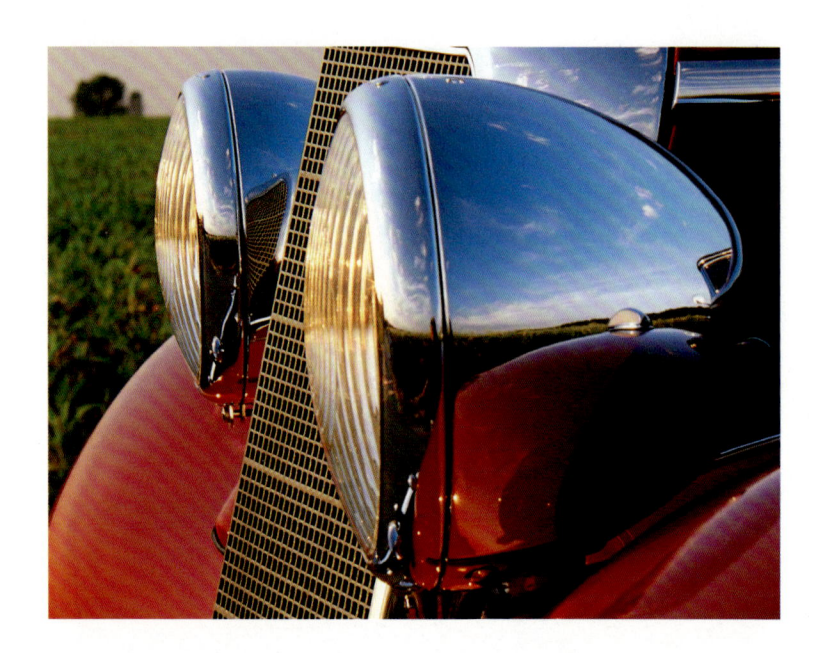

Before unibody construction brought about uniformity in car body design, the sum of a vehicle's parts sometimes, as here, contributed to the beauty of the whole. An abundance of chrome trim was regarded as a sure sign of exalted taste and ambition. To some extent it was a reflection of the owner himself. It was only later realized that the engine too could be an object of beauty.

Bevor sich mit der Pontonkarosserie Monotonie unter den Autoformen breitmacht, fügt sich manchmal wie hier die Summe der Details zum schönen Ganzen. Chromapplikationen in Hülle und Fülle gelten als Indiz für einen gehobenen Geschmack und einen gehobenen Anspruch. In ihnen bespiegelt der Besitzer gewissermaßen sich selbst. Dass auch die Maschine eine Augenweide sein kann, entdeckt man indes erst später.

Avant que la monotonie ne s'instaure dans le style automobile avec la carrosserie ponton, la somme des détails concourt parfois, comme ici, à donner un bel ensemble. Une débauche de chromes est considérée comme un signe de bon goût et de standing. Des chromes qui reflètent en quelque sorte l'ambition du propriétaire lui-même. En revanche, on ne s'apercevra que plus tard que le moteur, lui aussi, mérite d'être admiré.

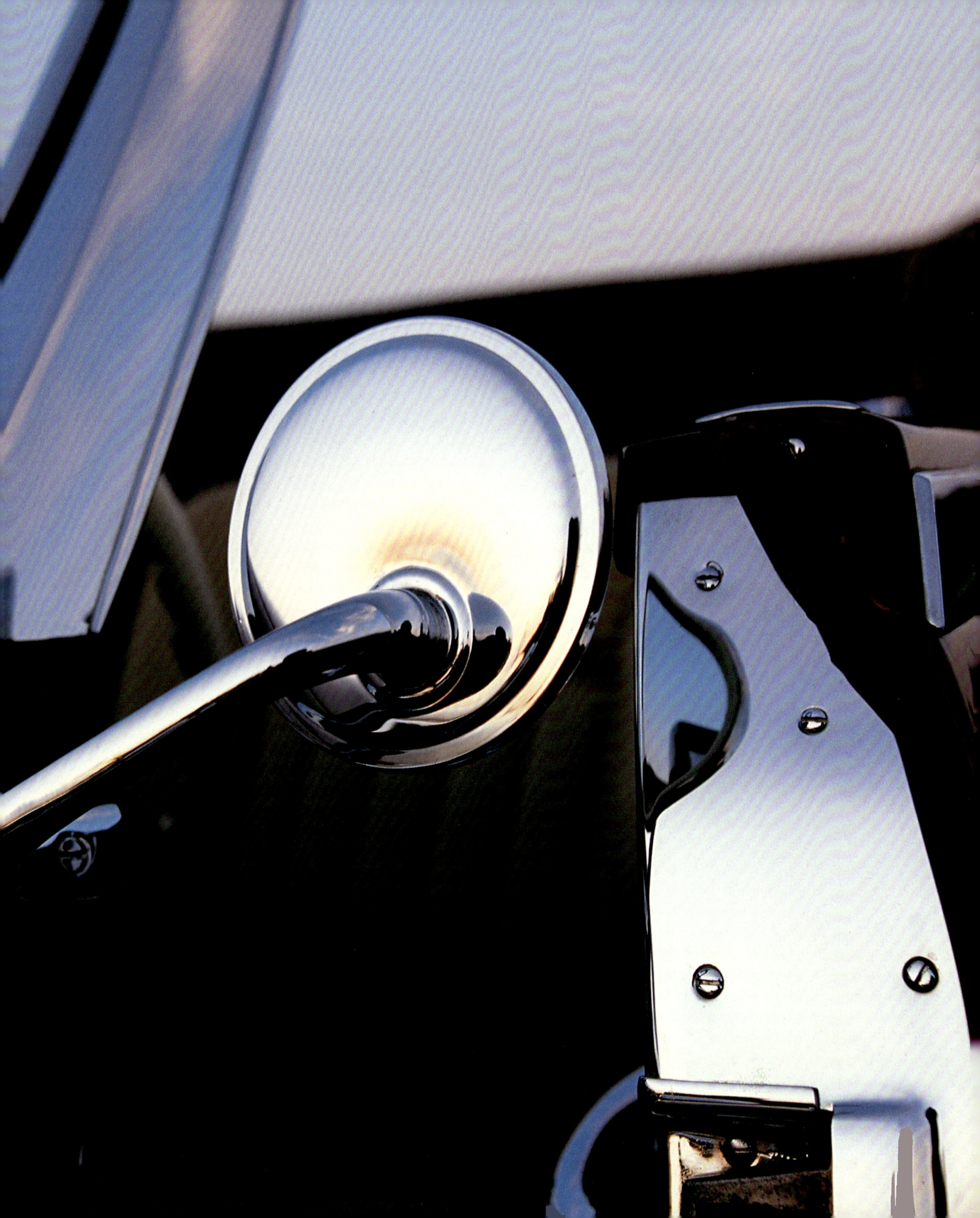

Six-cylinder engines have always been a defining feature of the company's history. The first record of such an engine at Daimler-Motoren-Gesellschaft came in 1906, and at Benz & Cie. AG in 1914. It was the six-cylinder engine in the Mercedes 220 which knocked the 170 s off its perch at the pinnacle of the company hierarchy when it was launched at the Frankfurt International Motor Show in April 1951.

It represented the latest in engine technology, and the racing input was unmistakable. It was an oversquare engine with valves operated by an overhead camshaft, with an oil cooler in the form of a cooling-water heat exchanger, thermostatic heating of the induction manifold and an "octane number compensator." Although the compression of 6.5:1 had deliberately been kept low because of the poor fuel quality, it was possible to adjust the ignition timing with a small hand lever. The 4-speed gearbox with its fashionable steering-column gearshift featured synchromesh on all gears. Its 80 bhp pushed the 220 to an impressive top speed of 87 mph, exactly the same as its contemporary, the Porsche 356 A 1100, which was regarded as extremely fast, and 11 mph quicker than the 170 s. The 220 had inherited its running gear and internal dimensions from the latter model, and the main difference between it and this older model was a stylistic one: the headlights were inset in the front of the fenders, the result of very painstaking and patient work.

Following the example of the 170 s, three body types were initially available, the sedan and the two cabriolets B and A, the respective prices of which—15,160 marks and 18,860 marks—had already secured them a niche in the elevated ranks of dream cars.

Pressure from prominent customers, as attested by a circular from the senior sales management, resulted in a coupé being added from May 1954 onwards which set its new owners back 22,000 marks if ordered with a sliding steel sunroof. With only 85 units sold, it remained a rarity, and its 85 bhp engine meant that, like the two contemporary cabriolets and the slightly later 220 a version, it was not exactly overpowered. In November 1953 the Cabriolet A was given a curved windshield which matched its gentle body curves. Despite the series' evident nobility, it could also be used for quite mundane tasks, as evidenced by the 41 open-top touring cars for the police manufactured between August 1952 and May 1953. These were not unlike the Cabriolet B, though they had four doors and a top without storm stays. No wonder they were much in demand for official business.

Sechszylinder prägen die Historie des Hauses seit jeher. Für 1906 notiert der Chronist ein erstes Vorkommen bei der Daimler-Motoren-Gesellschaft, für 1914 bei der Benz & Cie. AG. Der Sechszylinder im Mercedes 220 ist es, der auf der ersten Internationalen Automobilausstellung in Frankfurt im April 1951 den 170 s vom Sockel seiner Spitzenstellung in der Firmen-Hierarchie kippt.

Es ist ein modernes Triebwerk, und unverkennbar ist die Rückkoppelung vom Rennsport: ein Kurzhuber, dessen Ventile von einer obenliegenden Nockenwelle zur Arbeit angehalten werden, mit einem Ölkühler in Gestalt eines Kühlwasser-Wärmeaustauschers, thermostatischer Beheizung des Ansaugrohrs sowie einem »Oktanzahlkompensator«: Obwohl die Verdichtung mit 6,5:1 bewusst niedrig gehalten wurde wegen der schlechten Treibstoffqualität, lässt sich der Zündzeitpunkt noch einmal mit einem kleinen Handknebel verstellen. Das Vierganggetriebe mit der modischen Lenkradschaltung ist voll synchronisiert. Seine 80 PS befähigen den 220 zu stattlichen 140 Stundenkilometern, genausoviel wie der als ausgesprochen flink geltende Zeitgenosse Porsche 356 A 1100 und 18 Stundenkilometer schneller als der 170 s. Von diesem hat der 220 Fahrwerk und Innenmaße übernommen und hebt sich im wesentlichen durch einen stilistischen Gag von dem älteren Modell ab: Die Scheinwerfer sind als Intarsien in die Spitzen der Kotflügel eingelassen, Ergebnis geduldiger Tüftelarbeit.

Nach dem Muster des 170 s werden zunächst drei Karosserievarianten angeboten: die Limousine und die beiden Cabriolets B und A, die durch ihren Preis von 15 160 Mark beziehungsweise 18 860 Mark bereits in die entlegene Sphäre der Traumwagen entrückt werden.

Auf Drängen prominenter Kunden, wie ein Rundschreiben der Verkaufsleitung ausweist, sattelt man ab Mai 1954 mit einem Coupé drauf, dessen Anschaffung mit 22 000 Mark zu Buche schlägt, wenn man ein Stahlschiebedach ordert. Es bleibt in 85 Exemplaren eine Rarität, mit 85 PS motorisch mild aufgerüstet wie auch die beiden Cabriolets um die gleiche Zeit und wenig später die Version 220 a. Im November 1953 erhält das Cabriolet A eine gewölbte Frontscheibe, die mit seiner sanften Rundlichkeit harmoniert. Trotz der evidenten Noblesse der Baureihe kann sie auch durchaus profanen Alltagstätigkeiten zugeführt werden wie jene 41 offenen Tourenwagen für die Polizei, die zwischen dem August 1952 und dem Mai 1953 produziert werden, nicht unähnlich dem Cabriolet B, aber mit vier Türen und einem Verdeck ohne Sturmstangen. Kein Wunder, dass sie als Dienstwagen begehrt sind.

Les six-cylindres ont de tout temps ponctué la généalogie de la maison. Le chroniqueur relate leur première apparition à la Daimler-Motoren-Gesellschaft en 1906 et en 1914 pour la Benz & Cie. AG. C'est le six-cylindres de la Mercedes 220 qui, au premier Salon international de l'Automobile organisé à Francfort en avril 1951, fait perdre à la 170 s son statut de modèle haut de gamme dans la hiérarchie de la firme.

C'est un moteur moderne où l'on retrouve incontestablement les enseignements tirés de la compétition : un moteur à course courte dont les soupapes sont actionnées par un arbre à cames en tête, avec un radiateur d'huile sous la forme d'un échangeur thermique pour l'eau de refroidissement, un chauffage à thermostat du collecteur d'aspiration ainsi qu'un « compensateur d'octane » : bien qu'avec 6,5:1 le taux de compression ait été volontairement maintenu à un bas niveau à cause de la mauvaise qualité des carburants, il est encore possible de régler l'allumage à l'aide d'un petit levier manuel. La boîte à quatre vitesses avec la commande au volant alors à la mode est complètement synchronisée. Ses 80 ch permettent à la 220 d'atteindre la vitesse respectable de 140 km/h, soit autant que la Porsche 356 A 1100, considérée comme l'une de ses contemporaines particulièrement rapides, et 18 km/h de plus que la 170 s. De celle-ci, la 220 a d'ailleurs repris les trains roulants et les cotes intérieures, et elle se distingue du modèle le plus ancien essentiellement par un gag esthétique : les phares sont intégrés comme une marqueterie dans la pointe des ailes, résultat d'un patient travail de réflexion.

À l'instar de la 170 s, Mercedes propose tout d'abord trois variantes de carrosserie : la berline et les deux cabriolets B et A, que les prix respectifs de 15 160 et 18 860 marks situent déjà dans les sphères inaccessibles des voitures de rêve.

À la demande de clients célèbres, comme l'indique une circulaire émise par la direction des ventes, on y ajoute en mai 1954 un coupé dont le prix d'achat s'élève à 22 000 marks si l'on commande en plus un toit ouvrant en acier. Avec 85 exemplaires, il restera rarissime et, avec 85 ch, sa motorisation sera modeste, de même que celle des deux cabriolets de la même époque et, un peu plus tard, de la version 220 a. En novembre 1953, le cabriolet A reçoit un pare-brise galbé en parfaite harmonie avec ses lignes tout en rondeurs. Malgré l'évidente noblesse de la gamme, elle aussi peut parfaitement être consacrée à des activités quotidiennes banales comme le prouvent les 41 voitures de tourisme décapotables de la police produites d'août 1952 à mai 1953, des voitures semblables au cabriolet B, mais à quatre portes et une capote sans tiges de stabilisation. On envie les agents de la force publique.

Mercedes-Benz 220   1951

The 220 catered to the increased demand in West Germany for status symbols. Its powerful appearance and, in particular, the six-cylinder engine under the hood contributed to this effect.

Der 220 ist auf den vermehrten Bedarf der Bundesbürger nach Statussymbolik zugeschnitten. Dazu trägt sein stattliches Erscheinungsbild bei, vor allem aber der Sechszylinder unter der Haube.

La 220 va au-devant de l'Allemand qui veut donner une preuve de sa réussite. Sa stature déjà imposante y contribue encore plus quand un six-cylindres se trouve sous le capot.

Although the exterior design of the car was still largely classical, certain features were already reflecting the spirit of a new age, such as the column-mounted gearshift and the straight-six engine with its overhead camshaft.

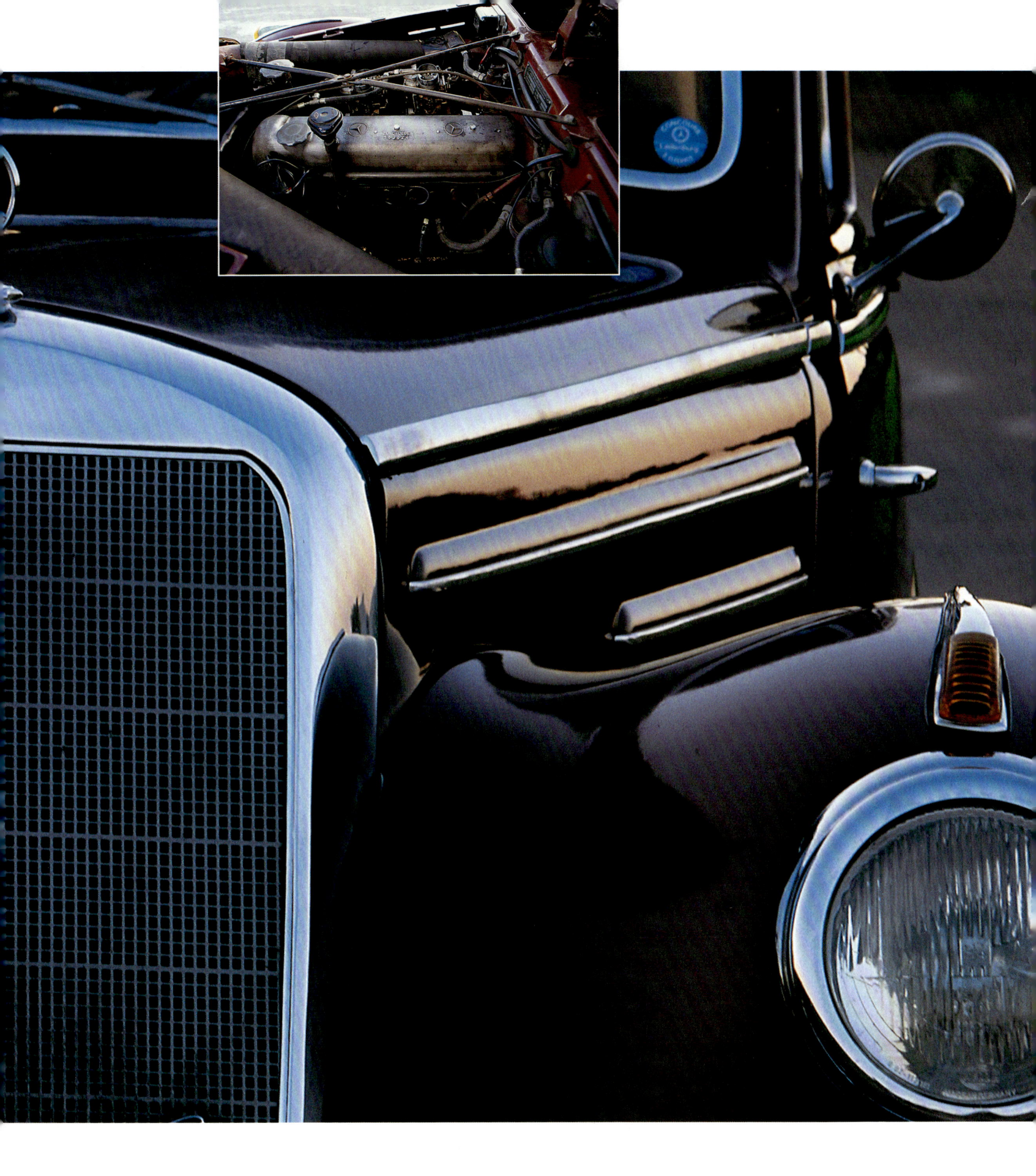

Noch ist das Exterieur überwiegend klassisch, schon atmen bestimmte Requisiten den Geist der neuen Zeit, die Lenkradschaltung, der Reihensechszylinder mit einer obenliegenden Nockenwelle.

Son extérieur est, encore, essentiellement classique, mais certains détails reflètent déjà l'esprit d'une époque nouvelle, par exemple l'existence d'un levier de vitesses au sol ou le six-cylindres en ligne à arbre à cames en tête.

It was either known as the "Adenauer Mercedes" after its most prominent customer, the German chancellor Konrad Adenauer, or simply as the "Three Hundred," and it represented much more than just a car. It was a metaphorical expression of an era, a symbol of the Federal Republic and its dignitaries. Like the 220, the 300 was also launched at the Frankfurt Motor Show in 1951, and its body was also mounted on a cruciform oval-tubed chassis. Like the 220 it had a twin-pivot swing axle with double coil springs at the rear, but also additional torsion bars for each wheel which could be actuated by a dashboard-mounted servo if heavy loads were being carried. Its shape already gave hints of future unit-construction designs. Its powerplant, 2996 cc and 115 bhp in original form, was an inline six-cylinder with an overhead camshaft. Apart from this, however, it had little in common with that of the 220 since its engine was rather longer in stroke and fed by two downdraft carburetors.

In its 11-year production life, the "Three Hundred," which was always very solidly equipped, underwent a comprehensive makeover. Three further generations emerged. In the 300 b of March 1954 the power was increased to 125 bhp, and stronger brakes took the speedy heavyweight in hand. The 300 c (from September 1955 onwards) had a single-pivot swing axle and a larger rear screen, and a Borg-Warner automatic gearbox was also available as an optional extra. From July 1956 there was a long version, made in response to a suggestion from Chancellor Adenauer, with a longer wheelbase (10 ft 4 in instead of 10 ft) and a longer rear section (length overall 16 ft 11 in instead of 16 ft 7 in), as a result of which 5½ in more legroom was created in the back. The 300 d of August 1957 with its substantially redesigned bodywork looked more angular when mounted on the long running gear of the Adenauer version, while a Bosch injection system helped the engine to develop 160 bhp.

A Cabriolet D, which was offered alongside the sedan from the word go, disappeared from the range for a time, though it became available again from July 1958 onwards on special request—for a handsome 35,500 marks compared with the 27,000 marks of the basic 300 model. Three special stretched models dating from 1960 (wheelbase 11 ft 10 in, overall length 18 ft 6 in) revelled in their air of cultivated and lovingly celebrated overstatement. One was purchased by Pope John XXIII as his official car, while the other two could be hired by the day from Mercedes together with a chauffeur. Meanwhile collective prosperity had obviously spread pretty far and wide. This was clear from the fact that 11,430 original owners were not put off such a purchase and wanted to call a Mercedes 300 their own.

Sie nennen ihn den »Adenauer-Mercedes« nach seinem prominentesten Kunden oder schlicht den »Dreihunderter«, und er ist viel mehr als nur ein Auto: sinnbildliche Ausprägung einer Ära, Symbol auch der Bonner Republik und ihrer Würdenträger. Wie der 220 debütiert der 300 auf der Frankfurter Ausstellung 1951, und wie bei jenem ruht sein Aufbau auf einem x-förmigen Ovalrohrrahmen. Analog zum 220 hat er hinten eine Zweigelenk-Pendelachse mit doppelten Schraubenfedern, aber auch zusätzliche Drehstäbe für jedes Rad, vom Armaturenbrett elektrisch aktivierbar für höhere Zuladungen. Seine Formen zeigen bereits Anklänge an künftige Pontonkarosserien. Sein Triebwerk mit 2996 cm³ und ursprünglich 115 PS ist ein Reihen-Sechszylinder mit einer obenliegenden Nockenwelle, im übrigen aber dem des 220 wenig verwandt, da eher langhubig konzipiert und von zwei Fallstromvergasern gespeist.

In den elf Jahren seiner Fertigung wird dem »Dreihunderter«, von Natur aus mit strotzender Robustheit ausgestattet, eine umfassende Modellpflege zuteil. Sie manifestiert sich in drei weiteren Generationen. Im 300 b vom März 1954 wird die Leistung auf 125 PS angehoben, und größere Bremsen nehmen das flinke Schwergewicht an die Kandare. Der 300 c (ab September 1955) hat eine Eingelenk-Pendelachse sowie eine größere Heckscheibe und wird wahlweise mit einer Automatik von Borg-Warner angeboten. Vom Juli 1956 an gibt es, einem Denkanstoß von Bundeskanzler Adenauer folgend, eine lange Variante mit mehr Radstand (3150 statt 3050 mm) und mehr Auto hinten (5165 statt 5065 mm), wodurch im Fond 140 mm Beinfreiheit gewonnen werden. Der 300 d vom August 1957 kommt mit kräftig retuschierter Karosserie kantiger daher auf dem langen Fahrwerk der Adenauer-Version, während eine Bosch-Einspritzung der Maschine zu 160 Pferdestärken verhilft.

Ein Cabriolet D, der Limousine von Anbeginn an zur Seite gestellt, verschwindet eine Zeitlang aus dem Angebot, ist jedoch ab Juli 1958 auf besonderen Wunsch wieder erhältlich – für stramme 35500 Mark gegenüber den 27000 Mark des Basis-300. Drei extra lange Sonderausführungen von 1960 (Radstand 3600 mm, Gesamtlänge 5640 mm) umfächelt ein Hauch gepflegten und genüsslich zelebrierten Overstatements: Eine bezieht Papst Johannes XXIII. als Dienstfahrzeug, die beiden anderen können beim Werk tageweise mit Chauffeur angemietet werden. Der kollektive Wohlstand ist indessen schon wieder recht weit gediehen. Das kann man daran erkennen, dass immerhin 11430 Erstbesitzer die Anschaffung nicht scheuen und einen Mercedes 300 ihr eigen nennen wollen.

Ils l'appellent la « Mercedes Adenauer » d'après son client le plus célèbre ou, simplement, la « Trois Cents », et elle est beaucoup plus qu'une simple voiture: c'est l'incarnation de toute une époque, le symbole, aussi, de la république de Bonn et de ses dignitaires. À l'instar de la 220, la 300 fait ses débuts au Salon de l'automobile de Francfort en 1951 et, comme celle-ci, sa carrosserie repose sur un châssis en tubes ovales en forme de x. Toujours à l'instar de la 220, elle a, à l'arrière, un essieu brisé à double articulation avec doubles ressorts hélicoïdaux, mais aussi des barres de torsion supplémentaires pour chaque roue, que l'on peut actionner électriquement depuis le tableau de bord en cas de charges élevées. Ses formes annoncent d'ores et déjà celles des futures carrosseries ponton. Son moteur de 2996 cm³ développant initialement 115 ch est un six-cylindres en ligne avec arbre à cames en tête, mais, pour le reste, il présente peu de similitudes avec celui de la 220, qui est plutôt à course longue et alimentée par deux carburateurs inversés.

Produite pendant onze ans, la « Trois Cents », dotée par nature d'une forte constitution, a bénéficié de remises au goût du jour permanentes. Il y en a ainsi eu trois autres générations. La 300 b de mars 1954 voit sa puissance partée à 125 ch et reçoit de plus gros freins qui ralentissent mieux cette voiture rapide, mais lourde. La 300 c (à partir de septembre 1955) a un essieu brisé à une articulation ainsi qu'une lunette arrière de plus grandes dimensions et est proposée avec une boîte automatique Borg-Warner. À partir de juillet 1956, sur une idée du chancelier fédéral Adenauer, il en est lancé une variante à empattement long (de 3150 au lieu de 3050 mm) et également plus longue à l'arrière (5165 au lieu de 5065 mm), ce qui permet de gagner 140 mm à l'arrière pour les jambes. La 300 d d'août 1957 possède une carrosserie plus anguleuse et sérieusement redessinée sur le châssis long de la version Adenauer, dont le moteur développe maintenant 160 ch grâce à une injection Bosch.

Le cabriolet D, qui a toujours été le compagnon de route de la berline, disparaît un certain temps du catalogue, mais est de nouveau disponible à partir de juillet 1958 sur demande expresse – pour le prix faramineux de 35500 marks alors que la 300 de base en coûte 27000. Trois versions spéciales à empattement extrêmement long sont produites en 1960 (empattement 3600 mm, longueur hors tout 5640 mm), d'apparence discrète et soignée: l'une est destinée au pape Jean XXIII comme voiture de service, les deux autres pouvant être louées à la journée avec chauffeur auprès de l'usine. Il est vrai que la période est à la prospérité collective. Ce dont témoigne le fait que pas moins de 11430 acheteurs n'ont pas hésité à débourser la somme exigée pour devenir propriétaire d'une Mercedes 300.

Mercedes-Benz *Adenauer*   1951

A familiar view for the political and financial elite of West Germany's early years: a Mercedes 300d from 1959 before the privileged classes took to the back seat and left the rest to the chauffeur.

Ein Anblick, welcher der Polit- und Geldaristokratie der frühen Bonner Republik vertraut ist: Ein Mercedes 300d von 1959, bevor man den Fond bezieht und sein bedeutendes Schicksal seinem Chauffeur anvertraut.

Une vue familière à l'élite politique et financière de l'ancienne république de Bonn : une Mercedes 300d de 1959 avant que l'on ne prenne place sur la banquette arrière et ne confie son destin à son chauffeur.

"If you've got something, you are something," was a well-known slogan of a bank group at the time, and those who owned this car really were something. The angular silhouette of the 300d from 1957 onwards was similar to contemporary unibody types. The windows could be lowered almost completely.

»Hast du was, so bist du was«, besagte ein Slogan der Sparkassen, und wer ihn hatte, der war in der Tat etwas. Die kantige Silhouette des 300d ab 1957 nähert sich bereits zeitgenössischen Pontonformen an. Die Fenster lassen sich fast durchgehend versenken.

« Si tu as quelque chose, tu es quelqu'un ! » proclamait un slogan des caisses d'épargne à l'époque. Avoir ce modèle faisait de vous quelqu'un. La silhouette anguleuse de la 300d à partir de 1957 se rapproche déjà des carrosseries ponton contemporaines. Les fenêtres se baissent presque complètement.

The generously-appointed cockpit of the 300d with the chromed column-mounted gearshift and the ubiquitous Becker Mexico radio.

Das reich besiedelte Cockpit des 300d mit dem Chromhebel für die Lenkradschaltung und dem allgegenwärtigen Radio Becker Mexico.

Le tableau de bord richement décoré de la 300d, avec le levier de vitesses chromé au volant et l'omniprésent autoradio Becker Mexico.

This was the apotheosis of classic automotive engineering, a cultural event that harmoniously married swelling shapes with noble simplicity. The 300 s did not gradually develop this aura; it was there right from the very beginning when the attractive trinity of coupé, cabriolet, and roadster was launched into the world of the beautiful and rich at the Paris Salon in October 1951 to crown the Mercedes range.

Reviewers went into immediate raptures; they spoke of the "car of the world's elite" and reckoned that the 300 s now represented "the standard for what could be achieved today in car making," that is, in a "traditional and, in this case, particularly noble form… without recourse to aerodynamics." There was scarcely any difference between the cabriolet and the roadster—the latter had a lighter top which could be completely retracted without storm stays, while the cabrio had a more opulent design which gave the impression of lavish coziness. The 300 formed the basis of the design, but its wheelbase was reduced by 6 in to 9 ft 6 in. The three-liter engine's compression was increased from 6.4:1 to 7.8:1, and three Solex downdraft carburetors did their bit, with the result that its power output rose to 150 bhp. At 109 mph, the 300 s was one of the fastest cars in Germany.

Since nothing and no-one is perfect, however, even the 300 s had to put up with its creators making further changes. The resulting 300 sc, which was shown together with the updated 300 c at the 1955 Frankfurt International Motor Show (IAA), had a single-pivot swing axle with a low center of gravity. With its Bosch direct injection system and a compression ratio which had been increased to 8.55:1, the six-cylinder engine developed 175 bhp, enough for a speed of 112 mph. Outwardly a second-generation 300 s can be recognized by its perforated chrome-plated disk wheels, vent windows, larger turn signals front and rear, two cooling slits sporting horizontal chrome-plated strips above the front fender, and the "Einspritzmotor" (injection engine) badge on the trunk lid. The fact that the mixture was no longer provided by carburetors did not in any way increase the cars's cruising range which still did not exceed 12–15 mpg.

The appearance of the 300 SL Roadster in 1957 brought interest in the antique beau which had sold 760 units to a sudden end. Whereas the 300 s tended to look to the past, the 300 SL was a taste of the future. To this must be added the fact that at 32,500 marks the newer model was 4000 marks cheaper than the old one. And even in the naturally limited circle of those who could afford such a price, this fact caught the attention.

Er ist die Apotheose klassischen Automobilbaus, ein Kulturereignis, das schwellende Formen in harmonischer Weise mit nobler Schlichtheit vermählt. Dieser Nimbus wächst dem 300 s nicht erst allmählich zu, sondern er ist sofort vorhanden, als er zur Krönung des Mercedes-Programms in der attraktiven Dreieinigkeit Coupé, Cabriolet und Roadster auf dem Pariser Salon im Oktober 1951 in die Welt der Schönen und der Reichen eingeführt wird.

Und so geraten seine Rezensenten umgehend ins Schwärmen, sprechen vom »Wagen der Weltelite« und davon, dass der 300 s nun »der Maßstab für das heute im Automobilbau Erreichbare« sei und zwar in einer »traditionellen und in diesem Fall besonders edlen Form… ohne Zuflucht zur Aerodynamik«. Cabriolet und Roadster unterscheiden sich kaum – letzterer hat ein leichteres und gänzlich versenkbares Verdeck ohne Sturmstangen, wo das Cabrio mit einer aufwändigeren Konstruktion den Eindruck üppiger Wohnlichkeit vermittelt. Basis ist der Typ 300, dessen Radstand um 150 mm auf 2900 mm zurückgenommen wird. Die Verdichtung des Dreiliter-Triebwerks wird von 6,4:1 auf 7,8:1 erhöht, und drei Solex-Fallstromvergaser tun das Ihrige, so dass seine Leistung auf 150 PS anwächst. Mit 176 Stundenkilometern Spitzengeschwindigkeit zählt der 300 s zu den Schnellsten im Lande.

Da aber nichts und niemand perfekt ist, muss selbst er sich gefallen lassen, dass seine Schöpfer noch einmal Hand an ihn legen: Der 300 sc, der zusammen mit dem überarbeiteten 300 c auf der Frankfurter IAA 1955 gezeigt wird, hat eine Eingelenk-Pendelachse mit tief liegendem Schwerpunkt erhalten, und mit einer Direkteinspritzung von Bosch sowie einer auf 8,55:1 gesteigerten Verdichtung gibt der Sechszylinder 175 PS ab, gut für Tempo 180. Nach außen hin verraten den 300 s der zweiten Generation verchromte Lochscheibenräder, Ausstellfensterchen, größere Blinkleuchten vorn und hinten, zwei mit Chromleisten verblendete waagerechte Kühlschlitze oberhalb der vorderen Kotflügel sowie der Schriftzug »Einspritzmotor« am Kofferraumdeckel. Dass die Gemischaufbereitung nicht länger von Vergasern besorgt wird, wirkt sich keineswegs mildernd auf den Durst des Motors aus, der allemal mit 16 bis 20 Litern verpflegt werden möchte.

Mit dem Erscheinen des 300 SL Roadsters 1957 lässt das Interesse an dem antikischen Beau, der es auf eine Verbreitung von 760 Exemplaren bringt, jäh nach: Die Vision 300 s ist doch eher nach hinten gewandt, die Vision 300 SL mehr nach vorn. Überdies kostet das neuere Modell mit 32 500 Mark 4000 Mark weniger als das alte. Und darauf achtet man selbst im naturgemäß begrenzten Kreis derer, die sich das alles leisten können.

C'est l'apothéose de la construction automobile classique, un événement culturel qui allie, dans la plus grande harmonie, des formes exubérantes et une sobriété pleine de noblesse. C'est une aura que la 300 s n'acquiert pas progressivement, mais qui la caractérise immédiatement lorsqu'elle est présentée, au Salon de Paris d'octobre 1951, dans le monde des riches et des célébrités pour couronner le programme Mercedes sous la forme d'une attrayante trinité : coupé, cabriolet et roadster.

Ainsi les critiques se répandent-elles immédiatement en éloges, parlant de «voiture de l'élite mondiale» et de ce que la 300 s était désormais «le critère de ce qui est aujourd'hui réalisable en construction automobile», à savoir dans une «forme traditionnelle et, dans le cas présent, particulièrement noble… sans fioritures aérodynamiques». Cabriolet et roadster sont presque identiques – ce dernier a une capote plus légère et totalement escamotable sans barreaux de rigidification alors que le cabriolet, au mécanisme plus sophistiqué, dégage une impression chaleureuse. Ils ont pour base la 300 dont l'empattement a été raccourci de 150 mm, à 2900 mm. Le taux de compression du moteur de trois litres est parté de 6,4:1 à 7,8:1 et trois carburateurs inversés Solex permettent à sa puissance d'offrir 150 ch. Avec une vitesse de pointe de 176 km/h, la 300 s est l'une des plus rapides voitures de son temps.

Mais comme rien ni personne n'est parfait, elle-même doit tolérer que ses créateurs lui fassent subir une cure de rajeunissement : la 300 sc, qui est dévoilée au Salon international de l'automobile de Francfort (IAA) de 1955 simultanément avec la 300 c retravaillée, possède un essieu brisé à une articulation avec centre de gravité abaissé et, grâce à une injection directe Bosch ainsi qu'à un taux de compression porté à 8,55:1, le six-cylindres délivre 175 ch qui lui permettent d'atteindre aisément 180 km/h. Extérieurement, la 300 s deuxième génération se distingue à ses roues chromées à jantes perforées, aux petits déflecteurs, aux plus grands clignotants à l'avant et à l'arrière, aux deux fentes de refroidissement horizontales décorées d'un jonc chromé au-dessus des ailes avant ainsi qu'à l'inscription «Einspritzmotor» (moteur d'injection) sur le couvercle de malle. Si la préparation du mélange n'est désormais plus assurée par des carburateurs, cela n'a en revanche absolument aucun effet bénéfique sur la soif du moteur, qui engloutit toujours ses 16 à 20 litres aux 100 km.

Avec l'apparition du roadster 300 SL, en 1957, l'intérêt manifesté pour cette beauté antique diffusée à 760 exemplaires s'évanouit instantanément : la vision 300 s est, il faut l'avouer, plutôt orientée vers le passé alors que la vision 300 SL est résolument tournée vers l'avenir. De plus, le nouveau modèle, à 32 500 marks, coûte 4000 marks de moins que l'ancien. Et c'est une somme non négligeable, même dans le gotha naturellement très élitaire de ceux qui peuvent se permettre un tel achat.

Mercedes-Benz 300 s 1951

Before horizontal lines and right angles finally seized power, traditional design philosophy bore its most exquisite fruit in the Mercedes 300S series. At the same time, however, it must be admitted that only very few people were fortunate enough to own such a car.

Vor der endgültigen Machtergreifung der Horizontale und des rechten Winkels treibt eine traditionell ausgerichtete Philosophie der Formen ihre schönste Blüte in der Mercedes-Baureihe 300S. Kein Zweifel aber auch, dass solche Automobile einigen wenigen Glücklichen vorbehalten bleiben.

Avant la prise du pouvoir définitive par l'horizontale et l'angle droit, une philosophie des formes éprise de traditions connaît son apogée avec la série Mercedes 300S. Le doute n'est pas permis: de telles automobiles seront restées l'apanage d'une élite.

Although the coupé was developed from the 300 model, which was the German government's official car of choice, it nonetheless evolved its own balanced proportions in which tastefully-rounded contours dominated.

Zwar wurde das Coupé aus der Staatslimousine 300 sublimiert, findet aber dennoch zu eigenständigen und ausgewogenen Proportionen, in denen die kunstvolle Rundung dominiert.

Bien qu'extrapolé de la limousine d'apparat 300, le coupé possède cependant des lignes personnelles et des proportions équilibrées dans lesquelles prédomine le galbe avec toute son élégance.

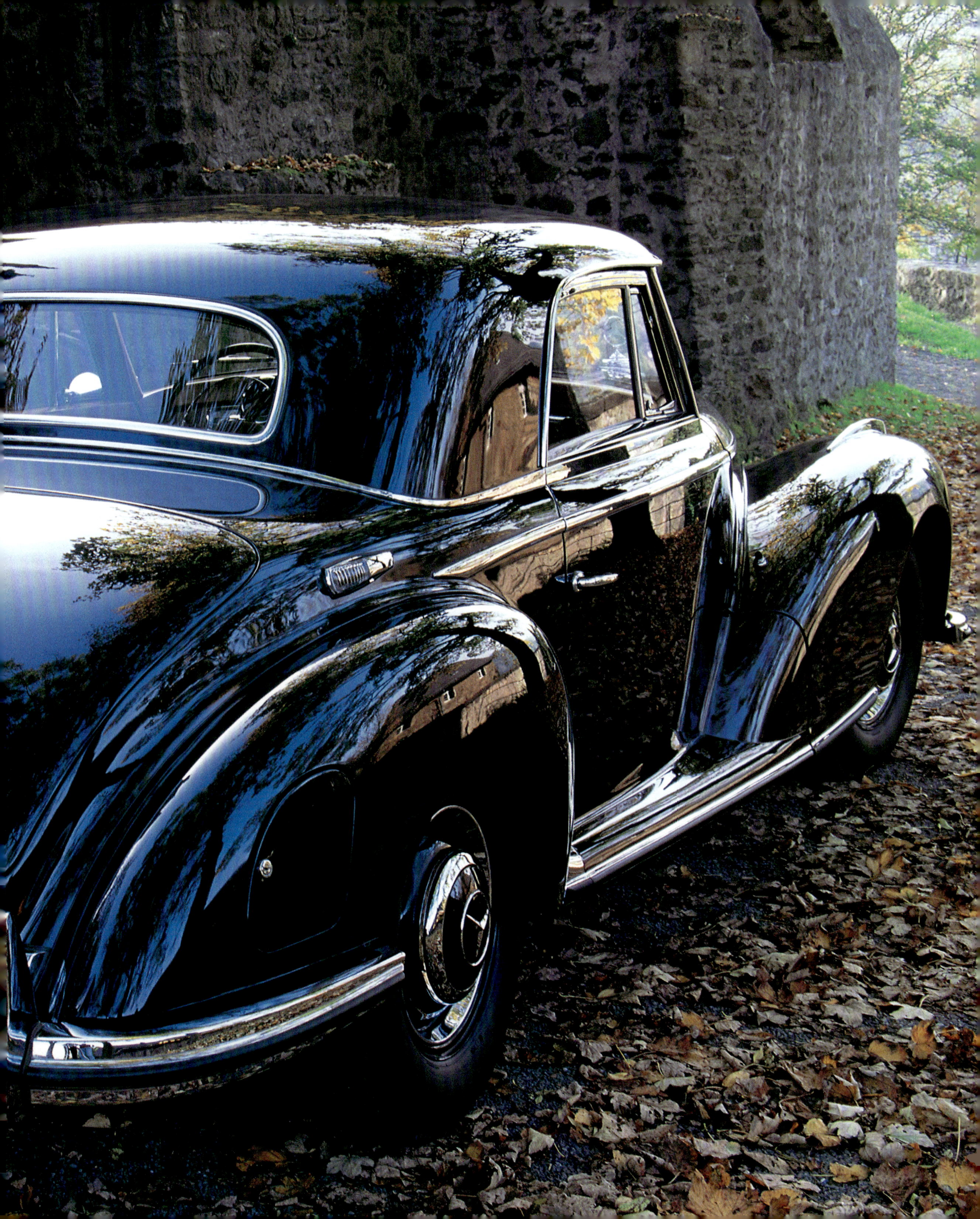

Once its lightweight fold-down top had disappeared into its recess, the 300S Roadster was an open declaration of war on all other cars on the road.

Sowie sein leichtes Klappverdeck in der Versenkung verschwunden ist, wird der 300S Roadster zur offenen Kriegserklärung an den Rest der Auto-Welt.

Une fois sa légère capote rangée dans son compartiment, la 300S Roadster est une déclaration de guerre au reste du monde automobile.

Mercedes-Benz 300 S   1951

Progress sometimes took its time at Daimler-Benz. Thus it was that the watershed between tradition and modernity did not really reveal itself in Untertürkheim until 1953. The unibody design, based on the American three-box model of engine, passenger, and luggage compartments, had already been imported into Germany in 1949 by Borgward with the Hansa 1500. Opel and Ford, as subsidiaries of US corporations, followed suit. Despite the esthetic sparseness of this concept, its benefits were obvious. While occupying the same floor area, it was much more economic than conventional bodies which squandered valuable space with generous fenders and wide running boards. Compared with the 170 s, the 180 had 20 per cent more cabin space and 75 per cent more luggage space. Its body, an absolute stronghold of the right angle, was still not a true monocoque; it provided support, combined with a sturdy floorpan chassis made of steel box sections with sheet metal welded between them, which was comparatively light and stiff. This helped the occupants in the event of an accident too as it had soft crumple zones positioned in front of and behind the rigid passenger cage.

An unusual feature of the 180, which was later to become standard, was that the engine, gearbox, steering gear, and the wishbones pressed from sheet metal were mounted at the front on a sub-frame that was connected to the rest of the running gear via three rubber bearings. Drivers of 180 s were greeted by a welcome increase in visibility on all sides, and even the traditional imposingly gothic radiator grille was perfectly in keeping with the new design configuration. Other than this, the car was rather conventional. It was not until September 1955 that the usual twin-pivot swing axle with additional longitudinal swing arms was replaced by a counterpart in which the two halves of the axle simply moved about a common low pivot. Design-instigated changes in camber were kept to a manageable minimum in this way.

The 52 bhp side-valve engine from the 170 s was a real workhorse, reliable and rugged, even if it lacked any touches of brilliance. In August 1957 it gave way to the 1.9-liter unit from its sister model, the 190, with an overhead camshaft and a solid 68 bhp. As far as the popular diesel engines were concerned, which cost an extra 500 to 1000 marks, the designers also opted for an in-house, off-the-shelf solution: the long-stroke engine from the 170 D was upgraded in 1955 to produce 43 bhp. A version with an overhead camshaft followed, and from 1962 onwards the 180 D used the engine from the 190 D which had been enlarged to a capacity of two liters. Mercedes diesel models still suffered from a high level of noise.

Their life expectancy, however, had taken on almost biblical proportions, and it was not unusual to find taxis, for example, with half a million kilometers (300,000 miles) on the clock.

Der Fortschritt nimmt sich bei Daimler-Benz manchmal Zeit. So wölbt sich die Wasserscheide zwischen Tradition und Moderne in Untertürkheim eigentlich erst 1953. Die Pontonkarosserie, fußend auf der amerikanischen Three-Box-Bauweise Motorraum, Passagiertrakt und Gepäckabteil, wird von Borgward mit dem Hansa 1500 bereits 1949 in Deutschland eingeführt. Opel und Ford als Töchter von US-Konzernen ziehen nach. Trotz der ästhetischen Kargheit dieses Konzepts liegen seine Vorzüge auf der Hand. Bei gleicher Grundfläche ist seine Ökonomie viel besser als die herkömmlicher Aufbauten, die mit schwellenden Kotflügeln und ellbogenbreiten Trittbrettern kostbaren Platz liberal verschwenden: Gegenüber dem 170 s gewinnt der 180 um die 20 Prozent Wohnraum und 75 Prozent Gepäckvolumen. Noch ist seine Karosserie, eine unumschränkte Domäne des rechten Winkels, nicht selbsttragend: Sie trägt mit, verquickt mit einer fahrfähigen Rahmen-Bodengruppe aus stählernen Kastenträgern und dazwischen geschweißten Blechen, vergleichsweise leicht und steif. Bei einem Unfall kommt den Insassen auch zugute, dass sich an die rigide Passagierzelle vorn und hinten weiche Knautschzonen anlagern.

Eine Eigentümlichkeit des 180, aber zukünftiger Standard: dass Motor, Getriebe, Lenkung sowie die aus Blech gepressten Querlenker vorn auf einem »Fahrschemel« zusammengefasst sind, der über drei Gummilager mit dem Rest des Fahrwerks verbunden ist. Den 180-Lenker erwartet ein erfreulicher Zuwachs an Überblick nach allen Seiten, und selbst der traditionelle gotisch aufragende Kühlergrill verträgt sich durchaus mit der neuen Form. Im Übrigen geht es im zeitgemäßen Gewande eher konventionell zu. Die übliche Zweigelenk-Pendelachse mit zusätzlichen Längslenkern wird erst im September 1955 durch ein Pendant abgelöst, bei dem sich die Achshälften nur noch um einen gemeinsamen tief gelegten Drehpunkt bewegen. So lassen sich die konstruktionsbedingten Sturzänderungen auf ein erträgliches Maß reduzieren.

Ein wahres Urgestein ist das seitengesteuerte Triebwerk aus dem 170 s mit seinen 52 PS, brav und zählebig, wenn auch ohne Brillanz. Im August 1957 weicht es dem 1,9-Liter-Aggregat aus dem Schwestermodell 190, mit einer oben liegenden Nockenwelle und 68 soliden PS. Was die volkstümlichen, aber stets mit einem Aufpreis von 500 bis 1000 Mark zu honorierenden Diesel-Aggregate anbelangt, bedient man sich ebenfalls aus den Regalen des Hauses: Der Langhuber aus dem 170 D wird 1955 auf 43 PS Leistung nachgerüstet. Eine Version mit einer oben liegenden Nockenwelle folgt, und ab 1962 gibt es den 180 D mit dem auf zwei Liter Hubraum vergrößerten Motor des 190 D. Noch ist das Geräuschniveau der Benz-Selbstzünder hoch.

Geradezu biblisch mutet dafür ihre Lebenserwartung an: Im Taxigewerbe zum Beispiel sind Laufleistungen von einer halben Million Kilometern nicht unüblich.

Chez Daimler-Benz, le progrès prend parfois beaucoup de temps. C'est ainsi que la ligne de partage entre la tradition et le modernisme n'est tracée définitivement, à Untertürkheim, qu'en 1953. La carrosserie ponton, qui reprend l'architecture *three-box* américaine avec compartiment moteur, cellule passagers et coffre à bagages, a déjà été introduite en Allemagne par Borgward avec la Hansa 1500 de 1949. Opel et Ford, toutes deux filiales de groupes américains, suivent elles aussi. Malgré l'aridité esthétique de ce concept, ses avantages sont patents. Pour un périmètre de sustentation identique, son économie est bien meilleure que celle des carrosseries traditionnelles qui gaspillent avec prodigalité une place précieuse : par rapport à la 170 s, la 180 offre un espace habitable majoré de 20 %, et de 75 % pour le volume de bagages. Sa carrosserie, domaine incontesté de l'angle droit, n'est pas encore autoporteuse ; elle est semi-porteuse, conjointement avec une plate-forme châssis en longerons caissons en acier et tôles soudés entre eux, à la fois relativement légère et rigide. Cela est aussi tout bénéfice pour les passagers en cas d'accident : à l'avant et à l'arrière, la cellule passagers rigide est précédée par des zones de déformation programmée.

Particularisme de la 180 qui deviendra vite un standard : le moteur, la boîte de vitesses, la direction ainsi que les leviers transversaux avant en tôle d'acier sont regroupés sur un « berceau auxiliaire » qui est relié au reste du châssis à l'aide de trois paliers en caoutchouc. Le conducteur de la 180 jouit d'un champ de vision nettement amélioré dans toutes les directions, et même la calandre traditionnelle de style gothique est parfaitement compatible avec la nouvelle forme. Pour le reste, sous une robe conforme à l'air du temps, tout est plutôt conventionnel. L'habituel essieu brisé à deux articulations avec leviers longitudinaux supplémentaires ne sera remplacé qu'en septembre 1955 par un train arrière où les demi-essieux ne sont plus ancrés que sur un seul point de rotation commun surbaissé. Cela permet de ramener à un niveau tolérable les modifications de déport dues au système.

Le moteur à commande latérale issu de la 170 s, avec ses 52 chevaux, brave et indestructible, mais sans le moindre prestige, est une véritable antiquité. En août 1957, il est donc évincé par le 1,9 litre de sa jumelle la 190, avec un arbre à cames en tête et 68 ch de bonne constitution. En ce qui concerne les populaires moteurs diesel, qui sont toujours facturés avec un supplément de prix de 500 à 1000 marks, on recourt aux ressources internes : le course longue de la 170 D voit sa puissance augmenter à 43 ch en 1955. Il est suivi d'une version à arbre à cames en tête et, à partir de 1962, il existe une 180 D avec le moteur majoré à deux litres de cylindrée de la 190 D. Les moteurs à auto-allumage de chez Benz se font encore entendre de loin. En revanche, leur espérance de vie permet de tabler sur un âge absolument canonique : dans l'industrie du taxi, par exemple, des kilométrages d'un demi-million de kilomètres n'ont rien de spectaculaire.

Mercedes-Benz *Ponton* 1953

A far-reaching measure: the unibody construction of the 180 with its mere hints of rear fenders made virtually optimum use of the footprint occupied by the first monocoque Mercedes.

Einschneidende Maßnahme: Die Pontonform des 180 mit nur noch angedeuteten Kotflügeln hinten nutzt fast optimal die Grundfläche, auf welcher der erste Mercedes mit einer selbsttragenden Karosserie steht.

Mesure décisive: la forme en ponton de la 180 aux ailes encore seulement esquissées à l'arrière exploite presque optimalement le périmètre de sustentation de la première Mercedes à carrosserie autoporteuse.

Mercedes-Benz *Ponton* 1953

The 180 used the powerplant of the 170 Sb, an inline four-cylinder engine with a lateral camshaft. The cockpit was also familiar.

Vom 170 Sb übernommen wird das Triebwerk des 180, ein Reihenvierzylinder mit seitlicher Nockenwelle. Vertraut wirkt auch das Cockpit.

La 180 reprend le moteur de la 170 Sb, un quatre-cylindres en ligne avec arbre à cames latéral. Le tableau de bord est lui aussi familier.

Mercedes-Benz *Ponton* 1953   157

Mercedes biographer Karl Ludvigsen called him the counterpart to Emil Jellinek. Max Hoffman, who had been the official Mercedes-Benz importer into the United States since 1952, was also Austrian and, like Jellinek, it was at his instigation—half a century later—that a model was created which caused a sensation. The dynamic businessman was highly impressed by the successes of the 1952 300 SL—and by its design. Something similar for the road, he told the Mercedes management in Stuttgart, could be just what was needed to open up the American market, and he put his money where his mouth was by ordering 1000 gullwing models.

A charismatic product was unveiled to an eager motor industry and countless fans at the International Motor Sports Show in New York on 6 February 1954: the road-going 300 SL coupé. That it had the SL racing car in its direct bloodline was undeniable, though, as was the case with this ancestor, a constructional necessity was turned into a positive virtue. The outer elements of the massive spaceframe, weighing in at a hefty 110 lbs, stood so high off the road as to make normal entry into the car impossible. Gullwings, which gave the car its name in the English-speaking world, were again the answer to the problem. And, as in the first-generation SL, the six-cylinder engine was canted to the left so that the front was low and streamlined.

Curiously the production engine delivered 40 bhp more than the racing engine. This was the result of the use for the first time by Mercedes of a high-pressure fuel-injection system developed by Dr. Hans Scherenberg, later the chief designer. The running gear was the same as that used on the 300—without additional springs and set up for sporty performance. However, the dynamics of the rear twin-pivot swing axle called for expert handling when pushed to the limit—the track width and camber changed constantly. Between August 1954 and May 1957, 1400 of the gullwinged coupés were sold, 29 of them with alloy bodies, and one with plastic bodywork.

As early as the summer of 1956 resourceful journalists at the German specialist publication *auto motor und sport* had tracked down a rolling chassis in the Stuttgart area which differed from the actual 300 SL only in respect of its low-slung longitudinal chassis tubes and a single-joint low-pivot swing axle *à la* 220. In October of that year the American sports-car champion Paul O'Shea unveiled the 300 SL Roadster at the Solitude track near Stuttgart. It was then officially launched at the 1957 Geneva Spring Motor Show with appropriate razzmatazz. The ball had again been set rolling by Maxi Hoffman who foresaw good sales prospects in the land of limitless opportunities for an open-top version of Stuttgart's finest. When production of the Roadster ceased in Sindelfingen on 8 February 1963, 1858 cars had left the line.

Major events in the history of this model include: from October 1958 onwards, just in time for the approaching

Mercedes-Benz 300 SL 1954

Mercedes-Benz 300 SL Coupé 1955

winter, an attractive, removable coupé hardtop was available for an extra 1500 marks; the already very effective bimetallic drum brakes, in which aluminum was coated with a thin layer of cast iron, gave way to Dunlop disk brakes in March 1961; and in March 1962 the SL was given a modified engine with an alloy block.

Einschneidende Vorkommnisse in der Modellgeschichte: Ab Oktober 1958, zeitgerecht zum nahenden Winter, ist ein attraktives abnehmbares Coupédach zum Mehrpreis von 1500 Mark erhältlich. Die bereits recht wirksamen Trommelbremsen in Verbundbauweise – Aluminium wird überzogen von einer dünnen Schicht aus Gusseisen – weichen im März 1961 Dunlop-Scheibenbremsen. Und noch im März 1962 spendiert man dem SL einen modifizierten Motor mit einem Block aus Leichtmetall.

Étapes décisives dans la généalogie du modèle: en octobre 1958, juste avant l'hiver menaçant, Mercedes propose un attrayant toit coupé démontable contre un supplément de prix de 1500 marks. Déjà assez efficaces avec leur structure mixte – aluminium recouvert d'une mince couche de fonte –, les freins à tambours sont remplacés en mars 1961 par des freins à disques Dunlop. Et, dès mars 1962, la SL bénéficie d'un moteur modifié avec bloc en aluminium.

At sports-car races in the mid-fifties, drivers like the German Walter Schock, Swede Bengt Martenson, or Belgian Willy Mairesse drove to the start with the gullwings raised, to get as much fresh air into the cockpit as possible, but also, it should be said, to make an impression.

Bei den Sportwagenrennen der Mittfünfziger rollen seine Piloten wie der Deutsche Walter Schock, der Schwede Bengt Martenson oder der Belgier Willy Mairesse mit erhobenem Flügel-Werk an den Start, wegen der frischen Luft und wohl auch ein bisschen wegen des Show-Effekts.

Lors des courses de voitures de sport du milieu des années 1950, ses pilotes comme l'Allemand Walter Schock, le Suédois Bengt Martenson ou le Belge Willy Mairesse roulent jusqu'au départ avec les portières relevées. Pour avoir un peu d'air frais, mais aussi, sans aucun doute, pour épater la galerie.

Mercedes-Benz 300 SL 1954

Mercedes-Benz 300 SL 1954

Chalk and cheese: the Roadster from 1959, with its comparitively gentle manners, and the Gullwing of 1955, a constant temptation to floor it—for those who could handle it...

Ungleiche Brüder: der Roadster von 1959, mit eher milden Manieren ausgestattet, vor dem Flügeltürer von 1955, einer ständigen Versuchung zum Schnellfahren – für den, der ihn beherrschte...

Des jumeaux bien dissemblables : le Roadster de 1959, aux manières plutôt policées, devant une « ailes de mouette » de 1955, une tentation permanente de conduire vite – pour celui qui savait la maîtriser...

Mercedes-Benz 300 SL 1954

Timeless designs. A striking feature was the Talbot rear-view mirror. The main feature that distinguished the roadster from the coupé was its vertical light units.

Formen, denen die Zeit nichts anhaben kann. Ein markantes Requisit: der Talbot-Rückspiegel. Das Gesicht des Roadsters unterscheidet sich von dem des Coupés vor allem durch die senkrechten Leuchteneinheiten.

Des formes à l'épreuve du temps. Un accessoire typique: le rétroviseur Talbot. L'allure du roadster se distingue surtout de celle du coupé par ses phares verticaux.

The fact that the 220a, launched in March 1954, and the 180 were closely related is unmistakable. Both were representatives of the new generation of unit-construction Mercedes. The difference, though, was that the 220 looked more stretched and elegant, while the 180, the unibody pioneer, came across as stocky and ungainly. Like the older model, the newer model's body was firmly welded to the floorpan chassis. The sub-frame and the front suspension using twin wishbones and coil springs were also re-employed. The rear axle, on the other hand, a single-joint low-pivot swing axle as fitted to the W196 Grand Prix car, represented the state of the art. It ensured that the driver was not caught out by severe changes in track widths and cambers. The extended wheelbase—lengthened by 6¾ in to 9 ft 3 in—gave more legroom to the rear passengers and to the six-cylinder engine under the stretched bonnet—a well-known feature of the 220 from 1951. Higher compression, a more positive camshaft, and a larger carburetor helped the car achieve a power output of 85 bhp. Much attention had been lavished on the brakes, with strongly ribbed drums to which cooling air was ducted via slits in the hubs. From September 1955 onwards a servo brake fitted as standard relieved the load on the driver's right foot.

The successor 220 s introduced in March 1956 was almost identical, though it developed 100 bhp, to which two governor carburetors contributed their mite. The engine now rested on four points on the sub-frame instead of two. An additional trim strip indicated the minor difference. At the same time the cut-down 219 was launched, a cross between the 190 and the engine of the 220 a. It cost 2000 marks less, and the clumsy type designation meant that it was already slightly devalued in the eyes of potential customers.

When Daimler-Benz decided in August 1957 to lavish free-of-charge upgrades on almost all the cars in its range, the main change to the 219 and 220 s was an increase in power, one by 5 and the other by 6 bhp. A Hydrak hydraulically-operated automatic clutch was available as an option at an extra cost of 450 marks, and it was available also on the 220 SE of September 1958 which was powered to 115 bhp by an intermittent induction-manifold fuel-injection system. With only 1974 cars built in a 10-month period, this model remained rare and exclusive. Even more exclusive were the most exquisite models in the series, the sumptuously appointed Cabriolet A/C, which appeared in the summer of 1956, and the coupé that followed in the autumn. Both underwent the same changes as the sedan and, although this was discontinued in August 1959, they were built for a little longer—though then fitted with the engine of the new 220 SEb.

Mercedes-Benz 219–220 SE   1954

The introduction of the Cabriolet A/C type 220 S in July 1956 represented in a sense the first appearance of unibody construction with its associated problems. For the time being, the monocoque body required the support of a hardtop.

Mit der Einführung des Cabriolets A/C vom Typ 220 S im Juli 1956 findet gewissermaßen die erstmalige Eröffnung des Pontonaufbaus statt mit den damit verbundenen Schwierigkeiten: Die selbsttragende Karosserie ist zunächst einmal auf die Unterstützung des Festdachs angewiesen.

Avec l'introduction du Cabriolet A/C de la 220 S, en juillet 1956, la première ouverture d'une carrosserie ponton a lieu avec les difficultés que cela implique: la carrosserie autoporteuse ne peut pas, en effet, se passer de la rigidité que confère un toit fixe.

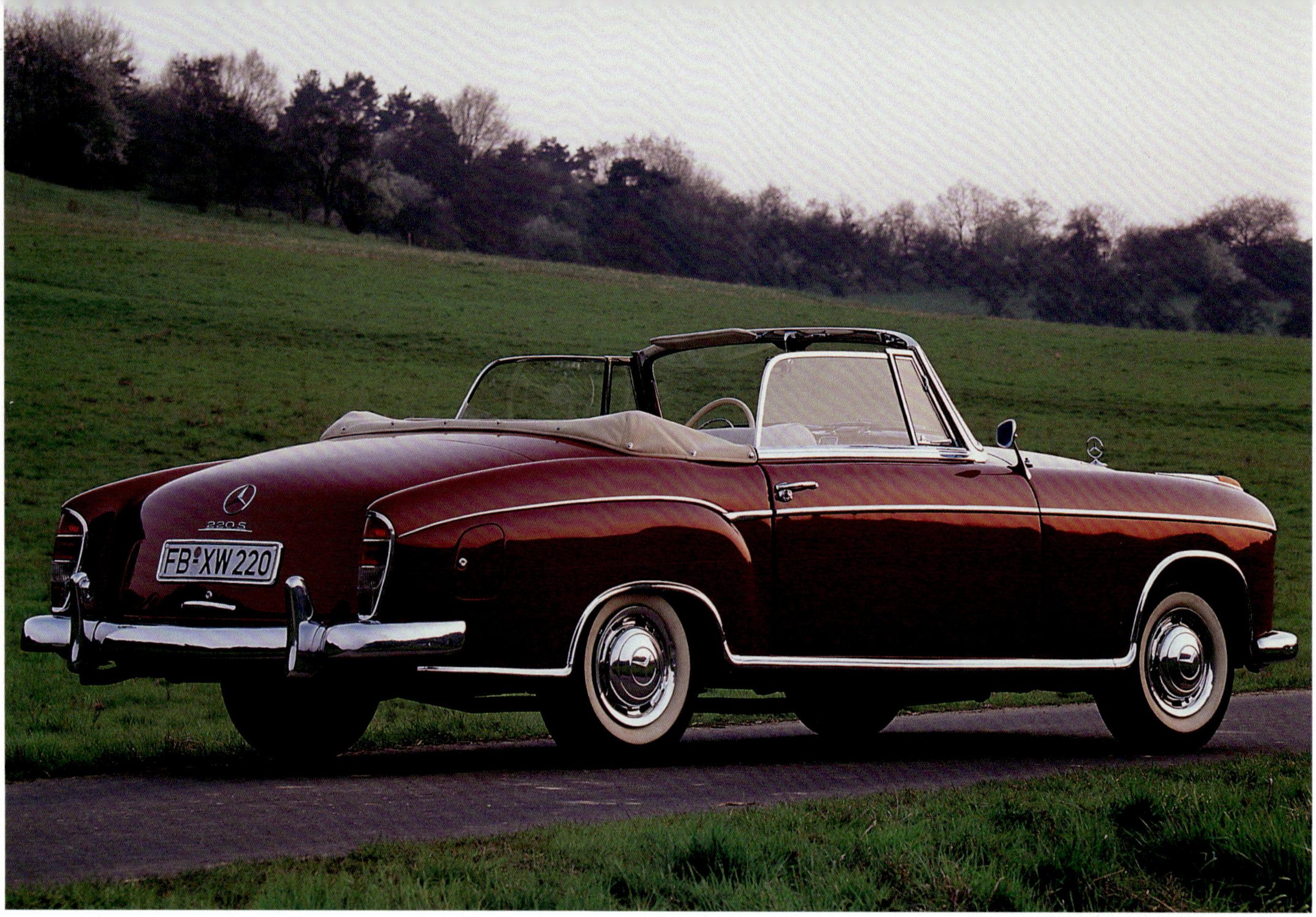
FB-XW 220

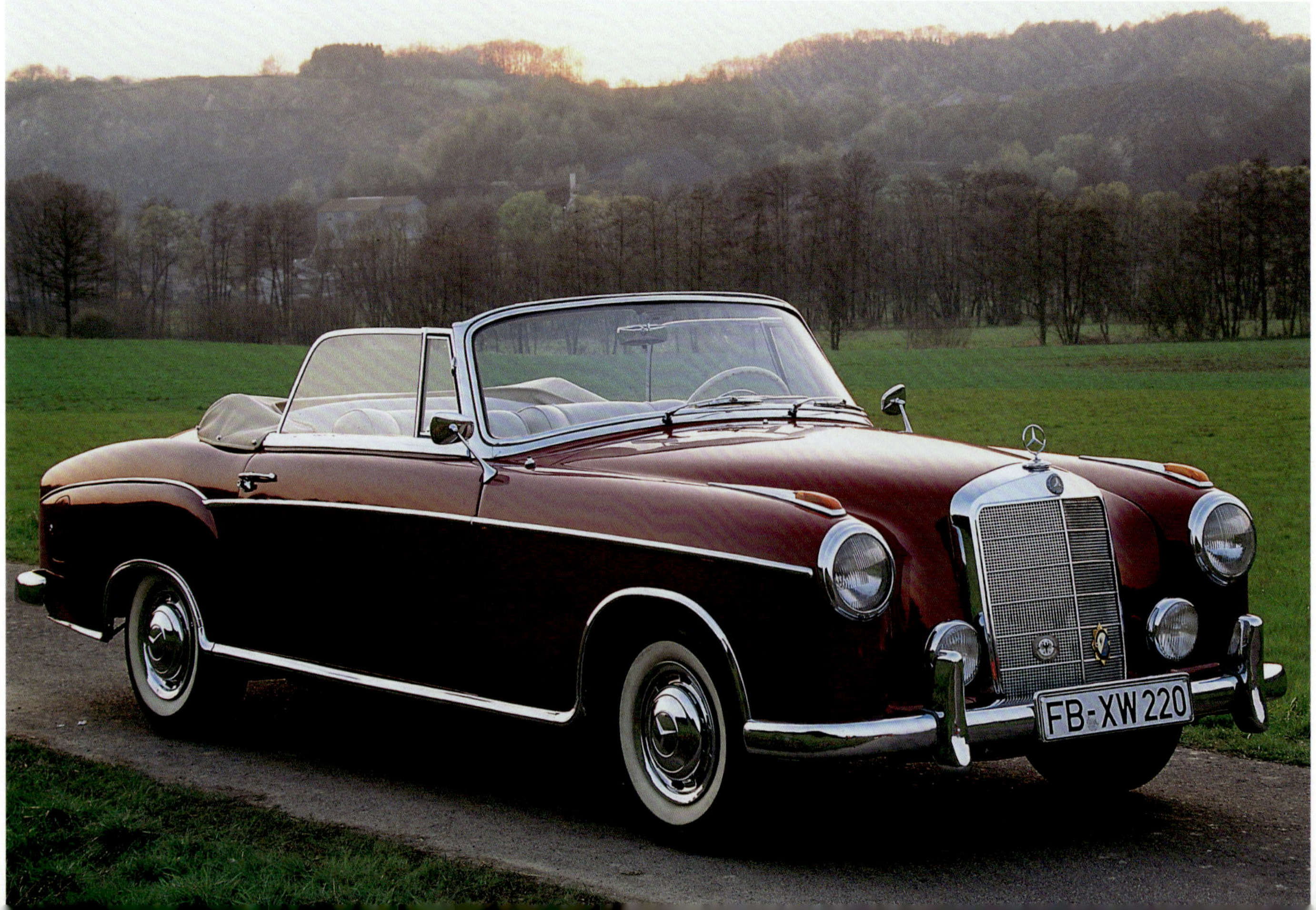
FB-XW 220

Experiments with a new design—the relative proportions of the front and rear were not all they might have been, and the chrome trim was a little overdone. The wide doors also gave access to the rear bench seat. It was rather a squeeze in the back.

Experimente mit einer neuen Form: Nicht unbedingt ausgewogen sind die Proportionen von Bug und Heck, etwas zu dick aufgetragen die Chromapplikationen. Die breiten Türen geben auch den Zugang frei zur hinteren Sitzbank. Im Fond geht es leicht beengt zu.

Expériences avec une nouvelle forme: les proportions de la proue et de la poupe ne sont pas très équilibrées et les applications de chromes sont un peu trop appuyées. Les larges portières donnent aussi accès à la banquette arrière, où l'espace est cependant un peu compté.

Mercedes-Benz 219–220 SE 1954

This car shared the same fate as all those whom fortune has blessed with charismatic siblings. While purely at a visual level the 300 SL conjured up a hint of drama and adventure at the New York International Motor Sports Show in February 1954, the impression given by the 190 SL alongside it was neat, certainly sporty and with dashing lines supplied by Mercedes designers Karl Wilfert and Walter Häckert, but—well—a little bit conventional. The statistics, however, tell their own tale; between May 1955 and February 1963, 25,881 of these cars were sold—it was a success.

Before that, however, there was still work to be done. Many aspects of the model exhibited in New York had not been thoroughly thought-out, and it was not until the Geneva Spring Motor Show in 1955 that the smaller SL appeared in its final form. It was available as a roadster, which was actually a cabriolet with its wind-down windows and a tough fabric top, or as a coupé which was basically a hardtop version with a removable alloy roof. Many reliable features of other series were incorporated in the 190 SL, which was only available in silver-grey until the end of 1956. Its engine, four inline cylinders with a chain-driven overhead camshaft and two governor downdraft carburetors, was in effect a part of the straight six from the "Three Hundred," delivering a respectable 105 bhp, even if it was rather rough beyond 3000 rpm. Its all-steel body was of monocoque design, welded to the shortened floorpan chassis of the type 180.

The engine was mounted on the sub-frame initially only at the front, though from January 1956 there were two further support points at the back. As with the 220 a, a single-joint, low-pivot swing axle counteracted any particularly severe changes in camber. A racing variant with aluminum doors and a small windshield was dropped in great secrecy. A series of minor modifications punctuated the 190 SL's lifetime. In March 1956 wider chrome trim strips bordered the area above the door; in June of the same year it was given the larger tail lights of the 220 a, 219, and 220 S sedans. In July 1957 the rear number-plate light was incorporated into the bumper overriders to make room for the larger number plates required by changes in legislation. And in October 1959 the coupé was given a new hardtop with an enlarged rear screen like those also found in the soft top of the roadster from this period.

The 190 SL's reputation was regrettably slightly tarnished. Admittedly it was regarded as an indispensable prop for films and fashion magazines. But the Frankfurt demi-mondaine Rosemarie Nitribitt also bought one to increase her appeal, and she enjoyed a rather dubious popularity in Germany which rubbed off on all the possessions with which she surrounded herself.

Er scheint das Los all derer zu teilen, denen das Schicksal charismatische Brüder und Schwestern an die Seite gestellt hat: Wo der 300 SL auf der New Yorker International Motor Sports Show im Februar 1954 schon rein visuell von einem Hauch von Drama und Abenteuer umgeben ist, wirkt der 190 SL neben ihm adrett, gewiss auch sportlich-schmissig mit seiner Silhouette, die die Mercedes-Mitarbeiter Karl Wilfert und Walter Häckert entworfen haben, aber eben ein bisschen bieder. Indessen sprechen Zahlen ihre eigene Sprache: Zwischen Mai 1955 und Februar 1963 bringt es das Modell auf eine Auflage von 25 881 Exemplaren – ein Erfolgstyp.

Bis dahin gibt es noch einiges zu tun: Vieles an dem New Yorker Exponat ist nicht ganz ins reine gedacht, und erst auf dem Genfer Frühlingssalon 1955 erscheint der kleinere SL in seiner endgültigen Form. Es gibt ihn als Roadster, der eigentlich ein Cabriolet ist mit seinen Kurbelfenstern und einem soliden Stoffverdeck, oder als Coupé, bei dem es sich im Grunde genommen um eine Hardtop-Version handelt, deren Leichtmetalldach man abnehmen kann. Viel Solides aus anderen Serien wird in den 190 SL eingespeist, der bis einschließlich 1956 nur in kleidsamem Silbergrau zu haben ist. Sein Motor, vier Verbrennungseinheiten in Linie mit einer kettengetriebenen obenliegenden Nockenwelle und zwei Register-Fallstromvergasern, ist praktisch ein Teil des Reihensechszylinders aus dem »Dreihunderter«, 105 anständige PS stark, wenn auch jenseits der 3000/min ein wenig knurrig. Sein Ganzstahlaufbau ist selbsttragend, verschweißt mit der verkürzten Rahmenbodengruppe des Typs 180.

Die Maschine ist auf dem Fahrschemel zunächst nur vorn gelagert, ab Januar 1956 gibt es zwei zusätzliche Auflagepunkte hinten. Wie am 220 a beugt eine Eingelenk-Pendelachse mit tiefgelegtem Drehpunkt allzu heftigen Sturzänderungen vor. Von einer Renn-Variante mit Aluminiumtüren und einer kleinen Windschutzscheibe nimmt man klammheimlich wieder Abstand. Die Modell-Vita des 190 SL ist gesäumt von sanften Retuschen: Im März 1956 fassen breitere Chromleisten den oberen Türabschluss ein, im Juni des gleichen Jahres erhält er die größeren Rückleuchten der Limousinen 220 a, 219 und 220 S. Im Juli 1957 wird die hintere Kennzeichenbeleuchtung in die Stoßstangenhörner eingelegt, so dass die vorgeschriebenen voluminöseren Nummernschilder Platz finden. Und im Oktober 1959 stülpt man dem Coupé ein neues Hardtop über mit einer vergrößerten Heckscheibe, wie sie von nun an auch im Stoffdach des Roadsters zu finden ist.

Da ist der Ruf des 190 SL schon leicht ramponiert. Gewiss muss er herhalten als schier unentbehrliches Requisit für Filme und Modejournale. Aber auch die Frankfurter Lebedame Rosemarie Nitribitt hat sich einen zum Kundenfang zugelegt, und die erfreut sich in Deutschland dubioser Popularität, mithin auch das Hab und Gut, mit dem sie sich schmückt…

Elle semble partager le sort de tous ceux auxquels le destin a fait côtoyer des frères et sœurs charismatiques : alors que la 300 SL présentée au New York International Motor Sports Show de février 1954 était déjà nimbée, sur le seul plan visuel, d'une aura de drame et d'aventure, la 190 SL semble comparativement jolie, certes sportive et élégante avec sa silhouette conçue par deux collaborateurs de Mercedes, Karl Wilfert et Walter Häckert, mais malheureusement aussi un peu banale. Les chiffres, en revanche, parlent une tout autre langue : de mai 1955 à février 1963, ce modèle a en effet été produit à 25 881 exemplaires. Un succès sans appel.

Mais, avant d'en arriver là, il aura fallu bien du travail : bien des détails du modèle exporté à New York restaient encore à régler et ce n'est qu'au Salon de printemps de Genève, en 1955, que la petite SL paraît sous sa forme définitive. Elle est proposée en roadster, mais c'est en réalité un cabriolet avec ses fenêtres à manivelle et sa solide capote de toit, ou en coupé, qui est en réalité une version à *hard-top* dont on peut ôter le toit en aluminium. On greffe en revanche sur la 190 SL, qui n'est disponible – jusqu'en 1956 compris – que dans un élégant gris métallisé, de nombreux organes solides provenant d'autres séries. Son moteur, un quatre-cylindres en ligne avec arbre à cames en tête entraîné par chaînes et deux carburateurs inversés à registre est pratiquement un fragment du six-cylindres en ligne de la « Trois Cents », avec 105 chevaux piaffants quoique légèrement lymphatiques au-delà de 3000 tr/min. Sa carrosserie tout acier est autoporteuse et soudée sur la plate-forme à empattement raccourci de la 180.

Le moteur reçoit, à partir de janvier 1956, deux paliers supplémentaires à l'arrière. Comme sur la 220 a, un essieu brisé à une articulation et ancrage surbaissé réprime les modifications de carrossage trop violentes. Une version course avec portes en aluminium et petit pare-brise coupe-vent disparaît discrètement aux oubliettes. Le curriculum vitae de la 190 SL est ponctué de discrètes retouches : en mars 1956, des joncs de chrome plus larges ornent l'arête de porte supérieure et, en juin de la même année, elle reçoit les feux arrière de plus grandes dimensions des berlines 220 a, 219 et 220 S. En juillet 1957, l'éclairage de la plaque signalétique arrière est placé dans les cornes de pare-chocs, ce qui permet de monter les plaques minéralogiques de plus grandes dimensions désormais prescrites. Et, en octobre 1959, le coupé reçoit un nouveau *hard-top* avec une lunette arrière plus vaste identique à celle du roadster.

Mais la réputation de la 190 SL est déjà légèrement entachée. Certes, elle a encore un beau rôle à jouer en tant qu'accessoire absolument indispensable pour les films et revues de mode. Mais la prostituée de luxe francfortoise Rosemarie Nitribitt s'est aussi fait, avec elle, une jolie clientèle et elle est victime en Allemagne d'une popularité douteuse, ce qui vaut également pour ceux qui se pavanent au volant de cette voiture…

Mercedes-Benz 190 SL   1955

The little brother. The similarity between the 190 SL and the 300 SL is clear to see. This too was a good-looking car and popular to boot. However, it did not find its way onto the racetracks.

Kleiner Bruder: Die Ähnlichkeit zum 300 SL steht dem 190 SL ins Gesicht geschrieben. Schön ist auch er und populär dazu. Das Ambiente der Pisten jedoch umfächelt ihn nicht.

Petite sœur: la similitude de la 190 SL avec la 300 SL est incontestable. Tout aussi jolie et, ce qui ne gâte rien, populaire. Mais elle n'a jamais reniflé l'odeur d'huile des circuits.

Mercedes-Benz 190 SL 1955

The 190 SL occupied the niche for a sporty touring car with good driving performance within the ever-expanding Mercedes range. Caressed by the summer heat of an Atlantic high, driving with the top down was unalloyed pleasure.

In der sich immer ausweitenden Typenpalette von Mercedes hat der 190 SL seinen Platz als sportliches Reisefahrzeug mit guten Fahreigenschaften. Bei offenem Verdeck in der Schmeichelwärme des Azorenhochs wird der Ausflug zum reinen Vergnügen.

Dans la gamme toujours plus diversifiée des Mercedes, la 190 SL a sa place bien à elle comme voiture de voyage sportive et sûre. Avec la capote ouverte pour accueillir les premières chaleurs du printemps, une excursion à la campagne est un plaisir sans mélange.

The robust four-cylinder engine did not necessarily need to be monitored by the tachometer. But it was all part of the sporty image.

Nicht unbedingt bedarf der kernige Vierzylinder der Überwachung durch den Drehzahlmesser. Aber der gehört zum sportiven Image.

Le compte-tours n'est pas absolument nécessaire pour surveiller le quatre-cylindres à la rauque sonorité. Mais il contribue à lui donner une touche sportive.

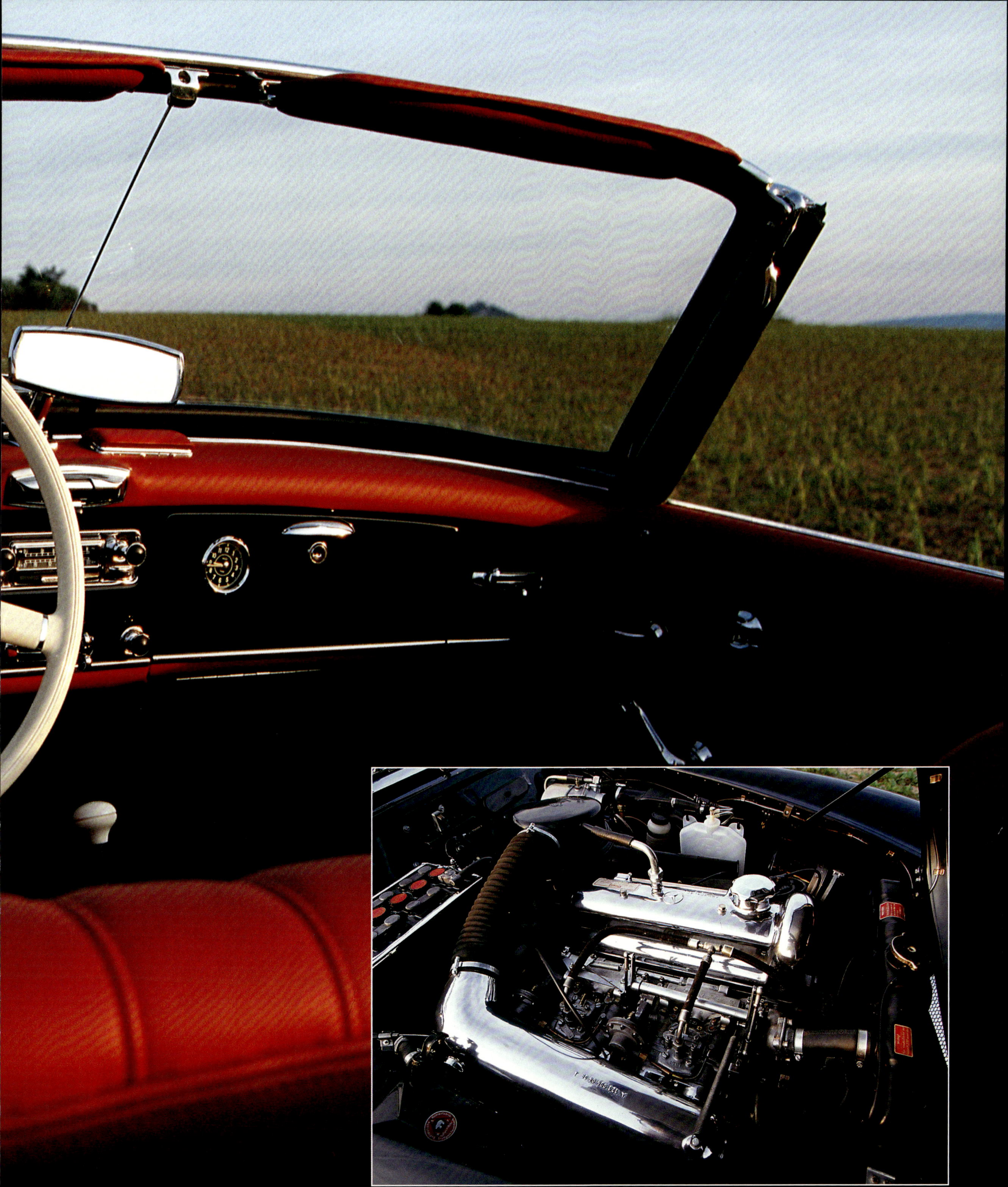

Design features sometimes inspire names that are much more memorable and enduring than the official company designations. Often they are vernacular terms that become part of the tradition. Thus it was that the earliest unibody type was known in German as the "Ponton"-Mercedes (or pontoon Mercedes), and this was followed in 1959 by the "Fin," so-called because of its gentle extensions at the upper ends of the rear fenders. These were concessions to contemporary taste that was greatly influenced by the United States, though they were much more restrained than, for example, the enormous protuberances of the Cadillac ("sharks fins") or Lincoln. And since Mercedes was determined that form should follow function, the new baby was given a matter-of-fact name: "Peilstege".

The motto for the 220 b, 220 sb and 220 sEb was "The new six-cylinders—a class of their own." Their quality showed particularly in the safety features. For the first time ideas from Mercedes employee Béla Barényi had been implemented with all their implications. In the event of an accident, a tough passenger cage would be protected by deformable zones at the front and rear. Safety consciousness also extended to the interior design—a cushioned pad was added to the steering wheel, and the dashboard was also cushioned. Notorious slashers and stabbers among the operating levers were flexibly mounted and some were also recessed. Wedge-pivot door locks were steps in the same direction.

Outwardly the two s models differed in that the 220 sb had more lavish chrome trim, and its engine was fed by two Solex carburetors, resulting in a power output of 95 bhp. The injection engine of the sEb was also retrofitted with linear induction manifolds, resulting in 120 bhp compared with its predecessor's 115 bhp. The sub-frame consisted of a simple cross-strut, flexibly connected to the chassis at two points. A compensating spring above the swing-axle pivot ensured even distribution of the axle load to the two drive wheels. Moving the four shock absorbers to the outside improved their accessibility and also their ability to damp vibrations. In April 1962 the s models were fitted with disk brakes. Sixteen months later so was the 220 b and a servo brake was fitted as standard at the same time. The Hydrak semi-automatic gearbox was an option until the beginning of 1962, when a fully automatic gearbox, a hydraulic clutch connected to a 4-speed planetary gear system, rendered it obsolete. This was available for the sEb from April onwards and from August 1962 onwards for an extra 1400 marks for the other two models. Like air suspension and power steering, this was fitted as standard from August 1961 onwards to the top-of-the-range model, the 300 SE, which was then joined by a stretched version, launched at the Geneva Spring Motor Show in March 1963 with a 4-in-longer wheelbase. When production of this series ended in the summer of 1965, the 230 s remained available for a time as a rebored derivative of the 220 b. However, the coupé,

Manchmal regen Designmerkmale zu Namen an, die einprägsamer und dauerhafter sind als die offizielle Nomenklatur einer Firma. Der Volksmund prägt sie, und schließlich gehen sie ein in die Überlieferung. So folgt auf den »Ponton«-Mercedes 1959 die »Heckflosse«, so genannt nach sanften Auswüchsen an den oberen Enden der hinteren Kotflügel. Es sind Konzessionen an einen Zeitgeschmack, der aus den Vereinigten Staaten gespeist wird, gleichwohl viel zurückhaltender als etwa die enormen Protuberanzen der Cadillac (»Haifischflossen«) oder Lincoln. Und da man bei Mercedes darauf bedacht ist, dass die Form der Funktion zu folgen habe, bekommt das Kind auch gleich einen sachlichen Namen: Peilstege.

Das Motto über der Baureihe 220 b, 220 sb und 220 sEb: Die neuen Sechszylinder – eine Klasse für sich. Das beginnt mit dem Bemühen um Sicherheit. Zum ersten Mal hat man Ideengut von Mercedes-Kostgänger Béla Barényi konsequent umgesetzt: Ein stabiler Passagiertrakt wird im Falle eines Unfalls abgefedert durch verformbare Zonen vorn und hinten. Mehr Sicherheit zugleich für den Innenraum: Auf das Lenkrad ist eine Polsterplatte gesattelt, auch das Armaturenbrett ist gepolstert. Notorische Schlitzer und Stecher unter den Bedienungselementen wurden elastisch und zum Teil versenkt angeordnet. Keilzapfen-Türschlösser sind Schritte in die gleiche Richtung.

Nach außen unterscheiden sich die beiden s-Modelle im wesentlichen durch üppigeren Chromzierrat vom 220 sb, dessen Triebwerk nun durch zwei Solex-Vergaser ernährt wird und 95 PS leistet. Auch beim Einspritzmotor des sEb wurde nachgerüstet mit geraden Ansaugrohren: 120 PS gegenüber den 115 PS des Vorgängers. Der Fahrschemel besteht nur noch aus einem simplen Querträger, an zwei Stellen elastisch verbunden mit dem Rahmen. Eine Ausgleichsfeder oberhalb des Drehpunkts der Pendelachse sorgt für gleichmäßige Verteilung der Achslast auf die beiden Antriebsräder. Dass alle vier Stoßdämpfer ganz nach außen gelegt wurden, verbessert ihre Zugänglichkeit sowie die Schwingungsdämpfung. Im April 1962 erhalten die s-Modelle Scheibenbremsen, der 220 b zieht 16 Monate später nach und wird zugleich mit einem serienmäßigen Bremskraftverstärker ausgestattet. Der Halbautomat Hydrak ist noch bis Anfang 1962 zu haben, schon obsolet angesichts einer vollwertigen Automatik, die bereits seit dem April für den sEb und ab August 1962 für einen Aufpreis von 1400 Mark für die beiden anderen erhältlich ist, eine hydraulische Kupplung mit nachgeschaltetem Viergang-Planetengetriebe. Sie gehört, wie Luftfederung und Servolenkung, zur Grundausstattung des Spitzenmodells 300 SE ab August 1961, dem im März 1963 auf dem Genfer Frühlingssalon eine Lang-Version mit 100 Millimetern mehr Radstand zur Seite gestellt wird. Als die Baureihe im Sommer 1965 ausläuft, bleibt noch eine Zeitlang der 230 s als aufgebohrtes Derivat des 220 b. Es bleiben aber auch das Coupé, präsentiert bei der

Il arrive que des caractéristiques de style donnent à une voiture un nom qui imprègne plus durablement les esprits que la nomenclature officielle d'une firme. Baptisées par le grand public, elles s'intègrent ensuite à la tradition de la marque. C'est ainsi que la Mercedes «Ponton» a été suivie, en 1959, par celle aux «dérives» ainsi nommée à cause des arêtes proéminentes de ses ailes arrière. Ce sont des concessions faites à la mode d'un moment en provenance des États-Unis, mais avec toutefois beaucoup plus de retenue que les énormes protubérances des Cadillac («ailerons de requin») ou des Lincoln. Et comme, chez Mercedes, on aspire toujours à ce que la forme obéisse à la fonction, l'enfant reçoit vite son surnom: le collimateur.

Un parti pris préside à la gamme 220 b, 220 sb et 220 sEb: les nouveaux six-cylindres – une classe à part. Principal champ d'action: la sécurité. Pour la première fois, on a transposé systématiquement la philosophie de Béla Barényi, l'apôtre de la sécurité chez Mercedes: une solide cellule passagers est amortie, en cas d'accident, par des zones à déformation programmée à l'avant et à l'arrière. Plus de sécurité également pour l'habitacle: le moyeu du volant est rembourré et le tableau de bord est, lui aussi, capitonné. Toutes les manettes et commandes proéminentes sont montées élastiquement et, en partie, affleurantes. Les serrures de portières à tourillon conique sont un autre pas dans la même direction.

Extérieurement, les deux modèles s se distinguent essentiellement par des chromes plus généreux de la 220 sb, dont le moteur est maintenant alimenté par deux carburateurs Solex et développe 95 ch. Le moteur à injection de la sEb fait, lui aussi, des progrès et, avec ses tubulures d'aspiration droites, développe 120 ch contre 115 pour l'ancien modèle. Le berceau auxiliaire ne consiste plus en une poutre transversale simple reliée élastiquement au cadre à deux endroits. Un ressort de compensation au-dessus du point de rotation de l'essieu brisé assure une répartition équilibrée de la charge d'essieu entre les deux roues motrices. Désormais placés tout à l'extérieur, les quatre amortisseurs sont plus accessibles, ce qui améliore aussi leur action. En avril 1962, les modèles s reçoivent des freins à disques, progrès dont bénéficie également, seize mois plus tard, la 220 b qui reçoit aussi en série un servofrein. La boîte semi-automatique Hydrak est proposée jusqu'au début de 1962, mais elle est déjà obsolète, compte tenu de la boîte complètement automatique déjà offerte depuis avril pour la sEb et, à partir d'août 1962, contre un supplément de prix de 1400 marks pour les deux autres modèles, un embrayage hydraulique avec boîte planétaire à quatre rapports en aval. Comme la suspension pneumatique et la direction assistée, elle fait partie de l'équipement de série du navire amiral, la 300 SE, à partir d'août 1961, voiture épaulée, en mars 1963, à partir du Salon de printemps de Genève, par une version à empattement long allongée de 100 mm. Lorsque la production de la gamme est suspendue durant l'été 1965, seule la 230 s

Mercedes-Benz *Heckflosse* 1959

Mercedes-Benz 220 Sb 1964

The 220 series had come of age, with a stretched body and a much greater window area. The headlights were mounted behind plexiglass covers.

Die Reihe 220 ist erwachsener geworden, mit einer gestreckten Karosserie und einer kräftig vergrößerten Verglasung. Die Scheinwerfer finden sich hinter Abdeckungen aus Plexiglas.

La Série 220 agrandie, avec une carrosserie aux lignes étirées et des surfaces vitrées beaucoup plus généreuses. Les phares se trouvent derrière un carénage en Plexiglas.

launched at the opening of the Daimler-Benz Museum on 24 February 1961, and the cabriolet, first unveiled in August of the same year, were still built. Their shapes were so elegant and timeless that they housed the engines of later model generations right up to the beautiful twins of the 280 SE 3.5 of September 1969 with their silky-smooth 200 bhp V8 engines and which were only distinguishable from their predecessors by their flatter radiators.

Eröffnung des Daimler-Benz-Museums am 24. Februar 1961, und das Cabriolet, zum erstenmal gezeigt im August desselben Jahres. So elegant und zeitlos sind ihre Formen, dass sie noch die Motoren späterer Modellgenerationen beherbergen bis hin zu den schönen Zwillingen 280 SE 3.5 vom September 1969 mit ihren seidig laufenden V8-Triebwerken von 200 PS, die sich ansonsten nur durch ihre flacheren Kühler von ihren Vorgängern unterscheiden.

est encore proposée un certain temps en tant qu'extrapolation de la cylindrée majorée de la 220 b. Mais il reste encore le coupé, présenté lors de l'inauguration du musée Daimler-Benz, le 24 février 1961, et le cabriolet, dévoilé en août de la même année. Leurs formes sont si élégantes et intemporelles qu'ils hébergeront encore les moteurs de générations ultérieures jusqu'aux admirables sœurs, les 280 SE 3.5 de septembre 1969 avec leurs moteurs V8 soyeux de 200 chevaux, qui ne se distinguent de leurs devancières que par leur seule calandre moins élevée.

The striking feature at the rear of the car—the wing extensions, popularly known as fins. The horn-ring, which was flattened out towards the top, was prone to breaking off if treated roughly.

Markantes Merkmal am Heck: die Peilstege, im Volksmund Heckflossen geheißen. Der nach oben abgeflachte Signalring bricht bei rüder Behandlung gerne ab.

Un arrière bien caractéristique : les ailes qui lui ont valu son surnom de « Mercedes à ailerons ». L'anneau de signalisation à pan coupé en haut se brise volontiers si on le brutalise.

The straight-six fuel-injected engine of the 220 SE was 10 bhp more powerful than the carburetor engine of the 220 S.

Der Reihensechszylinder des 220 SE ist als Einspritzer zehn PS stärker als der Vergasermotor des 220 S.

Le six-cylindres en ligne de la 220 SE à injection a dix chevaux de plus que le moteur à carburateur de la 220 S.

The body and running gear of the type 200 corresponded to that of the 220S. However, the hood was shorter, the fenders were more simple, and the headlights were round.

Karosserie und Fahrwerk des Typs 200 entsprechen dem 220S. Allerdings ist die Haube kürzer, sind die Stoßstangen einfacher und die Scheinwerfer rund.

La carrosserie et le châssis de la 200 sont identiques à ceux de la 220S, mais le capot moteur est plus court, les pare-chocs sont plus simples et les phares ronds.

Mercedes-Benz *Heckflosse* 1959

The fender extensions on the coupé and cabriolet in the series were discreetly rounded, which gave the design a certain timeless continuity.

An Coupé und Cabriolet der Baureihe sind die Peilstege dezent gerundet, was ihrer Formensprache eine gewisse zeitlose Beständigkeit verleiht.

Sur le coupé et le cabriolet de la gamme, les ailerons sont légèrement arrondis, ce qui confère à leur langage formel un certain caractère intemporel.

Mercedes-Benz *Heckflosse* 1959

Mercedes-Benz *Heckflosse* 1959

Mercedes-Benz *Heckflosse* 1959

The dashboard and steering wheel bore witness
to the importance now placed on safety:
deformability and a cushioned pad had arrived.

Armaturenbrett und Lenkrad zeugen vom
Streben nach Sicherheit: Deformierbarkeit
und Polsternabe haben Einzug gehalten.

Le tableau de bord et le volant
témoignent du désir de sécurité: ils
sont déformables et rembourrés.

It doesn't always go without saying—but even with the hood up the large cabriolet was a real looker. The front of the cabriolet was almost baroque in its splendor. The export model for the United States dropped the plexiglass headlight cover. The radiator grille was made wider and lower from 1969 onwards.

Nicht immer selbstverständlich – auch mit geschlossenem Verdeck macht das große Cabriolet eine gute Figur. Von geradezu barocker Pracht: die Frontpartie des Cabriolets. In der Exportausführung für die Vereinigten Staaten entfällt die Plexiglasabdeckung der Scheinwerfer. Seit 1969 ist das Kühlergitter breiter und niedriger.

Pas toujours évident – mais même avec la capote fermée, le grand cabriolet fait bonne figure. Magnificence baroque : la proue du cabriolet. La version destinée aux États-Unis ne comporte pas le carénage en Plexiglas des phares. Depuis 1969, la calandre est plus large et plus basse.

Mercedes-Benz *Heckflosse* 1959

Mercedes engineers were given three specifications in an attempt, as it were, to square the circle. A joint successor was sought for the very popular 190 SL and the 300 SL, which was a legend in its own lifetime. The design had to be absolutely contemporary. The new car had to be (1) bright, comfortable, and spacious, (2) use as many elements as possible of existing series, and (3) have a beautiful body.

The result, first seen at the Geneva Motor Show in March 1963, was what became popularly known as the "Pagoda" because of the concave bow in its roof. It was undoubtedly a gimmick with a touch of the avant-garde which cost the car a little in terms of top speed. However, it was also a safety factor which counteracted any possible instability caused by the lightweight construction. Safety was writ very large in the design of the 230 SL. The responsible expert, Béla Barényi, left his fingerprints all over this one—and more besides. Like modern-day sedans of the time, the new SL protected its occupants by means of a rigid cage with deformable sections to the front and rear.

Like the 190 SL, the 230 SL was available as a coupé with a removable roof and roadster top, or as a coupé with a removable roof, although four levers had to be released to remove the hardtop before two strong adults lifted it away. The elegantly flat body sat on the shortened, stiffened floorpan chassis of the 220 SEb, whose suspension was also used. Its engine had been rebored to increase its displacement by 100 cc, and increased compression and a Bosch six-stage pump also helped the luxury sports car to achieve 150 bhp. An automatic gearbox was available as an option, and a ZF 5-speed transmission from May 1966. The 230 SL proved its sporty qualities when the Stuttgart hotelier Eugen Böhringer, together with team-mate Klaus Kaiser, won the 1963 Liège-Sofia-Liège Rally in a well-prepared car.

On 27 February 1967 the 250 SL was launched as its replacement, unchanged outwardly, though fitted with elements from the 250 SE. Take the engine, for example: the SL's power output remained the same though it achieved ten per cent more torque. Or its brakes: like the sedan, the 250 SL now had disk brakes all round, rather than the rear drum brakes that it had made do with up till then. In addition, the disk size had been increased, and a servo brake relieved the driver of some of the work. The fuel tank had also been enlarged by 4½ gallons to 21¾ gallons. A further version offered to customers who could count on reliably good weather came to be known as the California model. The top and its box were replaced by a rear seat, but anyone caught out in a cloudburst without a coupé roof had to make a quick dash for cover.

The 250 SL had only been on the market for about a year when the "Pagoda" was treated to the general upgrading that top-of-the-range cars often enjoy. An increase in engine size to 2.8 liters yielded 20 bhp more and a further ten per cent more torque. The only external differences between the 280 SL and its predecessors were

Mercedes-Benz *Pagode*   1963

Mercedes-Benz 250 SL 1967

its hub caps and the badge on the trunk. When production ceased in March 1971, this series had sold 48,912 cars in eight years. Although the challenge of squaring the circle was still open, the sales statistics spoke volumes for its success.

Nicht einmal ein Jahr ist der 250 SL im Angebot, dann hat die »Pagode« teil an der allgemeinen Aufrüstung, die den Wagen der Oberklasse widerfährt. Eine Hubraumvergrößerung auf 2,8 Liter bringt 20 PS und erneut zehn Prozent mehr Drehmoment. Nur an seinen Radzierblenden und der üblichen Aufschrift auf dem Heck ist der 280 SL von seinen Vorfahren zu unterscheiden. Als die Produktion im März 1971 ausläuft, hat es die Baureihe in acht Jahren auf 48 912 Exemplare gebracht. Die Quadratur des Zirkels bleibt zwar nach wie vor eine Herausforderung. Aber wenn es um Erfolg geht, sprechen ja auch Zahlen Bände.

nément sous une averse doit immédiatement se mettre en quête d'un abri.

La 250 SL n'aura même pas été produite pendant un an puisque la « Pagode » participe à la course générale aux améliorations dont bénéficient les voitures du segment supérieur. L'accroissement de cylindrée à 2,8 litres lui donne vingt chevaux de plus et, de nouveau, 10 % de couple supplémentaire. La 280 SL ne se distingue de ses devancières que par de nouveaux enjoliveurs de roues et le patronyme traditionnel sur la malle arrière. Lorsque la production est suspendue en mars 1971, la gamme a donné naissance en huit ans à 48 912 exemplaires. La quadrature du cercle n'a, certes, toujours pas été résolue, mais, quand il est question de succès, les chiffres disent parfois plus que mille mots.

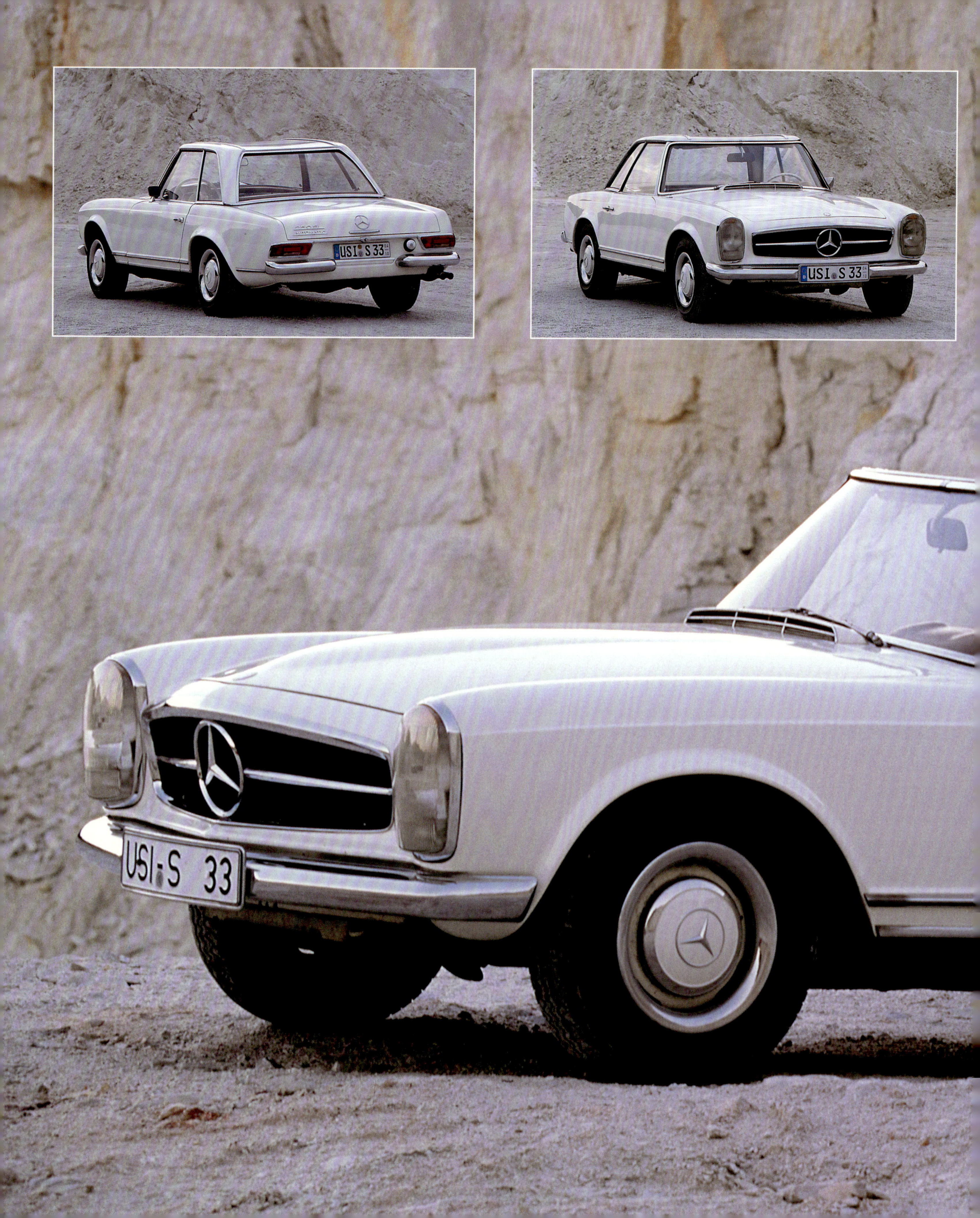
USI-S 33

Mercedes' interior stylists had a field day. The lavish interior trim and comprehensive instrumentation ensured that everything was taken care of. As with the 190 SL, the 230 SL was also available as a coupé with a removable roof and roadster top, or simply with a removable top. To remove the hardtop four levers had to be released before two strong adults lifted the roof off.

Die Innenarchitekten von Mercedes haben es gut mit ihm gemeint: Üppige Innenausstattung und umfassende Instrumentierung sorgen für behagliche Solidität. Wie den 190 SL gibt es den 230 SL als Coupé mit abnehmbarem Dach und Roadsterverdeck oder lediglich mit abnehmbarem Dach. Zum Entfernen des Hardtops müssen vier Hebel gelöst werden, bevor zwei kräftige Erwachsene zupacken können.

Les décorateurs intérieurs de Mercedes n'ont pas regardé à la dépense; équipement pléthorique et tableau de bord très complet donnent une impression de solidité accueillante. Comme la 190 SL, la 230 SL est disponible en coupé à toit escamotable et capote roadster ou seulement avec toit démontable. Pour ôter le *hard-top*, il faut desserrer quatre leviers avant que deux adultes vigoureux puissent l'enlever.

You either love it or hate it. Some regarded this car as a crude lump, a dire apotheosis of the right angle, while others saw it as the prestige car. Whatever, the Mercedes 600, which made its debut at the Frankfurt International Motor Show in September 1963, was an impressive phenomenon, a synthesis of all that had been achieved in automotive engineering to date. Its engine was a first for the company: a v8 injection engine with a capacity of 6.3 liters, developing 250 bhp and a maximum torque of 370 lb-ft. It powered the two-and-a-half-ton vehicle, which could well have been sluggish, to a performance that would not have disgraced a lively sports car of the time. It had a top speed of 127 mph, and 60 mph was reached in ten seconds without the automatic transmission seeming to be unduly troubled. The driver could adjust the hardness of the shock absorbers using a lever on the steering column. Its dual-circuit brake system was assisted by compressed air, and the front disk brakes were operated by two brake calipers each.

All-round comfort was a priority: air suspension, a comprehensive servo system, and the electrically regulated heating and ventilation system represented 1963 state-of-the-art. A sophisticated hydraulic system ensured ride comfort in every conceivable way. It helped to adjust the front seats horizontally and vertically and also changed the tilt of the back rest at the relevant input. It moved the rear seat longitudinally, assisted with the opening and closing of the doors, the trunk lid and the (optional) sunroof, and also raised and lowered the side windows.

The most common model sold was the 10 ft-6 in-wheelbase limousine which seated up to six passengers. There were also three Pullman versions with up to eight seats; one four-door model with facing rear seats, one Pullman limousine with six doors and a rear bench seat together with additional folding seats facing the direction of travel, plus a Landaulet model which normally had four seats and luxury individual seats in which the passengers faced one another. A rarer version of the Landaulet had six doors, the middle ones of which were supplied on request without handles as in the corresponding Pullman versions.

In the 17 years of manufacture up to 16 June 1981, 2677 Mercedes 600 units were built, including 429 Pullmans and 59 Landaulets. Highly customizable, hardly any two were identical. Nevertheless, three models stand out even from this host of individualists. In September 1965 a Pullman-Landaulet joined the Vatican fleet for Pope Paul VI, with four doors, individual rear seats, a raised roof, and a higher floor in the back which levelled out the transmission tunnel. It saw service for over 20 years, under two further Catholic pontiffs, before returning to Untertürkheim in 1985, its mission completed, and where it has been on display in the museum since February 1986. In May 1967 a sporty customer had the Landaulet body crossed with a chassis with the normal wheelbase. At the end of the Eighties this one-off was thoroughly restored

An ihm scheiden sich die Geister: Die einen halten ihn für einen kruden Klotz, die schlimme Apotheose des rechten Winkels, die anderen für das repräsentative Automobil schlechthin. In jedem Fall ist der Mercedes 600, Debütant auf der Frankfurter IAA im September 1963, eine eindrucksvolle Erscheinung, zugleich ein Kompendium all dessen, was zu diesem Zeitpunkt im Autobau erreicht worden ist. Eine hauseigene Premiere: sein V8, ein Einspritzer mit 6,3 Litern Hubraum, 250 PS und einem maximalen Drehmoment von 500 Nm. Er animiert den träge anmutenden Zweieinhalbtonner zu den Fahrleistungen eines gut im Saft stehenden zeitgenössischen Sportwagens: Er läuft 205 Stundenkilometer Spitze, und Tempo 100 ist nach zehn Sekunden erreicht, ohne dass die Automatik den Eindruck erweckt, rüde gefordert zu werden. Sein Chauffeur kann während der Fahrt die Härte der Stoßdämpfer von der Lenksäule aus regeln. Seine Zweikreis-Bremsanlage wird unterstützt durch Luftdruck, und je zwei Bremszangen nehmen die vorderen Scheibenbremsen in den Griff.

Ein Maximum an Komfort allüberall: Luftfederung, ein umfassendes Servosystem sowie die elektrisch regulierte Heizungs- und Lüftungsanlage verkörpern *state of the art* anno 1963. Eine aufwändige Komfort-Hydraulik verästelt ihre Dienstleistungen in alle erdenklichen Richtungen. Sie hilft, die Frontsitze horizontal und vertikal einzurichten, und verändert auf einen diesbezüglichen Impuls hin auch die Neigung der Rücklehne. Sie verstellt die hintere Bank in Längsrichtung, unterstützt das Öffnen und Schließen der Türen, des Kofferraumdeckels und des Schiebedachs (Option) und hebt und senkt die Seitenfenster.

Die größte Verbreitung erfährt die Limousine mit ihren 3200 Millimetern Radstand, in der bis zu sechs Passagiere Platz nehmen können. Dazu gibt es drei Pullman-Versionen mit bis zu acht Sitzen: einen Viertürer, dessen Fondsitze vis-à-vis angeordnet sind, eine Pullman-Limousine, die via sechs Türen betreten werden kann und eine Sitzbank hinten sowie zusätzliches Klappgestühl in Fahrtrichtung anbietet, sowie eine Landaulet-Variante: normalerweise mit vier Sitzen und Fond-Fauteuils, auf denen die Reisenden einander von Angesicht zu Angesicht gegenüberlagern. Im selteneren Falle eröffnen den Zugang zu diesem Landaulet sechs Türen, die mittleren auf Wunsch ohne Griff wie bei den entsprechenden Pullman-Limousinen.

In den 17 Jahren seiner Fertigung bis zum 16. Juni 1981 entstehen 2677 Mercedes 600, davon 429 Pullman und 59 Landaulet. Kaum zwei sind je identisch. Gleichwohl heben sich drei Exemplare selbst von dieser Schar von Individualisten ab. Im September 1965 wird ein Pullman-Landaulet dem Fuhrpark des Vatikans eingegliedert für den damaligen Pontifex maximus Paul VI., mit vier Türen, einzelnen Sesseln hinten, einem erhöhten Dachaufbau und höherem Boden im Fond, der den Kardantunnel nach oben hin abdeckt. Über 20 Jahre tut er Dienst auch

S'il est une voiture qui a divisé les esprits, c'est bien elle: les uns la considèrent comme taillée à la serpe, éloge de l'angle droit poussé au paroxysme, les autres, comme la limousine de représentation par excellence. Quoi qu'il en soit, la Mercedes 600, qui a fait ses débuts à l'IAA de Francfort en septembre 1963, est une voiture impressionnante et, simultanément, le parangon de ce qui est techniquement possible à cette époque en automobile. À commencer par son moteur: un V8 à injection de 6,3 litres de cylindrée, 250 ch et un couple maximum de 500 Nm. Il confère à ce pachyderme de 2,5 tonnes les performances d'une voiture de sport de son temps: elle atteint une vitesse de pointe de 205 km/h et passe de 0 à 100 km/h en dix secondes sans que la boîte automatique ne donne un seul instant l'impression d'avoir été mise à contribution plus qu'il ne convient. Tout en conduisant, son chauffeur peut régler la fermeté des amortisseurs depuis le volant. Son dispositif de freinage à double circuit possède une assistance pneumatique, et deux étriers de freins respectifs s'attaquent à chacun des freins à disque avant.

Le confort atteint un niveau inégalé: la suspension pneumatique, un système d'assistance exhaustif ainsi que le chauffage et la ventilation à régulation électrique incarnent une véritable avancée technique en cette année 1963. Tout aussi sophistiqué, un système hydraulique de grand confort assume toutes les fonctions que l'on puisse imaginer. Il permet de déplacer les sièges avant dans le sens horizontal et vertical et de modifier aussi, sur simple pression d'un bouton, l'inclinaison des dossiers. Il déplace la banquette arrière dans le sens longitudinal, facilite l'ouverture et la fermeture des portières, du couvercle de malle et du toit ouvrant (proposé en option) et, bien évidemment, il lève et baisse les vitres latérales.

C'est avec son empattement de 3200 mm que cette imposante limousine, qui peut alors transporter jusqu'à six passagers, est la plus diffusée. Mais il en existe aussi trois versions Pullman avec jusqu'à huit sièges: une quatre-portes, dont les sièges arrière sont placés en vis-à-vis, une limousine Pullman à laquelle on accède grâce à six portières et qui propose une banquette arrière et des strapontins supplémentaires dans le sens de la marche, ainsi qu'une version Landaulet: normalement avec quatre sièges et fauteuils arrière sur lesquels les voyageurs se font face. Dans quelques cas plus rares, six portières donnent accès à ce Landaulet, celles du centre, sur demande, sans poignée comme pour les limousines Pullman correspondantes.

Aux cours des dix-sept ans de sa fabrication jusqu'au 16 juin 1981, 2677 Mercedes 600 ont été construites, dont 429 Pullman et 59 Landaulet. Il est pratiquement exclu que deux soient identiques. Et pourtant, trois exemplaires se distinguent même de ce groupe d'individualistes. En septembre 1965, un Landaulet Pullman vient rejoindre la flotte du Vatican pour Paul VI, avec quatre portières, des fauteuils individuels à l'arrière, une superstructure de toit surélevée et un plancher plus haut à l'arrière qui

Mercedes-Benz 600   1963

Mercedes-Benz 600 Pullman-Landaulet 1971

and is now in private ownership, as is the prototype of a two-door coupé which is enjoying a well-deserved retirement in the land of its fathers after an intermezzo in the United States.

noch bei zwei weiteren obersten Seelenhirten der katholischen Christenheit und kehrt 1985 nach erfolgreicher Mission nach Untertürkheim zurück, wo er seit dem Februar 1986 im Museum zu besichtigen ist. Im Mai 1967 lässt ein sportlicher Kunde den Landaulet-Aufbau mit einem Chassis kreuzen, das den normalen Radstand aufweist. Ende der achtziger Jahre wird dieses Unikat gründlich restauriert und befindet sich heute in Privatbesitz ebenso wie der Prototyp eines zweitürigen Coupés, das nach einem Intermezzo in den Vereinigten Staaten im Land seiner Väter den verdienten Ruhestand genießt.

dissimule l'arbre de transmission. Pendant plus de vingt ans, il assure encore de bons et loyaux services à deux autres souverains pontifes de l'Église catholique avant, mission accomplie avec succès, de rentrer en 1985 à Untertürkheim où on peut l'admirer au musée depuis février 1986. En mai 1967, un client à la fibre sportive fait croiser une superstructure de Landaulet et un châssis possédant l'empattement normal.

    À la fin des années 1980, ce spécimen unique est restauré minutieusement et se trouve depuis dans une collection privée, au même titre que le prototype d'un coupé deux portes qui jouit d'une retraite bien méritée au pays de ses ancêtres après un bref intermède aux États-Unis.

Living in style. A sophisticated hydraulic system helped to adjust the front seats of the 600 horizontally and vertically, changed the tilt of the back rest, moved the rear seat longitudinally, and assisted with the opening and closing of the doors. This four-door Pullman-Landaulet, half limousine, half cabriolet, belonged to the fleet of the State President of Senegal.

Schöner Wohnen: Eine aufwändige Komfort-Hydraulik hilft, die Frontsitze des 600 horizontal und vertikal einzurichten, verändert die Neigung der Rücklehne, verstellt die hintere Bank in Längsrichtung und unterstützt das Öffnen und Schließen der Türen. Dieses viertürige Pullman-Landaulet, halb Limousine, halb Cabriolet, gehörte zum Fahrzeugpark des Staatspräsidenten von Senegal.

Confort intégral: un système hydraulique sophistiqué assiste à déplacer horizontalement et verticalement les sièges avant de la 600, à changer l'inclinaison des dossiers, à avancer ou reculer la banquette arrière et à ouvrir et fermer les portières. Ce Landaulet Pullman à quatre portes – semi-limousine, semi-cabriolet – a appartenu à la flotte du président de la république du Sénégal.

While Mercedes made a passing nod to contemporary taste with the "Fin" car, the new version of the s-Class, introduced in August 1965, made no such concession. Paul Bracq was the designer of this series, and the 250 s, 250 se, and 300 se had a restrained, timeless quality. The figures for the two smaller-engined models tell their story: their six-cylinder engines were of 2.5 liters, derived from the earlier 2.2-liter engines with a longer stroke and a larger bore. The injectors were fed by Bosch six-stage pumps.

The air suspension system of the 300 se was gone, and it only reappeared in the long-wheelbase 300 sel version from March 1966 onwards; its wheelbase was increased by 4 in to 9 ft 4 in. Like the other two members of the w108 model family, a hydropneumatic compensating spring on the rear axle ensured a constant ride level under changing loads and stresses. The 300 sel was given the in-house designation of w109, denoting its own series. Two cars, a Pullman and a Landaulet, graced the Vatican fleet which had long been a satisfied Mercedes customer, without any undue concern for Italian vanity.

The start of 1968 saw a changing of the guard with the introduction of the 280 s and the 280 se, in accordance with the time-honored maxim that there is only one thing better than a large engine, and that is an even larger engine. The carburetor engine now delivered 140 bhp, and the injection model 160 bhp, each 10 bhp more than previously, while the 170 bhp engine of the 280 sl replaced the expensive-to-manufacture 3-liter alloy engines in the 300 sel from January 1968 onwards. The series reached its zenith in March of the same year with the 300 sel 6.3. Connoisseurs guessed what was powering this car—the v8 from the luxury 600, coupled with its automatic 4-speed transmission. Despite its discreet appearance, this sedan could reach 137 mph. Eight seconds was all it took for the speedometer needle to pass 60 mph, and the 27.7-gal tank had to splash out nine gallons every 100 miles (11.2 mpg). Many of its 6526 owners took extra pleasure in helping this athlete of the automotive world take to the road like a wolf in sheep's clothing by completely removing any indications of its identity from the trunk, or by fitting misleading badges instead such as that for the 280 s.

From the autumn of 1969 onwards the 300 sel bore the suffix 3.5 on the trunk, an indication that a 3.5-liter v8 delivering 200 bhp had taken up residence. This powerplant, which was also the pilot for a new generation of engine, was available for the 280 se too from March 1971 and became the standard engine in the 280 sel as well as in the coupé and cabriolet. A further v8 of 4.5 liters was destined solely for the American market from May 1971 onwards, under the hoods of the 280 se and sel, and of the 300 sel.

The type designations had long since taken on a life of their own. Only the 280 s badge on the trunk lid of the

Mercedes-Benz S-Klasse 1965

Mercedes-Benz 300 SEL 3.5 1971

carburetor version, which survived all these metamorphoses until 1972, gave any reliable information about its engine size.

Maschine gibt nur noch die Aufschrift 280 s auf dem Kofferraumdeckel der Vergaser-Variante, die all diese Metamorphosen bis 1972 überdauert.

Il y a des lustres que les dénominations de série ont perdu toute signification véritable. Seule la mention 280 s sur le couvercle de malle de la version à carburateur dit encore la vérité quant à la cylindrée de son moteur, version qui survivra à toutes ces métamorphoses jusqu'en 1972.

The 3.5-liter V8 filled the entire engine compartment. The dashboard sported circular instruments which superseded the vertical arrangement that was fashionable for a time.

Eingebettet in den Kreis seiner Domestiken nimmt der V8 von 3,5 Litern den gesamten Motorraum in Anspruch. In der Armaturentafel haben Rundinstrumente das eine Zeitlang modische Vertikal-Arrangement abgelöst.

Le V8 de 3,5 litres occupe la totalité du compartiment moteur. Sur le tableau de bord, les instruments circulaires ont remplacé leurs homologues verticaux qui n'auront été à la mode que très peu de temps.

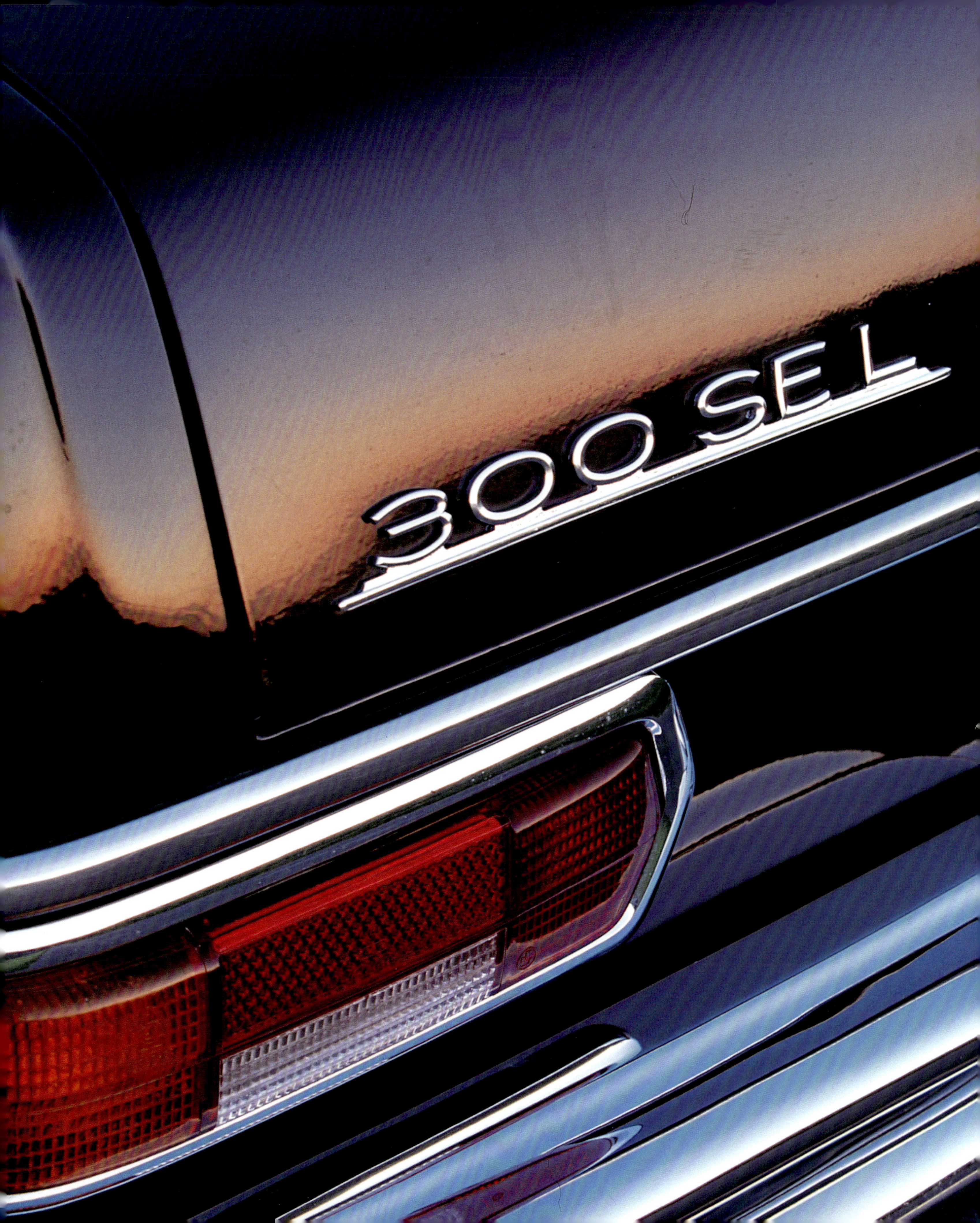
300 SEL

Although production of the new generation of mid-range Mercedes began in 1967, they were popularly known as the /8 models after the year of their first public appearance. Yet there was nothing remotely revolutionary about the Daimler-Benz /8 models apart from the chaotic series of abbreviations that was prodigally applied to them over the years. A tiny palace revolution was caused simply by their diagonal swing axle which improved drive performance without making any concessions in terms of comfort.

Introduced in January 1968, the series initially encompassed six types from the 200 D with 55 bhp up to the 250 with a six-cylinder carburetor engine delivering 130 bhp. In November of that year the series was crowned by the two coupés, the 250 C and 250 CE. And this really was an innovation, as this was the first time that this body variant had been available in a mid-range series. It immediately generated lively interest, although to a degree less car was being offered for more money, for example, it was identical to the sedans up to the a-pillar, with a flatter windshield and a 1¾-in-lower roof section, frameless and fully retractable side windows, and two large doors. The coupés from this series sold 67,048 units up to 1976. Another subsidiary line stands out because of the exclusivity of its lower sales figures: around 10,000 units were sold of models 220 D, 230, 240 D, and 230/6 with three rows of seats and eight places on a chassis which had been stretched by 2 ft 1½ in, a variant greatly welcomed by, for example, taxi companies and airlines.

In April 1972 the range was extended to include types 280 and 280 E and the corresponding coupés. Their new six-cylinder engines with double overhead camshafts delivered 160 bhp in the carburetor version and 185 bhp as injection engines, identifiable by the double bumpers at the front like the 250, and by rear bumpers that wrapped round as far as the wheel arches, as well as by twin muffler end pipes. At the same time the 250 and 250 C were fitted with the older 2.8-liter engine from the 280 s, reduced by 10 bhp to 130 bhp. The facelift that the series underwent in September 1973 was primarily concerned with safety considerations, involving movable external mirrors that could be adjusted from inside the car, trims on the a-pillars which kept dirt off the side windows, grooved tail lights, and a gutter above the rear screen. Headrests, inertia-reel belts, and a four-spoke safety steering wheel had been standard equipment for six months.

The cosmetic revamps undertaken at the same time as those in the s-Class did not always signal actual progress; for example the side vent windows had been discontinued or the hood had become lower and wider. Double bumpers were now a thing of the past, though to be honest they had always been a cosmetically effective and costly extra. At the same time two new four-cylinder cars were available, the 240 D as the largest diesel-engined model, and the 230/4 which replaced the 220. The 4 after the slash served to prevent confusion with the previous 230, a

Mercedes-Benz /8 1967

Mercedes-Benz 250C 1968

six-cylinder, which continued to be sold as the 230/6. In July 1974 there was another addition to the family in the form of the 240 D 3.0, a five-cylinder 3-liter engine delivering 80 bhp. The new generation was now turning into the older generation, but although the successors, type W123, had already been unveiled in January 1976, these predecessors proved hardy—and most continued to be built until the end of the year.

240 D als hubraumstärkster Diesel und der 230/4, der den 220 ersetzt. Die Vier hinter dem Schrägstrich dient dazu, Verwechslungen mit dem früheren 230 vorzubeugen, einem Sechszylinder, der als 230/6 weiterhin im Angebot bleibt. Im Juli 1974 bekommt die Modellfamilie noch einmal Zuwachs in Gestalt des 240 D 3.0, eines Fünfzylinders mit drei Litern und 80 PS. Da ist die neue Generation schon fast die alte Generation. Doch obwohl im Januar 1976 bereits die Nachfolger W123 vorgestellt werden, erweisen sich die Vorgänger als zählebig – die meisten werden noch bis Ende jenes Jahres weitergebaut.

diesel ayant la plus forte cylindrée, et le 230/4 qui remplace le 220. Le 4 derrière la barre oblique a pour but d'éliminer toute confusion avec l'ancien 230, un six-cylindres qui reste toujours au programme en tant que 230/6. En juillet 1974, la famille s'enrichit encore avec un 240 D 3.0, un cinq-cylindres de 3 litres développant 80 ch. Mais la nouvelle génération se confond presque déjà avec l'ancienne. En effet, bien que sa remplaçante la W123 ait déjà été présentée en janvier 1976, les anciens modèles semblent résister puisque la plupart sont encore construits jusqu'à la fin de cette année-là.

Mercedes-Benz /8 1967

While the engines of the /8 models already bore
the patina of distinguished age, the diagonal swing-
axle represented a minor palace revolution.

Während die Triebwerke der Strich-Acht-Modelle bereits mit
der Patina ehrwürdigen Alters behaftet sind, hat man mit ihrer
Diagonal-Pendelachse eine winzige Palastrevolte angezettelt.

Alors que les moteurs des modèles /8 arborent d'ores et
déjà la patine d'un âge vénérable, leur essieu brisé en
diagonale a déclenché une minuscule révolution de palais.

The launch of the 350 SL in April 1971 marked the beginning of the almost never-ending story of the 107 series. The fact that this spanned 18 years and a total of 237,387 cars was convincing evidence of the success of the design, and of the concept of a powerful and comfortable two-seater touring sports car with a convertible roadster top or a removable hardtop. The new car had only the abbreviation SL in common with the rugged gullwing coupé of earlier years, and even that was deceptive. It was nowhere near as sporty and at 3439 lbs it was certainly not light. After all, luxury and comprehensive protection had to be paid for in terms of weight.

Quite a number of the components again came from other series, for example the suspension from the /8 sedans, or the V8 from the 280 SE 3.5. The 350 SL was a safe car. The fuel tank was now in a protected position above the rear axle. The padded dashboard with its flexibly mounted or recessed switches and levers were safety features as was the four-spoke steering wheel with its baffle and wide cushioned pad. Cleverly designed wind deflector profiles on the A-pillars kept the side windows clear in rain. The turn-signal lights were wrapped around into the fenders and highly visible, while the tail lights were large and their ribbed profile kept them clear of dirt. The Paris Salon in the autumn of 1971 saw the launch of the stylistically related 350 SLC, intended to an extent as a family car, a four-seater coupé with a fixed roof and a 14-in-longer wheelbase. From April 1973 onwards both cars were available with a 4.5-liter V8, or, from July 1974 onwards in the shadow of the oil crisis, with a 2.8-liter six-cylinder with double overhead camshafts. The 280 SL could be recognized by its narrower tires, and the 450 SL by a front spoiler which also directed more air to the radiator. None was restrained in its drinking habits. The change to Bosch's mechanical K-Jetronic system at the beginning of 1975, which also entailed a slight drop in performance, made little change in this respect. At the same time a solid-state transistorized ignition system and a hydraulic compensator for valve play were introduced. The updated SL family was presented in Geneva in March 1980 with obvious influences in the interior deriving from the S-Class. The 3-speed converter automatic transmission had now given way to a 4-speed variant, while the 280 SL retained a 5-speed manual gearbox, standard equipment since 1981.

The engine of the 450 SLC 5.0 of September 1977 also found its way into the 500 SL from March 1980 onwards. The "Last Post" was also played for the 350 SL, which was replaced by the 380 SL, like its sister model with an alloy hood and a discreet front spoiler. The unveiling of the 380 SEC and 500 SEC coupés at the 1981 Frankfurt International Motor Show meant the end of the road for the SLC. The SL remained, however, with regular updates. In the autumn of 1985 a thoroughly revamped version was even exhibited again at the Frankfurt show. The

Mercedes-Benz SL & SLC   1971

Mercedes-Benz 500 SL 1986

2.8-liter engine was replaced by a 3-liter six-cylinder. This then ushered in the renaissance of a legend—the 300 SL— though in name only. The 420 SL's badge tacitly indicated that the previous 3.8-liter engine had been rebored to 4.2 liters. Modifications had been made to the 5-liter powerplant of the 500 SL, which developed 245 bhp with its Bosch KE-Jetronic electromechanical injection system and electronic ignition (compared with the previous 240 bhp). The 560 SL, whose potential was reduced to a mere 227 bhp when trimmed by the harsh regime of emissions legislation in some countries, was intended exclusively for export. Ultimately, SL no longer meant quite what it had in the early years. The rampant growth in engine size in the meantime had revealed one simple fact: even in the latter stages of the economic miracle, lots of people were still doing very well.

gezeigt. Wachablösung gibt es für den 2,8-Liter: einen Dreiliter-Sechszylinder. Damit kommt es zugleich zur Renaissance einer Legende, aber nur, was den Namen anbelangt: 300 SL. Das Sigel 420 SL verrät implizit, dass der bisherige 3,8-Liter auf 4,2 Liter aufgebohrt wurde. Modifiziert worden ist das 5-Liter-Triebwerk des 500 SL, das mit der elektronisch-mechanischen Einspritzanlage Bosch KE-Jetronic und elektronischer Zündung 245 PS leistet (bisher 240). Nur für den Export bestimmt ist der 560 SL, dessen Potential im scharfen Licht der Emissionsgesetzgebung einiger Länder auf lediglich 227 PS zusammenschmilzt. Am Ende heißt kein SL mehr so wie in den frühen Jahren. Das Wuchern der Hubräume in der Zwischenzeit verrät vor allem eines: Auch in der Spätphase des Wirtschaftswunders geht es noch sehr vielen Leuten sehr gut.

méritée et est remplacé par un six-cylindres de 3 litres. Cela pourrait faire croire à la renaissance d'une légende, mais ce n'est vrai que pour le nom: 300 SL. Le sigle 420 SL induit que l'ancien 3,8 litres a vu sa cylindrée majorée à 4,2 litres. Le 5 litres de la 500 SL bénéficie lui aussi de modifications puisqu'il reçoit l'injection électronique mécanique Bosch KE-Jetronic et un allumage électronique qui lui permet de développer désormais 245 ch contre 240 auparavant. La 560 SL est réservée aux exportations, mais sa puissance retombe à 227 ch par suite des sévères législations en matière d'écologie de certains pays. À la fin, aucune SL n'a plus le même nom que quelques années auparavant. L'inflation des cylindrées survenue entretemps prouve surtout une chose: même durant la phase ultime du miracle économique, il y a encore énormément de gens qui n'ont pas le moindre souci financier.

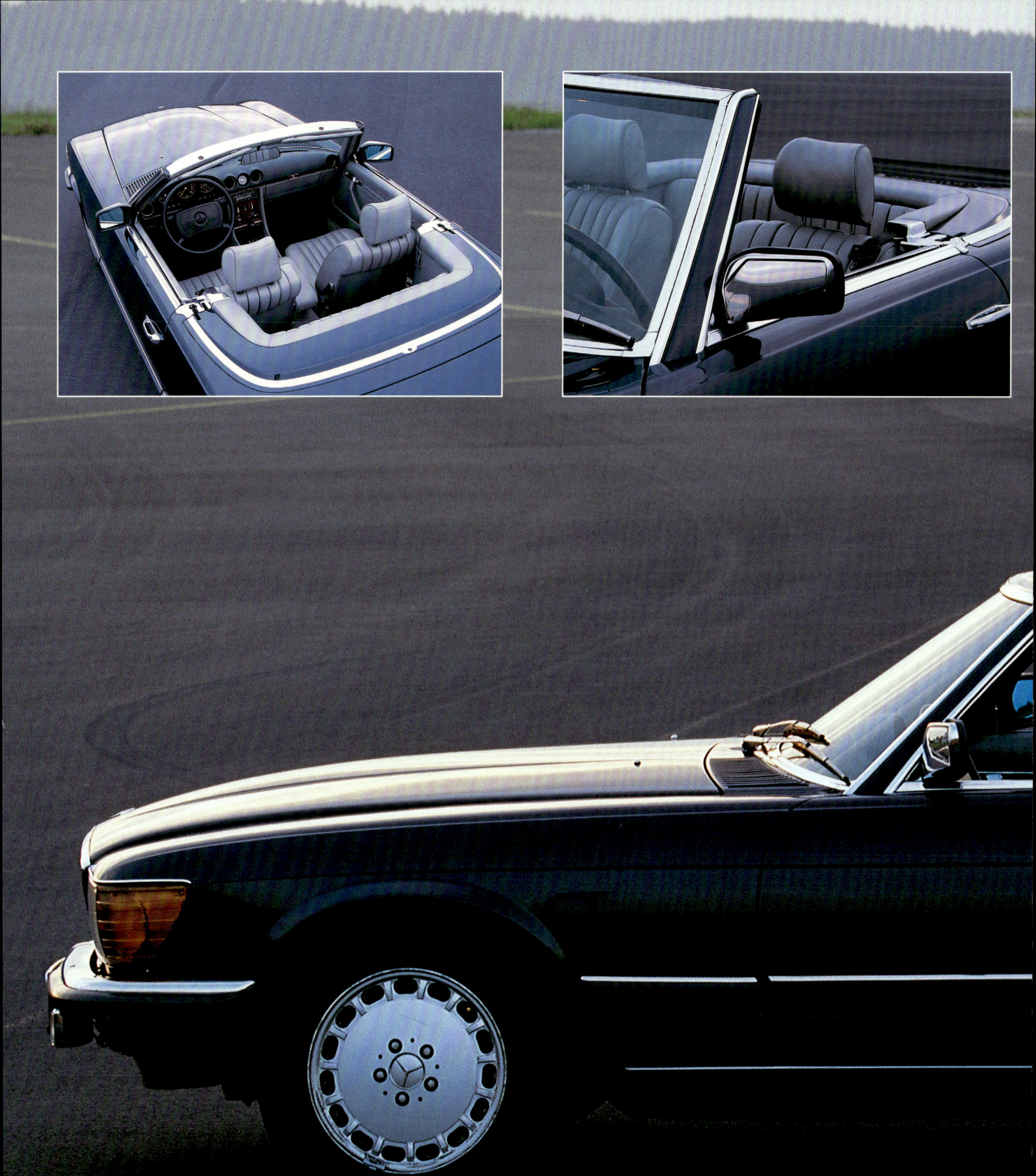

The series' comprehensive safety features included a dashboard on which you could not hurt yourself, together with a steering wheel with a baffle and cushioned pad. The turn signals and light units were ribbed to keep them clear of dirt. The roadster top disappeared completely under a metal cover. The rubber lip on the trunk was not to everyone's taste.

Zum umfassenden Sicherheitskonzept der Baureihe gehört ein Armaturenbrett, an dem man sich nicht wehtun kann, sowie das Lenkrad mit Pralltopf und Polsterplatte. Blinker und Leuchteneinheiten sind geriffelt, damit Schmutz von ihnen ferngehalten wird. Das Verdeck des Roadsters verschwindet zur Gänze unter einem metallenen Deckel. Die Gummilippe am Heck indessen trifft nicht jedermanns Geschmack.

Le concept de sécurité intégrale de la gamme comporte un tableau de bord parfaitement sécurisé ainsi qu'un volant à moyeu rembourré. Clignotants et feux arrière sont rainurés pour être moins sensibles à la saleté. La capote du roadster disparaît totalement sous un couvercle métallique. L'aileron arrière en caoutchouc n'est pas du goût de tous.

The SLC coupé was launched in October 1971 as a sister model to the SL. Its extended wheelbase offered space for a growing family of four. The 280 SLC owed its existence to the 1973 oil crisis. It proved a good buy, as its six-cylinder engine delivered the same performance as the 3.5-liter V8 but with lower fuel consumption.

Das Coupé SLC wird im Oktober 1971 als Schwestermodell zum SL herausgebracht und bietet über einem verlängerten Radstand Platz für eine knospende Familie von vier Köpfen. Der 280 SLC verdankt seine Existenz der Ölkrise von 1973. Der Käufer macht einen guten Fang: Bei geringerem Verbrauch schwingt sich sein Sechszylinder zu den gleichen Fahrleistungen auf wie der V8 von 3,5 Litern.

Le coupé SLC vient épauler son jumeau le cabriolet en octobre 1971. Grâce à un empattement allongé, il offre suffisamment de place pour une famille de quatre personnes. La 280 SLC doit sa naissance à la crise pétrolière de 1973. L'acheteur fait une bonne affaire : son six-cylindres affiche les mêmes performances que le V8 de 3,5 litres, tout en consommant moins.

Mercedes-Benz SL & SLC 1971

The name had long since been accepted in common parlance, and then it was finally adopted by the manufacturer too; the W116 series officially became known as the S-Class, launched in September 1972. The first models were the 280 S, 280 SE, and 350 SE. These were followed in March 1973 by the 450 SE and the 450 SEL which offered its rear passengers more space because of the 4 in increase in the wheelbase to 9 ft 9 in. Further long-wheelbase versions, which were popular as chauffeur-driven and company cars, appeared in November (350 SEL) and in April 1974 (280 SEL).

The front suspension had been inspired by the C111: double wishbones with a roll radius of 0 and an anti-dive mechanism. At the rear, tried-and-tested technology from the /8 sedans and the 350 SL—the tilted-shaft axle—was re-used. The standard set by the latter model was also applied to safety features too, both in detail and in overall design. The safety cage provided even greater protection for the occupants in the event of an accident, and the front and rear sections were even better at absorbing the kinetic energy of a collision. The 25½-gallon fuel tank was located above the rear axle. Wind deflectors on the A-pillars kept the side windows clear of water which might otherwise impair vision. The turn-signal lights wrapped round into the fenders, and the tail lights were grooved as a protection against soiling. The series again found its finest expression in a real supercar, the 450 SEL 6.9, unveiled in May, and produced from September 1975 onwards.

The engine, almost seven liters in displacement, developed 286 bhp. Even more impressive than its performance—top speed 140 mph, 0–62 mph in 7.4 seconds—was the manner in which the top Mercedes of its time achieved this with supreme coolness. Its 3-speed automatic transmission and pneumatic springing with hydraulic level control also contributed to this effect. Central locking, air-conditioning, and headlight washers all came as standard. 7380 owners of the 450 SEL 6.9 appreciated all these features, even though at 73,100 marks in March 1977 it cost twice as much as a 350 SE.

Towards the end of 1975 the electronic fuel supply of the injection versions was replaced by the mechanical K-Jetronic system. At the same time both V8 engines had a solid-state transistorized ignition system and hydraulic compensator for valve play fitted. Slight deteriorations in performance were cancelled out in the next two years.

Another new arrival joined the family in May 1978, and an innovation at that—the 300 SD was the first S-Class diesel model. The powerplant was familiar from the 240 D 3.0 and the 300 D, a 3-liter five-cylinder. Supercharged by a turbocharger, it reached the unfamiliar territory of 115 bhp, though it did have to shift a dry vehicle weight of 4000 lbs. However, only residents of Canada and the United States were able to enjoy these hybrids of luxury and economy. A tactical move was behind this; it was intended that the 300 SD should help to reduce fleet fuel consumption, a figure introduced by the Carter administration. The

Mercedes-Benz S-Klasse   1972

Mercedes-Benz 350 SEL 1979

average consumption of all a manufacturer's models was assessed as part of the authorization process for driving on American roads, and Mercedes had a little catching-up to do. Of the 473,035 cars of the W116 series, 28,634 were 300 SDs, including the last one to roll off the assembly line in Sindelfingen in September 1980.

Flottenverbrauch zu senken, eine Größe, die die Carter-Administration eingeführt hat: Der Durchschnitts-Konsum aller Modelle eines Herstellers ist Bestandteil ihrer Legitimation auf amerikanischen Straßen, und da gibt es bei Mercedes einigen Nachholbedarf. Immerhin sind 28 634 der 473 035 Exemplare der Serie W116 vom Typ 300 SD, auch der letzte, der im September 1980 in Sindelfingen vom Band rollt.

inhabituel une puissance de 115 ch qui sont bien nécessaires quand on sait que la voiture, à elle seule, accuse un poids de 1815 kg. Seuls les Canadiens et les citoyens des États-Unis profitent toutefois de cette symbiose de luxe et de sobriété. La stratégie qui se dissimule derrière cette décision est de bon aloi. La 300 SD a, en effet, pour but de diminuer une allègre consommation, suivant un paramètre introduit par l'administration Carter: la consommation moyenne de tous les modèles d'un constructeur conditionne son homologation pour circuler aux États-Unis, et, dans ce domaine, Mercedes a fort à faire. Des 473 035 exemplaires de la série W116, 28 634 appartiennent au type 300 SD, dont la dernière qui sort de chaîne à Sindelfingen en septembre 1980.

The 350 SEL, clothed in its smooth, solid lines, was one of the best cars of its era for performance, comfort, quality, and durability. The cockpit also bore witness to the notion of unobtrusive objectivity where only function determined form. The wheelbase, rear foot well and rear doors were four inches longer than in the standard version. It was decided to change the configuration of the lights from vertical to horizontal. The ribbed design of the tail lights prevented dirt from sticking to them.

Von ruhiger und gediegener Linienführung, zählt der 350 SEL zu den besten Autos seiner Zeit hinsichtlich Leistung, Komfort, Qualität und Langlebigkeit. Auch das Cockpit zeugt von jener unaufgeregten Sachlichkeit, bei der allein der Zweck die Formen bestimmt. Radstand, hinterer Sitzraum und hintere Türen sind zehn Zentimeter länger als bei der Normalversion. Bei der Anordnung der Lampen ist man von der Vertikalen zur Horizontalen übergegangen. Die Verrippung der hinteren Leuchten wirkt ihrer Verschmutzung entgegen.

La 350 SEL aux lignes pures, mais élégantes est l'une des meilleures voitures de son temps pour la puissance, le confort, la qualité et la longévité. Le tableau de bord affiche lui aussi cette sobriété reposante en vertu de laquelle seule la fonction dicte les formes. L'empattement, l'espace et les portières arrière mesurent dix centimètres de plus que dans la version normale. Pour l'agencement des phares, on a abandonné la verticale pour l'horizontale. Les rainures des optiques arrière maintiennent les feux plus propres.

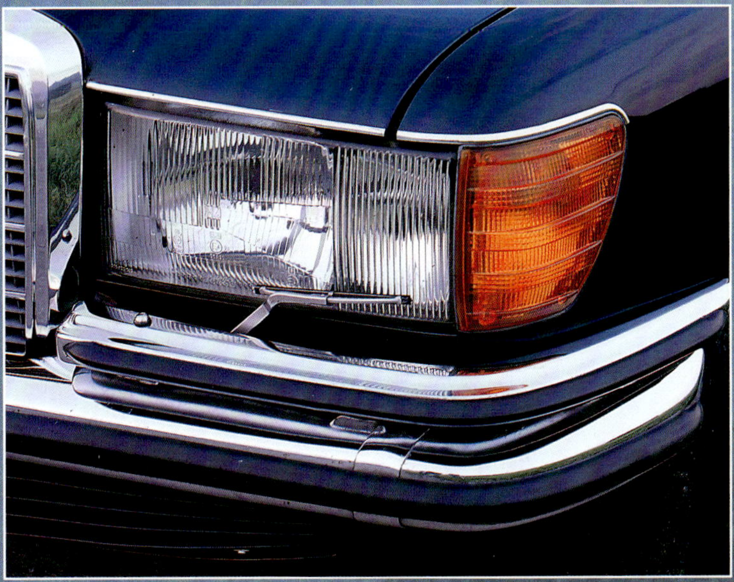
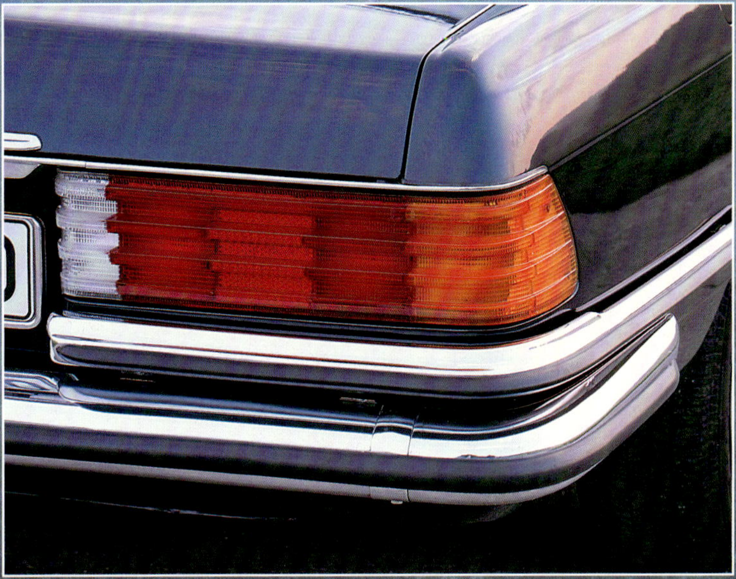
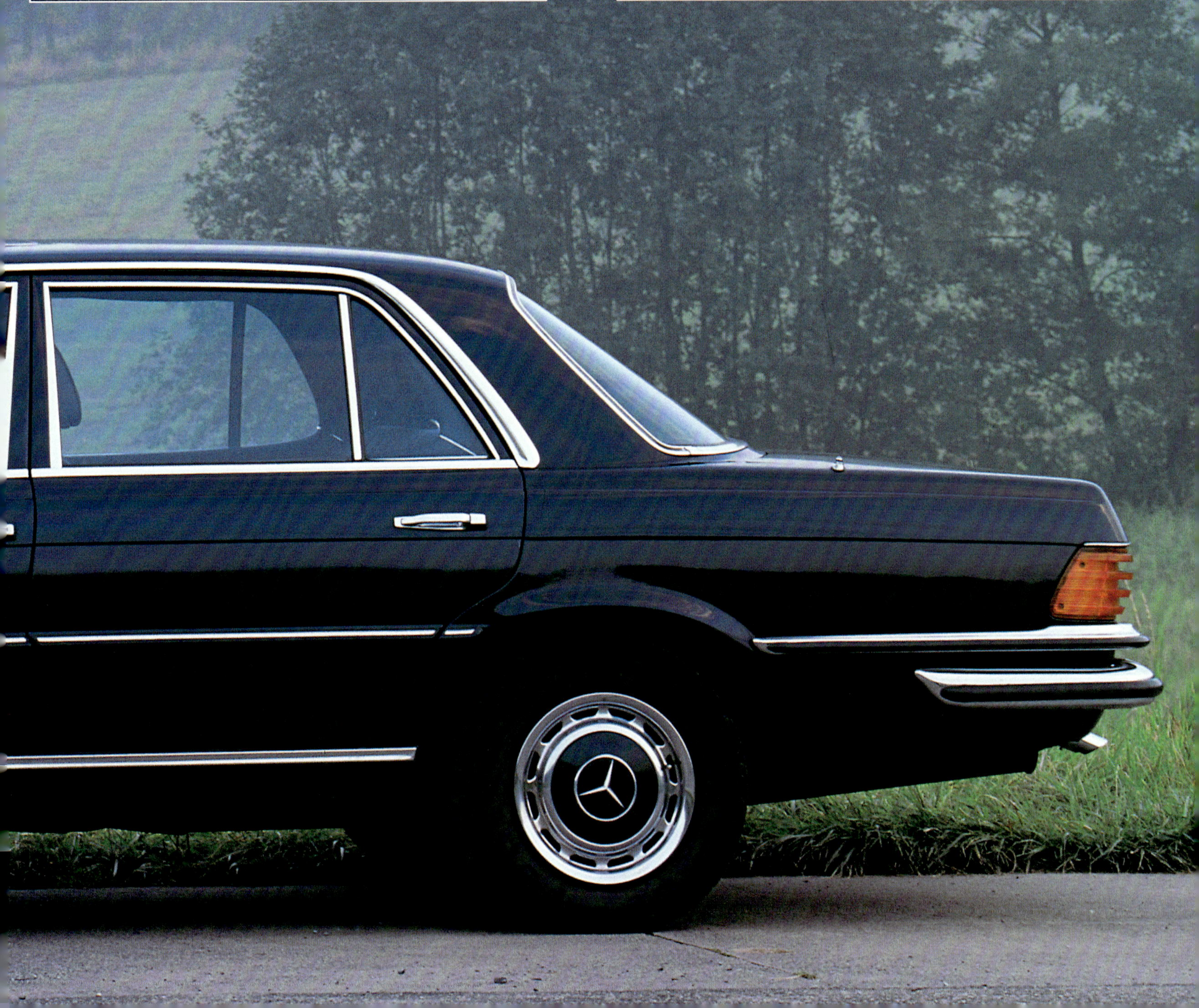

The transition was smooth—the /8 sedans were still rolling off the production line when the w123 series was introduced in January 1976, again a large family ranging from the rather rough-sounding 55 bhp 200 D to the powerful 280 E delivering 185 bhp. This was also mirrored by the price range, from 18,900 to 26,900 marks. The round lights, a main headlight located side-by-side with a small halogen light behind a common diffuser screen, were the most conspicuous external feature. The top-of-the-range models, the 280 and 280 E, were fitted with rectangular halogen wide-band headlights which were standard for the entire range from September 1982 onwards. The traditional sub-frame was dropped since the front wheels were now suspended from double wishbones with a roll radius of 0.

Furthermore, the Mercedes motto of "Safety First," which had been elevated to the status of a creed, was very much in evidence. Everyone is equal when faced with the trauma of a motor accident, and so passengers in Mercedes mid-range cars were not denied the safety features of the s and sL models. The passenger cage with its rigid roof frame, high-strength pillars, and reinforced doors had become even more stable, while the front and tail ends absorbed impacts more willingly thanks to "controlled deformability" as it was so inelegantly termed in the publicity literature. The safety steering column was an innovative feature. The steering linkage and steering column jacket were connected through a corrugated sleeve which reduced the risk of the steering column being thrust like a spear into the car interior in the event of an accident.

Initially there was little news to report in terms of the engines, except that the 250 was using a freshly developed 2.5-liter six-cylinder instead of the elderly 2.8 liters of previously. 1977 saw the range of bodies expand with three new types. There was the coupé launched in Geneva in March as the 230 C, 280 C, and 280 CE. There was the stretched version of the 240, 240 D, and 250 with three rows of seats, and a 25-in-longer wheelbase, unveiled in August. And there was the T-Sedan, a refined Mercedes term for a refined station wagon, first shown at the Frankfurt International Motor Show in September. The following three years saw the engines progressively beefed up: 185 bhp (previously 177 bhp) for the 280 E in April 1978, 72 bhp (originally 65 bhp) for the 240 D in August 1978, 60 bhp (previously 55 bhp) for the 200 D in February 1979. In June 1980 the series was offered with three new engines. There was a 5-cylinder, three-liter diesel with an exhaust-driven turbocharger available initially only in the wagon, though later also fitted to the sedan and coupé for export. There was a new 2-liter carburetor engine developing 109 bhp, to replace the earlier engines of the same size, and a corresponding 2.3-liter injection model delivering 136 bhp which was slightly canted to reduce the overall height. The 280 disappeared from the range in July 1981, as the 220 D had before it in February 1979.

Mercedes-Benz 200 D–280 CE 1976

Mercedes-Benz 280 E 1983

In profile there was little to distinguish the sedans of the 123 series from those of the earlier /8 generation. It was the details that made them better cars.

In September 1982 all the models were fitted with new wind deflectors on the A-pillars and power steering became standard, while ABS and a driver's airbag were available as options. When the W123 took its final bow in November 1985, 2,696,915 cars had left the factory in Sindelfingen, of which 2,375,440 had been sedans. The 240 D, whose purchase price brought with it a life expectation of almost biblical proportions, alone sold 454,679 units.

Im Profil unterscheiden sich die Limousinen der Baureihe 123 wenig von denen der Strich-Acht-Generation zuvor. Es sind die Details, die sie zu besseren Autos machen.

Im September 1982 erhalten alle Modelle neue Windleitprofile an den A-Säulen, und die Servolenkung wird der Grundausstattung zugeschlagen, während als Option ABS und Airbag auf der Fahrerseite zu haben sind. Als der W123 im November 1985 das Zeitliche segnet, haben 2 696 915 Fahrzeuge die Werkshallen in Sindelfingen verlassen, davon 2 375 440 Limousinen. Der 240 D allein hat es auf eine Population von 454 679 gebracht, wobei eine geradezu alttestamentarische Lebenserwartung im Kaufpreis mit einbegriffen ist.

Vues de profil, les berlines de la série 123 ne se distinguent guère de la génération /8 précédente. Ce sont des détails qui en font les meilleures voitures.

économiser de la hauteur. En juillet 1981, la 280 disparaît du programme, comme déjà la 220 D en février 1979.

En septembre 1982, tous les modèles reçoivent de nouveaux profilés déflecteurs sur les montants de pare-brise et la direction assistée fait désormais partie de l'équipement de série alors que l'ABS et le coussin gonflable côté conducteur sont proposés en option. Lorsque la W123 est retirée du marché en novembre 1985, 2 696 915 exemplaires sont sortis des chaînes de Sindelfingen, dont 2 375 440 berlines. À elle seule, la 240 D a été produite à 454 679 exemplaires avec une espérance de vie absolument canonique comprise dans le prix d'achat.

More function than form, with the emphasis on unobtrusiveness. In addition the company-specific sales argument that solidness and a long service life were included in the price. The round headlights located horizontally behind common diffuser lenses were the most striking feature. However, the top-of-the-range models, the 280 and 280 E, were fitted with rectangular halogen wide-band headlights.

Mehr sein als scheinen: Formen und Funktionsträger fern jeglicher Aufdringlichkeit. Dazu das firmenspezifische Verkaufsargument, dass Solidität und ein langes Autoleben im Preis inbegriffen sind. Auffälligstes Merkmal sind die waagerecht hinter gemeinsamen Streuscheiben untergebrachten runden Lichtquellen. Die Top-Typen 280 und 280 E sind allerdings mit rechteckigen Halogen-Breitbandscheinwerfern ausgerüstet.

Être, plus que paraître: des formes et fonctions aux antipodes de l'arrogance. Avec, en prime, l'argument commercial, spécifique à la marque, que solidité et longévité sont comprises dans le prix de la voiture. Principal signe distinctif: les phares ronds placés verticalement derrière une plaque de diffusion unique. Les modèles haut de gamme, 280 et 280 E, possèdent quant à eux des phares à iode rectangulaires.

217

While the coupés of the '68 generation looked like sedans with part of the roof sliced off, the new C models stood out as a result of their original, balanced design.

Während die Coupés der Achtundsechziger-Generation wie Limousinen ausschauen, aus denen man ein Teil ihres Dachs tranchiert hat, bestechen die neuen C-Modelle durch eine eigenständige, ausgewogene Form.

Contrairement aux coupés de la génération de 1968, qui ressemblaient à des berlines auxquelles on aurait ôté une partie du toit, les nouveaux modèles C se distinguent par des lignes personnelles et une forme équilibrée.

Mercedes-Benz 200 D–280 CE   1976

Mercedes-Benz 200 D–280 CE   1976

The station wagon, the T model, built in the Bremen factory from April 1978 onwards, combined an impressive appearance, robust practicality, and the prestige of the star marque.

In der Kombilimousine T, ab April 1978 im Werk Bremen hergestellt, verbinden sich Ansehnlichkeit, robuste Praktikabilität und das Prestige der Marke mit dem Stern.

Les breaks de la série T, fabriqués à partir d'avril 1978 à Brême, combinent l'élégance, un caractère robuste et pratique, et le prestige de la marque à l'étoile.

In many respects the new s-Class, premièred at the Frankfurt International Motor Show in September 1979, marked a watershed between the past and the future in its continued use of mature technology and its cautious acceptance of engineering innovations. Nevertheless, the w126 was a success, and the 818,036 units sold in 12 years have made it the bestselling large Mercedes to date.

The term s-Class again covered a broad spectrum. Initially there were seven models with four engines, ranging from the 280 s (six cylinders, carburetor, 156 bhp) to the 500SEL (v8, injection, 240 bhp). As was by now a standard feature, two variants were available, a normal and a stretched version with its wheelbase extended by 5½ in. Again it was the passengers in the rear who benefited, where wider doors were also provided. The designers had to meet three main specifications: the new car should be more comfortable, safer, and more economical. s-Class comfort has long been the benchmark worldwide. As far as safety was concerned too, this series was the result of state-of-the-art research and its passengers would survive unscathed even an offset crash at a speed of 34 mph.

There just remained the third specification: economy. Ten per cent lower fuel consumption was promised. The bodies were optimized in the wind tunnel, excess pounds were trimmed off wherever possible, for example by the use of plastics and alloy. These were the materials used for the crankcases of the two eight-cylinders, the 5-liter engine that had previously been used in the 450 SLC 5.0 and the 3.8-liter engine based on the previous 3.5-liter unit. The 2.8-liter six-cylinder engine with carburetor or injection system was unchanged for the moment.

The sedans on display at the 1981 Frankfurt International Motor Show shared the platform with a pleasingly shaped coupé which was only available with an eight-cylinder engine, which had again been made more economical as part of the Mercedes-Benz energy initiative for reducing consumption and pollution. It was again in Frankfurt, this time in September 1985, that a completely revamped s-Class was unveiled. Changes started with the external appearance, with lower skirts to exert more downforce at the front and better channeling of the air at the back, together with smooth side protection strips. The engines were new or substantially modified. Two six-cylinder injection engines of 2.6 and 3 liters were borrowed from the mid-range w124 to replace the 2.8-liter engine which had done such sterling service. The 3.8-liter engine was rebored to 4.2 liters. The 5-liter engine now with electronic ignition and the electromechanical Bosch Jetronic system now delivered 245 bhp, five more than at its most powerful previously. The first appearance of the designations 560 SEL and SEC attest to the existence of a new v8 with a capacity of 5.6 liters and 272 bhp, or 300 bhp at a higher compression.

Since unleaded gasoline could not be obtained everywhere, interim solutions were adopted to provide a flexible response. It was not until September 1986 that all

In vieler Hinsicht steht die neue s-Klasse, Premiere auf der IAA zu Frankfurt im September 1979, auf der Nahtstelle zwischen gestern und morgen im Rückgriff auf Gestandenes und im behutsamen Zugriff auf technisches Neuland. Gleichwohl ist der w126 ein Erfolgstyp und erweist sich in zwölf Jahren mit 818 036 Exemplaren als der auflagenstärkste große Mercedes bislang.

Wieder deckt der Begriff s-Klasse ein breites Spektrum ab: Am Anfang gibt es sieben Modelle mit vier Motoren, zwischen dem 280 s (sechs Zylinder, Vergaser, 156 PS) und dem 500 SEL (v8, Einspritzer, 240 PS). Wie längst eingespielt, stehen zwei Varianten zur Verfügung, eine Normal- und eine Langversion mit 140 mm mehr Radstand. Wiederum profitieren die Reisenden im Fond, der überdies durch breitere Türen betreten werden kann. Drei Leitlinien wurden den Konstrukteuren mit auf den Weg gegeben: Der Neue soll komfortabler, sicherer und sparsamer sein. Der s-Komfort setzt längst weltweit Maßstäbe. Auch was die Sicherheit anbelangt, verkörpert die Typenreihe den letzten Stand der Forschung, da die Passagiere selbst einen versetzten Frontalaufprall (*offset crash*) bei Tempo 55 unversehrt überstehen.

Bleibt das dritte Gebot: Sparsamkeit. Zehn Prozent Minderverbrauch werden verheißen. Die Karosserien sind im Windkanal optimiert, überflüssige Pfunde abgespeckt, wo immer das geht, etwa durch die Verwendung von Kunststoff und Leichtmetall. Aus diesem bestehen die Kurbelgehäuse der beiden Achtzylinder, des Fünfliters, der bereits im 450 SLC 5.0 Dienst getan hat, und eines 3,8-Liters, der auf dem bisherigen Aggregat mit 3,5 Litern fußt. Zunächst unverändert: der 2,8-Liter-Sechszylinder mit Vergaser oder Einspritzung.

Auf der IAA 1981 findet sich an der Seite der Limousinen ein wohlgeformtes Coupé, lediglich zu haben mit den Achtzylindern, denen man im Rahmen des Mercedes-Benz Energiekonzepts zur Reduzierung von Verbrauch und Schadstoff mehr Genügsamkeit anerzogen hat. Wieder in Frankfurt, im September 1985, präsentiert sich die s-Palette komplett renoviert. Das beginnt mit ihrem äußeren Erscheinungsbild, tiefer herabgezogenen Schürzen für mehr Abtrieb vorn und besserer Kanalisierung der Luft hinten sowie einem glatten Flankenschutz. Neu oder zumindest kräftig retuschiert sind die Maschinen. Zwei Sechszylinder-Einspritzer mit 2,6 und drei Litern werden der Mittelklasse w124 entlehnt und verdrängen den in Ehren ergrauten 2,8-Liter. Der 3,8-Liter wurde auf 4,2 Liter aufgebohrt. Der Fünfliter leistet nun mit elektronischer Zündung und der elektronisch-mechanischen Bosch-Jetronic 245 PS, fünf mehr als in seinen stärksten Zeiten zuvor. Das erstmalige Vorkommen der Bezeichnungen 560 SEL und SEC bezeugt die Existenz eines neuen v8 mit 5,6 Litern Volumen und 272 PS, mit höherer Kompression auch 300 PS.

Dass die Versorgung mit bleifreiem Benzin noch nicht flächendeckend ist, fängt man flexibel mit Zwischenlösungen auf. Erst im September 1986 haben alle Otto-

À de nombreux points de vue, la nouvelle Classe s qui fête sa première à l'IAA de Francfort en septembre 1979, à la ligne de césure entre hier et demain, recourt à des solutions éprouvées du passé et s'engage prudemment dans un no-man's-land technique. En fin de compte, la w126 sera un modèle largement plébiscité et, produite à 818 036 exemplaires en douze ans, ce sera le plus fort tirage de la grande Mercedes à ce jour.

La Classe s couvre de nouveau un large spectre : au début, il en existe sept modèles avec quatre moteurs allant de la 280 s (six-cylindres, carburateur, 156 ch) à la 500 SEL (v8, injection, 240 ch). On a le choix entre deux variantes d'empattement, normal et long avec 140 mm de plus d'empattement. Une fois de plus, les bénéficiaires en sont les passagers de la banquette arrière à laquelle on accède, en outre, par des portes plus larges. Trois préceptes ont été inculqués aux ingénieurs pour sa conception : la nouvelle voiture doit être plus confortable, plus sûre et plus économique. En ce qui concerne la sécurité aussi, cette gamme incarne un sommet de la recherche puisque les passagers sont censés ne pas subir la moindre blessure même en cas de collision frontale décalée (*offset crash*) à une vitesse de 55 km/h.

Pour ce qui est du troisième commandement (économique), la sobriété. Mercedes revendique une diminution de la consommation de 10 %. Les carrosseries ont été optimisées en soufflerie, la guerre a été déclarée aux kilogrammes superflus partout où cela a été possible, par exemple grâce à l'utilisation de matière plastique et d'alliage léger. C'est d'ailleurs dans ce matériau qu'à été réalisé le carter-moteur des deux huit-cylindres, le 5 litres qui officiait d'ores et déjà dans la 450 SLC 5.0 et un 3,8 litres extrapolé de l'ancien moteur de 3,5 litres. Tout d'abord inchangé, le six-cylindres de 2,8 litres est proposé au choix avec carburateur ou injection.

À l'IAA de 1981, les berlines sont rejointes par un coupé aux lignes élégantes propulsé exclusivement par les huit-cylindres auxquels, dans le cadre du concept d'économie d'énergie de Mercedes-Benz visant à réduire la consommation et les rejets de polluants, on a inculqué une plus grande sobriété. Toujours à Francfort, en septembre 1985, la série s est rénovée de fond en comble. Les moteurs sont nouveaux ou, tout au moins, sérieusement retravaillés. Deux six-cylindres à injection, de 2,6 litres et 3 litres de cylindrée, sont repris de la classe intermédiaire, la w124, et évincent le 2,8 litres après des années de bons et loyaux services. La cylindrée du 3,8 litres a été majorée à 4,2 litres. Grâce à l'allumage électronique et à l'injection d'essence électro-mécanique Bosch-Jetronic, le 5 litres délivre désormais 245 ch, soit 5 de plus qu'à sa meilleure époque. Un néologisme dans la nomenclature de Mercedes, 560 SEL et SEC, témoigne de l'existence d'un nouveau v8 de 5,6 litres cylindrée et d'une puissance de 272 ch, qui peut atteindre aussi 300 ch avec un taux de compression plus élevé.

L'approvisionnement en essence sans plomb n'étant pas encore garanti à l'échelle du territoire, Daimler

Mercedes-Benz S-Klasse   1979

Mercedes-Benz 300 SEL 1986

Daimler-Benz gasoline engines had a regulated catalytic converter. The innovative impetus of those years also extended to the exotic member of the S-Class family. The 300 SD, a special model for the North American market, yielded the 300 SDL with an extended wheelbase and a six-cylinder turbodiesel developing 150 bhp. After the Paris Salon a year later, the most powerful engine in the series was also available as a 560 SE, while the 350 SDL of June 1989 offered more capacity and better torque though delivering 14 bhp less, the victim of exhaust gas recycling and oxidizing catalytic converters. From June 1990 onwards the shortened form, the 350 SD, was available as an alternative, the last link in an evolutionary chain which had, let it not be forgotten, produced 97,546 S-Class diesels.

Motoren von Daimler-Benz den geregelten Katalysator. In den Innovationsschub jenes Jahres einbegriffen ist auch der Exot in der S-Familie: Aus dem 300 SD, Sonderangebot für den nordamerikanischen Markt, ist der 300 SDL geworden mit verlängertem Radstand und einem Turbodiesel mit sechs Zylindern, der 150 PS abgibt. Nach dem Pariser Salon ein Jahr später ist das stärkste Stück der Baureihe auch als 560 SE erhältlich, während der 350 SDL vom Juni 1989 mit mehr Hubraum und einem besseren Drehmoment, dafür aber mit 14 PS weniger aufwartet, die der Abgasrückführung und Oxidationskatalysatoren zum Opfer gefallen sind. Ab Juni 1990 gibt es als Alternative die Kurz-Form 350 SD, letztes Glied in einer evolutionären Kette, aus der immerhin 97 546 S-Diesel hervorgegangen sind.

compose tout d'abord avec cet aléa en proposant des solutions à la carte. Ce n'est qu'en septembre 1986 que tous les moteurs thermiques de Daimler-Benz posséderont un catalyseur réglé. Un modèle à part dans la famille S s'inscrit aussi dans la poussée d'innovation de cette année: la 300 SD, modèle spécial pour le marché nord-américain, s'est muée en une 300 SDL à empattement long et moteur turbodiesel six-cylindres développant 150 ch. Après le Salon de Paris, un an plus tard, le modèle le plus puissant de la gamme est aussi disponible en exécution 560 SE tandis que la 350 SDL de juin 1989 voit sa cylindrée et son couple majorés, mais sa puissance abaissée de 14 ch, victimes du recyclage des gaz d'échappement et des catalyseurs à oxydation. À partir de juin 1990, Mercedes propose à titre alternatif une version à empattement court, la 350 SD, dernier maillon d'une chaîne évolutive qui a tout de même généré 97 546 modèles S Diesel.

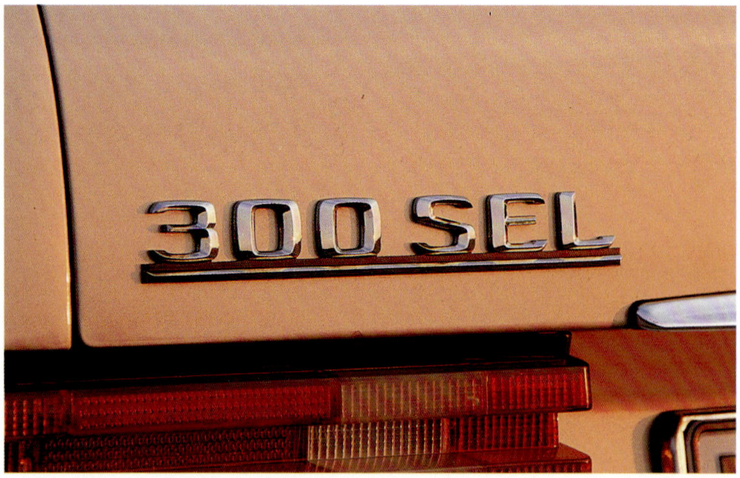
300 SEL

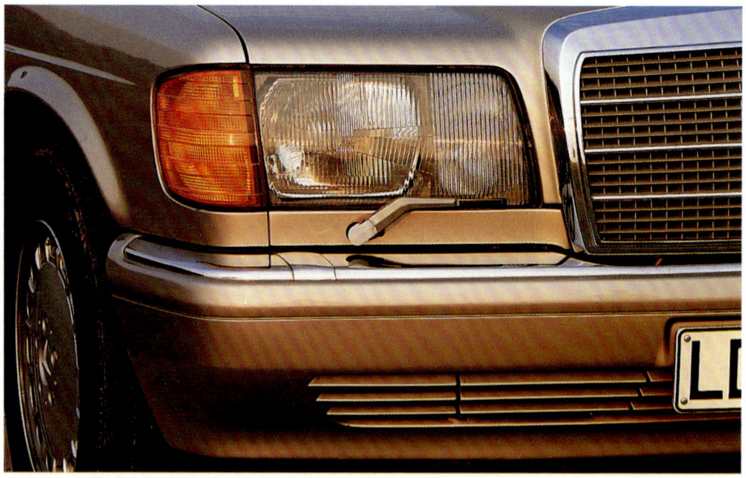

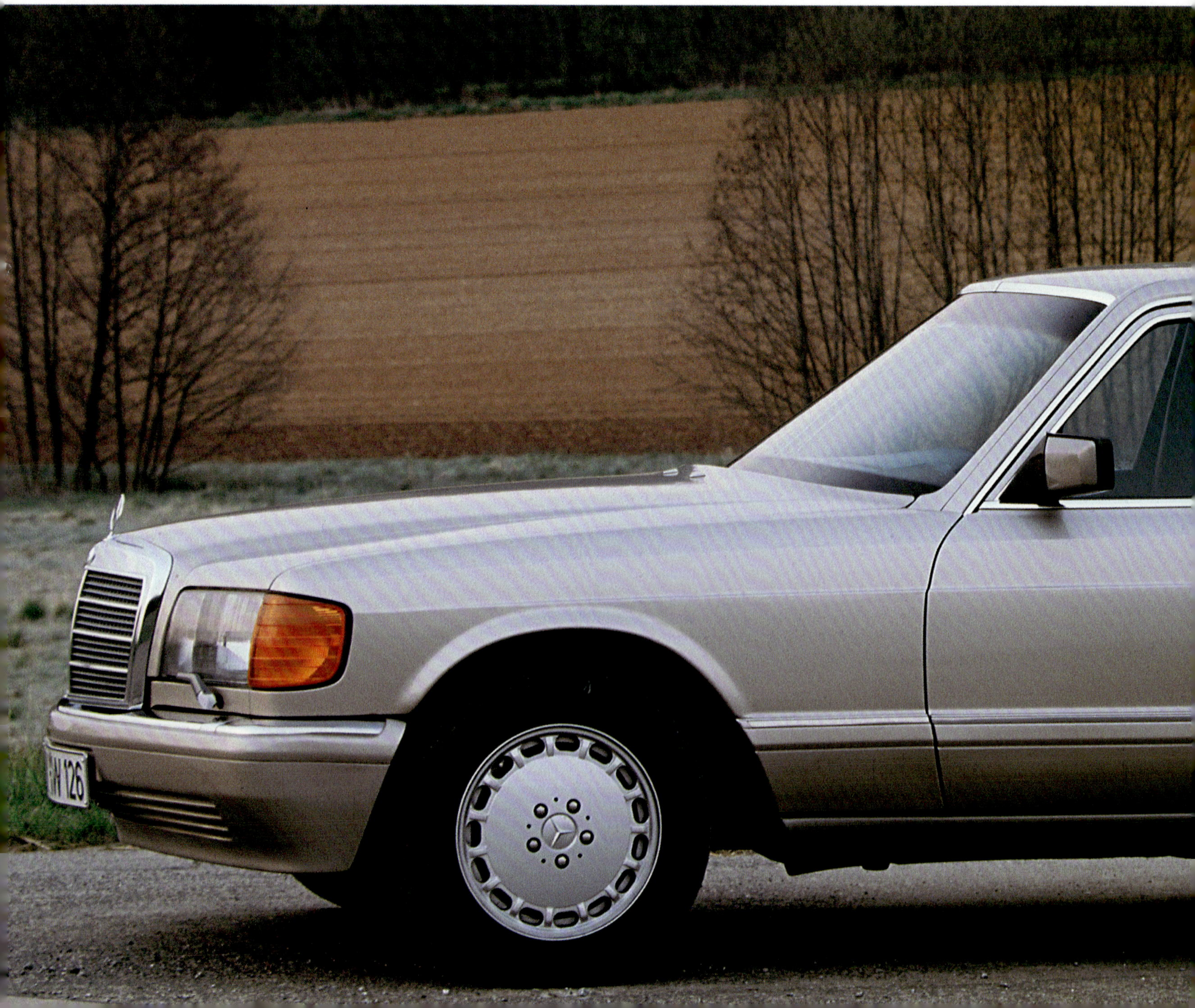

The bodies of the S-Class of 1979 were optimized in the wind tunnel, and excess pounds were trimmed off wherever possible, for example by the use of plastics and alloys. Nonetheless, they had a defiantly solid air.

Die Karosserien der S-Klasse von 1979 sind im Windkanal optimiert, überflüssige Pfunde abgespeckt, wo immer es geht, etwa durch die Verwendung von Kunststoff und Leichtmetall. Dennoch umfächelt sie ein Ambiente von trotziger Robustheit.

Les carrosseries de la Classe S de 1979 ont été optimisées en soufflerie et l'on a chassé les kilogrammes superflus, notamment en utilisant matières plastiques et alliages légers. Cela n'empêche pas une solidité à toute épreuve.

The driver of the top-of-the-range model, the 560 SEC available from 1985, could call on 242 bhp of sheer power which delivered throughout the engine's performance range. The level of comfort offered by the SEC extended to the seat-belt acceptors for the front-seat occupants, a rather complicated device that occasionally went on strike.

Im Spitzenmodell 560 SEC ab 1985 gebietet der Lenker über 242 PS, urige Kraft, die in allen Lebenslagen bereitwillig zur Verfügung steht. Zum Komfort, den der SEC offeriert, zählt für die vorderen Passagiere der Gurtanreicher, eine etwas komplizierte Vorkehrung, die gelegentlich in den Ausstand tritt.

Avec la 560 SEC haut de gamme de 1985, le conducteur est le maître de 242 ch, une force tranquille qui est docilement à sa disposition dans toutes les situations. L'un des accessoires de confort est le présentateur de ceintures pour les passagers avant, dispositif quelque peu compliqué qui a parfois le mauvais goût de ne pas fonctionner.

Mercedes-Benz S-Klasse 1979

The members of the W201 compact class, launched on 8 December 1982, were undoubtedly compact, but also in a class of their own. Apart from smaller dimensions, however, they embodied very traditional Untertürkheim virtues such as reliability, low depreciation, and safety.

New suspension systems guaranteed excellent handling—the MacPherson strut front axle with anti-dive mechanism, connected to individual triangular wishbones, the multi-link rear suspension, where each wheel was connected to five fixing points. Instead of Mercedes' typical foot-operated parking brake, there was a conventional handbrake in the center console. The new compact was initially offered as a 190 and a 190 E. Its powerplant came from the current type 200 with a carburetor, reduced to 90 bhp or with the Bosch KE-Jetronic system and increased to 122 bhp.

This base series was then extended in both directions in the autumn of 1983. This saw the introduction of the 190 D with 72 bhp whose engine was enclosed so that the familiar diesel knocking noise was reduced by a half, and of the sporty 190 E 2.3-16 with 185 bhp, a 16-valver with a wing spoiler on the trunk lid that sent shivers down the spine of even the most innocent observer. In 1985 the family grew by a further three models, the 190 D 2.5 with 90 bhp, very nimble with the five-cylinder engine from the 250 D, the 190 E 2.3 with the 136 bhp engine from the 230 E, and the aristocratic version, the 190 E 2.6, with a 166 bhp six-cylinder shoehorned into the engine compartment.

Various interim solutions were adopted to cope with the fact that unleaded fuel was not universally available until September 1985, when all Mercedes gasoline engines were supplied with a regulated catalytic converter. The 190 D 2.5 Turbo, whose 122 bhp powered the car to 118 mph, could be recognized by the six gills at the front right between the turn signal and the wheel arch.

At the Paris Salon a year later, a considerably revamped series was exhibited with wide plastic side strips, lower front and rear skirts for improved air channeling, and wider fenders. The first generation of 16-valvers was replaced by the 190 E 2.5-16 with 195 bhp. Before this could form the basis of a Group A touring car for race purposes, further preliminary work was necessary. Its long-stroke engine was not capable of further development. Consequently a new oversquare engine of the same volume was built, the power source for the 190 E 2.5-16 Evolution, which looked decidedly rough when unveiled at the Geneva Motor Show in March 1989. Stage II, which was revealed on the same occasion a year later, looked even more of a mess. Nevertheless, buyers were quickly found for the 500 units of each as required for homologation purposes. The young dynamic image was also served by two special editions, the Sportline package of June 1989 and the Avantgarde trim of March 1992, though these stood out more because of their fashionably weird design than any increased performance.

Kompakt sind sie, aber auch eine Klasse für sich, die Exponenten der Kompaktklasse W201, eingeführt am 8. Dezember 1982. Denn neben geringen Abmessungen bringen sie durchaus traditionelle Untertürkheimer Tugenden mit, Zuverlässigkeit, Wertbeständigkeit und Sicherheit.

Neue Lösungen bei der Aufhängung gewährleisten glänzende Fahreigenschaften: die Dämpferbein-Vorderachse mit Bremsnick-Abstützung, geführt an einzelnen Dreieck-Querlenkern, die Raumlenkerachse hinten, wo jedes Rad an fünf Stablenkern geführt wird. Anstelle der Mercedes-typischen Feststellbremse, die per Fußtritt aktiviert wird, findet sich eine normale Handbremse rechts neben dem Fahrer. Zunächst wird der neue Kompakte als 190 und als 190 E angeboten. Sein Triebwerk: das des aktuellen Typs 200 mit Vergaser und auf 90 PS gedrosselt oder mit der KE-Jetronic von Bosch und auf 122 PS gesteigert.

Im Herbst 1983 wird dieses Rumpfprogramm nach beiden Seiten ausgebaut. Da ist der 190 D mit 72 PS, dessen Motor so eingekapselt ist, dass das vertraute Diesel-Nageln um die Hälfte gedämpft wird. Und da ist die sportliche Offerte 190 E 2.3-16 mit 185 PS, ein Sechzehnventiler mit einem Flügelspoiler auf dem Kofferraumdeckel, bei dessen Anblick selbst dem arglosen Betrachter Unheil schwant. 1985 wächst die Kompakt-Familie um drei weitere Modelle, den 190 D 2.5 mit 90 PS, durchaus agil mit dem Fünfzylinder aus dem 250 D, den 190 E 2.3 mit der 136 PS starken Maschine aus dem 230 E und die Nobel-Variante 190 E 2.6, in deren Motorenabteil man einen 166 PS leistenden Sechszylinder gezwängt hat.

Dem Nebeneinander von verbleitem und bleifreiem Kraftstoff begegnet man mit diversen Zwischenlösungen, bis im September 1985 alle Mercedes mit Otto-Motoren mit geregeltem Katalysator geliefert werden. Den 190 D 2.5 Turbo, 122 PS kräftig und 190 Stundenkilometer schnell, erkennt man an sechs Kiemen vorn rechts zwischen Blinkleuchte und Radausschnitt.

Auf dem Pariser Salon ein Jahr später erscheint die Baureihe energisch retuschiert, mit breiten seitlichen Leisten aus Kunststoff, tiefer hängenden Bug- und Heckschürzen zu besserer Luftführung und voluminöseren Kotflügeln. Die erste Generation von Sechzehnventilern wird abgelöst vom 190 E 2.5-16 mit 195 PS. Bis dieser zur Basis eines Renntourenwagens der Gruppe A werden kann, ist indes noch Vorarbeit notwendig: Sein Triebwerk ist als Langhuber nicht entwicklungsfähig. Folglich konstruiert man einen neuen Kurzhuber mit gleichem Volumen, Kraftquelle des 190 E 2.5-16 Evolution, der sich auf der Genfer Show im März 1989 in entschieden halbstarkem Habitus präsentiert. Noch wüster treibt es visuell die Stufe II, die ein Jahr später bei der gleichen Gelegenheit gezündet wird. Gleichwohl finden sich rasch die Käufer für die jeweils 500 Exemplare, welche die Homologation fordert. Dem Image junger Dynamik sind auch zwei Sonderausstattungen dienlich, das Sportline-Paket vom Juni 1989 sowie die Avantgarde-Ausrüstung vom

Tout aussi compactes qu'elles soient, elles n'en ont pas moins une grande classe, les «petites» de la gamme compacte W201 introduite le 8 décembre 1982. En effet, malgré leur faible encombrement, elles possèdent les qualités que l'on attribue traditionnellement aux voitures d'Untertürkheim: fiabilité, stabilité et sécurité.

Des solutions inédites pour la suspension garantissent un comportement inégalé à ce jour : l'essieu avant à jambe élastique avec dispositif antiplongée au freinage, guidée par un triangle transversal respectif, et l'essieu arrière multibras où chaque roue est guidée par cinq tirants. À la place du typique frein de stationnement Mercedes à pédale, on trouve un frein à main normal situé à droite du conducteur. La nouvelle compacte est tout d'abord proposée en exécutions 190 et 190 E. Son moteur est celui de l'actuelle série 200 à carburateur, dont la puissance a été abaissée à 90 ch ou, avec l'injection KE-Jetronic Bosch, majorée à 122 ch.

À l'automne 1983, ce programme embryonnaire s'enrichit dans les deux directions. Vers le bas, avec la 190 D de 72 ch dont le moteur a été si bien encapsulé que les claquements familiers du diesel ne sont plus perceptibles qu'à moitié. Et, vers le haut, avec une version sportive, la 190 E 2.3-16 de 185 ch, un seize-soupapes avec un becquet sur le couvercle de malle qui laisse entrevoir, même au plus profane des observateurs, ce dont est capable cette voiture. En 1985, la famille des compactes s'enrichit de trois autres modèles, la 190 D 2.5 de 90 ch, à laquelle le cinq-cylindres de la 250 D confère une agilité surprenante, la 190 E 2.3 avec le moteur de 136 ch de la 230 E, et une version luxueuse, la 190 E 2.6 dont le compartiment moteur héberge à grand peine un six-cylindres de 166 ch.

Après septembre 1985, Mercedes ne fabrique plus que des moteurs thermiques à catalyseurs réglés. On reconnaît la 190 D 2.5 Turbo, avec ses 122 ch et ses 190 km/h, à six fentes d'aérations à l'avant droit entre le clignotant et l'arche de roue.

Pour le Salon de Paris, un an plus tard, la gamme a été profondément retravaillée avec de larges panneaux de carrosserie en matière plastique protégeant les portières, des boucliers avant et arrière descendant plus bas pour mieux canaliser l'air et des ailes plus volumineuses. La première génération de seize-soupapes est remplacée par une 190 E 2.5-16 de 195 ch. Mais bien du travail attend encore les ingénieurs avant que celle-ci puisse servir de base à une voiture du tourisme du Groupe A : à course longue, son moteur n'offre aucune perspective de développement. Logiquement, on construit donc un nouveau moteur à course courte de cylindrée identique, qui propulse la 190 E 2.5-16 Evolution, laquelle est présentée dans un accoutrement pour le moins tape-à-l'œil au Salon de l'automobile de Genève en mars 1989. L'Evolution II, présentée un an plus tard lors du même Salon, pousse le bouchon encore plus loin sur le plan «esthétique». Cela n'empêche pas qu'elle trouve rapidement les 500 preneurs

Mercedes-Benz 190   1982

Mercedes-Benz 190 E 2.5-16 Evolution II 1991

By March 1990 the 190 E 1.8 had replaced the original 190 which was the last Mercedes with a carburetor engine. And from January 1991 on the entire W201 range, apart from the entry models 190 E 1.8 and 190 D, had ABS brakes, a center console, and body-colored housings for the external mirrors. The designation 190 E had had a 2.0 added to it, and the car it referred to had become 4 bhp more powerful, as had the 190 E 2.3.

März 1992, die allerdings eher durch poppig-ausgefallenes Design glänzt als durch vermehrte Funktionalität.

Da hat bereits – im März 1990 – der 190 E 1.8 den ursprünglichen 190 abgelöst, mithin den letzten Mercedes mit einem Vergasermotor. Und seit dem Januar 1991 hat das gesamte W201-Spektrum außer den Einstiegstypen 190 E 1.8 und 190 D das Antiblockiersystem, eine Mittelkonsole und in Wagenfarbe lackierte Gehäuse der Außenspiegel. Die Bezeichnung 190 E hat ein 2.0 angesetzt, und das dazugehörige Auto ist um vier PS stärker geworden, ebenso wie der 190 E 2.3.

nécessaires pour son homologation. Deux éditions spéciales sont très bénéfiques à son image de jeunesse et de dynamisme, le pack Sportline de juin 1989 ainsi que la version Avantgarde de mars 1992, qui se distingue toutefois plus par son style coloré et tape-à-l'œil que par une fonctionnalité améliorée.

Pendant ce temps, en mars 1990, la 190 E 1.8 a déjà remplacé la 190 originelle, la dernière Mercedes à moteur à carburateur. Et, depuis janvier 1991, toute la série W201, sauf les modèles d'appel 190 E 1.8 et 190 D, possèdent le système d'antiblocage, une console médiane et des rétroviseurs extérieurs peints dans la couleur de la carrosserie. La dénomination 190 E a été complétée par un 2.0 et le moteur de la voiture correspondante a vu sa puissance augmenter de quatre chevaux, comme celui de la 190 E 2.3.

The 190 E 2.5-16 Evolution II was the wildest of the 190 models, offering 235 bhp and 155 mph. The combative look derived mainly from the huge rear spoiler. Inside, however, it was perfectly civilized as drivers expected to find almost all the comforts offered by the 201 series. The powerful engine—quite a dish.

Der 190 E 2.5-16 Evolution II ist der Wildeste unter den Hundertneunzigern, 235 PS stark und 250 Stundenkilometer schnell. Der martialische Eindruck rührt vor allem vom riesigen Luftleitwerk am Heck her. Drinnen geht es hingegen durchaus gesittet her: Da erwarten den Piloten fast ungeschmälert die Annehmlichkeiten, welche die Baureihe 201 zu bieten hat. Kulinarisch aufbereitet: das potente Triebwerk.

La 190 E 2.5-16 Evolution II est la plus sauvage des 190 avec ses 235 ch et ses 250 km/h. C'est surtout son gigantesque aileron arrière qui lui donne son air martial. L'intérieur, en revanche, est beaucoup plus conventionnel : ses pilotes y retrouvent presque tout le confort qu'offre la gamme 201. Revu par les hommes de l'art : le puissant moteur.

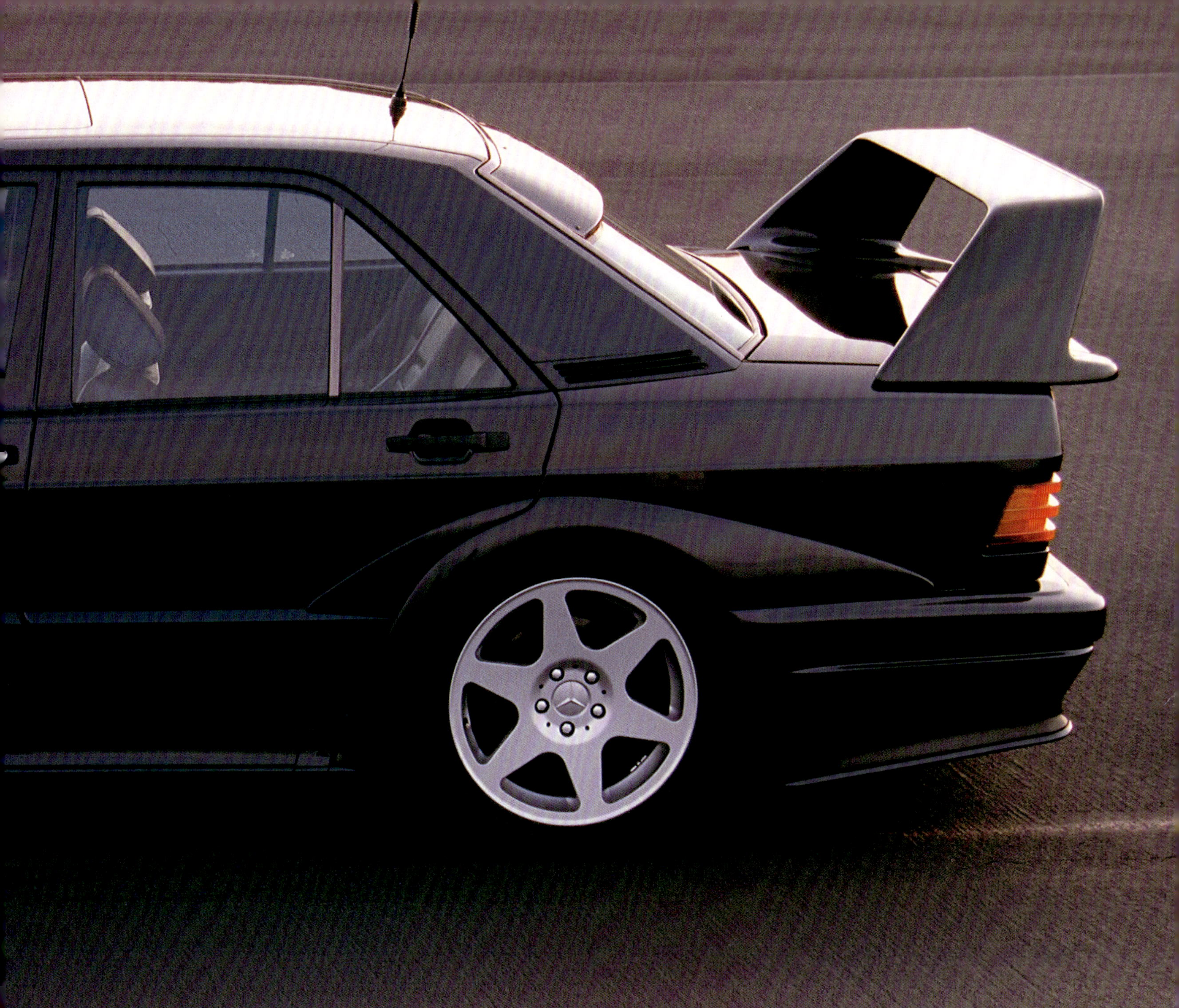

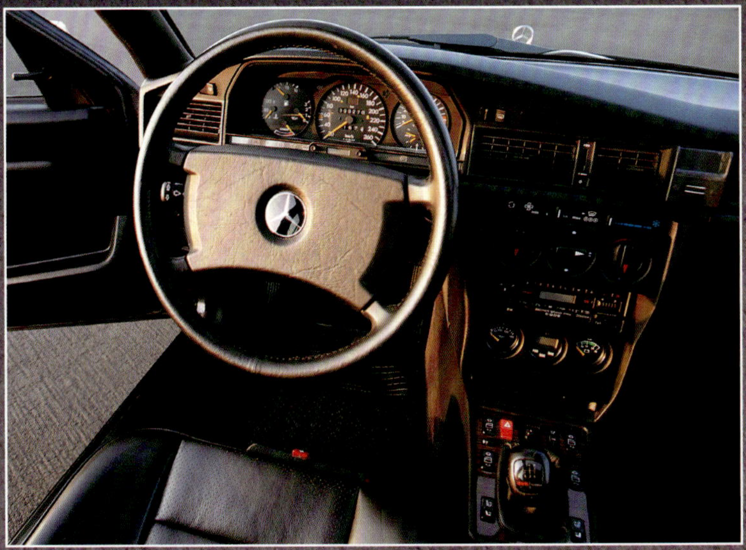

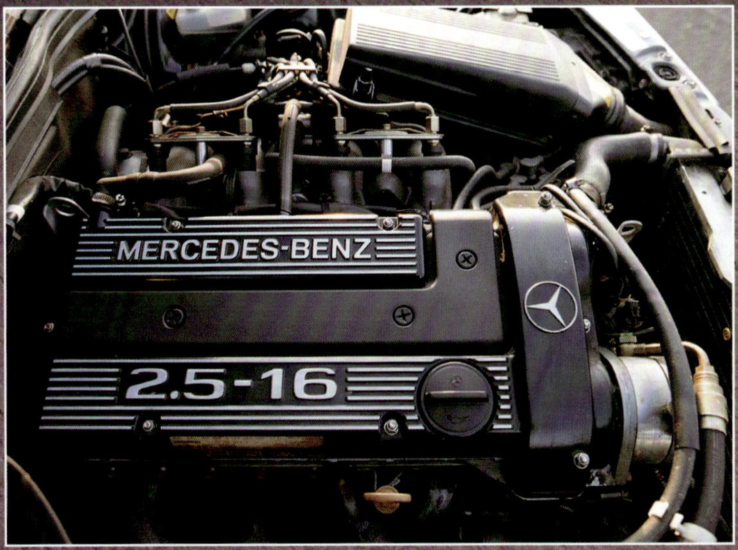
MERCEDES-BENZ
2.5-16

Cosmetically and technically the new Mercedes W124 mid-range series, launched in the final two months of 1984, revealed the influence of the company's compact cars. Nevertheless, it retained an individual profile, nowhere more noticeable than in the rounded tapering tail with a low loading edge below the trapezoidally extended trunk lid.

The four-cylinder engines came from the W123 series, and the diesel engines were also existing models, a four-cylinder of 2 liters, a five-cylinder of 2.5 liters and a six-cylinder of 3 liters. Two further six-cylinder gasoline engines were new, with displacements of 2.6 and 3 liters respectively. The T model made its debut at the 1985 Frankfurt International Motor Show. At the same time the 4matic system was introduced as an optional extra for the six-cylinder engines and convertibles. This was an automatically actuatable four-wheel-drive system of subtle refinement, the front differential of which was an integral part of the oil sump.

March 1987 saw the launch of a coupé in Geneva, and six months later, in Frankfurt, the turbo version of the 300 D, also available as a 4matic and identifiable by the five air-inlet slits in the right front fender. The range was further extended in September 1988 in Paris with the 200 E and the 250 D Turbo, effectively detoxified by the use of precombustion chambers with inclined injection like their old and bigger brother, the 300 D Turbo; each was 4 bhp more powerful as a result. Five months later the diesels with aspirated engines followed, again with a slight increase in power as a bonus. The most conspicuous external features of the cosmetic finish of the cars at the Frankfurt Motor Show in the autumn of 1989 were the plastic side-protection strips and the restrained use of chrome trim. All three body types were available with a 3-liter six-cylinder engine whose 24 valves produced a hefty 220 bhp, together with stretched versions with an 31½-in-longer wheelbase, six doors, and three rows of seats for the 250 D and 260 E.

The series reached its culmination in October 1990 in Paris with the 500 E, whose 5-liter V8 served up 326 bhp—at the handsome price initially of 134,520 marks. The construction of the body shell and the final assembly were handled by Porsche in Stuttgart-Zuffenhausen, while Mercedes in Sindelfingen was responsible for the paintwork and delivery. The significant features of this powerhouse were: lowered by ⅞ in, wider fenders, foglights in the front skirt, 16-inch wheels with wide tires of specification 225/55 ZR 16.

In Frankfurt in 1991 the four-seater 300 CE cabriolet was added to the series, while the revamping of the range a year later concentrated in particular on the engines. Four valves per cylinder became standard for all the gasoline engines, and two new six-cylinder engines of 2.8 and 3.2 liters were introduced which replaced the previous 3-liter units with the exception of the cabriolet and the four-wheel-drive version. The 400 E, which was available

Mercedes-Benz E-Klasse 1984

Mercedes-Benz 300 E 4matic 1986

from October 1992, was more within the financial reach of customers than the 500 E. It was 50,000 marks cheaper than the latter, but its 278 bhp meant that it was still agile enough, especially as both engines had a voluntary self-limiter system which intervened at a speed of 155 mph.

The diesel models with aspirated engines also began to go over to four-valve-per-cylinder technology provided they had more than four cylinders. In June 1993 this series was also stylistically updated in line with the marque's other models, with radiator badges, for example, in the form of narrow chrome strips, and new lights. The nomenclature was tidied up; the E was superfluous because only injection models were now manufactured, and C and T were dropped because the body shape was self-explanatory. The D was replaced by the terms Diesel and Turbodiesel. The Daimler-Benz mid-range was now called E-Class, however, with an E before the numerical symbol in contrast to previous practice.

liegt der 400 E ab Oktober 1992. Immerhin 50 000 Mark billiger als jener, gibt er sich mit 278 PS noch immer agil genug, zumal sich die Maschine bei Tempo 250 in beiden Fällen ohnehin in freiwilliger Selbstkontrolle einen Riegel vorschiebt.

Um die gleiche Zeit beginnen auch die Diesel-Modelle mit Saugmotoren ihren Stoffwechsel über vier Ventile zu vollziehen, sofern sie mehr als vier Zylinder haben. Im Juni 1993 präsentiert sich die Reihe stilistisch aktualisiert analog zu den anderen Modellen der Marke, mit Plakettenkühlern zum Beispiel, paspelliert von schmalen Chromstreifen, sowie neuen Leuchten. Zugleich entrümpelt man die Nomenklatur: das E erübrigt sich, denn es gibt nur noch Einspritzer, und C und T entfallen, weil die Karosserieform ja für sich spricht. Das D wird ersetzt durch die Begriffe Diesel und Turbodiesel. Der Mittelstand von Daimler-Benz aber nennt sich jetzt E-Klasse, mit einem E vor dem Zahlenkürzel im Gegensatz zur Praxis bisher.

roues motrices. La 400 E présentée en octobre 1992 coûte 50 000 marks de moins que la 500 E et, avec 278 ch, elle est presque aussi sportive que celle-ci, d'autant plus que la vitesse de pointe est de toute façon limitée dans les deux cas à 250 km/h en vertu d'un *gentleman's agreement* conclu entre les principaux constructeurs allemands.

À la même époque, les moteurs diesel atmosphériques commencent à bénéficier eux aussi d'une alimentation à quatre soupapes à condition d'avoir plus de quatre cylindres. En juin 1993, la gamme est remise au goût du jour sur le plan esthétique avec une calandre modifiée, soulignée de minces bandes chromées et de nouveaux phares. Parallèlement, la nomenclature est élaguée : le E est devenu superflu dès lors qu'il n'existe plus que des moteurs à injection, ce qui est aussi le cas du C et du T, pour lesquels la forme de carrosserie ne prête pas à confusion. Le T est remplacé par les notions Diesel et Turbodiesel. Le segment intermédiaire de chez Daimler-Benz se nomme dorénavant Classe E, avec un E précédant la série de chiffres contrairement à la pratique ancienne.

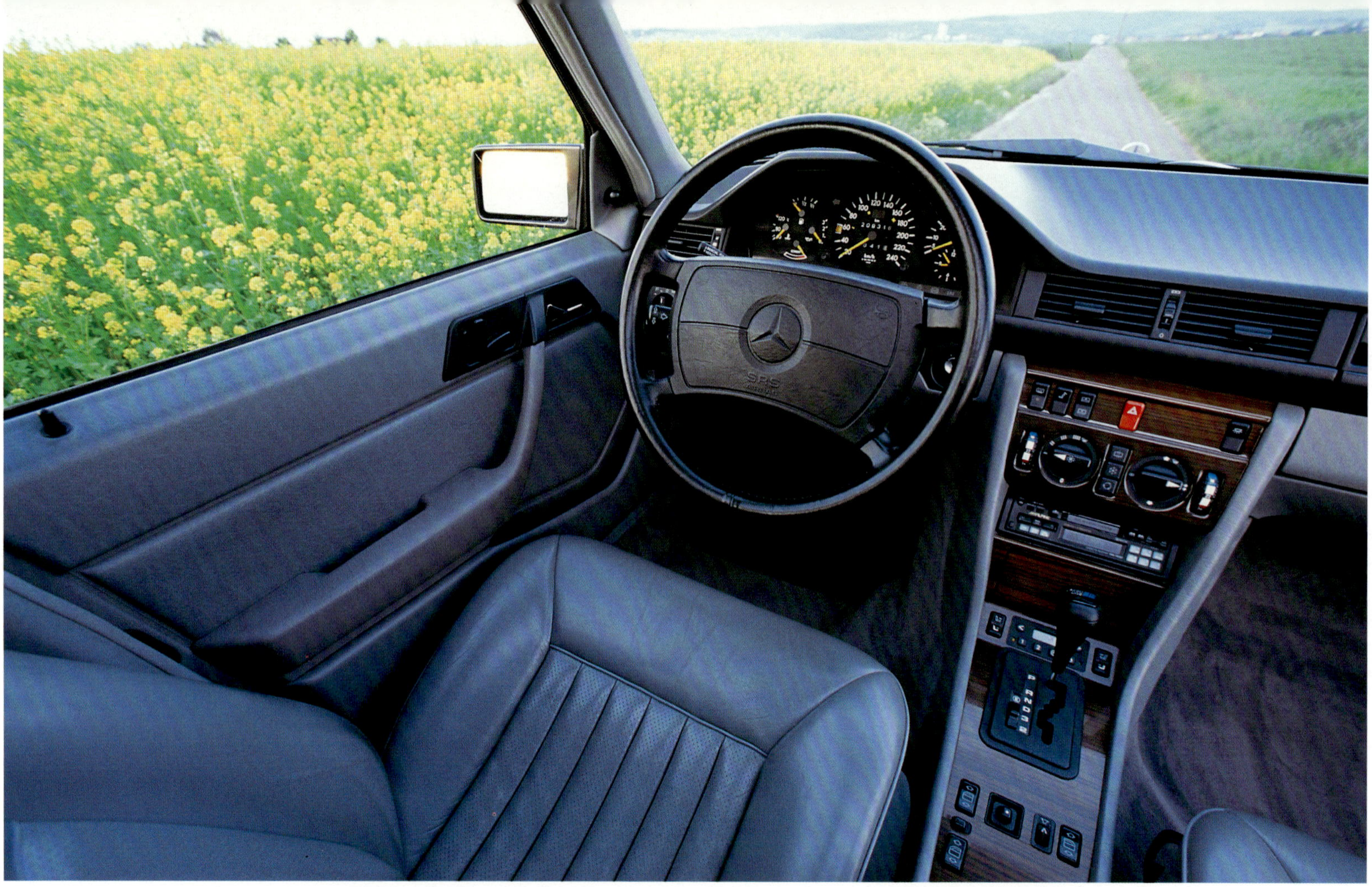

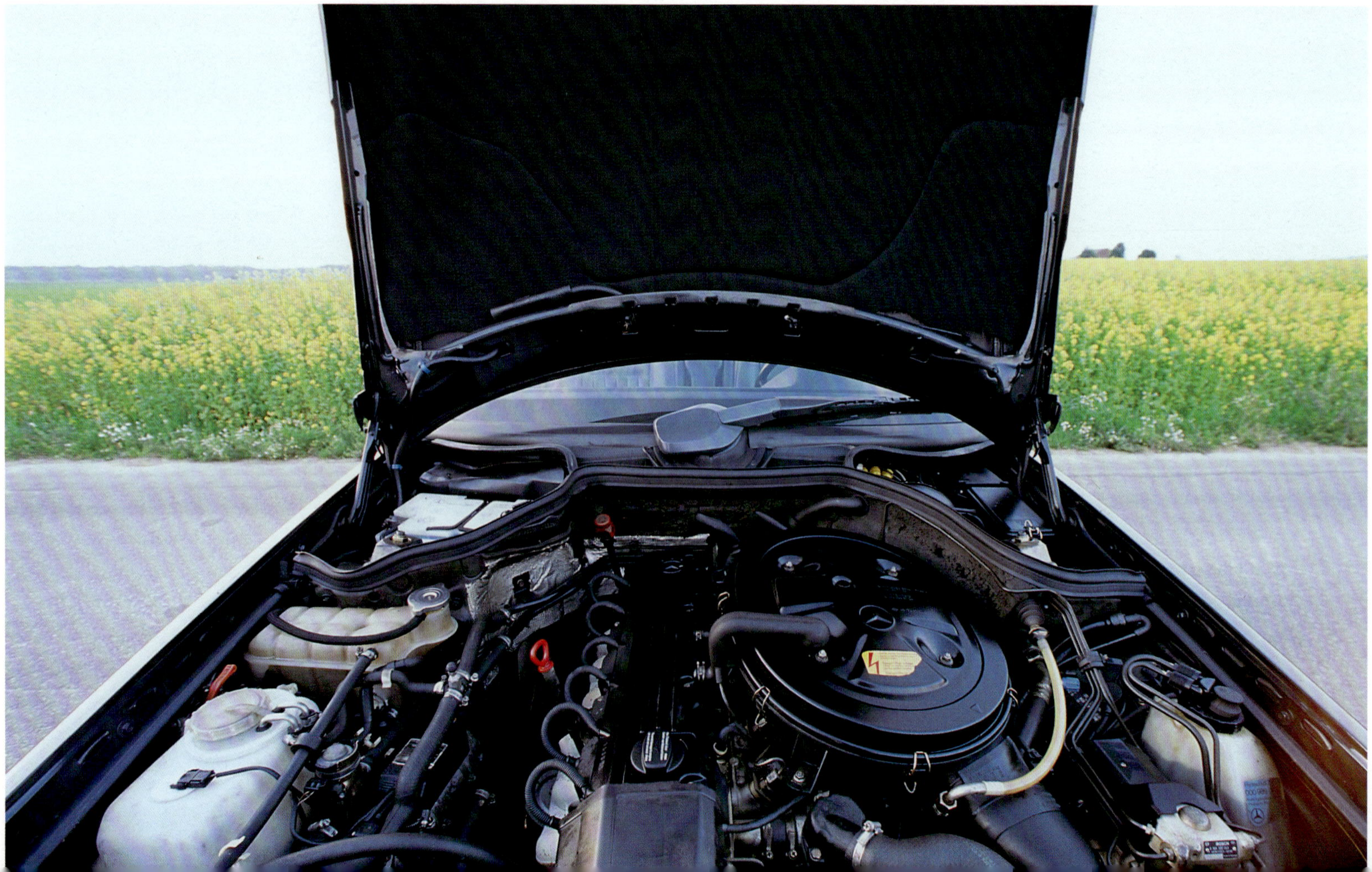

How times change: what was regarded as the non plus ultra amongst status symbols in the Fifties ranked only as an upper mid-range model in the Eighties—a Mercedes 300. The Mercedes-coined term "4matic" represented a four-wheel-drive system that engaged as soon as the car detected that it was required. In March 1987 the first six-cylinder cars were supplied with this system. Demand remained relatively low.

Wie sich die Zeiten ändern: Was in den fünfziger Jahren als Nonplusultra unter den Statussymbolen galt, wird in den Achtzigern der gehobenen Mittelklasse zugeordnet – ein Mercedes 300. Hinter dem kuriosen Kunstwort »4matic« verbirgt sich ein Vierradantrieb, der sich zuschaltet, sofern das Auto den Bedarf dazu verspürt. Im März 1987 werden die ersten Sechszylinder mit diesem System ausgeliefert. Der Bedarf bleibt relativ gering.

Comme les temps changent : ce qui était considéré comme le *nec plus ultra* parmi les symboles de réussite des années 1950 n'appartient plus, dans les années 1980, qu'au segment intermédiaire supérieur – une Mercedes 300. Derrière l'hermétique néologisme « 4matic » se dissimulent quatre roues motrices qui s'enclenchent dès que la voiture en ressent le besoin. Les premières six-cylindres sont équipées de ce système en mars 1987, mais la demande est décevante.

Mercedes-Benz E-Klasse 1984

The most powerful car in the series, assembled at Porsche: a 500 E with lowered running gear, the V8 of the new S-Class with four valves per cylinder, brakes from the SL, and 16-inch wheels. Owners of the high-speed eight-cylinder could expect to find tactile and visual treats both in the cockpit and under the hood. After all, if it is good, it should also look good.

Das stärkste Stück der Baureihe, bei Porsche montiert: ein 500 E mit tiefer gelegtem Fahrwerk, dem V8 der neuen S-Klasse mit vier Ventilen je Zylinder, den Bremsen des SL und 16-Zoll-Rädern. Handschmeichler und Augenweiden erwarten den Eigner des hurtigen Achtzylinders im Cockpit und unter der Motorhaube. Was gut ist, soll schließlich auch schön sein.

Le modèle le plus puissant de la gamme, monté chez Porsche : la 500 E à suspension surbaissée, avec le V8 de la nouvelle Classe S à quatre soupapes par cylindre, les freins de la SL et des roues de 16 pouces. Dans l'habitacle et sous le capot moteur, une main de fer dans un gant de velours attend les propriétaires de la puissante huit-cylindres. Ce qui est bon doit bien sûr être également beau.

Mercedes-Benz E-Klasse 1984

The second-generation T model, unveiled at the 1985 Frankfurt International Motor Show, was closely related to the series 124 sedan. However, the running gear, brakes, and other units were adapted to the higher payload, and the tail was designed to comply with the latest safety standards. The E 250 T Diesel from 1993 underwent a facelift to incorporate the latest features. The radiator grille, for example, was designed to match that of the S-Class, and the star was included separately on the hood.

Auf der Frankfurter IAA 1985 vorgestellt, lehnt sich das T-Modell der zweiten Generation eng an die Limousine der Baureihe 124 an. Allerdings sind Fahrwerk, Bremsanlage und Aggregate der höheren Nutzlast angepasst, und das Heck wird enstprechend dem neuesten Sicherheitsstandard gestaltet. Der E 250 T Diesel von 1993 wurde dem jüngsten Facelifting unterzogen. Die Kühlermaske zum Beispiel ist analog zur S-Klasse gestaltet, der Stern separat in die Motorhaube eingepflanzt.

Présenté pour l'IAA 1985, le modèle T deuxième génération est largement dérivé des berlines de la série 124. La suspension, le système de freinage et divers organes sont toutefois adaptés à la charge utile supérieure et l'arrière a été repensé en fonction des normes de sécurité les plus récentes. La E 250 T Diesel de 1993 vient de bénéficier de la dernière remise au goût du jour. La calandre, par exemple, s'inspire de celle de la Classe S et l'étoile, dissociée, est maintenant placée sur le capot moteur.

Mercedes-Benz E-Klasse 1984

Another four-seater: the series 124 coupé was essentially based on the template drawn up at Mercedes as the head of an aspirational family. The rear part of the roof merged gently with the midline.

Noch ein Fall für vier: Das Coupé der Baureihe 124 folgt grundsätzlich dem Baumuster, das man bei Mercedes für den Vater einer aufstrebenden Familie vorgesehen hat. Der hintere Teil des Dachs mündet dabei in sanfter Schräge in die Gürtellinie ein.

Encore une quatre-places : le coupé de la série 124 s'inspire par principe de l'architecture prévue par Mercedes pour le père d'une jeune famille en plein essor. La partie postérieure du toit se fond en une harmonieuse diagonale avec la ligne de ceinture.

Mercedes-Benz E-Klasse 1984

An open invitation: like all four-seater cabriolets, however, the E 200 version catered rather more for its front-seat occupants. It could be a little drafty in the back. A semi-automatic system to open the top was available as an optional extra. It concertina-ed backwards with much rustling and whirring until finally a solid metal cover descended with a definitive plop over the fabric.

Einladend geöffnet: Wie alle viersitzigen Cabriolets nimmt sich allerdings das vom Typ E 200 der Passagiere in der ersten Reihe behutsamer an. Hinten pfeift bald ein strammes Lüftchen. Eine Halbautomatik übernimmt gegen Aufpreis das Öffnen des Verdecks, das raschelnd und knisternd seinen Weg nach hinten antritt, bis sich am Ende ein Deckel aus dickem Blech mit ultimativem Plopp über allem Stofflichen senkt.

Ouverte et accueillante: comme tous les cabriolets à quatre places, la E 200 privilégie nettement les passagers des fauteuils avant. En effet, une brise fraîche ne tarde pas à se faire sentir à l'arrière. En option, un système semi-automatique se charge d'ouvrir et de fermer la capote qui se rabat presque silencieusement avant de disparaître dans un bruit distingué sous un épais capot de tôle.

Mercedes-Benz E-Klasse 1984 243

The fourth-generation SL, a star attraction at the Geneva Motor Show in March 1989 where it appeared as a 300 SL, 300 SL-24, and 500 SL, surpassed its predecessor in three aspects: assuredness of design, safety, and comfort.

The design, half with an eye to tradition, half forward-looking, had found a way back to a beautiful simplicity. Safety levels for the occupants matched those of the sedans, despite the lack of a roof. Many factors combined to ensure this; the rigid floorpan chassis, for example, with its high-strength panels and generously sized beam sections. The doors with their cleverly designed inner beading structure also made a contribution. A spectacular innovation was the automatic rollover bar made of high-tensile steel. At rest it was hidden in front of the box for the top, tensioned by springs, ready for action should the worst come to the worst. In that event, an electromagnetic system triggered deployment, ensuring that it was vertical within one-third of a second and locked in place with safety catches. Since the A-pillars were also solid pieces of high-tensile steel plate, reinforced with solid tubes, the SL formed a survival cell for its passengers in the event that the car should overturn.

The coupé roof, which had become 22 lbs lighter despite the large window area, thus had no load-bearing role any more. Opening and closing the electrohydraulic top, however, merely required a switch to be pressed. Everything else was taken care of within 30 seconds by 17 limit switches, 15 pressure cylinders, and 11 solenoids in movement sequences that were marvellously choreographed by microprocessors.

The suspension—MacPherson strut front axle and multi-link suspension rear axle—corresponded to that of the 210 and 124 series, and was tailored to the special requirements of the roadster. It was backed up by state-of-the-art supplementary systems such as a speed-dependent level control system and the ADS adaptive damping system, adjustable shock absorbers under electronic control which adapted them extremely rapidly to changes in the road surface under the wheels. The six-cylinder engines of the two 3-liter models came from existing engines but had undergone detailed modifications. The four-valve-per-cylinder system of the 300 SL-24, for example, had ignition-map-controlled adjustment of the inlet camshaft as did each cylinder bank of the 5-liter V8 in the 500 SL, at 326 bhp the most powerful Mercedes production engine.

This figure was surpassed by a 6-liter V12 in the 600 SL available from October 1992 onwards which developed 394 bhp. What buyers of this model received for their extra 60,000 marks was scarcely any increase in drive performance, but instead the turbine-like quietness of the V12 and a rather abstract quality—considerable social prestige.

From June 1993 onwards, the two top models were rebadged as the SL 500 and SL 600 during the Mercedes name reform, and the 3-liter engine models were replaced by an SL 280 and an SL 320, both using four-valves-per-cylinder technology. The SL 280 was the only model still

In drei Punkten überbietet der SL der vierten Generation, Attraktion des Genfer Salons im März 1989 als 300 SL, 300 SL-24 und 500 SL, seinen Vorgänger: hinsichtlich formaler Schlüssigkeit, Sicherheit und Komfort.

Das Design, halb der Tradition verpflichtet, halb nach vorn gewandt, hat zu einer schönen Schlichtheit zurückgefunden. Der Schutz der Insassen entspricht den Limousinen – trotz des fehlenden Dachs. Viele Faktoren wirken da zusammen, die rigide Bodenanlage zum Beispiel mit hochfesten Blechen und üppigen Trägerquerschnitten. Auch die Türen mit ihrer raffiniert ausgetüftelten inneren Sickenstruktur werden in das Konzept eingebunden. Eine spektakuläre Novität: der automatische Überrollbügel aus hochfestem Stahl. Im Ruhestand lagert er verborgen vor dem Verdeckkasten, von Federn vorgespannt für den Fall eines Falles. Tritt dieser ein, so schnellt er, elektromagnetisch ausgelöst, innerhalb einer Drittelsekunde in die Vertikale und wird durch Sperrklinken arretiert. Da auch die A-Säulen starke Stücke sind aus hochfestem Stahlblech, bewehrt mit massiven Rohren, schafft der SL bei einem Überschlag so einen Überlebensraum für seine Passagiere.

Keine tragende Rolle mehr fällt damit dem Coupé-dach zu, das trotz größerer Fensterfläche um zehn Kilogramm leichter geworden ist. Zum Öffnen und Schließen des elektrohydraulischen Verdecks genügt es, einen Schalter zu betätigen. Alles andere besorgen binnen einer halben Minute 17 Endschalter, 15 Druckzylinder sowie elf Magnetventile in Bewegungsabläufen, die durch Mikroprozessoren prächtig organisiert werden.

Die Aufhängung – Dämpferbein-Vorderachse und Raumlenker-Hinterachse – entspricht der der Baureihen 210 und 124, ist indes auf die besonderen Bedürfnisse des Roadsters zugeschnitten. Sie wird ergänzt durch Zusatzsysteme auf dem letzten Stand, eine geschwindigkeitsabhängige Niveauregulierung und das Adaptive Dämpfungs-System ADS, verstellbare Stoßdämpfer mit elektronischer Steuerung, die diese blitzschnell einem veränderten Untergrund anpasst. Die Sechszylinder der beiden Dreiliter stammen aus den Baukästen, wurden jedoch einer pingeligen Feinarbeit unterzogen. So verfügt etwa der Vierventiler des 300 SL-24 über eine kennfeldgesteuerte Verstellung der Einlassnockenwelle ebenso wie jede Zylinderbank des Fünfliter-V8 am 500 SL, dem stärksten Daimler-Serienmotor mit 326 PS.

Noch besser kann es ein Sechsliter-V12 von 394 PS im 600 SL vom Oktober 1992 an. Dessen Käufer handelt sich für 60 000 Mark mehr kaum höhere Fahrleistungen ein, dafür aber die turbinenartige Laufruhe des Zwölfzylinders sowie einen eher abstrakten Wert: viel Sozialprestige.

Ab Juni 1993 heißen die beiden Top-Modelle im Zuge der Mercedes-Namenreform SL 500 und SL 600, und die Dreiliter werden ersetzt durch einen SL 280 und einen SL 320, beide mit Vierventil-Technik. Nur noch der SL 280 hat ein Fünfgang-Schaltgetriebe. Auf der IAA im September 1995 zeigt sich die Baureihe technisch und optisch

La SL de la quatrième génération, attraction du salon de Genève de mars 1989, en versions 300 SL, 300 SL-24 et 500 SL, surclasse sa devancière à trois points de vue: son homogénéité esthétique, sa sécurité et son confort.

Le design, à la fois pétri de tradition et tourné vers l'avenir, est l'émanation d'une magnifique sobriété. La protection des passagers est égale à celle qu'offrent les berlines – malgré l'absence de toit. Mais cela est le fruit de nombreux facteurs, la plate-forme rigide, par exemple, aux tôles à haute résistance et aux généreuses poutres transversales. Nouveauté spectaculaire: l'arceau de sécurité automatique en acier à haute résistance. Comme les montants de pare-brise sont également en tôle d'acier à haute résistance, la SL offre donc un espace de survie à ses passagers même en cas de tonneau.

Le toit coupé ne joue plus aucun rôle structurel et, malgré des surfaces vitrées plus généreuses, il pèse 10 kg de moins. Pour ouvrir et fermer la capote électro-hydraulique, en revanche, il suffit d'appuyer sur un bouton. Tout le reste, ce sont 17 commutateurs de fin de course, 15 vérins hydrauliques et 11 électrovannes qui s'en chargent, en 30 secondes et en un processus admirablement orchestré par une ribambelle de microprocesseurs.

La suspension – avec essieu avant à jambes élastiques et essieu arrière multibras – correspond à celle des séries 210 et 124, mais toutefois adaptée aux besoins particuliers du roadster. Elle est complétée par des systèmes additionnels très en pointe, une correction d'assiette asservie à la vitesse et un système d'amortissement adaptatif ADS avec des amortisseurs réglables à commande électronique qui l'adapte instantanément à toute modification du revêtement. Les six-cylindres des deux 3 litres proviennent de chez Mercedes, mais ils ont été retravaillés dans les moindres détails. À titre d'exemple, le quatre-soupapes de la 300 SL-24 possède un variateur cartographique de l'arbre à cames d'admission au même titre que chaque banc de cylindres du V8 de 5 litres de la 500 SL, le moteur de série le plus puissant de chez Daimler-Benz avec 326 ch.

Mais tous ces chiffres font bien pâle figure comparés au V12 de 6 litres et 394 ch de la 600 SL présentée en octobre 1992. Pour un supplément de prix de 60 000 marks, ses acheteurs ne bénéficient guère de performances supérieures, mais, en revanche, de la montée en puissance du douze-cylindres digne d'une turbine ainsi que d'une valeur plutôt abstraite: un prestige social inégalable.

À partir de juin 1993, les deux modèles haut de gamme sont rebaptisés SL 500 et SL 600 tandis que les 3 litres sont remplacés par une SL 280 et une SL 320, toutes deux à culasse à quatre soupapes. Seule la SL 280 possède encore une boîte manuelle à cinq vitesses. À l'IAA, en septembre 1995, la gamme bénéficie des retouches mécaniques et esthétiques avec de nouveaux pare-chocs ainsi que des panneaux de carrosserie latéraux peints couleur carrosserie. Celui qui le désire peut obtenir à la place du *hard-top* en aluminium un toit en verre avec store pare-soleil et des

Mercedes-Benz SL 1988

Mercedes-Benz SL 500 1995

to use a 5-speed manual gearbox. At the Frankfurt Motor Show in September 1995 a technically and cosmetically updated series was unveiled with new bumpers which, like the side strips, were body-colored. On request buyers could have a glass roof with a sunblind in place of the aluminum hardtop, and xenon gas lamps with double the luminous efficiency. A cruise control for 30 kph zones helped avoid confrontations with the law.

The same month saw the replacement of the automatic gearbox used until then in the SL 500 and SL 600 by a compact, lightweight, 5-speed automatic transmission using a converter clutch and electronic transmission control. If the driver made errors while driving, the ESP electronic stability program, an optional extra in the SL 500 and fitted as standard to the SL 600, provided assistance. From June 1996 onwards the new automatic transmission was also available for the six-cylinders and it could be combined with the ESP from December 1996 onwards. In addition, SL drivers had the BAS brake assistance system. In 1998 the previous straight cylinder engines were replaced by V6 and V8 power units which are more compact, albeit not entirely refined.

retuschiert, mit neuen Stoßfängern wie auch den seitlichen Verkleidungen in Wagenfarbe. Wer das möchte, bekommt anstelle des Aluminium-Hardtops ein Glasdach mit Sonnenrollo und Xenon-Gaslampen mit doppelter Lichtausbeute. Ein Tempomat für 30-Kilometer-Zonen beugt Konflikten mit dem Gesetz vor.

Im gleichen Monat wird im SL 500 und SL 600 der bisherige Getriebeautomat ersetzt durch eine kompakte und leichte Fünfgang-Automatik mit Wandler-Überbrückungskupplung und elektronischer Getriebesteuerung. Bei Fahrfehlern geht dem Lenker das Fahrstabilitätsprogramm ESP zur Hand, Option beim SL 500, Serie am SL 600. Ab Juni 1996 ist die neue Automatik auch für die Sechszylinder verfügbar und kann vom Dezember des gleichen Jahres an mit dem Fahrdynamik-System ESP kombiniert werden. Zusätzlich greift nun dem SL-Piloten der Bremsassistent BAS unter die Arme. 1998 ersetzen V6- und V8-Triebwerke die bisherigen Reihenmotoren, kompakter, wenn auch nicht unbedingt kultivierter.

phares à décharge de gaz au xénon avec double rendement lumineux. Un régulateur de croisière pour les zones à 30 km/h prévient tout conflit avec les forces de l'ordre.

Le même mois, la boîte automatique équipant jusqu'alors la SL 500 et la SL 600 est remplacée par une nouvelle transmission automatique compacte et légère avec embrayage de pontage du convertisseur et commande de boîte électronique. En cas d'erreur de conduite, le programme de stabilité dynamique ESP vient au secours du conducteur; ce dispositif est proposé en option pour la SL 500 et offert en série sur la SL 600. À partir de juin 1996, la nouvelle boîte automatique est aussi disponible pour les six-cylindres et peut être combinée, à partir de décembre de la même année, au système ESP. Les pilotes de SL peuvent désormais compter sur l'aide supplémentaire du dispositif d'assistance au freinage BAS. En 1998, des moteurs V6 et V8, plus compacts, mais pas nécessairement plus perfectionnés, remplacent les anciens 6 et 8 en ligne.

The SL was at its best when completely open to the elements. However, to insure against the uncertainty of central European weather, occupants could have a top securely over their heads within 30 seconds—automatically.

Am liebsten präsentiert sich der SL in kompromissloser Offenheit. Den Wechselfällen und Schikanen mitteleuropäischer Witterung ausgeliefert, haben die Insassen indessen binnen 30 Sekunden ein Dach über dem Kopf – automatisch.

C'est décapotée que la SL fait la meilleure figure. Pour faire face aux aléas de la météorologie en Europe, les passagers peuvent refermer le toit en 30 secondes – automatiquement.

The cockpit of the SL500 with perfectly-designed seats under the steeply-inclined windshield, and its 326 bhp V8 engine which helped the roadster to deliver amazing performance figures.

Cockpit des SL 500 mit perfekt sitzendem Gestühl unter der starken Schräge der Windschutzscheibe und sein V8 von 326 PS, der dem Roadster zu souveränen Fahrleistungen verhilft.

L'habitacle de la SL500, avec ses fauteuils parfaits derrière le pare-brise fortement incliné et son V8 de 326 ch qui confère au roadster des performances souveraines.

The appearance of the S-Class at the Geneva Motor Show in March 1991 was not greeted exclusively by paeans of praise. Great lumps, moaned some, too large for most garages and many parking spaces. Future modifications were, therefore, often designed to correct this impression. The question of sheer size still remained, however: 16 ft 9 in × 6 ft 2 in × 4 ft 11 in for the standard version, 4 in more length and wheelbase for the longer version, and a thumping 20 ft 4½ in for the Pullman from September 1995.

In Germany the 140 series was initially offered with a choice of four engines, the first production V12 in the company's history at 6 liters and 408 bhp, the familiar 5-liter V8, and two other engines developed from existing units, a V8 of 4.2 liters and a six-cylinder of 3.2 liters. All used four-valves-per-cylinder technology and adjustable inlet camshafts and were fitted with state-of-the-art electronics: electronic injection and an ignition system that calculated the optimum ignition point for each cylinder individually from 300 ignition maps. The control modules of the engine and drive management system communicated with each other via a joint data channel.

The standard series was sumptuously appointed, including special features such as retractable external mirrors and a 2½-in-long reversing antenna at the rear which extended within two seconds once reverse gear was selected. The range was expanded at the Paris Show in October 1992 by the inclusion of the entry models 300 SE 2.8 and 350 SD. At the same time the eight- and twelve-cylinder engines had been made more economical, a development for which slight concessions had had to be made. The V12 now stood just under the magical 400 bhp threshold at 394 bhp. From May 1995 onwards the Parktronic system signaled distances at the front and rear ultrasonically; it was fitted as standard on the V12 and was available as an optional extra on the others.

From September of the same year onwards the previous 4-speed automatic gearbox was replaced by a 5-speed automatic transmission with a converter clutch that smoothly adapted to every driving situation, and that was also more compact and lighter. The ESP electronic stability program, which was fitted as standard in the S 600 or was an optional extra for the eight-cylinder models, used a sensor-controlled system to brake when required to counteract moments of instability. From June 1996 onwards the new automatic transmission was also available for the six-cylinder engines, as an optional extra in the S 280. Other new features included the front sidebags and a rain sensor which adjusted the wipe intervals to the amount of rain experienced. The side strips which had previously been in contrasting colors were now body-colored, though in a silk finish. A changing of the guard also took place in the S-Class diesels, from the S 350 Turbodiesel with 150 bhp to the S 300 Turbodiesel, a four-valves-per-cylinder model with intercooler and 177 bhp which was transmitted to the rear axle by the 5-speed automatic

Nicht nur wohlwollende Kommentare begleiten das Erscheinen der S-Klasse auf dem Genfer Salon im März 1991. Klötze seien das, grollen manche, zu groß für etliche Garagen und viele Parklücken. Und so dient künftige Modellpflege häufig dazu, diesen Eindruck zu verwischen. Dennoch bleibt schiere Größe: 5110 × 1890 × 1490 mm für die Normalversion, 100 mm mehr Länge und Radstand für die lange Variante, das Gardemaß von 6213 mm für den Pullman ab September 1995.

In Deutschland wird die Baureihe 140 zunächst mit vier Triebwerken angeboten, dem ersten serienmäßigen V12 in der Geschichte des Hauses mit sechs Litern und 408 PS, dem bekannten Fünfliter-V8 sowie zwei Maschinen, die aus existierenden Motoren entwickelt worden sind, einem V8 von 4,2 Litern und einem Sechszylinder mit 3,2 Litern. Sie alle haben Vierventil-Technik sowie verstellbare Einlassnockenwellen und sind mit den neuesten Segnungen der Elektronik versehen: elektronischer Einspritzung und einer Zündung, die den optimalen Zündzeitpunkt für jeden Zylinder einzeln aus 300 Kennfeldern errechnet. Die Steuermodule des Motor- und Antriebsmanagements kommunizieren über einen gemeinsamen Datenkanal miteinander.

Die Serienausstattung ist üppig und umspannt Besonderheiten wie abklappbare Außenspiegel und einen 65 mm langen Peilstab hinten, der binnen zwei Sekunden ausgefahren wird, nachdem der Rückwärtsgang eingelegt wurde. Auf der Pariser Show im Oktober 1992 wird die Palette bereichert um die Einstiegsmodelle 300 SE 2.8 und 350 SD. Zugleich hat man den Acht- und Zwölfzylindern mehr Genügsamkeit anerzogen, was mit geringen Aderlässen erkauft wird: Der V12 bleibt nun mit 394 PS knapp unter der magischen 400-PS-Grenze. Vom Mai 1995 meldet die Einparkhilfe Parktronic per Ultraschall die Abstände nach vorn und hinten, serienmäßig beim V12, auf Wunsch und gegen Mehrpreis bei den anderen.

Ab September des gleichen Jahres findet sich an der Stelle des bisherigen Viergang-Automaten eine Fünfgang-Automatik mit Wandler-Überbrückungskupplung, die sich schmiegsam in jede Fahrsituation einpasst und überdies kompakter und leichter ist. Als Grundausrüstung der S 600, Option bei den Achtzylindern, wirkt nun das Elektronische Fahrstabilitäts-Programm ESP bei Fahrfehlern sensorgesteuert durch gezielten Bremseingriff dem instabilen Moment entgegen. Ab Juni 1996 tut die neue Automatik auch in den Sechszylindern Dienst, beim S 280 auf Wunsch. Neu sind ebenfalls die vorderen Sidebags sowie ein Regensensor, der die Wischintervalle auf die Niederschlagsmenge abstimmt. Die seitlichen Anbauteile, vorher in Kontrastfarbe gehalten, schimmern jetzt in der Couleur des Wagenkörpers, allerdings seidig glänzend. Zugleich findet ein Wachwechsel bei den S-Dieseln statt, vom S 350 Turbodiesel mit 150 PS zum S 300 Turbodiesel, einem Vierventiler mit Ladeluftkühlung und 177 PS, welche von der Fünfgang-Automatik an die Hinterachse

La présentation de la Classe S, au Salon de Genève de mars 1991, ne recueille pas que des commentaires bienveillants. Quels horribles pachydermes, grognent certains, trop grands pour de nombreux garages et beaucoup de créneaux. Par la suite, Mercedes s'efforcera de dissiper cette impression. Imposante, elle l'est en effet: 5110 mm de long sur 1890 mm de large et 1490 de haut pour la version normale, 100 mm de plus en longueur et en empattement pour la version allongée et pas moins de 6213 mm pour la Pullman à partir de septembre 1995.

En Allemagne, la série 140 est tout d'abord proposée avec quatre moteurs, le premier V12 de série dans l'histoire de la maison, avec 6 litres et 408 ch, le V8 de 5 litres bien connu ainsi que deux nouveaux moteurs extrapolés de groupes préexistants, un V8 de 4,2 litres et un six-cylindres de 3,2 litres. Tous ont une culasse à quatre soupapes ainsi que des arbres à cames d'admission à décalage et sont dotés des dernières bénédictions de l'électronique: une injection électronique et un allumage qui calcule le moment optimal pour l'allumage de chaque cylindre à partir d'une cartographie à 300 paramètres. Le module de commande du moteur et de la chaîne cinématique communiquent entre eux grâce à un bus de données.

L'équipement de série est de grand luxe et comporte des particularismes comme des rétroviseurs extérieurs rabattables et une barre de visée de 65 mm à l'arrière qui se met en place en deux secondes dès que l'on enclenche la marche arrière. Au Salon de Paris, en octobre 1992, la gamme s'enrichit de deux modèles d'appel, la 300 SE 2.8 et la 350 SD. Pendant ce temps, on a insufflé plus de sobriété aux huit et douze-cylindres: avec 394 ch, le V12 reste désormais juste au-dessous du seuil magique des 400 ch. À partir de mai 1995, le système d'aide au stationnement Parktronic communique par ultrasons la distance vis-à-vis des obstacles à l'avant et à l'arrière, dispositif proposé en série pour la V12, mais sur demande et contre supplément de prix pour les autres modèles.

À partir de septembre de la même année, l'ancienne boîte automatique à quatre rapports disparaît au profit d'une transmission à cinq vitesses avec embrayage de pontage du convertisseur qui s'adapte aux différentes situations respectives et possède en outre l'avantage d'être plus compacte et plus légère. En équipement de base pour la S 600 et en option pour les huit-cylindres, le dispositif de stabilité dynamique électronique ESP gomme les erreurs de conduite à l'aide de capteurs qui répriment toute instabilité en freinant de façon ciblée une ou plusieurs roues. À partir de juin 1996, la nouvelle boîte automatique est aussi en service pour les six-cylindres, en option pour la S 280. Autres nouveautés, les airbags latéraux à l'avant ainsi qu'un détecteur de pluie qui calcule le rythme d'essuyage en fonction de la densité des précipitations. Les panneaux de protection latérale, autrefois ton sur ton, sont désormais dans la couleur de la carrosserie, mais avec une nuance plus soyeuse. Pour les Classe S à moteur diesel, une relève de la garde a lieu puisque la S 350 Turbodiesel de 150 ch fait

Mercedes-Benz S-Klasse & SEC/CL 1991

Mercedes-Benz S 320 1996

gearbox. From December 1996 onwards all S 280 and S 320 models with automatic transmission were fitted as standard with the ESP electronic stability program and, in line with the other models in the 129 and 140 series, with the BAS braking assistance system which cleverly detected emergency braking operations and determined the shortest braking distance. Although stylistically very much its own boss, the coupé, which was unveiled at the Motor Show in Detroit in January 1992 as the 500 SEC and 600 SEC, was greatly indebted in engineering terms to the S-Class sedans. The above models were joined by the S 420 coupé, launched in Geneva in 1994 for the slightly less well-off. All three were rebadged as CL 420, CL 500, and CL 600 in June 1996 and fitted with modified bumpers with integral sensors for the Parktronic system, which was fitted as standard. Other new standard features were the xenon lights and a cruise control with a limiter for 30 kph zones.

vermittelt werden. Vom Dezember 1996 an werden alle S 280 und S 320 mit Getriebeautomaten ausgestattet mit dem Fahrdynamik-System ESP sowie, analog zu den übrigen Modellen der Reihen 129 und 140, mit dem Bremsassistenten BAS, der Notbremsungen klug erkennt und den kürzesten Bremsweg ermittelt. Bei relativ großer formaler Eigenständigkeit technisch weitgehend den S-Limousinen verpflichtet ist das Coupé, im Januar 1992 bei der Motor Show zu Detroit eingeführt als 500 SEC und 600 SEC. Dazu gesellt sich in Genf 1994 das S 420 Coupé für die etwas weniger Wohlhabenden. Im Juni 1996 werden alle drei umbenannt in CL 420, CL 500 und CL 600 und ausgestattet mit überarbeiteten Stoßfängern, in die man die Sensoren für das serienmäßige System Parktronic integriert hat. Ebenfalls neu, aber im Grundpreis enthalten: Xenon-Licht sowie ein Tempomat mit einem Begrenzer auf 30 Stundenkilometer.

place à une S 300 Turbodiesel, avec un quatre-soupapes à intercooler développant 177 ch qui sont transmis à l'essieu arrière par une boîte automatique à cinq rapports. À partir de décembre 1996, toutes les S 280 et S 320 à boîte automatique reçoivent aussi le dispositif de stabilité dynamique ESP ainsi que, par analogie aux autres modèles des séries 129 et 140, le dispositif intelligent d'assistance de freinage BAS qui reconnaît les freinages d'urgence et calcule la distance de freinage la plus courte. Le coupé, qui se distingue par une personnalité esthétique relativement grande, mais est, techniquement, très proche des berlines de la Classe S, est présenté en janvier 1992 au Detroit Motor Show en versions 500 SEC et 600 SEC. Pour le Salon de Genève de 1994, ils sont rejoints par le coupé S 420 destiné à ceux qui ne sont pas tout aussi aisés. En juin 1996, tous trois sont rebaptisés en CL 420, CL 500 et CL 600 et reçoivent des pare-chocs d'une forme nouvelle dans lesquels on a intégré les capteurs pour le système Parktronic offert en série. Autres nouveautés toutefois comprises dans le prix de base, les phares au xénon ainsi qu'un régulateur de croisière avec un limiteur à 30 km/h.

Although of extremely solid proportions, the S-Class series 140 also proved surprisingly nimble. Steps were taken in 1994 to brighten up previously bare surfaces, so that the sedan did not look quite so imposing.

Von ungemein stattlichen Proportionen, gibt sich die S-Klasse Baureihe 140 gleichwohl erstaunlich behende. 1994 werden vormals kahle Flächen visuell belebt, so dass die Limousine weniger monumental erscheint.

Bien qu'extrêmement imposante, la Classe S série 140 n'en est pas moins étonnamment maniable. En 1994, les panneaux de carrosserie jusqu'alors lisses sont rainurés pour donner plus de légèreté à la berline.

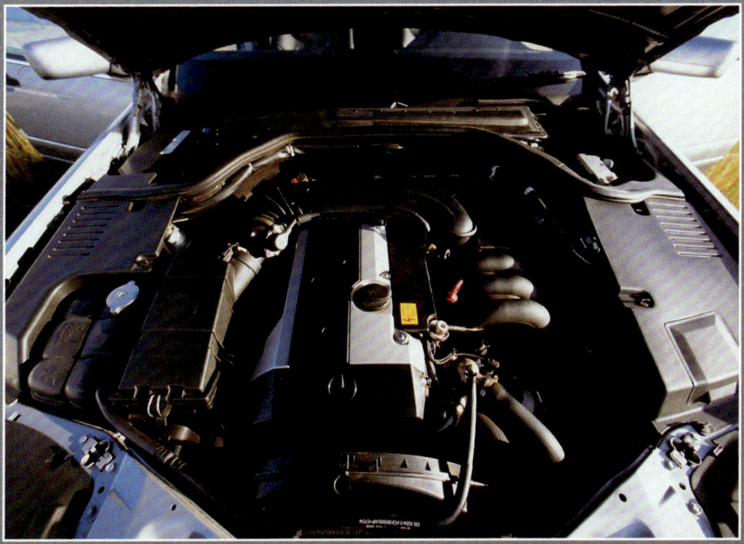

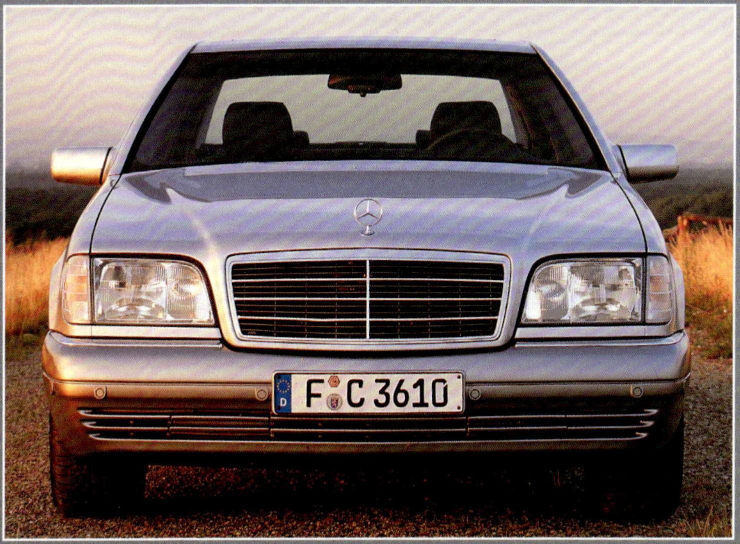
F C 3610

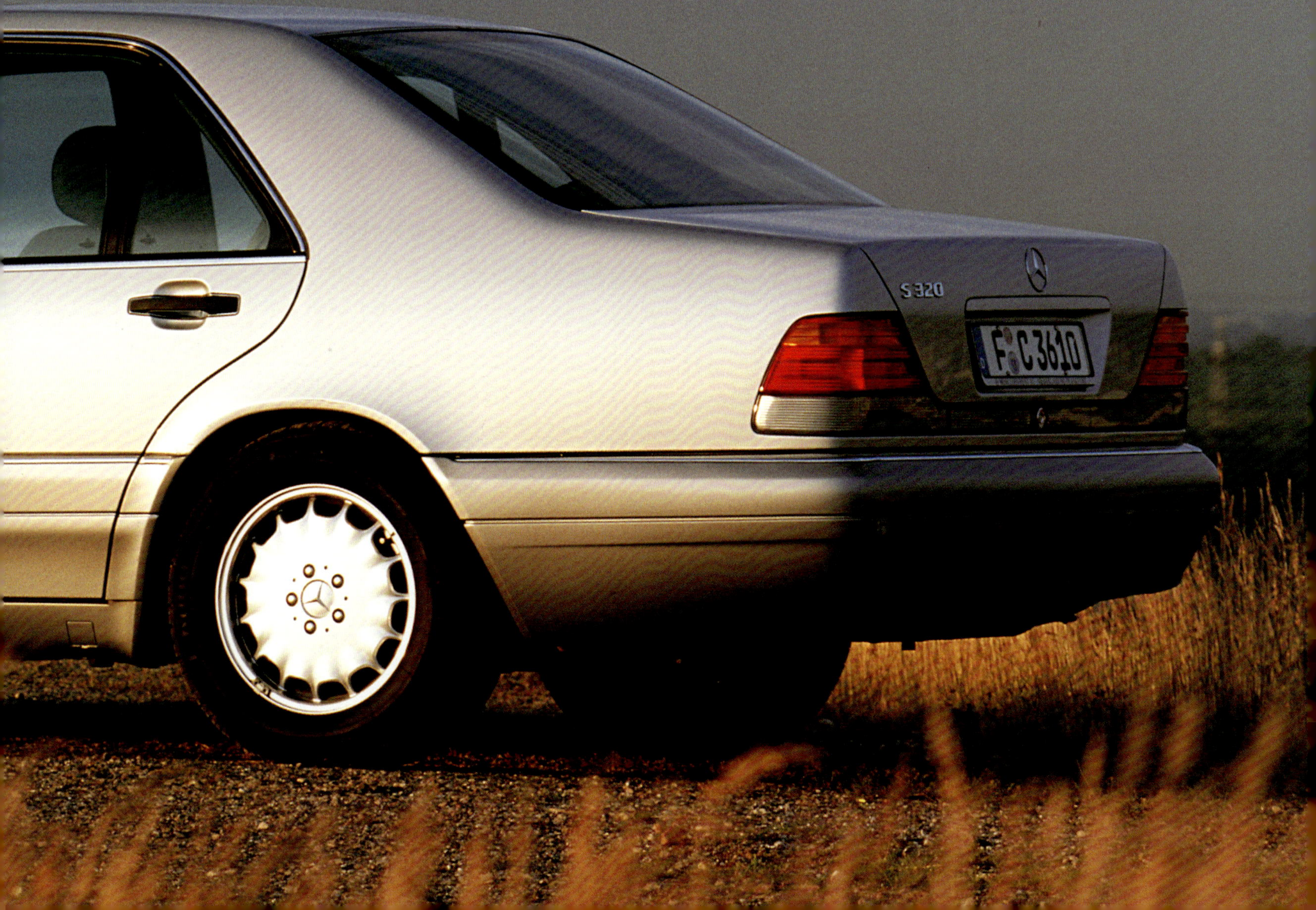
S 320
F C 3610

Mercedes-Benz S-Klasse & SEC/CL 1991

The entry-level model: a CL 420 from 1997 wearing the face adopted from the SL. The coupé did not attempt to hide its size, and offered its rear-seat passengers a comfortable ride below its broad C-pillars.

Einstiegsmodell: ein CL 420 von 1997 mit seinem vom SL übernommenen Gesicht. Das Coupé mag seine Größe ebenfalls nicht verhehlen und gestattet unter seinen breit ausgeprägten C-Säulen auch den hinten Sitzenden bequemes Reisen.

Modèle d'entrée de gamme: une CL 420 de 1997 avec sa proue inspirée de la SL. Le coupé ne cherche pas, lui non plus, à dissimuler sa grandeur et permet aussi aux passagers de l'arrière de voyager avec tout le confort dû à leur rang.

Mercedes-Benz S-Klasse & SEC/CL 1991

Like the S-Class models, the second generation of compact Mercedes, launched in May 1993, was given its own name. It was now known as the C-Class, with the C preceding the three-digit numerical code in accordance with the new Mercedes system. For about the same amount of money as for the W201 predecessor, the customer now got more car: more space, more safety, more comfort. A driver's airbag, integrated side-impact protection, ABS, power steering, 5-speed transmission, and central locking were included in the standard package. In addition to the standard version, there were also three special versions of the W202 that were obviously aimed at a younger clientele. The Esprit sat an inch lower and had a brightly colored interior; the Elegance was sumptuously appointed inside, and bore protective strips in contrasting colors, various chrome trims, and different lights; and the Sport, also with a lowered suspension, had harder running gear, wide tires and alloy wheels. Those whose thirst for a dynamic look was still not satisfied could turn to the AMG variant which offered a lowered sports suspension, different skirts, and side panels.

Four gasoline engines were available, the four-valves-per-cylinder types familiar from the 124 series and a new 1.8-liter engine with electronic injection, together with three diesel powerplants, the two-liter from the preceding model, and 2.2-liter and 2.5-liter engines, both using four-valves-per-cylinder technology for the first time. At the Frankfurt Motor Show in September 1993, collaboration with dynamic partner AMG in Affalterbach reached high C, as it were, with the C 36 AMG, which contributed a powerful helping hand in the form of a six-cylinder, 4-valve, 3.6-liter engine which delivered 280 bhp.

There were quite a number of innovations in the 202 series to report from the Frankfurt International Motor Show in the autumn of 1995. The standard model was now called Classic, and had new lights plus an updated interior, the whole series had been shod with 195/65 R 15 tires and its front track had been increased by ¼ in. Two new variants were pressurized in different ways: the C 230 Kompressor had a Roots supercharger that coaxed 193 bhp from its four-cylinder engine, and the C 250 Turbodiesel with four valves per cylinder by an exhaust-driven turbocharger that helped it to 150 bhp and so to a lively performance. Both engines offered a good torque response over a wide engine speed range. The introduction of their turbocharged counterpart signaled the disappearance without trace of the C 200 Diesel and the C 250 Diesel, while the C 220 was replaced in August 1996 by the C 230. From then on the whole range was available on request, and at an extra charge, with a 5-speed automatic transmission which reduced fuel consumption, noise, and also maintenance costs.

Three months earlier Mercedes had entered the sporty compact estate-car sector with the T model which had nevertheless proved to be unusually spacious. Measured in accordance with the VDA norm, it had a capacity of

Analog zu den S-Modellen bekommt die zweite Generation der kompakten Mercedes, vorgestellt im Mai 1993, einen eigenen Namen. Sie heißt nun C-Klasse, mit dem C vor dem dreistelligen Zahlencode nach neuem Benz-Brauch. Für ungefähr das gleiche Geld wie für den Vorgänger W201 erwirbt der Kunde mehr Auto: mehr Raum, mehr Sicherheit, mehr Komfort. Ins Serienpaket geschnürt sind Fahrer-Airbag, integrierter Seitenaufprallschutz, Servolenkung, Fünfganggetriebe, ABS sowie Zentralverriegelung. Neben der Standardausführung bietet man den W202 in drei Sonderversionen an, die offensichtlich an eine jüngere Klientel adressiert sind, als Esprit 25 mm tiefer und mit farbig-frohem Interieur, als Elegance mit üppiger Innenausstattung, Schutzleisten in Kontrastfarben, diversen Chromintarsien und anderen Leuchten und als Sport, wiederum tiefer gelegt, mit härterem Fahrwerk, Breitreifen und Leichtmetallfelgen. Wen es nach noch mehr visueller Dynamik dürstet, der kann mit der AMG-Variante zufriedengestellt werden, die mit einem abgesenkten Sportfahrwerk, anderen Schürzen und seitlichen Schwellern daherkommt.

Vier Ottomotoren stehen zur Verfügung, die aus der Baureihe 124 bekannten Vierventiler und ein neuer 1,8-Liter mit elektronischer Einspritzung, dazu drei Dieseltriebwerke: der Zweiliter aus dem Vorgänger sowie ein 2,2-Liter und ein 2,5-Liter, beide erstmals mit Vierventiltechnik. Auf der IAA im September 1993 zeitigt die Zusammenarbeit mit dem dynamischen Partner AMG in Affalterbach gewissermaßen das hohe C mit dem C 36 AMG, dem ein Sechszylinder-Vierventiler mit 3,6 Litern und 280 PS mächtig auf die Sprünge hilft.

Auf der Frankfurter Ausstellung im Herbst 1995 gibt es mancherlei Neues zu berichten von der Baureihe 202: das Standardmodell heißt nun Classic und hat neue Leuchten sowie ein aktualisiertes Interieur, die ganze Reihe ist mit Reifen des Formats 195/65 R 15 besohlt und hat sechs Millimeter mehr Spurweite vorn. Zwei neue Spielarten werden auf unterschiedliche Weise unter Druck gesetzt: der C 230 Kompressor von einem Roots-Gebläse, das seinem Vierzylinder 193 PS einhaucht, der C 250 Turbodiesel mit vier Ventilen je Zylinder von einem Abgaslader, der ihm zu 150 PS und damit ebenfalls zu munteren Fahrleistungen verhilft. Beide Maschinen warten mit einem guten Drehmoment über ein weites Drehzahlband auf. Mit dem Erscheinen ihres zwangsbeatmeten Pendants verschwinden der C 200 Diesel und der C 250 Diesel sang- und klanglos aus dem Programm, während der C 220 im August 1996 durch den C 230 abgelöst wird. Vom gleichen Zeitpunkt an gibt es die gesamte Palette auf Wunsch und gegen Aufpreis mit einer Fünfgang-Automatik, die Verbrauch und Geräuschemission ebenso mäßigt wie die Kosten für ihre Wartung.

Ein Vierteljahr vorher sind die Untertürkheimer in das Segment der sportlich-kompakten Kombis mit dem T-Modell vorgestoßen, das sich gleichwohl als ungewöhnlich geräumig erweist: mit 1510 Litern nach

À l'instar des modèles de la Classe S, la deuxième génération de la compacte Mercedes présentée en mai 1993 se voit dotée d'un nom spécifique. Elle s'appelle Classe C, le C se trouvant devant le code à trois chiffres selon les us et coutumes désormais en vigueur chez Mercedes. Pour une somme sensiblement identique à celle qu'il fallait débourser pour sa devancière la W201, le client en a maintenant plus pour son argent: plus d'espace, plus de sécurité, plus de confort. L'équipement de série comporte l'airbag conducteur, une protection intégrée anticollision latérale, l'ABS, la direction assistée, une boîte à cinq vitesses ainsi que le verrouillage centralisé. Outre l'exécution standard, la W202 est proposée en trois versions spéciales destinées à une clientèle plus jeune, l'Esprit à châssis surbaissé de 25 mm et habitacle haut en couleur, l'Elegance à l'aménagement intérieur très généreux, avec bandes de protection latérales de couleur contrastée, diverses applications de chrome et d'autres optiques, et, enfin, la Sport, elle aussi à châssis surbaissé, avec trains roulants plus fermes, pneus larges et jantes alliage. Celui qui souhaite plus d'esthétisme peut être comblé avec la version AMG caractérisée par un châssis sport surbaissé, d'autres boucliers et des jupes de bas de caisse.

La motorisation consiste en quatre moteurs à essence, les quatre-soupapes connus de la série 124 et un nouveau 1,8 litre à injection électronique, plus trois moteurs diesel: le deux litres de l'ancien modèle ainsi qu'un 2,2 litres et un 2,5 litres, dotés d'une culasse à quatre soupapes. À l'IAA de septembre 1993, la coopération avec le partenaire de Mercedes-Benz, AMG, à Affalterbach, porte ses fruits avec la C 36 AMG. Un six-cylindres à quatre soupapes de 3,6 litres et 280 ch lui confère des performances hors du commun.

Lors du Salon de Francfort, à l'automne 1995, les nouveautés de la gamme 202 ne manquent pas: le modèle standard s'appelle Classic et a de nouveaux phares ainsi qu'un intérieur remis au goût du jour, toute la gamme étant chaussée de pneus de 195/65 R 15 avec des voies élargies de 6 mm à l'avant. Deux nouvelles variantes sont mises sous pression de façon différente: la C 230 Kompressor avec un compresseur Roots qui confère 193 ch à son quatre-cylindres, ainsi que la C 250 Turbodiesel à quatre soupapes par cylindre avec un turbocompresseur qui lui insuffle 150 ch et la rend plus performante que la moyenne. Les deux moteurs se distinguent par un couple généreux sur une large plage de régime. L'apparition de son homologue turbochargé signifie pour la C 200 Diesel et la C 250 Diesel une disparition du programme alors que la C 220 est remplacée, en août 1996, par la C 230. Toute la gamme est disponible sur demande et contre supplément avec une boîte automatique à cinq rapports qui tempère aussi bien la consommation et le niveau sonore que les coûts d'utilisation.

Trois mois plus tôt, le constructeur de Stuttgart s'est lancé dans le segment des breaks sportifs et compacts avec le modèle T qui se signale par une habitabilité généreuse: avec un coffre de 1510 litres de capacité selon la norme VDA

Mercedes-Benz C-Klasse 1993

Mercedes-Benz C180 1996

53.3 cu.ft if loaded right up to roof level or 16.4 cu.ft in the normal luggage compartment. Initially two diesel engines and three gasoline engines could be ordered, the former being a four-cylinder, 2.2-liter model and the 2.5-liter turbodiesel with five cylinders, and the gasoline models of 1.8, 2.0, and 2.3 liters which were also fitted to the sedans in slightly modified form.

This illustrates a time-honored Daimler-Benz principle—a development spawns more offspring that in turn advance further development. 1997 saw quite far-reaching changes in the engine sector when tried-and-tested old friends were ditched to be replaced by new v6 engines with 18 valves, a 2.4-liter model to replace the previous inline four-cylinder in the C 230 and, almost at the same price, a 2.8-liter model in the C 280. And for those who like it hot, the AMG high-performance subsidiary in Affalterbach presented the top model in the series at the Frankfurt Motor Show in autumn 1997: the C 43 AMG, powered by a 4.3 liter v8 producing 306 horsepower.

VDA-Norm bei Beladung bis unters Dach, mit 465 Litern, die sich im normalen Gepäckabteil verstauen lassen. Zunächst können zwei Diesel- und drei Otto-Aggregate geordert werden, die Selbstzünder mit einem Vierzylinder von 2,2 Litern und dem 2,5-Liter Turbodiesel mit fünf Verbrennungseinheiten, die Benziner mit 1,8, 2,0 und 2,3 Litern, die etwas modifiziert und in ihrer überarbeiteten Form wieder in die Limousinen eingebracht werden.

So entlässt die Evolution ihre Kinder, die ihrerseits die Evolution vorantragen, Daimler-Benz-Prinzip von altersher. Massivere Eingriffe gibt es indessen 1997 im Motorensektor, als man Gestandenes und längst Bewährtes über Bord wirft und neue V6-Maschinen mit 18 Ventilen einführt, mit 2,4 Litern anstatt des bisherigen Reihen-Vierzylinders im C 230 und fast um den gleichen Preis, mit 2,8 Litern im C 280. Für alle aber, die es heiß mögen, hält die Hochleistungs-Filiale AMG seit der Frankfurter Ausstellung im Herbst 1997 den C 43 AMG bereit, in dessen Motorenabteil sich ein v8 von 4,3 Litern für 306 PS stark macht.

en étant chargé jusque sous le toit et avec 465 litres en configuration normale. On a le choix entre deux diesels et trois moteurs à essence, les moteurs à auto-allumage étant un quatre-cylindres de 2,2 litres et le 2,5 litres Turbodiesel à cinq-cylindres, alors que les moteurs à essence ont une cylindrée de 1,8, 2 et 2,3 litres et sont proposés pour les berlines avec de légères modifications.

C'est ainsi que l'évolution engendre ses enfants qui, eux-mêmes, génèrent de nouvelles évolutions, principe cultivé de tout temps par Daimler-Benz. Des interventions plus significatives sur les moteurs sont à l'ordre du jour en 1997, année qui voit l'abandon de solutions depuis longtemps éprouvées et l'apparition d'un moteur v6 à 18 soupapes, avec 2,4 litres pour l'ancien quatre-cylindres en ligne de la C 230 et, presque pour le même prix, avec 2,8 litres dans la C 280. Mais, pour tous ceux qui n'ont jamais assez de chevaux sous le capot, les ateliers d'AMG, le service Course, à Affalterbach, proposent aussi, depuis le Salon de l'automobile de Francfort, à l'automne 1997, une version C transcendée: la C 43 AMG équipée d'un moteur v8 de 4,3 litres délivrant 306 ch.

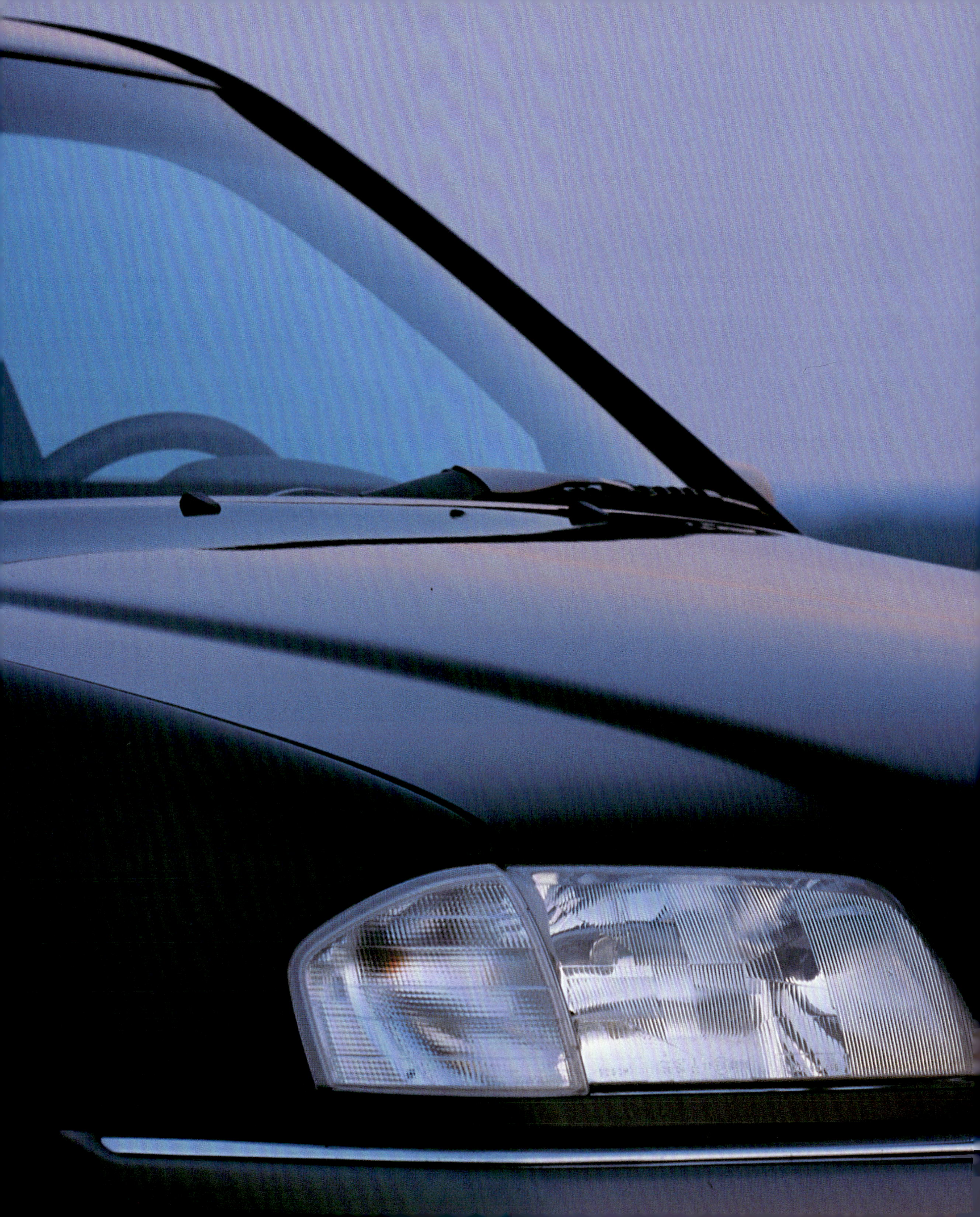

The compact Mercedes for the second half of the Nineties—technically, ergonomically, and aerodynamically refined. But perfectionists will always find something extra to improve.

Der kompakte Mercedes für die zweite Hälfte der neunziger Jahre: technisch, ergonomisch und aerodynamisch ausgefeilt. Aber für Perfektionisten gibt es immer noch etwas zu perfektionieren.

La compacte Mercedes de la seconde moitié des années 1990: sophistiquée sur le plan mécanique, ergonomique et aérodynamique. Mais pour les perfectionnistes, des améliorations sont toujours possibles.

Mercedes-Benz C-Klasse 1993

T time again: the C-Class station wagon was light and sporty, and intentionally so. Station wagons had long since rid themselves of the reputation of being merely functional.

Kennzeichen T: Der Kombi im C-Format gibt sich leicht und sportlich. Das ist beabsichtigt. Denn längst haftet dem Kombinationskraftwagen nicht mehr das Odium kühler Nützlichkeit an.

Sous le signe du T: le break de la Classe C se veut léger et sportif. Ce n'est pas le fait du hasard. En effet, il y a longtemps que le break n'est plus réservé aux seuls professionnels.

The new mid-range Mercedes, launched as the 210 series in June 1995, was unmistakably an Untertürkheim product. Stylistically, however, there were hints of independence; for example, the rear light assemblies which were parabolically rounded into the sides, and in particular the anatomic peculiarity of its four-eyed face, four discrete elliptical lights flanking the radiator grille.

The customer had the choice of eight powerplants, five gasoline and three diesel engines. The gasoline engines were as follows: four-cylinder with 2 liters (136 bhp) and 2.3 liters (150 bhp), six-cylinder with 2.8 liters (193 bhp) and 3.2 liters (220 bhp), a v8 of 4.2 liters (279 bhp), all with four valves per cylinder. Two of the diesels were old friends, the 2.2-liter model delivering 95 bhp and the turbocharged 3-liter with 177 bhp. A new five-cylinder engine of 2.9 liters delivering 129 bhp, with a turbocharger, intercooler and direct injection represented the state of the art. In one respect progress involved reverting to technology that was thought to have passed its sell-by date—the E 290 Turbodiesel's metabolism was controlled by only two valves per cylinder.

The more difficult market situation that obtained in the mid-Nineties meant that the basic price had long since become inclusive of a number of useful and desirable features, such as an electronic driver authority system, the ETS electronic traction system, electrically operated windows front and rear, a third brake light on the parcel shelf, seat-belt load limiters and sidebags. Making their first appearance in the 210 model line were a rain sensor, which adjusted wiper speed in accordance with the amount of rain, and the Parktronic ultrasonic parking aid.

The control of the injection, ignition, and exhaust gas functions was in the hands of the Bosch Motronic 1.0. Engine management in the E 420 also entailed electronic transmission control of the 5-speed automatic gearbox. Six months after the series launch, the E 500 was succeeded by the E 50 AMG, with a 5-liter v8 developing 347 bhp whose external appearance and suspension setup also betrayed that it was obviously on the warpath. Its gearbox was a new automatic 5-speed transmission that reduced fuel consumption, noise emissions, and the number of gear changes, while also being more robust and durable than in earlier generations. From June 1996 onwards, this was also available either as an optional extra or as standard equipment in the models with four, five, and six cylinders. The T model, based on the sedan but with massively reinforced structures particularly in the tail end where the fuel tank was located under the luggage compartment and behind the axle, had made its appearance one month previously. Apart from offering more comfort and freedom of movement for the occupants than its predecessor, this star-badged aristocrat among estate cars also offered an additional 2.5 cu.ft of load capacity. This was also available in three trim versions (Classic, Elegance, and Avantgarde) with the full range of engines of the sedans and 5-speed

Mercedes-Benz E-Klasse 1995

Mercedes-Benz E 230 1995

manual gearboxes in the four- and five-cylinder models. The automatic transmission with its slip-controlled converter clutch was fitted as standard to the top models with six or eight cylinders, and was otherwise available as an optional extra. 1997 saw novel features appear under the hood where newly developed v6 engines replaced the previous straight-six engines in two cases, namely in the E 280 with 204 bhp and in the E 320 with 224 bhp. At the same time these models saw the resurrection of the 4matic principle, though as a permanent four-wheel-drive with automatic braking of spinning wheels, instead of the conventional differential locks. According to the specialist publication *auto motor und sport*, there was no better system.

Automatik mit schlupfgesteuerter Wandler-Überbrückungskupplung bleibt als Serienausstattung den Top-Typen mit sechs oder acht Verbrennungseinheiten vorbehalten und ist ansonsten aufpreispflichtig. Das Jahr 1997 beschert Novitäten unter der vorderen Haube, wo in zwei Fällen neu entwickelte v6-Triebwerke die bisherigen Reihen-Sechszylinder verdrängen, im E 280 mit 204 PS, im E 320 mit 224 PS. Zugleich feiert in diesen Modellen das Prinzip 4matic Urständ, allerdings als permanenter Allradantrieb mit automatischem Bremseingriff an durchdrehenden Rädern statt der üblichen Differentialsperren. Ein besseres System, bescheinigt das Fachblatt *auto motor und sport*, gebe es nicht.

La transmission automatique avec embrayage de pontage du convertisseur commandé par patinage reste proposée en série uniquement pour les modèles haut de gamme à six ou huit-cylindres et facturée en sus pour les autres modèles. L'année 1997 se traduit par des nouveautés sous le capot moteur où, dans deux cas, de nouveaux moteurs v6 remplacent les anciens six-cylindres en ligne, dans la E 280 avec 204 ch et dans la E 320 avec 224 ch. Simultanément, le système 4matic fait sa réapparition sur ces modèles, mais en tant que traction intégrale permanente avec intervention automatique par freinage des roues qui patinent à la place des blocages de différentiel conventionnels. Selon la revue spécialisée *auto motor und sport*, il n'y a pas de meilleur système.

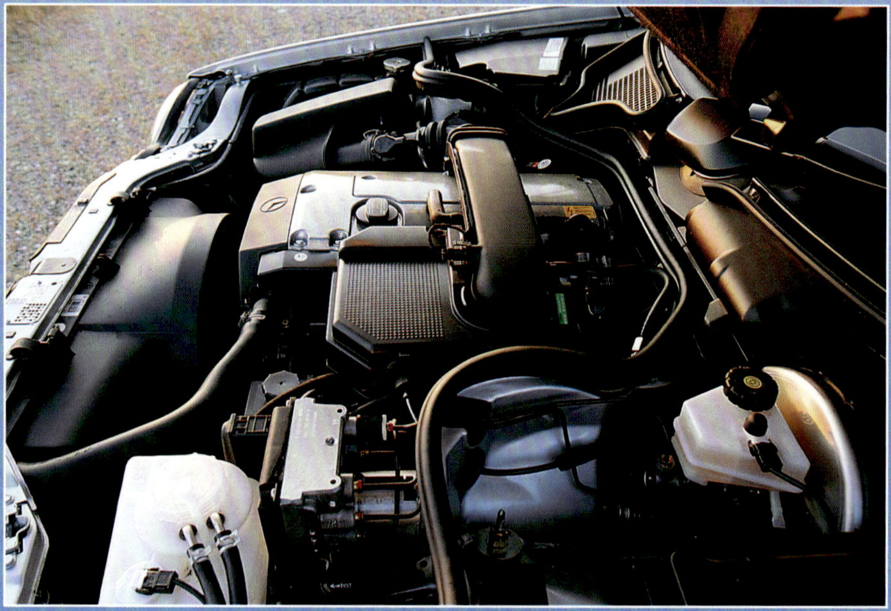

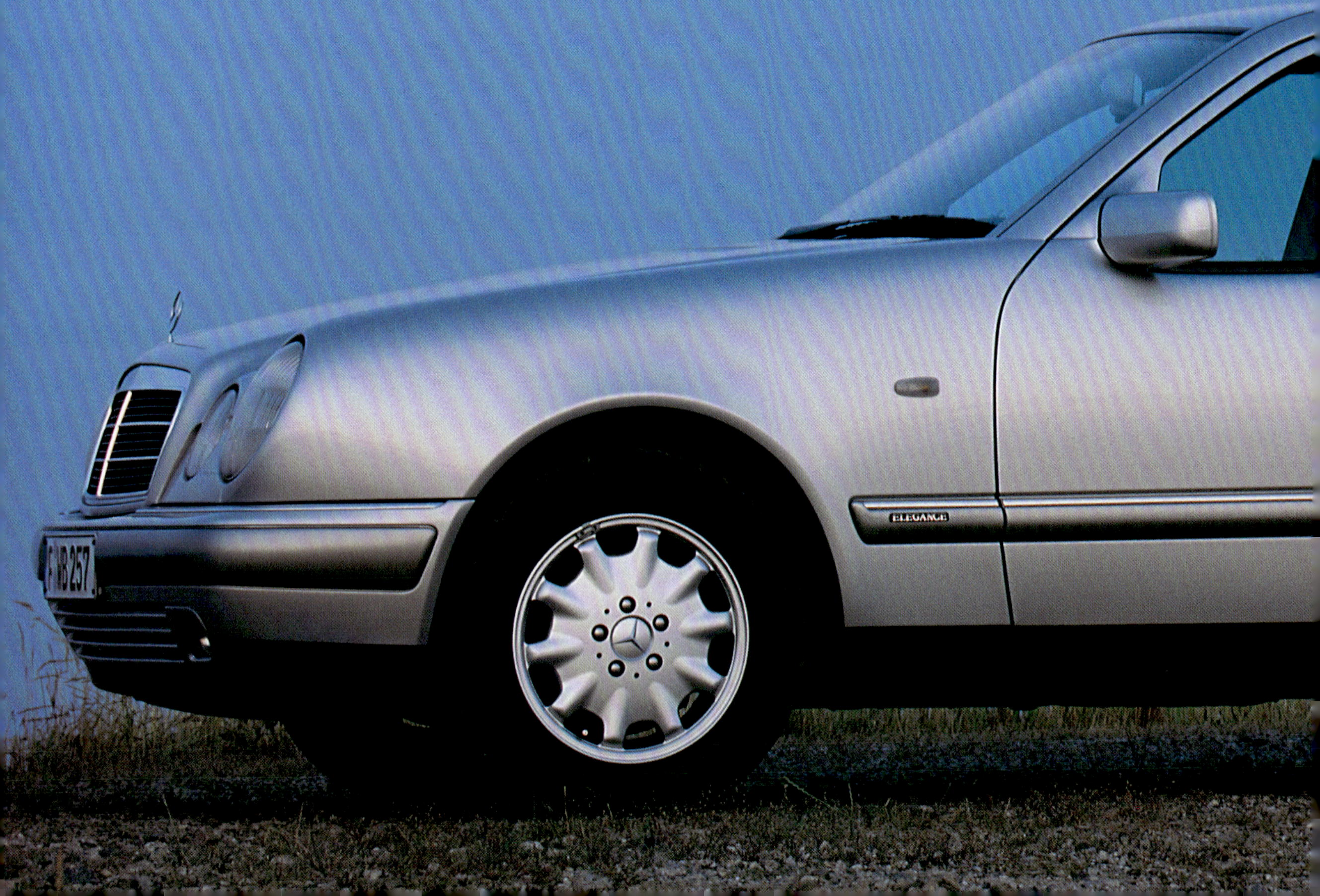
ELEGANCE

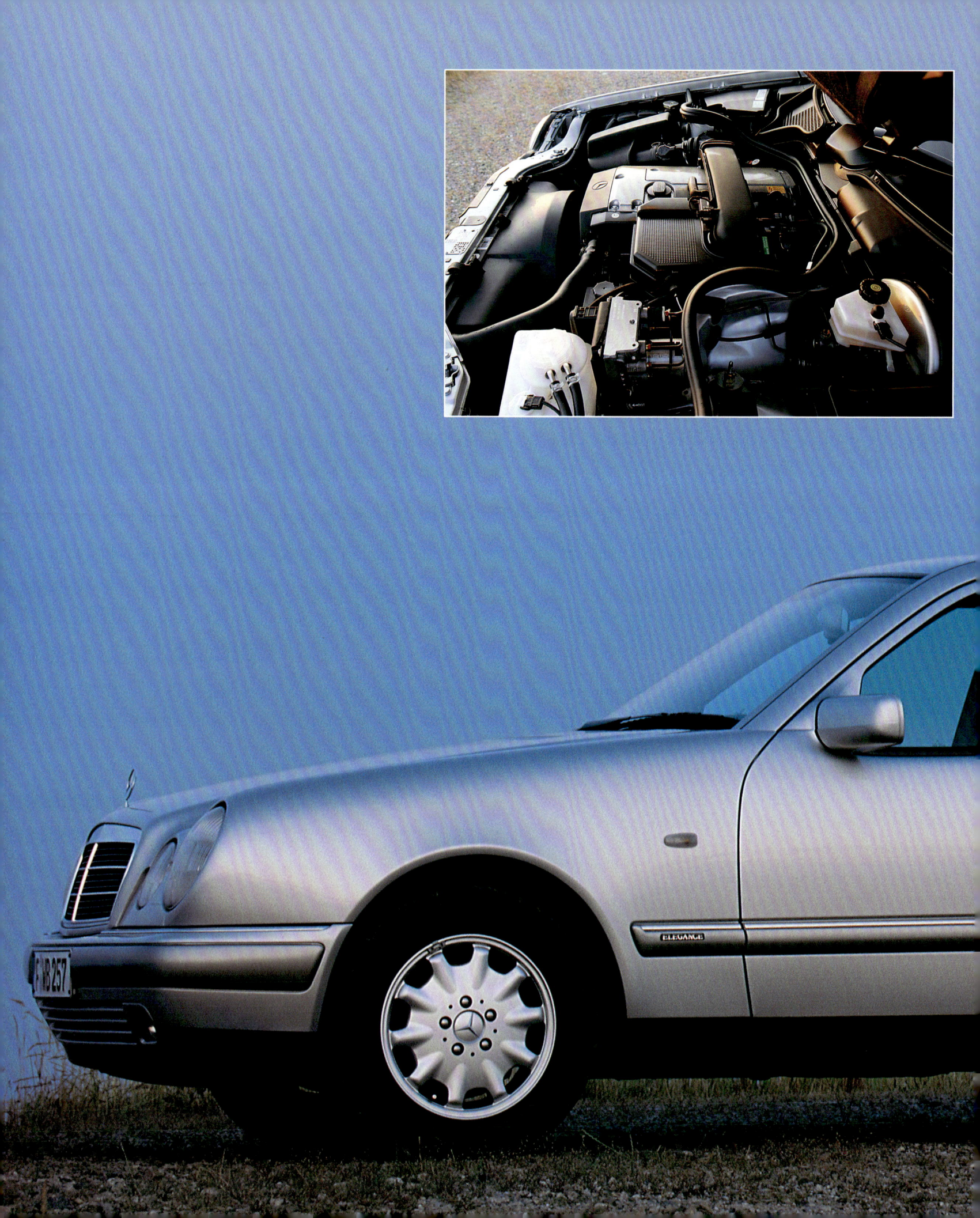

The tail section of the new mid-range Mercedes—represented here by the E 230—was reminiscent of the marque's coupés. Attractive plane-wood trim was included as standard.

Die Heckpartie des neuen Mercedes für die Mittelklasse – hier vertreten durch den E 230 – erinnert an die Coupés der Marke. Schmucke Intarsien aus Platanenholz gehören zur Serienausstattung.

La partie arrière de la nouvelle Mercedes du segment intermédiaire – ici celle de la E 230 – rappelle les coupés de la marque. Les élégantes applications de platane font partie de l'équipement de série.

"With this car we are experiencing a renaissance of automobile esthetics," declared Helmut Werner, chairman of the executive board of Mercedes-Benz AG, ignoring the hurricane of the wind tunnel resounding in everyone's ears.

"In a car like this the journey is the end in itself," added Jürgen Hubbert, board member and head of the passenger car section.

Of course all this is corporate hype to woo waverers and entice new customers. However, the SLK has no need of any such assistance. Launched at the Turin Exhibition in April 1996, it is half young Siegfried and half Don Juan reborn in the guise of a motor vehicle, the sweetest temptation to come out of Untertürkheim in living memory. It is love at first sight, as you gaze on the low windshield, the long hood, the wide doors and the defiant tail, with short valances at front and rear and a comparatively long wheelbase of 7 ft 10½ in, plus of course that certain indefinable something.

And then there's the price, throwing down the gauntlet to its competitors in this difficult market sector: precisely calculated at 60,950 marks for the more expensive of the two 2.3-liter models, with its supercharger generating 193 bhp. The version with the normally aspirated engine generating 136 bhp costs a modest 54,150 marks, and for this price the lucky owner gets two cars: press a little red button and in 25 seconds the SLK coupé you drove away from the show room retracts its roof to become a roadster. All material that could flap, flutter, judder, get wet, or spoil the elegant lines simply disappears.

Before the SLK reveals itself to the sun, moon, or stars, six precisely coordinated operations take place, all controlled by five hydraulic cylinders, two to drive the retractable roof, two for the loading action of the trunk lid, and one to fasten the roof when it is put up again. When the operation is complete the carefully folded hardtop is fully hidden from view in the trunk. That's the good news. The bad news is that this complex operation reduces the volume of the trunk from a reasonable 12.3 cu.ft to a somewhat miserly 5.1 cu.ft, so that for long journeys with plenty of luggage the roof has to stay up. Two steps have been taken in the factory to combat this problem: the fuel tank holds just 14 gallons and a spare wheel has been completely omitted (though a collapsible compact spare tire is available as an option): if the worst comes to the worst and you do have a puncture, and statistically this happens only once every 90,000 miles, a Tirefit tire repair kit, consisting of sealant and an electric pump, provides first aid.

SLK is a blend of well-known Mercedes designations of the past, and stands for *Sport, Leicht, Kurz* (Sport, Light, Short). "Light," as always with Mercedes, is somewhat economical with the truth: the SLK 230 Kompressor weighs in at 2921 lbs. "Short" is true enough, though: this mini Mercedes needs less parking space than a VW Golf. And it is definitely sporty, with a top speed of 144 mph, 0–62 mph in 7.5 seconds, and with agile, quicksilver steering, while

»Wir erleben mit ihm eine Renaissance automobiler Ästhetik«, sagt Helmut Werner, Vorstandsvorsitzer der Mercedes-Benz AG, so als sei die im alles glättenden Orkan des Windkanals verlorengegangen.

Und: »In einem solchen Automobil ist der Weg das Ziel«, sekundiert ihm Jürgen Hubbert, Mitglied des Vorstands und zuständig für das Geschäftsfeld PKW.

Das ist natürlich Konzernlyrik, Buhlen um Zaudernde, dazu bestimmt, neue Kunden zu betören. Nur: So was hat der SLK, vorgestellt auf dem Turiner Salon im April 1996, gar nicht nötig, halb Jung Siegfried, halb Don Juan in Autogestalt und die süßeste Verlockung aus Untertürkheim seit Menschengedenken. Liebe geht durch das Auge, und das sieht eine niedrige Frontscheibe, lange Motorhaube, breite Türen und ein trotziges Heck, dazu kurze Überhänge vorn und hinten und den vergleichsweise langen Radstand von 2400 Millimetern, versetzt mit einer Riesenportion gewisses Etwas.

Dazu der Preis, ein frecher Fehdehandschuh mitten ins Gesicht der Konkurrenten im fraglichen Marktsegment: laserscharf kalkulierte 60 950 Mark für die teurere der beiden Versionen mit 2,3-Liter-Triebwerk und Kompressor, 193 Pferdestärken stark. Die andere, mit einem Zweiliter-Saugmotor und 136 PS, kostet gar nur bescheidene 54 510 Mark. Um diesen Betrag kriegt der glückliche Besitzer zwei Autos: Ein Druck auf eine kleine rote Taste, und das Coupé, als das man den SLK vielleicht noch beim Händler abgeholt hat, weil das Wetter einfach unausstehlich war, wechselt in 25 Sekunden seinen Aggregatzustand und wird zum Roadster. Jegliches Stoffliche entfällt, mithin alles, was flattern, knattern, frösteln machen, durchnässen oder eine schöne Form schnöde verstümmeln könnte.

Bevor Sonne, Mond und Sterne Zugang zum Inneren des SLK haben, laufen sechs penibel koordinierte Arbeitsgänge ab, angezettelt und durchgeführt von fünf Hydraulikzylindern, zwei für den Antrieb des Variodachs, zwei für die einladende Bewegung des Kofferraumdeckels, ein weiterer für die Verriegelung des Dachs am Scheibenrahmen, wenn die Sache wieder rückgängig gemacht wird. Am Ende ruht das Hardtop sorgfältig zerknickt und dem neugierigen Blick radikal entzogen im Kofferraum. Soweit die gute Nachricht. Die schlechte: Dass sich durch dieses singuläre technische Prozedere das Gepäckvolumen von passablen 348 Litern auf dürftige 145 verringert – längere Reisen in angemessenem Outfit wird man hochgeschlossen antreten müssen. Mit zwei Maßnahmen ist man der Raumnot hinten bereits werksseitig begegnet: Das Tankvolumen beträgt lediglich 53 Liter, und auf ein Reserverad (ein Faltrad gibt es als Option) wird gänzlich verzichtet. Im Falle jenes Falles, der laut Statistik nur alle 150 000 Kilometer eintritt, leisten das Reifendichtmittel Tirefit und eine elektrische Luftpumpe erste Hilfe.

SLK, ein Mix aus bedeutsamen Mercedes-Kürzeln der Vergangenheit, bedeutet Sportlich, Leicht, Kurz. »Leicht«

«Nous assistons avec elle à une renaissance de l'esthétique dans l'automobile», déclarait Helmut Werner, président du directoire de Mercedes-Benz AG, comme s'il y avait eu un risque que l'on oublie tout cela dans l'ouragan dévastateur de la soufflerie.

Et, «dans une telle automobile, la route est la destination», lui réplique Jürgen Hubbert, membre du directoire au titre du secteur d'activité VP.

Ce n'est naturellement qu'un plaidoyer *pro domo*, pour rallier les faveurs des indécis, pour séduire de nouveaux clients. Cependant, elle n'a vraiment pas besoin de cela, la SLK, présentée au Salon de Turin en avril 1996, semi jeune Siegfried, semi Don Juan sous les traits d'une voiture, et, de mémoire d'homme, la tentation la plus irrésistible en provenance d'Untertürkheim: un pare-brise peu élevé, un long capot moteur, deux larges portes et une poupe rectiligne, avec de faibles porte-à-faux à l'avant et à l'arrière pour un empattement relativement long de 2400 mm, le tout assaisonné d'un certain «je-ne-sais-quoi».

Il y a particulièrement son prix, qui est une véritable gifle pour ses concurrents: 60 950 marks, prix calculé au plus juste pour la plus coûteuse des deux versions, à moteur de 2,3 litres et compresseur développant 193 ch. L'autre, avec moteur atmosphérique de 2 litres et 136 ch, ne coûte même que la somme modeste de 54 510 marks. Et, qui plus est, pour cette somme, l'heureux propriétaire bénéficie deux voitures en une: une simple pression sur un petit bouton rouge et le coupé SLK que l'on vient d'acquérir se métamorphose en un roadster en 25 secondes. En l'absence de tout tissu disparaît aussi tout ce qui peut claquer, vibrer, produire des courants d'air, laisser passer la pluie ou faire perdre tout son charme à une forme séduisante.

Avant que le soleil, la lune et les étoiles n'aient librement accès au cockpit de la SLK se déroulent six processus minutieusement coordonnés, déclenchés et exécutés par cinq vérins hydrauliques, deux pour le mécanisme du toit escamotable, deux pour l'ouverture accueillante du couvercle de malle et un cinquième pour le verrouillage du toit sur le cadre du pare-brise lorsque se termine la procédure dans le sens inverse. À l'issue du processus, le *hard-top* disparaît aux regards curieux, dissimulé dans le coffre. Voilà pour les bonnes nouvelles. Quant à la mauvaise, ce processus technique unique au monde ramène la capacité du coffre, *a priori* acceptable, de 348 à 145 litres – on ne peut donc partir en voyage prolongé avec une certaine quantité de bagages qu'avec le toit fermé. Deux mesures sont censées pallier le manque d'espace à l'arrière: la capacité du réservoir n'est que de 53 litres et il n'y a pas la moindre roue de secours (une roue galette est proposée en option): en cas de malheur – ce qui, selon les statistiques, ne se produit que tous les 150 000 km – la bombe anticrevaison Tirefit et une pompe à air électrique permettent de porter les premiers secours.

SLK, un cocktail d'abréviations Mercedes riches en tradition, signifie Sportive, Légère, Courte. «Légère» est, comme toujours dans l'histoire de la marque, un

Mercedes-Benz SLK 1996

Mercedes-Benz SLK 230 Kompressor 1996

remaining, whether the roof is up or down, as rigid and solid as the most stable Mercedes-Benz sedan.

And everybody wants one: "I've already ordered mine," declared Fritz B. Busch, the eloquent doyen of German automobile journalists, a man hardened and inured to anything that goes on four wheels, "I wasn't going to hang about." And no wonder: the demand far outstrips supply, despite the fact that the production plant in Bremen quickly took on 600 new employees. By the beginning of October 1996 41,300 German SLK fans had ordered one.

ist, wie schon immer in der Geschichte der Marke, eine charmante Schwindelei: Der SLK 230 Kompressor bringt immerhin 1325 Kilogramm auf die Waage. »Kurz« trifft zweifellos zu: Der Baby-Benz nimmt weniger Parkraum in Anspruch als ein VW Golf. Und sportlich ist er auch, 231 Stundenkilometer schnell, in 7,5 Sekunden auf Tempo 100 und wieselflink zu lenken, dabei offen wie geschlossen steif und rigide wie die stabilste Limousine aus dem gleichen noblen Hause.

Und so wollen ihn alle haben: »Ich habe mir gleich einen bestellt«, sagt etwa Fritz B. Busch, wortgewaltiger Nestor unter den deutschen Motor-Schreibern, mit allen Wassern gewaschen und abgebrüht gegen alles, was vier Räder hat, »da gab es überhaupt kein Vertun.« Kein Wunder: Die Nachfrage übersteigt entschieden das Angebot, obwohl im Produktionswerk Bremen flugs 600 neue Arbeitsplätze eingerichtet werden. Anfang Oktober 1996 haben bereits 41300 deutsche Mitbürger und SLK-Beflissene einen Kaufvertrag in der Tasche.

euphémisme: la SLK 230 Kompressor accuse tout de même un poids de 1325 kg. « Courte » est sans aucun doute vrai: la mini-Mercedes a besoin de moins d'espace pour se garer qu'une VW Golf. Et, sportive, elle l'est bel et bien avec une vitesse de pointe de 231 km/h, un temps de 7,5 secondes pour le 0 à 100 km/h et une maniabilité de feu follet, tout en étant tout aussi ferme et rigide, ouverte ou fermée, que la berline la plus solide de la même noble maison.

Et c'est pourquoi tous veulent en avoir une. « Je m'en suis commandée une tout de suite », déclare par exemple Fritz B. Busch, plume prestigieuse s'il en est parmi les journalistes spécialisés allemands, qui en a vu de toutes les couleurs et a pris le volant de tout ce qui a quatre roues. « On ne risque absolument pas de se tromper. » Et ce n'est pas un miracle: la demande est très largement supérieure à l'offre bien que 600 nouveaux emplois aient été créés spécialement pour sa ligne de production à Brême. Début octobre 1996, 41300 Allemands et adorateurs de SLK avaient d'ores et déjà un contrat en poche.

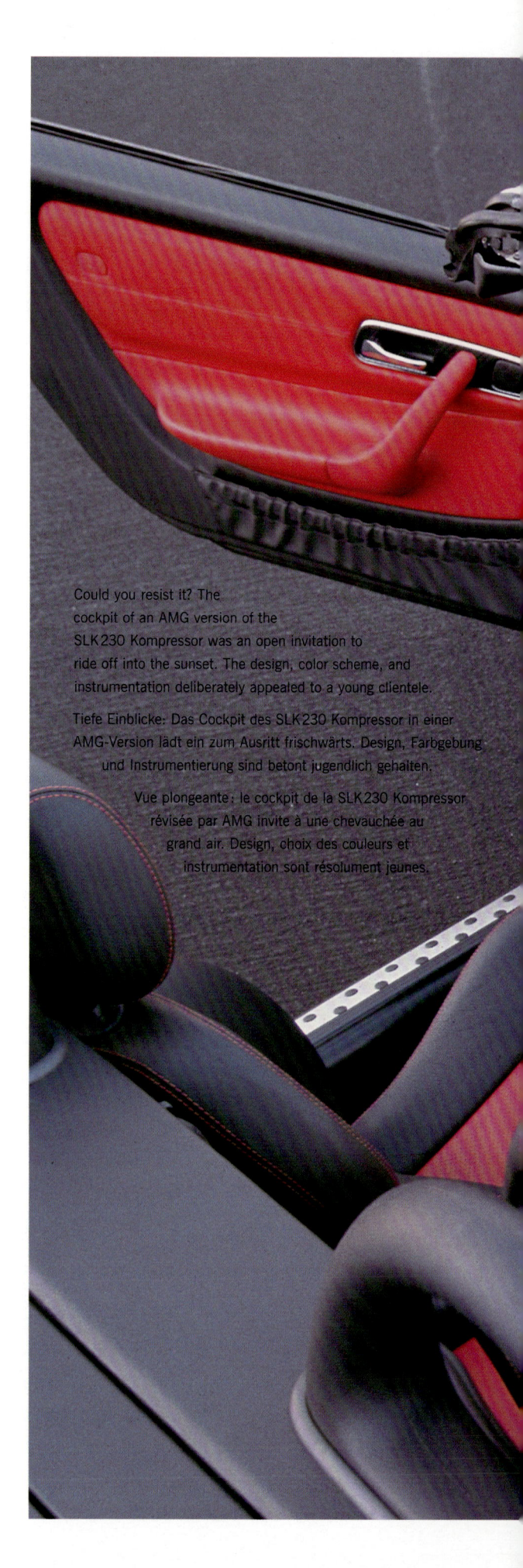

Could you resist it? The cockpit of an AMG version of the SLK 230 Kompressor was an open invitation to ride off into the sunset. The design, color scheme, and instrumentation deliberately appealed to a young clientele.

Tiefe Einblicke: Das Cockpit des SLK 230 Kompressor in einer AMG-Version lädt ein zum Ausritt frischwärts. Design, Farbgebung und Instrumentierung sind betont jugendlich gehalten.

Vue plongeante: le cockpit de la SLK 230 Kompressor révisée par AMG invite à une chevauchée au grand air. Design, choix des couleurs et instrumentation sont résolument jeunes.

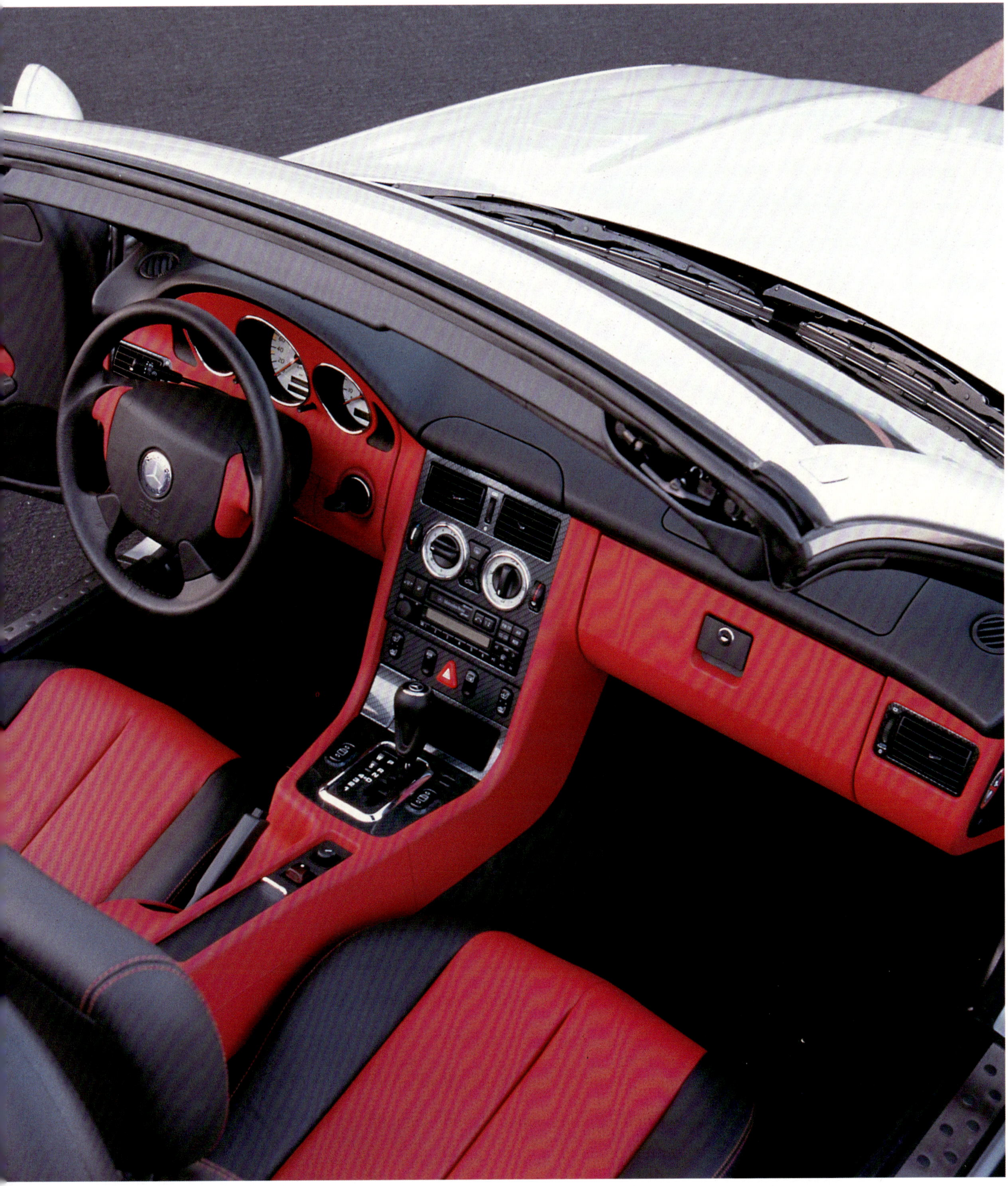

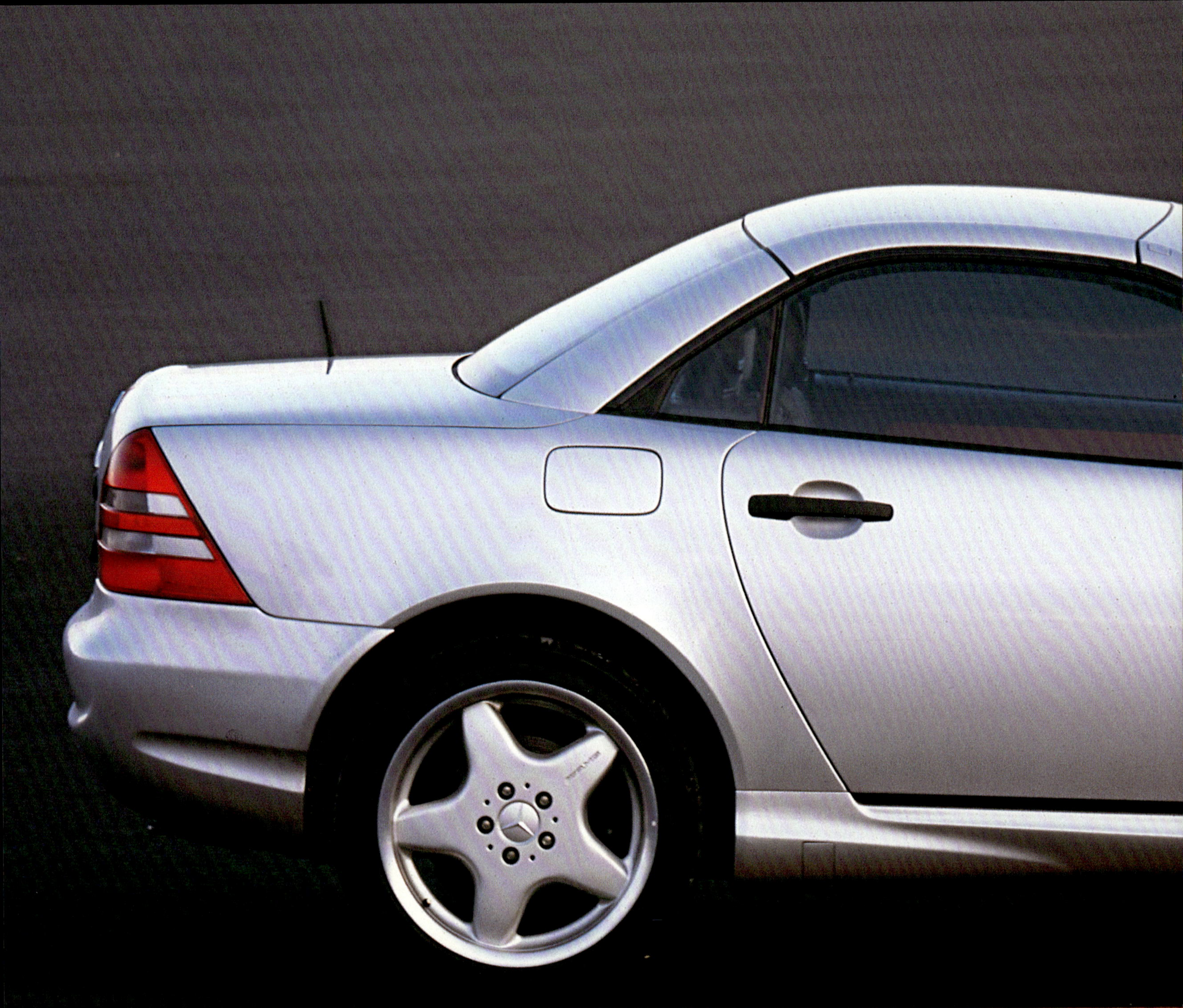

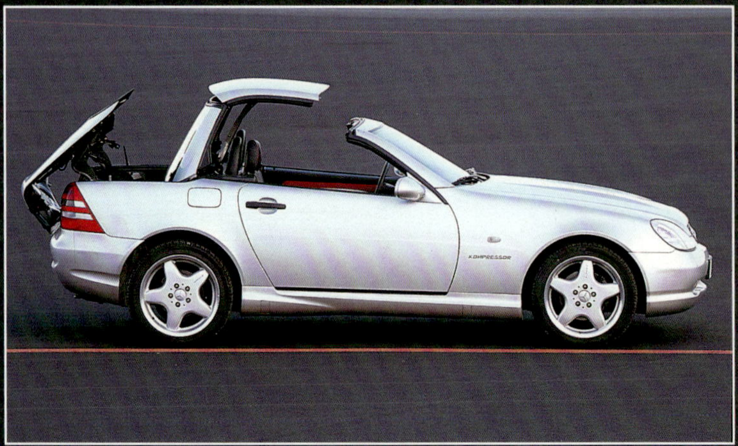

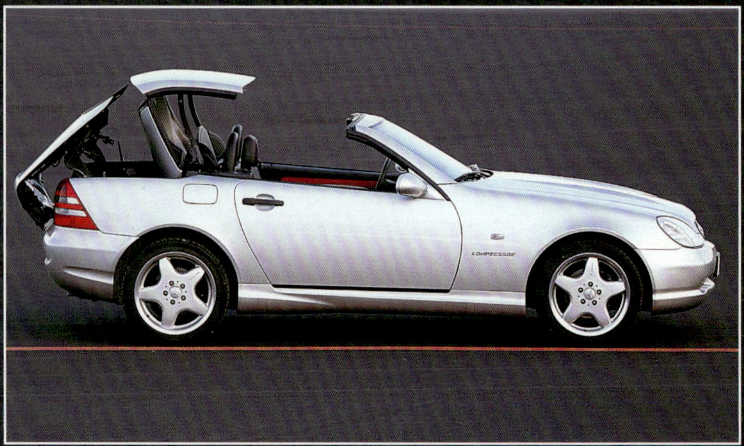

The aerodynamically-polished skirts and five-spoke wheels were specific to the AMG model. It took just 25 seconds before the mobile hardtop disappeared from view into its recess.

Spezifisch für die AMG-Variante sind die aerodynamisch durchgefeilten Schweller und fünfzackige Felgen. Bevor das mobile Hardtop von der Bildfläche und in der Versenkung verschwunden ist, vergehen 25 Sekunden.

Les bas de caisse aérodynamiques et les jantes en étoile sont caractéristiques de la version AMG. Il faut 25 secondes seulement pour voir le *hard-top* disparaître dans son compartiment où il sait se faire oublier.

This model was in many ways based on the C-Class, for example in terms of floor and engine. Over this, however, rose a completely self-contained superstructure. Design Chief Peter Pfeiffer—as was typical of Mercedes design theory in the late years of the last millennium—had stretched a bow over the waistline and stressed this by the underlying corrugation. And because the CLK (C-Class, Light, Compact) was so important, it was actually introduced three times over into the auto world: in January 1997 at the North American International Auto Show in Detroit, a month later at the Auto Show in Amsterdam, and finally at the Geneva Salon that March.

The customer immediately had a choice between the Sport and Elegance versions: the latter with chrome decoration on the side windows and door handles as well as the five-hole design alloy wheels, while the former came without such trappings and had wheels with seven perforations. The splendid standard equipment of both models included high-tech refinements such as ASR anti-skid control, the Elcode authorization system to ensure comfort and protection against theft with electronic door and ignition lock, and the BAS brake assist system to detect emergency braking and provide instant maximum support.

On the domestic market, the CLK was initially available with three engines: four cylinders in the CLK 200 (1998 cc, 136 bhp) and CLK 230 (2295 cc, 193 bhp, supercharger) and a V6 in the CLK 320 (3199 cc, 218 bhp). A CLK 200 Kompressor was available in Italy, Portugal, and Greece. There was further development in January 1998, again in Detroit, in the form of the CLK 430 with a V8 (4266 cc, 279 bhp). It was introduced on the market in June that year to coincide with the convertible, which had caused such a furore in Geneva three months before.

A full year later, the CLK presented itself in an updated form, with roof both open and closed. The current Sports line had been replaced by the exclusive Avantgarde version, recognizable from its 16-inch alloy wheels with seven spokes, birdseye maple veneer trim, and blue tinted glass. The five-speed automatic transmission, fitted as standard in the V6 and V8 models, facilitated manual selection—the driver simply needed to tap on the appropriate lever in position D. More expensive, but still popular, was the control and display system Comand, combining car radio, CD player and satnav. Really expensive (over 151,264 euros as against 61,480 euros for the entry-level CLK 200) was the muscle type CLK 55 AMG (5439 cc, 347 bhp), available from August 1999. It was an inch lower than the CLK 430 with more firmly tuned shock absorbers, modified springs, reinforced stabilizers, and internally ventilated pizza-sized disk brakes (13-in diameter), making a subdued and yet aggressive impact.

From June 2000, there was also the four-cylinder model with modified machinery and six-speed manual transmission, which stood out from previous models thanks to its short strokes and low settings. In the spring of 2002, the first generation of coupés in the newly developed series

Mercedes-Benz CLK 1997

Mercedes-Benz CLK 320 1997

209 (the convertible following one year later) was released, with 233,367 being produced. Now even diesel had become socially acceptable, as attested by the CLK 270 CDI (five cylinders, 2685 cc, 170 bhp). This was superseded by the CLK 320 CDI (2987 cc, 224 bhp) after another facelift in 2005; its v6 could also be found in the convertible, while a 2148 cc four-cylinder with 150 bhp remained the preserve of the CLK 220 CDI coupé. A policy of strength was also manifested in the petrol motors CLK 280 (v6, 2996 cc, 231 bhp), CLK 350 (v6, 3498 cc, 272 bhp) and CLK 500 (v8, 5461 cc, 388 bhp), and, before any of these, in spring 2006, the CLK 63 AMG, whose v8 produced a good, earthy 481 bhp from 6208 cc.

Generation von den Coupés der neu entwickelten Baureihe 209 (das Cabriolet folgt ein Jahr später) abgelöst wird, hat sie eine Verbreitung von 233 367 Exemplaren erfahren. Nun ist auch der Selbstzünder salonfähig geworden, bezeugt etwa durch den CLK 270 CDI (fünf Zylinder, 2685 cm³, 170 PS). Den löst nach einem weiteren Facelift 2005 der CLK 320 CDI (2987 cm³, 224 PS) ab, dessen v6 auch im Cabriolet vorzufinden ist, während ein Vierzylinder mit 2148 cm³ und 150 PS dem CLK 220 CDI Coupé vorbehalten bleibt. Eine Politik der Stärke manifestiert sich überdies in den Benzinern CLK 280 (v6, 2996 cm³, 231 PS), CLK 350 (v6, 3498 cm³, 272 PS) und CLK 500 (v8, 5461 cm³, 388 PS), allen voran ab Frühjahr 2006 der CLK 63 AMG, dessen v8 aus 6208 cm³ urige 481 PS gebiert.

été vendu à 233 367 exemplaires. L'allumage par compression était également devenu présentable au salon, comme en témoigne par exemple la CLK 270 CDI (cinq cylindres, 2685 cm³, 170 ch). Après un nouveau lifting facial, la CLK 320 CDI (2987 cm³, 224 ch) prit la relève. Son v6 est également présent dans le cabriolet alors qu'un quatre cylindres de 2148 cm³ et 150 ch est conservé pour le coupé CLK 220 CDI. La politique de la puissance se manifeste aussi dans les modèles à essence CLK 280 (v6, 2996 cm³, 231 ch), CLK 350 (v6, 3498 cm³, 272 ch) et CLK 500 (v8, 5461 cm³, 388 ch), tous disponibles depuis le printemps 2006 et précédant la CLK 63 AMG dont le v8 de 6208 cm³ abrite 481 ch.

The CLK 320's powerplant: a V6 with three valves per cylinder and double overhead camshafts. In performance terms it was scarcely inferior to a straight-six.

Das Triebwerk des CLK 320: ein V6 mit drei Ventilen je Zylinder und zwei oben liegenden Nockenwellen. In seiner Laufkultur steht es einem Reihensechszylinder kaum nach.

Le moteur de la CLK 320: un V6 à trois soupapes par cylindre et deux arbres à cames en tête qui ne le cède pratiquement en rien aux six-cylindres en ligne par sa douceur de fonctionnement.

273

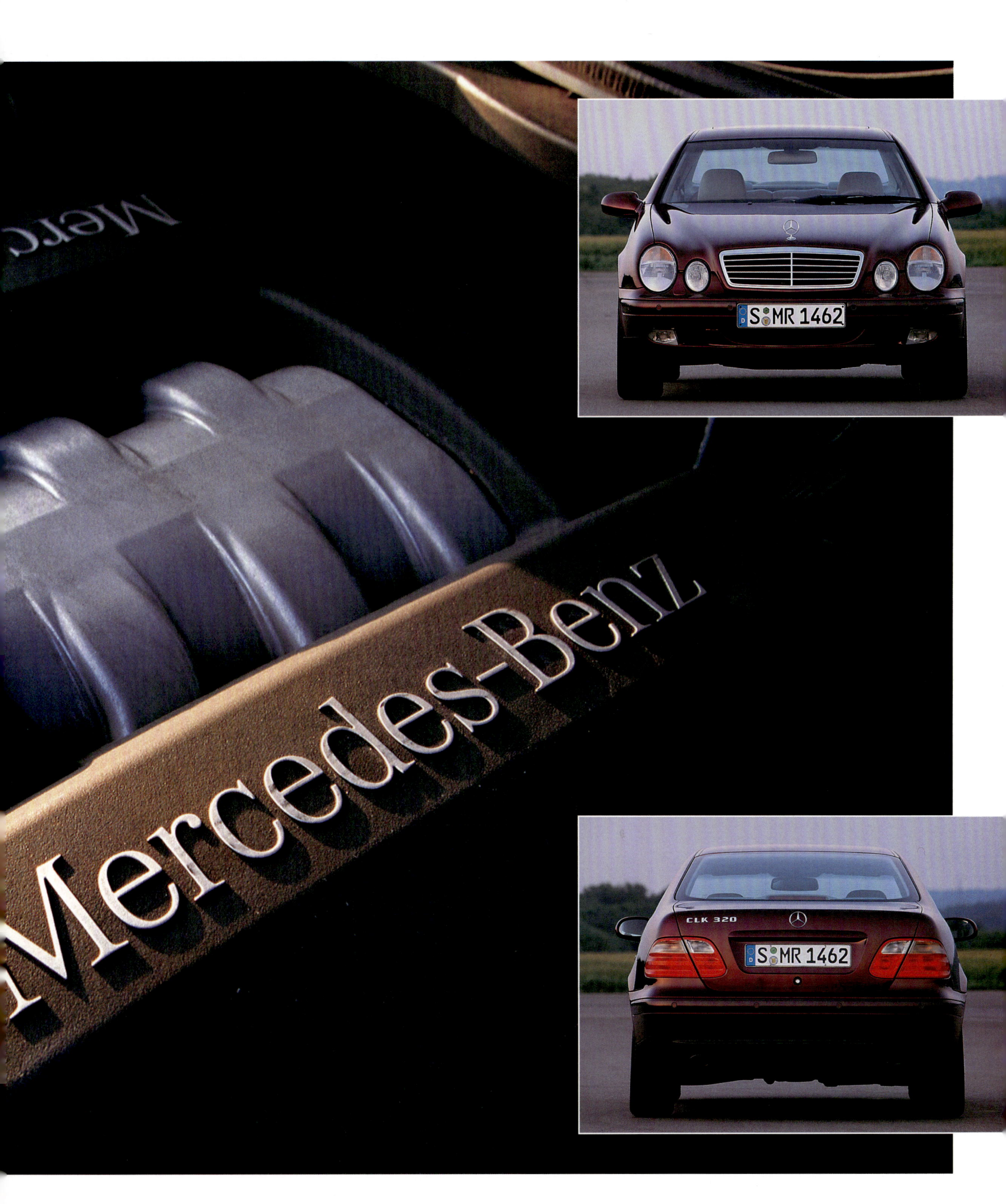

The formal 2005 update is extraordinarily reserved
and has of course been applied to the CLK
cabriolet: markedly curved front bumpers, expanded
air intakes, three-louver radiator grille.

Die formale Auffrischung Jahrgang 2005 fällt ungemein
behutsam aus und wird natürlich auch dem CLK-Cabriolet
anverwandelt: stärker gebogene Frontstoßdämpfer,
erweitere Lufteinlässe, dreifach lamellierte Kühlermaske.

Le rafraîchissement des formes de la version 2005 est
particulièrement soigné, et le cabriolet CLK a bien sûr
lui aussi été modifié : pare-chocs avant plus arqués,
prises d'air plus larges, calandre à trois lamelles.

Mercedes-Benz CLK 1997 275

The market launch in 1998 of what was the smallest car with the Mercedes star so far was prepared as if for the appearance of a superstar. Four years before, a study at the Frankfurt International Motor Show was carried out as a test of audience approval. Two years before, the data and details were revealed, with an apparent show of reluctance. The year prior to the launch, showmen did the rounds with their *A-Motion* show throughout Germany. Flashy brochures whetted the appetite, which became a real hunger: 375,000 curious potential customers phoned through to the dedicated hotlines, with an initial 75,000, caught in the finely woven marketing net, committing themselves to purchase. This tiny tot of a car, reported the press in unison, was a stunner.

It was actually a four-door car, but 11 ft 8 in short, with Mercedes-level safety and low fuel consumption, plus the maneuverability of a subcompact, spaciousness of a family car, comfort of a sedan, and versatility of a van. Customers were spoiled for choice: there were 72 variants. They were all mainly distinguished by the fact that the asymmetrically divided rear seats were separately adjustable: they could be folded down and quickly removed, as could (for an additional charge) the front passenger seat, which increased the load capacity to 61.4 cu.ft. Even with all seats occupied, there remained stowage capacity of 12.4 cu.ft in the trunk, plus an additional 1.4 cu.ft if, in place of a spare tire, the repair set Tirefit was chosen.

Squaring the circle was made possible by crossing a one-box design with a sandwich construction: axles, fuel tank, battery, and a larger portion of the engine and transmission were arranged under the car floor, so that the occupants were enthroned slightly above normal level. In the case of a frontal impact, the drive assembly completely dived down—a safety measure like the robust frame or the presence of four airbags, plus seat-belt tighteners and seat-belt force limiters as well as ABS.

The suspension, with front wheel drive, double wishbones and MacPherson struts in front and trailing arms behind, was rather conventional, but the four cylinders, all calculated to endow the little car with ferret-like agility, were completely new in design. To begin with, there were the two models A 140 and A 160 with a two-valve 1.4-liter engine and 82 bhp and a 1.6-liter engine and 102 bhp respectively. In 1998 there came the 1.7-liter turbodiesel with 60 or 90 bhp, direct injection with four valves per cylinder and intercooler. The common rail fuel injection system was new: fuel was supplied to the nozzles via a shared pipe serving as a pressure accumulator and dividing it up. An electronic calculator controlled timing and dosage for each cylinder according to engine load and speed, in the service of optimal combustion and uniform power delivery. Replete with 125 bhp, the A 190 was ready from June 1999. As an alternative to the five-speed gearbox, there was an automatic with the same number of levels and an automatic clutch.

Der Markt-Start des vorerst kleinsten Autos mit dem Stern anno 1998 wird vorbereitet wie der Auftritt eines Superstars: Vier Jahre zuvor treibt man eine Studie auf der Frankfurter IAA wie eine Sonde in die Gunst des Publikums. Zwei Jahre vorher sind alle Daten und Details scheinbar widerstrebend enthüllt. Im letzten Jahr tingeln Gaukler mit der Show *A-Motion* durch deutsche Lande. Poppiges Prospektmaterial steigert den Appetit zum Heißhunger: 375 000 Neugierige rufen auf eigens eingerichteten Hotlines an, und 75 000 verfangen sich vorab als Käufer im fein gewobenen Marketing-Netz. Der Winzling, meldet die Fachpresse unisono, sei eine Wucht.

Der Winzling: ein 3,57 Meter kurzer Viertürer, Sicherheit auf Mercedes-Niveau, günstiger Verbrauch, Wendigkeit eines Stadtwagens und Raumangebot eines Familienautos, Komfort einer Limousine und Variabilität eines Vans. Man hat die Qual der Wahl zwischen 72 Varianten. Sie ergeben sich etwa dadurch, dass sich die asymmetrisch geteilten Rücksitze getrennt verstellen, umklappen und flugs herausnehmen lassen wie gegen Aufpreis auch der Beifahrersitz, was das Ladevolumen auf 1740 Liter erweitert. Selbst bei voller Bestuhlung lassen sich im Kofferraum noch immer 350 Liter verstauen, dazu weitere 40 Liter, wenn anstelle eines Reserverads das Reparaturset Tirefit gewählt wurde.

Die Quadratur des Zirkels wird möglich durch eine Kreuzung von *One-Box*-Design und Sandwich-Bauweise: Achsen, Tank, Batterie sowie eine größere Portion von Motor und Getriebe sind unter dem Wagenboden angeordnet, wodurch die Insassen leicht erhaben über dem Normal-Niveau thronen. Bei einer Frontalkollision taucht die Antriebseinheit gänzlich nach unten ab, eine Sicherheitsmaßnahme wie der robuste Rahmen oder die Anwesenheit von vier Airbags, Gurtstraffern und Gurtkraft-Begrenzern sowie ABS.

Eher konventionell: das Fahrwerk, mit Frontantrieb, Dreieckslenkern und McPherson-Federbeinen vorn und Längslenkern hinten, völlig neu konstruiert hingegen die Vierzylinder, allesamt dazu angetan, den Kleinen mit wieselflinker Agilität auszustatten. Am Anfang stehen die beiden Modelle A 140 und A 160 mit Zweiventilern von 1,4 Litern und 82 PS und 1,6 Litern und 102 PS. 1998 folgen die Turbodiesel mit 1,7 Litern und 60 beziehungsweise 90 PS, Direkteinspritzer mit Ladeluftkühlung und Vierventiltechnik. Neu ist die Common-Rail-Einspritzung: Der Kraftstoff wird den Düsen über eine gemeinsame Leitung zugeführt, die als Druckspeicher dient und ihn verzweigt. Ein elektronischer Rechner steuert Zeitpunkt und Dosierung für jeden Zylinder gemäß Last und Drehzahl im Dienst von optimaler Verbrennung und gleichmäßiger Leistungsentfaltung. Mit urigen 125 PS wartet der A 190 ab Juni 1999 auf. Als Alternative zum Fünfganggetriebe gibt es eine Automatik mit derselben Anzahl von Fahrstufen und eine automatische Kupplung.

Le lancement en 1998 de ce qui fut la plus petite voiture de la marque à l'étoile fut préparé comme l'entrée d'une superstar : quatre ans auparavant, un prototype fut présenté au Salon de l'automobile de Francfort afin de sonder les réactions du public. Deux ans après, tous les détails et renseignements furent révélés, visiblement à contrecœur. La dernière année précédant la grande première, des saltimbanques parcoururent l'Allemagne afin de présenter le spectacle *A-Motion*. Des prospectus bariolés transformèrent les appétits en fringales : 375 000 curieux appelèrent sur des lignes créées tout spécialement et 75 000 acheteurs potentiels se firent prendre dans les filets finement tissés par le service marketing. La presse spécialisée fut unanime : cette puce est épatante.

La puce : une petite quatre portes de 3,57 mètres, la sécurité Mercedes, une faible consommation, la maniabilité d'une citadine et l'habitabilité d'une voiture familiale, le confort d'une berline et la modularité d'un monospace. On a l'embarras du choix entre 72 variantes. Il en résulte des sièges asymétriques pouvant être déplacés, rabattus ou enlevés séparément. Une option offre même la possibilité d'agir de même avec le siège passager avant. Cela permet d'obtenir un coffre de 1740 litres de volume. Même avec tous les sièges, le coffre offre encore une capacité de 350 litres auxquels on peut ajouter 40 litres si, à la place de la roue de secours, on opte pour le kit de réparation Tirefit.

La quadrature du cercle est rendue possible grâce au croisement du design monocorps et de la construction en sandwich : les essieux, le réservoir, la batterie ainsi qu'une grande partie du moteur et de la boîte de vitesses sont placés sous le plancher de la voiture, ce qui fait que les passagers trônent légèrement plus haut que le niveau normal. En cas de collision frontale, le moteur et la boîte de vitesses glissent sous la cellule passagers, une mesure de sécurité tout comme le cadre robuste ou la présence de quatre airbags, de rétracteurs et de limiteurs de tension des ceintures de sécurité ainsi que de l'ABS.

Plus conventionnels : le train de roulement à traction avant, les triangles transversaux et les jambes élastiques McPherson à l'avant ainsi que les bras longitudinaux à l'arrière. En revanche, les quatre cylindres sont entièrement nouveaux et tous destinés à donner à cette petite voiture l'agilité d'une puce. Les premiers modèles proposés furent la A 140 et la A 160, toutes les deux dotées d'un moteur à deux soupapes : 1,4 litre et 82 ch pour la première et 1,6 litre et 102 ch pour la seconde. En 1998, elles seront suivies par les turbodiesels de 1,7 litre et 60 ch ou bien 90 ch, à injection directe, échangeur d'air et culasse à quatre soupapes. Le système d'injection Common Rail est une nouveauté : le carburant est envoyé aux injecteurs par une durite commune qui sert de réservoir à pression et répartit le gasoil. Un calculateur électronique gère le moment et le dosage cylindre par cylindre en fonction de la charge et du régime afin de garantir une combustion optimale et une montée en puissance linéaire. La A 190 équipée de 125 vigoureux chevaux fut présentée en juin 1999. À la place de la boîte à

Mercedes-Benz A-Klasse   1997

Mercedes-Benz A160 1997

On 29 June 2004 on the club ship *AIDAaura* in Greece, a thoroughly modified A-metamorphosis was presented, its main new feature being a three-door version. Again, the haughty little car turned out to be a competitor: in early December 2006, in Rastatt, unit number 1,500,000 was celebrated. Everything flows, however. At the Leipzig International Motor Show in April 2008, a new high-tech generation paid its respects. The volume versions A 150/170 were available with the ECO start/stop function, while the three-door A 160 CDI with a "BlueEfficiency" package does not content itself with less than 55 mpg—in the light of really absurd diesel prices, this was, indeed, good news.

Am 29. Juni 2004 stellt man in Griechenland auf dem Clubschiff *AIDAaura* eine gründlich überarbeitete A-Metamorphose vor, Hauptneuerung: ein Dreitürer. Wieder wird der hohe Kleine zum Renner – Anfang Dezember 2006 lässt sich in Rastatt Exemplar Nummer 1 500 000 insgesamt feiern. Gleichwohl fließt alles. Auf der Leipziger Auto Mobil International im April 2008 macht eine neue Hightech-Generation ihre Aufwartung. Die Volumen-Versionen A 150/170 sind mit der ECO Start-Stopp-Funktion lieferbar, der dreitürige A 160 CDI begnügt sich dank eines Blue-Efficiency-Pakets mit 4,5 Litern je 100 Kilometer – angesichts schier absurder Dieselpreise fürwahr eine frohe Botschaft.

cinq vitesses, il existe une version automatique offrant le même nombre de rapports.

Le 29 juin 2004, une métamorphose complète de la Classe A fut présentée en Grèce au navire de croisière *AIDAaura*. Principale innovation : une trois portes. À nouveau la haute puce est devenue une championne. Début décembre 2006, on fêta à Rastatt l'exemplaire numéro 1 500 000. Mais tout passe. Lors du Salon de l'automobile de Leipzig d'avril 2008 fut présentée une nouvelle génération haute technologie. Les versions A 150/170 peuvent être livrées avec la fonction ECO Start-Stop ; la 3 portes A 160 CDI se contente de 4,5 litres aux 100 kilomètres grâce au pack BlueEfficiency. Étant donné le prix presque absurde du diesel, en vérité une bonne nouvelle.

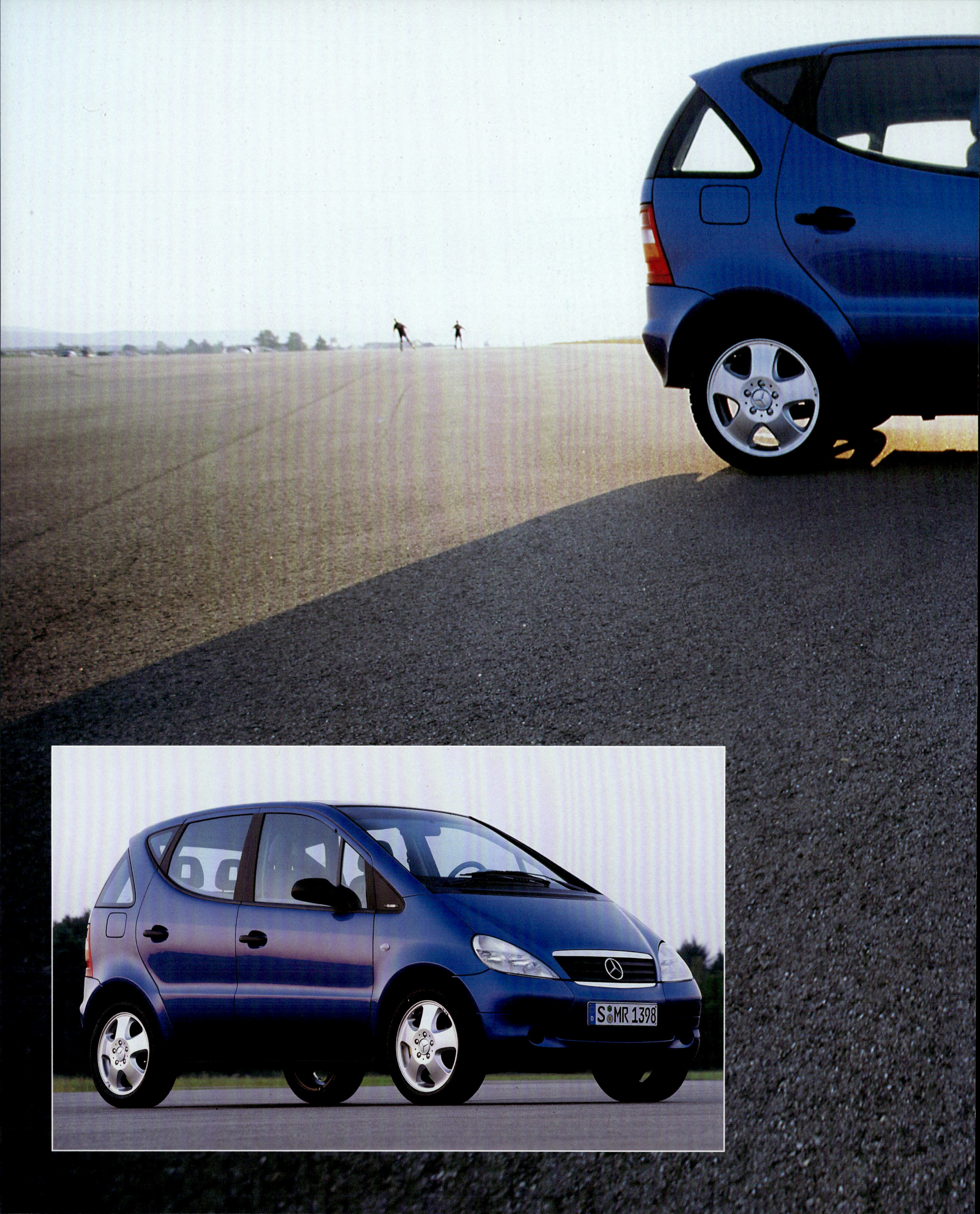
S MR 1398

What a car! The A-Class Mercedes with its footprint of 65 square feet combines a revolutionary space and safety concept with cunningly conceived details.

Tausendsassa: Auf sechs Quadratmetern Grundfläche verquickt der Mercedes der A-Klasse ein revolutionäres Raum- und Sicherheitskonzept mit listig ausgedachten Detaillösungen.

Coqueluche: sur six mètres carrés, la Mercedes Classe A allie un concept d'habitabilité et de sécurité révolutionnaire à des solutions de détails astucieuses et sophistiquées.

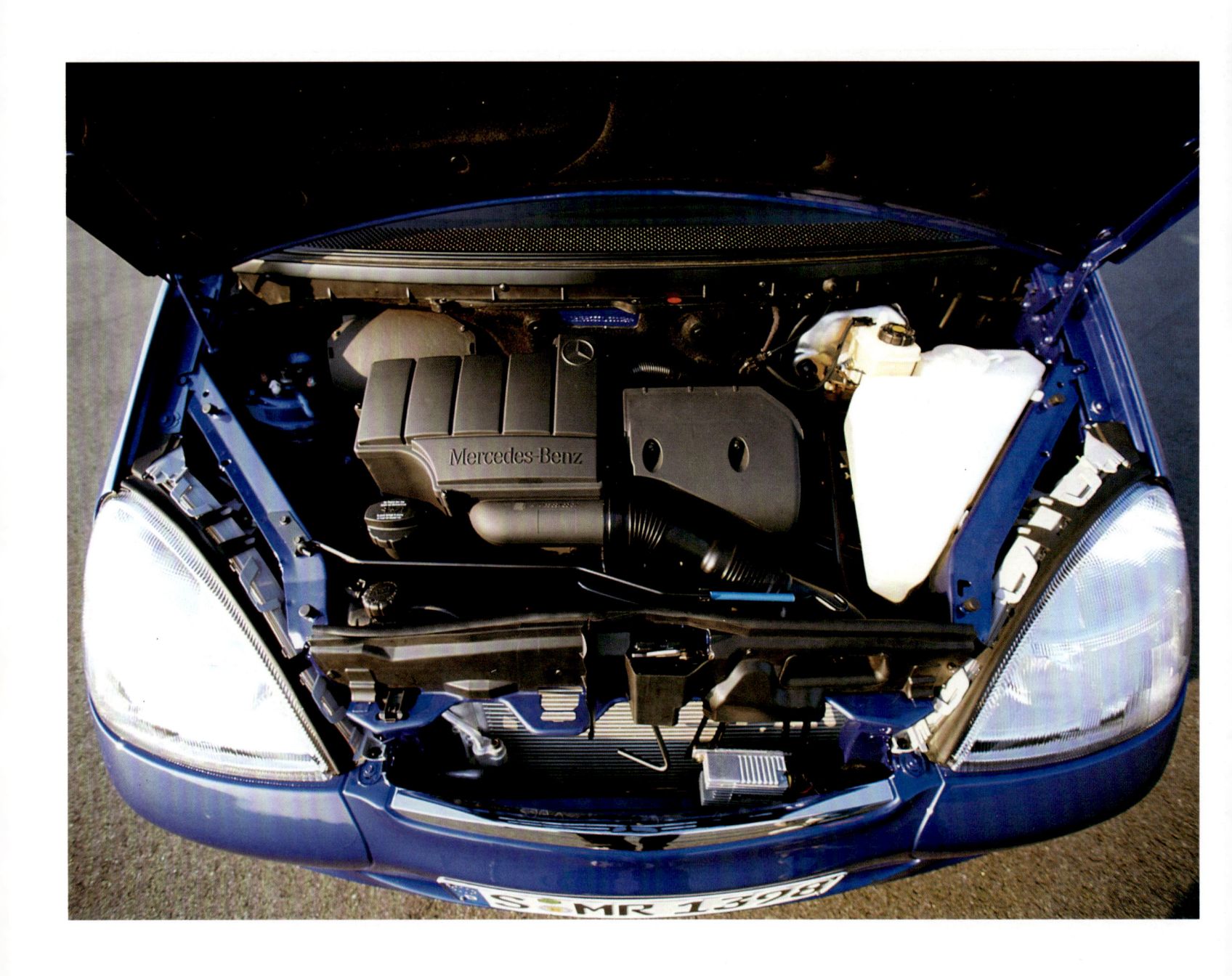

Thanks to its one-box design and the sandwich construction method, the drivetrain will be displaced downwards in the event of a frontal collision, ensuring more extensive crumple zones. The cockpit is unconventional. But the way the do-it-all multi-lever and various switches work conjures up that familiar Mercedes feeling. Note the unusually steep angle of the steering wheel.

One-Box-Design und Sandwich-Bauweise ermöglichen es: Bei einer Frontalkollision wird die Antriebseinheit nach unten weggestoßen und sichert so einen größeren Deformationsweg. Unkonventionell: das Cockpit. Aber die Betätigung des alles könnenden Multihebels und diverser Schalter vermittelt vertrautes Mercedes-Feeling. Auffällig steil: das Lenkrad.

Design monocorps et construction sandwich sont la clé de l'énigme : en cas de collision frontale, la chaîne cinématique glisse sous le plancher de la voiture et crée ainsi une plus grande zone de déformation programmée. Le cockpit a jeté par-dessus bord tout ce qui est conventionnel, mais l'utilisation de la multicommande à tout faire et des diverses manettes est dans le plus pur style de Mercedes. Noter la colonne de direction très verticale.

281

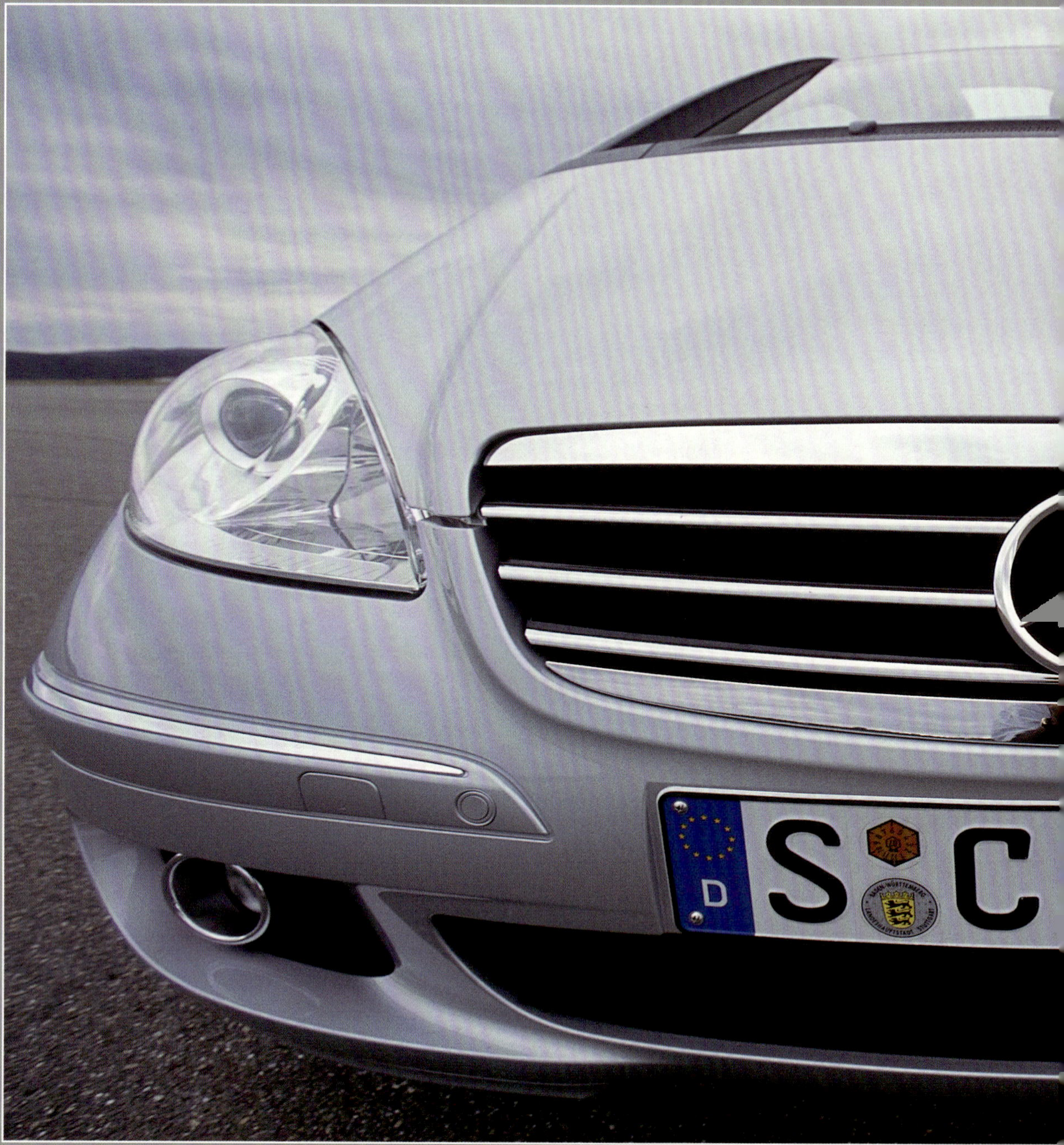
D
S C

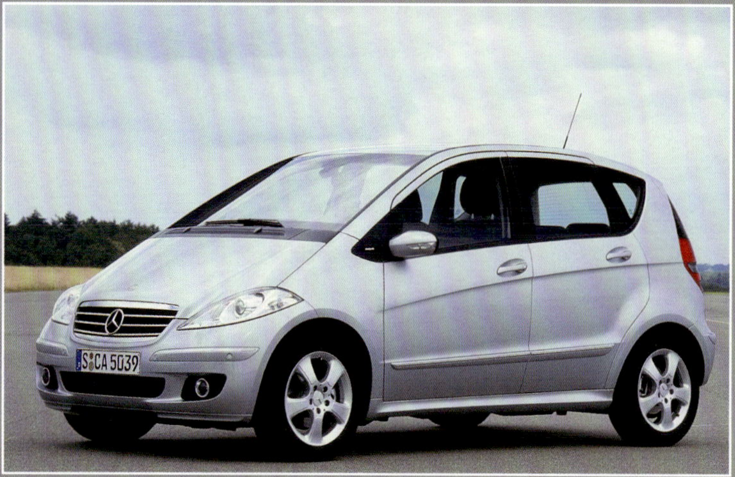
S CA 5039

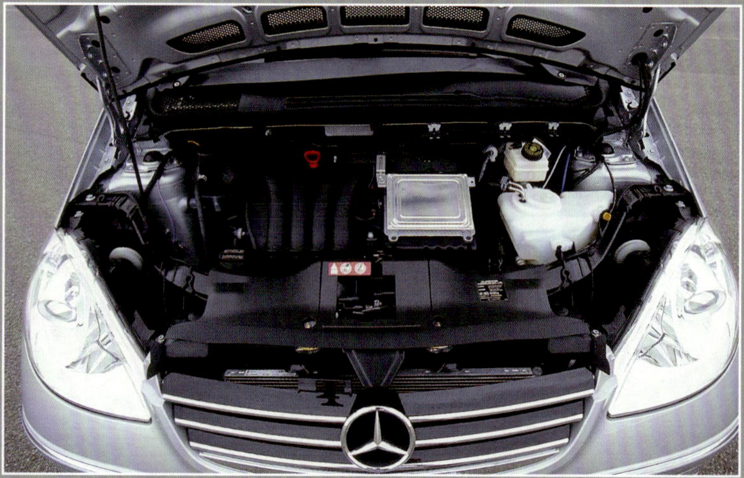

After seven fat A-Class years, a successor with just as many engine variations was presented in 2004. The palette of engines on offer for the new generation of 4-cylinders ranges from 95 bhp (A 150) to the Turbo with its 194 bhp (A 200, from June 2005). The small Mercedes is characterized by greater value, space, and variability despite its compact form.

Nach sieben ergiebigen A-Klassen-Jahren stellt sich 2004 ein Nachfolger mit ebenso vielen Motoren-Varianten vor. Die Triebwerkspalette der neuen Vierzylinder-Generation reicht von 95 PS (A 150) bis zum Turbo mit 194 PS (A 200, ab Juni 2005). Mehr Wertigkeit, Platz und Variabilität trotz aller Kompaktheit zeichnen den kleinen Mercedes aus.

Après sept années lucratives de Classe A, sa remplaçante se présente en 2004 avec un aussi grand nombre de variantes de moteurs. La palette de motorisations de la nouvelle génération de quatre-cylindres va de 95 ch (A 150) à un turbo de 194 ch (A 200, à partir de juin 2005). Plus grande qualité perçue, plus de place et variabilité en hausse malgré une compacité indéniable caractérisent la petite Mercedes.

In the Mercedes M-Class, everything was new, said Jürgen Hubbert, member of the board responsible for marketing passenger cars: the vehicle was in a new segment, the plant and its employees were at a new location, and even its entry into the market outside Europe was new. The first ML 320 premiered 21–23 July 1997 in Huntsville, Alabama. Production took place in the latest Mercedes plant in Tuscaloosa, Alabama. The product was an all-rounder, equally adept off and on the road, in everyday life, and in the world of adventure. It all started with an authoritative sedan-like appearance, dominated by smooth roundness, with no protrusions to impede wind flow. The interior was focused on comfort, with air conditioning fitted as standard, as were the variable rear seats and drive authorization Elcode (electronic code system) with remote central locking. Personal desires could be satisfied for an additional charge: they included leather upholstery, a third row of seats, and a slatted sunroof.

Ease of movement was provided (as in the E 320 and CLK 320) by an 18-valve V6, dual ignition, and 3.2 liters of displacement: 218 bhp. Another innovation replaced the three conventional differential locks: this was the electronic traction system 4-ETS. A microcomputer increased the brake pressure on the turning wheel until the difference ensured good grip on the wheels, thereby restoring traction. Even apart from that, the driver of the ML 320 had every kind of electronic magic within reach of hand or foot. As an extra, the electronic stability program ESP operated with brake intervention on individual wheels, as well as by additional action on the engine to prevent potential skidding and keep the car on track.

This species was called a Sport Utility Vehicle and the Mercedes was a trusted paradigm, with an extremely solid chassis frame, deformable crash boxes at the front ends of the side members, rigid transverse bearers, and full-size airbags for driver and front passenger as well as standard side bags. A special off-road ABS shortened the braking distance on loose surfaces. The electronic brake distribution EBV relieved the front brakes as needed without compromising stability. Brake Assist, available in conjunction with the ESP system, initiated automatic emergency braking. Of course, even the M-Class was not one of a kind. Depending on their needs and budgets, potential customers could very soon choose the ML 230 with four cylinders and 150 bhp, five-cylinder diesel ML 270 CDI with 163 bhp, or a V8 version: ML 430 with 272 bhp or ML 55 AMG with 347 bhp.

In 2001, the ML series appeared in completely revamped form, the range now including the V8 diesel ML 400 CDI (250 bhp), while the ML 500 (292 bhp) sent the ML 430 into retirement.

An der Mercedes M-Klasse sei alles neu, sagt Jürgen Hubbert, Mitglied des Vorstands für das Geschäftsfeld Personenwagen: das Fahrzeug in einem neuen Segment, das Werk und seine Mitarbeiter an einem neuen Standort, sogar die Markteinführung außerhalb Europas. Premiere des Erstlings ML 320: vom 21. bis zum 23. Juli 1997 in Huntsville, Alabama. Produktion: im jüngsten Mercedes-Werk in Tuscaloosa, Alabama. Das Produkt: ein Allrounder, gleichermaßen versiert *off road* und *on road*, in Alltag und Abenteuer. Das beginnt mit der limousinenhaften Verbindlichkeit seines Äußeren, in dem glatte Rundlichkeit dominiert, kein Klotz, der sich wütend gegen den Wind stemmt. Das Interieur ist durch und durch auf Komfort abgestellt, die Klimaanlage ebenso serienmäßig wie die variablen Fondsitze und das Fahrberechtigungssystem Elcode (für *Electronic Code System*) mit ferngesteuerter Zentralverriegelung. Persönliche Wünsche werden gegen Aufpreis befriedigt, etwa der nach Lederpolsterung, einer dritten Sitzreihe oder einem Lamellen-Schiebedach.

Für muntere Fortbewegung sorgt wie im E 320 oder CLK 320 ein V6 mit Dreiventiltechnik, Doppelzündung und 3,2 Litern Hubraum, 218 PS stark. Eine weitere Innovation ersetzt drei herkömmliche Differentialsperren: das elektronische Traktionssystem 4-ETS. Ein Mikrocomputer erhöht so lange den Bremsdruck am durchdrehenden Rad, bis die Differenz zu den Rädern mit guter Bodenhaftung ausreicht und somit seine Traktion wieder hergestellt ist. Auch sonst gehen dem Lenker des ML 320 allerlei elektronische Heinzelmännchen zur Hand oder unterstützen fürsorglich seine Beinarbeit. Als Extra wirkt das Elektronische Stabilitätsprogramm ESP durch Bremseingriff an einzelnen Rädern sowie durch zusätzliche Einwirkung auf den Motor möglichen Schleuderbewegungen des Wagens entgegen und hält ihn in der Spur.

Sport Utility Vehicles (SUV) nennt man diese Spezies, und der Mercedes ist ein sicheres Paradigma, mit einem besonders festen Fahrgestellrahmen, deformierbaren Crashboxen an den vorderen Enden der Längsträger, biegesteifen Querträgern, Fullsize Airbags für Fahrer und Beifahrer sowie serienmäßigen Sidebags. Ein spezielles Gelände-ABS verkürzt den Bremsweg auf losem Untergrund. Die elektronische Bremskraftverteilung EBV entlastet bei erkanntem Bedarf die Vorderradbremsen, ohne die Fahrstabilität zu schmälern. Ein in Verbindung mit dem ESP-System lieferbarer *Brake Assist* (Bremsassistent) leitet in Notfällen eine automatische Vollbremsung ein. Natürlich bleibt es auch im Falle der M-Klasse nicht bei einer Monokultur. Je nach Bedarf und Budget kann der potentielle Kunde sehr bald zusätzlich für den ML 230 mit vier Zylindern und 150 PS, den Fünfzylinder-Diesel ML 270 CDI mit 163 PS oder die beiden V8-Versionen ML 430 mit 272 PS sowie ML 55 AMG mit 347 PS votieren.

2001 zeigt sich der ML nachhaltig retuschiert, die Palette um den Diesel-V8 ML 400 CDI (250 PS) erweitert, während der ML 500 (292 PS) den ML 430 in den Ruhestand schickt.

Tout est neuf avec la Mercedes Classe M », a déclaré Jürgen Hubbert, membre du directoire au titre du secteur d'activités Voitures particulières : l'automobile dans un nouveau segment, l'usine et ses collaborateurs sur un nouveau site industriel de même que sa commercialisation en dehors de l'Europe. La jeune première, la ML 320, est dévoilée du 21 au 23 juillet 1997 à Huntsville en Alabama. Elle est produite dans l'usine la plus récente de Mercedes, à Tuscaloosa (Alabama). Le produit, une voiture à tout faire aussi à l'aise en tout-terrain que sur route, pour aller faire ses achats ou se lancer à l'aventure. Cela commence avec une présentation très proche d'une berline, où dominent les galbes et les rondeurs. L'intérieur est conçu pour un confort maximal et l'air conditionné est de série au même titre que les sièges arrière variables et le système d'habilitation à la conduite Elcode (pour *Electronic Code System*) avec verrouillage centralisé. Les options sont nombreuses, par exemple la sellerie cuir, une troisième rangée de sièges ou un toit coulissant.

Elle peut se targuer de performances flatteuses avec son V6 à culasse à trois soupapes, identique à celui qui équipe déjà la E 320 ou la CLK 320, avec double allumage, 3,2 litres de cylindrée et 218 ch. Une autre innovation remplace simultanément trois blocages de différentiel conventionnels : le système de motricité électronique 4-ETS. Un micro-ordinateur augmente la puissance de freinage sur toute roue qui risque de s'emballer jusqu'à ce que l'écart de régime par rapport aux roues ayant une bonne adhérence soit résorbé et la motricité, donc, rétablie. Le conducteur de la ML 320 peut faire appel aux magiciens électroniques qui lui épargnent du travail, notamment avec les pieds. Au nombre des options figurent l'*Electronic Stability Program* (ESP), qui freine une ou plusieurs roues et intervient sur le moteur pour réprimer d'éventuels mouvements incontrôlés de la voiture et la maintenir sur sa trajectoire.

Les Américains ont baptisé ces voitures « *Sport Utility Vehicles* » et la Mercedes en est un parfait exemple avec un cadre de châssis solide, des caissons de collision déformables aux extrémités avant des longerons longitudinaux, des poutres transversales résistant à la torsion, des airbags *full size* pour le conducteur et le passager avant ainsi que des coussins gonflables latéraux de série. Une triple innovation : un ABS tout-terrain raccourcit la distance de freinage sur revêtement peu adhérent ; le dispositif EBV de répartition électronique de la puissance de freinage diminue les sollicitations des roues avant sans porter préjudice à la stabilité dynamique ; en cas de freinage d'urgence, le système d'assistance au freinage *Brake Assist* proposé avec l'ESP déclenche un freinage d'urgence automatique. Le propriétaire de la M n'a plus qu'à conduire et choisir un terrain approprié pour ses ébats entre autoroute et chemin creux. La monoculture n'est pas de règle pour la Classe M non plus. Selon les désirs et le budget, le client potentiel peut choisir, à titre supplémentaire, entre la ML 230 à moteur à quatre cylindres de 150 ch ou les deux versions V8 ML 430 de 272 ch ou ML 55 AMG de 347 ch.

Mercedes-Benz ML 1997

Mercedes-Benz ML 320 1997

Its aristocratic exterior betrays it: although the ML 320
is equipped to handle any mudbath, metaled roads are
its preferred domain. The Mercedes family likeness
is evident in its radiator grille and headlights.

Sein nobles Äußeres verrät es: Obwohl der ML 320 für jede
Schlammschlacht gerüstet ist, zählen befestigte Straßen zu
seinem bevorzugten Operationsfeld. Die Familienähnlichkeit zu
anderen Mercedes zeigt sich in Kühlergrill und Scheinwerfern.

Le luxe de son aspect est sans équivoque. Bien que la ML 320 ne
craigne pas les chemins boueux, les routes asphaltées sont tout
de même son champ d'opération de prédilection. La parenté avec
les autres Mercedes s'exprime dans la calandre et les phares.

Functionality in a luxurious setting: the driver of the ML 320 can defy even the most inhospitable weather conditions surrounded by the usual Mercedes comfort.

Arbeiter im Frack: Der Lenker des ML 320 trotzt selbst der unwirtlichsten Natur umgeben vom gewohnten Mercedes-Komfort.

Travailleur en smoking: le chauffeur de la ML 320 défie même la nature la plus impénétrable dans le confort que l'on est en droit d'attendre d'une Mercedes.

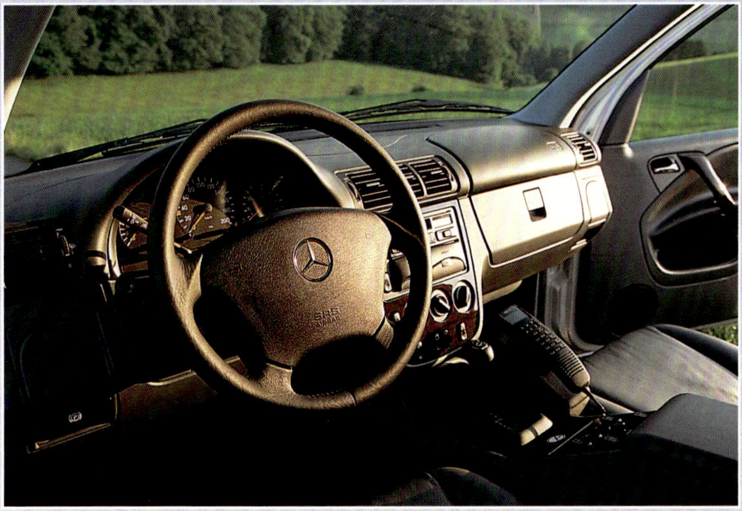

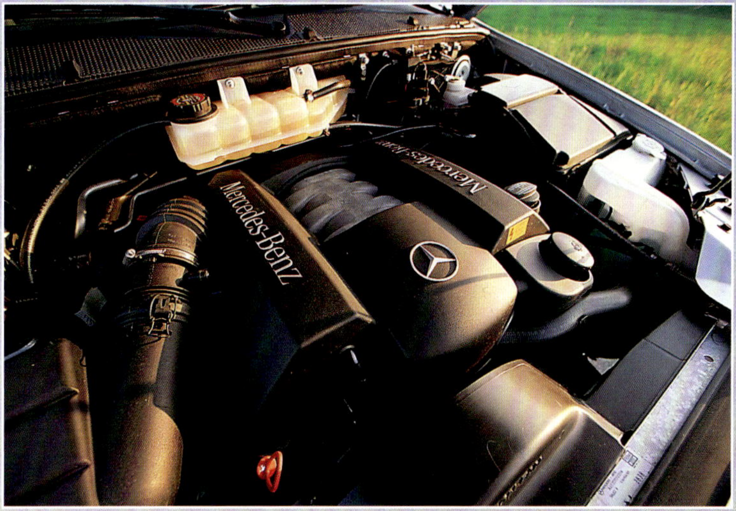
Mercedes-Benz

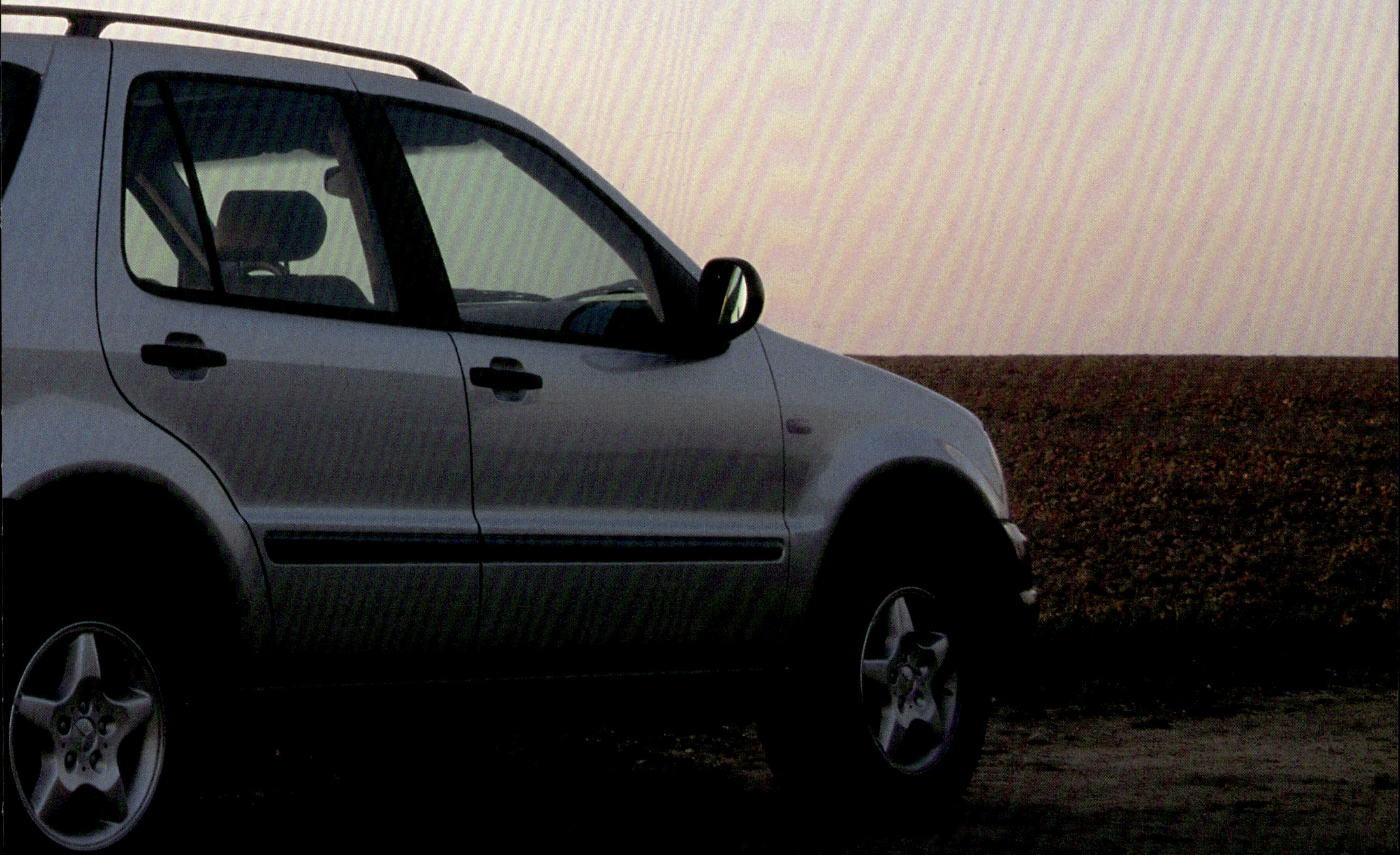

When the latest S-Class was unveiled at the Paris Motor Show in late September 1998, everyone was in agreement: the car was simply beautiful. Its predecessor had received little such praise. But its success—407,000 copies sold—justified both it and its forefathers.

The new model was not really much smaller: only three inches shorter, 1½ in narrower, and 1⅝ in flatter. With its flowing forms, which had been converted into the amazing drag coefficient of 0.27, however, it was almost delicate. Its elegant exterior was seamlessly continued inside, greeting its passengers with spaciousness and an abundance of controls and displays of extremely attractive design. The S-Class had to be the measure of all things. And so, the W220 had become the epitome of what was possible at the very cutting edge of science. Fears that its occupants might feel bewildered by an excess of new tasks to be learned were quickly dispelled. Buttons and switches were grouped into system-related entities. The operator guidance was very clear.

Traditional extras such as air conditioning or journey calculators were included in the basic package, while an additional sum was needed to secure such options as voice-controlled telephones or a multi-contour backrest that gently massaged the back at the push of a button.

The real revolution took place in the basement, where the refined Airmatic air suspension and an equally perfect adaptive damping turned driving into a trip on a flying carpet. At the start of production, the W220 was to be available as the S320 with a V6, and as the S430 and S500, both with whispering V8 engines. All were three-valve models. Six months later, the S55 AMG was introduced. Its engine was based on the five-liter version, but it had been drilled to 5439 cc and came with 54 more bhp, to the pleasure of many customers. Two petrol engines, the S280 and S600 (V12), and two diesel engines with six and eight cylinders rounded out the series. All engines were braced together with five-speed automatic transmission (and from the fall of 2003 with seven-stage on some V8 models) which had a nimble and discreet mode of action, though the accompanying Tiptronic actually made this redundant. Since fall 2002, a twin-turbo system had given the S600 a huge 500 bhp, just as the supercharger did to the S55 AMG, which, one year later, was accompanied by an S65 AMG twelve-cylinder (5980 cc, 612 bhp).

As established Mercedes custom dictated, the sedans were followed at the Geneva Salon 1999 by the coupés CL500, CL55 AMG, and CL600 and, from the summer of 2003, the CL65 AMG. They were rather similar to the CLK with their "four-eyed" faces and conspicuous elegance and came equipped with a conventional coil-sprung suspension, which was nevertheless controlled by a special hydraulic unit. Because of its sportier appearance, the CL was to break into the apparently secure fiefdoms of its rivals Porsche, BMW, and Jaguar.

Als die neueste S-Klasse auf dem Pariser Salon Ende September 1998 ihre Aufwartung macht, sind sich alle einig: Das Auto ist einfach schön. Dem Vorgänger wurde dergleichen Lob kaum zuteil. Sein Erfolg – 407000 verkaufte Exemplare – gab ihm und seinen Vätern gleichwohl Recht.

Der Neue ist nicht einmal viel kleiner: nur 75 mm kürzer, 37 mm schmaler und 41 mm flacher, und dennoch geradezu grazil, mit flüssigen Formen, die man in den erstaunlichen c_W-Wert von 0,27 umgemünzt hat. Seine äußere Eleganz setzt sich übergangslos nach innen fort, wo die Passagiere neben Raum in Hülle und Fülle Bedienelemente und Anzeigen von ungemein attraktiver Gestaltung erwarten. Die S-Klasse hat das Maß aller Dinge zu sein. Und so wird der W220 zum Konzentrat des Machbaren auf dem allerletzten Stand der Wissenschaft. Befürchtungen, man könne sich verlieren in einem Zuviel von Lernpensum, sind rasch zerstreut. Knöpfe und Schalter wurden in systembezogenen Einheiten zusammengefasst. Einleuchtend ist die Bedienerführung.

Traditionelle Extras wie Klimaautomatik oder Reiserechner sind ins Basispaket geschnürt, Optionen wie sprachgesteuerte Telefone oder eine Multikonturenlehne, die auf Knopfdruck mild den Rücken massiert, müssen dagegen anständig honoriert werden.

Die eigentliche Revolution findet im Souterrain statt, wo die raffinierte Luftfederung Airmatic sowie eine gleichermaßen perfekte adaptive Dämpfung die Fahrt zum Reisen auf einem fliegenden Teppich machen. Zum Produktionsstart wird der W220 angeboten als S320 mit einem V6 sowie als S430 und S500, beide mit wispernden V8-Triebwerken. Alle sind Dreiventiler. Ein halbes Jahr später stellt sich der S55 AMG ein. Seine Maschine fußt auf dem Fünfliter, wurde aber auf 5439 cm³ aufgebohrt und kommt mit 54 Mehr-PS der Lust mancher Kunden auf mehr Leistung entgegen. Zwei Benziner, der S280 und der S600 (V12), und zwei Diesel mit sechs und acht Zylindern runden die Baureihe ab. Alle Motoren sind zusammengespannt mit einer Fünfgangautomatik (ab Herbst 2003 für einige V8-Modelle mit einem 7-Stufen-Automaten) von flinker und diskreter Wirkungsweise, welche die dazugehörige Tiptronic eigentlich überflüssig macht. Ab Herbst 2002 bläst eine Biturbo-Anlage dem S600 satte 500 PS ein, ebenso viel wie ein Kompressor dem S55 AMG, dem man ein Jahr später den Zwölfzylinder S65 AMG (5980 cm³, 612 PS) zur Seite stellt.

Nach bewährtem Mercedes-Brauch folgen den Limousinen auf dem Genfer Frühjahrssalon 1999 die Coupés CL500, CL55 AMG und CL600, ab Sommer 2003 der CL65 AMG. Sie ähneln mit ihren Vier-Augen-Gesichtern und ihrer auffälligen Zierlichkeit eher dem CLK und sind ausgestattet mit einer konventionellen Stahlfederung, die gleichwohl über eine spezielle Hydraulikeinheit gesteuert wird. Auf Grund seiner sportiveren Anmutung soll der CL in die sicher gewähnten Erbhöfe der Rivalen Porsche, BMW und Jaguar einbrechen.

Quand la nouvelle Classe S tire sa révérence, au Salon de Paris à la fin du mois de septembre 1998, tous les spectateurs sont unanimes: la voiture est d'une beauté sculpturale. Et, au moment où est prononcée l'oraison funèbre de l'ancien modèle, s'élève une ultime fois le chœur de ses détracteurs qui n'ont jamais cessé de le critiquer: voilà bien la preuve que l'on aurait pu en faire une belle voiture! Le succès de l'ancien modèle leur aura donné raison, à lui-même et à ses concepteurs. Il aura tout de même été vendu à 407000 exemplaires.

La nouvelle n'est pourtant pas beaucoup plus petite: tout juste plus courte de 75 mm et plus étroite de 37 mm. Mais, sur un périmètre de sustentation revu à la baisse, se pavane en échange une voiture d'anthologie, plus basse de 41 mm, littéralement gracile, aux lignes fluides qui se traduisent par un étonnant c_x de 0,27. Son élégance extérieure se prolonge sans rupture à l'intérieur, où les passagers, qui disposent d'un espace pléthorique, ont aussi sous les yeux un tableau de bord et un aménagement intérieur que l'on peut légitimement qualifier de grande réussite. Le cahier des charges était pourtant ambitieux: la Classe S se devait d'être la référence dans sa catégorie. Et c'est ainsi que la W220 est le concentré de tout ce qui est réalisable sous réserve que cela représente le haut de gamme de la science. Ceux qui craignaient de devoir étudier en profondeur le manuel d'utilisation voient leurs réserves s'évanouir rapidement. Les boutons et les commandes ont été regroupés en ensembles logiques. Leur utilisation ne pose aucune difficulté. On se sent à l'aise dans la nouvelle grosse Mercedes.

Des équipements traditionnels comme la climatisation automatique ou l'ordinateur de bord font partie de l'équipement de base, alors que des options comme le téléphone à commande vocale ou le dossier de siège multicontours qui vous masse langoureusement le dos sur simple pression d'un bouton sont en revanche facturées contre espèces sonnantes et trébuchantes.

La révolution proprement dite s'est effectuée dans l'anonymat, en l'occurrence sous la carrosserie, où la suspension automatique Airmatic raffinée ainsi qu'un amortissement adaptatif tout aussi parfait transforment le moindre déplacement en une promenade sur un tapis volant. Pour le lancement de la production, la W220 est proposée dans trois versions: S320 à moteur V6 ainsi que S430 et S500, toutes les deux propulsées par un moteur V8 au murmure irrésistible. Tous ont une culasse à trois soupapes. Six mois plus tard, ce trio est rejoint par la S55 AMG. Son moteur est une évolution du V8 de 5 litres, mais réalésé à 5439 cm³ et qui, avec 54 ch supplémentaires, est destiné aux clients qui n'en ont jamais assez sous le pied. Deux autres moteurs à essence, le S280 et le S600 V12, et deux diesels, à six et huit cylindres, sont appelés à compléter la gamme. Tous les moteurs sont couplés à une boîte automatique à cinq vitesses au fonctionnement aussi rapide que discret, qui rend à proprement parler superflue la commande Tiptronic intégrée.

Mercedes-Benz S-Klasse & CL   1998

Mercedes-Benz S500 1999

Selon les bonnes vieilles habitudes de Mercedes, les berlines sont suivies, lors du Salon de printemps 1999 à Genève, par les deux coupés CL 500 et CL 600. Avec leur face avant à quatre yeux et leur gracilité flagrante, ils rappellent immédiatement la CLK et possèdent eux aussi une suspension conventionnelle à ressorts en acier, qui est toutefois commandée par une unité hydraulique spéciale. C'est le signe d'un changement de philosophie pour la politique de gamme: en raison de sa nature plus sportive, la CL est destinée à rouler dans les traces, sinon dans la chasse gardée, de ses rivales: Porsche, BMW et autres Jaguar.

Despite being compressed into the least possible space, the command center with its many features, from preset telephone numbers to controls for the GPS navigation system, is clearly laid out.

Auf knappstem Raum zusammengedrängt und dennoch übersichtlich ist die Kommandozentrale mit zahlreichen Funktionen von der Vorwahl fürs Telefon bis hin zum Bedienungszentrum für die GPS-Navigation.

Sur un espace extrêmement restreint, et pourtant clairement lisible, le poste de commande comporte de nombreuses fonctions avec la présélection pour téléphone et même la centrale de commande pour le système de navigation GPS.

While its predecessor's massive and monumental appearance put off some potential customers, the S-Class appeals at once with its more graceful lines. The five-liter engine runs with the quiet discretion of an English butler.

Während der Vorgänger so manchen möglichen Kunden durch wuchtige Monumentalität vergraulte, schmeichelt sich die S-Klasse durch rundum gefällige Formen sofort ein. Der Fünfliter unter der Haube arbeitet mit der Diskretion eines englischen Filmbutlers.

Alors que son prédécesseur a fait reculer maint client potentiel par son monumentalisme et sa lourdeur, la Classe S séduit immédiatement par l'élégance de ses lignes. Le moteur de cinq litres sous le capot travaille avec la discrétion d'un majordome britannique.

A liberating act: the lines of the new S-Class coupé are clearly distinguishable from those of the sedan, stressing its manifestly sporty intent.

Emanzipatorischer Akt: Das Coupé zur neuen S-Klasse setzt sich durch ein ganz eigenes Profil vom Basismodell ab. Manifeste Sportlichkeit ist angesagt.

Acte d'émancipation: la version coupé de la nouvelle Classe S se démarque du modèle de base par son profil bien spécifique. La sportivité est manifestement à l'ordre du jour.

Mercedes-Benz S-Klasse & CL 1998

Middle class when judged by its dimensions, upper middle class in its standard equipment, and in a class of its own in the range of potential individual variations: the new C-Class, presented in May 2000 (the T version was launched in spring 2001), was a thoroughly successful product. The clientele (ultimately the broadest group of buyers for a Mercedes model series) was delighted, and immediately helped itself with gusto to the new product. No fewer than twelve engine variants, from the initial 116-bhp four-cylinder up to the V6 AMG with 231 bhp, met all possible requirements. An AMG six-cylinder engine with 354 bhp was not long in coming. Amazing, too, was the variety of combinations of paint and upholstery recommended by the manufacturer. These covered even the most individual tastes, such as the special metallic varnish in amethyst violet for which the couturiers of the house had come up with only one matching seat color: anthracite.

Depending on budget, one could splash out on the so-called Classic finish, with the fabric design "York" plus the fine wood panels in "Calyptus Linea." Or perhaps on the Elegance, whose wood embellishments "Lauret" were prettily distributed throughout the interior. Alloy wheels, lots of chrome, and a leather steering wheel emphasized the distinguished character of this type. And, when it comes to conspicuous display, the fact that less is sometimes more was indicated by the matte black varnished slats of the radiator grille in the Avantgarde variant.

One striking Mercedes feature: the textured pedals in brushed stainless steel. Solid contact with the pedals cannot do without a certain justification, at least when handling considerable AMG power—especially with the C 55 AMG (available from 2004) with its 5.4-liter V8 that releases a sturdy 367 bhp and, with 376 lb-ft, a decent torque. To host this large-capacity engine, the front of the car had to be modified. Anyone who had laid out a cool 64,090 euros to purchase this model could use its five-speed automatic transmission with AMG Speedshift and steering wheel paddles to reach a speed of 62 mph within 5.2 seconds.

Let us stay, however, with the relatively modest C 220 CDI and its standard equipment, which turned out to be quite lush and included important components such as the electronic stability program ESP and braking system BAS. Some C-Class drivers complained that the extremely comfortable suspension was too soft. As part of the facelift, in 2004 Mercedes responded with stronger stabilizers, more direct steering, and modified axle bearings as well as the new standard tire size 205/55 R 16, which from the C 240 onward had figured among the top treads. In the context of this makeover, a good 7 bhp dropped away from the four-cylinder diesel engine of the C 220 CDI. Thanks to a particulate filter that regenerates itself without additives, the CDI has, since October 2003, met the strict EU-4 standards.

These technological interventions went hand in hand with smaller retouches in the interior. Thus the interlaced

Mittelklasse gemessen an den Dimensionen, gehobene Mittelklasse in der serienmäßigen Ausstattung und einsame Klasse in der Vielfalt individueller Variationsmöglichkeiten: Die neue C-Klasse, im Mai des Jahres 2000 präsentiert (T-Version Frühjahr 2001), ist ein rundum gelungenes Produkt. Die Klientel, immerhin die breiteste Käuferschicht für eine Mercedes-Modellreihe, ist entzückt und greift auch gleich herzhaft zu. Nicht weniger als zwölf Motoren-Varianten, anfänglich vom 116-PS-Vierzylinder bis hin zum V6 von AMG mit 231 PS, lassen keine Wünsche offen. Ein AMG-Sechszylinder mit 354 PS lässt nicht lange auf sich warten. Verblüffend auch die Vielzahl der Kombinationen von Lacken und Polster-Couleurs, die der Hersteller empfiehlt. Sie deckt selbst die kuriosesten Geschmäcker ab, wie etwa die Metallic-Sonderlackierung Amethyst-Violett, zu welcher den Couturiers des Hauses nur eine passende Sitzfarbe einfällt: anthrazit.

Je nach Geldbeutel darf geschwelgt werden: in der so genannten Classic-Ausführung mit dem Stoffdesign »York«, dazu die Edelholztäfelung »Calyptus Linea«. Oder beim Elegance: Hier heißt die Holzapplikation »Lauret«, hübsch im Interieur verteilt. Leichtmetallräder, viel Chrom und ein Lederlenkrad unterstreichen den noblen Charakter dieser Spielart. Dass weniger Pomp manchmal mehr ist, signalisieren schon die mattschwarz lackierten Lamellen des Kühlergrills bei der Variante Avantgarde.

Markantes Merkmal: die genoppten Pedale aus gebürstetem Edelstahl. Der feste Kontakt zur Pedalerie entbehrt zumindest im Umgang mit viel AMG-Power nicht einer gewissen Berechtigung – besonders bei dem ab 2004 erhältlichen C 55 AMG mit seinem 5,4-Liter-V8, der stämmige 367 PS und mit 510 Newtonmetern auch ein ordentliches Drehmoment freisetzt. Zur Aufnahme dieses großvolumigen Treibsatzes muss der Vorderwagen umgebaut werden. Wer den für seine Anschaffung erforderlichen Batzen von 64 090 Euro aufgebracht hat, vermag mit Hilfe seiner Fünfgang-Automatik mit AMG-Speedshift und Lenkradpaddeln Tempo 100 binnen 5,2 Sekunden zu erreichen.

Bleiben wir beim vergleichsweise bescheidenen C 220 CDI und seiner Serienausstattung, die durchaus üppig ausfällt und wichtige Komponenten wie das elektronische Stabilitätsprogramm ESP und den Bremsassistenten BAS beinhaltet. Einige C-Klasse-Lenker monieren, das äußerst komfortabel ausgelegte Fahrwerk sei zu schwammig. Im Rahmen der Modellpflege reagiert Mercedes 2004 mit stärkeren Stabilisatoren, direkterer Lenkung und überarbeiteten Achslagern sowie der neuen Standard-Reifengröße 205/55 R 16, die bislang vom C 240 aufwärts zur Werks-Besohlung zählte. Im Rahmen dieser Frischzellenkur fällt für den Vierzylinder-Diesel des C 220 CDI auch das milde Mehr von sieben PS ab. Dank eines Partikelfilters, der sich ohne Zusatzstoffe regeneriert, erfüllt der CDI seit Oktober 2003 die strengen EU-4-Normen.

Segment intermédiaire pour les dimensions, segment supérieur pour la richesse de l'équipement de série, mais nettement au-dessus pour la diversité des possibilités de personnalisation: la nouvelle Classe C présentée en mai 2000 (la version break au printemps 2001) est un produit tout à fait réussi. La clientèle est enchantée. Pas moins de douze motorisations, depuis une quatre cylindres à 116 chevaux jusqu'au V6 de AMG offrant 231 chevaux, satisfont toutes les envies. Une AMG six cylindres de 354 ch ne se fit pas attendre longtemps. Le nombre de combinaisons de peintures et de garnitures proposé par le constructeur est également stupéfiant. Elles satisfait les goûts les plus particuliers, notamment une peinture métallisée violet améthyste pour laquelle le couturier maison ne conseille qu'une seule nuance pour les sièges : anthracite.

Selon les porte-monnaie, le choix est large : dans la version dite Classic avec le tissu design « York », assorti à une boiserie en bois précieux « Calyptus Linea ». Ou dans la version Elegance : ici, le placage bois, joliment réparti à l'intérieur, s'appelle « Lauret ». Les roues en alliage léger, beaucoup de chrome et un volant en cuir soulignent le caractère noble de cette version. Dans la variante Avantgarde, les lamelles noir mat de la calandre prouvent que moins de faste est parfois le must.

Le signe distinctif du modèle réside dans un pédalier en acier inoxydable brossé, doté de petites boules en caoutchouc garantissant une bonne adhérence. En l'occurrence, faire corps avec son véhicule est fondamental, surtout avec la superpuissance de l'AMG – en particulier pour la C 55 AMG disponible à partir de 2004. En effet, son moteur V8 de 5,4 litres libère 367 robustes chevaux et un généreux couple de 510 Nm. Pour installer ce moteur de grosse cylindrée, il a fallu revoir toute la partie avant du véhicule. Celui qui est prêt à débourser la coquette somme de 64 090 euros pour son acquisition pourra, à l'aide de la boîte automatique cinq rapports dotée du speedshift AMG et du volant performance, atteindre les 100 km/h en 5,2 secondes.

Mais restons à la C 220 CDI comparativement modeste, et à son équipement de série qui est déjà imposant et intègre des composants importants tels que le programme de stabilité électronique ESP et l'assistance de freinage BAS. Certains conducteurs de la Classe C regrettaient une trop grande souplesse du châssis particulièrement confortable. Lors de l'actualisation de la Classe C en 2004, Mercedes réagit avec des barres antiroulis plus résistantes, une direction plus directe et des paliers d'essieu corrigés ainsi que des nouveaux pneumatiques standard 205/55 R 16 qui n'étaient proposés jusqu'alors qu'à partir de la C 240. Dans le cadre de cette cure de jouvence, le moteur diesel à quatre cylindres de la C 220 CDI bénéficia aussi d'un petit surplus de sept chevaux. Grâce à un filtre à particules se régénérant sans additifs, la CDI respecte les sévères normes UE 4 depuis octobre 2003.

Ces améliorations techniques vont de pair avec quelques petites retouches de l'habitacle. Ainsi, les cadrans

Mercedes-Benz C-Klasse 2000

Mercedes-Benz C 220 CDI 2003

clock-face fragments mutated into more readable, fully rounded fittings, and various switches became easier to handle. The lateral control of the seats—previously rather flabby—had been taken in hand by Mercedes orthopedists. Even in hard-cornering conditions they now offered a more secure purchase.

As always, these measures were accompanied with a rejuvenating facelift. The air intake, previously divided only by a bar in the rear bumper, was now divided by two strong ribs, and modern clear-glass optics gave the headlamps rather more transparency. The modified xenon spotlights with a special bending light cost extra, obliging customers to dig deep into their pockets. From spring 2005, in the C 320 CDI, as the forerunner of a new generation, a 224 bhp v6 diesel engine replaced the previous five-cylinder engine, which appeared to its best advantage combined with the optional seven-speed automatic.

Mit diesen Eingriffen in die Technik gehen kleinere Retuschen im Interieur einher. So mutieren die ineinander verschränkten Runduhr-Fragmente zu gut ablesbaren, komplett gerundeten Armaturen, und diverse Schalter sind griffbereiter angeordnet. Der seitlichen Führung der Sitze – bislang wenig energisch – nehmen sich die Orthopäden der Marke an. Auch bei scharfer Kurvenfahrt bieten sie jetzt sicheren Halt.

Wie stets gehen diese Verjüngungsmaßnahmen mit einem Facelift einher. Der nur durch einen Steg unterteilte Lufteinlass im Stoßfänger zeigt sich nun durch zwei kräftige Rippen gegliedert, und moderne Klarglas-Optik eröffnet den Scheinwerfern gewissermaßen mehr Durchblick. Das Verschreiben von Xenon-Strahlern mit speziellem Abbiegelicht ist kostenpflichtig und muss mit einem tiefen Griff in die Schatulle honoriert werden. Ab Frühjahr 2005 ersetzt – Vorläufer einer neuen Generation – im C 320 CDI ein 224 PS starker Diesel-V6 den bisherigen Fünfzylinder, der sich im Bunde mit der wahlweise verfügbaren Siebengang-Automatik am besten in Szene setzt.

circulaires jusqu'ici partiellement superposés se sont transformés en véritables armatures rondes et lisibles auxquels s'ajoutent diverses commandes bien positionnées. Les orthopédistes de la marque se sont occupés du guidage latéral des sièges, jusqu'ici relativement souples. Désormais, ils offrent un bon maintien même dans les virages serrés.

Comme toujours, ces mesures de rajeunissement s'accompagnent d'un lifting extérieur. La prise d'air dans le pare-chocs présentant un seul barreau montre désormais deux imposantes nervures. Quant aux optiques modernes en verre glace lisse, ils ouvrent nettement plus les yeux des phares. La prescription de projecteurs xénon directionnels adaptatifs est en option et oblige à plonger profondément la main dans son porte-monnaie. À partir du printemps 2005 dans la C 320 CDI un V6 Diesel de 224 ch, précurseur d'une nouvelle génération, remplace le cinq cylindres. Il est mieux mis en valeur avec la boîte automatique sept rapports disponible si on le souhaite.

The thrifty C 220 CDI engine whose 150 bhp are sufficient to provide the mid-range sedan with a mileage of 39 mpg and a top speed of 129 mph.

Knapp sechs Liter Diesel verbraucht das sparsame Triebwerk des C 220 CDI, dessen 150 PS aber ausreichen, um der Mittelklassen-Limousine eine Endgeschwindigkeit von 208 km/h zu verleihen.

L'économe moteur de la C 220 CDI se contente d'à peine six litres de diesel aux 100 km, mais ses 150 ch suffisent pour propulser, si besoin est, la berline du segment intermédiaire à une vitesse de pointe de 208 km/h.

The C-Class presents itself with an appealing exterior, spacious interior, functional dashboard, and seating with improved side design.

Mit ihrem ansprechenden Äußeren, dem geräumigen Innenleben, funktionellen Armaturen und Sitzen mit verbesserter Seitenführung empfiehlt sich die C-Klasse ebenfalls.

Avec sa présentation séduisante, son habitacle spacieux, son tableau de bord fonctionnel et ses sièges qui offrent un meilleur maintien latéral, on ne peut que recommander la Classe C.

As the name implies, the C coupé, introduced at the Paris Motor Show in the fall of 2000, was a close relative of the volume model C-Class. It filled a niche that its forefathers had in a sense created: a sporty hatchback alternative to the ever-popular range of four-door sedans for a wealthy, young clientele, though more suited to those without children. Its youthful, dynamic trimmings, a longer rear door in which a plexiglass pane ensured transparency, and a cheeky spoiler. With a mere 11.3 cu.ft the trunk was modest for the range, but this could be increased threefold for bulky goods by folding down the split rear seat. Getting into the rear seat demanded the flexibility and agility of youth.

The recipe seemed to work, especially as the little coupé compared favorably with the basic model owing to its increased maneuverability. It allowed the Mercedes star to shine in every road, its proud occupants reveling in its prestige. As had long been the custom, both the sheer range of its various facilities and the engine itself left nothing to be desired. Under the shortened hood there were no fewer than twelve gasoline engines, from the 1796 cc four-cylinder of the C160 Kompressor with 122 bhp to the 354 bhp of the powerful V6 with 3199 cc in the C32 AMG of 2003, and four diesel variants, from the four-pan engine of the C200 CDI with 2148 cc and 122 bhp to the five-cylinder (2850 cc, 231 bhp) in the C30 CDI AMG.

The 2004 vintage of the smallest Mercedes coupé was unveiled in completely renovated shape, however, theoretically as a result of the simultaneous transformation of the four-door model, but with even more of a sporty emphasis. The track, extended from 4 ft 10 in to 5 ft, made a particular contribution to this, as well as a new air intake in the bumper, where the traditional diamond lattice had been replaced by a more aggressive-looking slat structure. The radiator grille was also modified, with greater emphasis on the transverse ribs. Newly designed ornamental molding for the wheels and standard five-spoke alloy wheels for the C230 Kompressor and the C320 enhanced the sports coupé, as did the "diamond optics" of the tail lights, as Mercedes called it. The fresh and dynamic character of the model was also underlined by a new three-spoke steering wheel with silver-colored control buttons, aluminum decorative moldings in the central console, and sports seats. The basic package now included the automatic climate control Thermatic.

The short car was sent into retirement by the CLC, presented on 28 January 2008 at the Berlin Fashion Week. The platform and raw body from its predecessor have been retained, while the four-eyed face at the front has given way to the current C-Class' sports-orientated Avantgarde version with the star centered in the broad three-louver grille and large, low level air intake. The somewhat quirky rear has found its way to the style dump. The sporty steering wheel as part of the so-called Sports Package is well suited to the nippy two-door car. It reaches over 125 mph with all of the engines on offer, four gasoline

---

Wie bereits der Name besagt, ist das C-Coupé, eingeführt beim Pariser Salon im Herbst 2000, ein naher Anverwandter des Volumenmodells C-Klasse. Es füllt eine Nische aus, welche seine Väter gewissermaßen selber geschaffen haben: als sportive Schrägheck-Alternative zu der allseits beliebten Palette von viertürigen Limousinen, für eine wohlhabende jugendliche Klientel möglichst ohne Nachwuchs jung-dynamisch getrimmt, in der Verlängerung der Heckklappe, in der eine Plexiglas-Scheibe für Transparenz sorgt, ein kesser Spoiler. Der Kofferraum fällt mit 320 Litern Volumen artenspezifisch bescheiden aus, lässt sich indessen durch Umlegen der geteilten Fondlehne verdreifachen. Die hintere Sitzbank zu beziehen verlangt nach jugendfrischer Biegsam- und Behändigkeit.

Das Rezept scheint aufzugehen, zumal das kleine Coupé durch eine noch mal gesteigerte Handlichkeit gegenüber dem Basismodell glänzt und im Visier der Insassen stolz und statusträchtig den guten Stern auf allen Straßen trägt. Wie längst Usus, lässt ähnlich dem Spektrum seiner Ausstattungsvarianten auch seine Motorisierung keinerlei Wünsche übrig. Unter der kurzen vorderen Haube hausen nicht weniger als zwölf Benziner, vom 1796-cm³-Vierzylinder des C160 Kompressor mit 122 PS bis hinauf zum 354 PS starken V6 mit 3199 cm³ im C32 AMG von 2003, und vier Diesel-Varianten zwischen dem Viertöpfer des C200 CDI mit 2148 cm³ und 122 PS und dem Fünfzylinder (2850 cm³, 231 PS), der im C30 CDI AMG Dienst tut.

Der Jahrgang 2004 des kleinsten Coupés im Zeichen des Sterns gibt sich runderneuert, im Prinzip orientiert an der gleichzeitigen Metamorphose des Viertürers, aber mit noch stärkeren sportlichen Akzenten. Dazu trägt vor allem die von 1465 auf 1505 Millimeter erweitere Spur bei, ebenso wie ein neuer Lufteinlass im Stoßfänger, wo man das brave Rautengitterchen durch eine aggressiver anmutende Lamellenstruktur ersetzt hat. Ebenfalls einer Modifikation unterzogen wurde der Kühlergrill durch stärkere Betonung der Querrippen. Neu gestaltete Radzierblenden und serienmäßige Fünfspeichen-Leichtmetallräder für den C230 Kompressor und den C320 werten das Sportcoupé ebenso auf wie die Brillant-Optik der Rückleuchten, wie Mercedes das nennt. Der frisch-dynamische Charakter des Modells wird überdies unterstrichen durch ein neues Dreispeichenlenkrad mit silberfarbenen Bedientasten, Aluminium-Zierblenden in der Mittelkonsole sowie Sportsitze. Zum Basis-Paket zählt nun auch die Klimaautomatik Thermatic.

In Pension geschickt wird der Kurze durch den CLC, vorgestellt anlässlich der Berliner Fashion Week am 28. Januar 2008. Vom Vorgänger übernommen sind Plattform und Rohkarosse, während das Vieraugen-Gesicht der Frontpartie der aktuellen C-Klasse in der sportlich orientierten Variante Avantgarde mit Zentral-Stern im breit lächelnden Drei-Lamellen-Grill und großem Lufteinlass im Parterre wich. Die etwas verquast wirkende

---

Comme l'indique son nom, le coupé C présenté pour la première fois au salon de l'automobile de Paris à l'automne 2000, est un parent proche de la volumineuse Classe C. Il comble une niche que ses pères ont eux-mêmes créée dans une certaine mesure : modèle sportif à hayon, il est présenté comme une alternative à la gamme des berlines quatre portes appréciées de tous. Il vise une clientèle jeune et aisée, si possible sans enfants, et se donne un air jeune et dynamique grâce à l'allongement du hayon, sur lequel la vitre en plexiglas apporte de la lumière, et à un spoiler osé. Son moyen volume de 320 litres peut, en outre, être multiplié par trois pour un chargement volumineux. S'installer sur la banquette arrière nécessite cependant la souplesse et l'agilité de la jeunesse.

La recette semble prendre. Tout d'abord le petit coupé brille par une maniabilité encore plus grande que celle du modèle de base et porte fièrement la bonne étoile sur toutes les routes, montrant le statut social des passagers. Comme de coutume, l'étendue de ses versions et sa motorisation sont parfaites. Lecourt capot avant hébergeait pas moins de douze moteurs à essence depuis les 1796 cm³ du quatre cylindres C160 Kompressor de 122 chevaux, au C32 AMG de 2003 offrant les 354 ch d'un V6 de 3199 cm³ ; également quatre versions diesel depuis les quatre cylindres du C200 CDI de 2148 cm³ et 122 ch aux cinq cylindres (2850 cm³, 231 ch) fonctionnant dans le C30 CDI AMG.

Le millésime 2004 du plus petit coupé conçu sous le signe de l'étoile fut rénové, une métamorphose basée sur celle de la quatre portes mais avec une accentuation du caractère sportif. Y contribuent surtout l'écartement des roues qui passe de 1465 à 1505 millimètres, tout comme une nouvelle prise d'air dans les pare-chocs. La bonne vieille petite grille en losange a été également été remplacée par une structure en lamelles à l'aspect plus agressif. Également soumise à modification, la calandre a été dotée de barreaux horizontaux plus marqués. En option, le boîtier des phares antibrouillard héberge également l'éclairage de virage récemment mis au point. Les nouveaux enjoliveurs et les jantes en alliage léger de série de la C230 Kompressor et de la C320 Kompressor donnent de la valeur au coupé sport, tout comme l'aspect « diamant ciselé » des feux arrière, selon la description de Mercedes. Le caractère jeune et dynamique du modèle est encore souligné par le nouveau volant à trois branches aux touches de commande argentées, les éléments décoratifs en aluminium de la console centrale et les sièges sport. La climatisation automatique Thermatic fait partie également ment du pack de base.

La présentation du modèle suivant, la CLC, à la Fashion Week de Berlin le 28 janvier 2008 signe sa mise à la retraite. La CLC a repris la plateforme et la carrosserie de son prédécesseur tandis que le visage à doubles optiques a cédé la place à l'avant de l'actuelle Classe C en version Avantgarde orientée vers l'allure sportive, avec l'étoile centrale dans la large grille de la souriante calandre à trois lamelles et la

Mercedes-Benz C-Klasse Sportcoupé / CLC   2000

Mercedes-Benz CLC180 Kompressor 2008

engines, the two supercharged four-cylinders with 1796 cc, 143 bhp and 184 bhp, and the powerful v6 with 2496 cc and 204 bhp, and 3498 cc and 272 bhp, the latter in the CLC 350, its forward thrust being curbed electronically when a speed of 155 mph is reached. The diesel faction is represented by the common-rail four-cylinder with 2148 cc and 122 or 150 bhp. They all come with manual six-speed gearboxes or (at extra cost) five- or seven-speed automatic transmission.

Heckpartie wurde auf die stilistische Müllhalde entsorgt. Das Sportlenkrad im Rahmen des so genannten Sport-Pakets steht dem flinken Zweitürer gut an: Er läuft über 200 mit allen angebotenen Motoren, vier Benzinern, den beiden Kompressor-Vierzylindern mit 1796 cm³ und 143 PS und 184 PS und v6-Aggregaten mit 2496 cm³ und 204 PS und 3498 cm³ und 272 PS, letzterer im CLC 350, dessen Vorwärtsdrang bei Tempo 250 elektronisch Einhalt geboten wird. Die Diesel-Fraktion ist durch Common-Rail-Vierzylinder mit 2148 cm³ und 122 beziehungsweise 150 PS vertreten. Gepaart sind alle mit Sechsgang-Schaltgetrieben oder (gegen Aufpreis) Fünf- oder Sieben-Stufen-Automaten.

grande prise d'air en dessous. La partie arrière jusqu'alors assez confuse a été supprimée. Avec le pack sport est inclus un volant sport qui convient parfaitement à l'agile deux portes : il roule à plus de 200 km/h pour tous les moteurs proposés, quatre à essence, dont deux quatre cylindres à compresseur de 1796 cm³ et 143 ch ou 184 ch, et deux v6 de 2496 cm³ et 204 ch et 3498 cm³ et 272 ch pour la CLC 350 dont la soif d'avancer est limitée électroniquement à 250 km/h. Les versions diesel, avec 2148 cm³ et 122 ch ou 150 ch sont toutes deux équipées d'une injection Common-Rail avec quatre unités de combustion. Elles sont toutes dotées d'une boîte à six vitesses ou (en option) d'une boîte automatique cinq ou sept rapports.

A distinctive rear design and a compact wedge form: the sport coupé, fitted with a 6-gear switching transmission as standard, displays as the C 230 a red top above its four-cylinder supercharger engine. Reminiscent of the *testa rossa* from Maranello?

Unverwechselbar im Design der Heckpartie und der kompakten Keilform: Das Sportcoupé, serienmäßig mit einem 6-Gang-Schaltgetriebe ausgerüstet, zeigt als C 230 über seinem Vierzylinder-Kompressor-Motor einen roten Deckel. Etwa eine Reminiszenz an die *testa rossa* aus Maranello?

Unique par le design de sa poupe et ses lignes cunéiformes compactes : le coupé sport, équipé en série d'une boîte manuelle à six vitesses, est propulsé, en version C 230, par un moteur à compresseur et à quatre cylindres avec un couvercle de culasse de couleur rouge. Est-ce un clin d'œil à la *testa rossa* de Maranello ?

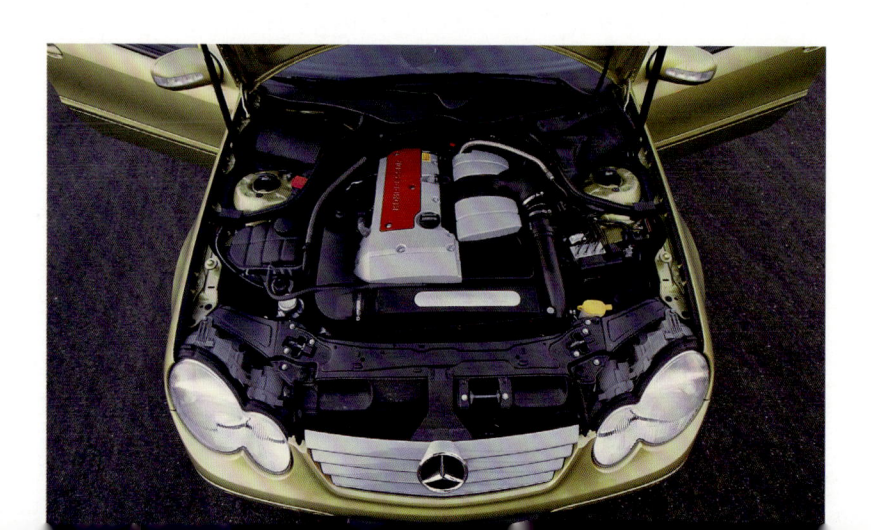

Mercedes-Benz C-Klasse Sportcoupé/CLC 2000

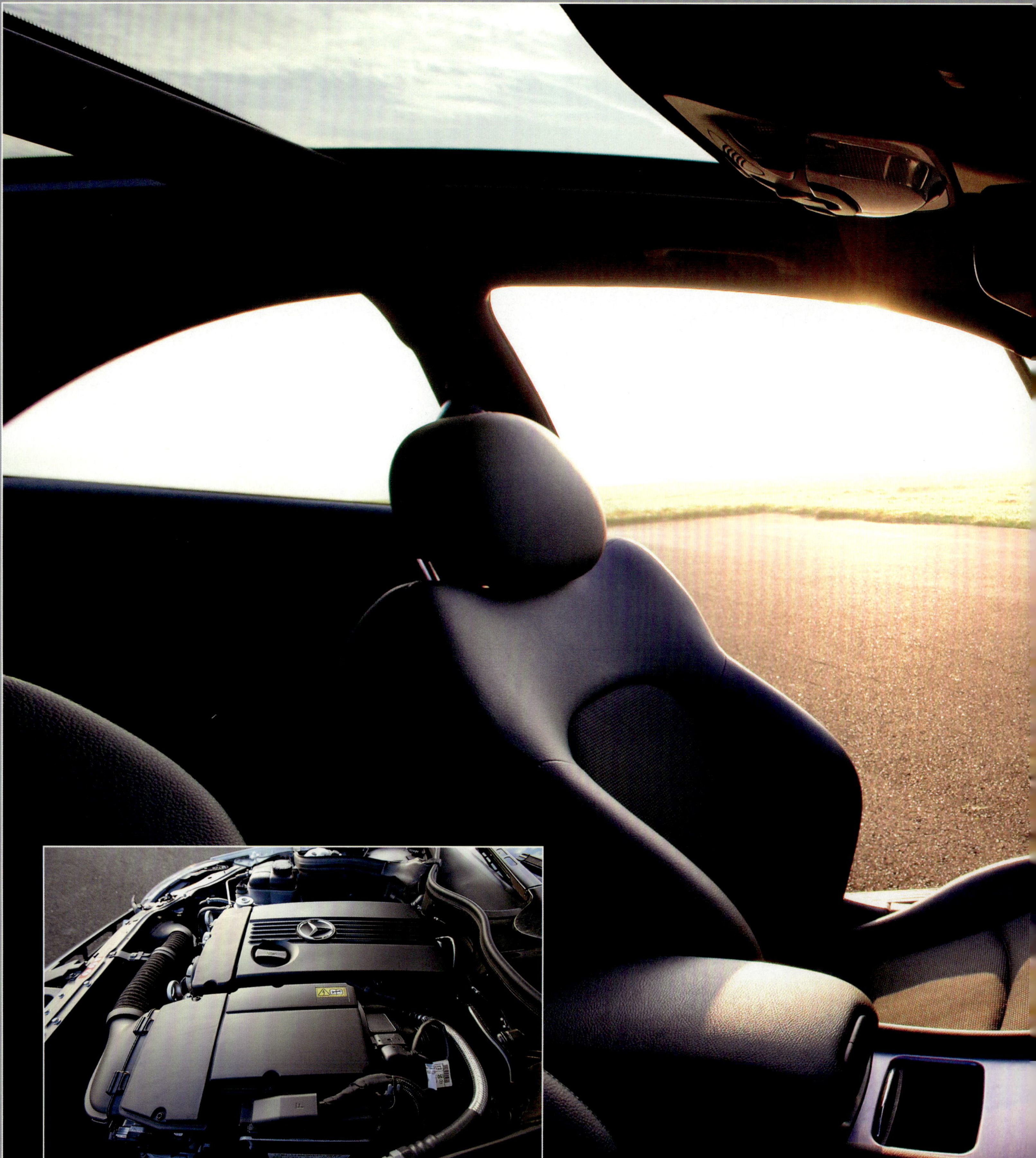

The modernization of the CLC exterior also took care of a couple of stylistic inconsistencies. The target group comprises the so-called Dinks (double income, no kids), and so the childless couple sits very comfortably and securely in the first row while things are seemingly cramped at the back—the usual drawback with smaller coupés in particular.

Bei der Modernisierung des Äußeren am CLC wurden nicht zuletzt ein paar stilistische Ungereimtheiten getilgt. Zielgruppe sind die so genannten Dinks (double income, no kids), und so sitzt das angepeilte kinderlose Paar in der ersten Reihe geborgen und überaus kommod, während es im zweiten Glied ziemlich beengt zugeht – das übliche Manko vor allem kleinerer Coupés.

La modernisation extérieure de la CLC prit également en compte deux ou trois incohérences stylistiques. Le public visé est constitué par les dinks (*double income, no kids,* c'est-à-dire les foyers à deux revenus et sans enfants). C'est pourquoi un couple peut voyager très confortablement à l'avant, tandis que les conditions sont beaucoup plus difficiles à l'arrière – inconvénient classique avec les petits coupés.

Produced since 2001 in the Mercedes plant in Bremen, the fifth-generation SL (R230, in-house code) must count among the most beautiful so far, and certainly the most innovative. The fact that even the seemingly perfect still offered room for improvement was nevertheless verified in the development of the long model vita 2006 and 2008.

Even more than its predecessor, the SL of the new species reconciled what had once seemed irreconcilable: it was both sporty and comfortable—the L (for light) in the model designation had, as everyone was aware, long since become an empty formula. The comfort of its occupants and the usefulness of the 2+2-seater in all four seasons was improved (somewhat following the lines of its little sibling, the SLK) by a fixed aluminum roof that could be taken off if desired and bedded down in the boot next to the glass rear window, thanks to a perfectly organized electro-hydraulic device. Its sporty character was emphasized by its ABC (Mercedes-speak for Active Body Control) chassis, which, with the help of sensor signals and specially designed hydraulic cylinders at the axles, almost completely eliminated pitching and rolling of the superstructure. What made it a sports car, however, was mainly its engine: an assortment of five juiced-up petrol motors, the diesel engine being simply incompatible with a car of this stamp. The new model made its appearance as the SL 500 with 4966 cc and 306 bhp generated by a V8, as well as a supercharger-enhanced SL 55 AMG (5439 cc with 500 bhp)—something really to make the mouth water.

In 2002 the model was upgraded and complemented, both above and below, by the SL 350 (V6, 3724 cc, 245 bhp) and the huskily whispering SL 600, boosted by a twin-turbo V12 (5513 cc, 500 bhp), while from 2004 what was theoretically the same engine released 612 bhp from 5980 cc in the SL 65 AMG. Given the reality of driving on the German autobahns, the prudent management of the SL put a categorical stop to any speeds faster than 155 mph. With the curious reporters from *auto motor und sport* on board, an unfettered AMG twelve-cylinder engine on the high-speed track in Nardo, Italy showed its true mettle, reaching 210 mph.

At the Geneva Motor Show in 2006, the handsome machine from Bremen made its appearance after a relatively gentle facelift. A new front bumper with three large cooling air intakes, greater sweep, and fog lights with chrome rings gave the appearance of greater width while visually emphasizing its potency. This harmonized with its radiator grille, now painted in matte silver and with three louvers plus chrome trim, and was finely tuned to the design of the new alloy wheels and horizontally divided rear lighting clusters with their red and clear glass covers. This markedly sporty appearance was carried forward in the interior, finding expression, for example, in the steering wheel control paddles of the special version 7G-Tronic Sport. It also manifested itself in even more muscular engines: a newly developed V8 engine with

Mercedes-Benz SL   2001

Mercedes-Benz SL500 2003

5461 cc, 388 bhp and 390 lb-ft in the SL 500 and an equally new V6 (3498 cc, 272 bhp) for the SL 350, while the output of the V12 in the SL 600 had increased to 517 bhp, with a huge maximum torque of 612 lb-ft.

In the second model metamorphosis of 2008, identifiable by two power domes on the hood and headlights pulled far back into the fenders, the 3.5-liter V6 produced 316 bhp, while a three-liter, six-cylinder engine in the SL 280 yielded 231 bhp; the V12 in the SL 65 AMG Black Series edition even came up with 670 bhp. A warm air system, integrated into the headrests if required, fanned the heads of the passengers with a pleasant breeze. Here, too, the SLK was godfather.

V8 mit 5461 cm³, 388 PS und 530 Newtonmetern im SL 500 sowie einem ebenfalls neuen V6 (3498 cm³, 272 PS) für den SL 350, während die Leistung des V12 im SL 600 auf 517 PS angeschwollen ist, bei einem maximalen Drehmoment von enormen 830 Newtonmetern.

In der zweiten Modell-Metamorphose von 2008, erkennbar an zwei Powerdomes auf der Fronthaube und weit in die Kotflügel gezogenen Scheinwerfern, wartet der 3,5-Liter V6 mit 316 PS, ein Dreiliter-Sechszylinder im SL 280 mit 231 PS und der V12 in der Edition SL 65 AMG Black Series gar mit 670 PS auf. Ein in die Kopfstützen integriertes Warmluftsystem umfächelt bei Bedarf die Häupter der Passagiere mit wohligen Winden. Auch hier stand der SLK Pate.

nouvellement développé de 5461 cm³, 388 ch et 530 Nm dans la SL 500 ainsi qu'un nouveau V6 (3498 cm³, 272 ch) pour la SL 350 alors que la puissance du V12 de la SL 600 a été gonflée à 517 ch, pour un énorme couple plafond de 830 Nm.

Dans la deuxième métamorphose du modèle en 2008, reconnaissable à deux bossages sur le capot et aux phares placés très loin dans l'aile, attend un V6 3,5 litres de 316 ch et un six cylindres trois litres dans la SL 280 d'une puissance de 231 ch. Quant au V12 de l'édition SL 65 AMG Black Series, il offre même 670 ch. En cas de besoin, un système de chauffage intégré dans les appuis-tête souffle un vent agréable sur la tête des passagers. On retrouve ici à nouveau la griffe de la SLK.

The SL 500 transforms itself in only 16 seconds from 2-seater sport coupé into a racy roadster, whose 306 bhp from 8 cylinders display refined power.

In nur 16 Sekunden verwandelt sich der SL 500 von einem zweisitzigem Sportcoupé in einen rassigen Roadster, dessen Achtzylinder mit 306 PS eine kultivierte Stärke entfaltet.

En seulement seize secondes, la SL 500 se métamorphose de coupé sport biplace en un roadster racé dont le huit-cylindres de 306 chevaux brille par sa culture et sa vigueur.

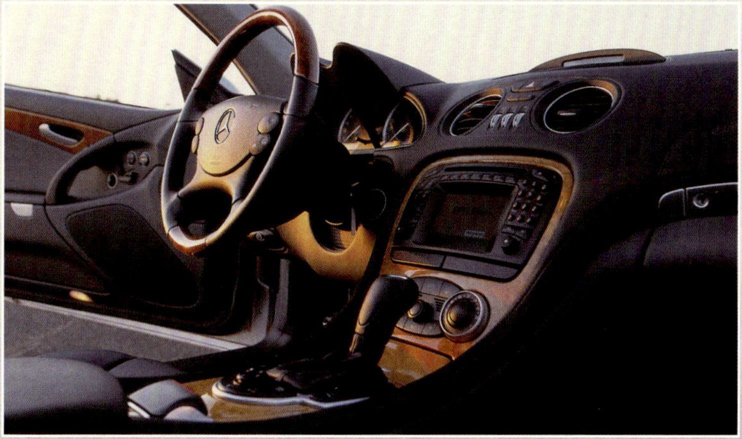

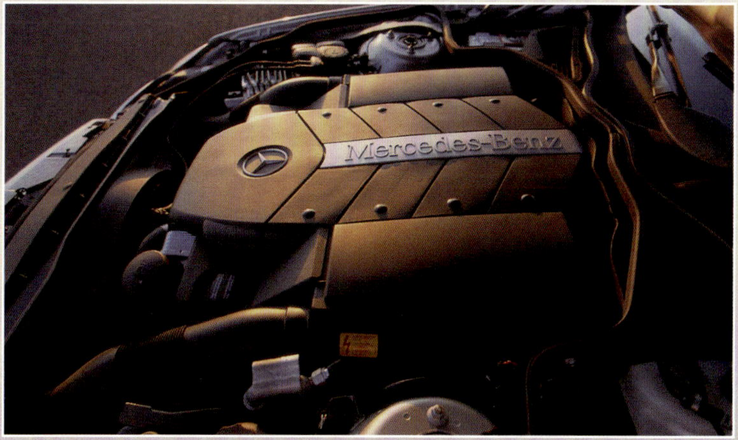
Mercedes-Benz

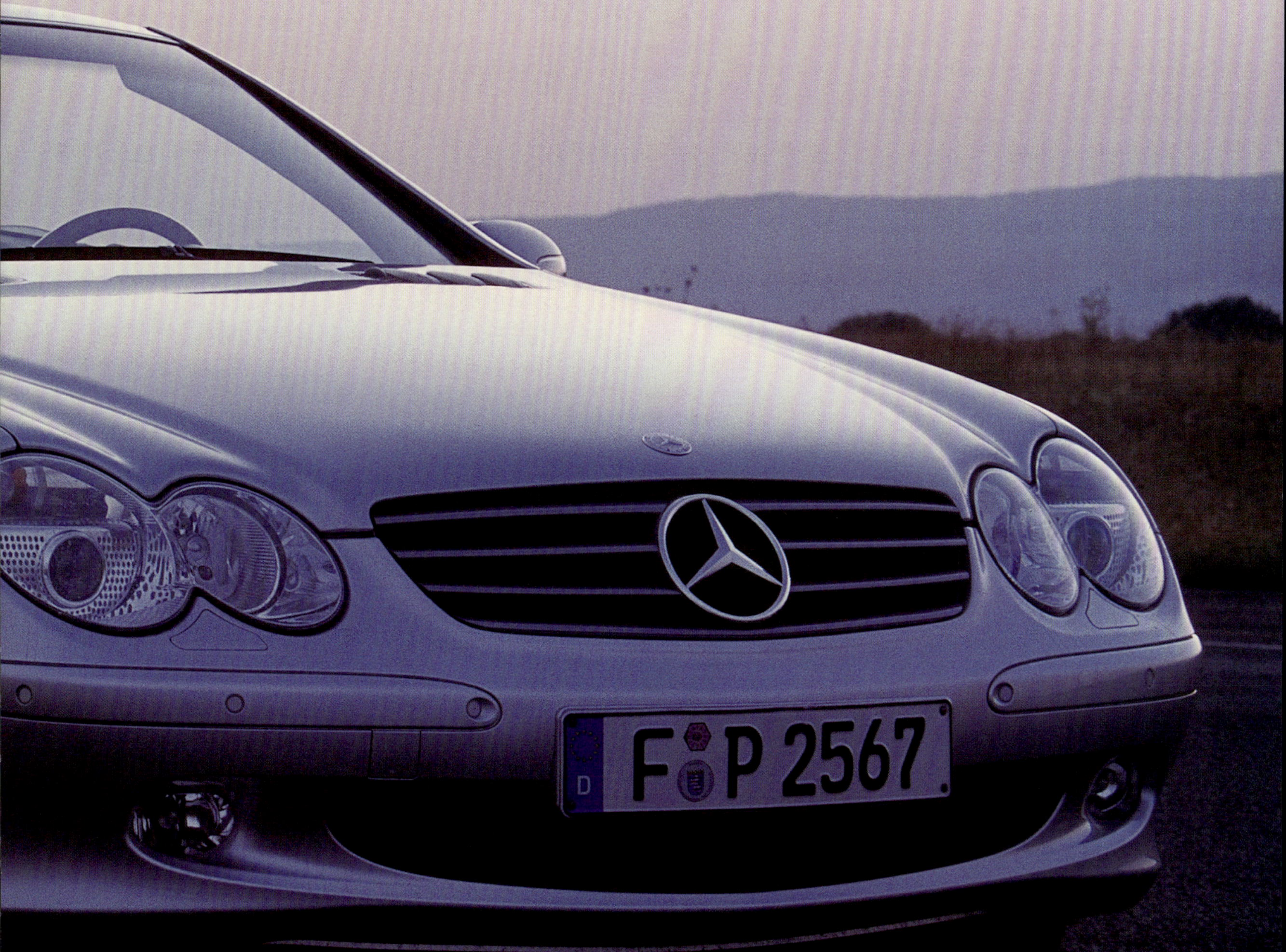
F P 2567

Mercedes-Benz SL   2001

The changes to the lights and the more spartan grille mean that the front of the 2008 SL is instantly recognizable, while remaining completely unchanged behind the A-pillar.

Am Bug ist der SL-Jahrgang 2008 wegen geänderter Lampen und schlichterem Grill sofort zu identifizieren, hinter der A-Säule hingegen ganz der alte.

Le millésime 2008 de la SL se reconnaît immédiatement à sa proue, en raison des nouveaux feux et de la grille plus simple. En revanche, au-delà du capot, il est similaire à l'ancien.

As the new E-Class was presented in the spring of 2004 after a four-year development phase and a total investment of more than two billion euros, Dr. Joachim Schmidt, Mercedes-Benz's marketing and sales boss took stock with satisfaction: "With about 1.4 million vehicles produced since 1995, the E-Class is the most successful Mercedes model. No other sedan in the top-of-the-range segment is as popular as the E-Class. That is proved by the high average worldwide market share of 24 percent". The "heart of the marque", as DaimlerChrysler executive and Mercedes leader Jürgen Hubbert calls this vehicle with its striking four-eyed visage, impresses with its dependability, esthetic, comfort, and high value stability. Apart from the most common model variation, the E 320, there are twelve further engines from which to choose, ranging from 123 to 477 bhp. In order to service the world market without exception, the E-Class is not only produced in Germany, but also in Egypt, India, Malaysia, Thailand, and the Philippines.

"To do the good even better", that was the task formulation for the bodywork development, according to the principle of "the right material in the right place". Therefore, principally steel and high-strength steel alloys are used, whereas the aluminum contribution is limited to the front wings, hood, trunk lid, as well as the front and rear modules. The side sections, welded together using laser-welding technology, offer even more impact safety than previously.

If the predecessor, the 210-model range from 1995 onward, was considered the most aerodynamic sedan series in the world, with its sensational aerodynamic drag coefficient of 0.27, this E-Class undercut its own record by a hundredth. Stylistically it embodies Mercedes design trend to a wedge-shaped, coupé-like side view with arched shoulder and waistline, rear with its subtle trailing edge, and more modern interpretation of the classical radiator grille.

The electro-hydraulic braking system developed by Mercedes-Benz, the Sensotronic Brake Control, a "thinking" brake, which belongs to the E-Class as a standard, displays a high technical standard. The new four-link front suspension and the principally aluminum multi-link independent rear suspension contribute to better road handling. The pneumatic suspension system of the E 500, which electronically steers both the suspension and shock absorbers at the same time, is a convenience available for all E-Class models on payment of a supplement.

Several airbags, the two-step seatbelt pressure inhibitor, in addition to an accident sensor system, ensure passenger safety. Teleaid can be installed, as an option, in connection with an integrated telephone system. An automatic emergency SOS signal is sent to the nearest emergency alarm center when the airbags are activated by a crash. There, an attempt is made to contact the unlucky driver by means of the intercom system. If unsuccessful, an ambulance is sent at speed. Of course, the automatic

Als nach vierjähriger Entwicklungszeit und einer Gesamtinvestition von mehr als zwei Milliarden Euro im Frühjahr 2002 die neue E-Klasse präsentiert wurde, zog Dr. Joachim Schmidt, Marketing- und Vertriebschef von Mercedes-Benz, zufrieden Bilanz: »Mit rund 1,4 Millionen Fahrzeugen, die wir seit 1995 produziert haben, ist die E-Klasse eines der erfolgreichsten Mercedes-Modelle. Keine andere Limousine im Segment der Oberklasse ist so beliebt wie die E-Klasse. Das beweist der hohe Marktanteil von weltweit durchschnittlich 24 Prozent,« Das »Herz der Marke«, wie DaimlerChrysler-Vorstand und Mercedes-Dirigent Jürgen Hubbert dieses Auto mit dem markanten Vier-Augen-Gesicht nennt, besticht durch Zuverlässigkeit, Ästhetik, Komfort und hohe Wertbeständigkeit. Neben dem E 320, der gängigsten Modell-Variante, stehen zwölf weitere Triebwerke – die Bandbreite reicht von 123 bis 477 PS – zur Auswahl. Um den Weltmarkt lückenlos bedienen zu können, wird die E-Klasse nicht nur in Deutschland, sondern auch in Ägypten, Indien, Malaysia, Thailand und auf den Philippinen produziert.

»Gutes noch besser machen«, so lautete die Aufgabenstellung an die Karosserie-Entwicklung, nach dem Prinzip »der richtige Werkstoff am richtigen Ort«. So werden vornehmlich Stahl und hochfeste Stahllegierungen verbaut, während sich der Aluminium-Anteil auf vordere Kotflügel, Motorhaube, Kofferraumdeckel sowie Front- und Heckmodule beschränkt. Mit Laser-Schweißtechnik zu einem Stück zusammengefügt, bieten die Seitenwände noch mehr Aufprall-Sicherheit als zuvor.

Galt der Vorgänger, Baureihe 210 ab 1995, damals als die strömungsgünstigste Serienlimousine der Welt, mit dem sensationellen Luftwiderstandsbeiwert von 0,27, so unterbietet diese E-Klasse den eigenen Rekord um ein Hundertstel. Stilistisch verkörpert sie den Design-Trend von Mercedes zu keilförmigen, Coupé-ähnlichen Seitenansichten mit bogenförmig gespannter Schulter- und Gürtellinie, Heck mit dezenter Abrisskante und modernerer Interpretation des klassischen Kühlergrills.

Höchstes technisches Niveau dokumentiert das von Mercedes-Benz entwickelte elektrohydraulische Bremssystem Sensotronic Brake Control, eine »mitdenkende« Bremse, die bei der E-Klasse zur Serienausstattung gehört. Zum besseren Handling tragen die neue Vierlenker-Vorderachse und die vornehmlich aus Aluminium gefertigte Raumlenker-Hinterachse bei. Das Luftfederungssystem des E 500, das gleichzeitig Federung und Dämpfer elektronisch steuert, ist gegen Aufpreis für alle E-Klassen-Vertreter wohlfeil.

Der Insassen-Sicherheit dienen mehrere Airbags, der zweistufige Gurtkraftbegrenzer sowie eine neue Unfall-Sensorik. Auf Wunsch – in Verbindung mit einer fest installierten Telefonanlage – kann Teleaid eingebaut werden. Mit der Aktivierung der Airbags bei einem Crash geht automatisch ein SOS-Signal an die nächste Notrufzentrale. Dort wird versucht, mit dem Unglücksraben über die Gegensprechanlage Kontakt aufzunehmen. Gelingt das

Quand, à l'issue de quatre ans de développement et au prix de plus de deux milliards d'euros d'investissements, la nouvelle Classe E est présentée, au printemps 2002, Joachim Schmidt, responsable du marketing et de la distribution chez Mercedes-Benz, dresse un bilan non sans satisfaction : « Avec environ 1,4 million de véhicules produits depuis 1995, la Classe E restera l'un des modèles de Mercedes qui aura connu le plus de succès. » Le « cœur de la marque » – comme le président du directoire de DaimlerChrysler et « grand timonier » de Mercedes, Jürgen Hubbert, qualifie cette voiture au visage à quatre yeux marquant – séduit par sa fiabilité, son esthétique, son confort et sa faible dépréciation. Outre la E 320, la variante de modèle la plus courante, douze autres moteurs sont proposés au choix – de 123 à 477 ch. Afin de desservir le marché mondial sans aucune lacune, la Classe E n'est pas seulement produite en Allemagne, mais aussi en Égypte, en Inde, en Malaisie, en Thaïlande et aux Philippines.

« Améliorer ce qui était déjà bon », telle est la consigne donnée aux ingénieurs chargés de concevoir la carrosserie selon le principe « le bon matériau au bon endroit ». Ainsi ont-ils utilisé essentiellement de l'acier et des alliages d'acier à haute résistance alors que l'aluminium est cantonné aux ailes avant, au capot moteur et au couvercle du coffre ainsi qu'aux modules de la proue et de la poupe. Assemblées en un seul bloc grâce à la technique de soudage au laser, les parois latérales offrent une protection contre les collisions latérales encore jamais vue à ce jour.

Tandis que sa devancière, la gamme 210 née en 1995, était réputée comme la berline de série la plus aérodynamique au monde avec un c_x exceptionnel de 0,27, cette Classe E bat son propre record d'un centième. Esthétiquement, elle incarne la tendance, actuellement en vogue pour le design chez Mercedes, du profil cunéiforme au style de coupé avec une ligne d'épaules et de ceinture tendue en arc de cercle, une poupe à l'arête de décrochement discrète et une interprétation moderne de la calandre classique.

Avec le système de freinage électrohydraulique Sensotronic Brake Control, un frein « intelligent » qui fait partie de l'équipement de série pour la Classe E, Mercedes-Benz offre une technicité inégalée à ce jour. Le nouveau train avant à quatre bras et l'essieu arrière multibras, essentiellement en aluminium, contribuent à l'amélioration du comportement. Le système de suspension pneumatique de la E 500, qui gère, simultanément, les ressorts et les amortisseurs à l'aide de l'électronique, est proposé pour toutes les versions de la Classe E contre un supplément de prix.

Plusieurs airbags, le limiteur à deux niveaux de la force de tension de la ceinture ainsi que tout un arsenal de nouveaux capteurs de détection d'un éventuel accident garantissent la sécurité des passagers. Sur demande – en combinaison avec un téléphone embarqué monté à demeure –, il est possible d'installer le dispositif Teleaid. Le déclenchement d'un ou de plusieurs airbags en cas de

Mercedes-Benz E-Klasse 2002

Mercedes-Benz E 320 CDI 2003

call for help is only of use when the crashed driver is to be found in a technologically highly developed region with the corresponding communication possibilities.

The fitting of a two-part panorama roof with its view from the front windscreen frame through to the rear roof section is a better prospect. At the press of a button, the front roof section slides slowly to the rear, while a transparent slat is raised at the front as a windbreak. Solar voltaic cells transform sunlight into energy for a cooling fan to prevent the vehicle from overheating unbearably when parked on a hot summer day. "Are you sitting comfortably?" This heretical question is answered by the multi-contoured seats with driving dynamics; the seat flanks pump themselves up—computer-controlled—in response to the driving situation of the E-Class vehicle, forming a stability pact with the seat occupant.

nicht, düst der Rettungswagen sofort los. Doch nützt der automatische Hilferuf natürlich nur, wenn man sich seinen Unfallpartner in einer technisch hoch entwickelten Zivilisation mit den dazugehörigen Kommunikations-Möglichkeiten sucht.

Bessere Aussichten verheißt die Bestückung mit einem zweiteiligen Panoramadach mit Durchblick vom Frontscheibenrahmen bis zum hinteren Teil des Daches. Auf Knopfdruck fährt das vordere Dachteil langsam nach hinten, während sich vorn eine durchsichtige Lamelle aufstellt, um als Windabweiser zu fungieren. Damit sich das Fahrzeug beim Parken an heißen Sommertagen nicht unerträglich aufwärmt, wandeln Solarzellen Sonnenlicht in Energie für ein Kühlluftgebläse um. »Sitzt du gut?« Diese ketzerische Frage beantwortet der fahrdynamische Multikontur-Sitz, denn je nach Fahrsituation des E-Klasse-Wagens pumpen sich computergesteuert die Sitzflanken auf und schließen mit dem Sitzbenutzer einen Stabilitätspakt.

collision a pour effet l'envoi automatique d'un sos à la centrale d'appel de détresse la plus proche. De là, les spécialistes s'efforcent de prendre contact par l'interphone avec le malheureux conducteur. En cas d'échec, une ambulance se rend immédiatement sur place.

Plus agréables sont les perspectives qu'offre le toit panoramique à deux panneaux, qui permet de scruter le ciel du haut du pare-brise jusqu'à la lunette arrière. Il suffit d'appuyer sur un bouton pour faire reculer lentement la partie antérieure du toit tandis qu'à l'avant, une lamelle transparente s'érige et sert de déflecteur. « Es-tu bien assis ? » Cette question insidieuse a sa réponse avec le siège multicontour dynamique, car, selon la situation de conduite de la Classe E, plusieurs coussins du siège – pilotés par ordinateur – se gonflent et se dégonflent à la demande et concluent un pacte de stabilité avec l'occupant du fauteuil.

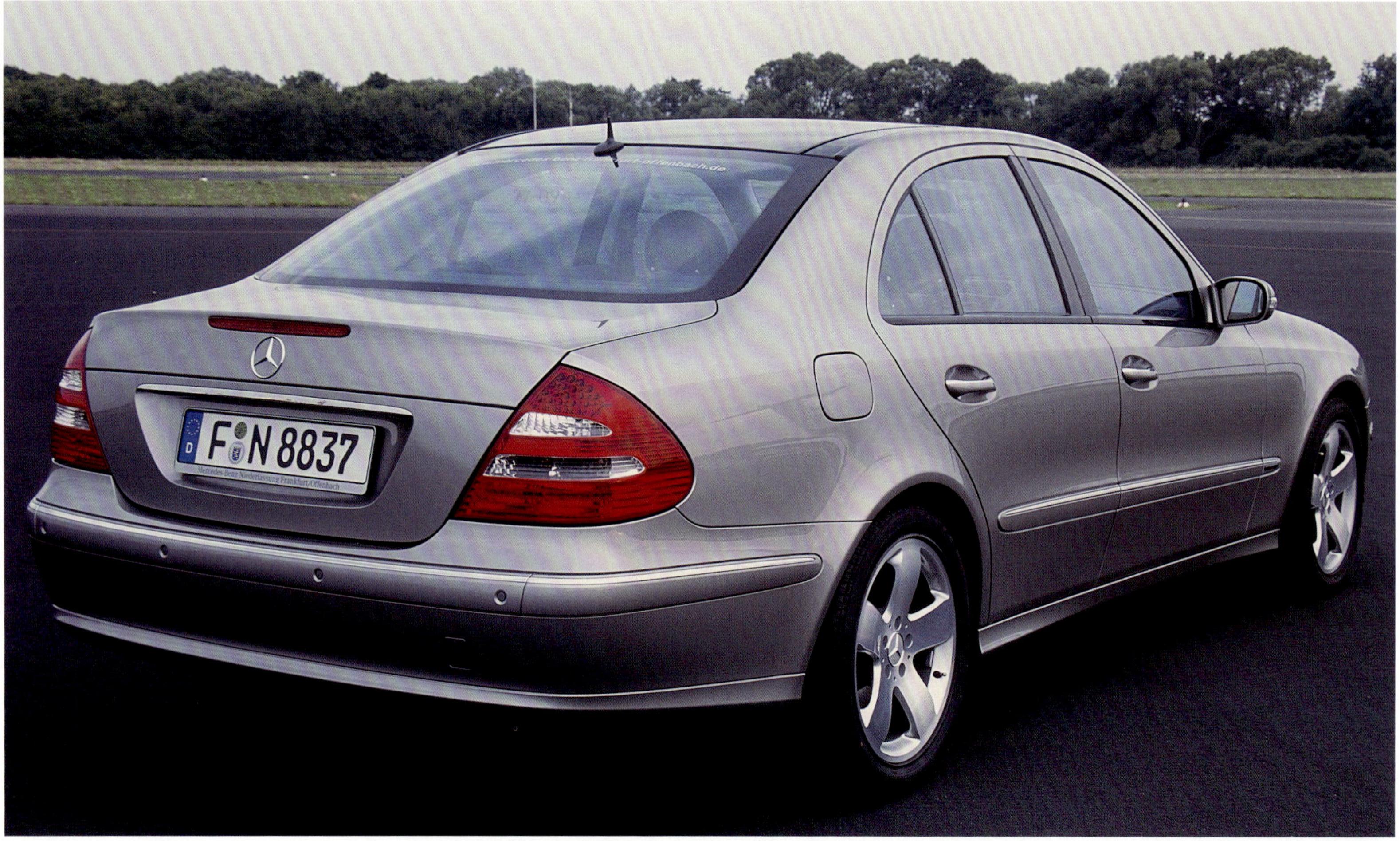
F N 8837

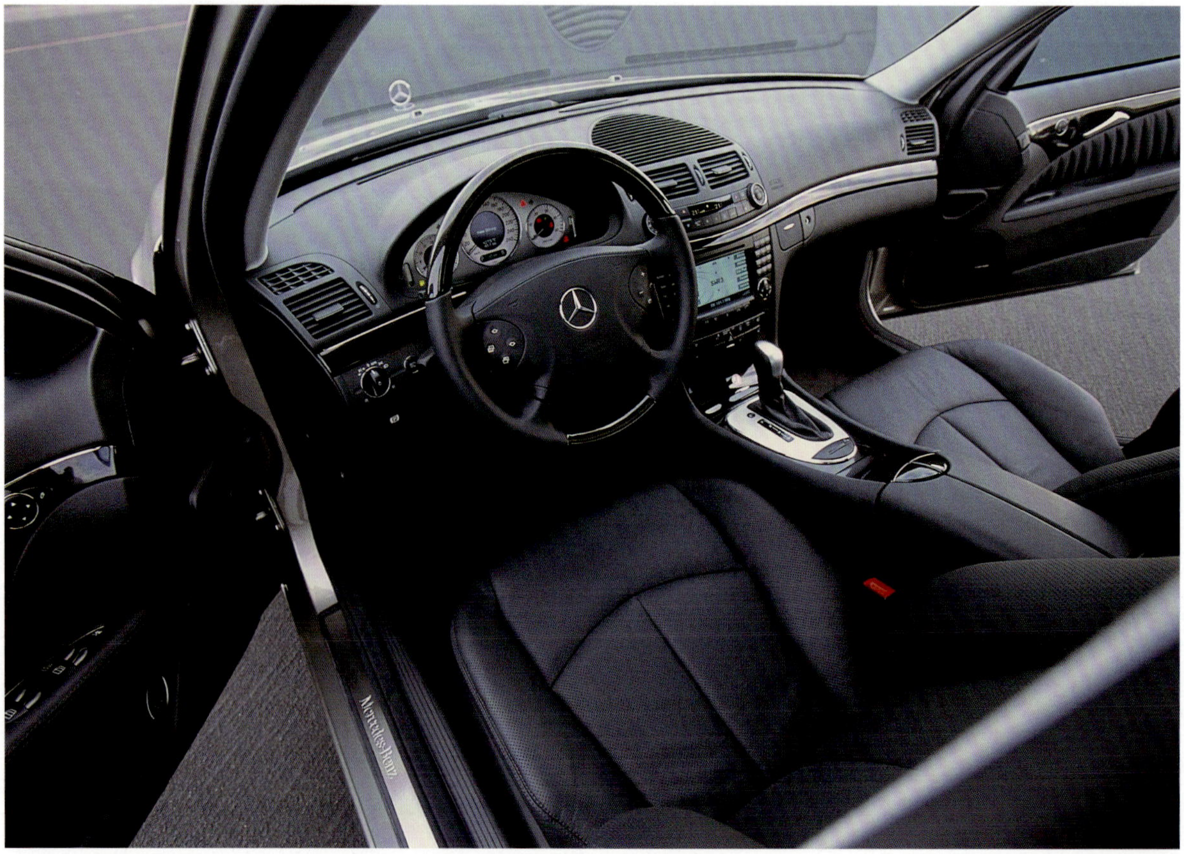
Mercedes-Benz

The buyer of an E-Class model has the choice of 48 color combinations for the exterior and diversity of interiors. Twelve further engine variations are available in addition to the V6 of the E 320 with its 224 bhp. *A la carte* power up to 500 bhp!

Beim Exterieur und der Vielfalt des Interieurs kann der Käufer eines E-Klasse-Modells zwischen 48 Farbkombinationen wählen. Zum V6 des E 320 mit 224 PS, ein Dreiventiler, gesellen sich noch zwölf weitere Triebwerks-Varianten. Kraft nach Wahl bis 500 PS!

Pour l'extérieur et la diversité de l'intérieur, l'acheteur d'un modèle de la Classe E a le choix entre 48 combinaisons de coloris. Au V6 de 224 ch de la E 320, un moteur à trois soupapes, s'ajoutent encore douze autres variantes de motorisation. Pour la puissance, on n'a que l'embarras du choix : jusqu'à 500 ch !

This elegant coupé, with its silhouette borrowed from the DTM racer, could not have been presented in a more spectacular manner: a joint presentation at the 2002 Geneva Salon of the CLK coupé with its motor sport derivate, the 470 bhp strong model for the German Touring Masters. In the same year, AMG came out with the steam hammer for the road: a CLK with a 5.5-liter engine and 367 bhp that enable an acceleration of 5.2 seconds. The sportiest manner to travel with a CLK captivates with its striking optic: an enormous air intake with spoiler lops in the fender, pronounced side rocker panels, lower back panel, wide-profile tires on alloy wheels all underline the claim to be leader of its class. The speedometer with its calibration up to 200 mph appears somewhat out of place considering that the concentrated power cannot be allowed free rein.

The engine palette for the CLK coupé is identical to that of the cabriolet except for a more economical common-rail diesel motor, which despite its 170 bhp reaches an average of 36 mpg. This CDI engine is not available for the open-air CLK. Instead, there is a choice of six aggregates: two four-cylinders and two six-cylinders, the CLK 500's 5-liter V8, and the previously mentioned fountain of power which the Mercedes daughter, AMG, lets gush in Affalterbach.

Design boss Peter Pfeiffer—formative of the latest Mercedes products—also drew a line along the waistband of the CLK, emphasized by the hollow beneath which runs out into the front wing. With the new CLS it is even more distinctive, while the new A-Class of 2004 displays it with a slight rear cut. The flowing lines are augmented by stylistic precision work such as the interlocking contours of the rocker panel series, the gentle hint of spoiler lips, as well as the analogue accentuation of the lower rear panel area. Well proportioned in this way, all CLKs were adorned with alloy wheels by the producer.

The external impression is strengthened by the ambience of the interior: noble and well thought-out into the smallest detail. The dashboard is dominated by the three round instruments. The central tachometer conceals a multifunctional display, whose eight menus can be activated by four buttons on the heated steering wheel. A "Comand APS" can be built into the center console on payment of a hefty supplement. This term covers a combination of navigation system, radio, CD player, and telephone with e-mail and messaging functions. The addition of a TV tuner is then a mere formality, as is the supplementation of the standard seven-speaker sound system with an "all-surround" sound for each of the four seats. A Linguatronic command is sufficient to mute the acoustic background when necessary. This optional extra, available on payment of a supplement, containing speech-control over radio, CD player, or navigation system, obviously requires a correspondingly modified and clear formulation. Dialects do not go down well at all.

Gemeinsame Präsentation des CLK-Coupés und seines Motorsport-Derivates, der 470 PS starken Ausführung für die Deutsche Tourenwagen Masters, auf dem Genfer Salon 2002: Spektakulärer konnte dieses elegante Coupé, von dem sich der DTM-Renner die Silhouette entliehen hat, nicht eingeführt werden. Noch im gleichen Jahr rückte AMG den Dampfhammer für die Straße heraus: einen CLK mit 5,5-Liter-Triebwerk und 367 PS, die eine Beschleunigung von 5,2 Sekunden ermöglichen. Die sportlichste Form, mit einem CLK unterwegs zu sein, besticht durch ihre auffällige Optik: Ein gewaltiger Lufteinlass im Stoßfänger mit Spoiler-Lippe, ausgeprägte seitliche Schweller, Heckschürze und Breitreifen auf den Leichtmetallrädern unterstreichen den Anspruch, Klassen-Primus zu sein. Da die geballte Kraft nicht ganz ausgetobt werden kann, wirkt der bis 320 Stundenkilometer reichende Tacho etwas deplatziert.

Die Motoren-Palette für CLK Coupé und Cabriolet ist bis auf einen sparsamen Common-Rail-Dieselmotor, der trotz seiner 170 PS lediglich 6,6 Liter im Schnitt schluckt, identisch. Dieses CDI-Triebwerk gibt es nicht für den Open-Air-CLK. Ansonsten stehen sechs Aggregate zur Auswahl: je zwei Vier- und Sechszylinder, der 5-Liter-V8 des CLK 500 und die bereits beschriebene Kraftquelle, die die Mercedes-Tochter AMG in Affalterbach sprudeln lässt.

Design-Chef Peter Pfeiffer spannt – prägnant für die jüngsten Mercedes-Jahrgänge – auch beim CLK einen Bogen über die Gürtellinie und betont diese durch eine darunter liegende Sicke, die im vorderen Kotflügel ausläuft. Beim neuen CLS ist sie sogar noch ausgeprägter, und auch die A-Klasse, Jahrgang 2004, trägt sie mit leichtem Hinterschnitt zur Schau. Stilistische Feinarbeit wie die ineinander greifenden Konturen der Serienschweller, die zarte Andeutung von Spoilerlippen sowie die analoge Betonung im unteren Heckschürzen-Bereich tragen zu der fließenden Form bei. Solchermaßen wohl proportioniert, dürfen sich alle CLK von Haus aus mit Leichtmetallrädern schmücken.

Das Ambiente des Interieurs bekräftigt den äußeren Eindruck: nobel und durchdacht bis ins kleinste Detail. Drei Rundinstrumente beherrschen das Armaturenbrett. Der zentrale Tacho beherbergt ein Multifunktionsdisplay, dessen acht Menüs durch vier Tasten am beheizbaren Lederlenkrad abgerufen werden können. Gegen saftigen Aufpreis kann in der Mittelkonsole »Comand APS« eingebaut werden. Hinter dieser Bezeichnung verbirgt sich eine Kombination aus Navigationssystem, Radio, CD-Player und Telefon mit E-Mail und SMS-Funktion. Die Addition eines TV-Tuners ist dann nur noch reine Formsache – wie die Ergänzung des serienmäßigen Sound-Systems mit sieben Lautsprechern durch einen Surround-Klang an jedem der vier Sitze. Selbst die Einfach-Ausführung, das Radio Audio 10, kommt nicht ohne 42-seitige Bedienungsanleitung – ohne Register, wohlgemerkt – aus. Um sich bei dieser akustischen Kulisse Gehör zu verschaffen, genügt ein Befehl in die Linguatronic, um sie zum Verstummen

Théâtre de présentation du coupé CLK et de sa version course, le modèle de 470 ch destiné au Deutsche Tourenwagen Masters (DTM) : le Salon de Genève 2002 – dévoiler de manière plus spectaculaire cet élégant coupé auquel le bolide du DTM a emprunté la silhouette aurait été difficile. La même année encore, AMG dévoile un « avion » pour la route : une CLK dotée d'un moteur de 5,5 litres développant 367 ch qui la catapulte en 5,2 secondes de 0 à 100 km/h. Le moyen le plus sportif – et le plus exclusif – de se déplacer en CLK séduit par son esthétique qui attire immédiatement le regard : une immense entrée d'air dans le pare-chocs avec lame d'aileron, de volumineux seuils de portière, un imposant tablier arrière et des pneus larges chaussant des jantes en alliage léger soulignent son ambition d'être la première de sa classe. Comme il n'est guère possible de laisser libre cours à un tempérament exubérant, le tachymètre indiquant jusqu'à 320 km/h semble quelque peu déplacé.

À l'exception d'un moteur diesel à rampe commune économique qui, malgré ses 170 ch, consomme seulement 6,6 litres aux 100 km en moyenne, la palette de moteurs pour les CLK Coupé et Cabriolet est identique. Ce moteur CDI n'est pas disponible pour la CLK open-air ; sinon, on a le choix entre six moteurs : respectivement deux quatre-cylindres et six-cylindres, le V8 de 5 litres de la CLK 500 et le groupe motopropulseur, source d'émerveillement que fait pétiller AMG, la filiale de Mercedes qui a son siège à Affalterbach.

Pour la CLK aussi, Peter Pfeiffer, responsable du design, étire un arc de cercle – caractéristique des tout derniers millésimes Mercedes – le long de la ligne de ceinture, que souligne un coup de gouge qui s'efface à l'extrémité de l'aile avant. Avec la nouvelle CLS, il est même encore plus creusé, et la Classe A du millésime 2004, elle aussi, arbore le même coup de griffe. Des détails esthétiques – qui témoignent d'une grande finesse – tels que les contours des bas de caisse s'emboîtant les uns dans les autres, la discrète ébauche de lame d'aileron ainsi que la légère accentuation du tablier arrière contribuent à la fluidité des formes.

L'ambiance qui règne dans l'habitacle confirme l'expression extérieure : noblesse de la finition et solutions pensées jusque dans les moindres détails sont au rendez-vous. Trois instruments circulaires monopolisent le tableau de bord. Le tachymètre central intègre un écran multifonction dont on peut appeler les huit menus grâce à quatre touches intégrées au volant chauffant gainé de cuir. Ceux qui peuvent se l'offrir trouveront dans la console médiane le système de navigation « Comand APS ». Derrière cette désignation se dissimule une combinaison de systèmes de navigation, d'autoradio, de lecteur de CD et de téléphone avec fonctions e-mail et SMS. Pour se faire entendre dans une telle débauche de raffinements acoustiques, il suffit de donner un ordre avec la commande vocale Linguatronic et le silence règne instantanément. Cette option, disponible contre paiement d'un

Mercedes-Benz CLK 2002

Mercedes-Benz CLK 320 2003

The CLK is not governed solely by high-tech and nobility, but also possesses highly practical lesser features. A wheel change after an irksome tire puncture can be avoided when the repair kit, which includes an electric air pump, is used. Both active and passive safety are written large with the CLK, as is the case with all Mercedes products. Window bags have been installed in addition to the two-part frontal airbags and side bags for driver and passenger. Self-tightening seat belts and seat belt force-limiters are standard. With the cabriolet, roll bars are extended in case of emergency. The chassis, with its front triple-link suspension and its multi-link independent rear suspension, is well balanced, and excuses little mistakes on the part of the driver thanks to ESP. Moreover, if it should come to a crash—for whatever reason—the strengthened side frame and rear-seating crossbeam do their job well.

zu bringen. Diese gegen Aufpreis erhältliche Sprachbedienung von Radio, CD-Player oder Navigationssystem setzt natürlich eine entsprechend angepasste und deutliche Formulierung voraus. Dialekte kommen ganz schlecht an. Im CLK regieren nicht nur Hightech und Nobilität, sondern er wartet auch mit kleinen, äußerst praktischen Dingen auf. So kann man sich bei einer lästigen Reifenpanne den Radwechsel ersparen, wenn man den Reparatur-Kit, zu dem auch eine elektrische Luftpumpe gehört, benutzt.

Wie bei allen Mercedes wird auch im CLK aktive und passive Sicherheit groß geschrieben. Neben den zweistufigen Frontairbags und Sidebags für Fahrer und Beifahrer sind auch Windowbags installiert. Gurtstraffer mit Gurtkraftbegrenzern für alle vier Sitze gehören zur Standardbestückung. Beim Cabrio fahren im Notfall Überrollbügel aus. Das Fahrwerk mit Dreilenkerachse vorn und Raumlenkerachse hinten ist ausgewogen und verzeiht dank ESP kleinere Fehler des CLK-Lenkers. Und wenn es wirklich – aus welchen Gründen auch immer – einmal krachen sollte, hält die in Seitenwand und Fondsitzquerträger verstärkte Karosserie, was sie verspricht.

supplément, comprenant la commande vocale de l'autoradio, du lecteur de CD ou du système de navigation, présuppose naturellement une élocution adaptée et, comme il se doit, bien audible.

Comme dans toutes les Mercedes, dans la CLK aussi la sécurité active et passive est écrite en lettres d'or. Outre les airbags avant à deux seuils de déclenchement et airbags latéraux pour le conducteur et le passager, elle offre aussi des airbags rideaux tête-thorax. Les tendeurs de ceintures avec limiteur de la force de tension à chacune des quatre places font partie de l'équipement de série. Sur le cabriolet, des arceaux de sécurité s'érigent instantanément en cas de danger. Les trains roulants avec essieu à trois bras à l'avant et essieu multibras à l'arrière sont équilibrés et, grâce à l'ESP, pardonnent les petites erreurs d'appréciation du conducteur de la CLK. Et si une collision devait malgré tout se produire, la carrosserie renforcée à hauteur des parois latérales et de la poutre transversale sous la banquette arrière tiendrait sans aucun doute ses promesses.

The CLK coupé, presented at the Geneva Motor Show of 2002, is an integral part of the long coupé tradition of Mercedes: fittings, technology, and road handling—hardly a wish is left unanswered. Distinctive: the arch that spans from the rear lights to the front headlights, and which underlines the flowing roof form without any disturbing B-pillar.

Coupés besitzen bei Mercedes eine lange Tradition, in die sich das CLK-Coupé, 2002 auf dem Genfer Salon vorgestellt, würdig einreiht: Ausstattung, Technik, Fahrverhalten – es bleiben wenig Wünsche übrig. Prägnant: der Bogen, den das Design von den Rückleuchten zu den Frontscheinwerfern spannt und den von keiner B-Säule gestörten Dachfluss unterstreicht.

Le coupé CLK, présenté au Salon de Genève en 2002, s'inscrit dignement dans la longue tradition du coupé de Mercedes : équipement, technique, comportement – difficile de formuler des critiques. Caractéristiques : le galbe tendu par les designers des optiques arrière aux phares et la ligne de toit qu'aucun pied central ne vient dégrader.

Mercedes-Benz CLK 2002

Motors were his life: along with Gottlieb Daimler, he was writing automotive history, and when Wilhelm Maybach (1846–1929) founded his own company in 1909, Count Zeppelin and the aviation industry had to queue up outside his factories. The real rivalry with Rolls-Royce began in 1921 when Karl Maybach Jr. (1879–1960), whose ingenuity wonderfully complemented that of Maybach Sr., successfully got a Spyker with a w2 Maybach engine to break the prestigious long-distance British record over 30,000 kilometers (18,640 miles). When, later that year, a complete luxury vehicle distinguished by its technical finesse was presented, the British were certainly not amused.

Ever since the Geneva Motor Show of 2002, the noble aura of the two-tone Maybach Zeppelin DS 8 with streamlined design in 1933 has been reflected by the Maybach of today, a vigorous Mercedes statement in the automotive upper class. Its luxurious quality goes without saying, and technical treats are presented on a silver platter. To achieve a maximum of stability with a minimum of material, the body is made of high-strength steel alloys. Fenders, hood, roof, and doors are made of aluminum, the boot lid of plastic. So in the Maybach 62—the type name reflects its length of 6.2 meters (20 ft 4 in)—just 22 percent of the total weight of 3.1 short tons falls into the outer envelope. The 3.5-short ton heavily armored Guard version (from September 2003), bullet- and shatter-proof to protect the occupants, can address any vulnerabilities with additional security components and tires with fail-safe running functions. Even the considerable extra weight of this design poses no problems for the chassis. The designers had fallen back on the technical benefits of the s-Class, such as air suspension and the adaptive damping system.

Like the 20-in shorter variant 57, the 62 lives up to its size in an individual and elegant manner. The low-noise twin-turbo v12 with 5513 cc and 550 bhp is conspicuous for its unfaltering smoothness and splendid torque of 664 lb-ft, even at 2300 rpm. If needed, the whole mass accelerates in 5.4 seconds to 62 mph, while the Guard manages this almost as nimbly in 5.7 seconds. The electronic management of the mega-Mercedes gives this car and its passengers no more than 155 mph, but a whole lot more could be achieved thanks to the advantageous drag coefficient of 0.30.

Anyone who wished to use this mansion on wheels as an office in the era of round-the-clock capitalism merely had to order the business package with a notebook, printer, and mobile Internet access. Electronic pastimes included an opulent radio, DVD player, and TV monitors in the backrests of the front seats, and could be enjoyed even more with a glass of champagne from the onboard bar. For a few dollars more, over a dream landscape of the finest leather and precious woods, curved a panoramic glass roof with a liquid crystal layer that became opaque at AC voltage, with incoming light diffused to a soft glow.

Maybach 2002

Maybach 62 2003

Progress did not come to a halt even in the face of this monument of automotive greatness, however. At the Frankfurt International Motor Show in September 2005, the 57 s was delivered: it had a six-liter V12 upgraded by AMG to 612 bhp and a modified suspension: "for the ambitious self-driver," as they said. However, the 62 s, first displayed to a forum of Chinese admirers 14 months later at the Auto China in Beijing, was declared to be "the world's most powerful chauffeur-driven saloon in series production." One year later, with a Landaulet study, the Daimler AG harked back to ancient tradition. Reception was favorable and so, in February 2008, at the factory in Sindelfingen, the handmade, swaggering Maybach was included in the program.

wölbt sich über einer Traumlandschaft aus feinstem Leder und edelsten Hölzern ein Panorama-Glasdach mit einer Flüssigkristallschicht, welche unter Wechselspannung undurchsichtig wird, während einfallendes Licht in diffusem Glanz erstrahlt.

Nicht einmal vor einem solchen Monument von Auto-Größe macht indessen der Fortschritt halt. Auf der Frankfurter IAA im September 2005 liefert man den 57 s nach mit einem von der Power-Dependance AMG auf 612 PS aufgerüsteten Sechsliter-V12 und modifiziertem Fahrwerk, »für den ambitionierten Selbstfahrer«, wie es heißt. Der 62 s hingegen, 14 Monate später bei der Auto China in Peking erstmalig einem Forum von staunenden Chinesen dargeboten, wird als »die leistungsstärkste in Serie gebaute Chauffeurlimousine der Welt« deklariert. Mit einer Landaulet-Studie entsinnt sich die Daimler AG nach einem weiteren Jahr einer uralten Tradition. Die Rezeption ist günstig, und so wird der in der Sindelfinger Manufaktur per Handarbeit gefertigte aufgeschnittene Maybach im Februar 2008 ins Programm aufgenommen.

s'étend un toit électrique panoramique doté d'une couche de cristaux liquides qui, sous courant alternatif, rend le vitrage opaque, laissant alors seulement pénétrer une lumière tamisée.

Le progrès n'arrête pas, même face à un tel monument automobile. Lors du salon de Francfort en septembre 2005, la 57 s fut présentée, équipée d'un six litres V12 AMG de 612 ch et d'une suspension modifiée «pour les ambitieux qui conduisent eux-mêmes», dit-on. La 62 s en revanche, présentée pour la première fois 14 mois plus tard lors du salon automobile de Pékin devant un parterre de Chinois ébahis, est considérée comme «la limousine avec chauffeur construite en série la plus performante au monde». Un an plus tard dans une étude de Landaulet, Daimler AG se rappela une autre tradition très ancienne. L'accueil fut favorable; par conséquent, la Maybach achevée à la main dans l'usine de Sindelfingen fut inscrite au programme en février 2008.

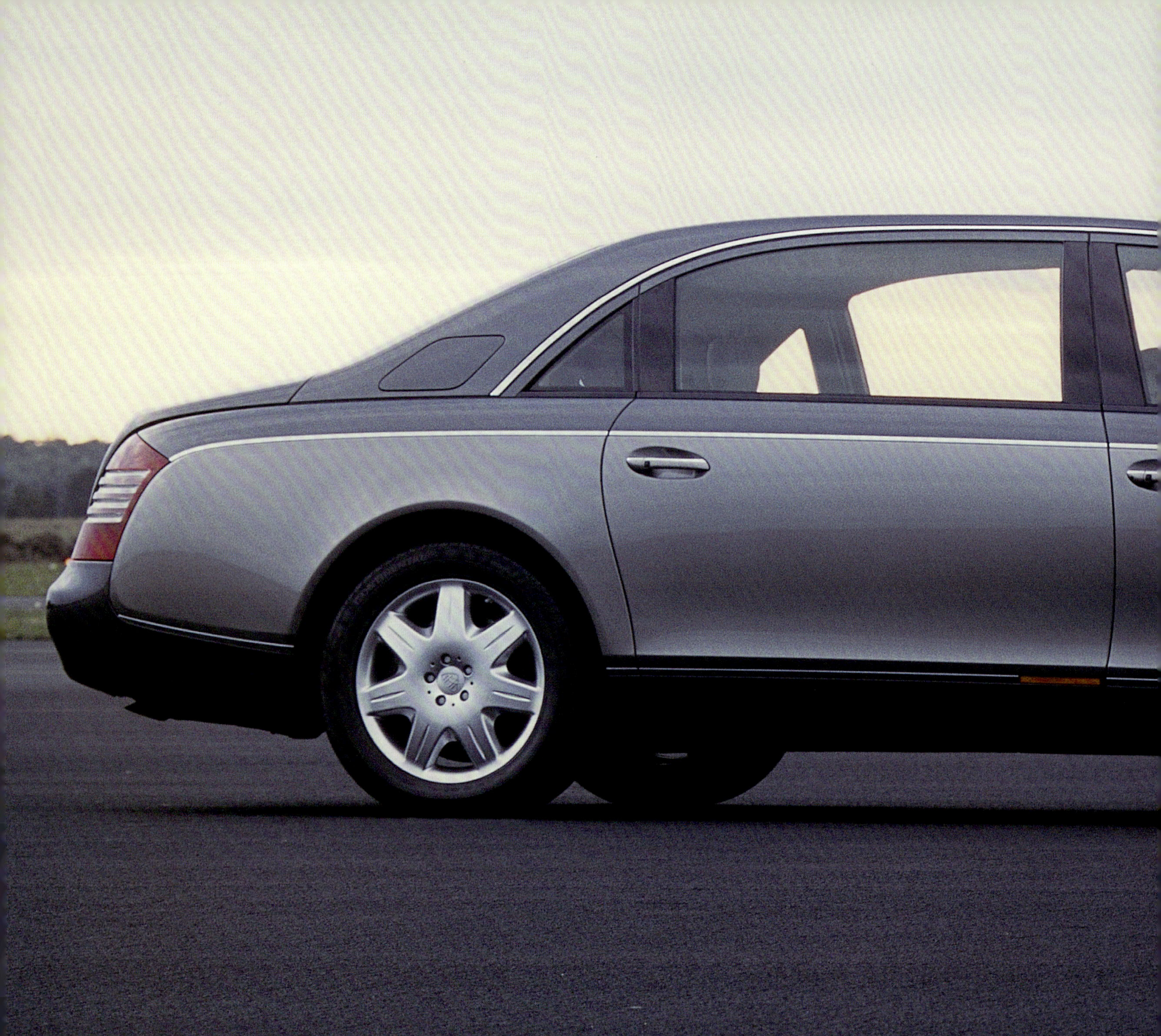

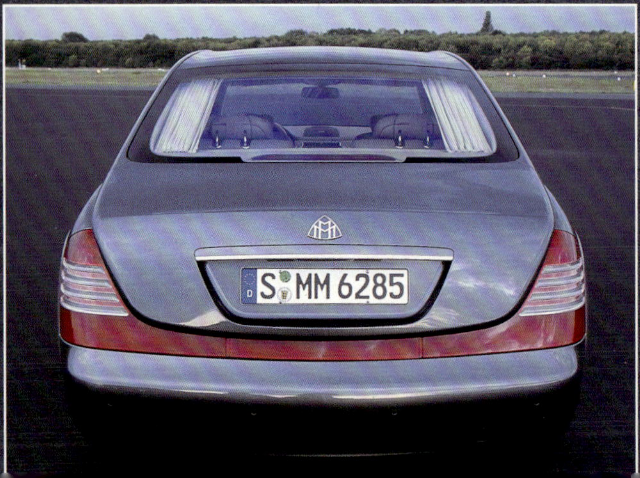
S MM 6285

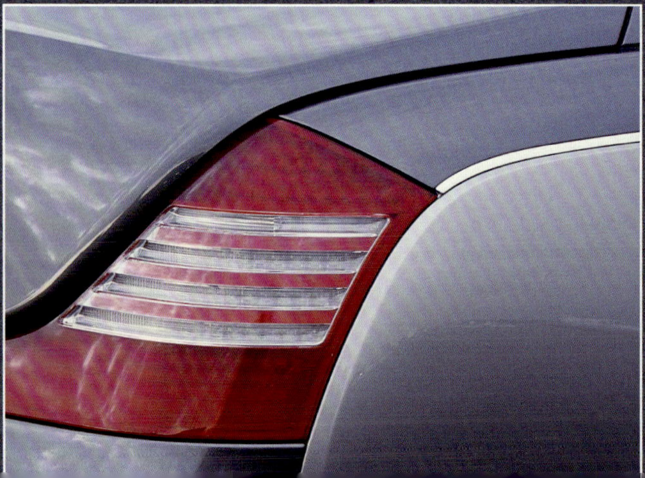

Nomen est omen: the Maybach 62's name is derived from its length of 6.2 meters (20 ft 4 in), while the smaller luxury limousine, the 57, correspondingly has a length of only 5.7 meters (18 ft 8 in). Good things take their time: in 2003, the annual production was only 702 vehicles.

Nomen est omen: Der Maybach 62 verdankt seine Typenbezeichnung seiner Länge von 6,2 Metern, während es die kleinere Luxus-Limousine, der 57, es analog »nur« auf 5,7 Meter bringt. Gut Ding will Weile haben: Die Jahresproduktion betrug 2003 lediglich 702 Exemplare.

Nomen est omen : la Maybach 62 doit sa désignation à sa longueur de 6,2 mètres à l'instar de la plus petite limousine de luxe, la 57, dont la longueur n'est «que» de 5,7 mètres. Toute bonne chose demande du temps : en 2003, la production annuelle a commencé avec seulement 702 exemplaires.

Over the finest leather armchairs, extendable as reclining seats with individually folding little tables in fine wood, flanked by the lush amenities of the rear section, curves an electromagnetic panoramic roof. Everything breathes distinction: from the threshold of stainless steel to the historic patina of the brand and status symbol on the cover of the V12 engine.

Über feinsten Leder-Fauteuils, auszufahren als Liegesitze mit individuell ausklappbaren Edelholztischlein, flankiert von den üppigen Annehmlichkeiten des Fonds, spannt sich ein elektromagnetisches Panoramadach. Überall Noblesse: von den Schwellen aus Edelstahl bis zur historischen Patina des Marken- und Status-Symbols auf dem Motordeckel des V12.

Au-dessus des fauteuils en cuir le plus fin, pouvant être transformés en sièges couchettes dotés d'une petite tablette individuelle et rabattable en bois précieux et entourés de toutes les commandes possibles à l'arrière, s'étend un toit panoramique électromagnétique. Partout des matériaux nobles : du seuil de portière en acier inoxydable à la patine historique du symbole de prestige de la marque sur le carénage du moteur V12.

Maybach 2002   323

Like its famous ancestors, the SSK of 1926 and 300 SL of 1954, the new mega-Mercedes with the unwieldy name was, from a commercial point of view, a piece of nonsense. But, like those, it gleamed like no other model of the brand name in the radiance of the Mercedes star. Besides, it was meant to seal the marriage of convenience between Mercedes-Benz and the British premium racing team and consolidate it through a common product, manufactured in the futuristic Paragon McLaren factory complex in Woking, England.

But this time something went wrong. The SLR study, introduced in January 1999 in Detroit, was still toasting its success from a few months earlier, when star pilot Mika Häkkinen had won his first world championship in a McLaren-Mercedes. By the time of its introduction as a marketable product—for the not inconsiderable price of 345,000 euros—at the Frankfurt International Motor Show 2003, however, a low-pressure area had long been hovering over the operations of joint ventures on the Grand Prix circuits. And the design of this Anglo-Teutonic supercar, in which current and historicizing quotations mingled with objective fact, did not necessarily encourage love at first sight.

There were good reasons for all of this. McLaren designer Gordon Murray had designed the SLR as a front mid-engine car, positioning the engine way down behind the front axle so as to balance weight distribution—hence the long stem. The high stump tail was involved in the generation of downforce, but also kept the very useful 9.6 cu.ft of trunk capacity available. Mounted flush above, a spoiler adapted variably to changing driving situations and rose with sharp braking to an angle of 65 degrees, while an aerodynamic counterpart underneath acted as a six-channel diffuser. To smooth the front undercarriage, emissions from the machine were expelled sideways. Through the angrily bared openings in the sides (a visual reminiscence of the SLR of 1955), two large exhausts discharged their heat.

The super sports car was clad in carbon fiber, five times stiffer than steel and much lighter. Weighing 3845 lbs when empty thanks to typical Mercedes luxury (including five-step automatic transmission, electric steering wheel adjustment, sophisticated airbag system, and left- and right-adjustable air conditioning), it was not exactly a featherweight.

Nobody was quick, however, to dispute the SLR driver's spot among the fastest in the country. This was ensured by its racing suspension with classic double wishbones and struts, brakes with massive ceramic disks, and, above all, the 626 bhp of its V8 with 5.4 liters of displacement, lovingly prepared by the company's subsidiary AMG. The similarity with the engine of the SL 55 AMG was reduced to appearances, the oil circuit converted to a dry sump and the IHI screw superchargers enlarged—11.3 seconds to 125 mph and 200 mph tops were not exactly to be sniffed at.

Wie seine berühmten Vorfahren SSK von 1926 und 300 SL von 1954 ist der aktuelle Mega-Mercedes mit dem sperrigen Namen aus kaufmännischer Sicht ein Unding. Aber gleich jenen poliert er wie kein anderes Modell der Marke an der Strahlkraft des Stuttgarter Sterns. Und überdies soll er die Vernunftehe zwischen Mercedes-Benz und dem englischen Premium-Rennstall besiegeln und festigen durch ein gemeinsames Produkt, gefertigt in dem futuristisch anmutenden McLaren-Werkskomplex Paragon in Woking (England).

Aber diesmal läuft einiges schief. Die Studie SLR, im Januar 1999 in Detroit vorgestellt, schöpft gleichsam noch aus dem Vollen, denn ein paar Monate zuvor hat Star-Pilot Mika Häkkinen auf McLaren-Mercedes seine erste Weltmeisterschaft gewonnen. Bei der Einführung als käufliches Produkt zum saftigen Preis von 345 000 Euro anlässlich der Frankfurter IAA 2003 lagert indessen längst ein Tiefdruckgebiet über den Einsätzen des Joint Ventures auf den Grand-Prix-Strecken. Und: Das Design des anglo-teutonischen Supercars, in dem sich aktuelle und historisierende Zitate mit Sachlichem mischen, lädt nicht unbedingt ein zu Liebe auf den ersten Blick.

Dabei hat das alles seine guten Gründe. McLaren-Konstrukteur Gordon Murray hat den SLR als Frontmittelmotorwagen ausgelegt, das Triebwerk zwecks ausgewogener Gewichtsverteilung tief hinter der Vorderachse eingelassen – daher der lange Vordersteven. Das hohe Stummelheck ist eingebunden in die Erzeugung von Abtrieb, hält indessen auch den durchaus nützlichen Kofferraum von 272 Litern Volumen bereit. Oben bündig eingelassen passt sich ein Spoiler variabel an die jeweilige Fahrsituation an und reckt sich etwa bei scharfem Bremsen im Winkel von 65 Grad empor, aerodynamisches Gegenstück unten: ein Sechskanal-Diffusor. Um den Unterboden davor gebührend zu glätten, werden die Emissionen der Maschine seitlich abgeführt. Durch die wütend gebleckten Öffnungen in den Flanken, visuelle Reminiszenzen an den SLR von 1955, entlassen die beiden großen Schalldämpfer ihre Hitze ins Freie.

Gewandet ist der Supersportler in CFK, fünfmal steifer als Stahl und viel leichter. Mit 1747 Kilo Leergewicht, bedingt durch Mercedes-typischen Luxus wie Fünfstufenautomat, elektrische Lenkradverstellung, ein ausgeklügeltes Airbag-System sowie eine links und rechts regelbare Klimaautomatik, ist er nicht eben ein Bruder Leichtfuß.

Den Spitzenplatz unter den Schnellsten im Lande wird dem SLR-Lenker dennoch niemand so rasch streitig machen. Dafür sorgen nachhaltig sein Rennfahrwerk mit klassischen Doppelquerlenkern und Federbeinen, Bremsen mit massiven Keramikscheiben, vor allem aber die 626 satt im Futter stehenden Pferdestärken seines Kompressor-V8 mit 5,4 Litern Hubraum, liebevoll aufbereitet von der Firmentochter AMG. Die Ähnlichkeit zum Triebwerk des SL 55 AMG ist auf Äußerlichkeiten reduziert, der Ölhaushalt auf Trockensumpfschmierung umgerüstet,

Comme ses célèbres ancêtres, la SSK de 1926 et la 300 SL de 1954, l'actuelle méga Mercedes au nom encombrant est une aberration commerciale. Mais tout comme ses aïeux, elle fait briller le charisme de l'étoile de Stuttgart comme aucun autre modèle de la marque. En outre, elle scelle et renforce le mariage de raison entre Mercedes-Benz et l'écurie anglaise de Formule 1 par un produit commun conçu dans le complexe McLaren aux allures futuristes à Woking en Angleterre.

Mais cette fois certaines choses sont allées de travers. L'étude SLR, présentée en janvier 1999 à Détroit, put en quelque sorte puiser dans la renommée car quelques mois auparavant, le pilote Mika Häkkinen avait remporté son premier championnat du monde sur McLaren-Mercedes. Lors de sa présentation comme produit commercial au prix exorbitant de 345 000 euros lors du Salon de l'automobile de Francfort en 2003, une dépression s'était installée depuis longtemps sur l'engagement de la coentreprise dans les courses de Grand Prix. De plus, le design du *supercar* anglo-germanique où des références actuelles et historiques sont mélangées à des objectifs concrets, n'invite pas au coup de foudre.

Tout cela a pourtant une bonne raison d'être. Le constructeur de McLaren Gordon Murray a conçu la SLR comme une voiture au moteur central et a installé la motorisation juste derrière le train avant afin de répartir le poids de façon équilibrée, d'où le capot allongé. La conception bicorps haute est associée à la génération de l'effet de dérive, celle-ci permettant cependant de disposer également d'un coffre au très utile volume de 272 litres. Un spoiler adaptable aux différentes situations de conduite est installé dessus et, en cas de freinage brutal, un diffuseur à six canaux situé près du sol se met à un angle de 65 degrés afin d'augmenter la résistance aérodynamique. Afin de caréner parfaitement le châssis à l'avant, le système d'échappement du véhicule a été logé sur le côté. Les deux gros pots d'échappement libèrent leur chaleur grâce aux ostentatoires ouvertures dans les flancs, réminiscences visuelles de la SLR de 1955.

Ce super-sportif est équipé de PRFC, cinq fois plus rigide que l'acier et beaucoup moins lourd. Avec 1747 kilos à vide, dus au luxe caractéristique de Mercedes comme sa boîte de vitesse cinq rapports, le réglage électrique de la colonne de direction, un système d'airbag alambiqué ainsi qu'une climatisation automatique réglable à droite et à gauche, elle est tout sauf nonchalante.

Parmi les plus rapides sur terre, personne ne lui disputera la pole position avant longtemps. Sa suspension de course avec ses doubles amortisseurs transversaux classiques et ses jambes élastiques, ses freins à disque en céramique, mais surtout les 626 chevaux bien alimentés par son moteur V8 de 5,4 litres à compresseur préparé avec amour par la filiale AMG y veillent. La similitude du groupe propulseur de la SL 55 AMG se réduit à des détails, la conversion du circuit d'huile en lubrification à carter sec et un plus grand dimensionnement du compresseur à

Mercedes-Benz SLR McLaren   2003

Mercedes-Benz SLR McLaren 2004

On 11 July 2006 DaimlerChrysler released the 722 Edition, a 650-bhp special version in a limited run of 150 units. A roadster was exhibited at the Frankfurt Show in September 2007. Later that year, 21 units of the sports version 722 GT (680 bhp) were made available, while finally, at the end of 2008 and in a limited run of 75, came the extreme SLR 722 Stirling Moss without roof or windshield, in a double tribute to the old Mille Miglia winner of 1955.

der IHI-Schraubenverdichter vergrößert. 11,3 Sekunden auf 200 km/h und 324 km/h Spitze sind schließlich kein Pappenstiel.

Am 11. Juli 2006 gibt DaimlerChrysler die Variante 722 Edition frei, ein 650 PS starkes Sonderangebot limitiert auf 150 Stück. Ein Roadster wird auf der Frankfurter IAA im September 2007 zur Schau gestellt. Kurz darauf offeriert man in 21 Exemplaren die Sportversion 722 GT (680 PS), Ende 2008 schließlich in einer Auflage von 75 den Extrem-SLR 722 Stirling Moss ohne Dach und Windschutzscheibe zur Doppel-Ehre des greisen Mille-Miglia-Siegers von 1955.

vis IHI. 11,3 secondes à 200 km/h et 324 km/h en vitesse de pointe, ce n'est pas une bagatelle.

Le 11 juillet 2006, DaimlerChrysler mit en service la variante Edition 722, un modèle de 650 chevaux limité à 150 exemplaires. Un roadster fut exposé lors du salon de Francfort de 2007. Peu après on a offert 21 exemplaires de la version sport 722 GT (680 ch), et finalement fin 2008 fut proposée dans une édition de 75 exemplaires, l'extrême SLR 722 Stirling Moss sans toit ni pare-brise, un double hommage au très âgé vainqueur du Mille Miglia de 1955.

Aimed at balanced weight distribution the engine in the SLR McLaren has been positioned way back from the front axle. This gives it its proportions, a thorn in the side of some esthetes: extremely long hood, tiny cabin for two, stubby rear.

Zwecks einer ausgewogenen Gewichtsverteilung ist das Triebwerk des SLR McLaren weit hinter der Vorderachse eingelassen. Daraus leiten sich seine Proportionen ab, so manchem Ästheten ein Dorn im Auge: ewig lange Fronthaube, winziges Kämmerchen für zwei, Stummelheck.

Pour une répartition équilibrée du poids, le moteur de la SLR McLaren est installé loin derrière l'essieu avant. Cela entraîne une dérive de ses proportions, insupportables pour certains esthètes : capot d'une longueur interminable, minuscule habitacle pour deux et partie arrière raccourcie.

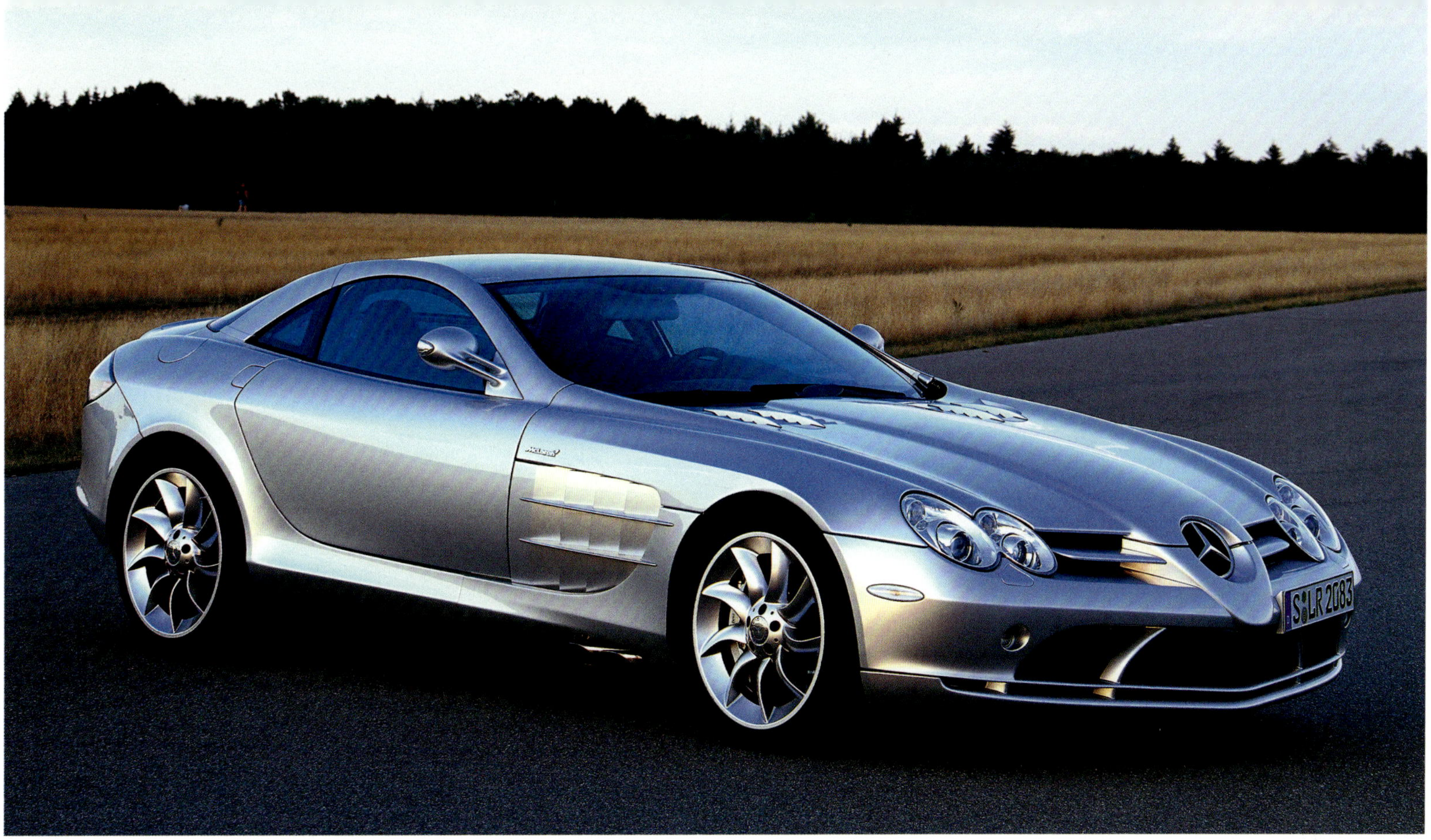
S LR 2083

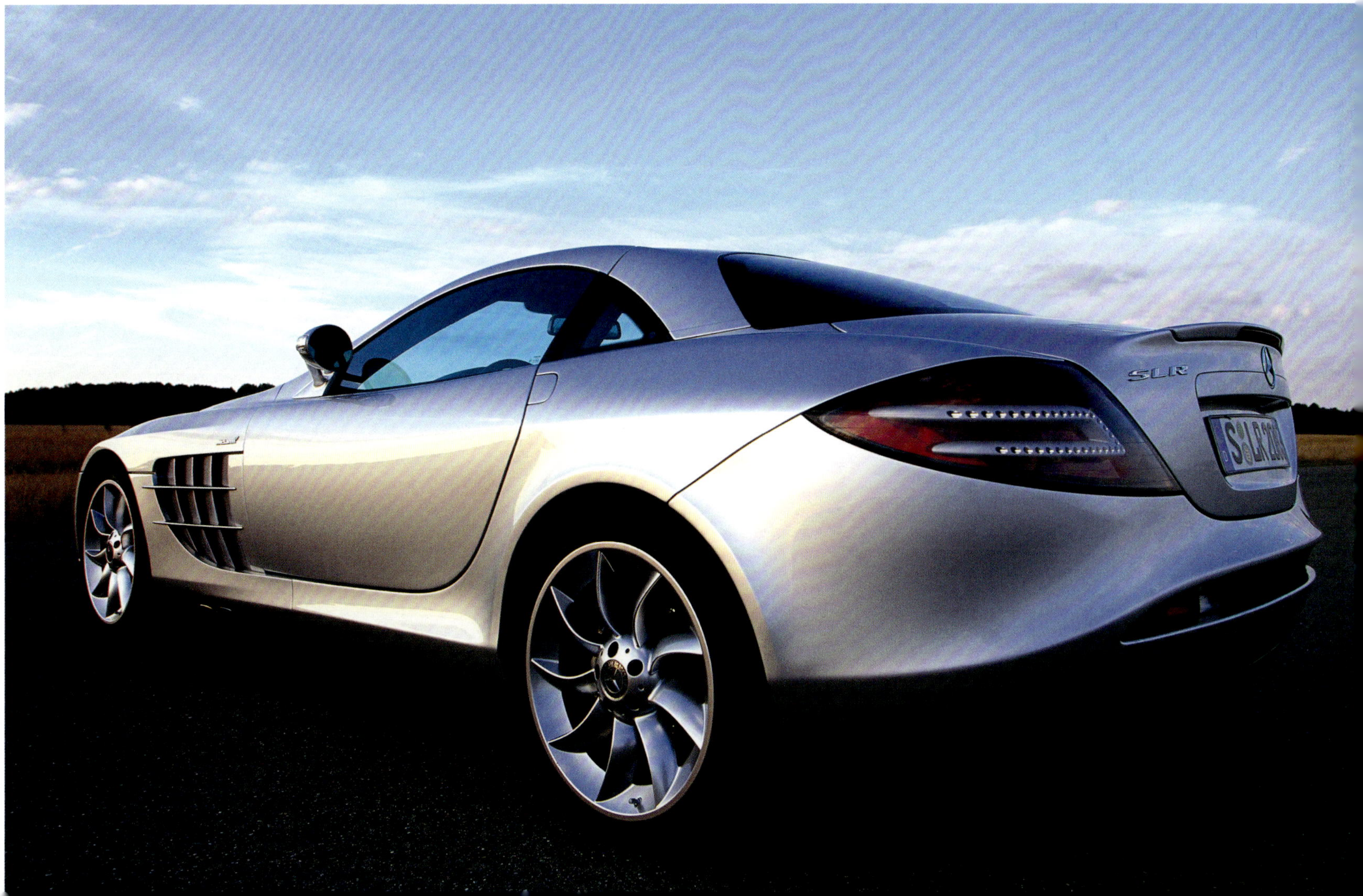

Mercedes-Benz SLR McLaren 2003

Its structural framework is so rigid that the SLR McLaren needs
only to have the top cut off to convert it into a roadster.

Um den SLR McLaren zum Roadster umzuwidmen, brauchte man ihn
eigentlich nur zu köpfen – so rigide ist die tragende Struktur.

Afin de transformer la SLR McLaren en roadster, il a suffi
de l'étêter, tant la structure porteuse est rigide.

"The most beautiful curves can be enjoyed even when standing still," enthuses a promotional brochure. And, indeed, the second-generation SLK, which was introduced in January 2004 and went on sale from May that year, wins everyone over straightaway—it is youthful, alluring, and pretty. Everything hits the spot: the overall proportions, the gentle slope of the high belt line curving up again behind the A-pillars, and the chunky rear end. Suddenly, even the sharp, jagged nose makes esthetic sense, reminiscent of the Formula 1 racers of the McLaren-Mercedes joint venture and its controversial big brother, the SLR. Even its much loved and highly praised predecessor fades in comparison.

Care was taken to improve the Vario roof, which now allows a gratifying view of the heavens in 22 seconds—three seconds faster than previously. The seemingly chaotic spectacle that precedes opening (or closing) the roof remains. By simply pressing a button on the right, in front of the hand brake, the system opens the trunk, pushing the C-pillar and roof segment over the roll bar, thus making the rear window describe a circle and locking the mechanism a little later, almost inaudibly. Of course, this transformation into a coupé is extremely welcome on long trips, when the weather is terrible, and especially in the winter. For anyone who cannot do without the joys of fresh air even then, however, the new model SLK can if requested—for an additional charge and only available in combination with heated leather seats—include the Mercedes specialty Airscarf. If necessary, and varying with the speed, a three-level neck-dryer blows hot air against the heads of the occupants through slats, a comfort that soon becomes indispensable. In its spacious cockpit for two (the wheelbase has increased by 1 3/16 in to 8 ft), even taller people can settle down comfortably in anatomically contoured sports seats, surrounded by beautifully embellished fittings such as the finely pitted matte black molding that contrasts attractively with the silver buttons and instrument trims.

With double wishbone and MacPherson strut suspension in front, multi-link suspension behind—a tried-and-tested Mercedes requisite since the 190 E—and brakes that always grip relentlessly, the SLK is itself brilliantly equipped for excursions into the further ranges of driving.

This was, indeed, something of an urgent necessity, the manufacturer having also splashed out on the engine. Even the entry-level model SLK 200 Kompressor happily manages 163 bhp, provided by a 1796 cc four-cylinder engine with double overhead camshafts, an Eaton supercharger, and an intercooler. Two balancer shafts keep it purring along smoothly. All the same, at high speeds the junior SLK allows itself a hoarse roar, carefully composed by specially commissioned Mercedes sound engineers. At around the same price, the SLK 350 is clearly superior to the BMW Z4 3.0 (originally 231 bhp), with its 272 bhp produced by a 3498 cc V6. Indeed, drivers of the SLK 55 AMG have over

Mercedes-Benz SLK 2004

Mercedes-Benz SLK 350 2008

360 bhp at their command, as under its hood sits a majestic 5439 cc v8—powerful, yet pleasantly restrained. In any case, the SLK 350 and SLK 55 AMG, as well as the SLK 280 (2996 cc, 231 bhp) that came on stream a little later, in the middle of 2005, and the SLK 55 AMG Black Series (400 bhp) from 2006, are kept in check at a speed of 155 mph through rev limiters, while the SLK 200, after all, can reach 143 mph. The five beauties accelerate to 62 mph in 8.3, 6.2, 5.5, 4.9, and 4.5 seconds, respectively.

At the North American International Auto Show in Detroit, the SLK made its debut in January 2008 in an updated form, with a new and more dynamic-looking front apron, thicker, trapezoidal exhaust tips and darker rear lights, a modified interior, and strengthened engines in the SLK 200 Kompressor (184 bhp) and SLK 350 (305 bhp).

der SLK 350 deutlich überlegen mit den 272 PS, welche ein v6 mit 3498 cm³ hervorbringt. Über 360 PS gebietet gar der Lenker des SLK 55 AMG, unter dessen Fronthaube ein v8 von 5439 cm³ mächtig und dennoch angenehm gezügelt waltet. Ohnehin werden SLK 350 und SLK 55 AMG ebenso wie der Mitte 2005 nachgelieferte SLK 280 (2996 cm³, 231 PS) und der SLK 55 AMG Black Series (400 PS) von 2006 bei Tempo 250 durch Drehzahlbegrenzer zur Raison gebracht, während es der SLK 200 auf immerhin 230 km/h bringt. Bei 100 sind die schönen Fünf in 8,3, 6,2, 5,5, 4,9 und 4,5 Sekunden angelangt.

Auf der North American International Auto Show in Detroit gibt der SLK im Januar 2008 in aktualisierter Form seinen Einstand, mit einer dynamischer anmutenden neuen Frontschürze, dickeren, trapezförmigen Endrohren und dunkleren Leuchten am Heck, modifiziertem Inneren und erstarkten Triebwerken im SLK 200 Kompressor (184 PS) und SLK 350 (305 PS).

aussi coûteuse, est déjà nettement dépassée par la SLK 350 de 272 ch développés par un v6 de 3498 cm³. Le moteur de la SLK 55 AMG offre même plus de 360 ch, son capot contenant un puissant mais néanmoins agréable v8 de 5439 cm³. De toute façon la SLK 350 et la SLK 55 AMG tout comme la SLK 280 (2996 cm³, 231 ch) livrée en 2005 et la SLK 55 AMG Black Series (400 ch) de 2006 sont ramenées à la raison par le bridage du moteur à 250 km/h alors que la SLK 200 arrive aux 230 km/h. Ce beau quinquet atteint les 100 km/h en respectivement 8,3, 6,2, 5,5, 4,9 et 4,5 secondes.

Lors du North American International Auto Show de Détroit en janvier 2008, la SLK a fait son entrée sous sa forme modernisée avec un nouveau tablier avant, des embouts d'échappement trapézoïdaux plus gros et des feux arrière plus foncés, un habitacle modifié et une motorisation plus puissante pour la SLK 200 Kompressor (184 ch) et la SLK 350 (305 ch).

The SLK presents itself as an appealing and comfortable vehicle irrespective of whether open or closed, for its electrically lowered roof leaves enough space in the luggage compartment for a trip with baggage.

Offen wie geschlossen präsentiert sich der SLK ansprechend und komfortabel, denn sein elektrisch versenkbares Dach lässt noch genügend Kofferraum für die Reise mit Gepäck übrig.

Ouverte ou fermée, la SLK est tout aussi séduisante et confortable, car son toit à commande électrique laisse suffisamment d'espace pour transporter les bagages nécessaires pour de longs voyages.

Mercedes-Benz SLK   2004   333

Provisionally hailed as Vision CLS, Mercedes exhibited an alluring synthesis of luxury sedan and sleek coupé at the Frankfurt International Car Show in 2003. Although they were still officially playing it down, insiders had long known that the CLS was a done deal. In fact, the voluminous hybrid celebrated its premiere six months later in Geneva, just ⅛ inch longer and a little deeper.

The many drawings from initial concept to finished product showed how creativity and imagination had dovetailed in a common design. The shoulder line of the spruce four-door sedan extends from the front wheel arch, with its dynamic appearance, along the entire flank, with a pleat running under it, ending in the rear lighting clusters. These assume the casual flow of the design, allowing it to meld gently into the bumper. Even more striking is the contour of the roof, which merges seamlessly into the sloping rear end. The small spoiler lip on the lid of the trunk is delicately emphasized and yet aerodynamically efficient. To underscore the momentum of the low side windows, these are bordered by a chrome strip, while the wide B-pillar (not found in a classic coupé) has been visually relegated to the background. The leather interior door linings and broad instrument panel with burl walnut trim carry the stylistic character of the exterior inside.

More new perspectives were opened up in the CLS 350 by the continuously variable stepless camshaft adjustment of the new lightweight V6 engine (3498 cc, 272 bhp). It regulates the 24 valves in the cylinder heads of aluminum in such a way that energy losses are reduced to a minimum. A special module alters the length of the intake manifold, depending on speed, and regulates air flow. Thus, the engine is already, at just 1500 rpm, enjoying 87 percent of the speed limit of 220 lb-ft. The CLS 500 is mobilized by the familiar five-liter V8 with 4966 cc and 272 bhp. Both engines, as standard, are combined with the new seven-speed 7G-Tronic automatic transmission with converter lockup clutch. This adjusts itself optimally to the speed, saves fuel, and operates very quietly. The CLS 500 offers S-culture in the form of the four-zone climate control Thermotronic and Airmatic DC air suspension—the abbreviation standing for Dual Control: it controls electrical springs and dampers, while rubber bellows on the struts, filled with compressed air, take over the work on site. With a level switch on the center console, the driver can determine the chassis setting. At higher speeds, however, the system automatically lowers the bodywork over both axles by ⅝ in, thus ensuring better road holding and lower fuel consumption.

As customary, the power variant CLS 55 AMG (5439 cc, 476 bhp) followed shortly thereafter; and, also in 2004, the diesel version CLS 320 CDI (2987 cc, 224 bhp), demonstrating the emancipation of diesel in this segment. A facelift in the second quarter of 2006 concerned not least three of the engines on offer: the six-cylinder was given a direct injection system, thus raising its output by 20 bhp, and

Provisorisch apostrophiert als »Vision CLS« setzt Mercedes auf der Frankfurter IAA 2003 als Lockvogel eine Synthese von Nobel-Limousine und schnittigem Coupé aus. Obwohl man offiziell noch abwiegelt, wissen Insider schon längst, dass der CLS beschlossene Sache ist. In der Tat feiert der voluminöse Hybride ein halbes Jahr später in Genf Premiere, lediglich drei Millimeter länger und etwas tiefer gelegt.

Die vielen Zeichnungen von der Konzeptidee bis hin zum fertigen Produkt belegen, wie sich Kreativität und Phantasie zu einem gemeinsamen Design gebündelt haben. In spannungsvollen Bögen zieht sich die Schulterlinie des schmucken Viertürers mit einer darunter laufenden Sicke aus der dynamisch anmutenden Rundung des vorderen Radkastens über die gesamte Flanke und endet im Ensemble der Rückleuchten. Dieses greift ihren lässigen Fluss auf und lässt ihn sanft in die Stoßfänger einmünden. Noch prägnanter verläuft die Kontur des Dachs, die nahtlos ins abgeschrägte Heck übergeht. Zart betont und dennoch aerodynamisch effizient: die kleine Abrisskante auf dem Deckel des Kofferraums. Um den Schwung der niedrigen Seitenfenster zu unterstreichen, werden diese von einer Chromleiste gesäumt und die bei einem klassischen Coupé nicht vorhandene breite B-Säule visuell in den Hintergrund relegiert. Die ledernen Innenverkleidungen der Türen und die großflächige Beplankung der Armaturentafel mit Wurzelnussholz zeichnen die stilistischen Elemente des Exteriors drinnen nach.

Ebenfalls neue Perspektiven eröffnet im CLS 350 die stufenlose, kontinuierliche Nockenwellenverstellung des neuen Leichtbau-V6 mit 3498 cm³ und 272 PS. Sie dirigiert die 24 Ventile in den Zylinderköpfen aus Aluminium dergestalt, dass Energieverluste auf ein Minimum reduziert werden. Ein spezielles Modul verändert die Länge des Saugrohrs je nach Drehzahl und reguliert die Luftströmung. So kommt das Triebwerk bereits bei lediglich 1500/min in den Genuss von 87 Prozent der Drehzahl-Obergrenze von 300 Newtonmetern. Den CLS 500 mobilisiert der bekannte Fünfliter-V8 mit 4966 cm³ und 272 PS. Beide Motoren arbeiten serienmäßig mit der neuen Siebengang-Automatik 7G-Tronic mit einer Wandler-Überbrückungskupplung zusammen. Sie richtet sich optimal nach der Drehzahl aus, spart Sprit und agiert überaus geräuscharm. Der CLS 500 bietet S-Kultur in Gestalt der Vierzonen-Klimatisierung Thermotronic und der Luftfederung Airmatic DC – das Kürzel steht für die Doppelfunktion Dual Control. Sie steuert elektrisch Federung und Dämpfung, wobei Gummibälge an den Federbeinen, gefüllt mit komprimierter Luft, die Arbeit vor Ort übernehmen. Mit einem Niveau-Schalter auf der mittleren Konsole bestimmt der Fahrer die Fahrwerks-einstellung. Bei höherem Tempo hingegen senkt das System die Karosserie über beiden Achsen automatisch um 15 Millimeter ab und sorgt somit für bessere Straßenlage und niedrigeren Verbrauch.

Lors du salon de l'automobile de Francfort en 2003, c'est sous le nom provisoire de Vision CLS que Mercedes présenta ce véhicule devant attirer les visiteurs. Il s'agit d'une synthèse de la berline de prestige et du coupé racé. Bien qu'officiellement on ait calmé les esprits, les initiés savaient déjà depuis longtemps que la CLS était chose faite. En effet, le volumineux hybride fêta sa première six mois plus tard, lors du salon de Genève, avec pour seules modifications, trois millimètres de plus en longueur et une hauteur légèrement diminuée.

Les nombreux dessins entre l'idée de départ et le produit fini prouvent combien la créativité et l'imagination ont été associées pour créer un design commun. En une courbure dynamique, la ligne de ceinture de la belle quatre portes dotée d'un épaulement prononcé au bas des vitres prend naissance dans les rondeurs dynamiques des passages de roues avant, soulignant les flancs sur toute leur longueur pour venir mourir au niveau de la poupe dans les blocs optiques arrière. Ceux-ci reprennent leur cours nonchalant et le laissent déboucher doucement sur les pare-chocs. Le contour du toit, qui à l'arrière prend une forme biseautée, est encore plus caractéristique. Discret mais pourtant efficace en termes d'aérodynamisme : le petit déflecteur sur l'arête de la porte du coffre. Pour souligner la surface galbée des vitres latérales, celles-ci sont entourées d'un liseré chromé tandis que le large montant central de la quatre portes, qui n'existe pas dans un coupé classique, est visuellement mis à l'arrière-plan. L'habillage en cuir de l'intérieur des portières et du large tableau de bord en ronce de noyer reprennent dans l'habitacle le style extérieur.

Le décalage en continu des arbres à cames du nouveau V6 de construction allégée (3498 cm³ et 272 ch) offre aussi de nouvelles perspectives. Il gère la cadence des 24 soupapes sous les culasses en aluminium de façon à réduire au maximum les pertes d'énergie. Un module spécial modifie la longueur du collecteur d'admission en fonction du régime et régule l'écoulement d'air. Ainsi, dès 1500 tours, le moteur bénéficie déjà de 87 % de son couple maximal de 300 Nm. La CLS 500 est mobilisée par le bien connu V8 de cinq litres (4966 cm³ et 272 ch). Les deux moteurs sont équipés en série de la nouvelle boîte automatique à sept rapports 7G-Tronic avec embrayage de prise directe. Elle s'adapte à la perfection aux différents régimes, économise le carburant, tout cela en silence. La CLS 500 offre la culture de la Classe S sous la forme de la climatisation quatre zones Thermotronic et de la suspension pneumatique Airmatic DC, abréviation de la double fonction *Dual Control*. Elle gère électriquement la suspension et les amortisseurs : des soufflets en caoutchouc remplis d'air comprimé à hauteur des jambes élastiques se chargent du travail. Avec un commutateur sur la console médiane, le conducteur détermine les réglages de châssis. En revanche, à grande vitesse, le système abaisse la carrosserie de 15 mm et assure ainsi une meilleure tenue de route et une consommation plus faible.

Mercedes-Benz CLS   2004

Mercedes-Benz CLS 320 2004

was now called CLS 350 CGI. In future, the CLS 500 would draw 388 bhp from 5461 cc, while the AMG variant could now reach a mighty 514 bhp, thanks to a 6208 cc V8: this was recognizable from its new name, the CLS 63 AMG. From April 2008, the entry-level version CLS 280 with 2996 cc and (still) 231 bhp rounded down the range.

Nach gutem Brauch folgt die Kraft-Variante CLS 55 AMG (5439 cm³, 476 PS) wenig später, und ebenfalls noch 2004 zeugt die Diesel-Version CLS 320 CDI (2987 cm³, 224 PS) von der Emanzipation des Selbstzünders auch in diesem Segment. Eine Modellpflege im zweiten Quartal 2006 betrifft nicht zuletzt drei der angebotenen Triebwerke: Der Sechszylinder erhält eine Direkteinspritzung, was seine Leistung um 20 PS anhebt, und heißt nun CLS 350 CGI. Der CLS 500 schöpft künftig 388 PS aus 5461 cm³, während die AMG-Spielart durch einen V8 mit 6208 cm³ zu mächtigen 514 PS befähigt wird, erkennbar auch am neuen Namen CLS 63 AMG. Ab April 2008 rundet die Einstiegs-Version CLS 280 mit 2996 cm³ und noch immer 231 PS die Palette nach unten ab.

Comme de coutume, la variante puissante, la CLS 55 AMG (5439 cm³, 476 ch) sortit peu de temps après et en 2004 la version diesel CLS 320 CDI (2987 cm³, 224 ch) prouva son émancipation de l'allumage par compression même dans cette gamme. Une révision du modèle durant le deuxième trimestre 2006 toucha surtout trois des motorisations proposées : le six cylindres fut équipé d'une injection directe, ce qui augmenta sa puissance de 20 chevaux ; il fut rebaptisé CLS 350 CGI. Le CLS 500 disposa de 388 ch provenant de 5461 cm³ alors que la série spéciale AMG fut capable d'atteindre 514 ch grâce à un V8 de 6208 cm³, reconnaissables à son nouveau nom : CLS 63 AMG. À partir d'avril 2008, la version d'entrée de gamme, CLS 280 (2996 cm³ et toujours 231 ch), vint compléter la gamme.

Power and functionality married to elegance and esthetics: the CLS also exudes the skill of the Swabian automobile constructor both under its hood and in its distinguished interior.

Kraft und Funktionalität, gepaart mit Eleganz und Ästhetik: Der CLS strahlt auch unter der Haube und im vornehmen Interieur das Können der schwäbischen Automobilbauer aus.

Quand vigueur et fonctionnalité vont de pair avec élégance et esthétique : sous le capot aussi et dans son habitacle distingué, la CLS traduit tout le savoir-faire du constructeur de Stuttgart.

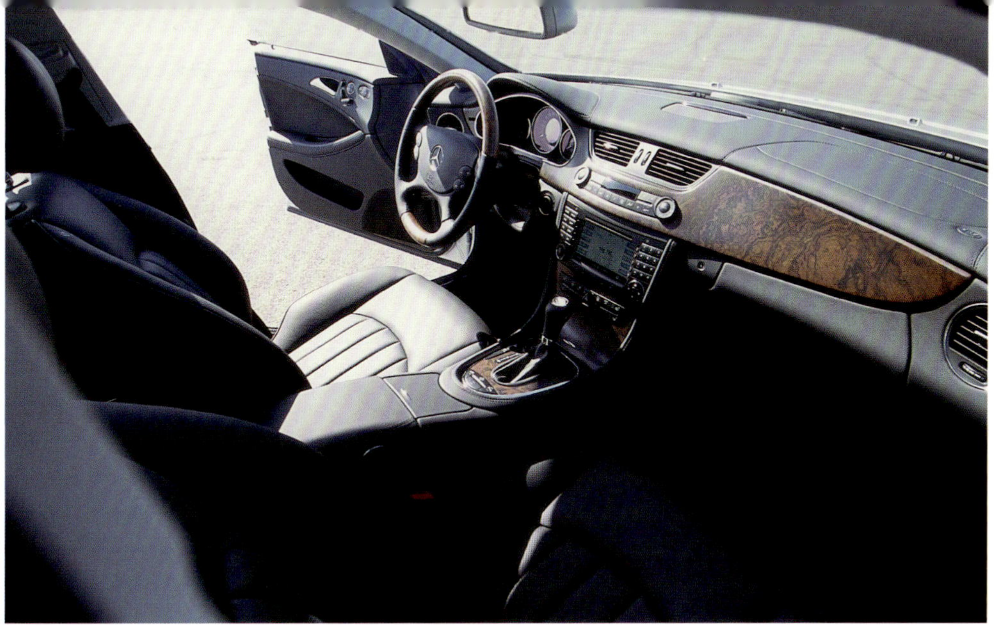

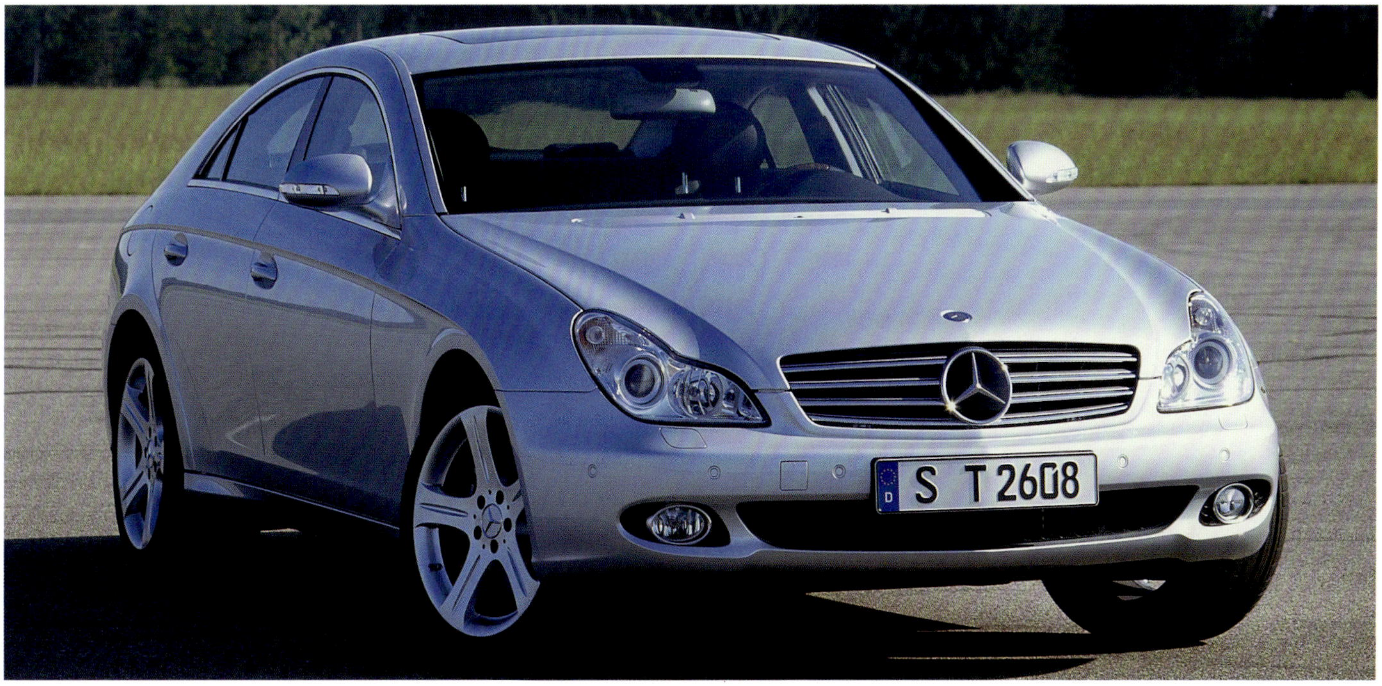
S T 2608

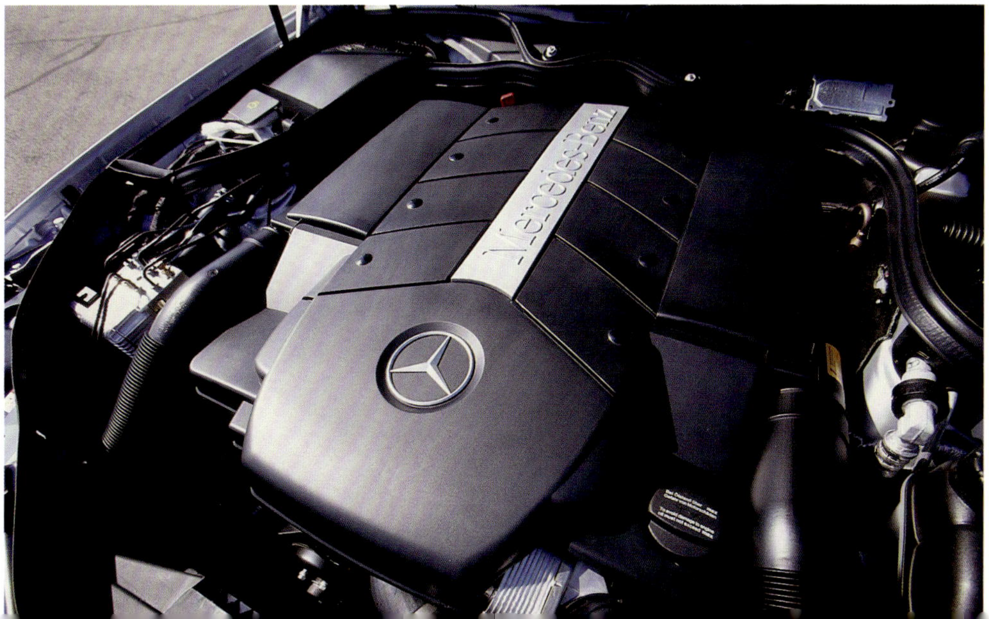
Mercedes-Benz

Sometimes a vision very quickly becomes reality. That is what happened with the Compact Sports Tourer named "Vision B," revealed at the Paris Motor Show in September 2004. The Vaneo, based like this one on the A-Class and designed as a hip family and leisure vehicle, was still—after three-and-a-half years and a feeble distribution of 57,000 units—on the verge of suffering infant death: then, at the Geneva Salon six months later, the finished product marked a new departure in the same direction. A successful marketing campaign mused eloquently on the "value-added experience in terms of design and dynamism," and the new car turned out to be a great success.

On 22 March 2005 in the Rastatt plant, "Job Number One"—a B 200 CDI (1991 cc, 140 bhp) in polar silver—rolled off the assembly line, the first series B car. From now on, the customer was spoiled for choice between a chrome (standard on more powerful models) and a sports package with leather and aluminum finish and five other variants of motor in the gasoline engines B 150 (1498 cc, 95 bhp), B 170 (1699 cc, 115 bhp), B 200 (2034 cc, 136 bhp), B 200 Turbo (193 bhp) and the B 180 CDI diesel (1991 cc, 109 bhp). With the B 170 NGT BlueEfficiency (2034 cc, 116 bhp) of 2008, the brand paid tribute to the spirit of the new age: with natural gas, it can achieve 190 miles per tank, or 440 miles if gas is tapped from its 13-gallon tank. The change can be effected by pressing a key on the multifunction steering wheel.

The intention behind the new model can, indeed, be read from its shape: in evident similarity with the A-Class, and even in unmistakable kinship with the R-series located a whole level higher, it seeks to make a lot more space available. At about the same height and width as the Baby Benz, with which it contrasts in shape (for example in its exposed wheel houses and horizontally positioned tail lights), the B-type is almost twenty inches longer and has eight inches more wheelbase. In fact, the occupants of this front-wheel drive are greeted, after making a comfortable entry through wide-opening doors, with an opulent feeling of space. This is due not least to the placing of the transverse engine and transmission, housed partly in front of and partly under the passenger compartment, which on frontal impact reveals safety margins in terms of space that are typical of the model. Travelers in the rear also have a comfortable journey. Some experience, however, is required for B-drivers to ascertain where their car actually begins and where it ends.

In any event, they have around 19.2 cu.ft of storage space at their disposal, which can easily be extended to 79.2 cu.ft if they do not mind the (quite reasonable) extra cost of removable front passenger and rear seats. Otherwise, split folding rear seats and an adjustable two-level load area make it easier to use the standard luggage compartment. Even with a full load, the B-type, cheerfully able to understeer at the limits, stubbornly holds its own. This is thanks in no small measure to the suspension it

Manchmal wird aus Vision ganz schnell Wirklichkeit. So geschehen beim Compact Sports Tourer namens Vision B, enthüllt auf dem Pariser Automobilsalon im September 2004. Der wie dieser auf der A-Klasse fußende Vaneo, als hippes Familien- und Freizeitmobil eingeplant, ist noch im Begriff, nach dreieinhalb Jahren und der schwächlichen Verbreitung von 57 000 Exemplaren, den frühen Kindstod zu erleiden, da macht man auf der Genfer Frühjahrsshow ein halbes Jahr später mit dem fertigen Produkt einen neuen Anlauf in die gleiche Richtung. Eine blühende Marketing-Lyrik verheißt »Erlebnis-Mehrwert in Design und Dynamik«, und in der Tat stellt sich beträchtlicher Erfolg ein.

Am 22. März 2005 rollt im Werk Rastatt »Job Number One«, ein B 200 CDI (1991 cm³, 140 PS) in Polarsilber, vom Band, der erste Serien-B. Der Kunde hat künftig die Qual der Wahl zwischen einem Chrom- (serienmäßig bei den stärkeren Modellen) und einem Sportpaket mit Leder- und Aluminium-Zierrat sowie fünf weiteren Varianten der Motorisierung in den Benzinern B 150 (1498 cm³, 95 PS), B 170 (1699 cm³, 115 PS), B 200 (2034 cm³, 136 PS), B 200 Turbo (193 PS) und dem Selbstzünder B 180 CDI (1991 cm³, 109 PS). Mit dem B 170 NGT BlueEfficiency (2034 cm³, 116 PS) von 2008 wird die Marke dem Geist der neuen Zeit Tribut zollen: Mit Erdgas wartet er mit einem Aktionsradius von 300 Kilometern je Füllung auf, mit 700 Kilometern, wenn aus seinem 54-Liter-Tank Benzin gezapft wird. Bewerkstelligen lässt sich der Wechsel per Tastendruck am Multifunktionslenkrad.

Schon aus der Form kann man die Intention hinter dem Neuen ablesen: bei augenscheinlicher Ähnlichkeit mit der A-Klasse, übrigens auch unverkennbarer Nähe zur ein ganzes Stück höher angesiedelten R-Baureihe, eine Menge mehr Platz zur Verfügung zu stellen. Ungefähr gleich hoch und breit wie der Baby-Benz, von dem er sich formal beispielsweise durch ausgestellte Radkästen und horizontal angesiedelte Rückleuchten abhebt, ist der B-Typ fast einen halben Meter länger und weist 210 Millimeter mehr Radstand auf. In der Tat erwartet die Insassen nach dem kommoden Betreten des Fronttrieblers durch weit öffnende Türen ein opulentes Raumgefühl. Dafür ist nicht zuletzt die Platzierung von Quermotor und Getriebe verantwortlich, teils vor, teils unter der Fahrgastzelle untergebracht, was bei einem Frontalaufprall modelltypische Sicherheitsspielräume eröffnet. Auch hinten reist man gut. Gleichwohl bedarf es einiger Routine, bis der B-Lenker ermittelt hat, wo genau sein Auto aufhört und wo es eigentlich anfängt.

Auf jeden Fall gebietet er über 544 Liter Stauraum, der sich locker auf 2245 Liter erweitern lässt, wenn er den verkraftbaren Aufpreis für herausnehmbare Beifahrer- und Rücksitze nicht scheut. Ansonsten erleichtern geteilt klappbare Rücksitze und ein in zwei Höhen zu verstellender Ladeboden die Nutzung des Standard-Gepäckabteils. Selbst bei voller Beladung hält der B-Typ, im Grenzbereich gutmütig untersteuernd, stur Kurs. Dafür sorgen nicht

Parfois une vision devient très vite réalité. C'est ce qu'il s'est passé avec le *Compact Sports Tourer* portant le nom de Vision B, révélé lors du salon de l'automobile de Paris en septembre 2004. Cette voiture, comme le Vaneo basé sur la Classe A, est conçue comme un véhicule à la mode pour les familles et les loisirs. Après trois ans et demi et étant donné sa faible diffusion, 57 000 exemplaires, ce modèle promettait de ne pas durer. Il prit cependant un nouveau départ six mois plus tard, lors du salon de l'automobile de Genève, avec le produit fini. Les sirènes du marketing promettaient un «résultat à valeur ajoutée dans le design et la dynamique». Le succès fut effectivement considérable.

Le 22 mars 2005 sortit de la chaîne de l'atelier de Rastatt «Job Number One», une B 200 CDI (1991 cm³, 140 ch) argent polaire, le premier de la gamme B. Le client a maintenant l'embarras du choix entre un pack chromé (de série sur le haut de gamme) et un pack sport doté d'un décor en cuir et aluminium, ainsi que cinq autres motorisations essence B 150 (1498 cm³, 95 ch), B 170 (1699 cm³, 115 ch), B 200 (2034 cm³, 136 ch), B 200 Turbo (193 ch) et diesel B 180 CDI (1991 cm³, 109 ch). Avec la B 170 NGT Blue-Efficiency (2 034 cm³, 116 ch) de 2008, la marque paie son tribut à l'air du temps: le modèle est disponible avec du gaz naturel et une autonomie de 300 kilomètres par plein, 700 kilomètres lorsqu'on puise dans son réservoir d'essence de 54 litres. Le changement s'effectue par pression sur une touche située sur le volant multifonctions.

La forme de la petite nouvelle indique clairement l'intention du constructeur: offrir beaucoup plus de place tout en conservant les ressemblances avec la Classe A, de même qu'avec une grande partie de la Classe R, haute sur roues. Presque aussi haute que large, comme la Baby-Benz, dont elle se distingue par exemple par ses passages de roue évasés et ses feux arrière placés à l'horizontale, la gamme B est plus longue de presque 50 centimètres et offre 210 millimètres d'empattement supplémentaire. En effet, après l'accès facile en raison de portes s'ouvrant largement, une grande sensation d'espace attend les passagers de la traction avant, principalement due à l'implantation transversale du moteur et de la boîte de vitesses: en partie devant, en partie sous l'emplacement de la cellule passager, ce qui en cas de choc frontal augmente la sécurité, une caractéristique du modèle. À l'arrière de ce véhicule compact, on voyage bien. Il faut toutefois un peu d'entraînement pour le conducteur de la série B qui doit se familiariser avec les dimensions du véhicules.

Dans tous les cas, la Classe B offre plus de 544 litres d'espace de rangement qui se transforrment facilement en 2245 litres lorsqu'on ne redoute pas l'onéreuse option permettant de retirer les sièges passagers avant et arrière. Les sièges arrière rabattables facilement et les deux niveaux du plancher de la malle facilitent l'utilisation du coffre standard. Même entièrement remplie, la Classe B maintient la trajectoire et s'inscrit facilement en courbe. Son train de roulement bien rodé issu de la Classe A veille à son bon

Mercedes-Benz B-Klasse   2005

Mercedes-Benz B 180 CDI 2008

has inherited from the A-Class, with MacPherson strut suspension in front, a parabolic rear axle, and adaptive shock absorbers all around.

On 20 October 2006, B-class candidates emerged from the European NCAP (New Car Assessment Program) crash tests with brilliant results. In April 2008, at the AMI (Auto Mobil International) show in Leipzig, a thoroughly renovated B-generation made its debut.

zuletzt sein von der A-Klasse her geläufiges Fahrwerk mit einer McPherson-Achse vorn, einer Parabel-Hinterachse sowie adaptiven Stoßdämpfern ringsum.

Am 20. Oktober 2006 gehen Kandidaten der B-Klasse aus Crashtests nach dem europäischen NCAP (für *New Car Assessment Programme*) mit glänzendem Ergebnis hervor. Auf der Auto Mobil International AMI in Leipzig im April 2008 schließlich gibt eine gründlich renovierte B-Generation ihr Debüt.

comportement. Il est équipé d'un essieu McPherson à l'avant, d'un essieu arrière parabolique ainsi que d'amortisseurs adaptatifs.

Le 20 octobre 2006, les candidats de la Classe B passèrent les essais de choc selon le NCAP (pour *New Car Assessment Programme*) européen brillamment. Une génération B entièrement rénovée fit ses débuts en avril 2008 lors de l'Auto Mobil International AMI à Leipzig. Les puissantes versions B 150 et B 170 sont livrables avec la fonction Start-Stop qui arrête le moteur lorsqu'on est au point mort.

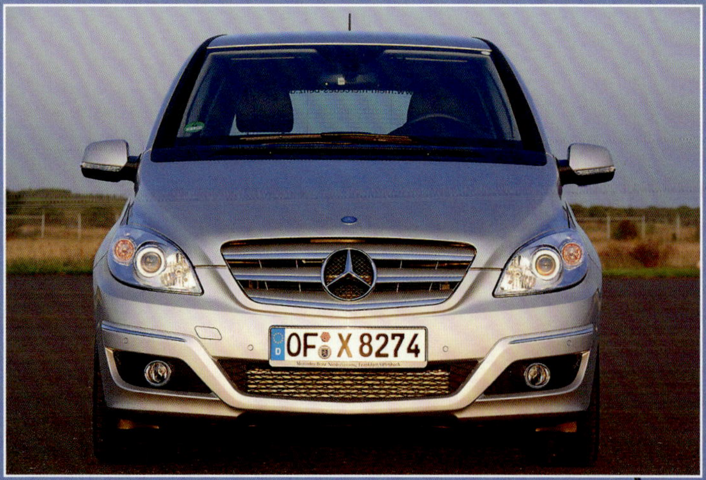
OF X 8274

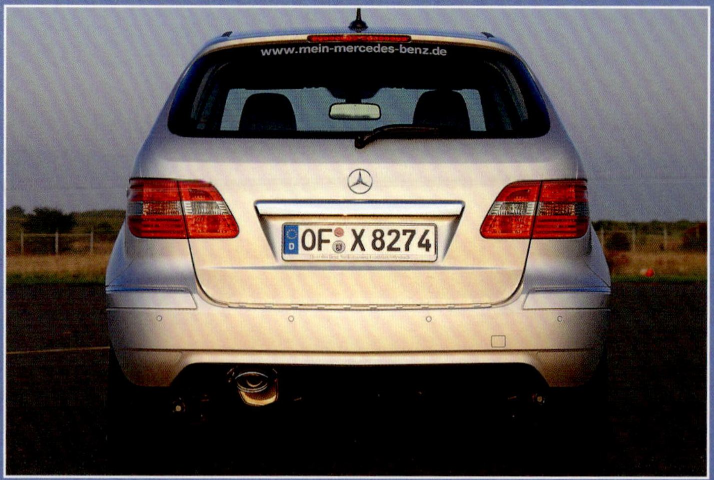
www.mein-mercedes-benz.de
OF X 8274

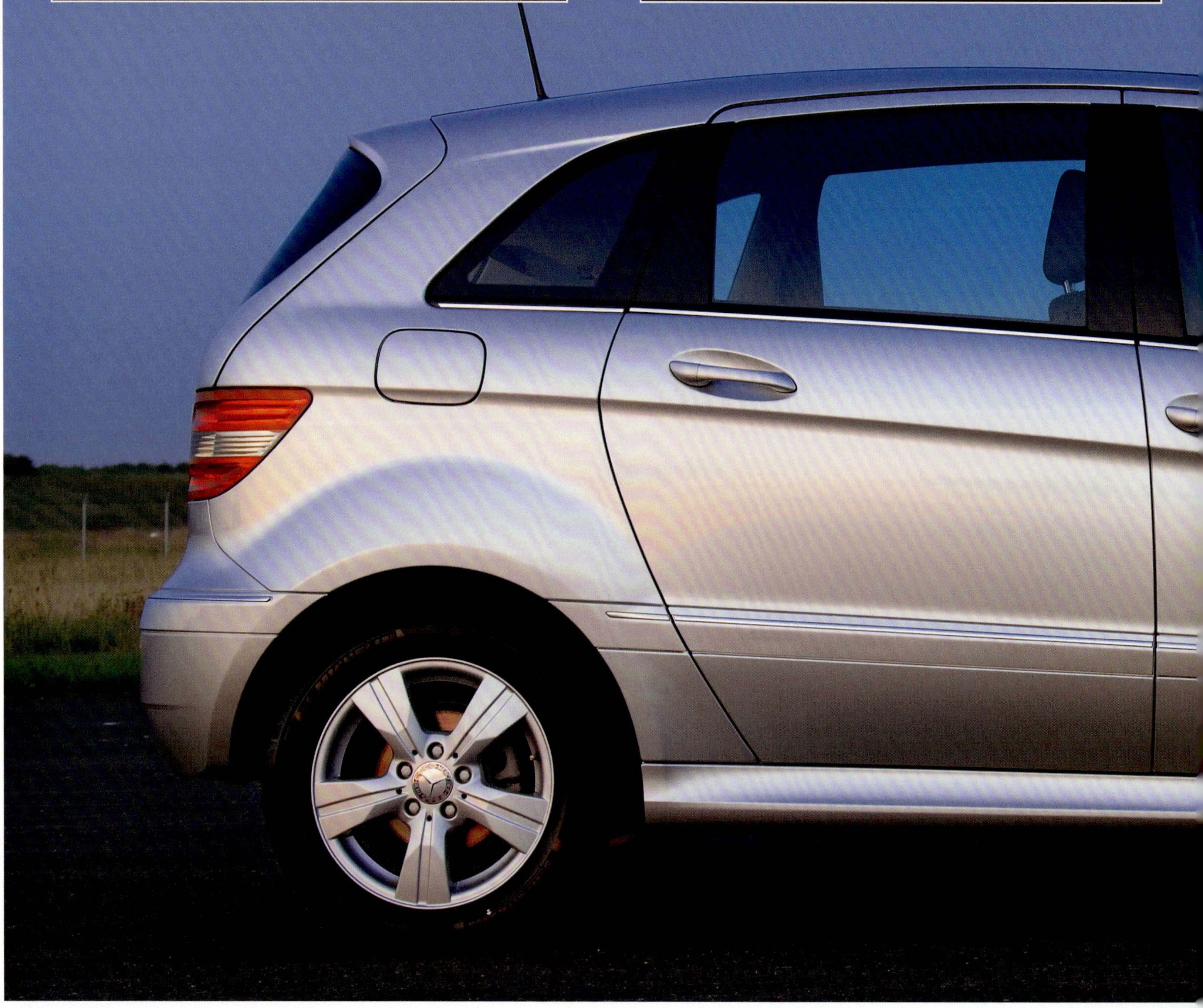

Exposed wheel housings and horizontal tail lights underline the departure from
the related A-Class. Despite the good field of vision and the significantly reduced
front, the B-driver can only speculate as to where his car begins and ends.

Ausgestellte Radhäuser und horizontale Rückleuchten unterstreichen die Abgrenzung zur
wesensverwandten A-Klasse. Wo genau sein Auto anfängt und aufhört, das kann der
B-Lenker trotz guter Übersicht und deutlich abgesetzter Front indessen nur erahnen.

Des passages de roue évasés et des blocs optiques arrière horizontaux soulignent
la différence avec la Classe A, très similaire. Malgré une bonne allure générale
et une proue nettement fuyante, le conducteur de la classe B ne peut
que deviner où commence et où se termine sa voiture.

Mercedes-Benz B-Klasse 2005

Something of an American affair, and—like the ML-series—produced in Tuscaloosa, Alabama, the Mercedes R-Class was exhibited to the public for the first time on 23 March 2005 at the New York International Auto Show before being given, in September of that year, its European premiere at the Frankfurt International Motor Show. Called, in Daimler house jargon, the Grand Sports Tourer, it perfectly filled a niche that had needed first to be spotted. The aim was to create, in this model, a "very luxurious way of traveling for up to six people," as noted by Wolf-Dieter Kurz, Mercedes director of marketing and sales, in an attempt to define the truly indefinable. He added that it bore "the positive characteristics of three vehicle types: the status and dynamics of a premium sedan, the all-wheel drive of an SUV, and the spatial concept of a multi-purpose vehicle."

Out of all this there emerged a powerful vehicle 17 ft long, 6 ft 4 in wide, and 5 ft 6 in high, with a wheelbase of 10 ft 6 in. Even the shorter version produced for European markets, available from 2006, was 16 ft 2 in long and had a 9-ft-9-in wheelbase—still an intimidating chunk of metal, despite excursions into a more sporty design language including the long bonnet, coupé-like sloping lines of the flat roof, and dagger-sharp rear tapering wheel curve below. Four passengers were splendidly raised on comfortable individual seats, even in the rear, with individual air-conditioning facilities and a comprehensive entertainment center in the form of a CD and DVD player, and—at additional cost—screens in the headrests of the front seats to satisfy the electronic desires of restless offspring.

Sitting in the rear row, however, could be annoying for teenagers, even more so in the short variant. Full occupation of the Mercedes spaceship also definitely came at the cost of potential luggage volume, pared down to a paltry 11 cu.ft. Again the magic word was flexibility. All four rear seats could be easily lowered by hand, so that a flat load floor over 6 ft 6 in in length with a capacity of 84.2 cu.ft could rapidly be created.

The R-Class shared with the ML, produced on the same assembly line, the chassis, drive train, and four-wheel drive. Rear air suspension was included in the basic price: all-round Airmatic, however, came as an extra, as did the huge two-part glass roof, designed as a front sunroof. Like an SUV, the superstructure with this configuration could be raised if desired by two inches, while from a speed of 75 mph upward it automatically sank ¾ in. Another similarity with its ML counterparts was the seven-speed automatic with direct gear selector lever at the wheel, while the Pre-Safe system operated to forestall injury in case of an accident, in tandem with the so-called Neck-Pro active head restraints borrowed from the S-Class.

From fall 2007 there was the generally refurbished 2.5-short-ton model, either five- or seven-seater, with significantly remodeled styling to front and rear. The entry models R 280 CDI (V6 turbodiesel, 2987 cc, 190 bhp), R 280 (V6, 2996 cc, 231 bhp) and R 350 (V6, 3498 cc, 272 bhp)

Irgendwie eine amerikanische Angelegenheit und wie die ML-Modellreihe in Tuscaloosa, Alabama, gefertigt, wird die Mercedes R-Klasse dem verehrten Publikum erstmalig am 23. März 2005 bei der New York International Auto Show vorgestellt, bevor sie im September jenes Jahres auf der Frankfurter IAA ihrer Europa-Premiere zugeführt wird. Im Daimler-Hausjargon Grand Sports Tourer geheißen, füllt sie perfekt eine Nische, die gleichwohl erst einmal aufgespürt werden musste. Mit diesem Typ habe man »eine besonders luxuriöse Reisemöglichkeit für bis zu sechs Personen« schaffen wollen, definiert Wolf-Dieter Kurz, bei Mercedes Leiter für Marketing und Vertrieb, das eigentlich Undefinierbare. Er verbinde »die positiven Eigenschaften von drei Fahrzeug-Gattungen: den Status und die Dynamik einer Premium-Limousine, den Allradantrieb eines SUV und das Raumkonzept einer Großraumlimousine«.

Dabei herausgekommen ist ein mächtiges Mobil von 5175 mm Länge, 1920 mm Breite, 1665 mm Höhe und einem Radstand von 3215 mm. Selbst die für europäische Märkte vorgesehene und ab 2006 angebotene Kurzversion, 4940 mm lang und mit 2980 mm Radstand, kommt noch als einschüchterndes Trumm daher trotz Ausflügen in eine sportliche Formensprache wie die langgezogene Fronthaube, die coupéartig abfallende Linienführung des flachen Dachs und der hinten dolchspitz zulaufende Scheibenbogen darunter. Vier Reisende sind auf kommoden Einzel-Fauteuils glänzend aufgehoben, auch im zweiten Glied mit individuellen Klima-Möglichkeiten und einem umfassenden Unterhaltungs-Angebot in Gestalt eines CD- und DVD-Players und – gegen Aufpreis – Bildschirmen in den Kopfstützen der Vordersitze zur elektronischen Besänftigung des unruhigen Nachwuchses.

Der Aufenthalt der letzten Reihe hingegen dürfte bereits Halbwüchsigen Verdruss bereiten, in der kurzen Variante noch mehr. Volle Besatzung des Mercedes-Raumschiffs geht überdies entschieden auf Kosten des möglichen Gepäckvolumens, das dann auf mickrige 314 Liter eingedampft wird. Wieder heißt das Zauberwort Variabilität: Alle vier Rücksitze lassen sich mit einfachen Handgriffen flachlegen, so dass flugs eine ebene Ladefläche von über zwei Metern Länge und einer Kapazität von 2385 Litern erzeugt werden kann.

Mit dem ML, auf dem gleichen Band zusammengesetzt, teilt die R-Klasse das Fahrwerk, den Antriebsstrang und somit das Allradkonzept. Luftfederung hinten ist im Basispreis inbegriffen, Rundum-Airmatic hingegen aufpreispflichtig wie das riesige zweiteilige Glasdach, vorn als Schiebedach konzipiert. SUV-mäßig lässt sich der Aufbau mit dieser Konfiguration bei Bedarf um 50 Millimeter anheben, wogegen er sich ab Tempo 120 automatisch um 20 Millimeter absenkt. Eine weitere Gemeinsamkeit mit den ML-Kollegen bildet die Siebengang-Automatik mit Direktwahlhebel am Volant, während das Pre-Safe-System, im Falle eines Unfalls prophylaktisch zusammenwirkend

---

Dans tous les cas, une histoire américaine fabriquée à Tuscaloosa, Alabama, comme la gamme ML. La Mercedes Classe R fut d'abord présentée au public admiratif lors du Salon international de l'automobile de New York le 23 mars 2005 avant d'être introduite en septembre de la même année en Europe lors du Salon de Francfort. Appelée *Grand Sports Tourer* dans le jargon de Daimler, elle remplit parfaitement une niche qui pourtant devait tout d'abord être inventée. Avec cette gamme, on a voulu créer «une possibilité de voyager particulièrement luxueuse pour six personnes», explique Wolf-Dieter Kurz, chef du marketing et des ventes chez Mercedes. Elle associe «les caractéristiques positives de trois types de véhicules : le statut et la dynamique d'une berline premium, les quatre roues motrices d'un SUV et l'habitacle généreux d'un monospace».

Il en résulte une automobile puissante de 5175 mm de long, 1920 mm de large, 1665 mm de hauteur et un empattement de 3215 mm. Même la version courte prévue pour les marchés européens et proposée à partir de 2006, 4940 mm de long et 2980 mm d'empattement, reste donc encore un monstre intimidant malgré des incursions dans les lignes sportives, tels le capot allongé, les lignes plongeantes du toit plat rappelant un coupé et les courbes des vitres arrière se terminant en pointe. Quatre voyageurs sont très bien installés dans les fauteuils individuels, même au deuxième rang avec les possibilités de climatisation individuelle et une large palette de divertissements sous la forme d'un lecteur de CD et de DVD et, en option, des écrans dans les appuis-tête des sièges avant afin d'étancher la soif d'électronique des enfants turbulents.

Le voyage au dernier rang en revanche devrait réserver des désagréments, même aux adolescents, et encore plus dans la version courte. L'occupation totale du navire Mercedes se fait largement aux dépens de l'éventuel volume des bagages car il se réduit alors à 314 petits litres. Le mot magique est à nouveau «modularité»: les quatre sièges arrière peuvent être encastrés en quelques gestes simples si bien que rapidement on peut générer une surface de chargement plane de plus de deux mètres de long et une capacité de 2385 litres.

La Classe R est assemblée sur la même chaîne que la ML avec laquelle elle partage le châssis, le train de roulement et donc tout le concept quatre roues motrices. La suspension pneumatique à l'arrière est incluse dans le prix de base ; par contre l'Airmatic complet est en option, tout comme l'immense toit en verre en deux parties, conçu à l'avant comme un toit ouvrant. Comme pour un tout-terrain, avec cette configuration la structure s'élève de 50 mm en cas de besoin, mais en revanche à partir de 120 km/h, elle s'abaisse automatiquement de 20 mm. Un autre point commun avec sa collègue ML est la boîte automatique à sept rapports avec un levier de commande direct au volant alors que le système Pre-Safe agissant de façon préventive en cas d'accident simultanément avec les appuis-tête actifs appelés Neck-Pro est emprunté à la Classe S.

Mercedes-Benz R-Klasse 2005

Mercedes-Benz R 320 CDI 2008

would also be available in the future with rear-wheel drive, the R 320 CDI (V6 turbodiesel, 2987 cc, 224 bhp) and the top R 500 (V8, 5461 cc, 388 bhp) only as a 4WD. The most powerful model, the R 63 AMG (V8, 6208 cc), a real sports tourer with 510 bhp, was available for only one year, from 2006.

mit den Neck-Pro genannten aktiven Kopfstützen, der S-Klasse entlehnt ist.

Seit Herbst 2007 gibt es den 2,2-Tonner runderneuert, wahlweise fünf- oder siebensitzig, mit markant überarbeitetem Styling an Front und Heck. Die Einstiegsmodelle R 280 CDI (V6-Turbodiesel, 2987 cm³, 190 PS), R 280 (V6, 2996 cm³, 231 PS) und R 350 (V6, 3498 cm³, 272 PS) sind künftig auch mit Heckantrieb erhältlich, der R 320 CDI (V6-Turbodiesel, 2987 cm³, 224 PS) sowie der Top-R 500 (V8, 5461 cm³, 388 PS) lediglich als Allradler. Dem stärksten Stück R 63 AMG (V8, 6208 cm³), mit 510 PS wahrlich ein Sports Tourer, ist ab 2006 nur ein Jahr Verweildauer beschieden.

Depuis l'automne 2007 il existe la version 2,2 tonnes entièrement reconfigurée, cinq ou sept sièges au choix, avec un style fortement remanié à l'avant et à l'arrière. Les modèles d'entrée de gamme, les R 280 CDI (V6 turbo diesel, 2987 cm³, 190 ch), R 280 (V6, 2996 cm³, 231 ch), et R 350 (V6, 3498 cm³, 272 ch) sont désormais disponibles avec traction arrière; par contre la R 320 CDI (V6 turbo diesel, 2987 cm³, 224 ch) et l'excellence, la R 500 (V8, 5461 cm³, 388 ch) n'existent qu'en quatre roues motrices. Le plus beau morceau, la R 63 AMG (V8, 6208 cm³), véritable Sport Tourer avec ses 510 ch fut disponible seulement un an à compter de 2006.

Mercedes-Benz R-Klasse 2005

With six seats in three rows like a van, four-wheel drive like a SUV, and carrying space like a station wagon, the R-Class combines a lot of advantages under one roof. Cultured, powerful, and yet economical: the three-liter V6 diesel.

Mit sechs Sitzen in drei Reihen wie ein Van, Allradantrieb wie ein SUV und Laderaum wie ein Kombi bringt die R-Klasse viel Erstrebenswertes unter einen Hut. Kultiviert, kraftvoll und dennoch genügsam: der Dreiliter-V6-Diesel.

Avec six sièges sur trois rangées, comme un van, quatre roues motrices comme un SUV et l'habitacle d'un break, la Classe R réunit de nombreux atouts. Élégant, puissant et néanmoins sobre: le trois litres V6 diesel.

Its arch-rival, the BMW Seven, had—from the point of view of the company—forced its way unduly to the foreground. As a result, the Mercedes empire waved its magic wand, unveiling the new edition of the flagship s-Class on 22 June 2005 and exhibiting it to an interested public at the Frankfurt Motor Show in mid-September that year.

The novice had a rather graceful appearance in spite of markedly muscular wheel arches. It had increased overall in size and was available in two variants, with lengths of 16 ft 8 in (10 ft wheelbase) and 17 ft (wheelbase 10 ft 4 in), corresponding to an increase of 1¼ in and 1¾ in in length, ⅝ in in width, and 1⅛ in in height. Of course this was done for the benefit of the passengers who were now, in the back seats of the longer version, able to enjoy ½ in more legroom: the trunk capacity had also expanded by 2.1 cu.ft to 19.8 cu.ft. Its torsion resistance had increased by twelve percent, its rigidity by six percent, and its weight by 66–110 pounds. Maneuverability and ease of driving conspired, however, to make the driver forget size and weight, and set new active and passive safety standards.

Traveling in comfort had always been the main concern of this high-tech vehicle and status symbol, the s-Class. Already, the s 350 (v6, 3498 cc, 272 bhp), an early offering together with the four-valve engine s 500 (v8, 5461 cc, 388 bhp) provided, for the basic price of 70,760 euros, cultural and security enhancements such as the seven-speed automatic with its smooth-as-silk transitions, connected via a lever behind the steering wheel, and a second-generation Pre-Safe system.

The s-driver found willing electronic fairies at hand, alert to each and every bidding. For an additional sum, active suspension Active Body Control (ABC), standard in the s 63 AMG (v8, 6208 cc, 525 bhp), s 600 (twin-turbo v12, 5513 cc, 517 bhp), and s 65 AMG (twin-turbo v12, 5980 cc, 612 bhp), all since 2006, controlled the suspension by means of sensors, high-pressure hydraulics, and sophisticated microprocessors so as to detect with lightning speed the state of the road and combat faltering or pitching of the heavy superstructure. The distance control Distronic Plus, supplemented by radar for short range, automatically kept the correct distance from the vehicle ahead, between 0 and 125 mph. Sensors in the apron enabled Brake Assist Plus to perceive obstacles at 8 in–500 ft and provide support for the braking process, up to a complete halt, with the brake lights flashing as warning signs. Night View Assist, aided by infrared light in conjunction with the dimmed beam, extended the driver's field of vision to over 500 ft.

The model and engine range of the top Daimler was expanded within one year to include the s 450 (v8, 4663 cc, 340 bhp) and the thoroughly refined diesels s 320 CDI (v6 twin turbo, 2987 cc, 235 bhp) and s 420 CDI (v8 twin turbo, 3996 cc, 320 bhp). The two twelve-cylinder engines could be purchased only with five-speed automatic transmission. On 16 October 2006, the s-range was completed by

Mercedes-Benz s-Klasse 2005

Mercedes-Benz S 420 CDI 2008

the armored s 600 Guard with a long wheelbase and, in January 2007 in Detroit, by the four-wheel drive variants. At the Frankfurt IAA in September of that year, the firm pointed the way to a climate-friendly future with the showpiece s 300 Bluetec Hybrid, and in Paris in October 2008 it repeated the trick with the s 400 Hybrid. Technically and visually refreshed, the s-Class was exhibited in March 2009 in the Palais des Expositions in Geneva.

Biturbo, 3996 cm³, 320 PS) ergänzt. Die beiden Zwölfzylinder sind nur im Bunde mit einem Fünfstufen-Automaten zu haben. Am 16. Oktober 2006 wird das s-Spektrum komplettiert durch den gepanzerten s 600 Guard mit langem Radstand, im Januar 2007 in Detroit durch die Allrad-Spielarten. Auf der Frankfurter IAA im September desselben Jahres weist man mit dem Schau-Stück s 300 Bluetec Hybrid den Weg in eine klimafreundliche Zukunft, in Paris im Oktober 2008 mit dem s 400 Hybrid. Technisch und optisch aufgefrischt zeigt sich die s-Klasse im März 2009 im Genfer Palais des Expositions.

320 ch) à allumage par compression. Les deux douze cylindres ne sont disponibles qu'avec une boîte automatique à cinq rapports. Le 16 octobre 2006, la gamme s fut complétée par une version blindée, la s 600 Guard à empattement long, et en janvier 2007 à Détroit par les versions quatre roues motrices. Lors du Salon de l'automobile de Francfort en septembre de la même année, on montra avec la spectaculaire s 300 Bluetec Hybrid le chemin d'un avenir moins dommageable pour le climat et on fit de même à Paris en octobre 2008 avec la s 400 Hybrid. Lors du salon de Genève en mars 2009, la Classe s apparut techniquement et visuellement rafraîchie.

The Mercedes heavy weight S-Class has remained heavy. It notches up 2.3 short tons despite the aluminum doors and hood. Self-ignition and yet still a cultural experience: the 420 CDI V8.

Das Mercedes-Schwergewicht S-Klasse ist auch schwer geblieben. Trotz Aluminiums für Türen und Hauben bringt sie 2,1 Tonnen auf die Waage. Selbstzünder und dennoch ein Kulturereignis: der V8 des 420 CDI.

La Classe S, poids lourd de Mercedes, n'a pas été allégée. Malgré l'aluminium des portes et du capot, elle pèse encore 2,1 tonnes. Allumage par compression et pourtant un événement culturel : le V8 de la 420 CDI.

Mercedes-Benz S-Klasse 2005

In the second-generation M-Class, unveiled at the Detroit Show in 2005, Mercedes decisively shifted its balancing act between off-road and on-road driving toward travel comfort, luxury, and sedan models à la S- or R-Class. It was no longer a requisite that such a vehicle could cavort like a fish in mountain-clear spring water even in rough terrain. After all, hardly anyone goes there.

There was still an ML for difficult surfaces, however, but only if splashing out on an off-road package (optional extra). A two-stage transfer case with low-range gearing was delightfully included, as was a manual or automatic switchable differential lock (100 percent) between the front and rear axles and on the rear axle, as well as the Airmatic air suspension specially installed for cross-country driving, which increased the ground clearance by 4⅜ in to 11½ in and the fording depth to 2 ft. The standard ML for the street, however, protected itself and its occupants against injury from below by means of conventional coil springs, while distributing the force of its power source in the same way as its predecessor, with a center differential normally divided equally between the axles. The suspension was new, too: at the front it was on highly placed aluminum double wishbones, in the rear on a four-link suspension.

The measurements of the new model were also tailored to the demands for comfort: it was, at 15 ft 8 in, six inches longer than the previous model; at 6 ft 3 in, 2¾ in wider; and therefore ¼ in lower—6 ft, including the roof rails. The increase in wheelbase by 3¾ in to 9 ft 7 in especially benefited the passengers in the second row, where the distance from the front passenger had increased by 1⅜ in. Behind it opened up a colossal trunk that could swallow up 19.4–72.4 cu.ft of luggage, on a loading area which, thanks to a removable seat cushion in the back, now appeared as smooth as a lid. The squat appearance of the ML also obeyed a different criterion: it needed to look sportier, with other elements such as its flat windshield, the markedly luxurious curve of the wheel arches, and the shoulder line rising toward the rear all contributing to this.

As usual, the elegant new SUV set new standards in active and passive safety, such as the optional Pre-Safe protection system. In conjunction with ABS, Brake Assist and ESP, this recognized potential accident situations, tightened the seat belts, brought the passenger seat into an optimal position, and if necessary even closed the sunroof. One comfortable note was definitely the standard automatic transmission, which operated the seven gears as smoothly as if they were made of butter, with hardly noticeable transitions, electronically operated via a steering-column selector lever. It was initially connected to four engines, three of them new V6 four-valves: a diesel with 2987 cc in two power levels of 190 and 224 bhp (ML 280 CDI and ML 320 CDI), a gasoline engine with 3498 cc and 272 bhp (ML 350), and the familiar V8 with three valves per cylinder, 4966 cc and 306 bhp (ML 500). The potent ML 63 AMG with 6208 cc and 510 bhp had to wait only until

Bei der M-Klasse der zweiten Generation, vorgestellt bei der Detroiter Show 2005, verlagert Mercedes den Spagat zwischen Off- und Onroad entschieden wieder in Richtung auf komfortables Reisen, Luxus, das Limousinenhafte à la S- oder R-Klasse. Dass sich ein solches Fahrzeug in rauem Gelände zu tummeln vermag wie ein Fisch in gebirgsklarem Quellwasser ist nicht mehr gefragt: Da fährt nämlich kaum jemand mehr hin.

Gleichwohl gibt's den ML fürs Grobe noch immer, aber nur durch den Erwerb eines aufpreispflichtigen Offroad-Pro-Pakets. Liebevoll hineingeschnürt sind ein Zweistufen-Verteilergetriebe mit Low-Range-Untersetzung, eine manuell oder automatisch zuschaltbare Differentialsperre (100 Prozent) zwischen Vorder- und Hinterachse und an der Hinterachse sowie die speziell fürs Gelände eingerichtete Luftfederung Airmatic, welche die Bodenfreiheit um 110 bis zu 291 mm und die Wat-Tiefe bis zu 600 mm anhebt. Der Standard-ML für die Straße hingegen schützt sich und seine Insassen gegen Unbill von unten mittels konventioneller Schraubenfedern und verteilt die Kraft seiner Antriebsquelle wie der Vorgänger durch ein Mittendifferential im Normalfall je zur Hälfte auf die Achsen. Auch die Aufhängung ist neu: vorn an hoch angeordneten Dreiecks-Querlenkern aus Aluminium, hinten an einer Vierlenkerachse.

Auf den Komfort-Anspruch des Neuen sind nicht zuletzt seine Maße zugeschnitten: mit 4780 mm 150 mm länger als das Vorgängermodell, mit 1911 mm nun 71 mm breiter, dafür mit 1815 mm inklusive Dachreling fünf Millimeter niedriger. Dass der Radstand um 95 auf 2915 mm zugelegt hat, kommt vor allem den Passagieren in der zweiten Reihe zugute, wo der Abstand zu den Vordersitzen um 35 mm gewachsen ist. Dahinter tut sich ein kolossaler Kofferraum auf, der zwischen 550 und 2050 Liter schluckt, auf einer Ladefläche, die sich dank herausnehmbarer Sitzkissen im Fond nun topfeben präsentiert. Der geduckte Auftritt des ML gehorcht zugleich einem anderen Parameter: Er soll sportlicher daherkommen, wozu weitere Elemente wie seine flache Frontscheibe, die markant üppig ausgewölbten Radhäuser und die nach hinten ansteigende Schulterlinie ihr Scherflein beisteuern.

Wie gewohnt setzt der neue Nobel-SUV Maßstäbe hinsichtlich aktiver und passiver Sicherheit, etwa mit dem optionalen prophylaktisch wirkenden Schutzsystem Pre-Safe. Es erkennt im Zusammenwirken mit ABS, Bremsassistent und ESP potentielle Unfall-Situationen, strafft die Gurte, bringt den Beifahrersitz in eine optimale Position und schließt notfalls sogar das Schiebedach. Unbedingt ein Komfort-Attribut: die serienmäßige Automatik, welche die sieben Gänge butterweich mit kaum spürbaren Übergängen einlegt, elektronisch bedient mittels eines lenkradnahen Wählhebels. Im Bunde steht sie anfangs mit vier Triebwerken, drei davon neue V6-Vierventiler: ein Selbstzünder mit 2987 cm³ in zwei Leistungsstufen von 190 und 224 PS (ML 280 CDI und ML 320 CDI), ein Benziner mit 3498 cm³ und 272 PS (ML 350), dazu der bekannte

Avec la deuxième génération de la Classe M présentée lors du salon automobile de Détroit en 2005, Mercedes transpose clairement le grand écart entre le tout-terrain et la routière à nouveau dans la direction des voyages confortables, du luxe, des berlines de style Classes S ou R. Que sur un terrain accidenté, un tel véhicule puisse s'ébattre comme un poisson dans les eaux vives des montagnes n'est plus demandé: après tout, presque plus personne n'y va.

Pourtant la ML est toujours bon pour tout, mais seulement grâce à l'achat d'une option: le pack Offroad-Pro comprenant une boîte transfert à deux étages avec une assistance Low-Range, un blocage de différentiel manuel ou automatique (100 %) entre le train avant et le pont arrière et sur ce dernier également la suspension pneumatique Airmatic spécialement conçue pour les tout-terrains, qui permet une garde au sol allant de 100 à 291 mm et une guéabilité de 600 mm. En revanche, la ML standard pour la route se défend, et par conséquent protège ses passagers, contre les irrégularités du terrain à l'aide de ressorts hélicoïdaux. Comme ses prédécesseurs, dans des conditions normales il distribue sa force motrice à l'aide d'un différentiel central répartissant celle-ci à parts égales sur chaque essieu. La suspension est également nouvelle: à l'avant des triangles transversaux superposés en aluminium, à l'arrière un essieu à quadruple bras.

Les dimensions du dernier-né ont été conçues pour favoriser le confort: une longueur de 4780 mm, 150 mm de plus que son prédécesseur, largeur de 1911 mm, soit 71 mm de plus mais une hauteur de seulement 1815 mm, y compris les barres de toit, soit cinq millimètres de moins. L'empattement ayant augmenté de 95 mm pour atteindre 2915 mm, cela est surtout appréciable pour les passagers arrière car la distance avec les sièges avant a augmenté de 35 mm. Derrière se trouve un immense coffre pouvant absorber 550 à 2050 litres sur une surface de chargement entièrement plane grâce aux sièges arrière amovibles. La forme compacte de la ML obéit également à un autre paramètre: elle devait paraître plus sportive. Son pare-brise plat, ses passages de roue exagérément bombés et ses lignes qui remontent à l'arrière y contribuent aussi.

Comme d'habitude, le nouveau SUV de luxe mise sur les mesures de sécurité active et passive, par exemple avec le système optionnel de sécurité Pre-Safe qui agit de façon préventive. En agissant simultanément avec l'ABS, l'assistance au freinage et l'ESP, il reconnaît les éventuelles situations d'accident et tend les ceintures de sécurité, relève le siège du passager avant dans une position optimale et ferme même le toit ouvrant si nécessaire. Élément indispensable au confort, la boîte automatique de série passe les sept rapports de manière à peine perceptibles. Elle est commandée électroniquement avec un levier de sélection intégré au volant. Cette gamme existait au début en quatre motorisations, dont trois équipées du nouveau V6 quatre soupapes: un allumage par compression pour 2987 cm³ en deux puissances 190 et 224 ch (ML 280 CDI et ML 320 CDI),

Mercedes-Benz ML 2005

Mercedes-Benz ML 320 CDI 2008

the 2005 Frankfurt Show, while the ML 420 CDI joined the diesel fraternity a year later: its v8 with 3996 cc and 306 bhp was likewise not stingy. This applied *a fortiori* to the 388 bhp produced by the 5461 cc of the ML 500 in 2007— the name was preserved and the 10th anniversary of the ML family celebrated with a special-type Edition 10. At the end of April 2008, it emerged afresh from the Mercedes fountain of youth after a facelift, with remodeled bumpers and a larger radiator, positioned lower down.

v8 mit drei Ventilen je Zylinder, 4966 cm³ und 306 PS (ML 500). Nur bis zur IAA 2005 lässt der potente ML 63 AMG mit 6208 cm³ und 510 PS auf sich warten, während der Diesel-Fraternität ein Jahr später der ML 420 CDI beitritt, dessen v8 mit 3996 cm³ und 306 PS sich ebenfalls nicht lumpen lässt. Das gilt erst recht für die 388 PS, geboren aus 5461 cm³ des ML 500 von 2007 – den Namen behält man bei und feiert im selben Jahr mit dem Sonder-Typ Edition 10 das zehnjährige Bestehen der ML-Familie. Ende April 2008 taucht sie modellgepflegt aus dem Mercedes-Jungbrunnen wieder auf mit überarbeiteten Stoßfängern und einem größeren und tiefer angesetzten Kühlergrill.

une essence de 3498 cm³ et 272 ch (ML 350), plus le célèbre v8 avec trois soupapes par cylindre, 4966 cm³ et 306 ch (ML 500). Seul le viril ML 63 AMG de 6208 cm³ et 510 ch se fit attendre jusqu'au salon automobile de Francfort de 2005 alors que son frère diesel est apparu un an après le ML 420 CDI. Son v8 de 3996 cm³ et 306 ch fait bien les choses. C'est particulièrement vrai pour les 388 ch issus des 5461 cm³ de la ML 500 de 2007. On a conservé le nom et fêté la même année avec la série limitée Édition 10 les dix ans d'existence de la famille ML. Fin avril 2008, elle est sortie de la fontaine de jouvence de Mercedes avec des pare-chocs retouchés et une calandre placée plus bas.

Following the exit by the former market leader, the 2005 ML is positioning itself as the head of the SUV family. Its wider track benefits both the sporty look and its handling characteristics. The 320 CDI V6 diesel has little problem with the multipurpose giant.

Nachdem der ehemalige Marktführer abgetreten ist, wirft sich der ML Jahrgang 2005 zum neuen Oberhaupt der SUV-Familie auf. Von seiner breiteren Spur profitieren sowohl die sportive Optik als auch sein Fahrverhalten. Der V6-Diesel des 320 CDI hat mit dem Vielzweck-Trumm wenig Mühe.

Après que l'ancien leader du marché eut été retiré, la ML millésime 2005 est devenue le nouveau chef de la famille SUV. Tant les blocs optiques que sa tenue de route profitent de sa voie plus large. Le V6 diesel de la 320 CDI est plutôt à l'aise avec ce solide polyvalent.

Mercedes-Benz ML 2005

Presented, with some deliberation, at the January 2006 show in the Motor City of Detroit, the Mercedes GL-Class proved the truism that all size is relative. Promoting it as a "premium full-size sport utility vehicle," strategists of the firm gave the GL a market position while forcing the seemingly irreconcilable together in five words. The super-SUV was a macho vehicle in XXL format, built in the Tuscaloosa branch of Mercedes and, so it was said, 80 percent of the sales were aimed at the market in America—the land of opportunity.

In fact, when placed alongside the ML, itself a far from ramshackle piece of work that had been reissued the year before, the latter positively faded into insignificance in visual terms. For Big Brother was a bigger car: at 6 ft 10 in, it had a 6-in longer wheelbase and total length of 16 ft 8 in (12 in longer), a width of 6 ft 3 in (⅜ in wider) and a height of 6 feet (one inch higher). The new arrival had more rough edges and a classic side view that dispensed with the fashionably curved C-pillar. Before long, the off-roader G presented its compliments; since 1979 it had figured in the portfolio as the apotheosis of the right angle, and a paragon of good, honest cross-country driving.

The GL, however, intended to provide up to seven people with a comfortable ride, together with up to 81.2 cu.ft of moveable property. The third row of seats, an optional extra in Europe and standard in North America, could be electrically folded down at the push of a button and then modestly fitted away into a huge smooth-surfaced luggage compartment. The U.S. equipment featured, as standard, screens in the rear, on the headrests. An efficient air-conditioning system provided a temperate and comfortable atmosphere in the rear seats, through air diffusers in the car roof.

As a mark of respect, the European version of the GL was launched in the Old Continent a little later. It found itself at odds with many a customary garage, but it did make a splash with its fine technology, including a transfer gearbox with cross-country ratios and a 100-percent lock in the central differential and rear axle. The reference 4matic on the rear, as with all Mercedes four-wheel drive vehicles, made its presence felt. The tauter Airmatic air suspension, included in the basic package, produced amazing results. It not only provided excellent and comfortable suspension, but also had another attribute to offer: the ground clearance of the GL could be raised via a rotary knob from 7¾ in to 12 in, giving 2 ft of fording depth. With sufficient tire grip, the theoretical climb capability increased to 45 degrees. Lateral tilt occurred in the GL only from an angle of 35 degrees.

Especially suitable for the temperament of the light-footed 2.5-tonner was the eight-cylinder turbodiesel of the GL 420 CDI version with 3996 cc, yielding an earthy 306 bhp at 3600 rpm, and a beefy torque of 516 lb-ft at 2200 rpm. No more diesel noise: the relaxed and smooth running resulted not least from the generally low rev level. Next to it, in congenial company, stood the seven-speed

Im Januar 2006 mit Bedacht präsentiert auf der Auto Show in der US-Motor-City Detroit belegt die Mercedes GL-Klasse die Binsenweisheit, alle Größe sei relativ. Als *Premium Fullsize Sport Utility Vehicle* haben die Strategen der Marke den GL positioniert und dabei das scheinbar Unvereinbare in fünf Vokabeln zusammengezwängt. Der Super-SUV ist ein Macho-Mobil im XXL-Format, in der Mercedes-Zweigstelle Tuscaloosa gebaut und, so heißt es, zu ungefähr 80 Prozent auch für den Markt im Lande der unbegrenzten Möglichkeiten bestimmt.

In der Tat: Seite an Seite mit dem keineswegs rachitischen ML, im Vorjahr neu aufgelegt, dampft der andere visuell regelrecht ein. Denn Big Brother bietet mit 3075 mm 160 mm mehr Radstand und insgesamt mit einer Länge von 5090 mm 310 mm, einer Breite von 1920 zehn Millimeter und seiner Höhe von 1840 mm stattliche 25 mm mehr Auto. Der Neue kommt statt mit gefälligen Rundungen mit mehr Ecken und Kanten daher und einer klassischen Seitenansicht, die auf die modisch geschwungene C-Säule verzichtet. Da lässt beinahe schon wieder der Offroader G grüßen, seit 1979 im Portfolio als Apotheose des rechten Winkels und Exponent rechtschaffener Geländigkeit.

Der GL indes möchte bis zu sieben Personen kommodes Reisen ermöglichen, in Begleitung von bis zu 2300 Litern beweglicher Habe. Die dritte Sitzreihe, Extra in der Europa- und Standard in der Ami-Version, lässt sich elektrisch falten und fügt sich dann demütig in ein riesiges glattflächiges Gepäckabteil. Die US-Ausstattung sieht serienmäßig Bildschirmchen hinten in den Kopfstützen vor. Auf ihnen lässt sich dann die zur Landschaft passende John-Wayne-DVD oder ein Road Movie genießen. Eine effiziente Klimaanlage fördert unterdessen durch Ausströmer im Wagenhimmel wohl temperiertes Behagen in den Fond.

Der GL für den Alten Kontinent hingegen, mit leichtem zeitlichem Respektabstand in den europäischen Markt eingespeist und hierzulande sicher auf Kriegsfuß mit so mancher handelsüblichen Garage, glänzt eher durch feine Technik, ein Verteilergetriebe mit Geländeübersetzung zum Beispiel mit hundertprozentiger Sperre im Zentraldifferential und in der Hinterachse. Der Hinweis 4matic am Heck weist wie bei allen Mercedes-Allradlern auf seine Anwesenheit hin. Straffer abgestimmt, bewirkt die im Basispaket enthaltene Luftfederung Airmatic Erstaunliches. Sie sorgt nicht nur für exzellenten Federungskomfort, sondern hat auch abseits gebahnter Straßen einiges zu bieten. Die Bodenfreiheit des GL kann per Drehknopf von 197 mm bis zu 307 mm angehoben werden, was für 600 mm Wattiefe gut ist. Bei genügend Reifengrip beläuft sich die theoretische Steigfähigkeit auf 45 Grad. Seitlich abkippen wird der GL erst ab einem Winkel von 35 Grad.

Besonders gut zum Naturell des leichtfüßigen 2,5-Tonners passt der Achtzylinder-Turbodiesel der Version GL 420 CDI mit 3996 cm³, 306 rustikalen PS bei 3600/min und dem bulligen Drehmoment von 700 Nm

Présentée de façon avisée à l'occasion du Salon de l'automobile de Détroit, la ville américaine de l'automobile, la Mercedes Classe GL justifi a une vérité de La Palisse: toutes les tailles sont relatives. En tant que *Premium Full Size Sport Utility Vehicle* (gros véhicule utilitaire sportif haut de gamme), les stratèges de la marque ont positionné la Classe GL et ont, en cinq mots, réussi à réunir ce qui semblait incompatible. Le super SUV, tout-terrain de loisir, est un véhicule de macho format XXL fabriqué dans la filiale Mercedes de Tuscaloosa. Selon Mercedes, il est destiné à 80 % au marché des États-Unis.

En fait, lorsqu'il se trouve à côté de la Classe ML pourtant pas rachitique, présentée l'année précédente, cette dernière disparaît purement et simplement. Car avec 3075 mm, «Big Brother» offre 160 mm d'empattement en plus. Il procure globalement plus d'espace en raison de sa longueur de 5090 mm, soit 310 mm supplémentaires, de sa largeur de 1920 mm, donc 10 mm de plus, et une hauteur de 1840 mm, gagnant ainsi 25 mm. Ces deux classes ne sont pas sans similitudes mais la nouvelle présente plus d'angles et d'arêtes à la place des rondeurs habituelles et une vue de côté classique, plus angulaire, a renoncé aux formes galbées de la Classe C. Au catalogue depuis 1979, le tout-terrain G tira bientôt sa révérence après avoir représenté l'apothéose de l'angle droit.

La GL permet le transport confortable de sept personnes, d'un chargement pouvant atteindre 2300 litres. La troisième rangée de sièges, en option dans la version européenne et standard dans la version américaine, se replie à l'aide d'un mécanisme électrique et s'encastre facilement dans un compartiment à bagages plat. L'aménagement américain prévoit à l'arrière, de série, des écrans installés dans les appuis-tête. Un système de climatisation efficace permet, grâce à l'arrivée d'air situé dans le plafond du véhicule, d'obtenir une température tempérée au fond.

La GL destinée au vieux continent est arrivée sur le marché européen avec un léger décalage et rencontre certainement des problèmes avec les dimensions des garages habituellement utilisés. Elle brille surtout par sa technique de pointe, une boîte de transfert avec mode tout-terrain équipée, par exemple, d'un blocage total de différentiel sur la boîte et le pont arrière. Comme pour toutes les Mercedes quatre roues motrices, l'indication 4matic à l'arrière signale la présence de ce système. Réglée de façon rigoureuse, la suspension pneumatique Airmatic, incluse dans la version de base, est d'une surprenante effi cacité. Elle n'offre pas seulement une suspension au confort exceptionnel mais également des avantages sur les petits chemins. La garde au sol de la GL peut passer de 197 mm à 307 mm, ce qui permet une guéabilité de 600 mm. Avec une adhérence suffisante des pneus, la capacité en pente est théoriquement de 45 degrés. La GL ne versera sur le côté qu'à partir d'un angle de 35 degrés.

Le turbo diesel huit cylindres de la version GL 420 CDI – 3996 cm³, 306 ch à 3600 tr/min et un puissant couple moteur de 700 Nm à 2200 tr/min – convient parfaitement

Mercedes-Benz GL   2006

Mercedes-Benz GL 320 CDI 2008

automatic, whose activity was hardly perceptible. It was standard equipment and blended beautifully with the other three engines available: the two v8 petrol engines in the GL 450 (4663 cc, 340 bhp) and in the GL 500 (5461 cc, 388 bhp) and a further diesel variant, the GL 320 CDI (2987 cc, 224 bhp). At the Detroit Show in 2007, the Concept Car Vision GL 420 Bluetec was introduced: its 290 bhp v8 went 24 miles to the gallon of diesel and thus met the strict U.S. ULEV emissions standards.

bei 2200/min. Vom Selbstzünder ist nichts mehr zu hören. Kongenial zur Seite steht ihm dabei die Siebengang-Automatik, deren Tätigkeit man kaum wahrnimmt, prächtig abgestimmt auch auf die beiden v8-Benziner im GL 450 (4663 cm³, 340 PS) und im GL 500 (5461 cm³, 388 PS) sowie eine weiteren Diesel-Variante, dem GL 320 CDI (2987 cm³, 224 PS). Auf der Detroiter Schau 2007 wird das Concept Car Vision GL 420 Bluetec vorgestellt, dessen 290 PS starker v8 nur 9,8 Liter Dieselöl pro 100 Kilometer schluckt und die strenge US-Abgasnorm ULEV erfüllt.

à la nature de cet agile 2,5 tonnes. On n'entend plus parler d'allumage par régime. La boîte automatique à sept rapports le soutient de façon extrêmement efficace et s'harmonise également de façon parfaite avec les trois autres motorisations proposées: les deux moteurs v8 à essence de la GL 450 (4663 cm³, 340 ch) et la GL 500 (5461 cm³, 388 ch) ainsi qu'une autre variante diesel, la GL 320 CDI (2987 cm³, 224 ch). Le *concept car* Vision GL 420 Bluetec a été présenté à l'occasion du salon de Détroit 2007. Les 290 ch de son moteur v8 ne consomment que 9,8 litres de gasoil aux 100 km. Il satisfait la très stricte loi américaine ULEV sur les gaz d'échappement.

The visual orientation of the four-wheel drive GL is the contemporary spatial wonder ML. The hatchback accommodates a third row with additional single fold-up seats and—either way—the space for a huge quantity of luggage.

Visuell orientiert sich der Allradler GL am zeitgenössischen Raumwunder ML. Im Steilheck verbergen sich eine dritte Reihe mit zusätzlichen klappbaren Einzelsitzen und – in jedem Falle – das Volumen für eine enorme Menge Gepäck.

L'apparence du tout terrain GL est moins proche de la Classe G que de la ML, contemporaine à l'espace miraculeux. Dans le coffre se cachent une troisième rangée de sièges individuels supplémentaires rabattables et, dans tous les cas, un très grand volume pour les bagages.

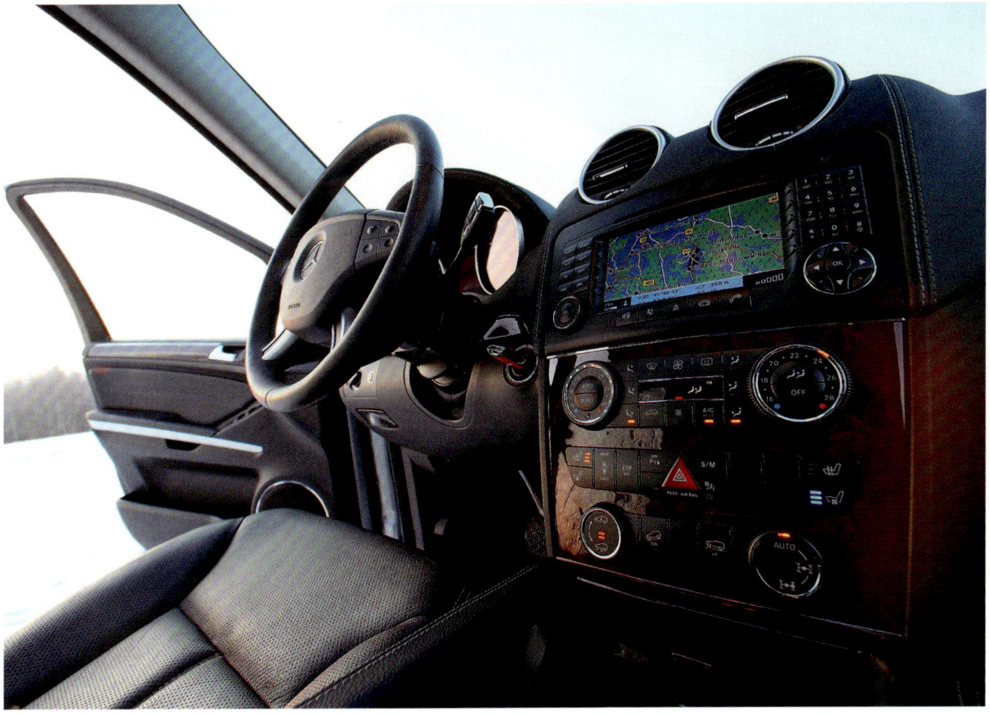

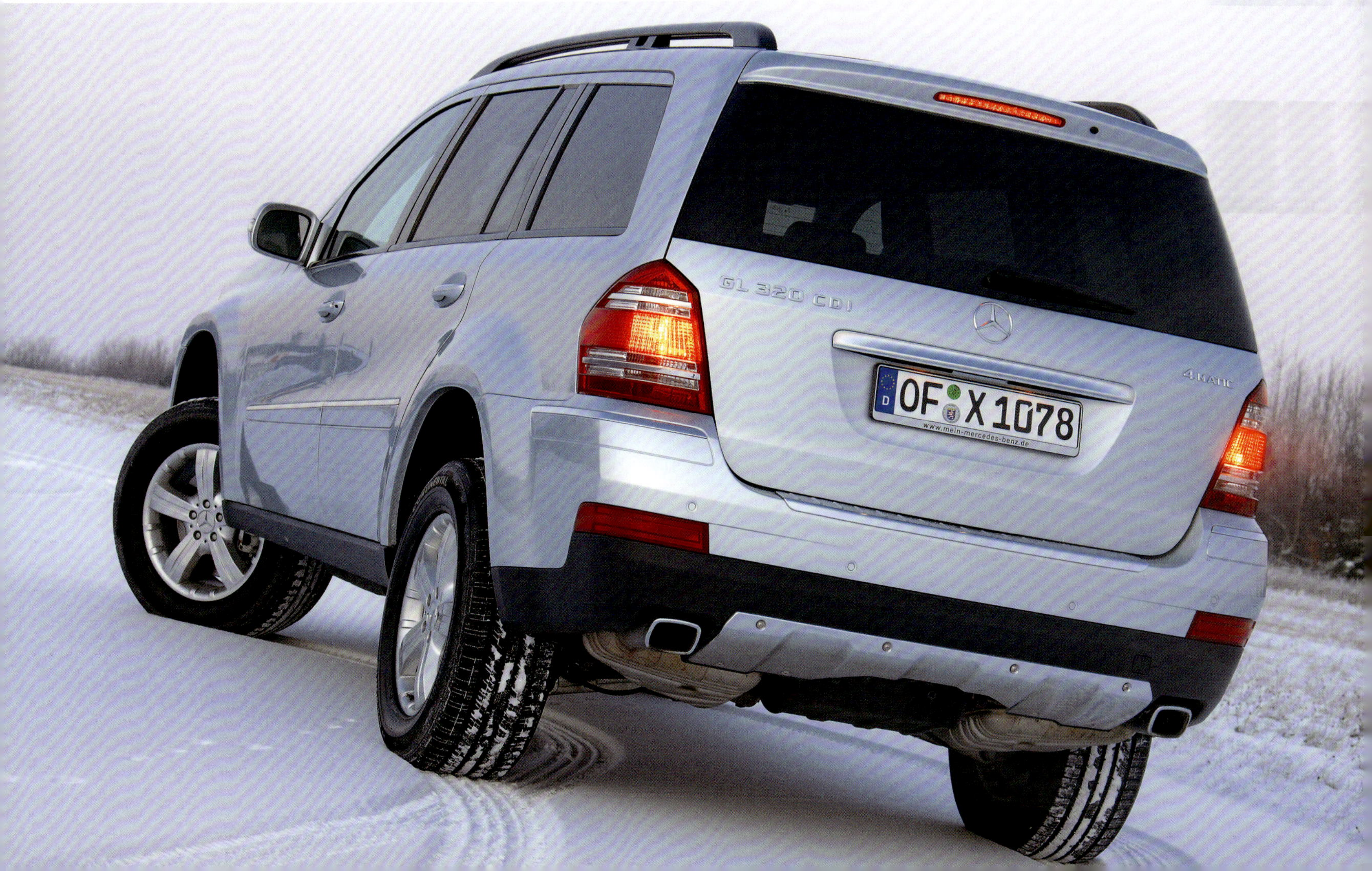
GL 320 CDI
4MATIC
OF X 1078
www.mein-mercedes-benz.de

A selected few eye witnesses were able to discover the CL "cultural event" for the first time in June 2006 at the Daimler garrison in Untertürkheim, and the general public at the Paris Motor Show on 29 September of that year.

Still, the luxury habit had been integral to the big coupés from the Mercedes works in Stuttgart since the fifties, except that sportiness was now factored into the equation as well, as inherent in the generic name. The recipe was simple and basically remained the same: three inches had been cut from the wheelbase of the donor S-Class, two doors eliminated, and, on the suitably modified chassis, a superstructure of pleasing fluidity and virile beauty created. The majestic appearance of the CL was more than adequately refined with an interior boasting all the blessings of civilization. With the snappy swing of its roof line, the continuous side window surfaces, and the generous use of fine wood, leather, and chrome metal trim, the new car fitted seamlessly into the gallery of its ancestors. Since the 2.4-short-ton vehicle reached an impressive length of just over 16 ft 5 in, its coupé configuration was not necessarily achieved at the expense of the occupants in the rear seat.

Throughout, the driver has small electronic aids to hand, or within easy reach. With a gentle purr the doors close by themselves, should they have been negligently left ajar. The Pre-Safe protection system, designed to prevent accidents through a three-fold radar (fitted as standard), as well as the Intelligent Light System, the operating system COMAND with its central push-button control dial, nano-paint and adaptive brake light, automatically decelerate at 40 percent of potential braking power should the driver start heading toward an obstacle without taking evasive action. Optional (though not cheap) is the radar-based parking guidance system, which provides assistance when maneuvering into parking spaces, and constitutes a vigilant sensory system at speeds of up to 25 mph.

The sporting component of the CL is increased by its amazingly light-footed agility. This is due not least to its newly tuned ABC (Active Body Control) suspension, based on coil springs, and even more tautly configured than in the sedan. Unwanted body movements are permanently blocked. On the other hand there is the strength of its engine, which is sublime beyond doubt: as mighty as King Kong, yet light as a cat's paw, a V8 with 5461 cc and 388 bhp in the CL 500 and a V12 twin-turbo in the CL 600. Its 5513 cc releases 517 bhp and a powerful torque of 612 lb-ft at 1900 rpm, sounding like an angry speedboat disappearing into the distance in a cloud of spray.

Those who wish to inflict this on such a superb car, let alone on themselves and their innocent passengers, can reach 62 mph in 5.4 or 4.6 seconds, via five-speed automatic transmission in the twelve-cylinder and seven-stage in the eight-cylinder respectively.

Vom Kulturereignis CL konnten sich erstmalig handverlesene Augenzeugen im Juni 2006 in der Daimler-Garnison Untertürkheim und die interessierte Allgemeinheit beim Pariser Autosalon im September jenes Jahres einen Eindruck verschaffen.

Der luxuriöse Habitus ist den großen Coupés aus Stuttgart gleichwohl seit den fünfziger Jahren ins Stammbuch geschrieben, nur dass am Ende auch noch die Sportlichkeit hinzukommt, die in der Gattungsbezeichnung eigentlich ja angelegt ist. Die Rezeptur ist ganz einfach und bleibt grundsätzlich die gleiche: Man tranchiert aus dem Radstand des Spenders S-Klasse 80 Millimeter heraus, streicht zwei Türen und errichtet über dem angemessen modifizierten Fahrwerk einen Aufbau von gefälliger Flüssigkeit und viriler Schönheit. Adäquat unterfüttert wird der majestätische Auftritt des CL von einer Inneneinrichtung mit allen Segnungen der Auto-Zivilisation. Mit dem schmissigen Schwung seiner Dachlinie, den durchgehenden seitlichen Fensterflächen sowie der großzügigen Verwendung von Edelholz, Leder und verchromtem Metall fügt sich der Neue nahtlos in die Galerie seiner Ahnen ein. Da der 2,2-Tonner mit der stattlichen Länge von knapp über fünf Metern aufwartet, geht sein Coupé-Layout im Übrigen nicht unbedingt auf Kosten der Insassen im zweiten Glied.

Überall gehen dem Chauffeur elektronische Helferlein zur Hand oder greifen ihm unter die Arme: Mit sanftem Schnurren ziehen sich etwa die Türen von selber ins Schloss, wenn sie nur nachlässig angelehnt wurden. Die prophylaktisch via Dreifach-Radar wirkende Schutzvorkehrung Pre-Safe, hier serienmäßig wie das Intelligent Light System, das Bediensystem COMAND mit seinem zentralen Dreh-Drück-Schiebesteller, Nanolack und das adaptive Bremslicht, verzögert selbsttätig mit 40 Prozent der potentiellen Bremskraft, sobald sich der Fahrer auf ein Hindernis zubewegt, ohne zu reagieren. Optional und nicht eben billig: die radargestützte Parkführung, die Hilfestellung leistet beim Einfädeln in Parklücken, die eine wachsame Sensorik beim Vorbeifahren bis zu 40 Stundenkilometern ausmacht.

Die sportliche Komponente wächst dem CL zum einen durch seine verblüffend leichtfüßige Behändigkeit zu. Zu danken ist diese nicht zuletzt dem auf einer Stahlfederung basierenden und neu abgestimmten ABC (Active Body Control)-Fahrwerk, noch straffer konfiguriert als in der Limousine. Unerwünschte Karosseriebewegungen werden nachhaltig unterbunden. Zum anderen ist da die über jeden Zweifel erhabene, auf Katzenpfötchen daherkommende Bullenstärke seiner Triebwerke, eines V8 mit 5461 cm³ und 388 PS im CL 500 oder eines Biturbo-V12 im CL 600. Dessen 5513 cm³ setzen 517 PS und das mächtige Drehmoment von 830 Newtonmetern bei 1900/min frei, im Zorn mit dem Sound eines am Horizont dahingischtenden Sportboots.

Wer das dem schönen Auto, sich selbst und arglosen Mitreisenden antun möchte, ist bei Tempo 100

Les premiers témoins oculaires, triés sur le volet, ont découvert ce modèle en juin 2006 dans le bastion de Daimler à Untertürkheim et le public intéressé du Salon de l'automobile de Paris, en septembre de la même année.

Le luxueux aspect extérieur des gros coupés est inscrit dans le livret de famille depuis les années 1950, seule vient s'ajouter finalement la sportivité, qui est tout de même inscrite dans le nom. La recette est toute simple et reste globalement la même: on retire 80 mm à l'empattement de la Classe S, inspiratrice du modèle, on enlève deux portes et on érige autour du véhicule ainsi modifié une carrosserie d'une fluidité agréable et d'une beauté virile. La majestueuse entrée en scène de la CL est doublée de façon adéquate d'un aménagement intérieur doté de tous les bienfaits de la civilisation automobile. Avec l'élan entraînant de ses lignes, les surfaces vitrées ininterrompues sur les côtés ainsi qu'une utilisation généreuse de bois précieux, de cuir et de métaux chromés, la nouvelle s'intègre sans problème dans la galerie de ses ancêtres. Car le véhicule de 2,2 tonnes à la longueur imposante d'un peu plus de cinq mètres ne sacrifie pas obligatoirement son aspect coupé aux dépens des passagers arrière.

Les lutins électroniques sont partout à portée de main ou sous le bras du conducteur: les portières se ferment toutes seules avec un léger ronronnement lorsqu'elles ont été laissées entrebâillées par négligence. Le système de mesures préventives Pre-Safe fonctionnant grâce à trois radars est ici de série; il ralentit tout seul à 40 % du potentiel de freinage dès que le conducteur avance vers un obstacle sans réagir. De série également, le système d'éclairage Intelligent Light System, le système multimédia COMAND avec son bouton-poussoir rotatif central, le vernis ultra-résistant et les feux de stop adaptatifs. En option et pas vraiment donné: le guidage au stationnement qui aide à s'insérer dans une place de parking et qui à l'aide de senseurs, détecte une place de stationnement lorsqu'on passe devant à moins de 40 km/h.

D'une part, l'époustouflante agilité de la CL lui donne un aspect sportif. Cela est principalement dû au système de train de roulement actif ABC (Active Body Control) dernière génération basé sur une suspension en acier dont la configuration est encore plus rigoureuse que pour une berline. D'autre part, sa motorisation, dont la puissance ne fait aucun doute, s'approche sur des pattes de velours: un V8 de 5461 cm³ et 388 ch pour la CL 500; un biturbo V12 pour la CL 600. Ses 5513 cm³ libèrent 517 ch et un puissant couple de 830 Nm à 1900 tr/min; lorsqu'il vrombit, il fait le bruit d'un hors-bord écumant à l'horizon. Celui qui veut se faire plaisir ou charmer ses passagers peut atteindre les 100 km/h en respectivement 5,4 et 4,6 secondes avec pour complice une boîte automatique cinq vitesses pour le douze cylindres et sept rapports pour le huit cylindres. Pour les insatiables les deux versions sport, la CL 63 AMG (6208 cm³, 525 ch) et la CL 65 AMG (5980 cm³, 612 ch) peuvent faire un peu mieux.

Mercedes-Benz CL   2006

Mercedes-Benz CL 500 2008

The insatiable can get even more, in the way of two corresponding power variants, the CL 63 AMG (6208 cc, 525 bhp) and the CL 65 AMG (5980 cc, 612 bhp).

At the Geneva Motor Show in 2008, the CL range was unveiled in a somewhat updated form, enhanced with all-wheel drive and air suspension for the entry model CL 500 and with 10 percent reduced fuel consumption. Its consumption habits, however, are still on the liberal side.

in 5,4 beziehungsweise 4,6 Sekunden angelangt, mit einer Fünfgang-Automatik beim Zwölfzylinder und einem Sieben-Stufen-Automaten beim Achtzylinder als Helfershelfer.

Noch etwas besser können es die beiden entsprechenden Power-Varianten für die Nimmersatten, der CL 63 AMG (6208 cm³, 525 PS) und der CL 65 AMG (5980 cm³, 612 PS).

Auf der Genfer Show 2008 bietet sich die CL-Baureihe milde aktualisiert dar, bereichert um Allradantrieb und Luftfederung für das Einstiegsmodell CL 500 und mit um zehn Prozent reduziertem Verbrauch.

Lors du Salon de l'automobile de Genève en 2008, la gamme CL a été présentée légèrement modernisée, enrichie d'une traction intégrale et d'une suspension pneumatique pour le modèle d'entrée de gamme, la CL 500, et une consommation diminuée de 10 %.

CL customers are not looking for experiments. Hence it literally exudes a classic profile and sense of tradition. The attractive fittings are not all that is based on the style of the S-Class. The excellent finish of the big Mercedes coupé is omnipresent.

CL-Käufer wollen sich auf keine Experimente einlassen. Deshalb atmen seine Linien förmlich Klassik und Traditionsbewusstsein. Am Stil der S-Klasse orientieren sich nicht zuletzt die schönen Armaturen. Überall präsent: das exzellente Finish des großen Mercedes-Coupés.

Les acquéreurs de CL ne veulent pas s'aventurer dans de nouvelles expériences. C'est pourquoi les lignes de ce modèle respirent le classicisme formel et la tradition. Les belles armatures s'inspirent beaucoup du style de la Classe S. Les excellentes finitions du gros coupé Mercedes sont partout présentes.

Mercedes-Benz CL   2006

With the third generation C-Class, first revealed to the press on 18 January 2007 in the Mercedes museum in Stuttgart and to the rest of the world in March at the Geneva Motor Show, the brand soared to a pinnacle of perfection. No wonder: its goal was nothing less than the title of bestseller in the program. Since the launch of the series in 2000, sales of over two million units have been achieved worldwide, inclusive of the T variant, the latest version of which went on sale in December 2007.

The third edition is in every way handsomer, larger, more technically sophisticated, more imposing, safer, and usually more powerful than the previous generation. Its claim to sit a few rungs higher in the in-house hierarchy is underpinned by echoes of the s-Class, such as the chubby wheel housings on display. With the Mercedes star inlaid into the grille, as in the coupés and its SL siblings, the Avantgarde version immediately produces a strong visual contrast with the entry-level Classic version and the refined fittings of the Elegance, thus targeting a younger and sportier-minded clientele. The new kind of C-type is differentiated from its predecessor by much larger air intakes, the significantly more aggressive grille, a more streamlined form with a markedly clearer lateral line, a move away from all-round protection strips, trapezoidal headlamps, and larger exterior mirrors and turn signals. The higher hood, a legal requirement, is easier on pedestrians in the event of an accident.

The new size manifests primarily in the 1½-in wider track, making entry easier, and 1¾-in increase in the wheelbase to nine feet, to the delight of rear-seat passengers. The inviting interior, both tasteful and lovely, now includes three round instruments in the driver's field of vision, with a fold-back color display on the right for the control system COMAND III (optional extra). Another optional extra is the improved interpretive voice system Linguatronic II, capable of understanding complete sentences, now also with satnav, the accident-preventive PreSafe system or the Intelligent Light System.

Despite its conventional steel springs, the comfort of the suspension is exemplary, as is the handling of the most recent C-Class, which can again be improved by sports suspension (extra). Four-wheel drive is also on offer, always combined with the seven-speed automatic, an advantage for some of the higher-positioned C-types. Otherwise, automatic transmission with six speed levels or an automatic with five are available. In addition, as befits the much-touted general impact of the model, the customer can choose from a wide range of engines.

BlueEfficiency: this is the magic phrase for a package of measures to reduce fuel consumption. It includes, for example, overall lowering of ⅝ in, full cladding of the undercarriage in diesel models, partial coverage of the grille, sealing of joints around the headlights, tires

Mercedes-Benz C-Klasse 2007

Mercedes-Benz C 200 Kompressor 2008

with less rolling resistance, and weight reduction: for example, 42 lbs relative to 70 lbs in the case of a thinner windshield. The spirit of the new age is clearly blowing in the wind.

Diese umfassen zum Beispiel eine Tieferlegung um 15 mm, die vollständige Verkleidung des Unterbodens bei den Diesel-Modellen, eine Teilabdeckung der Kühlermaske, die Abdichtung von Trennfugen im Umfeld der Scheinwerfer, Reifen mit weniger Rollwiderstand und 19 beziehungsweise 32 Kilo weniger als Folge einer Schlankheitskur, etwa durch eine dünnere Windschutzscheibe. Da weht spürbar der Geist der neuen Zeit.

trouve de nombreux modèles à essence et à allumage par compression.

BlueEfficiency – telle est la formule magique pour une série de mesures réduisant la consommation, par exemple un abaissement de 15 mm, l'habillage du dessous de caisse pour les modèles diesel, un recouvrement partiel de la calandre du radiateur, le colmatage des joints à proximité des phares, des pneus avec moins de résistance au roulement et 19 à 32 kilos de moins suite à une cure d'amaigrissement, notamment à l'aide d'un pare-brise plus fin. Ici souffle nettement le vent d'une époque nouvelle.

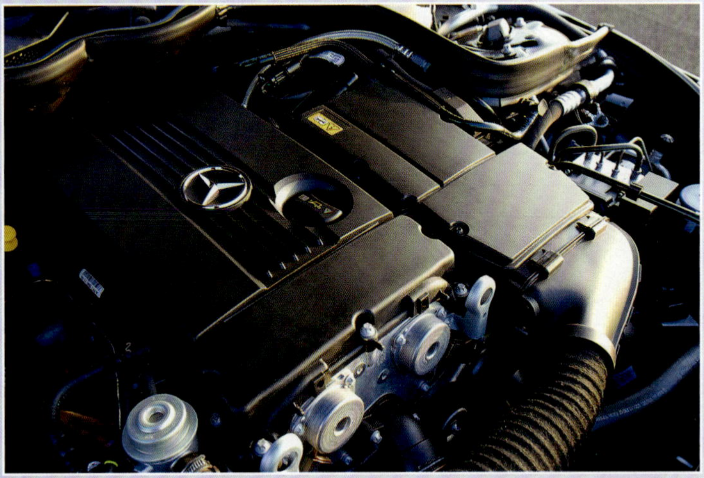

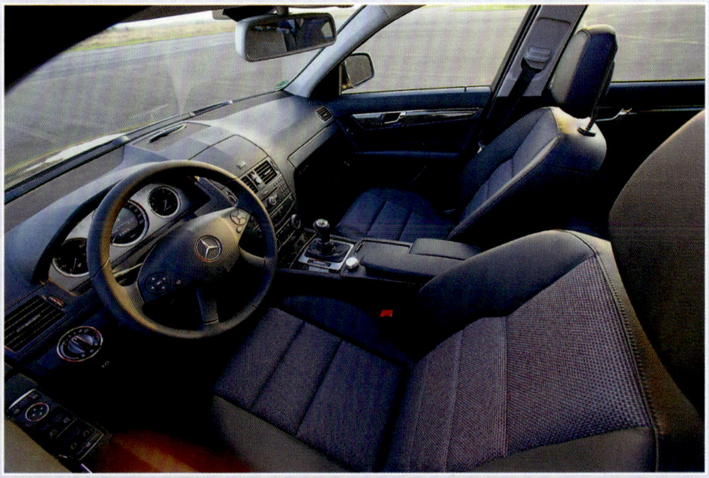

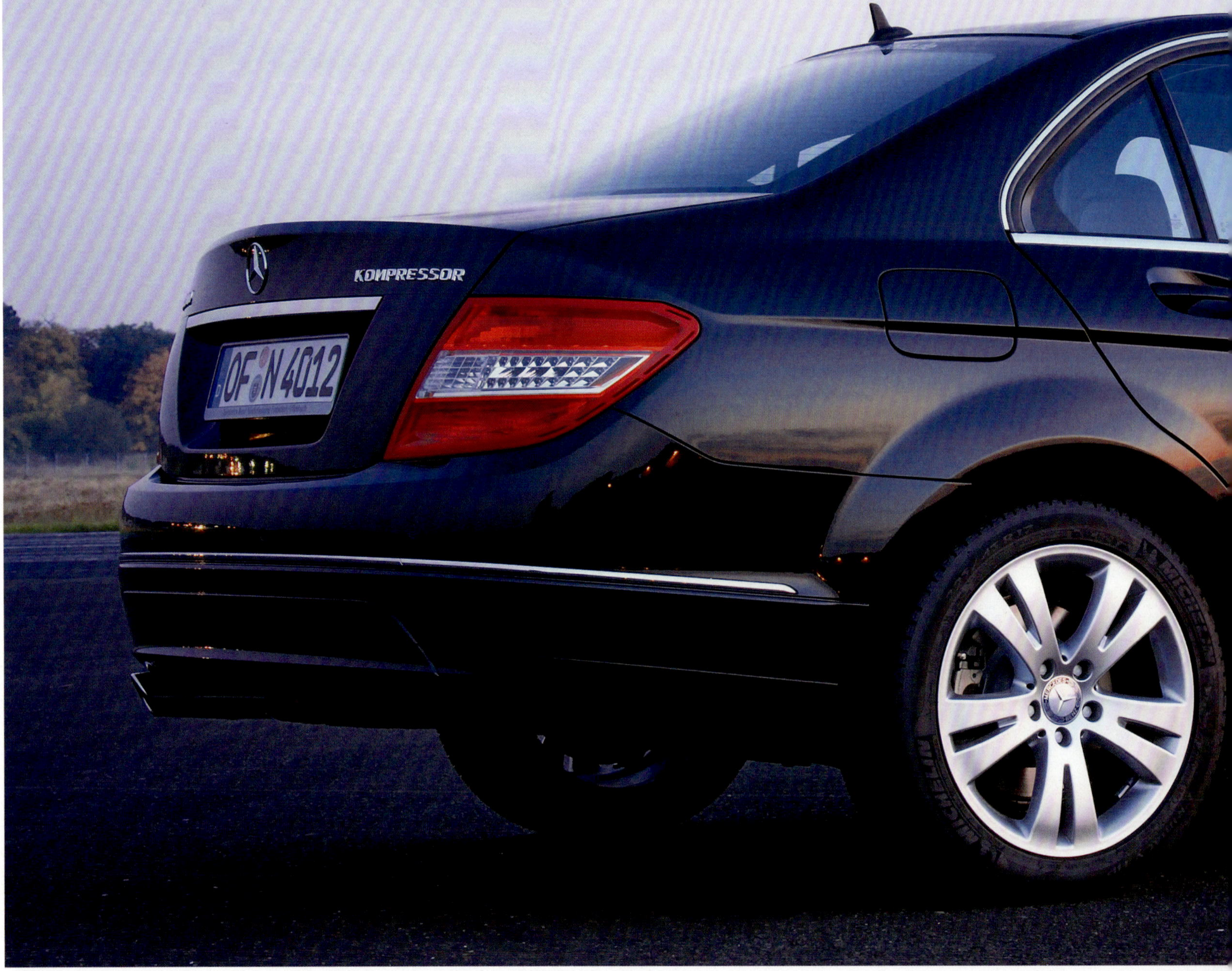
KOMPRESSOR
OF N 4012

The added value claims of the new C-Class are substantiated by elements taken from the majestic S series, such as the gently rounded fenders, as well as the large star centered in the new grille of the Avantgarde version—once a feature of the marque's sports models.

Den Mehr-Wert-Anspruch der neuen C-Klasse belegen Zitate aus der majestätischen Baureihe S wie die sanft und rundlich ausgestellten Kotflügel ebenso wie der mittig im neuen Grill eingelassene große Stern der Linie Avantgarde – einst Merkmal der sportlichen Modelle der Marke.

Des réminiscences de la majestueuse Classe S étayent les ambitions de la nouvelle Classe C : par exemple, les ailes douces et arrondies ainsi que la grosse étoile installée au centre de la nouvelle grille de calandre de la ligne Avantgarde, jadis un signe distinguant les modèles sportifs de la marque.

Before its premiere as Vision GLK at the Detroit Motor Show in January 2008, this model had already made a film appearance—a supporting role in the cult movie *Sex and the City*. So its edgy appearance had already made a subliminal impression, aroused curiosity, and spurred initial enquiries. Stylistically, it seemed to lean on its out-of-doors big brother, the G-Class. But the GLK (the K stands for "kompakt" because of its relatively short length of 14 ft 10 in) wanted more.

It was based on the T variant of the C-Class, near which it was also produced at the Bremen plant. As with the 4matic versions of its bourgeois siblings, its permanent four-wheel drive gets by without massive mechanical locks, both to economize on space and because the solution actually found weighs only about 88 pounds more. The power of the engine is divided among the four wheels through a multi-plate clutch in the central differential. It is usually distributed by the drive torque in a ratio of 45 to 55 percent between the front and rear axles. If conditions turn bad, it intervenes with a locking effect of 37 lb-ft. In support of this, the ESP also kicks in to keep wheel-spin under control.

All this has led to remarkable agility in the compact SUV, even in harsh and inhospitable terrain, in spite of only eight inches of ground clearance and the gently sloping angles of 23 degrees forward and 25 degrees backward. Having to cope with such difficulties, however, would be the exception rather than the rule. The GLK can halt if it wants to—like its distant relative the SLR on the prestigious terrain of speed, in the main country targeted for export, the U.S.A., with its rigid speed limits everywhere. Apart from a rough-and-ready categorization into *Freeside,* with huge 20-inch wheels and massive roof rails, and *Townside* with its smaller track, the character of the GLK can be adapted to circumstances by means of two switches in the bottom center of the cockpit. One of these is responsible for uphill and downhill assist and allows steep gradients to be attacked at between two and eleven mph. The other activates the off-road mode, permitting the gas pedal to respond less sensitively, extending the range of the gears, and attuning the ABS to slippery surfaces.

Proof that the GLK is also a pleasant companion and accomplice on normal roads can be found in the way its supple suspension operates with longer strokes than in the C-Class. The housing and work unit is reminiscent of the interior of the C-Class, though it has been given a more pleasing shape with its doughty cockpit with rotary push button on the center console and stand-alone instrumentation. As in the T-type, the large rear hatch gives access to a voluminous luggage compartment for at least 15.9 cu.ft, to a maximum of 54.7 cu.ft of load capacity. At its market launch in autumn 2008, the GLK came with three V6 engines, ensuring that the reality lived up to the expectations. They were all associated with a seven-speed automatic: a 3- and a 3.5-liter gasoline

Vor seiner Premiere als Vision GLK bei der Detroit Auto Show im Januar 2008 hat er bereits einen Filmauftritt, eine automobile Nebenrolle in dem Kino-Kultstreifen *Sex and the City*. So prägt sich sein kantiges Erscheinungsbild schon mal unterschwellig ein, erweckt Neugier und erste Nachfrage. Stilistisch scheint er sich an den großen, naturburschenhaften Bruder G-Klasse anzulehnen. Aber der GLK (das K steht für kompakt wegen seiner relativen Kürze von 4520 mm) will mehr.

Er fußt auf der T-Variante der C-Klasse, in deren Nachbarschaft er auch im Werk Bremen gefertigt wird. Wie bei den 4matic-Versionen seiner bürgerlichen Geschwister verzichtet sein permanenter Allradantrieb, schon aus Gründen der Raum-Ökonomie und weil die tatsächlich gefundene Lösung nur rund 40 Kilo mehr auf die Waage bringt, auf massive mechanische Sperren. Die Kraft des Triebwerks wird den vier Rädern durch eine Lamellenkupplung im Zentraldifferential zugemessen. Gewöhnlich verteilt sie das Antriebsmoment im Verhältnis 45 zu 55 Prozent zwischen Vorder- und Hinterachse. Wenn die Umstände widrig werden, interveniert sie mit einer Sperrwirkung von 50 Newtonmetern. Flankierend greift überdies das ESP ein und nimmt etwa durchdrehende Räder in den Griff.

All das führt zu einer bemerkenswerten Agilität des kompakten SUV in rauem und unwirtlichem Gelände, trotz lediglich 200 Millimetern Bodenfreiheit sowie den milden Böschungswinkeln von 23 Grad vorn und 25 Grad hinten. Nur: Ihn dergleichen Schikanen zu unterziehen wird eher der Ausnahmefall bleiben. Der GLK könnte halt, wenn er wollte – wie der weitläufige Verwandte SLR auf dem Prestige-Feld der Geschwindigkeit in dem ebenfalls anvisierten Haupt-Exportland USA mit seinen rigiden Tempolimits allüberall. Abgesehen von einer Grob-Sortierung als *Freeside* mit riesigen 20-Zoll-Rädern und massiver Dachreling und *Townside* mit kleinerem Geläuf lässt sich der Charakter des GLK vermittels zweier Schalter im unteren Zentrum des Cockpits den Gegebenheiten anpassen. Der eine ist zuständig für Hilfestellung bergan und bergab und gestattet, kräftige Gefälle mit zwischen vier und 18 Stundenkilometern in Angriff zu nehmen. Der andere aktiviert den Offroad-Modus, lässt das Gaspedal weniger alert ansprechen, verlängert die Reichweite der Gänge und stimmt das ABS auf rutschigen Untergrund ein.

Dass sich der GLK auch auf normalen Verkehrsstraßen als angenehmer Begleiter und Helfershelfer erweist, dafür macht sich bereits seine geschmeidig agierende Federung mit längeren Wegen als in der C-Klasse stark. An deren Interieur erinnert der Wohn- und Arbeitstrakt, nicht ohne dass es gefällig sublimiert worden wäre mit einem Cockpit von wertiger Anmutung mit Dreh-Drücksteller in der Mittelkonsole und eigenständiger Instrumentierung. Wie im T-Typ eröffnet die große Heckklappe den Zugang zu einem voluminösen Kofferabteil für mindestens 450, maximal 1550 Litern Gepäck. Zum Marktstart

Avant la première présentation de la Vision GLK lors du salon automobile de Détroit en janvier 2008, elle avait déjà fait une apparition cinématographique en tenant un second rôle automobile dans la version grand écran de la série culte *Sex and the City*. Ainsi son aspect anguleux s'était déjà imprimé dans le subconscient, avait éveillé la curiosité et déclenché les premières demandes.

Son style semble s'inspirer de sa grande sœur, la Classe G. Mais la GLK (K signifiant compact en raison de sa longueur – 4520 mm – relativement réduite) veut plus.

Elle se base sur la version break de la Classe C aux côtés de laquelle elle sera fabriqué dans l'usine de Brême. Comme pour les versions 4matic de ses sœurs citadines, ne serait-ce que pour des raisons de gain de place et parce que la solution réellement trouvée ne pèse qu'environ 40 kg supplémentaires, sa traction intégrale renonce au volumineux blocage mécanique. La puissance de la motorisation est distribuée sur les quatre roues grâce à un embrayage multidisques dans le différentiel central. Habituellement, le couple moteur se répartit dans des proportions allant de 45 à 55 % entre les trains avant et arrière. Lorsque les conditions deviennent difficiles, il intervient avec un effet bloquant de 50 Nm. À ses côtés, le système ESP intervient et prend en charge les roues qui patinent.

Tout cela engendre une agilité remarquable du SUV compact sur les terrains abrupts et inhospitaliers malgré une garde au sol de seulement 200 millimètres et une inclinaison moyenne de 23 degrés à l'avant et 25 degrés à l'arrière. Le confronter à de telles conditions devra plutôt rester une exception. Tout comme sa cousine éloignée la SLR, modèle du prestigieux secteur de la vitesse dans le principal pays d'exportation visé, à savoir les États-Unis aux limites de vitesse draconiennes, la GLK peut se maîtriser, si elle le veut ! Exceptée la vague différence entre le *Freeside,* doté de grandes roues 20 pouces et de massives barres de toit, et le *Townside* avec une assiette plus basse, le caractère de la GLK s'adapte aux conditions à l'aide de deux boutons au centre du tableau de bord. L'un est responsable de l'assistance pour escalader et descendre les pentes. Il est conçu pour prendre en charge les déclivités importantes à une vitesse allant de quatre à 18 km/h. L'autre active le mode tout-terrain : il fait réagir la pédale d'accélérateur de façon moins vive, prolonge la course d'accès des rapports et adapte l'ABS à un sol glissant.

La GLK se révèle également un compagnon et un complice agréable sur des routes normales en grande partie grâce à sa suspension réagissant de façon souple avec un débattement plus long que sur la Classe C. L'intérieur rappelle le coin salon et bureau mais pas sans que cela ait été agréablement sublimé avec un tableau de bord de qualité doté d'actionneurs rotatifs à pression sur la console centrale et une instrumentation autonome. Comme pour la version T, le grand hayon donne accès à un coffre volumineux d'au moins 450 litres, pouvant aller jusqu'à 1550 litres. Pour sa mise sur le marché à l'automne

Mercedes-Benz GLK   2008

Mercedes-Benz GLK 320 CDI 2008

engine with 231 (GLK 280) or 272 bhp (GLK 350) and 3-liter diesel engines in the GLK 320 CDI, in which 224 bhp could still turn out a very nice speed. In 2009, the GLK 220 CDI four-cylinder engine (2143 cc, 170 bhp) was introduced, also available from the second quarter of the year as a BlueEfficiency model.

im Herbst 2008 tritt der GLK mit drei V6-Triebwerken an, die Anspruch und Wirklichkeit auf Augenhöhe halten. Alle stehen sie mit einer Siebengang-Automatik im Bunde: ein drei- und ein 3,5-Liter Benziner mit 231 (GLK 280) respektive 272 PS (GLK 350) sowie der Dreiliter-Diesel im GLK 320 CDI, in dem noch immer 224 PS muntere Beweglichkeit auslösen. 2009 wird draufgesattelt mit dem Vierzylinder GLK 220 CDI (2143 cm³, 170 PS), ab dem 2. Quartal auch als BlueEfficiency-Modell lieferbar.

2008, la GLK sera proposée avec trois motorisations V6 qui offrent l'équilibre entre promesses et réalité. Elles sont tous équipées de série d'une boîte automatique sept rapports : deux versions essence, l'une de 3 litres (GLK 280) de 231 ch et l'autre de 3,5 litres (GLK 350) de 272 ch ; une version diesel trois litres, la GLK 320 CDI dont les 224 ch offrent une bonne mobilité. 2009 proposera le quatre cylindres GLK 220 CDI (2143 cm³, 170 ch) qui à partir du deuxième trimestre sera également livrable en modèle BlueEfficiency.

When spaces come true: wide-opening doors and a huge tailgate make for generously free access to the all-purpose GLK. Refined optical appeal: the 320 CDI V6 diesel.

Wenn Räume wahr werden: Weit öffnende Türen und eine riesige Heckklappe machen den Zugang zum Allzweckler GLK generös frei. Optisch süffig aufbereitet: der V6-Diesel des 320 CDI.

Quand l'espace devient réalité : des portières qui s'ouvrent en grand et un immense hayon offrent un accès généreux au tout-terrain GLK. Traité visuellement de façon agréable : le V6 diesel de la 320 CDI.

In purely numerical terms alone, this model saw itself up against a real challenge: its predecessor had since 2002 achieved sales of some 1.3 million units. Now the new E-Class, after a stopover in January 2009 on the eve of the North American International Auto Show in Detroit and its premiere at the Geneva Salon that spring, had become the representative of Mercedes interests among the upper echelons of society.

Boldly designed by the new head of design Gorden Wagener, who succeeded Peter Pfeiffer in mid-2008, it conquered new terrain in practically every respect. The ingratiating roundedness of the previous generation was abandoned. The new model made its entrance with a sharper profile and more prominent flaring and edges, without losing much in the way of streamlining. The novelty began with the updated version of its "four-eyed" face: lamps whose sharp corners were now turned back and daytime lights, inlaid into the air intakes in front of the front wheels below the bumper, now almost completely absorbed into the body work. With its new silhouette, sloping up gradually toward the rear and visually enhanced by two energetically rising grooves, this E-type still has a somewhat classical appearance. A dynamically accentuated curvature over the rear wheel arches points to the rear wheel drive.

Of course, it had, quite in the spirit of its occupants, increased in dimensions: ¾ in in the wheelbase, ½ in in respect of length, and 1⅜ in in terms of width, while being ⅜ in lower. Head and elbow room for travelers used to high-class comfort and elegance had also slightly increased. To prevent such improvement involving more weight, the hood is made of aluminum and the instrument panel from magnesium and high-strength steel, which make the superstructure 30 percent more rigid.

Radical progress, almost always signaled by the magic fuel-efficient formula BlueEfficiency, was also apparent in the engine compartment. Here, combined with corresponding six-speed gearboxes and automatic gears with five or seven speeds, were an optional nine engines: two petrol, with four and six combustion units and direct injection system, a turbo four-cylinder engine with 1796 cc and 184 bhp in the E 200 CGI (with start-stop function) and 204 bhp in the E 250 CGI, a V6 engine with 3498 cc and 292 bhp in the E 350 CGI, plus the V8 in the E 500, with 5461 cc and 388 bhp—until the appearance of the AMG variant the strongest in the series. With five members, the widely popular diesel complement already had the upper hand, with an impressive range from the E 200 CDI (four cylinders, 2143 cc, 136 bhp) to the E 350 CDI (V6, 2987 cc, 211 bhp).

Such obvious strength was more than counterbalanced by a newly developed suspension with an electronically controlled adaptive damping system. Upon request, and in return for a significant extra outlay, there was also a continuously adjustable air suspension. But the Mercedes whiz-kids had showered a veritable cornucopia

Schon rein zahlenmäßig gesehen sieht sie sich mit einer echten Herausforderung konfrontiert: Der Vorgänger der neuen E-Klasse, die nach einem Zwischenhalt im Januar 2009 am Vorabend der North American International Auto Show in Detroit seit ihrer Publikums-Premiere beim Genfer Frühlingssalon die Mercedes-Interessen in der oberen Mittelklasse vertritt, wurde seit 2002 in rund 1,3 Millionen Einheiten abgesetzt.

Vom neuen Designchef Gorden Wagener, seit Mitte 2008 Thronfolger von Peter Pfeiffer, mit kühnem Strich gezeichnet, betritt sie fast überall neues Terrain. Abgekommen ist man von der einschmeichelnden Rundlichkeit der Generation davor. Der Nachfolger setzt sich mit einem geschärften Profil voller ausgeprägter Sicken und Kanten in Szene, ohne deshalb viel an windschlüpfiger Glätte zu verlieren. Das beginnt mit der aktuellen Version seines Vieraugen-Gesichts mit Lampen, in welche der spitze Winkel eingekehrt ist, und die wie Intarsien in die Lufteinlässe vor den Vorderrädern eingelegten Tagfahrlämplein unterhalb der nun fast völlig von der Karosserie absorbierten Stoßfänger. In seiner Silhouette mit ihrer Aufwärts-Tendenz nach hinten, durch zwei energisch ansteigende Sicken visuell unterstützt, gibt sich der aktuelle E-Typ gleichwohl eher klassisch. Eine dynamisch akzentuierte Rundung über den hinteren Radläufen verweist auf den Heckantrieb.

Natürlich hat er ganz im Sinne seiner Insassen wieder zugelegt, 20 mm mehr beim Radstand, 13 mm hinsichtlich seiner Länge, 34 mm in puncto Breite, während er zehn Millimeter niedriger daherkommt. Kopf- und Ellbogenfreiheit für die in schöner und hochwertiger Wohnlichkeit Reisenden sind leicht gewachsen. Dass sich dergleichen nicht in mehr Gewicht niederschlägt, dafür sorgen Hauben aus Aluminium, ein Instrumententräger aus Magnesium sowie hochfester Stahl, der den Aufbau zugleich um 30 Prozent steifer macht.

Radikaler Fortschritt, fast durchweg signalisiert durch die magische Spritspar-Formel BlueEfficiency, ist auch im Motor-Abteil eingekehrt. Dort wirken, vermählt mit entsprechenden Sechsgang-Schaltgetrieben und Automaten mit fünf oder sieben Fahrstufen, wahlweise neun Triebwerke. Zwei davon sind Benziner mit vier und sechs Verbrennungseinheiten und direkter Einspritzung, ein Turbo-Vierzylinder mit 1796 cm³ und 184 PS im E 200 CGI (mit Start-Stopp-Funktion) und 204 PS im E 250 CGI, ein V6 mit 3498 cm³ und 292 PS im E 350 CGI, dazu der V8 im E 500, mit 5461 cm³ und 388 PS bis zum Erscheinen der AMG-Variante stärkstes Stück der Baureihe. Mit fünf Mitgliedern hat bereits die allseits beliebte Diesel-Fraktion die Oberhand mit einer stattlichen Bandbreite zwischen E 200 CDI (vier Zylinder, 2143 cm³, 136 PS) und E 350 CDI (V6, 2987 cm³, 211 PS).

Mehr als austariert wird soviel manifeste Stärke durch ein neu entwickeltes Fahrwerk mit einem elektronisch geregelten adaptiven Dämpfungssystem. Auf Wunsch und gegen kräftigen Aufpreis gibt es überdies

Déjà numériquement, elle se trouve confrontée à un véritable défi: son prédécesseur s'est vendu à 1,3 million d'exemplaires depuis 2002. Après une étape intermédiaire à Detroit en janvier 2009 à la veille du North American International Auto Show, la nouvelle Classe E représente les intérêts de Mercedes dans la classe moyenne supérieure depuis sa première présentation au public lors du Salon de l'automobile de Genève au printemps.

Dessinée de façon audacieuse par le nouveau chef designer Gorden Wagener qui a succédé à Peter Pfeiffer mi-2008, elle pénètre presque partout sur un nouveau terrain. On s'éloigne des rondeurs généreuses de la précédente génération. Le successeur s'impose avec un profil plus aiguisé plein de nervures et d'arêtes bien marquées sans pour autant perdre beaucoup de son aérodynamisme. Cela commence avec la version actuelle de son visage à doubles optiques doté de feux dans lesquels se termine l'angle aigu de l'optique, et l'éclairage diurne installé comme une marqueterie dans les prises d'air devant les roues avant sous les pare-chocs presque entièrement absorbés par la carrosserie. La puissante silhouette aux lignes ascendantes vers l'arrière, soulignées visuellement par deux nervures montant fortement, l'actuelle gamme E est plutôt classique. Une rondeur accentuée au-dessus des passages de roue arrière indique une traction arrière.

Bien sûr, elle en a rajouté pour ses passagers: 20 mm d'empattement en plus, 13 mm quant à la longueur, 34 mm concernant la largeur alors qu'elle perd dix millimètres en hauteur. L'espace pour la tête et les coudes des passagers installés dans un bel habitacle de qualité, a légèrement augmenté. Que cela ne se manifeste pas par un supplément pondéral, est dû au capot en aluminium, à un combiné d'instruments en magnésium ainsi qu'à l'acier très résistant qui rend la carrosserie 30 % plus solide.

Un progrès radical, presque entièrement signalé par la formule magique pour l'économie de carburant BlueEfficiency, s'est également installé dans la partie moteur. Neuf motorisations sont proposées associées à une boîte six vitesses et à des boîtes automatiques cinq ou sept rapports. Deux fonctionnent à l'essence avec quatre et six unités de combustion et injection directe, un quatre cylindres turbo de 1796 cm³ et 184 ch pour la E 200 CGI (avec la fonction start-stop) et 240 ch pour la E 250 CGI ; un V6 de 3498 cm³ et 292 ch pour la E 350 CGI ainsi qu'un V8 pour la E 500 avec 5461 cm³ et 388 ch, jusqu'à la sortie de la version AMG, le plus puissant de la classe. Avec cinq membres, la fraction diesel très appréciée de tous a déjà le dessus avec une large gamme allant de la E 200 CDI (quatre cylindres, 2143 cm³, 136 ch) à la E 350 CDI (V6, 2987 cm³, 211 ch).

Une telle puissance manifeste est plus que compensée par une régulation des trains de roulement nouvellement mise au point et dotée d'un système de suspension adaptatif réglé électroniquement. Si on le souhaite et contre un important supplément, il existe également une suspension pneumatique à réglage continu. Mais surtout

Mercedes-Benz E-Klasse 2009

Mercedes-Benz E 250 CDI 2009

of brilliant support systems into the new type of E-Class. There is a night-view assist that can make out even living objects, sensitively cross-linked with the Brake Assist Plus. And the main-beam assist: thanks to a camera on the windscreen, the E-Class controls the cone of light so that overtaking cars, or oncoming traffic, are not inconvenienced. This is just as true for the T version from the end of 2009 and for the E-Class Coupé as the successor to the CLK.

eine stufenlos einstellbare Luftfederung. Vor allem aber hat die Denkfabrik im Zeichen des guten Sterns ein wahres Füllhorn voller blitzgescheiter Hilfssysteme über der E-Klasse neuer Art ausgegossen. Da sind etwa ein Nachtsicht-Assistent, der auch lebende Objekte ausmacht, einfühlsam vernetzt mit dem Brems-Assistenten Plus. Oder der Fernlicht-Assistent: Mittels einer Kamera an der Windschutzscheibe steuert die E-Klasse den Lichtkegel so, dass er vorausfahrende oder entgegenkommende Autofahrer nicht inkommodiert. Ähnliches gilt für die T-Version ab Ende 2009 und für das E-Klasse Coupé, den Nachfolger des CLK.

l'usine pensante sous le signe de la bonne étoile a déversé sur la nouvelle version de la Classe E une véritable corne d'abondance pleine d'assistants très intelligents. Ainsi il y a l'assistant de vision de nuit qui rend visible les objets vivants, intelligemment relié au Freinage d'urgence assistée BAS Plus. Ou l'assistant des feux de route : à l'aide d'une caméra sur le pare-brise, la Classe E gère le faisceau lumineux de façon à ne pas incommoder le conducteur du véhicule qui la précède ou la croise. Tout cela sera similaire pour la version break qui sortira à partir de fin 2009 ainsi que pour le successeur de la CLK, la Classe E Coupé.

"Defiantly provoking design discussion, the W212 displays its edges and angles like a Cubist image, while its passengers flow through the landscape as softly and roundly as a Rubens beauty" rhapsodized an enchanted poet in *auto motor und sport*. That says it all.

»Trotzig um Design-Diskussionen buhlend, stellt der W212 seine Ecken und Kanten wie ein kubistisches Bild zur Schau, während die Insassen mit ihm weich und rund wie eine Rubens-Schönheit durch die Landschaft fließen«, schwärmt ein entzückter Poet in *auto motor und sport*. Dem ist nichts hinzuzufügen.

« Obstinée dans la recherche de la discussion sur le design, la W212 expose ses angles et ses arêtes comme une toile cubiste alors que les passagers traversent les paysages en son sein offrant la douceur et la rondeur d'une beauté de Rubens », s'extasie un poète subjugué dans *auto motor und sport*. Il n'y a rien à ajouter.

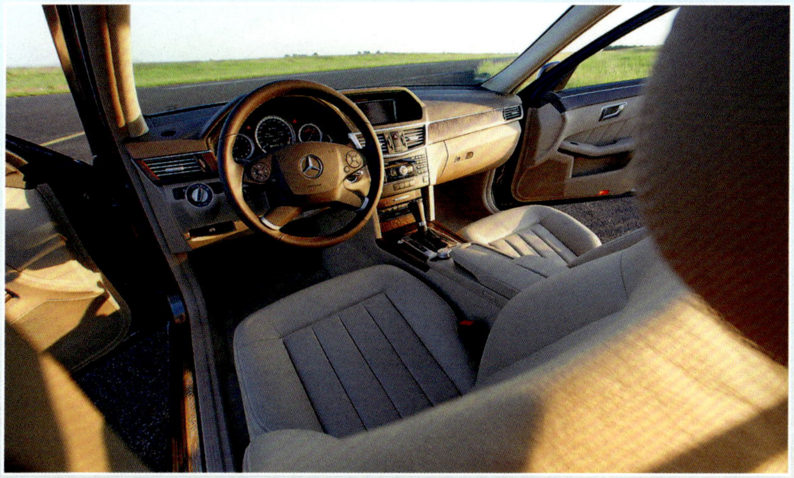

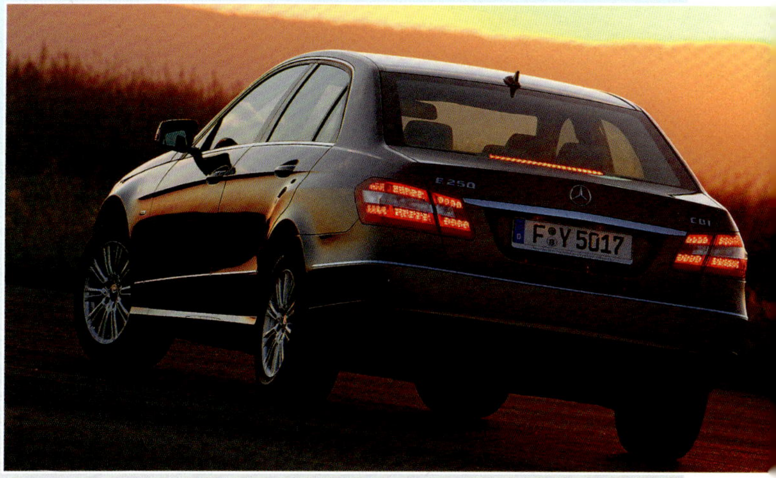
E 250
F·Y 5017

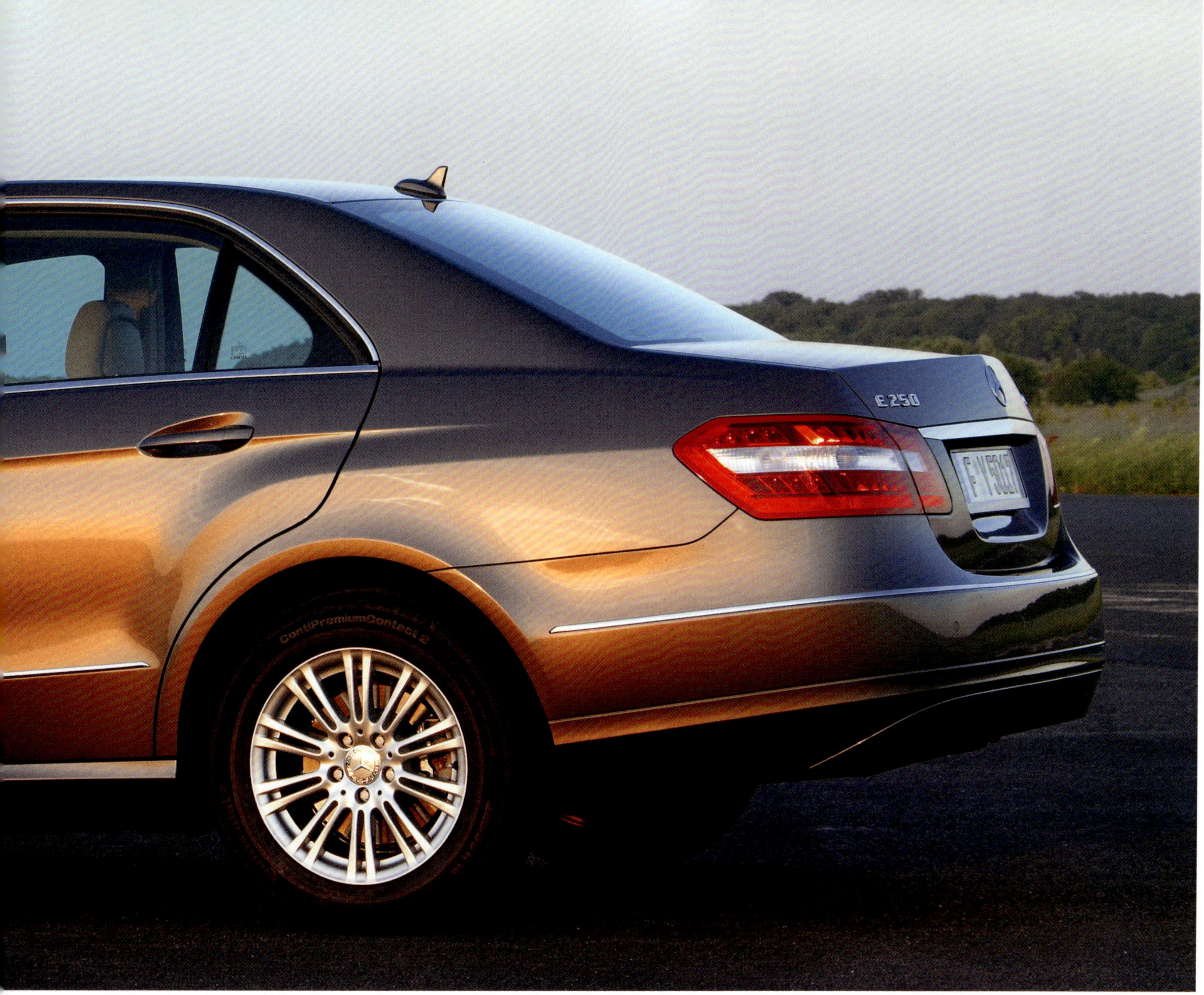
E250

Visually, there is no denying the E-Class coupé's origins. Its streamlining sets a world record, however: its drag coefficient is 0.25. The tiny triangular windows at the rear allow the side windows to be wound down completely.

Optisch mag das E-Klasse-Coupé seinen Stammbaum nicht verleugnen. Dennoch stellt es einen Weltrekord in Windschlüpfigkeit auf: Sein c_w-Wert liegt bei 0,25. Die winzigen Dreiecksfenster hinten gestatten, die Seitenscheiben voll zu versenken.

Visuellement, le coupé de la Classe E ne peut pas renier ses origines. Pourtant, il détient un record mondial en matière d'aérodynamisme: sa valeur c_x est de 0,25. Les minuscules fenêtres triangulaires à l'arrière permettent d'abaisser complètement les vitres latérales.

Mercedes-Benz E-Klasse 2009

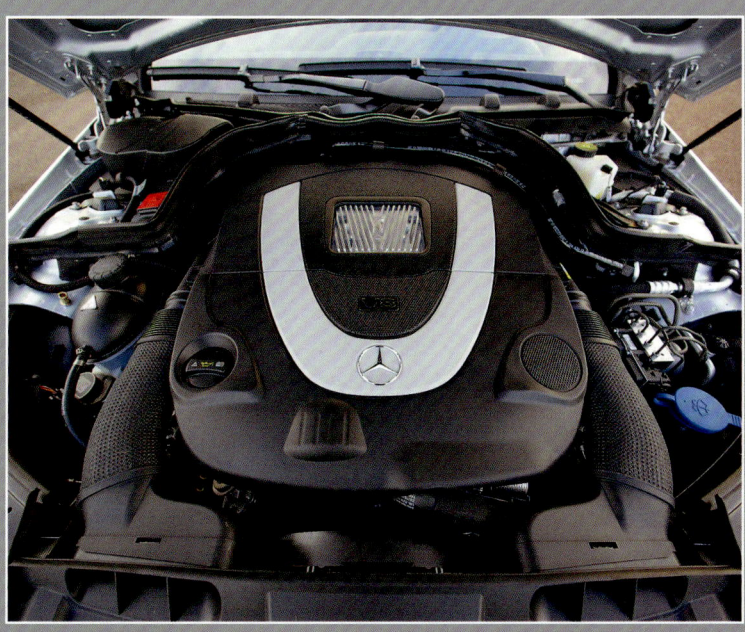

Production of the 300 SL may have ceased in 1963, at which point it entered into automobile legend, but the dream of the perfect Mercedes sports car remained. And although the C111 of 1969 had what it takes, it withdrew from the reach of a willing and well-off potential clientele like the apple from the hand of Tantalus. The SLR McLaren, which was the result of a collaboration with the renowned English motor sports specialist in Woking, was more of a hybrid. Not many people considered it their idea of a "dream car" with the famous three-pointed star.

Eventually, the legend returned in the form of the SLS, designed in 2009 and introduced in 2010 to the Grand Prix community and the world—on site and to TV audiences—as the Formula 1 safety car. The idea of a joint venture had not been entirely abandoned: the SLS was developed by AMG in Affalterbach, the first independent product by the Mercedes subsidiary, and built at its works in Sindelfingen. It is a classic that shines with timeless beauty. Even half a century later, it is still something to be proud of, and referencing can't do any harm—especially if the copyright-holder is doing the copying. The SLS was adapted from the "gullwing" of 1954, and thus the racing SL of two years before. It has the long hood and the passenger cabin right next to the rear axle, the rounded rear end, the broad mouth of the radiator grille adorned with the three-pointed star— but most important of all, it has the spectacular upward-swinging doors.

The historic similarities are far from insignificant. Form followed function, as it used to in the "old days." The doors, for example, were connected to the roof edge, and rise above the sills to provide an entrance height of 17¾ inches. The component parts of the aluminum space frame spread out beneath them, which means that an old problem has reemerged: now, as then, ladies wearing tight skirts find it difficult to sit up and to exit the car in a ladylike fashion—as Heinz-Ulrich Wiedermann, editor-in-chief of *auto motor und sport,* once put it in the 1950s. Furthermore, beneath the seemingly endless front hood a V8 rules in front mid-engine architecture, courtesy of a carbon-reinforced plastic cardan shaft that weighs a mere 8¾ pounds and is connected to the seven-gear dual clutch transmission of the rear axle. The 6.2-liter V8, embedded deeply in the chassis and fed by a dry sump with 3½ gallons of lubricant, weighs a modest 454 pounds.

Pressing the red-lettered button on the center console starts up an orgy of power, orchestrated by the impressive V8 rumble. Performance is undoubtedly more than required—the thirsty beast is greedy for revs. It finally releases its 572 bhp at 6800 rpm. But 480 lb-ft underscore this peak with a sturdy foundation, manually by means of a switch on the steering wheel or automatically to the rear. This lends the vehicle a sovereignty that borders on the virtual. Unlike safety car driver Bernd Mayländer, only very few SLS drivers opt for the muted potency of this Mercedes super sports car. As with the clientele for the Roadster version that became available in 2011, this is

Mercedes-Benz SLS-AMG 2009

Mercedes-Benz SLS-AMG 2009

not least because of the price of $250,000 for the basic version. At over twice the price is the good-looking SLS GT3, the racing version that arrived on the world's tracks in 2010.

schon ans Virtuelle reichende Souveränität. Im Gegensatz zu Safety-Car-Pilot Bernd Mayländer werden gleichwohl nur sehr wenige SLS-Piloten sehr selten auf die gebändigt lauernde Potenz des Mercedes-Supersportlers zurückgreifen.

    Eingebremst wird ihre Schar, ebenso wie die Klientel für die Roadster-Version ab 2011, schon durch den Grundpreis von 177 310 Euro. Mehr als doppelt so teuer: die Rennvariante SLS GT3, die ab 2010 auf den Pisten der Welt eine gute Figur macht.

rétrogradage, ce qui offre une souveraineté frôlant le virtuel. Contrairement au pilote du *safety car* Bernd Mayländer, seuls très peu de conducteurs de la SLS auront recours au potentiel disponible de la supersportive de Mercedes. Ses admirateurs, de même que les clients de la version roadster à partir de 2011, seront sans doute freinés par son prix de base de 177 310 euros. La SLS GT3, version de course, qui fait bonne figure sur les circuits depuis 2010, coûte près de deux fois plus cher.

Mercedes-Benz SLS-AMG 2009

Highlights on the inside come from the sports-style steering wheel, which is flattened at the bottom, and the wide center console. Designer Hartmut Sinkwitz was inspired by the jet plane, with elements that are purist, expressive, suitable for daily use and sporty. Engine: front-middle.

Ein unten abgeflachtes Sportlenkrad sowie ein breiter Mittelbau setzen innen die Akzente. Designer Hartmut Sinkwitz hat sich vom Jet inspirieren lassen, mit Elementen, die puristisch, ausdrucksstark, fit für den Alltag und sportlich sind. Motor: front-mittig.

Un volant aplati à la base ainsi qu'une large console centrale donnent le ton dans l'habitacle. Son designer, Hartmut Sinkwitz, s'est inspiré d'un jet, avec des éléments épurés, puissants, adaptés au quotidien et sportifs. Le moteur ? En position centrale avant.

The CLS of 2011 appeals for its skillful style elements that, according to the design department, give it an expressive look. Edgier and more spirited than before, a crimp runs from the expressive bi-xenon headlight "eye" over the wheelbase to the rear flank. There, it meets up in solidarity with a wing arch that flows elegantly into the rear LED lights. The contours of the flat downward-drawn hood and roof line blending smoothly with the rear bring to mind a modern interpretation of the streamlined shape with an unmistakable touch of the sculptural. The front of the CLS radiates power and dynamism with its aerodynamically shaped front apron, although the rear apron, underside and wing mirrors also carry the signature of a wind tunnel.

Five powertrains of emission class Euro 5—two self-igniting and three gas—fight for the customer's favor. Choosing is difficult, starting with the 4-cylinder straight engine of the CLS 250 CDI BlueEfficiency, with the latest common-rail diesel technology. Its 204 bhp move the 16 feet 2 inches vehicle at up to 153 mph. The 3-liter V6 version is more powerful, already reaching its maximum torque of 457 lb-ft at between 1600 and 2000 rpm. Thanks to the ultimate progress turbo technology, this CLS 350 CDI has surprisingly low fuel consumption. The 4Matic version with permanent all-wheel drive takes an extra pint of diesel.

Spray-guided combustion with piezo injectors, effectively high-pressure injection, is one of the tricks used by the Mercedes engine men to reduce the thirst of the V6 and V8 gasoline engines. The factory happily boasts that this enhances fuel efficiency by 20 percent. In the light of the potential of these compact powertrains—306 bhp on the V6 and 408 on the V8 in the CLS 500—the occasional fall from grace is permissible so that you can at least feel the acceleration to 62 mph—5.2 seconds in the CLS 500. Those who prefer to drive more conscientiously at around 2000 rpm—with no loss in torque—will be rewarded with fuel savings of 40 percent. However, it is unlikely that anyone buying a CLS 63 AMG will be too concerned with these considerations; all that will matter is the brute strength of the 525 bhp V8 twin-turbo that demands to be fed premium fuel.

However, the technology inside the chic exterior of the CLS offers enough attractions to prevent the foot throttle food from tiring. The chassis is ready for almost any eventuality: a selective damping system is provided for all CLS models with an engine having fewer than eight cylinders. The Airmatic air suspension of the V8s will have the occupants floating on cloud nine. The direct steering also contributes to the unadulterated driving pleasure. Its servo support is electronically adapted to the current driving speed.

The safety features begin with the extremely stable passenger cell—a sandwich of energy-absorbing front and rear crumple zones—and end with the special headrests that activate a mechanism to protect the cervical

Mercedes-Benz CLS 2011

Mercedes-Benz CLS 350 CDI 2012

vertebrae of driver and passenger in the event of a rear collision. The exclusive ambience of the interior can be enjoyed to the full, knowing that measures such as these are in place. Mercedes pampers its CLS clientele with all kinds of special features and the finest materials. Those of a sporty bent will find the world-famous combination of three letters AMG offers them a comprehensive program for dynamic individuality.

Das Thema Sicherheit beginnt bei einer äußerst stabilen Fahrgastzelle – im Sandwich von Energie absorbierenden vorderen und hinteren Knautschzonen – und endet bei speziellen Kopfstützen, die bei einem Heckaufprall einen Mechanismus zum Schutz der Halswirbel von Fahrer und Beifahrer aktivieren. Solchermaßen geschützt, darf die hochherrschaftliche Atmosphäre des Innenraums genossen werden. Mit Sonderausstattungen aller Art und feinsten Materialien verwöhnt Mercedes die CLS-Klientel. Den sportlich Ambitionierten bietet die weltbekannte Kombination von drei Buchstaben ein umfangreiches Programm zur individuellen Dynamisierung: AMG.

l'avant et à l'arrière entre des zones déformables qui absorbent l'énergie en cas de choc. En cas de collision arrière, des appuie-têtes spéciaux activent un mécanisme destiné à protéger les cervicales du conducteur et du passager avant. Ainsi protégés, on peut profiter au mieux de l'atmosphère luxueuse de l'habitacle. Mercedes chouchoute la clientèle de la CLS avec une vaste gamme d'équipements spéciaux et les matériaux les plus nobles. AMG – la marque aux trois célèbres initiales offre aux amateurs de sensations sportives un programme complet pour dynamiser personnellement leur véhicule.

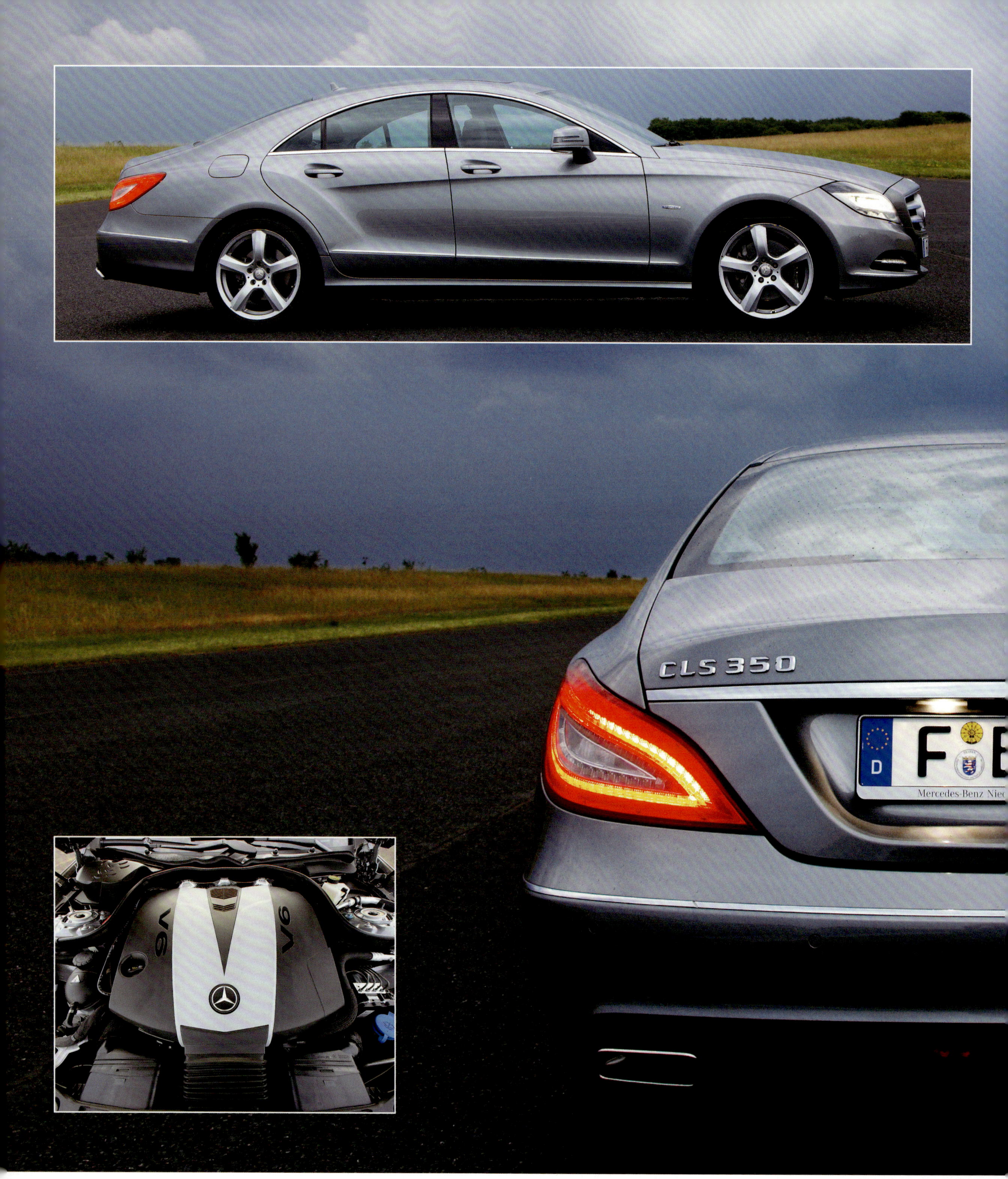
CLS 350
D
F
V6
V6

Edgy but full of swing: the CLS—seen here as a 350 CDI with a powerful diesel engine—
appeals for its design language and the tasteful ambience of the interior.

Kantig aber schwungvoll: Der CLS – hier als 350 CDI mit kraftvollem Diesel-Triebwerk –
besticht durch seine Formensprache und sein geschmackvolles Ambiente im Interieur.

Tout en courbes et en arêtes : la CLS, ici la version 350 CDI dotée d'un puissant
moteur diesel, séduit par ses formes et l'ambiance raffinée de son habitacle.

The dramaturgy looks like this: it can be ordered from 17 January 2011, and collected from the dealer from the end of March of the particular year. And its future is no less shining than that of the earlier generations, 1996 and 2004. This sporty little Mercedes is chic, hip, and will hold its value like glue.

Its creators still call it a roadster. But the term has long since become a cliché. Having it open is only one option. Its folding hardtop makes it a coupé at all times. And the Mercedes strategists have come up with two other forms of "being" in between these two alternatives. Called a panorama vario roof in the company jargon, it consists of a dome of tinted glass and *Magic Sky Control:* like certain types of eyewear, the front part of the cockpit darkens when desired, perhaps when the sun is particularly strong, a process that is initiated and reversed at the touch of a button.

Those who prefer to be truly at one with nature can create the conditions for this in less than 20 seconds. A new wind deflector with movable plastic panes positioned on the back of the headrests guides the remaining driving wind off and away. Meanwhile, as before, Airscarves pamper the passengers' necks with pleasant warmth. Once the apparent chaos when folding back the overhead cover has calmed down, the trunk shrinks from a capacity of 12 to just under 8 cubic feet—still plenty if the occupants are genuinely fond of themselves, each other, and the car.

The 2011 SLK is more virile than its predecessors, both of which have the reputation of being "ladies' cars," just like their distant ancestor, the 190 SL. This is due in no small part to the elongated front section, luscious rear, and added-on strips with the generous LED lights. Gone is the nose section with its gentle longing to resemble that of the Formula 1 racing car of the McLaren-Mercedes joint venture. In form, it was in some respects based more on its big brother, the SLS, such as with the large radiator grille with the embedded star, the design of the center console, and the chrome-clad ventilation rosettes. The "shorty" has also become a little longer and wider, by approximately 1¼ inches.

The appearance is exciting, and the same emotion is also experienced behind the multifunction steering wheel with the flattened bottom. The cockpit is clearly laid out, high quality, and appealing both to the eye and touch, with large round instruments and a beautifully arranged Comand system.

The SLK also has the full range of modern features found on the Mercedes shelves, including LED daytime running lights, bi-xenon cornering headlights with nine different light profiles, pre-safe brake, traffic sign recognition and attention assist. It kicks off with three different petrol engines: the SLK 200 of 1796 cc and 184 bhp has a top speed of 147 mph; the SLK 250 with the same turbo four-cylinder and 204 bhp, and the SLK 350 with 3498 cc and a 305 bhp v6. A manual six-speed or a seven-speed automatic gearbox with a long transmission ratio—standard

Die Dramaturgie sieht so aus: Ab 17. Januar 2011 darf er bestellt, ab Ende März des nämlichen Jahres beim Händler abgeholt werden. Und eine glanzvolle Zukunft ist ihm in die Wiege gelegt wie schon den Generationen von 1996 und 2004. Denn der kleine Mercedes-Sportler ist chic, hip und überdies von zäher Wertbeständigkeit.

Noch immer nennen ihn seine Väter einen Roadster. Aber der Begriff ist längst zur Worthülse verkümmert. Offen zu sein ist nur eine Option. Sein faltbares Hardtop macht ihn seit jeher auch zum Coupé. Dazwischen haben die Mercedes-Strategen zwei weitere Möglichkeiten des Seins angesiedelt. Im Jargon des Hauses heißen sie Panorama-Variodach, eine Kuppel aus dunkel getöntem Glas, und *Magic Sky Control:* Nach Art bestimmter Brillen verdüstert sich der vordere Teil der Kanzel, falls etwa bei intensiver Sonneneinwirkung gewünscht, ein Effekt, der sich per Knopfdruck herstellen und rückgängig machen lässt.

Wer seinen Blick dankbar, aber unbehindert zum Himmel richten möchte, kann die Voraussetzung dazu binnen 20 Sekunden schaffen. Ein neues Windschott mit drehbaren Scheiben aus Kunststoff an der Rückseite der Kopfstützen lenkt den verbleibenden Fahrtwind gänzlich ins Abseits. Wie bisher indessen schmeicheln Airscarfs dem Nacken der Passagiere mit wohltuend austretender Wärme. Wenn sich das scheinbare Chaos beim Zusammenfalten der Kopf-Bedeckung geglättet hat, ist der Kofferraum von 335 Liter auf 225 Liter Volumen geschrumpft – immer noch genug, wenn die Insassen sich selbst, einander und dem Auto von Herzen zugetan sind.

Der SLK Jahrgang 2011 kommt viriler daher als seine Vorgänger, beide in dem Ruf, sie seien Damen-Autos wie einst der entfernte Vorfahr 190 SL. Zu dieser Anmutung tragen das längere Vorderschiff und ein knackiges Hinterteil nebst aufgesetzter Abreißkante, in das sich voluminöse LED-Leuchten einlagern, ihr Scherflein bei. Ein Ding der Vergangenheit ist die zart verquaste Anspielung der Nasenpartie auf die Formel-1-Rennwagen des Joint Ventures McLaren Mercedes. Formal Pate steht vielmehr der große Bruder SLS, in mancherlei Hinsicht wie etwa der großen Kühlermaske mit dem darin eingebetteten Stern, der Gestaltung der Mittelkonsole sowie den in Chrom gefassten Lüftungsrosetten. Etwas länger und breiter ist der Kurze ebenfalls geworden, 31 beziehungsweise 33 Millimeter.

Mit Gusto betrachtet man ihn nicht nur, sondern setzt sich auch hinter das unten abgeflachte Multifunktions-Lenkrad. Das Cockpit gibt sich übersichtlich, wertig und visuell und haptisch attraktiv, mit großen Rundinstrumenten und einem einleuchtend-übersichtlichem Comand-System.

Auch der SLK hält das ganze Spektrum der Moderne aus den Mercedes-Regalen wie LED-Tagfahrleuchten, Bi-Xenon-Kurvenscheinwerfer mit neun verschiedenen Lichtprofilen, Pre-Safe-Bremse, Verkehrszeichen-Erkennung oder

Le scénario est le suivant: on peut la commander à partir du 17 janvier 2011 et la récupérer chez le concessionnaire à la fin du mois de mars de la même année. On lui prédit déjà un avenir radieux, à l'instar des millésimes 1996 et 2004. En effet, la petite sportive Mercedes est chic, tendance et c'est avant tout une valeur stable.

Ses concepteurs continuent de la qualifier de roadster, mais le terme semble depuis longtemps galvaudé. La conduite à ciel ouvert n'est qu'une option. Son toit rigide escamotable en fait naturellement aussi un coupé. Entre les deux, les stratèges de Mercedes ont inventé deux nouveaux concepts. Dans le jargon de la maison, il s'agit du toit escamotable panoramique, une coupole de verre teinté, et du système *Magic Sky Control:* comme certaines lunettes, le toit s'assombrit ou s'éclaircit sur simple pression d'un bouton, lorsque l'ensoleillement est trop intense par exemple.

Il faut à peine 20 secondes pour créer les conditions optimales d'une conduite à ciel ouvert et profiter d'une vue imprenable sur le ciel. Le tout nouveau pare-vent en plexiglas fixé à l'arrière des appuie-têtes et réglable à l'aide d'une molette élimine totalement les courants d'air. De plus, les Airscarfs, littéralement «écharpes d'air», viennent réchauffer le cou du conducteur et du passager en soufflant un courant d'air chaud bienfaisant. Une fois le toit replié dans un chaos tout relatif, le volume du coffre passe de 335 à 225 litres – ce que les occupants sauront trouver suffisant si leur ego est à la mesure de leur amour pour cette voiture.

La SLK millésime 2011 se montre donc sous un jour plus viril que ses prédécesseurs, toutes deux ayant la réputation d'être des voitures de femme comme autrefois leur lointaine aïeule, la 190 SL. La proue allongée et la poupe musclée dans laquelle viennent se loger les volumineux feux arrière à DEL apportent leur modeste contribution à cette allure sportive. Élément emprunté au passé, la partie inférieure du bouclier semble imiter confusément le museau de la F1 McLaren Mercedes. L'influence de sa grande sœur, la SLS, est beaucoup plus évidente et se traduit à divers endroits: la grande grille de la calandre où vient se loger l'étoile de la marque, la forme de la console médiane ou encore les buses d'aération chromées. Le petit roadster a pris un peu d'envergure en gagnant respectivement 31 et 33 mm en longueur et en largeur.

Le bon goût ne s'arrête pas à l'extérieur, mais se poursuit derrière le volant multifonctions à méplat. L'habitacle est ergonomique, élégant, séduisant visuellement, avec de gros instruments ronds et un système Comand lumineux très clair.

La SLK possède aussi toute la gamme des équipements de pointe Mercedes: feux de jour à DEL, projecteurs bi-xénon à éclairage actif dans les virages avec neuf profils d'éclairage, freins Pre-Safe, système de reconnaissance des panneaux de signalisation ou système de détection de somnolence. À son lancement, la SLK est proposée

Mercedes-Benz SLK 2011

Mercedes-Benz SLK 200 Sport 2011

in the SLK 350—are available to choose from. Available since January 2012: the mighty SLK 55 AMG with a 421 bhp V8, and a 2.1-liter diesel version with 204 bhp. So there's also room for the culture diesel in this series.

Aufmerksamkeits-Assistent bereit. An den Start rollt er mit drei verschiedenen Otto-Triebwerken, als SLK 200 mit 1796 cm³ und 184 PS bereits 237 Stundenkilometer flink, als SLK 250 mit dem gleichen Turbo-Vierzylinder und 204 PS, als SLK 350 mit einem 306 PS starken V6 von 3498 cm³. Geschaltet wird mit sechs Gängen oder einer lang übersetzten Siebengang-Automatik, ab SLK 350 Serie. Seit Januar 2012 erhältlich: der Kraftprotz SLK 55 AMG, dessen V8 mit 421 PS aufwartet, und eine Selbstzünder-Variante mit 2,1 Litern und 204 PS. Damit hat der Kultur-Diesel auch in diese Baureihe Einzug gehalten.

avec trois motorisations différentes : la SLK 200 avec une cylindrée de 1796 cm³ développant 184 ch pour une vitesse maximale de 237 km/h, la SLK 250 avec le même moteur turbo 4 cylindres de 204 ch, et la SLK 350 avec un V6 de 306 ch et d'une cylindrée de 3498 cm³. Le moteur est couplé à une boîte six vitesses ou à une boîte automatique à sept rapports, en série à partir de la SLK 350. La SLK 55 AMG, un roadster ultrasportif doté d'un V8 de 421 ch, ainsi que la version diesel de 2,1 litres et 204 ch, sont disponibles depuis janvier 2012. Le diesel fait ainsi également son entrée dans cette série.

The profile and character of the sporty little Mercedes have basically been left untouched apart from a few minor metamorphoses toward a more masculine look. The third-generation SLK is based on the principle of the reciprocal progressive character of its speedy big brother, the SLS. Everything is clearly arranged: the cockpit with the large round instruments, multifunction steering wheel that is flattened at the bottom, and the Comand system. Both cycles of the folding hardtop take just 20 seconds.

Mercedes-Benz SLK 2011

Im Prinzip sind Profil und Charakter des kleinen Mercedes-Sportlers unangetastet geblieben trotz milder Metamorphosen zum mehr Maskulinen hin. Der SLK der dritten Generation orientiert sich nach dem Prinzip der wechselseitig fortschreitenden Prägung am großen und schnellen Bruder SLS. Klar und übersichtlich: sein Cockpit mit großen Rundinstrumenten, unten flachem Multifunktionslenkrad und Comand-System. Das faltbare Hardtop benötigt für beide Arbeitstakte 20 Sekunden.

La silhouette et le caractère de la petite sportive Mercedes n'ont pas fondamentalement changé malgré quelques métamorphoses légères aboutissant à une virilité renforcée. Suivant le principe de l'inspiration mutuelle, la SLK troisième génération emprunte des traits de caractère à sa grande sœur, la SLS, plus rapide. Clarté et ergonomie: habitacle aux grands instruments ronds, volant multifonctions à méplat et système Comand. Le toit escamotable se déploie et se replie en 20 secondes.

Lots of SUVs tend to be heavy drinkers—but not so the third generation of the M-Class. With economical, well-designed powertrains, refined aerodynamics, and considerable weight reductions, the ML appeals to many drivers who eye the fuel gauge on the dash with concern. *Magna cum laude* honor is due the 204 bhp diesel engine of the ML 250 BlueTec, which runs 39 miles per gallon, and so will happily travel more than 680 miles on a single tank of fuel. With its low emission rating, this Mercedes proves with ease that a modern SUV masterpiece can also be eco-friendly. By the same token, the two-ton machine achieves a top speed of more than 130 mph. This could partly be due to the vehicle's favorable drag coefficient. Its much improved contours are flatter, wider and longer than those of its predecessor. A greater use of aluminum—in particular for the hood, fenders and some of the powertrain components—compensates for the weight of the added technology and luxury on the inside.

The 3.5-liter V6 of the ML 350 4Matic BlueEfficiency produces 306 bhp at 6500 rpm. With an average mileage of some 26 miles per gallon of premium petrol, it is undeniably a piggy bank. Its wider tires—255s—might provide a little more aerodynamic drag, but its power is enough for 145 mph. Beyond good and evil is a beefcake called the ML 63 AMG with a V8 that pushes 525 bhp through its pipes. A further 32 bhp are activated in conjunction with the AMG performance package. This enables the electronic 155-mph lock to be deactivated. So this power pack that rockets to 62 mph in just 4.7 seconds is allowed to unfold almost without restraint. With a peak that is only limited to 174 mph, this SUV lies within the sports car range.

Mercedes offers no fewer than 16 alloy wheel designs for the M-Class. The particular highlight is, of course, the five twin-spoke design, lacquered in titanium grey and with a high-gloss finish—designed for 295-type tires—for the ML 63 AMG. The chassis (double wishbones at the front, multi-link suspension at the rear) with coil springs and gas pressure shock absorbers creates a harmonious unit for road use that is optimized by the "Active Curve System" roll stabilization system. An appropriate driving program is available at the touch of a button for true off-road use of the ML. It adjusts all the components—from engine output to automatic drive to ESP, ABS and 4ETS—to the particular conditions. However, it is a good idea to add appropriate items to protect the underside of the 4WD when driving off-road. Cruise control regulates the downhill speed from 2 to 11 mph on very steep slopes, undoubtedly an extremely useful facility—as is the brake assist, which comes as standard.

In the event of a frontal collision, bumper sensors activate a mechanism that lifts the hood, which reduces the impact energy and thus the risk of injury.

The exterior of the ML has been completely refined and enhanced, with a tremendous feeling for detail, especially the front and rear lights. This nifty package houses elegant,

So mancher SUV neigt zum Suff, nicht so die dritte Generation der M-Klasse. Sparsame, ausgereifte Triebwerke, verfeinerte Aerodynamik und erhebliche Gewichtseinsparungen machen den ML attraktiv für so manchen Lenker, der ängstlich auf die Tankuhr-Rotunde im Tacho schaut. *Magna cum laude* gebührt dem 204-PS-Dieselmotor des ML 250 BlueTec, der sich mit durchschnittlich sechs Litern auf 100 Kilometer begnügt, gut genug für eine Tankfüllungs-Reichweite von mehr als 1100 Kilometern. Eingestuft in die Emissionsklasse Euro 6, demonstriert dieser Mercedes mit Leichtigkeit, dass ein modernes Masterpiece im SUV-Segment auch umweltfreundlich sein kann. Andererseits erreicht der Zweitonner eine Spitzengeschwindigkeit, die deutlich jenseits der 200-km/h-Marke zu suchen ist. Das mag auch an dem günstigen Luftwiderstandsbeiwert dieses Fahrzeuges liegen. Seine stark überarbeiteten Konturen fallen gegenüber dem Vorgänger flacher, breiter und länger aus. Vermehrte Verwendung von Aluminium – besonders bei der Motorhaube, den Kotflügeln und einigen Fahrwerks-Komponenten – gleicht gewichtsmäßig mehr Technik und Interieurs-Luxus aus.

306 Pferdestärken bei 6500 Touren schöpft der V6 (Euro 5) des ML 350 4Matic BlueEfficiency aus 3,5 Litern Hubraum. Mit durchschnittlich weniger als neun Litern Super auf 100 Kilometer ist er ein Sparschwein. Breiter besohlt – mit 255er Reifen – bietet er zwar etwas mehr Luftwiderstand, doch seine Potenz reicht für 235 km/h. Jenseits von Gut und Böse präsentiert sich ein Muskelprotz namens ML 63 AMG, dessen V8 525 PS durch die Rohre jagt. Weitere 32 PS werden in Verbindung mit dem AMG-Performance-Paket aktiviert. Dieses erlaubt auch, die elektronische Sperre bei 250 km/h außer Kraft zu setzen. So darf sich dieses Kraftei, das innerhalb von 4,7 Sekunden aus dem Stand auf 100 Sachen beschleunigt, fast ungezügelt entfalten. Mit einer erst bei 280 km/h abgeregelten Spitze liegt dieser SUV im Sportwagen-Bereich.

Nicht weniger als 16 Leichtmetallräder-Designs bietet Mercedes für die M-Klasse an. Aus diesem Angebot hebt sich natürlich das 5-Doppelspeichen-Design, titangrau lackiert und glanzgedreht – zur Aufnahme von 295er-Puschen – für den ML 63 AMG besonders hervor. Das Fahrwerk (Doppelquerlenker vorn und Mehrlenker hinten) mit Schraubenfedern und Gasdruck-Stoßdämpfern bildet eine harmonische Einheit für den Straßengebrauch, optimiert durch die Wankstabilisierung »Active Curve System«. Für den wirklichen Offroad-Gebrauch des ML steht auf Tastendruck ein entsprechendes Fahrprogramm zur Verfügung. Es stellt sich mit allen Komponenten – von der Motorleistung bis zum Automatikgetriebe sowie ESP, ABS und 4ETS – auf den jeweiligen Untergrund ein. Zum Unterboden-Schutz des Allradlers im Gelände empfiehlt sich jedoch eine Nachrüstung. Ein Tempomat reguliert die Bergab-Geschwindigkeit von zwei bis 18 Stundenkilometer bei stark abschüssigen Hängen: gewiss eine hilfreiche Einrichtung – wie auch der serienmäßige Bremsassistent.

Si tant de SUV ont tendance à la gloutonnerie, ce n'est pas le cas de la troisième génération de la Classe M. Des moteurs économiques et aboutis, une aérodynamique optimisée et une perte de poids considérable rendent la ML attractive pour tous les conducteurs qui scrutent avec angoisse le niveau de la jauge sur le tableau de bord. Le moteur diesel 204 ch de la ML 250 BlueTec, qui se contente de 6 l/100 km en moyenne, permettant une autonomie de plus de 1100 km, mérite une mention spéciale. Répondant à la norme antipollution Euro 6, cette Mercedes démontre aisément qu'un chef-d'œuvre moderne dans le segment du tout-terrain de loisirs (SUV) peut être compatible avec une démarche de développement durable. Par ailleurs, ce modèle de deux tonnes atteint une vitesse de pointe largement supérieure à 200 km/h, prouesse qu'il doit peut-être à son excellent coefficient de traînée. Ses contours fortement modifiés semblent, par rapport aux modèles précédents, plus lisses, plus larges et plus longs. L'utilisation accrue de l'aluminium, en particulier au niveau du capot, des ailes et de certains composants du châssis, compense le poids de l'augmentation des éléments techniques et de confort dans l'habitacle.

Le V6 (Euro 5) de la ML 350 4Matic BlueEfficiency délivre 306 ch à 6500 tr/min pour une cylindrée de 3,5 litres. Avec en moyenne moins de 9 litres de super aux 100 km, il est vraiment sobre. Avec des pneumatiques plus larges (255), la résistance à l'air de la ML 350 est plus grande, mais sa puissance suffit pour 235 km/h. Un concentré de muscles baptisé ML 63 AMG, dont le V8 développe 525 ch, est également présenté. Avec le pack Performance AMG, 32 chevaux supplémentaires sont offerts au conducteur. Il permet également de désactiver le bridage automatique de la vitesse à 250 km/h. Ce bolide qui abat le 0 à 100 km/h en 4,7 secondes peut donc s'épanouir pratiquement sans retenue. Avec un bridage de la vitesse maximale à 280 km/h, ce SUV appartient indéniablement au segment des voitures de sport.

Pour la Classe M, Mercedes propose 16 modèles de jantes alliage. Le modèle à 5 doubles branches peint en gris titane, finition brillante, dédié à l'accueil de pneus de largeur 295, en série sur la ML 63 AMG, se démarque particulièrement dans cette offre. Le châssis (doubles bras transversaux à l'avant et essieu arrière multibras) à ressorts hélicoïdaux et amortisseurs à gaz compose une unité harmonieuse pour une utilisation routière, optimisée par l'« Active Curve System », appelé aussi système de stabilisation antiroulis. Pour emmener la ML hors des sentiers balisés, une molette permet de choisir le programme de conduite adapté. Les caractéristiques du moteur, de la boîte de vitesses automatique et de l'ESP, de l'ABS et du système 4ETS s'adaptent au type de chaussée. Pour protéger le soubassement de ce tout-terrain, il est néanmoins conseillé de l'équiper d'un habillage renforcé. Un limiteur de vitesse en descente régule automatiquement la vitesse entre 2 et 18 km/h dans les pentes raides : un équipement bien utile, comme l'assistant de freinage de série.

Mercedes-Benz M-Klasse   2011

Mercedes-Benz ML 350 BlueTec 2012

all-electric upholstered seats, the front ones divided by a neat, tidy, sensibly equipped center console that blends with the dashboard screen. This is where the night vision device also displays its functions.

ML could also stand for "medium load capacity," as there are just 24.4 cubic feet behind the second row of seats. However, with the seats down this figure rises to 71 cubic feet. Perhaps the abbreviation really means "mega load capacity."

Bei einem frontalen Zusammenprall lösen Sensoren im Stoßfänger einen Mechanismus aus, der die Motorhaube anhebt, was die Aufprallenergie und damit die Verletzungsgefahr reduziert.

Gut in Form präsentiert sich die verfeinerte und gleichzeitig markanter aufbereitete Gewandung des ML – mit viel Liebe zum Detail, besonders bei den Front- und Heckleuchten. In diesem Outfit steckt nobles, vollelektrisch bewegbares Polster-Gestühl, vorn geteilt durch eine aufgeräumt gestaltete und sinnvoll bestückte Mittelkonsole, die in den Bildschirm des Armaturenbretts mündet. Hier visualisiert auch das Nachtsichtgerät seine Empfindungen.

ML könnte auch für »mittlere Ladekapazität« stehen – hinter der zweiten Sitzreihe sind es lediglich 690 Liter. Doch legt man diese flach, kommen immerhin 2010 Liter unter. Nichts gegen neue Wortschöpfungen, doch der ML verdient eine weitere: »Mega-Ladekapazität«.

En cas de collision frontale, des capteurs situés dans le pare-chocs déclenchent un mécanisme qui déplace le capot moteur vers le haut. L'énergie cinétique est ainsi mieux absorbée et le risque de blessure, réduit.

L'extérieur de la ML s'affiche sous un jour plus raffiné et athlétique avec des contours plus marqués et révèle un grand amour du détail, en particulier au niveau des feux avant et arrière. Sous cette livrée élégante, on découvre des sièges rembourrés harmonieux à réglage entièrement électrique, séparés à l'avant par une console médiane bien conçue et intelligemment équipée qui se termine dans l'écran du tableau de bord. C'est ici que l'assistant de vision de nuit entre en jeu.

La ML n'est toutefois pas synonyme de grand volume de chargement : derrière les sièges arrière, seuls 690 litres sont en effet disponibles. Néanmoins, lorsque l'on rabat les sièges, on obtient un généreux espace de 2010 litres.

The third generation of the successful M-Class is sporty throughout and economical in consumption.

Rundum sportlich und sparsam im Verbrauch präsentiert sich die dritte Generation der erfolgreichen M-Klasse.

La troisième génération de la célèbre Classe M révèle son caractère sportif, mais économique.

Mercedes-Benz M-Klasse 2011

Momentum in the German family car genre of minivans, a domain of the Volkswagen Group, really started to pick up in January 2010. That month, Mercedes's new B-Class established itself directly behind VW's successful Touran with 3911 new vehicles registered. It was a little spatial miracle on wheels: folding down the back seats increases the load capacity from 17.2 to a generous 54.6 cubic feet. And there's already plenty of headroom in the five-seater, which is 5 feet 1 inch high. Achieving a drag coefficient of 0.26 (B 180 BlueEfficiency) in this "space" segment is a testimony to the aerodynamic sensitivity that went into designing it. Whether you have it with or without the chrome package, or opt for the sporty version, the converging creases below the beltline that end virtually in the rear lights add design accents that are even more distinctive on the so-called "night package" with tinted side windows. This impression is further enhanced by the innovative clear lacquer with an extra dense molecular structure. There is little doubt that the love for the design of this metal clothing will not always be returned.

Mercedes offers two diesel and two gasoline environmentally friendly, economical four-cylinder engines. All make important contributions toward the added value that the group calls "BlueEfficiency." By the end of 2012, this optimized, energy-saving yet powerful technology will be included in no fewer than 140 Daimler AG vehicle models. The 1.8-liter diesel powertrain impresses for its exceptionally low consumption figures, which are achieved with high injection pressures and the variable turbine geometry, so its 109 or 136 bhp are not expensive. The newly developed 1.6-liter gasoline engine with high-pressure direct injection and turbocharger is more powerful: 122 and 156 bhp.

Instead of the standard 6-speed gearbox, the B-Class driver can also order a 7-gear dual-clutch transmission for an additional $2330 before tax.

The catalog of sporty attributes, exclusive and practical accessories, and special features leaves nothing to be desired. Mercedes offers a sliding panorama sunroof for a clear view of the sky. Aircon with separate temperature controls for driver and passenger is only available with the chrome or sports package.

Like almost all front-wheel drives, the B-Class tends to understeer, although that is no bad thing. And there's a whole range of assist systems for those who value safe driving: sensors to detect driver fatigue, distance warning systems, and a "modular driving dynamics control system". The latter consists primarily of safety and comfort functions that complement the anti-blocking system.

As "crossovers," the B-Class models belong to a category that is not concerned with proving itself either in terms of acceleration or top speeds—unless you are dealing with the B 200 BlueEfficiency. This one hits 62 mph in 8.9 seconds and has a top speed of 136 mph. And depending on driving style and load, a tank of gas is

Im Januar 2012 gerät Bewegung in das deutsche Familien-Auto-Genre der Mini-Vans, eine Domäne des Volkswagenwerks. Direkt hinter dem VW-Erfolgsmodell Touran etabliert sich in jenem Monat die neue B-Klasse von Mercedes mit 3911 Zulassungen. Ein kleines Raumwunder auf Rädern, denn durch Umklappen der Fondsitze vergrößert sich das Ladevolumen von 486 auf ergiebige 1545 Liter. An Kopffreiheit mangelt es dem 155,7 Zentimeter hohen Fünfsitzer ohnehin nicht. In diesem »Raumfahrt«-Segment einen Luftwiderstands-Beiwert von 0,26 (B 180 BlueEfficiency) zu erzielen, zeugt von viel aerodynamischem Fingerspitzengefühl beim Fahrzeug-Design. Ob mit oder ohne Chrom-Paket oder als sportliche Variante angeboten: Das gegenläufige Faltenspiel unterhalb der Gürtellinie, das virtuell in den Rückleuchten mündet, setzt gestalterische Akzente, die beim sogenannten »Night-Paket« mit dunkel getönten Seitenscheiben noch deutlicher hervortreten. Ein innovativer Klarlack mit extrem dichter Molekularstruktur verstärkt diesen Eindruck. Sicherlich trifft dieses Seitenflächen-Design des Blechkleides nicht nur auf Gegenliebe.

Mit je zwei Diesel- und Benzin-Motoren offeriert Mercedes umweltfreundliche und sparsame Vierzylinder. Sie leisten einen wesentlichen Beitrag zu einer Wertschöpfung, die der Konzern als »BlueEfficiency« bezeichnet. Diese optimierte, energiesparende und gleichermaßen leistungsfähige Technologie hält bis Ende 2012 bei nicht weniger als 140 Fahrzeug-Modellen der Daimler AG Einzug. Das 1.8-Liter-Diesel-Triebwerk beeindruckt durch außerordentlich niedrige Verbrauchswerte, erzielt durch hohen Einspritzdruck und die variable Turbinengeometrie. Wohlfeil sind 109 oder 136 PS. Stärker motorisiert gibt sich der neu entwickelte 1.6-Liter-Benziner mit Hochdruck-Direkteinspritzung und Turboaufladung: 122 und 156 PS.

Statt des serienmäßigen 6-Gang-Schaltgetriebes kann der B-Klassen-Fahrer auch ein 7-Gang-Doppelkupplungsgetriebe ordern, Aufpreis: 1820 Euro zuzüglich Mehrwertsteuer.

Der Katalog sportlicher Attribute, exklusiver Accessoires und diverser Sonderausstattungen sowie praktischen Zubehörs lässt keine Wünsche offen. Für einen ungetrübten Blick nach oben bietet Mercedes ein Panorama-Glasschiebedach an. Nur in Verbindung mit dem Chrom- oder dem Sport-Paket ist der Erwerb einer Klimaautomatik mit getrennter Temperaturwahl für Fahrer und Beifahrer möglich.

Wie fast alle Fronttriebler neigt die B-Klasse zum Untersteuern, was der Fahrstabilität keinen Abbruch tut. Wem besonders sicheres Fahren am Herzen liegt, der kann sich über eine Fülle von Assistenz-Systemen freuen. Keinen zusätzlichen Griff in den Geldbeutel verlangen Sensoren zur Müdigkeitserkennung des Fahrzeuglenkers, Abstands-Warneinrichtungen und ein »modular aufgebautes Fahrdynamik-Regelsystem« (Werksjargon). Letzteres

En janvier 2012, un vent de changement souffle sur le segment allemand des monospaces familiaux compacts, domaine habituel de la firme Volkswagen. Ce même mois, la nouvelle Classe B de Mercedes s'établit immédiatement derrière la célèbre Touran de Volkswagen, avec 3911 immatriculations en Allemagne. Véritable prodige sur roues en termes d'espace, le volume de chargement passe de 486 à 1545 litres en rabattant les sièges arrière. L'habitacle de cette voiture cinq places d'une hauteur de 155,7 cm offre de fait suffisamment de place aux passagers. Le c_x exceptionnel de seulement 0,26 (B 180 BlueEfficiency) dans ce segment des voitures spacieuses témoigne du soin apporté à l'optimisation de l'aérodynamisme lors du design. Avec ou sans pack chrome ou encore en version sport, les lignes dynamiques sous la ligne de ceinture qui débouchent virtuellement dans les feux arrière, sculptent les flancs que souligne encore plus le «pack Night» avec vitres surteintées. Un vernis innovant à la structure moléculaire particulièrement épaisse renforce cette impression. Ce design latéral de la tôle ne recevra sans doute pas un accueil unanimement favorable.

Avec deux moteurs diesel et deux moteurs essence, Mercedes propose des quatre-cylindres éco-compatibles et peu gourmands. Ils apportent une contribution considérable à ce que le groupe appelle la technologie «BlueEfficiency». D'ici fin 2012, plus de 140 modèles du groupe Daimler AG seront équipés de cette technologie optimisée, économique mais efficace. Le moteur diesel 1,8 litre séduit par une consommation extraordinairement faible obtenue grâce à l'action conjuguée d'une pression d'injection élevée et d'une géométrie de turbine variable. À un prix accessible, on retrouve les moteurs 109 ou 136 ch. Le nouveau moteur essence 1,6 litre à injection directe haute pression et suralimentation par turbocompresseur est quant à lui plus puissant : 122 et 156 ch.

En lieu et place de la boîte mécanique à six rapports de série, l'acheteur d'une Classe B peut commander une boîte de vitesses sept rapports à double embrayage pour un surcoût de 1820 euros hors TVA. Le catalogue des attributs sportifs, sans compter les multiples accessoires pratiques et équipements divers répond à tous les désirs. Pour bénéficier d'une vue imprenable sur le ciel, Mercedes propose aussi un toit panoramique ouvrant électrique. La climatisation automatique avec choix individuel de la température pour le conducteur et le passager n'est disponible que pour les packs Chrome et Sport.

Comme presque tous les modèles à traction avant, la Classe B présente une tendance innée au sous-virage ce qui ne nuit pas à la stabilité. Ceux à qui la sécurité tient particulièrement à cœur pourront se réjouir de l'abondance des systèmes d'assistance. Nul besoin de porter la main au porte-monnaie pour disposer du système de détection de somnolence du conducteur, d'un régulateur de distance et d'un «système modulaire de régulation de la dynamique de marche intégré» (jargon interne). Ce dispositif propose essentiellement des fonctions supplémentaires au service

Mercedes-Benz B-Klasse 2011

Mercedes-Benz B 180 CDI 2012

good for over 430 miles. All this, and it produces less than 225 grams of CO_2 per mile. In summary: top of its class!

bezieht sich primär auf Sicherheits- und Komfort-Funktionen zur Ergänzung des Anti-Blockier-Systems.

Als »Crossover« gehören die B-Klasse-Modelle zu einer Kategorie, die sich weder beim Beschleunigen noch in der Endgeschwindigkeit Meriten verdienen will, es sei, man tritt mit dem B 200 BlueEfficiency an. Dieser erreicht die 100-km/h-Marke nach 8,9 Sekunden und bringt es immerhin auf 220 Stundenkilometer. Mit einer Tankfüllung lassen sich – je nach Fahrstil und Beladung – über 700 Kilometer zurücklegen. Dabei werden pro Kilometer weniger als 140 Gramm CO_2 ausgestoßen. Fazit: Ein Klassen-Primus!

de la sécurité et du confort pour améliorer les performances du système antiblocage de roues.

En tant que «crossover», les modèles de la Classe B appartiennent à une catégorie qui ne cherche à gagner des lauriers ni en termes d'accélération, ni en termes de vitesse de pointe. Prenons l'exemple de la B 200 BlueEfficiency. Elle accélère de 0 à 100 km/h en 8,9 secondes et atteint tout de même une vitesse de pointe de 220 km/h. Avec le plein, on peut, selon le style de conduite et le chargement, parcourir plus de 700 km, pour une émission au kilomètre de moins de 140 g de CO_2. Bilan: premier de la classe!

"Seats for five people, and room for a whole family" is how Mercedes-Benz advertises the spacious new B-Class that is making a name for itself in the small van segment.

»Sitze für fünf Personen und Platz für eine ganze Familie«, so lautet die Mercedes-Benz-Laudatio auf die geräumige, neue B-Klasse, die sich im Segment der kleinen Vans breit macht.

« Cinq places et espace pour toute la famille. » Tel est le slogan utilisé par Mercedes-Benz pour vanter les mérites de la nouvelle et spacieuse Classe B qui s'installe dans le segment des monospaces compacts.

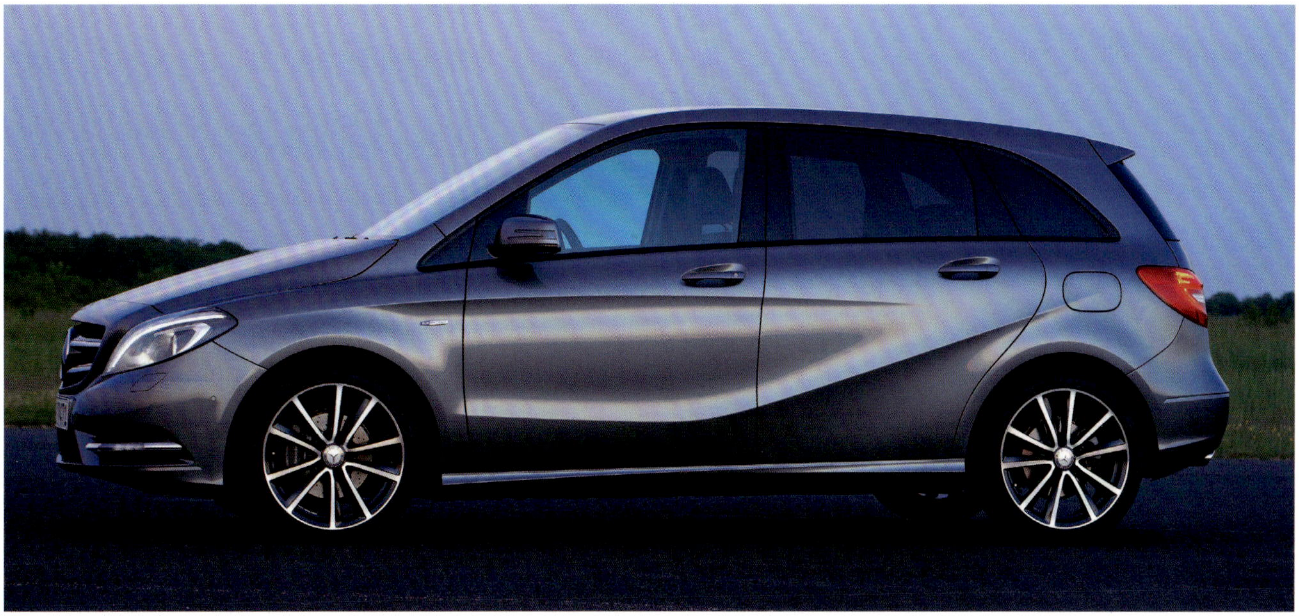

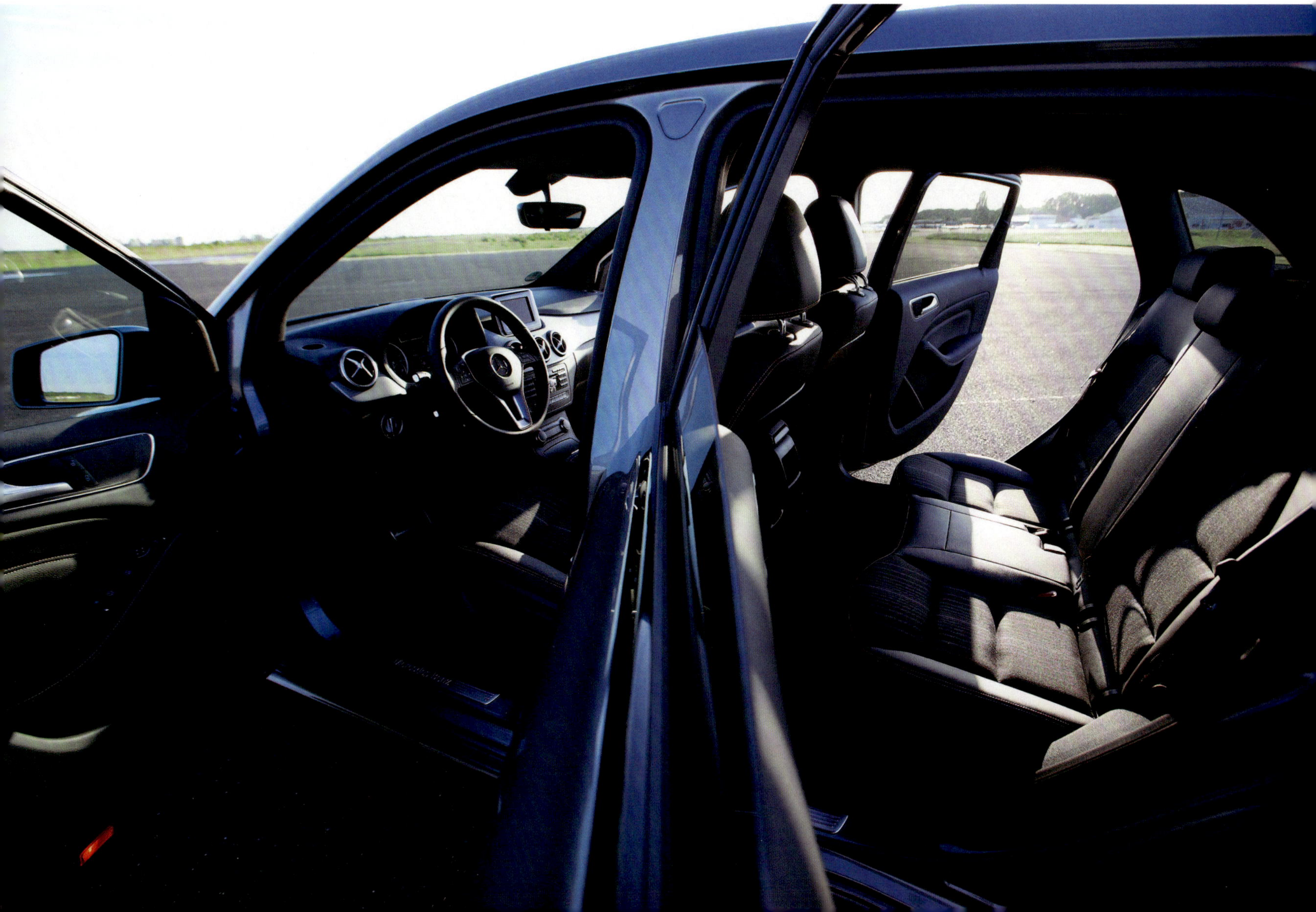

Made for a decade, the sixth generation of the SL basks in the glory of all its predecessors. Of course, this roadster still has to earn itself the additional accolade of "icon" or even "legend," like the famous gullwing of the early 50s. But it has to be said that this luxurious two-seater not only has a sporty character, but also lives up to the second letter in the abbreviation "SL." After more than 40 years of constantly putting on weight—the SL 63 AMG recently topped the scales at 4310 pounds—Mercedes-Benz is now offering a consistent lightweight aluminum construction with lots of intelligent detail solutions. Thanks to a tube-in-tube concept, thin-walled but extremely strong hollow profiles and weight reductions all over, this AMG SL has slimmed down to 3935 pounds. This is not the weight when empty, because the corresponding European Union standard is based on an almost full tank, a fictional person weighing 150 pounds behind the wheel, and a baggage allowance of 16 pounds. So it's lucky that more than a briefcase will fit in the trunk when the top is up. And if you can get your belongings down to a volume of 17.8 cubic feet, you'll even be able to get two golf bags in. Once the plastic vario roof which is molded over a lightweight magnesium frame, is retracted, 12.9 cubic feet remain.

Although the new SL (factory name R 231) has been stretched by 1¾ inches, it looks more bullish and more masculine than its direct predecessor. This could be thanks to its wide hips and the steeper slope to the nose— a "soft nose" for better impact absorption in the event of minor collisions. Eye-catching air inlets add a special touch to the front of the vehicle.

Under the SL hood are magnificent powertrains that, despite the increase in performance, are amazingly economical. While the V6 of the SL 350 BlueEfficiency had to make do with the customary capacity of 3498 cc and 306 bhp, the SL 500 has a 4.7-liter twin-turbo that offers an additional 47.5 bhp. The SL 36 AMG has more power, too: from 525 to 537 bhp. Almost as compensation for the high prices of premium fuels, these engines are less thirsty: city and highway combined over 23.5 mpg. This means that with a fuel tank capacity of 21 gallons and electronic speed limitation to 155 mph, the range of the SL is surprisingly large.

The SL 63 AMG is a particularly impressive sprinter: 62 mph in 4.3 seconds, and the SL 500 accelerates at a rate only three-tenths slower than this version. The electromechanical power-assisted direct steering that adapts to the driving speed is a particular delight on winding roads. The SL chassis with adaptive absorbers easily gobbles up road bumps, and rolling motions caused by load changes are neutralized even without the optional Active Body Control. The SL's headlights with variable light cone react to extreme weather situations and the corresponding poor visibility. The windshield washer system is connected to the wiper blades, and thus works more efficiently.

Ganz im Glanze seiner Vorgänger sonnt sich die nunmehr sechste Generation des SL, geschaffen für eine Dekade. Freilich muss sich dieser Roadster noch das schmückende Attribut »Ikone« oder gar »Legende« wie der berühmte Flügeltürer der frühen fünfziger Jahre verdienen. Immerhin muss man diesem luxuriösen Zweisitzer attestieren, dass er nicht nur sehr sportlich agiert, sondern auch den zweiten Buchstaben des Kürzels SL erfüllt. Nach mehr als 40 Jahren permanenter Gewichtszunahme – zuletzt brachte es der SL 63 AMG auf 1955 Kilo – präsentiert Mercedes-Benz 2012 einen konsequenten Aluminium-Leichtbau mit vielen intelligenten Detaillösungen. Dank eines Rohr-in-Rohr-Konzepts, dünnwandiger aber äußerst stabiler Hohlprofile und Gewichtseinsparungen rundum, speckte eben dieser AMG-SL auf 1785 Kilo ab. Kein Leergewicht, da die entsprechende EU-Norm einen fast vollen Tank, eine fiktive 68-Kilo-Person hinter dem Volant sowie ein Gepäck-Zugeständnis von sieben Kilo integriert. Ein Glück, dass in den Kofferraum bei geschlossenem Verdeck mehr als eine Aktentasche passt. Wenn man seine Mitbringsel geschickt auf das Volumen von 504 Litern verteilt, finden sogar zwei Golfbags Platz. Hat sich das über einen leichten Magnesiumrahmen gezogene Kunststoff-Variodach im Heck versenkt, bleiben noch 364 Liter.

Obwohl der neue SL (werksintern R 231 genannt) um 45 Millimeter gestreckt worden ist, wirkt er bulliger und maskuliner als sein direkter Vorfahr. Das mag an seinen breiten Hüften und dem steiler abfallenden Bug – einer »Soft Nose« zur besseren Aufprall-Absorbtion bei nicht allzu heftigen Auffahrunfällen – liegen. Markante Lufteinlässe verleihen der Fahrzeugfront einen besonderen Touch.

Unter den SL-Hauben verbirgt sich die Kraft und Herrlichkeit von Triebwerken, die trotz gestiegener Leistung erstaunliche Verbrauchswerte offerieren. Muss sich der V6 des SL 350 BlueEfficiency mit dem gewohnten Hubraum von 3498 cm³ und 306 PS begnügen, wartet der SL 500 nun mit einem 4,7-Liter-Biturbo auf, der zusätzliche 47,5 PS entfaltet. Power-Plus auch beim SL 63 AMG: von 525 auf 537 PS. Quasi als Entschädigung für die hohen Super-Plus-Preise an der Zapfsäule entwickeln die Motoren weniger Sprit-Durst: inner- und außerorts kombiniert unter zehn Liter. Angesichts eines Tankinhalts von 80 Litern und einer elektronischen Geschwindigkeitsbegrenzung auf 250 km/h fällt die Reichweite des SL somit recht groß aus.

Seine Sprinterqualitäten dokumentiert besonders der SL 63 AMG: 4,3 Sekunden auf Tempo 100, und nur drei Zehntel langsamer beschleunigt der SL 500 auf diese Marke. Besondere Fahrfreude auf kurvenreichem Terrain beschert die elektromechanische Direktlenkung mit einem Servosystem, das sich an der Fahrgeschwindigkeit orientiert. Fahrbahn-Unebenheiten schluckt das SL-Fahrwerk mit adaptiven Dämpfern locker – selbst ohne das optionale Active Body Control, das lastwechselbedingte Wankbewegungen neutralisiert. Auf extreme Wettersituationen mit entsprechend schlechten Sichtverhältnissen

La désormais sixième génération de la SL, conçue pour durer une décennie, savoure encore la gloire de ses prédécesseurs. Pourtant, ce roadster doit encore faire ses preuves pour mériter le titre honorifique d'«icône», voire de «légende», comme le célèbre coupé «papillon» du début des années 1950. Néanmoins force est d'admettre que ce luxueux roadster biplace très sportif porte à merveille les deux initiales de son nom, SL. Après plus de 40 ans de prise de poids permanente – la dernière SL 63 AMG affichait 1955 kg sur la balance – Mercedes-Benz présente en 2012 une caisse légère en aluminium agrémentée de nombreux détails «gain de poids» astucieux. Grâce à une conception tubulaire, des profilés creux à paroi fine extrêmement stables et d'autres pertes de poids ça et là, la SL AMG est descendue à 1785 kg. Ce n'est pas exactement son poids à vide, puisque la norme européenne en vigueur inclut dans le calcul un réservoir quasiment plein, un conducteur fictif de 68 kg derrière le volant et des bagages de sept kilogrammes. Lorsque le toit est fermé, le coffre offre fort heureusement suffisamment de place pour caser plus qu'un porte-documents. Si l'on dispose habilement les souvenirs rapportés de vacances dans le volume de chargement de 504 litres, on pourra encore y loger deux sacs de golf. Une fois le toit escamotable replié sur un cadre léger en magnésium, il reste encore un volume de 364 litres.

Bien que la nouvelle SL (baptisée R 231 en interne) ait été rallongé de 45 mm, elle semble plus robuste et plus virile que la précédente, sans doute à cause de ses hanches élargies et de son museau plongeant – un «soft nose» pour une meilleure absorption des chocs en cas de collision modérée. Les impressionnantes prises d'air confèrent une allure particulière aux ailes avant de ce véhicule.

Le capot de la SL abrite toute la force et la souveraineté de moteurs qui, malgré une puissance accrue, restent très raisonnables en matière de consommation. Si le V6 de la SL 350 BlueEfficiency doit se contenter d'une cylindrée usuelle de 3498 cm³ pour 306 ch, la SL 500 dispose désormais d'un bi-turbo 4,7 litres qui développe 47,5 ch supplémentaires. Gain de puissance aussi avec la SL 63 AMG: on passe de 525 à 537 ch. En guise peut-être de dédommagement face aux prix élevés du super à la pompe, ces moteurs sont peu gourmands: moins de 10 l/100 km en moyen urbain/extra-urbain. Compte tenu de la capacité du réservoir de 80 litres et du bridage électronique de la vitesse à 250 km/h, l'autonomie de la SL est très enviable.

La SL 63 AMG présente de véritables qualités de sprinter: il lui faut 4,3 secondes pour passer de 0 à 100 km/h, mais la SL 500 accélère en seulement trois dixièmes de plus. La direction paramétrique à fonctionnement électromécanique asservie à la vitesse offre un véritable confort de conduite dans les virages. Le train de roulement à système d'amortissement adaptatif de la SL absorbe les défauts de la chaussée, même sans la suspension active ABC (Active Body Control) en option qui neutralise les mouvements de roulis dans les virages. En conditions climatiques extrêmes avec visibilité réduite, les phares de

Mercedes-Benz SL   2012

Mercedes-Benz SL 500 2012

Despite the sporty genes of the SL, the interior with its luscious leather covers, elegant woods, and finely brushed aluminum parts are irresistible to passers-by. After all, a status-conscious SL driver wants everyone to know what his classy vehicle has to offer: a tasteful, practically equipped cockpit with a joystick for automatic drive; an electric wind deflector that controls the turbulence when driving with the top down; and, for cooler days, warm air blowers in the headrests that provide a pleasant temperature at the highest level.

As with the SLK, a panoramic window that can be darkened is also available for the vario roof. This is another SL attribute that underscores the vehicle's claim to belong to the automotive *haute couture*.

reagieren beim SL Scheinwerfer mit variablem Leuchtkegel. Ohne Streuverlust arbeitet die Scheibenwaschanlage, die an die Wischerblätter gekoppelt ist.

Trotz aller sportlichen Gene des SL animiert das Interieur mit üppigen Lederbezügen, edlen Hölzern und fein gebürsteten Alu-Teilen zum offenen Defilieren. Schließlich will ein standesbewusster SL-Lenker zeigen, was sein nobles Gefährt zu bieten hat: nämlich ein geschmackvoll und praktisch ausgestattetes Cockpit mit einem Joystick für die Automatik. Ein elektrisches Windschott reguliert die Turbulenzen beim Open-Air-Fahrvergnügen. An kühleren Tagen sorgen Warmluftgebläse in den Kopfstützen für angenehme Temperierung auf höchster Ebene.

Wie beim SLK wird für das Variodach eine abdunkelbare Panoramascheibe angeboten. Auch dieses SL-Attribut unterstreicht den Anspruch, zur automobilen Haute Couture zu gehören.

la SL réagissent en adaptant le cône lumineux. Le système d'essuie-glace associant balai et lave-glace nettoie les vitres en utilisant juste la quantité nécessaire de liquide.

Malgré l'ADN sportif de la SL, l'habitacle s'offre aux regards avec des selleries cuirs raffinées, du bois précieux et des éléments en aluminium brossé. Pour conclure, le conducteur de SL peut être fier de ce que sa noble monture a à offrir : un cockpit sophistiqué et ergonomique avec levier sélecteur pour la boîte de vitesses. Un pare-vent électrique protège des courants d'air en conduite à ciel ouvert. Lorsque la température baisse, le chauffage de nuque intégré dans les appuie-têtes garantit une chaleur agréable dans les plus hautes sphères.

Comme pour la SLK, le toit escamotable est proposé avec une vitre panoramique qui peut s'assombrir au besoin. Cet attribut de la SL souligne sa volonté d'appartenir à la haute couture de l'automobile.

Mercedes-Benz SL 2012

Masculine: the lightweight SL 500 achieves the speed-strength of a sprinter from its new 4.7-liter twin-turbo combined with the tremendous torque of 516 lb-ft.

Maskulin: Aus einem neuen 4,7-Liter-Biturbo schöpft der Leichtbau-SL 500 die Schnellkraft eines Sprinters, gepaart mit dem enormen Drehmoment von 700 Newtonmetern.

Virile : avec son nouveau bi-turbo 4,7 litres, la SL 500 à la structure légère atteint des performances dignes d'un bolide de course, associé à un couple énorme de 700 Nm.

"We have also transferred our new design language into the A-Class," Professor Gorden Wagener, head of Mercedes-Benz design, explained at the presentation at the 2012 Geneva Motor Show. By this he meant the expressive play of line in the structural edge that sloped gently to the rear starting at the top of the front fender, and the crimp below it that is bent upward, analogous to the side section design of the new B-Class (W 246).

However, unlike this design, the A-Class (W 176) has moved away from its original configuration as a minivan with a sandwich construction base. Stretched from 11 feet 9 inches to 12 feet 9 inches (2004) and now 14 feet 1 inch, and 6¾ inches lower in height, the dimensions already indicate that this little Mercedes-Benz intends to fight the corresponding Volkswagen and Audi models and the BMW 1 series for its share of the market. Dieter Zetsche, President of Daimler AG, sums it up: "A is for attack." And his development director Thomas Weber adds: "The design is absolutely cool—but this compact car also has S-Class safety technology and the latest telematics, which turns the A-Class into an iPhone on wheels. Alternative drive concepts are in preparation." The engine co-operation with Renault-Nissan should help.

Mercedes will be well equipped as it approaches the compact car front in the summer of 2012 with six four-cylinder engines, three diesel and three petrol. The bandwidth of the diesel versions ranges from 108 to 170 bhp. The gasoline trio offer 122 to 210 bhp. A special version of the A 180 CDI is particularly environmentally friendly: in economy mode, it ejects just 159 grams per mile of carbon dioxide into the atmosphere. The start-stop function, which is as much a part of daily life in the A-Class as the radar emergency brake assist or the choice of six gears and the dual clutch automatic with seven soft-as-butter meshing forward gears, are all aids to economy.

Wagener's "dynamic new style" on the inside, demonstrated in the Concept A-Class at the 2011 IAA in Frankfurt, hasn't yet established itself in the A-Class. It still has a functional cockpit with no frills or fancies. The screen, which still comes down below the ventilation slits on the center console on the predecessor, becomes a real feature in the new A-Class. It reigns supreme over three jet-like air circulation nozzles. Styled for aerodynamics right through to the extended ridge, the new A-Class reveals its sporty nature.

Low air resistance and a lower center of gravity plus an optimized four-link rear axle, together with the sports suspension and optional direct steering, make the well-powered A 250 shock the GTIs. This model shows its potency in the red stripe around the middle air inlet above the front spoiler—as if it had tasted GTI blood—and an aggressive-looking "diamond" grille, which includes an exhaust system with twin tailpipes, embedded in the rear apron of the AMG. And there's another red stripe on the rear, which one can do without. To the practically

»Wir haben unsere neue Formensprache auch in die A-Klasse übertragen«, doziert Mercedes-Benz-Designchef Professor Gorden Wagener am Rande der Präsentation auf dem Genfer Salon 2012. Damit meint er sein expressives Linienspiel einer nach hinten leicht abfallenden Strukturkante, die oberhalb des vorderen Kotflügels beginnt, und einer darunter liegenden gegenläufigen, nach oben abgeknickten Sicke – analog zum Seitenflächen-Design der neuen B-Klasse (W246).

Doch im Gegensatz zu dieser bewegt sich die A-Klasse (W176) weg von ihrer ursprünglichen Konfiguration als Mini-Van mit Sandwich-Boden. Von 3,57 über 3,88 (2004) auf nunmehr 4,29 Meter gestreckt und 17 Zentimeter flacher nivelliert, verraten schon die Abmessungen, dass der kleine Mercedes-Benz den entsprechenden VW- und Audi-Modellen sowie dem 1er-BMW Marktanteile streitig machen will. Dieter Zetsche, Vorstandsvorsitzender der Daimler AG, bringt es auf den Punkt: »A steht für Angriff«. Und sein Entwicklungs-Vorstand Thomas Weber fügt hinzu: »Das Design ist absolut cool, wir bieten mit diesem Kompaktwagen aber auch Sicherheitstechnologien aus der S-Klasse und versehen ihn mit neuester Telematik, welche die A-Klasse zum iPhone auf Rädern macht. Alternative Antriebskonzepte sind in Arbeit.« Dabei soll eine Motoren-Kooperation mit Renault-Nissan hilfreich sein.

Mit sechs Vierzylindern – je drei Diesel- und Benzinmotoren – marschiert Mercedes im Sommer 2012 gut gerüstet an die Kompaktwagen-Front. Die Bandbreite der Diesel-Einheiten reicht von 108 bis 170 PS. Die Benziner-Truppe formiert sich von 122 bis 210 PS. Mit einer speziellen Version des A 180 CDI ist man besonders umweltfreundlich angetreten: Sie pustet im Sprit-Spar-Modus gerade mal 99 Gramm Kohlendioxid in die Luft. Im Dienste der Sparsamkeit arbeitet auch die Start-Stopp-Funktion, die ebenso zum Alltag der A-Klasse gehört wie der Notbremsassistent auf Radar-Basis oder die Wahl zwischen einer 6-Gang-Schaltung und der Doppelkupplungs-Automatik mit sieben butterweich ineinander übergehenden Vorwärtsgängen.

Wageners »neuer dynamischer Stil« im Interieur, demonstriert im Concept A-Class auf der IAA 2011 in Frankfurt, hat bei der A-Klasse noch nicht Fuß gefasst. Sie präsentiert sich mit einem funktionellen Cockpit ohne Schnörkel. Der Bildschirm, beim Vorgänger noch in der Mittelkonsole unter den Belüftungsschlitzen versenkt, rückt bei der neuen A-Klasse voll in den Blickpunkt. Er thront freistehend über drei Jet-ähnlichen Düsen zur Luftzirkulation. Bis zur verlängerten Abrisskante des Daches aerodynamisch durchgestylt, lässt die neue A-Klasse ihren sportlichen Habitus erkennen.

Niedriger Luftwiderstand und tief liegender Schwerpunkt sowie eine optimierte Vierlenker-Hinterachse: Diese Kriterien machen zusammen mit einem Sportfahrwerk und der optionalen Direktlenkung den an sich gut motorisierten A 250 zum GTI-Schreck. Mit einem roten Streifen über dem Frontspoiler im Bereich des

«Nous avons aussi appliqué notre nouveau langage formel à la Classe A», expliquait Gorden Wagener, responsable du département design chez Mercedes-Benz, lors de la présentation de ce modèle au salon de Genève en 2012. Il fait sans doute référence au jeu des lignes expressif structurant les surfaces: une ligne propulsive qui parcourt les flancs et s'élance vers l'arrière dans un mouvement plongeant et, juste en dessous, un coup de crayon dynamique tiré vers le haut, en sens contraire – rappelant le dessin des flancs de la nouvelle Classe B (W 246).

Toutefois, contrairement à cette dernière, la Classe A (W 176) s'écarte de sa configuration monospace compact initiale à architecture sandwich. Allongée de 3,57 m, puis 3,88 (2004) à désormais 4,29 m et rabaissée de 17 cm, ses dimensions annoncent la couleur: la petite Mercedes-Benz veut contester les parts de marché des modèles Volkswagen et Audi similaires, ainsi que de la BMW Série 1. Dieter Zetsche, président du groupe Daimler AG, va droit au but: «Classe A, comme Attaque». Et le directeur de la R&D, Thomas Weber, de renchérir: «Le design est résolument cool, cependant avec cette voiture compacte, nous proposons aussi des technologies issues de la Classe S pour la sécurité. Nous l'équipons de systèmes télématiques de pointe, ce qui fait de la Classe A un véritable iPhone sur roues. Nous travaillons enfin sur de nouveaux concepts de motorisation alternative.» La coopération avec Renault-Nissan pour les moteurs devrait porter ses fruits dans ce domaine.

Avec six moteurs quatre cylindres – trois diesel et trois essence –, Mercedes se présente bien armée sur le front des voitures compactes à l'aube de l'été 2012. L'escadrille diesel offre des puissances allant de 108 à 170 ch, l'escouade essence de 122 à 210 ch. Une version spéciale de la A 180 CDI est particulièrement respectueuse de l'environnement: en mode économie de carburant, elle rejette tout juste 99 grammes de CO_2 dans l'air. La fonction stop/start œuvre aussi au service de cette frugalité: elle équipe la Classe A de série au même titre que le système d'assistance au freinage d'urgence avec radar anticollision ou le choix entre une boîte six vitesses et la boîte automatique à double embrayage sept rapports de marche avant qui se distingue par son grand confort de passage.

Le «nouveau style dynamique» de l'habitacle imaginé par Gorden Wagener et présenté avec la Concept A-Class en 2011 à l'IAA à Francfort, ne s'est pas encore imposé dans la Classe A. Elle possède un cockpit fonctionnel sans fioritures. L'écran, encore ancré dans la console médiane en dessous des buses d'aération sur le modèle précédent, remonte dans le champ de vision sur la nouvelle Classe A. Il trône en suspension au-dessus de trois buses d'air de style emprunté au cockpit des avions. La nouvelle Classe A révèle son allure sportive et aérodynamique jusque dans la moulure sculptée dans le toit qui allonge sa silhouette.

Faible coefficient de pénétration dans l'air, centre de gravité bas, essieu arrière à quatre bras optimisé: l'ensemble de ces critères associés au réglage sport du

Mercedes-Benz A-Klasse   2012

Mercedes-Benz A250 2012

minded, the continuous rear lights that constrict the loading bay of the rear tailgate will undoubtedly be like a red flag to a bull.

mittleren Lufteinlasses – als habe er GTI-Blut geleckt – und einem aggressiv wirkenden »Diamant«-Gesicht visualisiert dieses Modell seine Potenz. Dazu gehört auch eine Auspuffanlage mit Doppelendrohren, eingebettet in die AMG-Heckschürze. Roter Streifen auch am Heck: ein verzichtbares Attribut. Dass die Heckleuchten, da ungeteilt, die Ladebucht der Heckklappe einengen, dürfte für Pragmatiker freilich wie ein rotes Tuch auf einen Stier wirken.

train de roulement et à la direction paramétrique en option font de la A 250, déjà bien motorisée, la terreur des GTI. Avec une bande rouge au-dessus du spoiler avant au niveau de la calandre – comme si elle avait sucé le sang d'une GTI – et sa calandre diamant, ce modèle fait étalage de sa puissance. On peut mentionner encore la double sortie d'échappement intégrée dans le tablier arrière AMG. On aurait sans doute pu se passer des lignes rouges à l'arrière. Les feux arrière pour ainsi dire collés au seuil de chargement du hayon arrière, pourraient évoquer aux plus pragmatiques d'entre nous la cape rouge brandie par les toreros pendant la corrida.

402 Mercedes-Benz A-Klasse 2012

Pure driving dynamics: the A 250 Sport, top speed 149 mph—"engineered by AMG"—makes clear at which competitors Mercedes-Benz is aiming the new A-Class.

Fahrdynamik pur: Der 240 km/h schnelle A 250 Sport – »engineered by AMG« – deutet an, auf welche Konkurrenten Mercedes-Benz mit der neuen A-Klasse zum Angriff bläst.

Le dynamisme à l'état pur : l'A 250 Sport – « engineered by AMG » – dont la vitesse de pointe atteint 240 km/h, laisse deviner contre quels concurrents Mercedes-Benz sonne la charge.

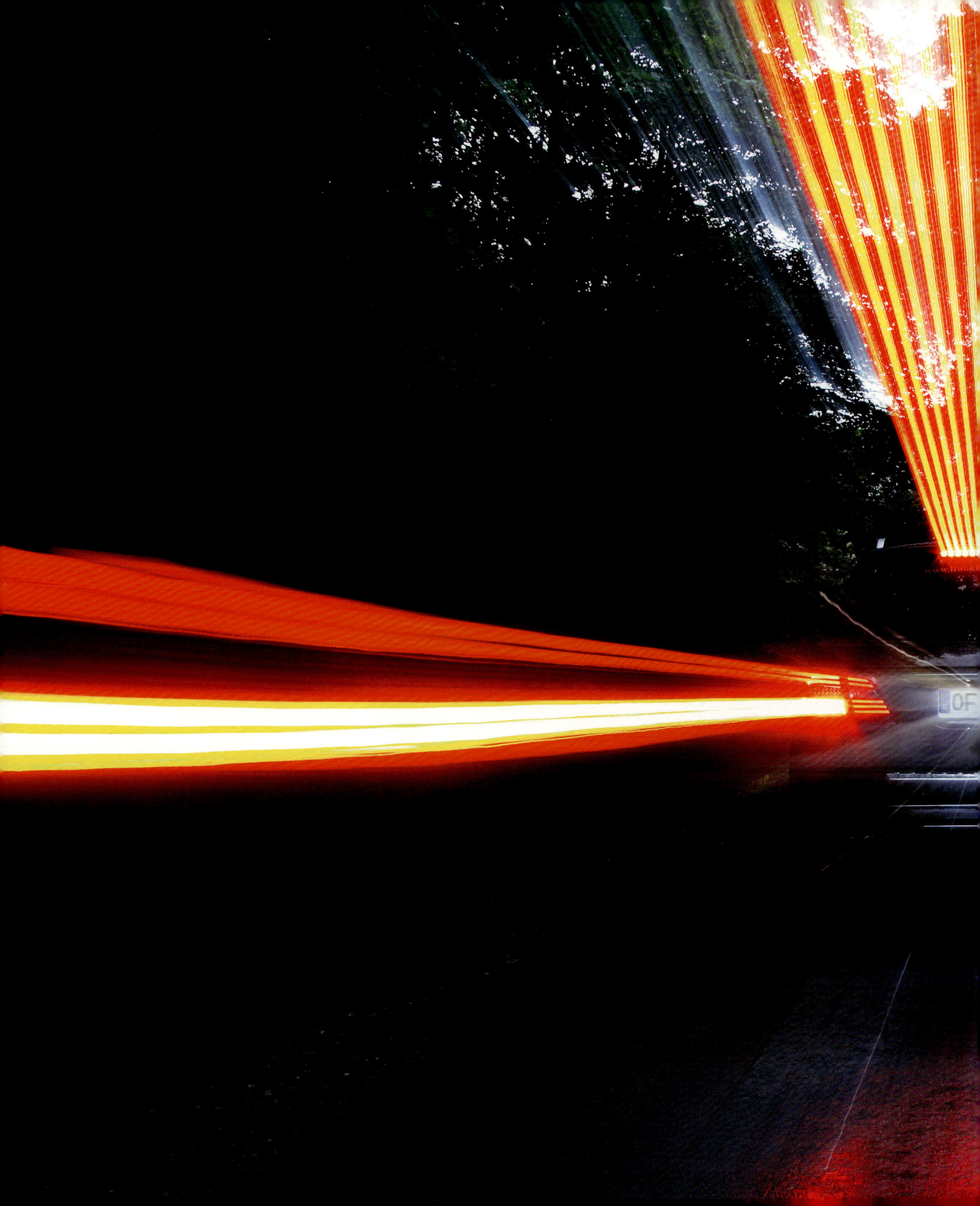
OF

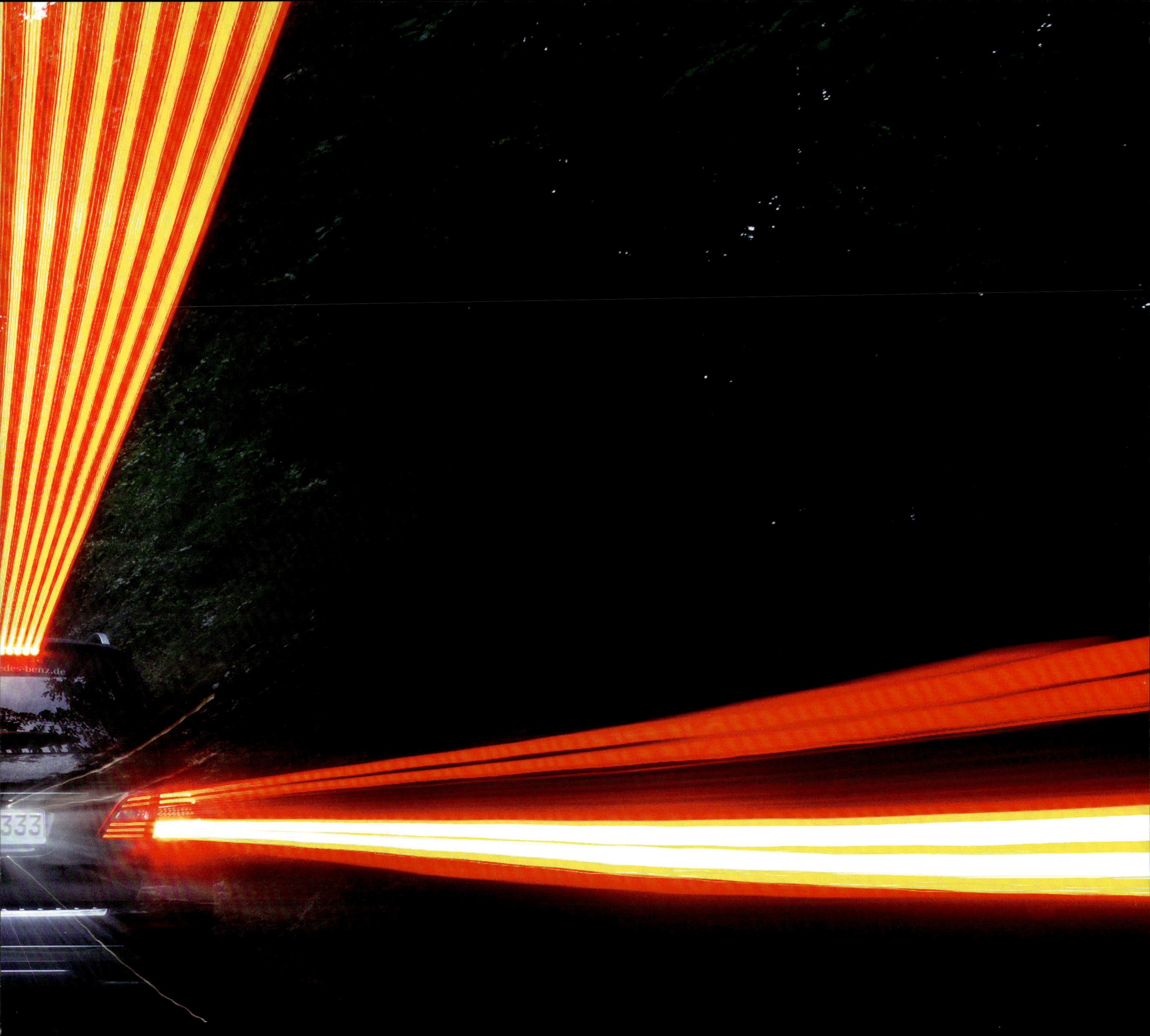
333

Bibliography · Bibliografie · Bibliographie

Daimler-Benz – Das Unternehmen/Die Technik, Kruk/Lingnau/Bartels (Hase & Koehler) Mainz 1986

Der Stern ihrer Sehnsucht: Plakate und Anzeigen von Daimler-Benz. Zeitdokumente der Gebrauchskunst von 1900 bis 1960, Simsa/Sproß/Wendt (Cantz) Ostfildern-Ruit 1995

Magnificent Mercedes – The Complete History of the Marque, Graham Robson (Chevprime) 1988

Mercedes-Benz Grand Prix 1934–1955, George C. Monkhouse (Orell Füssli) Stuttgart 1986

Mercedes-Benz Catalogue Raisonné 1886–1986, Jürgen Lewandowski (Edita)

Mercedes-Benz Personenwagen 1886–1986, Werner Oswald (Motorbuch) Stuttgart 1994

Deutsche Autos seit 1945, Werner Oswald (Motorbuch) Stuttgart 1992

Mercedes-Benz Quicksilver Century, Karl E. Ludvigsen (Transport Bookman) Isleworth 1995

Quicksilver, An Investigation into the Development of German Grand Prix Racing Cars 1934–1939, Cameron C. Earl (hmso) London 1996

Mercedes-Benz: A History, W. Robert Nitske (Motorbooks International) Osceola 1978

Sterne, Stars und Majestäten – Prominenz auf Mercedes-Benz, Simsa/Lewandowski (Stadler) Konstanz 1985

Mercedes-Benz Automobile 1–6, Schrader/Hofner (blv) München 1985 etc.

Kataloge der *Automobil Revue* 1952–2009 (Hallwag) Bern

Die große Automobilgeschichte Mercedes-Benz, Die multimediale Enzyklopädie aller Typen und Modelle auf CD-ROM (United Soft Media) München 1996

Personenwagen von Mercedes-Benz, Harry Niemann (Motorbuch) Stuttgart 2006

Mercedes-Benz Personenwagen seit 1996, Günter Engelen (Motorbuch) Stuttgart 2003

Das Mercedes-Benz Rennfahrer-Lexikon, Hartmut Lehbrink (Heel) Königswinter 2009

www.daimler.com

www.mercedes-benz.com

Acknowledgements · Danksagung · Remerciements

I wish to record my very sincere thanks to the following persons, without whose commitment this book could not have got off the ground, for making their cars available and for their active support for this project as a whole:

Für die Bereitstellung ihrer Fahrzeuge und die Unterstützung des Gesamtprojekts durch Rat und Tat danke ich ganz herzlich folgenden Personen, ohne deren Engagement dieses Buch nicht hätte entstehen können:

Je remercie très cordialement les personnes mentionnées ci-dessous pour la mise à disposition de leurs véhicules et leur appui en paroles et en actes pour l'ensemble du projet, car ce livre n'aurait pas pu être produit sans leur engagement:

Michael Allner, Erhard Aumüller, Helmut Baaden, Marina Bernert, Stefan Bisiani, Waldemar Boroz, Frank Bracke, Stefan Diehl, Andreas Ditzenbach, Dieter Fröbe, Dieter Götz, Thomas Guth, Thomas Hartmann, Heinz Haueisen, Ulrike Hörl, Matthias Jung, Klaus Keck, Peterheinz Kern, Wolfgang Knauth, Hardy Langer, Hermann Layher, Peter Lehmann, Friedhelm Loh, Markus Mahler, Kay Mertens, Dr. Harry Niemann, Horst Nies, Max von Pein, Steffen Pisoni, Günter Reinhard, Thomas Riedinger, Martin Röder, Stefan Röhrig, Wolfgang Rolli, Berthold E. Rückwarth, Bruno Sacco, Heinz Schacker, Heinrich Schäffler, Horst Schickedanz, Karl-Heinz Schleisick, Heinz Schlosser, Peter Schoene, Uwe Schüler, Oliver Schwarz, Peter Schwarz, Winfried A. Seidel, Klaus Seybold, Alois Singvogel, Markus Stapp, Ditmar Stehr, Norbert Szielasko, Jürgen Tauscher, Willi Vogel, Peter Völker, Ingo Waldschmidt.

I also extend my thanks to the following for their willing cooperation:

Ebenso danke ich für die hilfreiche Kooperation:

Je remercie également pour leur précieuse collaboration:

Mercedes-Benz Museum & Mercedes-Benz Classic, Stuttgart; Flughafen Siegerland; Flugplatz Egelsbach & Flugplatz Michelstadt.

Rainer W. Schlegelmilch

Photo credits · Fotonachweis · Crédits photographiques

All photographs by Rainer W. Schlegelmilch except:

Alle Fotos von Rainer W. Schlegelmilch außer:

Toutes les photos sont de Rainer W. Schlegelmilch sauf:

DaimlerChrysler-Konzernarchiv: pp 10, 11, 12tl, 12tr, 12br, 13tr
© Daimler AG: pp 13bl, 13br, 14tl, 14tr, 15
© Bundesarchiv, Bild 101I-732-0117-06, Foto: o. Ang.: p 12bl

t: top, b: bottom, l: left, r: right

© h.f.ullmann publishing GmbH

Original title: *Mercedes*
ISBN 978-3-8331-1056-6

Photography: Rainer W. Schlegelmilch
Text: Hartmut Lehbrink, Jochen von Osterroth (Updates)
Layout: Rainer W. Schlegelmilch, Oliver Hessmann
Project management: Sally Bald, Joachim Schwochert
Typography: Oliver Hessmann
Translation into English: Les Telford, Stephen Hunter, Mike Daly, Russell Cennydd
Translations into French: Jean-Luc Lesouëf

© for this updated edition: h.f.ullmann publishing GmbH

Special edition

Project management for h.f.ullmann: Lars Pietzschmann

Translations into English: Andrew Brown and Mo Croasdale in association with First Edition Translations Ltd, Cambridge, UK.
Edited by Sally Heavens and David Price in association with First Edition Translations Ltd, Cambridge, UK.

Translations into French: Florence Lecanu and Marion Villain-Richaud in association with Intexte Édition, Toulouse

Cover design: Oliver Hessmann

Overall responsibility for production: h.f.ullmann publishing GmbH, Potsdam, Germany

Printed in China, 2013

ISBN 978-3-8480-0438-6

10 9 8 7 6 5 4 3 2 1
X IX VIII VII VI V IV

www.ullmann-publishing.com
newsletter@ullmann-publishing.com